THE HISTORY OF SOVIET AIRBORNE FORCES

CASS SERIES ON SOVIET MILITARY THEORY AND PRACTICE

Series Editor – David M. Glantz
Ft. Leavenworth, Kansas

This series examines in detail the evolution of Soviet military science and the way the Soviets have translated theoretical concepts for the conduct of war into concrete military practice. Separate volumes focus on how the Soviets have applied and refined theory in combat and on how they have structured their forces to suit the requirement of changing times.

1. David M. Glantz, *Soviet Military Deception in the Second World War*

2. David M. Glantz, *Soviet Military Operational Art: In Pursuit of Deep Battle*

3. David M. Glantz, *Soviet Military Intelligence in War*

4. David M. Glantz, *The Soviet Conduct of Tactical Maneuver: Spearhead of the Offensive*

5. David M. Glantz, *The Military Strategy of the Soviet Union: A History*

6. David M. Glantz, *The History of Soviet Airborne Forces*

THE HISTORY OF
SOVIET AIRBORNE
FORCES

DAVID M. GLANTZ

FRANK CASS

First published 1994 in Great Britain by
FRANK CASS & CO. LTD
Newbury House, 900 Eastern Avenue,
Newbury Park, Ilford, Essex IG2 7HH

and in the United States of America by
FRANK CASS
c/o International Specialized Book Services, Inc.,
5804 N.E. Hassalo Street,
Portland, Oregon 97213-3644

The views expressed here are those of the author.
They should not necessarily be construed as those
of the U.S. Department of Defense or the United
States Army.

British Library Cataloguing in Publication Data

Glantz, David M.
  History of Soviet Airborne Forces. –
  (Cass Series on Soviet Military Theory &
  Practice; Vol.6)
  I. Title II. Series
  356.1660947

  ISBN 0 7146 3483 2 (cloth)
  ISBN 0 7146 4120 0 (paper)

Library of Congress Cataloging-in-Publication Data

Glantz, David M.
    The history of Soviet airborne forces / David M. Glantz.
        p.   cm. — (Cass series on Soviet military theory and practice
  ; 6)
    Includes index.
    ISBN 0-7146-3483-2 (cloth); 0-7146-4120-0 (paper)
    1. Soviet Union. Sukhoputnye voiska. Vozdushno–desantnye voiska–
  –History. I. Title. II. Series: Glantz, David M. Cass series on
  Soviet military theory and practice ; 6.
  UA776.V69G53 1994
  356'.166'0947—dc20   03-10289
                                                        CIP

Typeset by Regent Typesetting, London
Printed in Great Britain by
Bookcraft Ltd, Midsomer Norton, Avon

Contents

List of Figures   viii

Abbreviations   xi

Preface   xiii

1. The Interwar Years (1919–1941)   1
   The Genesis of Airborne Concepts   1
   Experimentation with Airborne Forces, 1929–1932   4
   Formation of Air Assault Forces, 1932–1937   11
   On the Eve of War, 1938–1941   38

2. Airborne Forces During the Second World War:
   Initial Operations, Subsequent Reorganization,
   and Changes in Employment Concepts   47
   Initial Operations, 1941   47
   Organization and Employment in Theory and Practice
      1941–1945   60

3. The Moscow Operation (December 1941–January 1942)   74
   Strategic Context, November–December 1941   74
   Teriaeva Sloboda, December 1941   75
   Medyn, January 1942   78
   Strategic Context, January 1942   86
   The Zhelan'e Operation, January 1942   94

4. The Viaz'ma Operation, Phase 1: 8th Airborne
   Brigade Operations (January–February 1942)   104
   Planning   104
   8th Airborne Brigade Assault   113
   8th Airborne Brigade Operations with 1st Guards
      Cavalry Corps   123
   Conclusions   143

5. The Viaz'ma Operation, Phase 2: 4th Airborne
   Corps' Operations (February–March 1942)   145
   Strategic Context   145
   Operational Planning   146
   4th Airborne Corps' Assault   152
   The February Offensive   160
   The March Offensive   169
   Conclusions   186

6. The Viaz'ma Operation, Phase 3: 4th Airborne
   Corps' Operations (April–June 1942)   188
   Strategic Context   188
   The April Offensive   189
   Encirclement and Breakout   201
   Conclusions   219

7. Rzhev and Demiansk: 1st Airborne Corps Operations
   (February–April 1942)   228
   Strategic Context   228
   Rzhev, February 1942   229
   Demiansk, February–April 1942   231

8. Across the Dnepr (September 1943)   262
   Strategic Context   262
   Operational Planning   263
   Dnepr Assault   273
   5th Guards Airborne Brigade Operations   278
   Conclusions   286

9. To War's End   289
   Introduction   289
   The Polotsk Operation, November 1943   290
   The Slovak Operation, September 1944   298

10. Reconnaissance and Diversionary Operations   305
    General   305
    Odessa, September 1941   305
    Kerch–Feodosiia, December 1941   308
    Maikop, October 1942   311
    Novorossiisk, February 1943   314
    Manchuria, August 1945   316

11. The First Postwar Years (1946–1953)   322
    Context   322
    Postwar Airborne Reorganization   324
    Theoretical Writings   325
    Airborne Force Employment   329
    Conclusions   334

12. The Revolution in Military Affairs (1953–1970)   336
    Context   336
    Theoretical Writings   338
    Airborne Force Employment   345
    Conclusions   348

13. On the Threshold of a New Technological
    Revolution (1971–1985)   350
    Context   350
    Theory and Practice to 1975   351
    Theory and Practice, 1975–1985   359
    Conclusions   368

14. On the Eve of the Twenty-First Century   369
    Growing Problems – Tentative Solutions   369
    The Role of Airborne and Air Assault Forces in
        Non-Linear Battle   373
    Dilemmas of the 1990s   376
    Defensiveness and Air Assault Concepts and Forces 379
    Into the Future   382

15. Conclusions   385

Notes   393

APPENDIX 1
    Logistical Support of the Viaz'ma Operation   424

APPENDIX 2
    Known Fate of Commanders and Staff Officers,
        4th Airborne Corps   426

Index   430

Figures

1. The Kiev Maneuvers of 1935: Overview — 15
2. The Kiev Maneuvers, 14 September 1935 — 16
3. The Moscow Maneuvers of 1936: The First Day — 24
4. The Moscow Maneuvers of 1936: The Second and Third Days — 25
5. Use of Airborne Forces on the Offensive, 1936 — 31
6. Airborne Brigades, 1936 — 36
7. Airborne Regiments, 1936 — 36
8. Airborne Forces, 1939 — 36
9. Airborne Force Employment, 1940 — 42
10. Airborne Brigade, 1940 — 43
11. Intelligence Assessment of Location of Soviet Airborne Forces, December 1940 — 44
12. Airborne Corps, 1941 — 45
13. Airborne Corps and Brigades, May 1941 — 45
14. Airborne Corps Dispositions, June 1941 — 48
15. 4th Airborne Corps Operations, June–September 1941 — 53
16. Operations around Mtsensk, October 1941 — 58
17. Airborne Brigade, 1941 — 61
18. Soviet Airborne Operations in the Moscow Region, 1941–42 — 63
19. Conversion of Airborne Units, Summer 1942 — 64
20. Selected German Intelligence Reports on Soviet Airborne Forces — 66
21. Airborne Brigade, 1943 — 67
22. Separate Airborne Army, 1944 — 68
23. German Third Panzer Group Situation Map, 16 December 1941 — 77
24. Medyn Area of Operations — 80
25. Medyn Operational Plan — 81
26. Medyn Operation, 3–20 January 1942 — 83
27. First Phase of Soviet Winter Offensive, 5 December–7 January 1942 — 87
28. Western Front Situation, 2 January 1942 — 93
29. Zhelan'e Operational Plan: Overview — 96
30. Zhelan'e Operational Plan: In Detail — 97
31. Zhelan'e Operation, 18–20 January 1942 — 99
32. Zhelan'e Operation, 21–31 January 1942 — 102
33. Western Front Situation, mid-January 1942 — 105
34. 4th Airborne Corps Operational Plan — 106

35. Viaz'ma–Dorogobuzh Area of Operations   107
36. 1st Guards Cavalry Corps Operations, 28 January–3 February
    1942   110
37. 8th Airborne Brigade Operations, 27 January–2 February 1942   114
38. 8th Airborne Brigade Operations, 2–10 February 1942   124
39. 8th Airborne Brigade Operations, 10–14 February 1942   130
40. 8th Airborne Brigade Operations, 14–16 February 1942   134
41. 8th Airborne Brigade Operations, 18–25 February 1942   137
42. 8th Airborne Brigade Operations, 2–5 March 1942   141
43. 8th Airborne Brigade Operations, 7–9 March 1942   142
44. Western Front Situation, 16 February 1942   147
45. 4th Airborne Corps Operational Plan   149
46. Viaz'ma–Iukhnov Area of Operations   151
47. 4th Airborne Corps Operations, February–June 1942: Soviet
    View   155
48. 4th Airborne Corps Operations: Overview   156
49. 4th Airborne Corps Operations, 17–24 February 1942   157
50. 4th Airborne Corps Operations, 25–28 February 1942   161
51. 4th Airborne Corps Operations, 1–20 March 1942   170
52. German 137th Infantry Division Defensive Area   173
53. 4th Airborne Corps Operations, 21–31 March 1942   182
54. 8th Airborne Brigade and 1st Guards Cavalry Corps
    Operations, 21–31 March 1942   184
55. Situation, 31 March 1942   190
56. 4th Airborne and 1st Guards Cavalry Corps Operations, 3–10
    April 1942   191
57. 4th Airborne and 1st Guards Cavalry Corps Operations, 11–20
    April 1942   195
58. Situation, 20 April 1942   202
59. Operation Hannover: A German Perspective   205
60. 4th Airborne and 1st Guards Cavalry Corps Operations, 30
    April–30 May 1942   206
61. 4th Airborne and 1st Guards Cavalry Corps Operations, 1–11
    June 1942   212
62. 4th Airborne and 1st Guards Cavalry Corps Operations, 11–23
    June 1942   215
63. Rzhev Operation, February 1942   230
64. Northwestern Front Operations, 7 January–1 March 1942   233
65. German Situation Map of the Demiansk Encirclement, 25
    February 1942   235
66. Demiansk Area of Operations   239
67. 1st Airborne Corps Plan of Operations   240
68. 204th Airborne Brigade Landing at Iasski, 15 February 1942   243

69. 1st Airborne Corps Operations, 6–23 March 1942   245
70. German Intelligence Map, 20 March 1942   251
71. 1st Airborne Corps Operations, 23 March–9 April 1942   252
72. Voronezh Front Advance to the Dnepr River   264
73. Rzhishchev–Kanev Area of Operations   266
74. Dnepr Airborne Operational Plan, 20 September 1943   267
75. Revised Dnepr Airborne Operational Plan, 23 September 1943   271
76. Dnepr Airborne Operation, 24 September–13 October 1943   275
77. 5th Guards Airborne Brigade Operations, November 1943   282
78. Operations in the Vitebsk–Gomel' Sector through October
       1943   291
79. Nevel' Offensive Operation, 6–10 October 1943   292
80. Situation, 10 November 1943   295
81. Begoml'–Ushiachi Operational Plan, November 1943   296
82. Slovak Uprising Area of Operations, August–September 1944   299
83. Dukla Operation, September 1944   302
84. Odessa Operation, September 1941   307
85. Kerch–Feodosiia Operation, December 1941–January 1942   310
86. Maikop Operation, October 1942   312
87. Novorossiisk Operation, February 1943   315
88. Air-landings in Manchuria, August 1945   317
89. Airborne Division Organization, 1946   324
90. Airborne Division Organization, 1968   346
91. Airborne Division Organization, 1975   358
92. Air Assault Brigade Organization, 1982   364
93. Airborne Forces Organization, 1978–82   365
94. Airborne Forces in the ATTU Region, 1991   382
95. Air Assault Forces in the ATTU Region, 1991   383
96. Airborne Division, 1991   383

Transliteration note: In general, this volume employs the Library of Congress transliteration system. In some maps and quotations, other transliteration systems will be encountered. Place names containing ia, iu, or e may be written ya, yu, and ye (or in German style).

Abbreviations

A	Army
AC	Army corps
AF	Army force (division)
AbnB	Airborne brigade
AbnC	Airborne corps
AbnDet.	Airborne detachment
AbnR(Regt)	Airborne regiment
AR	Artillery regiment
B	Brigade
Bde	Brigade
Bn	Battalion
CC	Cavalry corps
CD	Cavalry division
CR	Cavalry regiment
Co	Company
D	Division
Gp	Group
GA	Guards Army
GCC	Guards cavalry corps
GCD	Guards cavalry division
Gds	Guards
GMC	Guards mechanized corps
GRD	Guards rifle division
GTA	Guards tank army
GTB	Guards tank brigade
GTC	Guards tank corps
ID	Infantry division
IR	Infantry regiment
JD	Jäger (light) division
MC	Mechanized corps
MD	Motorized division
PartDet	Partisan detachment
PzA	Panzer army
PzD	Panzer division
PzR	Panzer regiment
PolR(Regt)	Police regiment

RB	Rifle brigade
RC	Rifle corps
RD	Rifle division
SA	Shock army
SB	Ski brigade
TA	Tank army
TB	Tank brigade
TC	Tank corps

On maps, numerals with no abbreviations attached are divisions (German and Soviet)

Preface

The historical record of Soviet development and employment of airborne forces in peace and war has been marred by neglect and misinformation. Until the early 1960s Soviet historians and military analysts concealed the historical record of these forces with a virtually impenetrable veil of secrecy, as they did with so many of the more unpleasant aspects of their military experiences. At the same time, their former and current adversaries in the West did little to set the historical record straight.

The tone of Western reporting was set by an important Western historical assessment of wartime airborne operations which was published by the United States Army in 1951. This ostensibly accurate survey compiled by prestigious former German wartime commanders contained the following judgement:

> It is surprising that during World War II the USSR did not attempt any large-scale airborne operations. Although Soviet Russia was the first country in the world which during peacetime had experimented with landing troops by air and had organised special units for this purpose, its wartime operations were confined to the commitment of small units which were dropped back of the German front for the purpose of supporting partisan activities and which had no direct tactical or strategic effect.[1]

This study attributed wartime Soviet airborne inactivity to numerous causes, including: their lack of air superiority, which 'persisted until the final stages of the war'; a failure of Soviet confidence in the utility or necessity of airborne operations; and the ill effects of the military purges of the 1930s, which had decimated the ranks of those who had originally created the airborne force. Finally, the study judged that 'The Russians are primarily at home on the ground and are not in their element on the water or in the air.'[2]

Although the German authors acknowledged rumors that a small Soviet airborne operation may have taken place along the banks of the Dnepr River in late summer 1943, it asserted that all knowledgeable German military authorities 'unanimously and independently stated that no large-scale airborne operations had been carried out by the Russians during World War II.'[3] The study concluded with the judgement that:

> The impression prevails that tactically and technically the Russians

could not meet the requirements of such an enterprise. Further reasons may be that the Russian soldier as a rule is not a good individual fighter but prefers to fight in mass formations, and that the junior Russian commanders lacked initiative and aggressiveness, two qualities that are basic requirements in a parachute officer.[4]

The German analysts who reaached these conclusions may be forgiven for their mistaken judgement, for within a year they carefully corrected their mistakes. In 1952 a second study, prepared by a new group of German veterans, disclosed that major Soviet airborne operations had indeed taken place.[5] This study revealed basic details about large-scale Soviet air drops, which had taken place during the Moscow operations of 1942 and added substance to the story of the Dnepr operation of September 1943. The study did, however, belittle the military significance of both airborne operations. Unfortunately, despite ultimate German candor, the more accurate of the two studies remained in unpublished manuscript form while the first, inaccurate version developed a life of its own and is today still published as 'history.'

Soviet historiography concerning their own airborne experiences is more thorough, although belated, but it is also marred by inaccuracies and seemingly deliberate oversights regarding the more unpleasant aspects of their historical record. The motive force behind their revelations was the imperative to study and learn from concrete war experiences, a time-honored Soviet procedure. Once the impenetrable veil of Stalinist secrecy about virtually all negative aspects of the Soviet wartime record had been lifted in the late 1950s, military analysts and scholars began studying those wartime procedures and techniques that seemed applicable to future warfare. The nuclear era of the 1960s accorded airborne forces new and expanded combat roles. Necessity then dictated that previous wartime use of these forces be reinvestigated and debated in both closed and open forums.

Since the early 1960s, airborne operations had been a recurring theme for the work of Soviet military analysts. A series of standard works that capture the essence of the wartime Soviet airborne record have appeared (authored by G. P. Sofronov, I. I. Lisov, and D. S. Sukhorukhov). In the main, the information in these works is accurate. But, as has usually been the case in Soviet historiography, the works reveal only enough material to promote educated discussion and no more. For example, the authors cover most, but not all, of the major airborne operations. Information regarding the timing, location, sequence of ground actions, and general outcome of each operation is likewise mostly accurate. The authors, however, have availed themselves of considerable literary license as they described the specific flow and outcome of these combats. Individual and group heroics mask problems of tragic proportions, and the often catastrophic losses experienced in these operations have been inferred, but seldom candidly revealed. More importantly, some of the more tragic and futile operations, like that at Demiansk, have been conveniently neglected and, hence, erased from the historical record.

To their credit, Soviet military analysts did keep records, albeit secret, of these airborne experiences, and they have recently begun releasing this archival material to public view. The many volumes of official General Staff war experiences, which have been recently released, contain candid and revealing reports and assessments of the more famous Moscow (Viaz'ma) airborne operations of 1942. This material does not contradict material in previously published Soviet open-source accounts. It does, however, illuminate many of the more sordid aspects of the operations, including their problems and casualties and losses. Sadly, the Russians have not released all pertinent archival materials. Therefore, the historian has been, and still is, forced to undertake the vastly more difficult task of ferreting out the truth through thorough examination of mountains of German wartime records. Only then does the scope and ubiquitousness of Soviet airborne operations become apparent.

There can be no questioning of the importance which Soviet military theorists have attached to the subject of airborne operations. From the 1930s vertical maneuver in the form of airborne, air assault, air-landing, and air mobile actions have formed an integral and increasingly significant role in Soviet fixation on maneuver in general.[6] There was an important vertical dimension to the twin 1930s concepts of 'deep battle' and 'deep operations' as well as to the 1970s and 1980s concepts of modern operational and tactical maneuver. Most recently, Soviet and Russian (Commonwealth) theorists have focused on theories of air-mechanization and postulated the combat employment of a distinct 'air echelon.' For generations, in fact, the theory and practice of airborne operations have seemed to offer at least a partial solution to the problem of escaping from the adverse effects of accelerating changes to combat weaponry in ground combat.

Thus, there has been, and still is, basic continuity in how the Soviets and their Russian descendants perceive the utility of vertical envelopment in warfare. It is likely that the experiences of the past in this regard will continue to play a significant part in determining the role of airborne and air assault operations in future war.

Finally, I hope that the search for historical truth and candor in the realm of Soviet (Russian) military experience will serve not only practitioners of military science and art. To be fully justified it must also be of service to the memory of those history has ignored – those who perished in combat without recognition. While study goes on to better prepare armies to cope with the realities of future combat, I hope the study will also reveal the failures of the past and the suffering of those engaged in the many airborne experiments and operations, successful and unsuccessful alike. At the least, full revelation of the details of the Soviet historical record can become the ultimate test of *glasnost'* and Russian historical accuracy and candor.

NOTES

1. 'Airborne Operations: A German Appraisal', *Department of the Army Pamphlet No. 20-232* (Washington, DC: Department of the Army, October 1951), 36. Reissued by the United States Army Center of Military History, 1982.
2. Ibid.
3. Ibid, 37.
4. Ibid.
5. H. Reinhardt, ed., 'Russian Airborne Operations' (Draft translation), *Chief of Military History, MS# P-116* (Historical Division, Headquarters, United States Army, Europe, 1952).
6. For the purposes of this study the terms airborne, air assault, and air-landing are used interchangeably and take their ultimate meaning from context. The Soviets themselves use air-landing [*vosdushno-desantnyi*] to describe the delivery of forces into combat both by parachute and by air-landing. Recently they have also begun to employ the term landing-assault [*desantno-shturmovoi*] to describe operations by certain types of helicopter-delivered forces. The Soviets have often described forces subordinate to air-landing formations as parachute-landing [*parashiutno-desantnyi*] units. Here, for the sake of understanding, I have often used the Western term 'airborne' to describe operations by parachute forces and 'air assault' to relate to actions of helicopter-delivered forces.

CHAPTER 1

The Interwar Years (1919–1941)

THE GENESIS OF AIRBORNE CONCEPTS

The concept of committing forces into combat from the air or, as it came to be known, vertical envelopment, originated during the early post-World War years, which was a period characterized by intense intellectual ferment in Soviet as well as Western military affairs. In the early 1930s, rampant industrialization and the adoption of modern technology intensified to produce a renaissance in military thought within the Soviet Union. A generation of military leaders and thinkers, conditioned by a revolutionary philosophy and participation in the Russian Civil War and Allied intervention and eager to elevate the Soviet Union into a competitive military position with the rest of Europe, gave shape and focus to that renaissance. They were imaginative men, infused with ideological zeal, encouraged by their political leaders to experiment, and willing to learn from the experiences of military leaders abroad. Their efforts produced a sophisticated military doctrine, advanced for its time, and an elaborate, if not unique, military force structure to implement that doctrine.

It is one of the major ironies of history that the work of these men – the Tukhachevskys, the Triandafilovs, the Issersons, and a host of others – would be eclipsed and almost forgotten. Their efforts for the Soviet Union earned for them only sudden death in the brutal purges of the late 1930s. The formidable armed force they had built and the sophisticated thought that had governed use of that force decayed. The brain of the army dulled, and imagination and initiative failed. The military embarrassments of 1939–40 and the debacle of 1941 blinded the world to the true accomplishments of Soviet military science in the 1930s, and an appreciation of those accomplishments never really returned. The military leaders of 1943–45 resurrected the concepts of their illustrious predecessors and competently employed them to achieve victory over Europe's most vaunted military machine. Yet the memories of the Soviets' poor performance in 1941 never faded and have since colored Western attitudes toward Soviet military art. Thus, it is appropriate to recall the realities of Soviet military development unblemished by the images of 1941. One of those realities was Soviet experimentation with airborne forces in the 1930s.

Soviet receptivity to the idea of air assault was but a part of greater Soviet interest in experimentation with new military ideas to restore offensive dominance to the battlefield. The World War had seen the offensive fall victim to static defensive war. In positional warfare, the firepower of modern weaponry stymied the offense and exacted an excruciating toll in human lives. Those wedded to the idea of the dominance of the infantry – the ultimate elevation of men to preeminence on the battlefield – saw the infantry slaughtered in the ultimate humiliation of man's power to influence battle. Infantry, the collective personification of man, dug antlike into the ground, overpowered by impersonal firepower and the crushing weight of explosives and steel.

New weapons – the tank, the airplane – emerged during wartime, but most military theorists saw these weapons as demeaning to the infantry and as an adjunct to the existing technological dominance of fire. Yet there were those who experienced war in a different context. For three years after 1918 in the vast expanse of Russia, regiments, brigades, divisions, and armies engaged in a seesaw civil war – a chaotic confrontation over vast territories, a war in which the zeal of man and his ability to act counted more than human numbers on the battlefield. Shorn of advanced weaponry, separate armies joined a struggle in which imaginative maneuver paid dividends, in which rudimentary operational and tactical techniques could once again be tested without prohibitive loss of life. It was a different sort of struggle, one that conditioned many of its participants to be receptive to new concepts of warfare. The credibility of the offense emerged supreme, and to that new faith in the offense was added the imperative of an ideology that inherently embraced the offensive.

The Red Army (*Raboche-Krest'ianskaia Krasnaia Armiia* [Workers and Peasants Red Army – RKKA]) as it emerged from the civil war was crude by Western standards. Large, ill-equipped, and relatively unschooled in military art, the Red Army was simultaneously the shield of the Soviet state and the sword of revolutionary socialism. Although Soviet ardor for international revolution waned in the face of harsh economic and political realities, and the army shrank in the immediate postwar years as it provided manpower for factories and fields, the revolutionary foundation of the army remained. The writings of Mikhail Frunze enunciated the uniqueness of the Red Army. The attitudes and actions of the leading commanders and theorists better characterized the reality of the army. Theoretical debates within the army over the nature of war and the role of man and modern weaponry began in the 1920s. At first, these debates expressed mere hopes, kept so by the reality of Soviet industrial and technological backwardness. But as that industrial development began to accelerate, goaded by Stalin's ruthless 'Socialism in One Country,' and as technological proficiency rose, either generated from within or imported from abroad, abstract hopes turned into concrete policies and programs. These new doctrines sought to combine the offensive potential of new weapons with the ideological zeal and faith in the offensive which was born of revolution and civil war experience. Thus, while the victors of the World War sought to make new weapons the slave of the defense and guarantor of the status quo, those defeated – Germany and the U.S.S.R. – turned to the new weaponry as a means of overturning the status quo. In this sense, it is not surprising that German and Soviet military thought evolved in so similar a manner during the interwar years.

The shape of future Soviet military thought began to take form in the late 1920s. Frunze's postulation of a proletarian military doctrine reflecting the classless nature of the Socialist state gave focus to that thought. Soviet officers began to ponder the implications of Frunze's 'Unified Military Doctrine,' a doctrine that dictated dedication to maneuver, *activnost* [activity], and the offensive in the real world of battle. These new principles rejected the concepts of defensive, static, positional warfare so dominant in Western European and American military thought.[1]

Although Frunze died in 1925, other thinkers expanded his theories, deriving first an intellectual basis in doctrine and then specific methods and techniques to translate that doctrine into practice. The Field Regulation [*USTAV – Ustavlenie* (regulation), Russians routinely refer to regulations as *USTAVs*] of 1929 reflected this mixture of theory and experiment. It established the objective of conducting deep battle [*glubokyi boi*] to secure victory at the tactical depth of the enemy defense by using combined arms forces, specifically infantry, armor, artillery, and aviation, acting in concert.[2] Deep battle, however, remained an abstract objective that could be realized only when technology and industry had provided the modern armaments necessary for its execution. The 1929 regulation was a declaration of intent, an intent that would begin to be realized in the early 1930s as the first Five Year Plan ground out the heavy implements of war.

Among those implements of war were tanks and aircraft, each symbolizing an aspect of potential deep battle. The tank offered prospects for decisive penetration, envelopment, and the exploitation of offensive tactical success to effect greater operational success, the latter dimension conspicuously absent in the positional warfare of the World War. Aircraft also added a new dimension to the battlefield. Besides the potentially devastating effects of aerial firepower, aircraft offered prospects for vertical envelopment, a third dimension of offensive maneuver. Vertical envelopment, of potential value even in isolation, would supplement the offensive action of mechanized forces and further guarantee the success of deep battle. Thus, the emerging doctrinal fixation on deep battle gave impetus to experimentation with airborne forces, experimentation that began in earnest in the late 1920s.

EXPERIMENTATION WITH AIRBORNE FORCES, 1929–1932

The first recorded Soviet use of air-landed forces occurred in 1929, when the Red Army landed a small detachment to relieve a small force besieged by a larger Basmach band in the Tadzhik town of Garm. The landing was made by 15 men transported by three trimotor aircraft, and the operation led to the defeat of the Basmach force and relief of the encircled garrison.[3]

Subsequent experimentation with airborne forces went hand in glove with doctrinal research. Although many theorists examined the uses of airborne forces, in particular the problems and their potential missions, M. N. Tukhachevsky played the leading role. In 1928, as commander of the Leningrad Military District, he conducted trial exercises and prepared a study on the 'Operations of an Air Assault Force in an Offensive Operation.' The following year Tukhachevsky conducted an exercise employing a reinforced rifle company as an air-landed assault force. As a result of his critiques of exercises conducted in 1929 and 1930, he proposed to the *Revoensovet* [Revolutionary Military Soviet – RVS] a sample air-motorized division TOE (table of organization and equipment) for use as an operational-strategic air-landing force.[4]

Supplementing Tukhachevsky's work, A. N. Lapchinsky, chief of staff of the Red Army's air force [*VVS (voenno-vozdushnyi sil')*], and N. P. Ivanov wrote an article in the journal *War and Revolution* [Voina i revoliutsiia], for the first time discussing combat use of air assault forces. Reflecting on experiences of the World War when aircraft had landed individuals in the enemy rear, Lapchinsky trumpeted the feasibility of harnessing aircraft to the task of large-scale delivery of combat forces into the enemy rear. Modern passenger aircraft, he argued, 'Now permitted expectations of stronger *desants* in the enemy's dispositions.'[5] Citing further air assault experiences in battle with the Basmachy, he and Ivanov investigated such finite airborne problems as timing and location of landings, joint operations with both aircraft and land forces, calculation of requisite force size relative to mission, and landing times for air assault forces from battalion to regimental size.

Lapchinsky calculated that a detachment of 15 aircraft could land 450 combat soldiers in a single trip, along with requisite ammunition, supplies, and equipment. It followed that two trips by three such detachments could land 2,700 men. Specially prepared aircraft could transport one to two artillery pieces with ammunition with the only limitation being the need to develop means to tow the artillery once landed. He recognized the necessity of selecting and preparing a landing area of up to one square kilometer to accommodate the aircraft. Further calculations indicated that it would take up to three hours to land 3,000 men, although use of multiple landing strips could reduce the time.

To provide security for the landing, forces had to conduct careful reconnaissance and provide adequate protection in the form of fighter aircraft to deal with air threats and support assault troops against any enemy troops in the landing region.

Lapchinsky assessed that a regimental air landing so organized could have tactical significance and would have to operate in conjunction with frontal ground forces. He detailed three appropriate missions for an airborne force:

1. *desant* to create an unexpected threat to an enemy's open flank;
2. *desant* at the time of and in the region of the main attack of our offensive to penetrate the enemy front and, in some instances, a *desant* to force a river crossing;
3. *desant* during an enemy withdrawal to occupy restricted access areas which the enemy could not mine (defiles between lakes or swamps and crossings of rivers).[6]

Such assaults would be parallel to the enemy route of withdrawal or directly across his routes of egress. In all cases, the air-landing missions would be an integral part of the overall operational plan. The first echelon of air-landing forces had the principal mission of reconnaissance, selection of landing sites for heavier equipment, and establishment of initial communications. In all instances, timing of the assault and its coordination with ground forces was most critical and difficult to effect.

These theoretical discussions paralleled practical exercises in both countryside and classroom. Simultaneously, other agencies worked on developing all types of airborne equipment as evidenced by the first Soviet domestic production of parachutes in April 1930. Active experimentation grew in scope when, on 2 August 1930, a major test occurred near Voronezh in the Moscow Military District.[7] To test landing techniques rather than tactics, three R-1 aircraft dropped two detachments of 12 parachutists, each armed with machine guns and rifles; their mission was to perform a diversionary mission in the enemy rear. The detachment commanders, L. G. Minov and Ia. D. Moshkovsky, would play a leading role in future airborne experimentation. The Voronezh test drop, from heights of 500 and 300 meters, focused on solution of such technical problems as preventing dispersal of dropped personnel, determining visibility on the part of airborne troops, and calculating the time necessary for those troops to reform and become combat capable. The exercise was repeated at the same location in September 1930 when ANT-9 aircraft dropped an 11-man detachment under Moshkovsky's command.[8] While the military district commander, A. I. Kork, looked on, the detachment successfully seized documents from an 'enemy' division headquarters. The success of these experiments was noted in a decree of the *Revoensovet* on the results of combat training. The decree mandated conduct of additional airborne exercises in 1931, to emphasize both technical and tactical aspects of an air assault.[9] From 1933 on, virtually all Soviet field exercises included airborne operations.

Early experimentation in various military districts gave rise to the formation of an experimental aviation motorized landing detachment in Tukhachevsky's Leningrad Military District in March 1931. This detachment consisted of a rifle company; sapper, communications, and light vehicle platoons; a heavy bomber aviation squadron; and a corps aviation detachment. Ia. D. Lukin commanded the 164 men, under the staff responsibility of D. N. Nikishev. The unit had two 76-mm guns, two T-27 tankettes, four grenade launchers, three light machine guns, four heavy machine guns, 14 hand machine guns, and a variety of light vehicles. Twelve TB-1 bombers and ten R-5 light aircraft provided aviation support. Tukhachevsky charged the detachment to conduct airborne operations to achieve tactical aims; specifically, a parachute echelon would seize airfields and landing strips in the enemy rear to secure an area for landing the main force.[10] At first, the unit tested organizational concepts and equipment for airlanding but did not address the issue of airdrop.

In June 1931, Tukhachevsky ordered the creation of an experimental non-TOE parachute detachment in the 1st Aviation Brigade to test the airdrop dimension of airborne operations.[11] This new unit became the parachute echelon of the combined airborne force and, with 46 volunteers under Minov, practiced airdrops in exercises at Krasnoe Selo and Krasnogvardeisk, outside Leningrad, and at Mogilevka, in the Ukraine, during August and September 1931. At Mogilevka, I. E. Iakir, the Kiev Military District commander, supervised the drop of Minov's 29 men from several ANT-9 aircraft.[12]

On 14 December 1931, I. P. Belov, Tukhachevsky's successor as the Leningrad Military District commander, reported on the airborne exercises to the *Revoensovet*. Belov lauded the success of airborne troops in working with ground and naval forces in the enemy's rear areas. In particular, the exercises accented the paratroopers' ability to capitalize on their inherent element of surprise. Belov echoed Tukhachevsky's earlier call to create TOE [establishment] airborne divisions based on existing detachments. Specifically, Belov argued that an airborne division should consist of a motor-landing brigade, an aviation brigade, a parachute detachment, and essential support units.[13]

Though positive in general, air force assessments of the more than 550 airborne exercises pointed out several noticeable shortcomings in the use of airborne forces. All the drops had taken place in summer, and few had occurred at night. Drops were small-scale and usually resulted in considerable dispersion of forces. The air force command criticized the haphazard study of foreign parachute equipment and urged accelerated work on Soviet domestic chutes.[14]

On 5 January 1932, on the basis of these and other reports, the *Revoensovet* issued its own report, 'Concerning the Air-Motorized Detachments of the Leningrad Military District.' That report mandated the creation of four aviation motorized detachments, one each in the Moscow, Leningrad, Belorussian, and Ukrainian military districts, and the establishment of a squadron of TB-1 bombers to transport the airborne troops. The Leningrad detachment, stationed at Detskoe Selo, designated the 3d Motorized Airborne Landing Detachment, was formed from two existing aviation landing units. Commanded by M. V. Boitsov, the detachment had 144 men organized into three machine gun companies and three aviation squadrons, supported by an aviation park (aviation support units). These units would deploy on a functional basis as a parachute battalion of two companies and a landing group of one company and one artillery battery. The detachment had six 76-mm guns, 18 light machine guns, 144 automatic pistols, and light vehicles. For transportation, the aviation squadrons contained six ANT-9, six R-5, three TB-1, and three U-2 aircraft.[15] The grandiose plans of the *Revoensovet* to create four of these detachments failed, probably because of shortages of equipment and trained personnel. Only the Leningrad detachment was complete, although the Ukrainian Military District formed a 30-man parachute platoon. No units appeared in other districts. Consequently, exercises involving the Leningrad detachment would be the focus for further experimentation.[16]

The conceptual framework for use of airborne forces became more elaborate in February 1932 when a Red Army order, 'Temporary Regulation on the Organization of Deep Battle,' recognized that the 1929 hope of being able to conduct such battle was becoming a reality. Although the basic regulation emphasized the role of mechanized forces in the success of deep battle, the Red Army discussed the utility of airborne forces in a companion draft document, 'Regulation on the Operational-Tactical Employment of Air-Motorized Landing Detachments,' which was accompanied by a list of subjects for tactical training during the 1932–33 training year. The new regulation declared that aviation motorized detachments were 'army operational-tactical units that coordinated closely with ground forces.' When mobilized, the detachments would perform diversionary missions, such as destroying enemy rail and road bridges, ammunition warehouses, fuel dumps, and aircraft at forward airfields. They would also support ground offensive operations by destroying enemy lines of communication, supply depots, headquarters, and other important objectives in the enemy rear areas. In addition, they would block withdrawal or reinforcement by enemy forces. During defensive operations, the detachments would perform similar functions by striking enemy command and control facilities, disrupting enemy troop movements, and securing airfields in the enemy rear area.[17]

Having articulated the concept of airborne operations, the Red Army addressed the issues of training and equipment development. The Red Army Training Directorate issued a series of directives that outlined training requirements for airborne units and subdivided training into four categories: parachute, glider, air-landing, and combined operations. Training in each category occurred in close coordination with aviation units. In April 1932, the 'Regulations Governing the Special Design Bureau [*OKB*] of the Red Army Air Force [*VVS, RKKA*]' addressed equipment requirements and entrusted the *OKB* with planning and developing air assault equipment, in particular gliders, parachute platforms for transporting guns and vehicles and with modifying the TB-1 bomber to transport airborne troops by use of cabins suspended beneath the aircraft.[18] By November 1932, the *OKB* had worked out and submitted to the People's Commissariat of Defense (NKO) specific equipment requirements for the aviation motorized detachments, including modifications to the TB-1 and TB-3 bombers. Each modified aircraft could carry 32 assault troops with parachutes or 50 without.

While the Red Army issued its specific regulations, exercise experience and theoretical writings continued to refine practices and concepts of airborne force use. An exercise of the Leningrad 3d Motorized Airborne Landing Detachment on 29 September 1932 at Krasnogvardeisk, conducted under the watchful eyes of the *Revoensovet* chairman, K. E. Voroshilov, included a full cycle of airborne activities. Drop, attack, and withdrawal were all rated successful.[19] A 17 November 1932 *Revoensovet* order assessing the year's exercises noted that problems of airborne assault still existed by again emphasizing the importance of the unit.

Two important contributions to airborne theory appeared in 1932, fueling the movement toward fielding larger and more numerous airborne units. Tukhachevsky published an article investigating the 'New Question of War' [*Novye voprosy voiny*], which articulated the role and missions of airborne forces. He stressed the operational and tactical missions of such forces by stating that 'air assault forces must operate between deployed enemy corps, army, and front reserves, arresting the action of the forces throughout the operational depth of the defense.'[20] The Chief of Airborne Service of the Red Army air force staff, I. E. Tatarchenko, seconded the views of Tukhachevsky with an article in *War and Revolution [Voina i revolutsiia]* titled 'Technical, Organizational, and Operational Questions of Air Assault Forces.' Tatarchenko argued for creation of separate, uniquely armed airborne forces to operate in close coordination with aviation units in attacks on enemy rear areas. He wrote, 'Indeed, to achieve surprise, air assaults will often be conducted in very bad weather, perhaps at night and possibly in fog, etc. As a rule, after landing, assault forces at once must conduct most decisive operations.'[21] The extreme demands of such operations placed high premium on quality training and equally effective equipment support.

Tatarchenko recommended employment of multiple air-landings in a single operation to lessen the vulnerability of a single landing and to confuse the enemy. Operations should begin with the advanced parachute landing of special reconnaissance and engineer parties supported by assault aviation to prepare landing sites. Communications in these early stages was particularly important. The initial 'vertical envelopment' secured the overall landing site. Thereafter, the *avangard* of the main forces landed by parachute or air-landing, equipped with machine guns and light (20–37mm) field and antitank guns. Using firepower and, if necessary, smoke, the *avangard* supported the main force landing operation which followed. With the main air-landed force arrived heavier guns, vehicles, and light tanks, followed by supplies and ammunition. After the time-phased insertion of air assault forces, those forces would commence operations in close coordination with main *front* forces. The February regulations and the theoretical articles of 1932 paved the way for more concrete measures for the development of an effective airborne force.

Western intelligence monitored Soviet experimentation with air assault forces and the growing body of theoretical writing concerning their possible wartime use. A July 1934 report to Washington from the U.S. attaché in Riga entitled *Transport of Troops by Air* surveyed exercises in the Leningrad Military District against the backdrop of earlier Red Army use of air-landing. Regarding a 1933 exercise, it read 'It was learned from a reliable source that such an experiment [the air transport of a complete infantry battalion with modern equipment] was carried out in the outskirts of Leningrad [date not stated] and that 100 planes participated in it.'[22] The attaché added, 'As the personnel of such a battalion does not exceed 800 men and as they were transported in two flights, it is believed that the number of planes is greatly exaggerated.'

As background, the attaché reviewed Soviet experiences using landing parties to combat Basmach insurgents in Turkestan. He then went on to report the present state of Soviet air-landing theory, stating that landing parties were trained in all air brigades. 'For this purpose there is usually detailed a special group of bombers with observation and pursuit (or more often, attack) planes as a reconnaissance detachment.'[23] These groups participated in maneuvers of nearby rifle divisions. In one such maneuver during 1932, a rifle landing company was transported in 16 attached AN T-9 transport aircraft. The following year a full rifle battalion was transported in two aircraft detachments on the same night, using transport planes, land torpedo bombers of the Baltic Fleet, and heavy bombers. During the same two-year period, the attaché noted that during the transfer of rifle units to camps near Luga and Krasnoarmeis-kyi, near Pskov, rifle landing parties previously trained and organized for this purpose were transported by air as leading elements. In addition, when air force units were switched from one airdrome to another, he noted, 'It is required that personnel, equipment, tanks, ground radio stations, fuel, lubricants, etc. be transported by air.'[24]

Several months later, another attaché report addressed the transfer of machine gun units by air. Reporting from Riga in November 1934 the attaché quoted a news item from Berlin published by an Italian news-paper, which summarized Soviet press releases concerning the use of parachutists in the fall maneuvers of 1933. It read:

The Russian press has just published the first particulars about the results of the last fall maneuvers which were especially important because experiments were made for the first time in combined ground and air exercises with the new corps of parachute jumpers. These units have been specially trained in making parachute jumps in the enemy rear areas from great heights. The parachute jumpers were carried by airplanes behind the enemy lines and made their jumps from a height of from 6,000 to 8,000 meters. At this height it is rather difficult to distinguish airplanes and almost impossible to bring them down by anti-aircraft artillery fire.

The parachutists jumped from large machines in groups of 300 or 400 men. They were trained to descend with closed parachutes until a distance of a few hundred meters from the ground. The later the parachutes open, the greater is the possibility of surprise. More-over, by this method greater precision is obtained in reaching the desired objective because the parachutists remain only for a few seconds exposed to the effect of the drift of the wind. As soon as they have touched the ground, the parachutists, who are all armed with special very light machine guns and supplied with adequate ammunition, form small groups which have the mission of surprising the enemy troops by attacking them from the rear and of disorganizing traffic in the rear areas.

The Soviet General Staff is certain that the descent of thousands of soldiers on the flanks of a combatant army will be such an element of surprise and of amazement that it may be decisive in a battle. In the first year of existence of the corps of parachutists there have been already trained several thousand men who will constitute quite a new element which will play an unknown role in future warfare.[25]

The attaché, Major W. E. Shipp, commented that the reference to 'several thousand' trained parachutists was probably an exaggeration. Subsequent reports, however, indicated Shipp's caution was probably unwarranted.

FORMATION OF AIR ASSAULT FORCES, 1932–1937

The growing sophistication of air assault theory and the development of new equipment paralleled Soviet appreciation of the need to create larger air assault units to operate at the division, corps, and army levels. An 11 December 1932 *Revoensovet* decree directly responded to the need by creating a special-purpose air assault brigade from the existing detachment in the Leningrad Military District.[26] The new brigade was to train an airborne cadre and establish operational norms for all Soviet airborne units. In addition, by 1 March 1933, special-purpose air-landing detachments were to be formed in the Belorussian, Ukrainian, Moscow, and Volga military districts, and non-TOE air assault battalions were to be established in rifle corps and cadre rifle divisions throughout the Soviet Union. To implement the *Revoensovet* order, a directive of the Commissariat of Military and Naval Affairs transformed the Leningrad Military District's 3d Motorized Air-Landing Detachment into the 3d Airlanding Brigade (Special-Purpose), commanded by Boitsov.

Unlike the earlier detachment, the new brigade was a combined arms unit organized with both peacetime and wartime TOEs. It had a parachute detachment (battalion-size), a motorized/mechanized detachment (battalion-size), an artillery battalion, and an air group comprising two squadrons of TB-3 modified bombers and one squadron of R-5 aircraft. Initially, four such special purpose air-landing detachments (1st through 4th) were formed in the Volga, Belorussian, Ukrainian, and Moscow military districts, each with peacetime and wartime TOEs. Throughout 1933, the *Revoensovet* created 29 additional non-TOE special purpose air-landing battalions in the rifle corps and cadre rifle divisions of other military districts so that, by year's end, the 29 existing air-landing battalions totaled more than 8,000 men. By 1 January 1934, the airborne force structure included one air-landing brigade, four air-motorized detachments, 29 separate air-landing battalions, and several company- and platoon-size elements totaling 10,000 men.[27] To train air assault cadres, the *Revoensovet*, in March 1933, initiated a special airborne combat training course that focused on the precise techniques required by parachute, air-landing, and combined operations. Combat training focused on the basic tasks associated with air assaults, such as parachute training, landing techniques, and actions conducted after the landing, including assembly, movement to the objective, and the performance of standard operational-tactical tasks in the enemy rear.[28]

Thus, while units formed, staff responsibilities governing their use also emerged. The Red Army staff was responsible for training and overall use of airborne forces. In wartime, the Red Army air force would deliver units to combat, but, once in combat, airborne units would be under the operational control of the *fronts* and armies. The 1933 air assault organization remained unchanged until 1936.

Western intelligence kept only sketchy track of the process of formation of parachute and air-landing forces within the Red Army. Distinguishing between regular infantry and air-landed infantry was a particularly difficult task. In October 1935, however, the US military attaché in Riga submitted a report on air units situated in the Leningrad Military District. In it he identified air-landing forces based at Detskoe Selo, just outside Leningrad. Noting that the Soviets prominently displayed such units in military reviews, he described two such examples. On 1 May 1934, 36 trucks carrying 16 parachutists each (500 men) appeared in the parade. Each man was equipped with two parachutes, and the trucks had light and heavy machine guns. During the 7 November parade the same year, 48 trucks participated, each with six to nine men equipped with parachutes and light and heavy machine guns (350 men, 70 light machine guns, and 30 heavy machine guns).[29]

Civilian organizations helped provide the manpower for Soviet airborne units. *Komsomol* [Communist Union of Youth] and *OSOAVIAKHIM* [Society for the Promotion of Defense and the Furthering of Aviation and of the Chemical Industry of the U.S.S.R.] sponsored sport parachuting, popular in the Soviet Union in the 1930s, and created a large pool of trained youth parachutists.[30]

Western intelligence reports supported the well-documented claims of Soviet writers regarding *OSOAVIAKHIM's* role in integrating the military and society. This role was clearest in promotion of air assault-related activities and training, in particular, glider and parachute training. According to these reports, by 1935 *OSOAVIAKHIM* had founded 2,000 glider schools associated with towns, cities, factories, and state farms, which trained 140,000 pupils in the art of gliding. The training was capped by summer glider competition at Koktebel in the Crimea for the best of the students. During the same period, an extensive *OSOAVIAKHIM* parachute sports training program prepared thousands of jumpers for future military service.[31] Although the attaché who forwarded the report to Washington admitted the absolute number participating in both programs were probably exaggerated, the real figures were likely to have been imposing.

Meanwhile, theoretical work on air assault force employment continued, punctuated by increasingly elaborate practical exercises. On 15 June 1933, the Red Army deputy chief of staff, S. A. Mazheninov, issued 'Provisional Instructions on the Combat Use of Air-Landing Units.'[32] This regulation, broader than its 1932 predecessor, categorized air assaults as either operational (conducted by a regiment or brigade against objectives in the operational depth of the defense) or tactical (carried out by one to two companies or a battalion against objectives in its tactical depth). The regulations also defined the specific functions of each command level in an air assault operation. Combined arms headquarters staffs, the chief of the air group, and the air assault commander were jointly to work out employment plans after conducting a systematic air and photographic reconnaissance and a careful assessment of force requirements and objectives. Then, the commander of the air assault operation would fully coordinate the actions of the air and air assault units and also ensure that airborne force plans were coordinated with the plans of the ground force commander in whose sector the assault force operated. The aviation unit commander was in command of the air assault force from the time it loaded on the aircraft to the time of its descent or landing. The regulation also required that air assault forces engage in 'daringly bold' maneuvers to capitalize on the element of surprise and to effect speedy employment and rapid concentration of forces. Because air assault units were equipped with only light weapons, the regulations emphasized the decisive importance of using assault forces *en masse*.

In consonance with the new instructions, exercises involving air assault forces intensified. In September 1933, at Luga in the Leningrad Military District, the 3d Air-Landing Brigade conducted a tactical exercise under Tukhachevsky's supervision. Operating in poor weather (strong winds and low clouds), the paratroopers dropped in a heavily defended enemy rear area to block enemy withdrawal and movement of reserves. The surprise drop, after the lifting of a friendly artillery barrage, succeeded in driving off the enemy, occupying the objective, and repulsing enemy reserves. Tukhachevsky was pleased with the results.[33] In September the following year, near Minsk in the Belorussian Military District, multiple air assaults supported a ground force offensive exercise. On 7 September, a 129-man force participated in a tactical parachute assault to secure a section of highway west of Minsk and a key crossing over the Svisloch River where, in coordination with an advancing motorized regiment, it blocked enemy withdrawal routes from the city. On 9 September near Trostianets, northeast of Minsk, a second and operational-scale assault by 603 men, in close coordination with an advancing mechanized brigade, blocked movement of enemy reserves from Smolevichi into the city. The two airborne operations emphasized coordination between ground and airborne units operating in the enemy rear.[34]

Capitalizing on the success of the 1934 maneuvers, more extensive airborne activity occurred during maneuvers in 1935. Held from 12–15 September 1935 in the Kiev Military District, under the supervision of Army Commander First Rank I. E. Iakir, Kiev Military District Commander, the exercise tested techniques for conducting deep battle. Also watching were such luminaries as K. E. Voroshilov, people's commissar of defense; S. M. Budenny, inspector of Cavalry Forces; Ia. B. Gamarnik, deputy commissar of defense; M. N. Tukhachevsky, deputy commissar of defense; A. I. Egorov, chief of the General Staff. The 8th Rifle Corps, 45th Mechanized Corps, and 9th Cavalry Division participated on the 'Red' side, and the 17th Rifle Corps and 2d Cavalry Corps fought under the 'Blue' banner. Attached to these forces were four T-28 tank battalions, eight T-26 tank battalions, four BT tank battalions, the 137th Artillery Regiment of the High Command Reserve (RGK) and an air assault group consisting of one parachute and two rifle regiments.[35]

The scenario involved the penetration of a strong Blue defense by the Red 17th Rifle Corps reinforced by a tank battalion and RGK [High Command reserve] artillery (see Figures 1 and 2). The 2d Cavalry Corps developed that penetration, and a large airborne assault supported their efforts to encircle and destroy the enemy. An attaché report elaborated on the role of the air-landing:

> On September 14 only small outpost engagements took place along the front line. The serious operations were transferred far into the rear of the Reds. Even early in the morning the airplanes of both sides made reconnaissance raids. At 9 o'clock the Blues landed by air a strong detachment into the rear of the Reds. Part of the personnel were dropped by means of parachutes, while other airplanes landed and after having unloaded a party again rose into the air. The detachment, having landed, attacked the Reds. About noon a hard fight began between this Blue and a strong Red counterattack detachment.
>
> This well-planned and excellently carried out air attack failed,

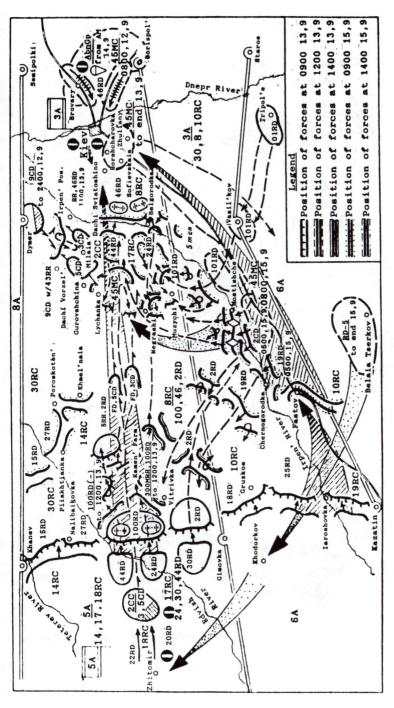

1. The Kiev Maneuvers of 1935: Overview

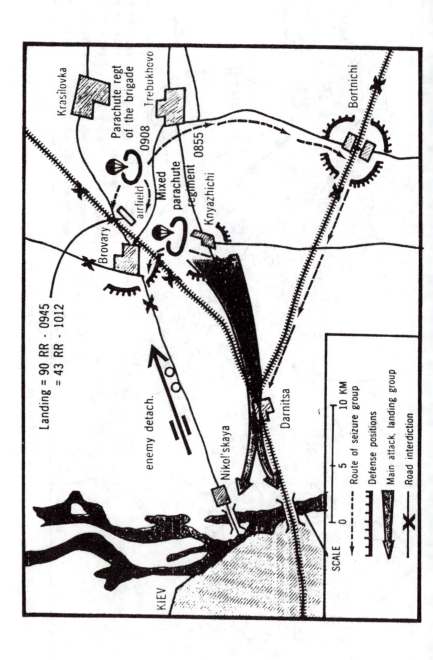

SCALE

0   5   10 KM

Route of seizure group

Defense positions

Main attack, landing group

Road interdiction

Landing = 90 RR - 0945
        = 43 RR - 1012

Krasilovka

Parachute regt
of the brigade
0908

Trebukhovo

Bortnichi

airfield

Mixed
parachute
regiment 0855

Knyazhichi

Brovary

enemy detach.

Nikol'skaya

Darnitsa

KIEV

however, as the Blue detachment was incapable of occupying the selected points of attack, owing to superiority of force of the Red detachment which comprised motorized infantry and cavalry supported by a tank unit and armored trains.[36]

The airborne force of two parachute regiments (1,188 men) and two rifle regiments (1,765 men), under control of a rifle division, had to land at Brovary (northeast of Kiev), secure a landing area and crossings over the Dnepr River, block the approach of enemy reserves from the east, and cooperate with cavalry and rifle corps units attacking Kiev from the west. More than 1,000 troops of the parachute echelon, flying in from bases 280 kilometers away, participated in a simultaneous drop and secured the landing area. Troops of the main force rifle regiments followed and, together with the parachute echelon, strove to accomplish their assigned mission.[37]

Western attachés accorded the exercise considerable attention. The British attaché, Maj. Gen. (later Field Marshal) A. P. Wavell reported:

We were taken to see a force of about 1,500 men dropped by parachute; they were supposed to represent a 'Blue' force dropped to occupy the passages of a river and so delay the advance of the 'Red' Infantry corps which was being brought up for the counter-offensive. This parachute descent, though its tactical value may be doubtful, was a most spectacular performance. We were told that there were no casualties and we certainly saw none; in fact the parachutists we saw in action after the landings were in remarkably good trim and mostly moving at the double. They are, of course, a specially picked force and had had some months training. It apparently took some time to collect the force after the first descent began landing; about one and a half hours after the first descent began a part of the force was still being collected, though the greater part had already been in action for some time. The personal equipment seemed to consist of a rifle or a light automatic with a small supply of ammunition. The less experienced parachutists, we were told, landed without rifles, their rifles being parachuted separately. No mechanical vehicles were landed by plane as was done at Kiev in 1933.[38]

The U.S. attaché in Moscow, Major Philip R. Faymonville, sent several dispatches to Washington detailing the role of Soviet parachute and air-landing forces in the exercise. After sketching out the scenario and course of the 11–15 September maneuvers, he noted:

The most important feature of the maneuvers was undoubtedly the mass parachute jumps executed from bombing planes in the space of three minutes by 500 infantrymen and machine gunners. The mass parachute jump took place at dawn approximately 20 kilometers behind the 'enemy' lines. The parachute jumpers entrenched themselves in a strongpoint and were ready for defense within a very few minutes. Supplies of ammunition were launched from parachutes shortly after the machine gunners jumped.

The defending forces immediately assembled and dispatched to the strongpoint established by the parachutists, a strong detachment of fast tanks (apparently 40 Christies). The tanks, according to the umpires, put out of commission all the machine guns in the strongpoint and completely cleaned the rear areas of hostile parachutists. ...

Under the plan of maneuver, it was the defending side which rushed a force of tanks to the strongpoint and destroyed it. There is reason to believe, however, that under Soviet tactics a strong tank detachment would be combined with the air attack and would attempt a break-through simultaneously with the launching of a mass parachute jump. Deep penetration by such a tank detachment would permit it to arrive at a rendezvous in the enemy's rear areas and act as a security detachment while the strongpoint established by parachute jumpers is being reinforced by additional flights of parachutists.[39]

Faymonville added parenthetically that, 'It seems evident that the tactics of the Red Army seriously contemplates mass parachute jumps combined with deep tank attacks in order to create strongpoints in enemy rear areas.'[40] Faymonville added to the report a copy of a 23 September 1935 official order of the Commissariat of Defense praising participants in the Kiev maneuvers. Among the accolades Voroshilov accorded the troops was the comment, 'I make special mention of the mass aviation landing, which was excellently fulfilled, both organizationally as well as from the technical and tactical standpoint, and the exemplary military operations of the landing units on the ground immediately after the descent.'[41]

In several subsquent reports, Faymonville quoted from French, Czech, and Italian observers at the exercises. General L'Oiseau, Assistant Chief of the French General Staff, had extensive comments published in Pravda. When commenting on the role of Soviet aviation, L'Oiseau stated:

I am full of admiration. During the whole time of maneuvers, aviation forces were working uninterruptedly in great masses, in small groups, and with separate planes. The aid they rendered to the land forces was worthy of great praise. And aviation itself has grown up in your country into a menacing weapon. The parachute descent of a great troop unit which I saw near Kiev, I find a world unprecedented event. This was not only a mass review. The parachutists are qualified, organized, fighters. They conduct combat just a few minutes after their landing! What surprising new arms! I find especially important General Yakir's information that parachute units are formed strictly voluntarily. This provides an excellent morale level for the units. Representatives of the French Aviation Mission, directed by me, received useful lessons from the Kiev maneuvers.[42]

The Czech military mission, headed by General Kreichi, Chief of the Czechoslovakian Army General Staff, spent three days after the Kiev maneuvers at a Red Army glider base in the Crimea. There they observed glider training and took part in a glider assault. Regarding the maneuvers themselves, Kreichi added plaudits similar to those of his French counterpart, writing:

> We are amazed at the multitude of problems which were intended to be solved at these maneuvers. We followed them with great interest and satisfaction. During the maneuvers the newest weapons and the most modern technical materiel were made use of in masses in modern warfare and in a multitude of various situations with the closest cooperation of different arms.
>
> Our attention was especially drawn to the employment of masses of parachutes and to descents from airplanes on so large a scale, as well as to the operative and tactical employment of so large motor-mechanized units.[43]

A 4 October German press notice appended to Faymonville's report added a more sober appreciation of Soviet parachute activity:

> Of all countries Soviet Russia pays the most attention to the landing of troops behind the hostile front. Formerly preference was given to the landing of troops by transport planes and during an exercise a whole infantry battalion with all arms and equipment was carried in 100 transport planes. Recently, however, parachute jumps have been favored. The efforts made by Soviet Russia to train large numbers of parachute jumpers and the propaganda carried on in order to introduce parachute jumping as a popular sport, therefore, deserve serious attention. It should be also noted that Soviet Russia intends to land not only troops but also spies and first of all political propagandists in the hostile rear areas because she hopes that sabotage and subversive propaganda will easily undermine the hostile power of resistance.[44]

Faymonville placed the comments of foreign observers in perspective by adding to his last report the note that, 'The statements by the chiefs of the Czechoslovakian and French military missions to the Kiev maneuvers should not be taken *au pied de la lettre* as they were undoubtedly made in order to persuade their own countrymen that their Red allies could be depended upon.'[45] As a prudent analyst, however, he continued to ferret out information on the operation. His last recorded report on the maneuver, prepared in December, read:

> 1. Further information has just become available with reference to the maneuvers of the air units which participated in the general maneuvers at Kiev on September 14–17, 1935.
> 2. The numbers of parachutists landed behind enemy lines (reported in Report No. 333, Sept. 18, 1935) now appear to have been understated by observers. The Commissar for Defense states that 1,200 parachutists leaped simultaneously at one stage of the maneuvers and that in the course of 40 minutes 2,500 men were landed from airplanes.
> 3. The Commissar has also stated in public that in another Military District, 1,800 parachutists have jumped simultanously and that a force of 5,700 men were landed from airplanes within a brief period of time.
> 4. At the Kiev maneuvers, armored cars and two different types of light tanks were carried by bombers and successfully landed behind enemy lines, moving off under their own power, a few seconds after being released from the racks which secured them to the bombers.
> 5. Complete batteries of artillery were also landed by bombers behind enemy lines.
> 6. Machine guns with disassembled carts and wheels, made up into tarpaulin bundles, cigar-shaped and about ten feet long, were parachuted down from planes in flight.[46]

In the fall of 1936, yet another large exercise in Belorussia validated the results of preceding summer exercises. I. P. Uborevich, the military district commander, supervised the exercise along with Voroshilov, Tukhahchevsky, and Budenny. Combined mechanized, rifle, cavalry, aviation, and airborne forces practiced deep operations and surmounting water obstacles. A combined air assault began with a landing of the 47th Special Purpose Air Assault Brigade; follow-on tanks, artillery, and heavy equipment landed thereafter. From the airborne perspective, maneuver controllers gave a favorable evaluation to key aspects of the operation, namely, preparations for the assault and control of the battle after landing.[47]

Attachés observed and made extensive comment on the 1936 Belorussian maneuvers. In his summary of 1936 exercises, Major G. B. Guenther, U.S. attaché to Riga, reported:

The largest maneuvers of the training season were organized in the White Russian Military District in the vicinity of Minsk from September 8–11. All the troops of the District, i.e. 4 Infantry and one cavalry corps, a motorized division, a great number of mechanized units, air force and air infantry detachments took part in them. The maneuvers were conducted by the Commander of the White Russian Military District, First Category Army Commander, Uborevich; the Commander of the Western side was Army Commander, Apenasenko, and of the Eastern side Army Commander, Kovtyukh. The chief object of the maneuvers was to experiment with the employment of large troop formations supported by ample mechanized units and air force.[48]

Commenting on air-landing activities on the second day of the maneuvers, Guenther added:

The air infantry unit under the command of Brigade Commander Karmelyuk was assigned the mission of preventing the advance and arrival of the reinforcements by occupying the passages across Plitsch River in the rear of the Red defense (about 25 km. behind the front). A Red airdrome occupied by hostile bombers and pursuit planes was designated as the landing place. Observation planes were first detailed to accurately reconnoiter the vicinity of the hostile airdrome, its forces and AA weapons. After a rapid estimate of all the reconnaissance data the first echelon, consisting of several light bomber squadrons, moved out and covered by pursuit squadrons, arrived at the airdrome and dropped bombs. Strong units of attack planes supported the action of bombers by flying low enough to attack the personnel of the airdrome. Nevertheless, the Red pursuit planes succeeded in taking off in a very short time in order to avoid destruction on the ground. They immediately organized and attacked the Blue bombers which were supposed to have suffered serious casualties. A desperate aerial struggle ensued. While both sides were fighting to gain air superiority above the airdrome, the Blue main air force consisting of heavy bombers covered by pursuit planes arrived at the airdrome at 5:00 pm. The landing of 1,200 men, 150 MGs and 18 guns was carried out in 7–8 minutes by means of parachutes at the completion of a flight of 170 km. Immediately after the occupation of the airdrome by parachute troops other squadrons of large transport planes arrived which landed the air infantry on the airdrome.[49]

Guenther also recorded the reactions of some of the observers and the Soviet Commissar of Defense, Voroshilov:

The Chief of the British military delegation is reported to have said: 'One who has not seen it with his own eyes would never regard such an operation as possible.' Voroshilov stated to the foreign delegations: 'A great deal naturally depends on exercises of this type in order to obtain team work in such a remarkable body of men'. The last word has not yet been spoken about air landings but the problem undoubtedly deserves serious consideration.[50]

The subsequent Moscow maneuver of 19–22 September 1936 involved a joint airdrop of a mixed parachute regiment, four non-TOE battalions of the Moscow Military District, and a reserve parachute detachment. To add to the exercise's uniqueness, the Soviets flew the 84th Rifle Division from Tula to an airfield in the Gorki region, which had already been secured by more than 5,000 airborne troops. Guenther, the U.S. military attaché in Riga, commented extensively on the Moscow Military District maneuvers. He recorded in his summary:

> The maneuvers of the Moscow Military District were held in the area Kovrovo – Gorokhovets – Murom – Vyaznikov from September 19–22. In these maneuvers there were two infantry divisions on one side and three on the other. One of the latter divisions was motorized and reinforced by mechanized and air units, and by air infantry.
>
> During the first day and during the approach march great attention was paid to the operation and functioning of the communications and to the proper organization of the signal service.
>
> On the following day the two forces fought a meeting engagement during which two attempts were made at landing air infantry. The first one failed at the very beginning; during the second, 500 men were landed and it was reported that they had a decisive effect upon the later development of the situation.
>
> On the third day the main forces of the combatants met and were engaged in a fight on heavily wooded terrain. The program of the day included the crossing of a river under the protection of smoke screens, and the arrival and employment of a motorized division which arrived from the rear. In connection with the combat a small 'tank force' assisted an infantry unit amply equipped with automatic weapons, to cross difficult terrain which was under heavy hostile fire.
>
> During the last day the chief feature was the fighting by the air units to make it possible to gain air superiority so that 2,000 men could be dropped from airplanes. After the first descent another group of 3,000 men with artillery were dropped. These descents were the decisive operations of the maneuver. The Marshals

Voroshilov, Egorov and Tukhachevski, the Commanders of the Moscow, White Russian, Kharkov and Ural Military Districts and many other high ranking officers were present at these maneuvers.[51]

An enclosure provided a more detailed account of air assault activities. For the first time, the Soviets attempted to use air-landed forces in the critical stage of operations (see Figures 3 and 4). Thus, on the first day, Guenther recorded the following:

First Day (September 20) Both parties thus had the opportunity of making use of the night September 19/20 for extensive reconnaissance activities. Very little information being available of the enemy, the principal mission of all reconnaissance agencies was to determine as soon as possible the hostile organization, location and strength; air reconnaissance was particularly successful on both sides. The Reds intended to gain an advantage over the Blues by attempting to put the Blue observation units out of action by attacking the Blue airdrome, the location of which had become known to the Reds. Soon after the declaration of war Red forces made a raid on the Blue airdrome by landing air infantry. Before the air infantry could initiate any action they were discovered by the Blue troops and repelled.[52]

Later on the first day, a Red motor-mechanized division outflanked a Blue cavalry division and reached a village in the Blue rear area where a major tank battle ensued. The Red advance was facilitated by the landing of 500 Red air-infantry in the rear of the cavalry division.

On the third day of the maneuvers, Red forces employed an even larger air assault force. According to Guenther:

In order to complete the envelopment of the Blues the Red commander decided to employ strong air infantry forces because at this time its metereological service reported that weather conditions were favorable for such an operation. Early in the morning of September 22 the parachute jumper units started toward Gorochowez. At 8:45 a.m. the forward echelon airplanes arrived above Wyjesd Village, the prescribed place of landing. The first person to jump off was the commander of the forward echelon. He dropped a considerable distance before opening his parachute in order to arrive first as a regulating officer and to watch the landing of his unit from the ground. The Blue pursuit planes attempted to interfere with the landing. They made repeated attacks but were repulsed by the Red covering airplanes.

The Red unit of the forward echelon of parachute jumpers landed

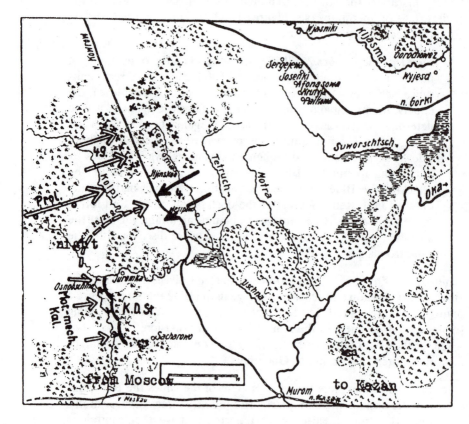

3. The Moscow Maneuvers of 1936: The First Day

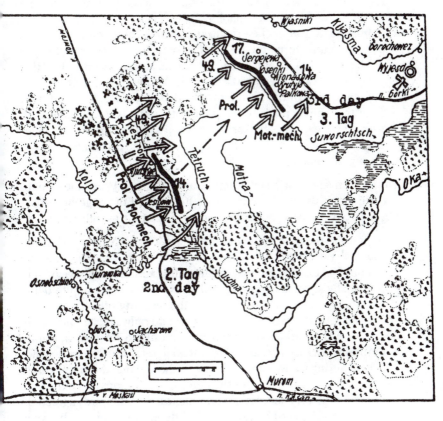

4. The Moscow Maneuvers of 1936: The Second and Third Days

at the prescribed place. They were succeeded by the main body of the parachute jumper unit which were transported in squadrons. Guns and ammunition reached the ground by means of parachutes. After a short time the whole unit with all of its weapons and numbering 2,200 men was at the disposal of its commander for the execution of his combat mission.

Immediately after the organization into a combat formation the parachute unit occupied the fords across Kljasma River in the rear of the Blue forces and prepared for an attack against the Blue positions toward Suworschtsch River. About one hour afterwards the main body of the air infantry landed at a place 40 km. distant from the landing place of the parachute jumpers. Over 3,000 men with their weapons were carried by means of large transport planes over a distance of 420 km. It is reported that no accidents occurred during the landing.[53]

Guenther then commented on Commissar of Defense Voroshilov's published critique of the maneuvers, which highlighted the ongoing debate within the Red Army over the role and utility of air assault forces:

Following the fall maneuver in the Moscow Military District, Marshal Voroshilov conducted a critique in which he said that the military district maneuvers, training and exercises of the year were principally devoted to problems of transportation. He admitted that the results were not satisfactory in the majority of cases.

Criticizing the extremely poor roads and railways, he said that in case of war aviation would have to be utilized for transportation purposes to a much greater extent than heretofore. The experience gained during the Moscow maneuvers showed that the employment of large transport planes for the movement of troops and parachute jumpers was very successful and practical. The umpires agreed on this point. There was, however, a difference of opinion between Marshal Egorov and Marshal Tukhachevski. The former has only advocated the employment of large transport planes and recommended the use of parachute jumper units for reconnaissance and demolition purposes. Marshal Tukhachevski has been for two years of the opinion that the parachute jumper units could also be employed as an efficient fighting force.

The Moscow maneuvers were so planned as to demonstrate a mass employment of parachute troops as a fighting force and during envelopment operations. Voroshilov and all umpires believed that the landing of 500 men in the rear of the Stalin Cavalry Division and the landing of over 2,000 parachute jumpers near Wyjesd were decisive operations and highly successful. He admitted this and sided with Tukhachevski. In view of this statement it is likely that this branch of combat training will receive particular attention in the future.

Voroshilov emphasized the necessity of having a large Air Force which could not only be employed for landing troops in the hostile rear but which could also be employed for the rapid transportation of reinforcements to check a hostile breakthrough. He believed that serious breakthroughs similar to those which repeatedly happened during the World War would in the future be rendered less effective. The difficulties presented by the obstacle zones created many problems for the motor-mechanized troops, but Voroshilov stated that every attempt will be made to motorize the major portion of the Army.[54]

Guenther noted Voroshilov's estimate that the Red Army then possessed over 15,000 well-trained parachute jumpers and that a doubling of that number was planned for 1937. Guenther's report on the 1936 maneuvers, as a whole, ended with the following judgement:

It is noteworthy that in the maneuvers of the Red Army, motor-mechanized units and air infantry were employed on a large scale. With respect to the landing of large bodies of troops by means of parachutes and transport planes it is doubtful whether such operations can be carried out in actual warfare with terrain conditions which prevail in Central or Western European countries. Germany has an excellent network of hard surfaced roads, a dense population and a well organized air intelligence service. It will very likely be possible to land small parties of men to destroy installations or to carry out demolition work at critical points but it is the opinion of the undersigned that the attempt to land whole battalions or regiments in a country like Germany would result in such heavy casualties that this method of conducting operations and moving troops would have to be abandoned. Articles expressing a similar opinion have appeared in the German military press but it is interesting to note that the Western Allies of Soviet Russia, France and Czechoslovakia, are experimenting along the same lines. So far there is no detailed information about the results attained by these countries. Of course, terrain conditions in Soviet Russia are favorable for the landing of large units of air infantry. The Soviets emphasize an aggressive war doctrine and only a war can show to what an extent the landing of troops from the air can be utilized.[55]

Other exercises conducted during 1936 focused on questions of unit organization and tactical employment after landing.[56]

Prompted by the extensive use of parachute forces in the 1936 maneuvers, in late 1936 U.S. attachés dispatched an increasing number of assessments to Washington analyzing what they had seen. In late September attaché Faymonville wrote a memorandum concerning the tactics of mass parachute descents based on what he had read in Soviet journals and what maneuver observers had seen. In part, the memorandum stated:

2. It is evident that the present expectations envisage the launching of groups of jumpers numbering several thousand at points deep in the enemy rear areas. During recent maneuvers in various military districts parachute jumpers have been landed as much as 430 kilometers behind the assumed enemy lines.

3. In the case of the maneuvers within the Moscow Military District 2,200 parachutists were landed within a half hour and these were followed within 15 minutes by a reinforcing group of 3,000 infantrymen, machine gunners, and artillerymen landed from planes.

4. Soviet commanders evidently believe that the proper time to effect mass parachute jumps is just after sunset. The place of landing is selected after intensive air reconnaissance. The first aim of the parachutists is to take possession of telegraph and telephone stations, or when unsuccessful to destroy all communications lines and isolate the region in which the descent has taken place.

5. Before complete darkness sets in an appropriate rallying point is selected which can be strengthened by field fortifications during the night. This rallying point serves as a base to which ammunition, supplies, and reinforcing personnel are parachuted down as soon as the first light of dawn permits the approach of planes.

6. As soon as practicable the invading force is reinforced by light tanks and trucks landed from airplanes (this operation was actually carried out successfully at the Kiev maneuvers of 1935). Having built up a small moto-mechanized force the invaders thence proceed to raid enemy communications, to seize strongpoints which can be defended with small detachments and to enlarge the area of occupation.

7. Meanwhile the advancing daylight hours permit a continuous procession of planes to land reinforcements by parachuting, or, when the area has been enlarged to include suitable landing fields, to land reinforcements direct from bombers and transport planes. In theory, hostile aviation has been swept aside by swarms of powerful fighting planes.

8. Many possible defense measures which could be taken to offset the effectiveness of parachute invasions at once come to mind.

There is little probability that parachute operations could ever be undertaken in warfare under the ideal conditions which surround them during maneuvers, but at least the following facts which have been actually demonstrated by performance indicate that parachute descents may prove to be an effective means of interrupting at least temporarily the enemy's communication systems and of spreading confusion in his rear areas:

a. Over 2,000 parachutists have been landed in the course of half an hour at a point more than 400 kilometers from the take-off.

b. A ring of field fortifications has been constructed by parachutists using tools carried during parachute descent within a half hour of the landing.

c. Machine guns, complete with ammunition, have been ready for action three minutes after the descent. Wrecking parties have succeeded in destroying all wire communications within a radius of five miles in a half hour.

d. All important bridges and culverts in the vicinity have been theoretically destroyed by demolition squads within a half hour of the descent.[57]

At the same time, Guenther in Riga forwarded to Washington a detailed German technical report on the state and implications of Soviet parachute technology and air assault training together with a French assessment that 100,000 parachute jumpers would be available to the Soviet government by the end of 1937, which 'will be organized into military units and will be under army control.'[58]

Experiences of the 1937 maneuvers did not allay the attachés' fears. The largest of these maneuvers occurred in September, near Vitebsk, in the Belorussian Military District. At the invitation of Assistant People's Commissar of Defense, Marshal Egorov, military delegations from Latvia, Lithuania, and Estonia attended and afterwards prepared extensive reports, which they shared with U.S. attachés. The maneuver, which included two rifle corps each reinforced by special troops and tank brigades, concentrated on the themes of extended marches, meeting engagements, and tactical combat across an extended front. Regarding parachute operations, Faymonville noted:

8. Large numbers of parachutists participated in the maneuvers. This feature is now expected as part of any large-scale operations of the Red Army.

9. In the past, parachute operations have in general been landings deep in the enemy rear with a professed object of seizing and holding points as much as 300 kilometers behind the enemy lines. During the past year, articles in the Soviet press have discussed the

possibility of parachute descents in the immediate rear of the enemy army with a view to supporting a break-through. Both the deep attack and the near supporting attack by parachutists were attempted at the Vitebsk maneuvers. The most spectacular appears to have been that of 1,200 infantrymen, mostly machine-gunners, who landed about 10 kilometers behind the enemy front lines in order to support a break-through of approximately 400 tanks. Although observers judged the descent to have been impracticable, it is probable that the possibilities of parachute descents in support of major attacks will be further explored by the Red Army. In any case, parachute attacks deep in the enemy rear areas seem to be held practicable by Red Army authorities.[59]

Exercises conducted from 1934 to 1937 confirmed both the utility of air assault forces and the doctrinal concepts for their use. As expected, the exercises surfaced many problem areas that future practice would have to address, such as tactics for operating in the enemy rear area, waging battle while encircled, and escaping from encirclement. Only superior tactics and timely employment of such forces could compensate for the inherent weakness of the forces' light infantry weaponry. Exercises conducted before 1938 did not exploit the possibilities of close co-operation between airborne troops and diversionary forces, and, although there were some spectacular long-distance drops, most of the operations extended to relatively limited depths in the enemy defense. Equipment problems still hindered air assault operations, and a larger, more versatile fleet of aircraft was essential if larger air assault forces were to conduct deeper operations. Soviet military theorists directly confronted these problems in a detailed 1937 report, 'The Course of Preparing Parachute Landing forces,' which focused on equipment deficiencies and their remedies.[60]

While the Soviets validated their airborne techniques in these and other exercises, theoretical work continued. Exercises and maneuvers, in turn, permitted more complete articulation of the theory of deep battle. In March 1935, the Red Army issued its 'Instructions on Deep Battle,' which more clearly defined the concept:

> Deep battle is battle involving massive use of new mobile and shock means for a simultaneous attack on the enemy to the entire depth of his combat formation with the aim of fully encircling and destroying him...The new means and tactics of deep battle increase the importance of surprise.[61]

One of the new shock means was the fledgling air assault force.

The 1936 Field Regulation represented the epitome of Soviet pre-

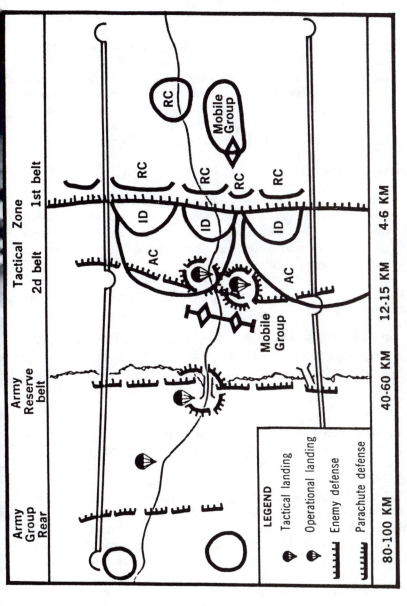

5. Use of Airborne Forces on the Offensive, 1936

Second World War doctrinal development (see Figure 5). It expanded upon the tactical concept of deep battle contained in the 1935 'Instructions' and broadened it into the operational concept of deep operations [*glubokaia operatsiia*], which it defined as:

> the simultaneous assault on enemy defenses by aviation and artillery to the depth of the defense, penetration of the tactical zone of the defense by attacking units with wide use of tank forces, and violent development of tactical success into operational success with the aim of complete encirclement and destruction of the enemy. The main role is performed by the infantry, and in its interests are organized the mutual support of all types of forces....[62]

This was possible because:

> Present day destructive agents, principally tanks, artillery, aircraft, and mechanized [air] landing parties, when employed in masses render it possible to attack the enemy simultaneously throughout the entire depth of his combat zone with the object of isolating, encircling, and destroying him....[63]

Article 7 of the Field Regulation specifically outlined the role of air assault forces:

> Parachute landing units are the effective means... disorganizing the command and rear services structure of the enemy. In coordination with forces attacking along the front, parachute landing units can go a long way toward producing a complete rout of the enemy on a given axis.[64]

Thus, while success in deep battle relied primarily on mechanized and tank forces, the air assault arm played a considerable supporting role.

Soviet theorists, writing in military journals, also pondered the role and significance of air assault forces in contemporary battle. A.Vol'pe, in a 1937 article in the General Staff journal, *Military thought [Voennaia mysl']*, described the potential contribution of an air assault force in achieving surprise in war. Within the context of the increasingly important role aviation could play in contemporary combat, Vol'pe emphasized the beneficial role airborne forces could perform:

> In its highest form independent action of air forces is manifested in the operations of air assault units. There, where today one can succeed in landing a combined assault (parachute and landing) in division strength, tomorrow one can land a corps. Therefore the

new French Field Service Regulation of 1936, which focuses on the close conditions of the Western European Theater of War, had to foresee the possibility for the active use of air assaults and measures to combat them.[65]

A year later A. Ia. Ianovsky wrote on the same subject in the same journal. Regarding air assaults, he first stressed the utility of such operations:

> If in former wars one could land forces in the enemy rear only with the help of the fleet, then today they can be landed with the help of aviation. In doing so, air forces evidence a whole range of advantages over naval forces. The navy is limited to sea coasts and, it follows, is also limited in the selection of objectives for its actions. An air assault has no such limits, as it can be landed at any time in the enemy rear to attack any objective.[66]

Ianovsky identified four types of air assault, distinguished from one another by assault means – landing assault, parachute assault, thrown out (non-parachute), and mixed. The landing assault involved the delivery of combat troops and equipment by aircraft landing in the enemy rear. This type of assault could land larger forces than could be inserted by other means, and forces so landed could carry with them heavier weaponry, such as heavy machine guns, light field guns, antitank weapons, mortars, tankettes, and light tanks. A major problem associated with such a landing was the necessity for identifying and securing a large enough and well enough prepared landing site.

Assault by parachute, involving personnel and cargo chutes, could deliver some heavier weapons as well but suffered from the problems of dispersion during the drop and the necessity of the force fighting its way back through enemy lines once it had achieved its objectives. Non-parachute air assaults (literally thrown out) were effected by 'special carts with shock absorbers on their wheels (in winter, on skis).'[67] The carts were carried under an aircraft fuselage and dropped by mechanized means from a height of two to three meters. Troops could also be landed from gliders, towed behind light aircraft. One must assume certain technical problems and risks associated with this means of delivery. The fourth and last technique for air assault was the mixed *desant*, which usually involved an initial parachute drop to secure landing areas and subsequent aircraft landing of troops on the secured airstrip.

Ianovsky also categorized air assault operations by their scope and objective. Tactical assaults, usually by parachute into the immediate enemy rear area, were integrated closely with ground operations and required quick link-up between the two forces. Operational assaults into the deep enemy rear sought to 'demoralize the enemy rear and seize railroad bridges, etc.' Recognizing that 'an air assault is a difficult operation,' Ianovsky stressed the necessity for detailed and thorough planning and preparation of the force to accomplish such a mission. In particular, it required expert advanced reconnaissance of the landing area and suppression of enemy aircraft and anti-aircraft weaponry before and during the operation.[68] Reconnaissance was best conducted by parachute landed detachments, and strong air force cover was necessary throughout the operation.

The air assault itself, according to Ianovsky, would take place in four stages: preparation; flight and actual landing; operations of the assault force in the enemy rear area; and return flight of the force or penetration of enemy lines for link-up with main forces. The force to perform such a complex mission had to consist of dedicated air transports, fighter aviation for defensive cover, and a *desant* assault detachment, if possible under unified command. Selection of the proper size unit to perform the mission was particularly challenging in light of the paucity of actual combat experiences. To maintain maximum secrecy and security, Ianovsky recommended the flight to the landing area be made at night, and the actual landing occur at first light. He identified fog as the worst enemy of an air assault.[69]

By virtue of this theoretical work, by 1938 the missions of air assault forces were well defined. Based on mission, force composition, and depth of operations, air assaults could be operational or tactical. Operational assaults embraced both parachute and air-landed forces, attacking deep in the enemy rear. Cooperating with main forces, usually deep-operating mechanized forces, assault forces played a critical role in fulfilling operational objectives. Usually whole formations [*soedineniia*] of ground forces made up the assault force.

Tactical air assaults usually comprised parachute forces from platoon to regiment strength, equipped with light weaponry, operating in the shallow enemy rear area in close cooperation with frontal ground forces.

Prewar Soviet field service regulations (in particular, those of 1941) assigned air assault forces the following missions:

1. Disruption of enemy command and control and rear area work by striking staff organs;
2. Destruction of means of communications and blocking the approaches to the front of enemy forces, ammunition, and supplies;
3. Seizure and destruction of enemy airdromes and air bases;
4. Securing of regions to facilitate the landing of an air assault;
5. Strengthening of encircled forces or mobile formations, fulfilling missions in the enemy's operational depth;

6. Combat with enemy air assault forces.[70]

Soviet theorists were well aware of the problems associated with air assault. For example, a 1938 article from *Military Thought* emphasized the importance of reconnaissance if air assaults were to succeed, stating:

> Landing troops from planes is the chief method of transferring military activities to the other side of a fortified border. It is not without reason that all countries, without exception, are devoting special attention to aerial descents of troops. But such operations cannot count upon success without careful preparations, which in modern war is not to be thought of without a photographic map of the area of the descent and the area of action. In selecting from the map suitable areas for the descent, reconnaissance aviation must look for the following: (1) areas upon which may be landed transport planes of a special type, or suitable for landing descent groups by parachute; (2) the distance from these areas of enemy units which may oppose resistance to the landing, their composition and strength; (3) commanding points in the surrounding terrain suitable for detachments covering the landing; (4) cover which will be suitable for concentrating the landing groups to protect them from aerial attack; (5) condition of the roads from the landing points to the objectives. Besides this, there should be exhaustive information of the objectives themselves with regard to their defense capacity, the approaches to them, etc.[71]

With airborne forces accepted as a full participant in deep battle, the airborne force structure continued to become more sophisticated and to grow in size. In 1936, two new airborne brigades (aviation landing and special purpose) were organized on the basis of existing TOE and non-TOE units in the Belorussian and Kiev military districts, thus raising the number of brigades to three (see Figure 6). To augment airborne forces in the increasingly dangerous climate of the Far East, the *Revoensovet* created three airborne regiments from existing smaller units (see Figure 7). As part of the 1936 force expansion, one separate special purpose battalion was formed in each of the Moscow, Volga, and Trans-Baikal military districts, and three non-TOE parachute regiments of 1,660 men each were organized in the Moscow Military District.[72]

As the overall Soviet force structure expanded significantly in the late 1930s, so did the airborne structure. In 1938, existing aviation landing units were transformed into six airborne brigades of 3,000 men each. A year later, three new special aviation landing regiments were created in the Moscow Military District. These 1938–39 units were organized on a uniform TOE (see Figure 8).[73]

FIGURE 6.   AIRBORNE BRIGADES, 1936

Unit	Commander	Location
3d Abn Bde	I. S. Kokhansky	Leningrad MD
13th Abn Bde	A. O. Indzer	Kiev MD
47th Abn Bde	A. F. Levashov	Belorussian MD

Source: Sukhorukov, *Sovetskie vozdushno*, 35.

FIGURE 7.   AIRBORNE REGIMENTS, 1936

Unit	Commander	Location
1st Abn Regt	M. I. Denisenko	Far East
2d Abn Regt	I. I. Zatevakhin	Far East
5th Abn Regt	N. E. Tarasov	Far East

Source: Sukhorukov, *Sovetskie vozdushno*, 35.

FIGURE 8.   AIRBORNE FORCES, 1939

Unit	Commander	Location
201st Abn Bde	Col. I. S. Bezugly	Leningrad MD
202d Abn Bde	Maj. M. I. Denisenko	Far East
204th Abn Bde	Maj. I. I. Gudarevich	Kiev MD
211th Abn Bde	Maj. V. A. Glazunov	Kiev MD
212th Abn Bde	Maj. I. I. Zatevakhin	Far East (later in the Odessa MD)
214th Abn Bde	Col. A. F. Levashov	Belorussian MD
1st Rostov Regt		
2d Gorokhovets Regt		
3d Voronezh Regt		

Source: Sukhorukov, *Sovetskie vozdushno*, 36.

Little information exists about the precise impact of the military purges of the late 1930s on the airborne forces. It is reasonable to assume that the execution during the purges of the leading theorists of deep battle and the generation of military leaders who had created the concept and form of airborne and mechanized warfare crippled further improvement of doctrine and imaginative work in perfecting airborne tactics. Airborne units, however, continued to expand in size and number, and doctrine for their use reflected the pattern established in the Field Regulation of 1936. As late as January 1941, Lt. Gen. A. Eremenko described a controversial military council meeting in Moscow during which the air force commander, Lt. Gen. Pavel Rychagov, discussed the use of airborne forces.[74] At the same meeting, however, the debate over the use of mechanized forces to effect deep battle reflected the shift of the pendulum away from the dynamic views of Tukhachevsky and toward the views of the less imaginative or the views of those for whom the Spanish Civil War experience had raised doubts about prospects for wartime success using large mechanized forces. The partial eclipse of men who advocated the creation of a force envisioned by the earlier planners of deep battle had to affect adversely further improvement of airborne doctrine and refinement of airborne techniques. The airborne forces grew, and the Field Regulations of 1940 and 1941 parroted the ideas of the 1936 Field Regulations, but the vigor of thought and performance waned. Only future years of struggle would revive that vigor.

The Soviets were pioneers in the development of airborne forces during the interwar years. Although other nations gave thought to such forces, only the Germans came close to matching Soviet achievements in the field. Italy conducted early experiments in the late 1920s and, in 1928, formed a company of trained parachutists before its interest waned. The British took note of Soviet experiences in the 1933 and 1936 maneuvers, but concern over the light nature of airborne forces and an absence of lift aircraft thwarted British development of airborne units. In essence, the primarily defensive concerns of Great Britain argued against the development of an offensive airborne force. French experimentation was limited to the creation in 1938 of two airborne companies, but even this small force was disbanded after war began. Similarly, no serious airborne experimentation occurred in the United States before 1940.[75] Only the use of a German airborne force on Crete in May 1941 prompted Great Britain and the United States to create their own airborne units.

The Germans, however, more concerned with offensive theory, accepted the potential value of airborne units and, in the 1930s, began building an airborne force. Airborne forces, in German eyes, 'offered great possibilities for surprise attack, which was something occupying the minds of the German Army planners, and it looked to be a suitable way of speeding up the armored thrust of the Blitzkrieg.'[76] Formation of a German airborne force began in secret in 1938. Maj. Gen. Kurt Student formed the first airborne division (7th Air Division), which consisted of a mixture of parachute battalions and airlanding battalions with integrated air units. Yet, by 1940, the German airborne force was still limited to a single division.

Thus, the Soviets and Germans alike accepted the validity of airborne concepts. Although both nations formed airborne units, the scale was far greater in the Soviet Union. The ensuing war would test the effectiveness of that large force.

During the crisis-ridden years of 1938–41 the Red Army continued to grow and played an increasing role in the prewar incidents that would forecast the coming of more difficult times. The airborne force grew apace with the army and gained combat experience in those crises. When tension rose in the Soviet Far East between the Soviet Union and Japan and finally erupted in the major battle at Khalkhin-Gol in July and August 1939, Soviet airborne forces were sucked into the conflict. Dispatched from the Far East into eastern Mongolia, Col. I. I. Zatevakhin's 212th Airborne Brigade, participating in a ground role as part of Army Group Commander G. K. Zhukov's force, earned fame in the assaults on Mount Fui that smashed the Japanese right flank.[77] During the Soviet – Finnish War in the winter of 1939–40, which began with a series of striking Soviet failures, airborne forces again participated as infantry, performing diversionary missions while operating with motorized rifle forces. The 201st Airborne Brigade operated with the 15th Army, and the 204th Airborne Brigade was in 15th Army reserve until committed to combat in the final stages of the conflict.

The first use of airborne forces in their proper role occurred during the Soviet occupation of Rumanian Bessarabia in June 1940. The Bessarabian operation called for rapid advance by tank and cavalry forces, followed by rifle units to seize and annex the territory from a recalcitrant Rumanian government. Airborne forces had the missions of capturing important positions to cut the lines of withdrawal of advancing Soviet mobile forces. Moreover, airborne forces would prevent retreating Rumanian forces from destroying property and supplies and would secure the key cities of Bolgrad and Izmail. The planned operation commenced with a ground force advance on 28 June. While ground operations proceeded, the 201st, 204th, and 214th Airborne brigades, under control of the air force commander, moved by rail to airfields 350 kilometers from their drop zone. There they joined the four heavy bomber regiments (comprising 170 TB-3 aircraft) that would convey them to their drop areas. On 29 June, the 204th Airborne Brigade dropped 12 kilometers north of Bolgrad, advanced to the city, and occupied it that evening. The following day, the 1st Battalion, 204th Airborne Brigade, secured the city of Kagul at the mouth of the Danube River. That same day, the 201st Airborne Brigade received orders to airland at Izmail and secure both that city and the vital road network passing through it. Because an air reconnaissance had confirmed the inadequacy of the airfields to accommodate so large a force, the brigade landed instead by parachute in the Izmail area. By the evening of 30 June, against no opposition, the brigade occupied the city.[78] The Bessarabian operation was unopposed and was a more realistic repeat of the many exercises Soviet airborne forces had engaged in during the previous years.

Soviet experiences with air assault during the Finnish War were less than satisfactory. Accordingly, Soviet writers avoid any mention of them. Finnish reports passed to U.S. intelligence provide a sketchy picture of Soviet air assaults, most of which were apparently of a small-scale or diversionary nature. Prisoner-of-war reports confirmed the brigade organization of Soviet air assault forces. Each brigade had two parachute-rifle battalions and a headquarters company. Battalions, in turn, consisted of two companies, a reconnaissance and sapper platoon, and an artillery battery for a strength of about 500 men. According to these reports, Soviet personnel wore air force uniform without flyers' insignia and were, for the most part, Komsomol members.[79] Parachutists jumped from TB-3 bombers in groups of up to 15 men. When operating in the Finnish rear area, personnel wore uniforms similar to the Finns'. Air assault forces were equipped with carbines, machine pistols, rifles, and rifle grenades. Some carried explosives, and most had skis.

Although Finnish authorities were uncertain of the air assault forces' missions, some groups probably engaged in reconnaissance, and others sought to destroy facilities in the Finnish rear. Most experienced distinct lack of success. Of the two known groups, one was 'annihilated when it attempted to retire across the ice and the other at an earlier stage.' None of the troops apparently spoke Finnish. Finnish reports ended with the admission that:

> The men were apparently selected from members of the Komsomol or Communist Party. Some of them displayed, even singly, an extraordinary stubbornness in attempting to reach important military objectives. Therefore it is of importance that friendly posts should be vigilant both in the theater of operations and in the home area.[80]

In the wake of Soviet military confrontations during 1939 and 1940 and in light of the generally poor performance of the Red Army, in particular in Finland, a major reappraisal began. The program was overseen by S. K. Timoshenko, the new commissar of defense; and it directly affected airborne forces because new regulations had appeared, and the airborne corps had undergone a major expansion. Regulations published in 1940 and 1941 redefined and enlarged the role of airborne forces in offensive operations. Article 28 of the 1941 Field Regulation specified the role of airborne forces:

> Air assault forces are an instrument of higher command. They are

used to decide those missions in the enemy rear area which within a specified period cannot be satisfied by other types of forces, but the decision of which can have a serious impact on the outcome of the entire operation (battle). Air assault forces must be used as a surprise for the enemy, in large masses, independent or in coordination with land, air and sea forces....[81]

Additional instructions and regulations governing all aspects of the wartime use of airborne forces appeared. Taken together, these documents accorded the airborne forces a list of specific missions: disruption of army command and control and supply functions; destruction of communications routes; interruption of enemy troop, arms, and supply movements; capture and destruction of airfields and bases; seizure of coastal areas in support of naval landings; reinforcement of troops in encirclement and of mobile units operating in the enemy rear; and fighting against enemy airborne landings in one's own rear area, among others. The Soviet High Command would invoke these regulations when it called upon Soviet airborne forces to perform these types of missions within the next two years.

The performance of the German Army in Poland and France in 1939 and 1940 did not go unnoticed by Soviet observers. Col. A. I. Starunin, writing in *Military Thought*, assessed German success with surprise and concluded that the air assaults played a considerable role. While 'the actions of German aviation and motor-mechanized forces against the Polish Army were one of the characteristic features of surprise' in the case of Belgium and Holland, so were 'the massive strikes of aviation on enemy airfields and the landing of large air assaults.' Starunin then described the basic air assault missions: 'The air assault has the missions of securing airdromes, destroying lines of communications, various structures on the roads, attacking transports, and seizing and holding important objectives (Rotterdam airfield, the rail bridge across the Maas River, etc.).'[82] In combination with deep operating aviation and mobile units, air assaults secured the initiative for the Germans and earned them rapid and decisive victory in the initial period of war.

Col. A. Kononenko, in the same month in *Military-historical Journal*, described the German operation in France in detail. He noted that the German Army, 'having used the factor of surprise, developed the blow by massive aviation strikes on enemy airfields and by organizing penetrations of the fortified lines by tank divisions and by parachutist landings in the rear of Allied forces.' The Germans supplemented air and ground operations with large-scale air assault operations in both Holland and Belgium. Specifically, 'to secure "fortress Holland" in the rear of the Dutch Army, the parachute assault divisions of General Student and the air transport division of General Eponek were landed.' Kononenko remarked that while some assaults suffered 'substantial casualties, nevertheless they played a large role in disorganizing enemy opposition.'[83] The assessments of Starunin, Kononenko, and others convinced the Soviet command that its earlier commitment to deep operations was correct, prompted re-creation of large mechanized units, and produced a wholesale expansion of the airborne force structure.

In December 1940 Timoshenko surveyed the panoply of 1939–40 combat experiences of both the Soviets and Germany and concluded, 'The experience of the recent wars of 1939–40 show that great shifts have occurred in the realm of military art caused by the use of new and improved earlier known combat means of armed struggle.' Specifically, Timoshenko declared:

> First of all, it is important to note that the massive use of such means as tanks and bombers, in combination with motorized and motorcycle forces, and in cooperation with parachute and airlanded assaults and massive aviation, secures in spite of other reasons, high tempo and the strength of a contemporary operational offensive.[84]

Timoshenko noted that German forces operating in the West used air assault forces to fill the critical gap between aviation attacks and the approach of fast mobile ground units. Thus, while of limited use in a penetration of heavy defenses, airborne forces could play a significant role in deep mobile operations (see Figure 9). Timoshenko concluded by stating: 'Air assaults in recent wars in the West played a positive role. Being well-prepared not only to jump from aircraft, but also independent combat action, these forces can disorganize the enemy by their appearance on the ground and by energetic operations.' Thus: 'In the combat training of air assault units and formations we have to concern ourselves with the demands of contemporary battle. We must train ourselves in what is practical to fulfill in combat in the enemy rear area.' Ominously, he warned: 'In this question we must make great progress beyond the West, for the experience of air assaults the Germans first borrowed from us.'[85]

As dark clouds of war descended over Europe, the Soviet Union heeded Timoshenko's words and the evidence provided by German combat experiences as it rushed to put its forces on a wartime footing. Large and cumbersome mechanized units reappeared (at least on paper), and airborne forces underwent massive expansion. In the first step toward expansion in November 1940, Timoshenko approved a new airborne brigade organization. The new brigade contained parachute, glider, and airlanded groups, as well as a brigade school to teach combat personnel airborne techniques. The refurbished brigades numbered

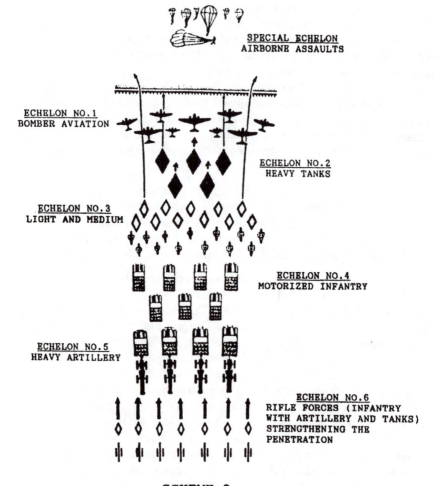

SPECIAL ECHELON
AIRBORNE ASSAULTS

ECHELON NO.1
BOMBER AVIATION

ECHELON NO.2
HEAVY TANKS

ECHELON NO.3
LIGHT AND MEDIUM

ECHELON NO.4
MOTORIZED INFANTRY

ECHELON NO.5
HEAVY ARTILLERY

ECHELON NO.6
RIFLE FORCES (INFANTRY
WITH ARTILLERY AND TANKS)
STRENGTHENING THE
PENETRATION

SCHEME 8

FORMATION OF A MOBILE SHOCK GROUP OF FORCES
FOR THE PENETRATION

(ONE OF THE POSSIBLE VARIANTS)

9. Airborne Force Employment, 1940

3,000 personnel and had 67 motorcycles; 54 bicycles; and improved artillery, antitank, and antiaircraft capabilities (see Figure 10).[86]

Western intelligence reports confirmed the growth in the airborne force structure, but conflicted with Soviet accounts regarding unit locations. A December 1940 U.S. attaché report from Helsinki, quoting 'reliable' German sources, gave the locations for airborne brigades and regiments (each brigade was said to consist of two regiments as listed in Figure 11). [87]

Although the airborne brigade structure was strengthened, the total number of brigades remained at six. The 201st, 204th, and 214th Airborne brigades were stationed in European Russia and the 202d, 211th, and 212th in the Far East. In 1940, the 211th and 212th brigades moved to the Ukraine. The 202d Airborne brigade remained at Khabarovsk until

FIGURE 10. AIRBORNE BRIGADE, 1940

Airborne Brigade – Parachute Group
    2 parachute battalions (546 men each)
     3 parachute rifle companies (141 men each)
     1 mortar platoon (50-mm mortars)
     1 control squad (12 men)
     1 signal platoon
     1 reconnaissance platoon (37 men)
     1 sapper demolition platoon
     1 combat rations and supply platoon
     1 medical squad
    1 motorcycle-bicycle reconnaissance company
    1 signal company

    Glider Group – same as parachute group

    Airlanded Group – same as parachute group plus:
    1 mortar company (9×82-mm)
    1 air defense company (12× heavy antiaircraft machine guns)
    1 tank company (11×T40 or T38)
    1 artillery battalion
     1 artillery battery (4×45-mm)
     1 artillery battery (4×76-mm)

Strength – 3,000 men
  11 tanks
  4 guns (over 50-mm)

Source: Lisov, *Desantniki*, 37–8.

March 1944, when it moved to Moscow.[88] Further expansion of the airborne force occurred in March and April 1941, when the Soviets formed five airborne corps around the nucleus of the existing 201st, 204th, 211th, 212th, and 214th Airborne Brigades. Each airborne corps had about 10,000 men and a significant number of supporting weapons organized into three airborne brigades, a separate tank battalion, and control and logistical support elements (see Figure 12).[89] The new corps

(1st through 5th) were positioned in the Pre-Baltic Special (5th), Western Special (4th), Kiev Special (1st), Kharkov (2d), and Odessa (3d) military districts (see Figure 13[90]). All were at full personnel strength by June 1941; however, equipment stocks were incomplete, especially critical light tanks and radios.

German intelligence estimates prepared in anticipation of Operation Barbarossa had only an imperfect picture of Soviet air assault force

FIGURE 11.   INTELLIGENCE ASSESSMENT OF LOCATION OF SOVIET AIRBORNE FORCES, DECEMBER 1940

Unit	Location	Military District
Unknown Regiment	Dvinsk	Baltic
Unknown Regiment	Siauliai	Baltic
3d Regiment	Pushkino	Leningrad
Unknown Regiment	Baranovichi	Belorussian
7th Regiment	Kishinev	Kiev
1st Regiment	Monino	Moscow
2d Regiment	Navtlug	Transcaucasian
212th Brigade	Kuibyshev	Siberian
208th Brigade	Chita	Trans-Baikal
Unknown Brigade	Guron	Trans-Baikal
211th Brigade	Muchnaia	1st Sep. Far Eastern Army
202d Brigade	Khabarovsk	2d Sep. Far Eastern Army

strength and dispositions. A 15 January 1941 assessment of Soviet forces made no mention of the airborne brigades or corps. A subsequent report date 11 June 1941 noted the existence of seven parachute brigades based on information obtained from agents and radio intercepts. The Germans assumed all seven brigades could operate in the Western Theater. Of these, three parachute-rifle regiments threatened Army Group Center. German reports concluded that, 'Having paid attention to the success of German parachute forces, the Russians are also devoting considerable attention to the preparation of their parachute units. These Russian forces, to all appearances, have a battalion organization.'[91]

To further increase the stature of airborne forces and make them more responsive to the High Command, the Ministry of Defense, in June 1941, established a special airborne [*VDV – Vozdushno desantnye voiska* (airborne forces)] administration, thus taking airborne forces away from the control of the Red Army air force.[92] On the eve of war, the Soviet airborne force appeared formidable: five airborne corps, one airborne brigade, and smaller airborne units with a growing administrative staff totaling about 100,000 men. The Field Regulations expressed well-developed theory, and numerous exercises tested it. Thus, guidance existed for the operations of this force. Yet, in spite of the numbers and sophisticated theoretical employment concepts, severe shortages of organizational equipment hindered prospective combat employment of the force. Airborne forces lacked tanks heavy enough to withstand modern antitank and artillery fire; vehicles; radios for command and control; and aircraft to transport the units, particularly aircraft modified for carrying paratroopers.[93] Work to build new aircraft progressed, but total war would intervene before it was completed.

Beyond the equipment shortages loomed the question of leadership, especially at the higher levels. The purges had eliminated from the High

FIGURE 12.   AIRBORNE CORPS, 1941

Airborne Corps – 3 airborne brigades
          4 parachute battalions (458 men each)
             3 parachute rifle companies (24 flamethrowers)
             brigade artillery (6×76-mm, 12×45-mm, 6×82-mm)
             1 reconnaissance company (113 bicycles)
             1 antiaircraft machine gun company (6-mm, 12-mm, 7-mm)
             1 signal company (4 PO-2 radios) (never formed)
          1 separate tank battalion (50×T-37) (later reduced to 32)
             3 tank companies
             1 long-range reconnaissance platoon (4-RSB)
          1 control aircraft flight
          1 mobile equipment platoon (15 motorcycles)

    Strength – 10,419 men
             50 tanks
             18 guns (over 50-mm)
             18 mortars

Source: Lisov, *Desantniki*, 38–9.

FIGURE 13. AIRBORNE CORPS AND BRIGADES, MAY 1941

Location	*Airborne Corps*	*Airborne Brigades*
Pre-Baltic MD	5th	9th, 10th, 201st
Western Special MD	4th	7th, 8th, 214th
Kiev Special MD	1st	1st, 204th, 211th
Kharkov MD	2d	2d, 3d, 4th
Odessa MD	3d	5th, 6th, 212th

Command those men with the potential vision and ability to articulate deep operations involving close coordination among mechanized, airborne, and major ground forces. Yet, while lamenting the loss of the generation of Tukhachevsky, one must ask whether even those personalities could have coped with all the problems associated with command and control of the immense force structure the Soviet Union had built. The size of the units and the absence of modern command and control equipment would have severely tested the capacities of even gifted men, just as it did the commanders of 1941. The least one can say is that the new military leaders, by virtue of their inherent abilities, limited experience, and the political climate, had less chance to adjust to the realities of war than their purged predecessors might have enjoyed. This situation condemned the airborne force to bitter struggles and a long, harsh education on the battlefield.

CHAPTER 2

Airborne Forces During the Second World War: Initial Operations, Subsequent Reorganization, and Changes in Employment Concepts

INITIAL OPERATIONS, 1941

War struck the Soviet Union suddenly, like a breaking storm of unexpected severity. Many saw the storm clouds, in particular the Soviet military leaders who commanded divisions, corps, and armies on the western border, as well as those in the higher commands who remained attuned to the military situation in Europe. While they recognized the ominous storm warnings, the political leadership denied the portents to the very moment the storm broke. Paralyzed by an inability to act, the military were the first to pay the price for the blindness of their political leaders.[1]

The incompetence of the political leadership was not the only burden the military had to shoulder on the eve of war. The new Soviet military force structure still existed largely on paper only. Large units existed in name and number, but manpower strength and, most notably, equipment production lagged. Concepts for employment of the elaborate force existed, but it had not been tested. Also, the military leadership, still suffering from the stifling effects of the purges, had not matured sufficiently to perform capably in new command positions. Rearmament programs were incomplete, a problem compounded by the obsolete equipment. Furthermore, the wholesale expansion of the military exacerbated the twin defects of incompetent leadership and equipment shortages. Deployment problems added to the dilemma of the Soviet military. Acquisition of new lands in the west (the Baltic States, Eastern Poland, and Bessarabia) and political insistence that these lands be defended, forced the military to abandon fortified border positions prepared before 1939 and to move westward to occupy new, as yet largely unfortified, positions. New fortification construction programs were incomplete, as

was the construction of new logistical and communication systems leading west from the Soviet Union's former borders. Adding to these
problems was the political injunction not to mass large Soviet troop
concentrations on the border to avoid unduly provoking Nazi Germany.
Soviet forces thus deployed in dispersed order deep behind the still
unfinished border fortifications. Lacking equipment, suffering from
weak leadership, and enjoined from prudent readiness preparations,
they would soon face the onslaught of Europe's most well-trained army,
blooded in war and intent on utterly destroying its unwary Soviet
opponent.

A microcosm of the Soviet force structure, airborne forces suffered
similar basic problems. Principal among these was the lack of experience

FIGURE 14.   AIRBORNE CORPS DISPOSITIONS, JUNE 1941

Military District	Location	Corps	Airborne Brigades
Pre-Baltic Special	Field exercises SE of Daugavpils	5th	9th, 10th, 201st
Western Special	Marina Gorka	4th	7th, 8th, 214th
Kiev Special	Kiev	1st	1st, 204th, 211th
Khar'kov	Khar'kov	2d	2d, 3d, 4th
Odessa	Unknown	3d	5th, 6th, 212th

Source: Kostylev, 'Stanovlenie,' 82.

at higher command levels. Few senior commanders were capable of
conducting strategic operations requiring the integration of airborne
forces into the complex overall combat scheme of deep battle. Airborne
forces also suffered from the general equipment deficiencies of the Red
Army and the deployment problems of other forces. Elite and well
trained airborne units did, however, manage to avoid some of the
problems that plagued other Soviet units. Airborne unit commanders
generally led well in combat, and many of the original airborne leaders
rose to prominence in later war years.[2] The nature of airborne units, as
well as their prewar deployments, resulted in their immediate commitment to combat in 1941 as ground infantry units. On several occasions,
airborne units were ordered to join special formations designed to block
German advances in critical sectors. Only after six months of war would
airborne units begin to perform, on a large scale, those special tasks for
which they had been formed and trained.

In June 1941, four airborne corps were positioned in the four western
border military districts, and a fifth corps was close by in the Khar'kov
Military District (see Figure 14).[3]

When the German attack swept across the border on 22 June 1941, airborne forces, although only partially prepared for combat, had to be thrown into the fray. The brigades deployed forward as motorized rifle units to support crumbling Soviet units on the border and to block deep penetration of advancing German panzer units. The surprise of the German offensive and the Soviet command's general paralysis during the first few weeks of war prevented a concerted Soviet counteroffensive using Soviet airborne units. Consequently, airborne units went into combat in piecemeal fashion as reinforcements in critical areas. Few had the opportunity to conduct airborne missions for which they had trained.

The first airborne units to see combat were those of the 5th Airborne Corps in the Pre-Baltic Military District. In the midst of field maneuvers when the Germans attacked, the airborne troops, under Gen. I. S. Bezugly, cooperated first with the 21st Mechanized Corps and then with the 27th Army in unsuccessful attempts to halt the slashing German armored advances. After suffering heavy casualties south of Daugavpils, the corps, on High Command orders, moved from the Northwestern Front (formerly Pre-Baltic Military District) to the Moscow Military District on 15 August.[4]

Maj. Gen. A. S. Zhadov's 4th Airborne Corps of the Western Special Military District fought a bitter six-day defensive action, attempting to hold German Army Group Center at the Berezina River. Zhadov, former commander of the 21st Mountain Cavalry Division of the Central Asian Military District, was *en route* to his new command during the first few days of war. In his absence, the corps Chief of Staff, Colonel A. F. Kazankin, commanded the 4th Airborne Corps.

Shortly after the outbreak of war, 4th Airborne Corps units attempted to carry out air assault missions but were unsuccessful. Typical was the case of 4th Airborne Corps' 214th Airborne Brigade, commanded by Colonel A. F. Levashov. The 4th Corps, created in 1941 on the base of the 214th Airborne Brigade, had completed its formation only on 15 May. It was composed largely of hand-picked soldiers, its commanders were party members, and its non-commissioned officers Komsomol members. Like other formations, the corps lacked its full complement of trucks, weapons, and other equipment.

Initially, after the outbreak of war, the 214th Brigade was stationed at Marina Gorka airfield to prepare for eventual parachute assaults. Faced with the rapid advance of German panzer forces, on 27 June the Western Front commander, General D. G. Pavlov, ordered Kazankin's corps to withdraw eastward and erect defenses in the Berezino region. During the two-day march, on 28 June Pavlov ordered the corps to employ its 214th Airborne Brigade in an air assault to support a counterattack by 20th Mechanized Corps based in Minsk against German lines of communications west of Bobruisk. The order read:

To the Commander, 4th Airborne Corps
To the Commander of Western Front Airborne Forces
From the receipt of this order bring the 214th Airborne Brigade to full combat readiness and having loaded its personnel and equipment on all available corps transport, transfer it for a subsequent air landing at Lubnishche and Tumanovka (12 km. northwest and southwest of Mogilov) in the forests near these points...

At first light on 29.6.41, the 214th Airborne Brigade, under control of the commander of Western Front Airborne Forces, will conduct a parachute assault in the Slutsk region with the mission of cutting the roads running from Baranovichi, Timkovichi and Siniavka to Bobruisk and preventing the approach of reinforced enemy forces from the west to forward units in Bobruisk. Subsequently the brigade will cooperate with 210th Motorized Division, which is being transferred to the Slutsk region to destroy the enemy Bobruisk group, while disrupting work in the rear and command and control by blowing up bridges, destroying lines of communications, and by diversionary activity. All attempts of the enemy to penetrate back to the west toward Slutsk will be thwarted by all means available to the brigade....

Western Front Commander   Member of the Western Front
Army General D. Pavlov   Military Council
                       Corps Commissar Fominikh

Western Front Chief of Staff
Major General Klimovskikh[5]

On the same day, a Western Front order to 20th Mechanized Corps confirmed the airborne brigade's mission, stating:

To the Commander of 20th Mechanized Corps
The latest confirmed data affirms that the enemy, having occupied Bobruisk with his forward units, has stretched out too far his large mechanized units and tank forces (about 70 tanks in all) a great distance along the road from Siniavka to Bobruisk. In order to prevent the concentration of main enemy forces and destroy the overextended enemy tank units in the Bobruisk region –
I order:
– Bring the 210th Motorized Division to full alert and while bringing it to full combat readiness, on night-fall 28.6.41 begin an offensive in the general direction of Slutsk with the mission of

cutting routes from Baranovichi, Timkovichi, and Siniavka to Bobruisk.

– Reinforce the division with all available tanks. Subsequently, having secured Slutsk, and together with the 214th Airborne Brigade, landed at first light on 29.6.41 in the Slutsk region, establish a covering force to the west and, having cut off reserves approaching from Baranovichi and Timkovichi, destroy enemy forward units occupying Bobruisk.... The airborne brigade is subordinated to 210th Motorized Division.

Western Front Commander
Army General D. Pavlov

Member of Western Front
Military Council
Secretary of Central
Committee, Communist
Party
Ponomarenko
Corps Commissar Fominikh

Western Front Chief of Staff
Major General Klimovskikh[6]

No sooner had 4th Airborne Corps reached Berezina late on 28 June than the planned air assault went awry. For undisclosed reasons, sufficient aircraft to lift the 214th Brigade into combat were unavailable. Hence, early on 29 June, *front* dispatched Kazankin new orders, subordinating his corps to 4th Army and requiring two brigades to occupy defenses along a line running from Berezino to Svisloch. The 214th Airborne Brigade received orders to 'travel by trucks along open march routes in the general direction of Slutsk and secure the Grusha, Slutsk, Staraia Doroga regions. Deprive the enemy of all lines of supply, destroy crossings and bridges, by night actions smash [enemy] transport and individual vehicles and burn and destroy tanks.' The order then underscored the precariousness of the situation, stating, 'Remain in that area until the full destruction of the enemy Bobruisk group and upon the fulfillment of these missions independently rejoin our forces, depending on conditions.'[7] Further, the brigade was to live off the land and co-operate with elements of another airborne brigade (the 204th), then operating in small teams further south in the Parichi region.

The brigade began fulfilling its orders that day, although it was forced by lack of sufficient truck transport to leave over one battalion and its artillery behind. Despite the fact that the 214th Airborne brigade was mentioned in Western Front operational summaries through 1 July, it failed to accomplish its principal mission of disrupting the German advance on Bobruisk. The brigade failed to link up with the 210th Motorized Division, and, in the end, its remnants operated in the German rear area for more than three months.

After the Germans had forced the Berezina and Dnepr Rivers, 4th Airborne Corps was attached to 13th Army to help defend the approaches to Smolensk. It was involved in heavy fighting throughout the duration of the Smolensk operation (July–August) and defended in the Krichev region until dislodged by Guderian's Second Panzer Group's September attack, which resulted in the massive encirclement of Soviet forces at Kiev and eastward.

During the early phases of the Smolensk operation, the airborne corps was again called on to attempt a small-scale airborne operation. Early on 13 July, the Western Front ordered Kazankin to launch a parachute assault against German forces assembled near Gorki, northwest of Mogilev (see Figure 15). Air reconnaissance had detected a force of about 300 German tanks and vehicles, out of fuel in the town. Kazankin assigned the mission to Senior Lieutenant N. Romanenko's 10th Company of the 214th Airborne Brigade's remaining (4th) battalion. Romanenko's force consisted of 64 well-trained parachutists armed with automatic weapons and two gasoline bottles each. Flying from Klimovichi airfield in four TB-3 bombers, after bombing by the aircraft, the force was to burn or otherwise destroy the German equipment. The attack was to take place at 0100 on 14 July, with landings on three sides of the town.

After a lengthy delay in bomb loading, the flight finally took off after noon on 14 July. At the target area, the force took casualties from heavy antiaircraft fire but, nevertheless, conducted its parachute drop. Two of the three groups successfully engaged and burned some tanks. A second group landed 30 miles from the target and was forced by heavy machine gun fire to withdraw into the forests. By evening the force reassembled at a prearranged location in the nearby forests, and by morning the force numbered 36 men. Reportedly having destroyed *many tanks and vehicles,* they thereafter operated in partisan fashion, recording in their activities destruction of a German railroad train at Temnyi Les station. This raid, which terminated in late July, is the earliest recorded Soviet airborne action of the Great Patriotic War.[8]

The 4th Mixed Parachute Battalion of 214th Airborne Brigade was subordinated to the Western Front High Command on 31 July and moved by rail to Sukhinichi, near *front* headquarters, where it established a camp and training area. A nearby airdrome provided support. By late August the battalion was again ready for action. At the direction of the Western Front, on 22 August the battalion received the mission of supporting Soviet forces fighting in the Iartsevo area by seizing and

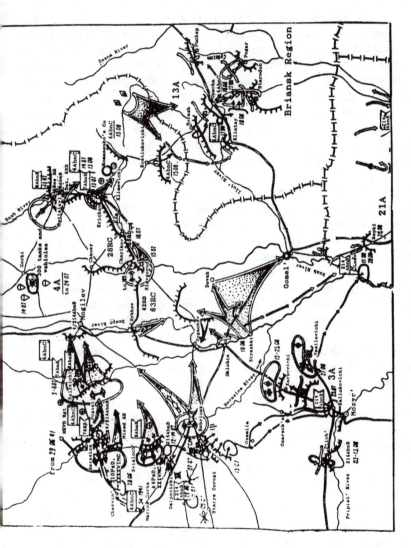

15. 4th Airborne Corps Operations, June–September 1941

destroying two bridges over the Khmost' River near the city of Dukhovshchina and by blocking roads west of Demidov.

The 11th Company with 72 men flying in six TB-3 aircraft launched the attack on the bridges, while the aircraft flew on to bomb a nearby airfield. Dropping from a height of 500 meters in the dark on the night of 22 August, the company commander, Senior Lieutenant P. Tereshchenko, assembled 62 men by morning. His plan was to launch two groups in attacks on two bridges the following night. At 0400 the next morning, under cover of the two groups, sappers mined and destroyed both bridges. After operating for more than 45 days in the enemy rear, the remnants of Tereshchenko's company broke through enemy lines and joined General L. M. Dovator's cavalry group (consisting of 50th and 53d Cavalry Divisions). Ultimately, they traveled by rail to Engels airfield, where they joined the newly reformed 4th Airborne Corps (second formation).[9]

The second parachute company, the 12th Company of Senior Lieutenant Kulitsky, also began its operations on the night of 22 August, landing in the fog near Demidov, when one platoon lost its bearings and was lost. Kulitsky's company engaged several German vehicle columns on the road and succeeded in 'holding up the movement of enemy reserves for six hours.'[10] Ultimately, with a group of another 1,000 men encircled in earlier operations, they broke through to Russian front-line positions near Rzhev. The Western Front staff assigned the parachutists to a newly-formed airborne force, the so-called Western Front Parachute-Assault Detachment commanded by Captain I. G. Starchak, then operating along the front near Iukhnov. Later, in December, that detachment operated in the German rear south of Kalinin, subordinated to the 201st Airborne Brigade of the reformed 5th Airborne Corps.

The 214th Airborne Brigade's mixed battalion's 10th Company, under Senior Lieutenant N. Romanenko, began yet another mission on 25 August. The force was to block the road and rail line near Torop and, for two weeks, disrupt transport of German reserves to the front. The assault took place over three evenings by platoon, and, although the company commander did not arrive at the appointed assembly area, his subordinates took over. After conducting reconnaissance with troops dressed in civilian dress, the groups destroyed several trains on the Velikie Luki – Western Dvina rail line. The group continued operating in the enemy rear until 14 December, when its survivors crossed the ice on Lake Seliger and rejoined Kalinin Front forces. The remainder of the 214th Airborne Brigade's mixed battalion, some 200 men, reunited with its parent corps on 28 September at Engel's airfield near Moscow, secure in the knowledge that it was the only corps unit to have routinely operated in airborne fashion.

The fate of the main body of 214th Airborne Brigade is poorly documented but covered in detail in the 4th Airborne Corps' unit history. A recently discovered journal of the brigade provides fascinating details of the unit's hegira. Finally, on 25 July Levashov's men (grown to 1,200 with the addition of other victims of encirclement) reached the Central Front's 3d Army near Kalinkovichi, where it reorganized and joined the defense. In late September it again fell into encirclement east of Kiev. Again the brigade fled eastward seeking to escape encirclement. On 24 September the brigade's 200 survivors reached Soviet lines near Lebedin, after almost three months of harrowing combat. Thereafter the brigade traveled by rail to Engel's, where it rejoined its parent 4th Airborne Corps.[11]

German intelligence reports, relying primarily on prisoner of war interrogations and captured documents, corroborate official Soviet accounts of 4th Airborne Corps' operations. A comprehensive report dated March 1942 identified 4th Airborne Corps' subordinate brigades as the 7th, 8th, and 214th Airborne Brigades. It provided the following narrative of corps operations to that date:

> The following is known about the deployment of the 4th Airborne Corps in the summer of 1941: The 214th Airborne Brigade, under its commander, Colonel Lewaschow, went through the German lines south of Smolensk in July. There they deployed in partisan operations. Their deployment as partisans occurred for the most part in civilian clothing. The brigade operated for three months in the rear of the German front. They maintained radio communications with the high command of the Red Army from which they received their guidance. During this time, the brigade commander passed through German lines to the east five times. Two companies which had remained behind the Russian front were deployed by parachute in mid-August 1941 in the vicinity of Smolensk. Their mission was to conduct partisan warfare. Several air transports belonging to these units landed in the vicinity of 5th Corps near Tjapolowo (northwest of Duchowschtschina). The bulk of 4th Airborne Corps was deployed on the front as infantry at Mogilew where it sustained heavy casualties.[12]

The same German assessment properly judged that 5th Airborne Corps was used almost entirely as infantry in the Baltic and Moscow regions.

In general, the combat record of 4th Airborne Corps in the initial period of war typified operations of all existing airborne corps. Although their operations are not well documented, other corps probably employed small forces similarly to 4th Corps.

Farther south, in the Kiev Special Military District (Southwestern

Front), Maj. Gen. M. A. Usenko's 1st Airborne Corps fought defensive battles alongside the Soviet 5th and 6th Armies as German Army Group South battered its way toward Kiev. Reinforced by 2d and 3d Airborne Corps, the 1st also participated in the futile defense of Kiev. Both the 1st and 2d Airborne corps were caught in the German encirclement of Kiev in August–September 1941 and suffered such grievous losses that they were dis-established (only to be re-created later). The 3d Airborne Corps, also encircled at Konotop, fought its way out. In November it was reorganized into the 87th Rifle Division under Col. A. I. Rodimtsev (former commander of 5th Airborne Brigade).[13] The 87th Rifle Division, later redesignated 13th Guards Rifle Division, achieved lasting fame at Stalingrad and combat later in the war. In summary, during the initial period of war, actual airborne operations were limited to occasional diversionary airdrops, as elite Soviet airborne troops fought as infantry-men.

As summer passed into fall and German forces developed their strategic drive to threaten Moscow, airborne forces left undestroyed after three months of war played an increasing role in ever more desperate Soviet attempts to halt the German onslaught. The two surviving air-borne corps (4th and 5th) and the newly regrouped 1st Airborne Corps figured prominently. At this stage airborne forces engaged in intense diversionary actions or were shifted to the most critical frontal sectors, often by air, to meet this or that crisis.

In late September 1941, remnants of brigades subordinate to 4th Airborne Corps assembled near Engel's airfield and began the process of accepting replacements, regrouping, and forming a new corps structure. Improved equipment included anti-tank rifles (24 per company) for an anti-tank and heavy machine gun company in each battalion. Each brigade now included a sapper-explosive company. New command personnel included Colonel A. F. Levashov as corps commander and Lieutenant Colonel N. E. Kolobovnikov as 214th Airborne Brigade commander. During the German drive on Moscow in October and November, 4th Airborne Corps forces continued their training program in preparation for a prominent role in the impending counteroffensive. Finally, between 21 and 23 December, the corps entrained at Apisovka and disembarked at Ramenskoe airfield southeast of Moscow. There, at their final staging area, they were joined by Senior Lieutenant Romanenko and the long-missing 10th Company, 214th Brigade, which had conducted the August assault on Torop Station. All then awaited new missions.[14]

From early September, re-formed 1st Airborne Corps conducted train-ing in the Volga Military District around the city of Saratov. The training of 1st Corps' 1st, 204th, and 211th Airborne Brigades lasted fully three months. According to Soviet sources, 'During that time, units and subunits were almost fully reformed and armed, and some thousand of the troops began to conduct actions in the enemy rear.' This action probably involved small-scale diversionary operations.[15] On 24 November 1st Airborne Corps received orders subordinating it to the Western Front High Command. A medical service officer reported in his memoirs, 'The next day at 0700 we left the city and marched on foot to the railhead located a considerable distance away.'[16] The following night the corps arrived at the railhead. A lengthy rail trip began the next day toward the Moscow region. The corps detrained at Gorbachevo station and marched 15 kilometers to its new camp near Moscow. The corps headquarters was located at A. V. Ukhtomsky State Farm and the subordinate brigades in the villages of Dzerzhinsky and Kapotna (1st Brigade), and Liubertsy and Malakhovki. All were near the Liubertsy airfield, which would soon become the principal launching pad for major airborne operations. Throughout the first week of December, the force waited, anticipating a likely Soviet counteroffensive in the Moscow region.

The 5th Airborne Corps, transferred into the Moscow region from the Baltic Military District on 15 August, played a far more active role in opposing the German Army's drive on Moscow. In fact, two of its brigades participated in one of the Soviets' more successful ground actions midst a period of cascading operational disasters. Moreover, air movement of Soviet forces figured prominently in Soviet successes.

On 30 September 1941, the German High Command commenced its long-expected operation to seize Moscow, codenamed 'Typhoon.' As a part of the operation, General Guderian's Second Panzer Group attacked the Soviet Briansk Front and drove on toward Moscow via Orel. To halt Guderian's rapid advance, the *Stavka* rapidly concentrated reserve forces in the Mtsensk region, many of which were relatively elite forces. These were unified under command of the newly-formed 1st Guards Rifle Corps commanded by Major General D. D. Leliushenko. Despite strenuous *Stavka* attempts to raise a sizeable force and hurl it into Guderian's path west of Orel, there was insufficient time to do so, and, by 3 October, German tanks had penetrated into the city, secured it, and commenced an advance down the Orel – Tula highway toward Mtsensk. As German XXIV Panzer Corps raced down the highway, Leliushenko frantically erected defenses at Mtsensk (see Figure 16). To assist his effort, the *Stavka* ordered 5th Airborne Corps and its two combat-ready brigades (10th and 201st) to fly into the Orel and Mtsensk area and join 1st Guards Rifle Corps.[17]

At 0510 3 October, 5th Airborne Corps commander, Colonel S. S. Gur'ev received an order to fly via Kolomna and Tula to Orel, land at the Orel airfield, halt the movement of enemy tanks along the road to Tula,

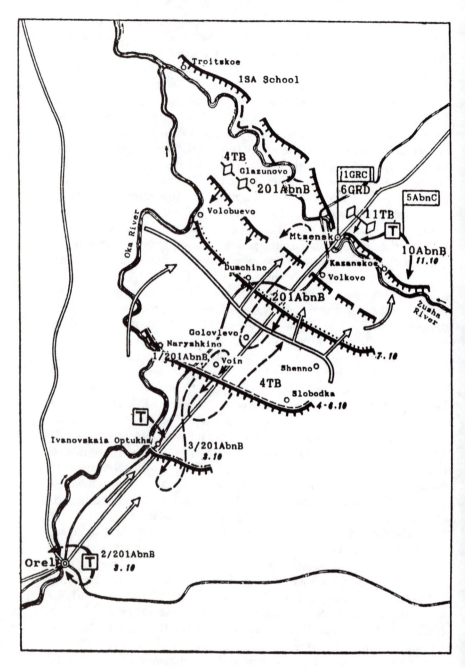

16. Operations around Mtsensk, October 1941

support the concentration of 1st Guards Rifle Corps, and thereafter become subordinate to that corps. At 0630 that day, the 'S. M. Kirov' 201st Airborne Brigade, commanded by Lieutenant Colonel S. M. Kovalev, took off in TB-3 bombers and transport aircraft. The brigade's lead elements began landing at Orel airfield at the very moment the airfield came under Germany artillery fire. Despite heavy ground fire, under cover of lead airborne units, the remainder of the brigade landed and immediately entered battle. Midst the chaos of heavy combat and some burning aircraft, the 201st Brigade's three battalions cleared the airfield of German troops and moved to the northwestern section of Orel to support Soviet ground forces attempting to hold the city. The 3d Battalion, 201st, Airborne Brigade, the last arriving battalion, diverted and landed at the more peaceful Optukha airfield eight kilometers northeast of Orel and quickly moved southwestward to cut the Orel – Mtsensk road between Optukha and Ivanovskaia. Under constant attack by German aircraft, the 10th Airborne Brigade also landed its forces on 3 and 4 October, followed by corps support subunits and equipment.

In assessing the scope of the air movement, Soviet critics later stated, 'The aviation-technical group, carrying out the transport of 5th Corps and disposing of only 80 PS-84 and TB-3 aircraft, succeeded in a short period in transporting more than 5,000 airborne forces with their arms and equipment and two complete loads of ammunition a distance of up to 500 kilometers.'[18]

Late on 4 October, Colonel M. E. Katukov's 4th Tank Brigade arrived from Moscow and joined the airborne defense. Battle raged until 10 October on the southwestern outskirts of Mtsensk as both airborne brigades cooperated in the 1st Guards Rifle Corps' defense. Late on 10 October, German forces finally succeeded in entering the city, only to be repelled in a counterattack the following day. Action around Mtsensk endured until 24 October, when German forces were finally able to cross the Zusha River and continue the advance on Tula. A Soviet assessment noted the impact of the Mtsensk battle:

Up to 24 October that obstacle remained insurmountable for the Germans. The Soviet command gained time to erect defenses at Tula. In the main, the withdrawal of the Briansk Front's 50th Army to the Tula region was completed as was the conduct of the necessary regrouping of forces on the Western Front's left wing to permit covering of the Briansk axis. The enemy plan on that axis was spoiled. With heavy losses, the 24th Panzer Corps of Guderian's 2d Panzer Group was able to overcome the distance of 45–50 km separating Orel and Mtsensk only in nine days. The resistance of Soviet forces at Mtsensk was totally unexpected by the

Germans. The transport of the airborne forces by air played a large role in this.[19]

On 17 October the *Stavka* ordered 5th Airborne Corps to disengage and immediately travel by road and rail to the Podol'sk region. By 20 October the corps had already occupied a defensive sector along the Nara River west of Moscow, where, in the ensuing two months, it engaged in defensive fighting north of Maloiaroslavets and on the approaches to Moscow. After 17 December the corps took part in offensive operations to retake Maloiaroslavets. During those operations the 201st Airborne Brigade was detached from the corps to participate with elements of 4th Airborne Corps and 250th Airborne Regiment in airborne operations near Medyn. Finally, on 26 January, the remainder of 5th Airborne Corps withdrew from battle to assemble on 30 January at the Podol'sk Artillery School, where it underwent reorganization. In early February it gave up its 9th Airborne Brigade to 4th Airborne Corps and, in return, received from that corps 7th Airborne Brigade.

While 1st, 4th, and 5th Airborne Corps operated or trained during the fall of 1941, another airborne force took form. In August Western Front began forming its own parachute-landing detachment in a camp near Iukhnov, 200 kilometers southwest of Moscow along the Moscow–Warsaw highway. This detachment, consisting initially of Komsomol members, party members, and troops from *front* airfield units, was commanded by Captain I. G. Starchak. Soon the detachment swelled in size to 400 men by the addition of remnants of 214th Airborne Brigade's mixed battalion, whose companies had conducted airborne assaults around Smolensk in August and September. Throughout October Starchak's detachment engaged in defensive ground fighting. By December, however, they were ready to conduct operations in the enemy rear in support of the Soviet counteroffensive, which had begun on 5 December.[20]

ORGANIZATION AND EMPLOYMENT IN THEORY AND PRACTICE, (1941–1945)

After the tragic border battles, only the 4th and 5th Airborne Corps in the Moscow region remained relatively intact. In August and September 1941 the High Command reorganized its airborne forces and redefined the guidelines for their future employment. A 4 September order of the People's Commissariat of Defense created the higher level Administration of the Command of Airborne Forces to replace the older lower level airborne force administration. The order also withdrew all airborne forces from *front* command and subordinated them to the new administration, now commanded by Maj. Gen. V. A. Glazunov. Henceforth, airborne units would be used only with specific *Stavka* (Supreme head-quarters – in essence, Stalin) approval to perform the following missions:

- Cooperate with ground forces in encircling and destroying large enemy groups.
- Disorganize enemy command and control and rear area logistics facilities.
- Secure and hold important terrain, crossings, and points in the enemy rear.
- Secure and destroy enemy airfields.
- Secure landings of naval infantry and river crossings.[21]

To bolster the depleted airborne force structure, a new airborne brigade organization strengthened the parachute battalion (see Figure 17), and five new airborne corps (6th through 10th) were organized on the basis of this new brigade organization.

FIGURE 17. AIRBORNE BRIGADE, 1941

4 parachute battalions (678 men each)
3 parachute companies
1 mortar company
1 sapper demolition platoon
1 machine gun platoon
1 signal platoon
Strength: About 3,000 men

Source: Lisov, *Desantniki*, 39.

The Soviets reorganized or reinforced the older corps (1st through 5th) with additional personnel and equipment and created five new maneuver airborne brigades. By June 1942, creation of these new units was completed. The new administration also established schools and courses to train cadre for these units.[22] The *Stavka* formed nine separate aviation transport squadrons and five separate aviation detachments to perform the critical function of transporting airborne units. During 1942, these units combined to form two separate aviation-glider regiments and two aviation transport regiments equipped with U-2, R-5, TB-1, TB-3, and PS-84 aircraft.[23] Because of heavy aircraft losses early in the war, the lack of aircraft posed a serious problem for the airborne forces.

German reports confirmed the general nature of this reorganization, stating:

The High Command of the Red Army established its own High Command for Airborne Forces. Its scope went beyond the scope of an Army High Command, it includes a Commander of Airborne Troops, a member of the Military Council, a Chief of Staff, a War Commissar for Airborne Forces, an Operations Division, and a 2d, 3rd, 4th, 5th, and Political Department.[24]

The Germans identified the corps (presumably 2 through 5) and 250th Airborne Regiment as subordinate to the Airborne High Command, stating:

> According to information known to this point, as of early March 1942, the following corps consisting of the following subordinate units were in existence or being organized:
> 1st Airborne Corps with headquarters in Saratow,
>   subordinate brigades unknown
> 4th Airborne Corps established in the Volga Republic
>   7th, 8th, and 204th Airborne Brigades
> 5th Airborne Corps established in the Volga Republic
>   9th, 10th, and 201st Airborne Brigades
> 10th Airborne Corps location unknown
>   23d Airborne Brigade
> 250th Airborne Regiment
> The existence of a 1st Airborne Brigade and a 6th Airborne Brigade at Kupanna, 40 kilometers east of Moscow is unconfirmed.[25]

According to German intelligence, the reorganized and surviving airborne corps of fall 1941 consisted of three airborne brigades, one artillery regiment, signal and transportation subunits, and an optional tank battalion of 45 tanks. The artillery regiment consisted of three batteries of mortars and anti-tank guns. The brigade contained the following:

4 airborne infantry battalions
1 artillery battalion (76mm guns)
1 machine gun company (24 light machine guns)
1 reconnaissance company (on bicycles and equipped with automatic weapons)
1 signal company (with abundant radios)
1 transportation company
1 anti-aircraft machine gun company (optional)
1 sapper company.[26]

As a result of these reorganization measures, Soviet airborne forces numbered about 200,000 personnel by the end of 1941. While the formation of the new airborne force was under way, the first concerted large-scale use of those forces occurred (see Figure 18). During the Soviet counteroffensive at Moscow in December 1941 and January 1942 the *Stavka* marshaled all available forces in an attempt to drive German Army Group Center away from Moscow and destroy them. While committing the bulk of its rifle forces in an offensive against the Germans, the *Stavka* marshaled its scarce mobile forces in an attempt to convert tactical successes into operational success and even strategic victory. Into the boiling cauldron of battle around Moscow, the *Stavka* threw mobile groups consisting of ski battalions, cavalry divisions and corps, its few

FIGURE 18
SOVIET AIRBORNE OPERATIONS IN THE MOSCOW REGION, 1941–42

Date	Location	Airborne Force
14–15 Dec 1941	Teriaeva Sloboda	One Bn. 214th Abn Bde, 4th Abn Corps
2–4 Jan 1942	Medyn	One Bn, 201st Abn Bde, 5th Abn Corps
		One Bn, 250th Rifle Regt
18–22 Jan 1942	Zhelan'e	1st and 2d Bns, 201st Abn Bde, 5th Abn Corps
		250th Abn Regt
27–31 Jan 1942	Ozerechnia-Tabory	8th Abn Bde, 4th Abn Corps
13–23 Feb 1942	Velikopol'e-Zhelan'e	One Bn, 201st Abn Bde,
		5th Abn Corps
		9th and 214th Abn Bdes, 4th Abn Corps
16–17 Feb 1942	Rzhev	4th Bn, 204th Abn Bde, 1st Abn Corps
17–18 Feb 1942	Ilomlia, north of	2d Bn, 204th Abn Bde, 1st Airborne Corps
	Demiansk	
March 1942	Demiansk region	Elements of 1st, 2d and 204th Airborne
		Brigades, 1st Airborne Corps
16–18 Apr 1942	Svintsovo	4th Bn, 23d Abn Bde, 10th Abn Corps
29–30 May 1942	10 km south	23d Abn Bde, 10th Abn Corps
	of Dorogobuzh	211th Abn Bde, 1st Abn Corps

precious tank brigades, and its airborne forces, as well. In addition to the role played by airborne forces in conducting minor tactical and diversionary operations on main army attack axes, ultimately an entire airborne corps dropped into German Army Group Center's rear near Viaz'ma to aid in the encirclement and destruction of the enemy. At this stage of the war, the limited mobility and staying power of Soviet forces thwarted *Stavka*'s ambitious plans, and airborne forces ultimately had to fight a four-month battle of encirclement before breaking free of the German rear and rejoining Soviet main forces. While major airborne operations went on near Moscow, a smaller tactical drop occurred at Kerch in the Crimea.

Finally, in late February and March 1942, the Soviet Northwestern Front employed 1st Airborne Corps in both air assault and ground roles to dislodge German forces from the Demiansk salient in a spectacular operation, which ultimately failed.

After the extensive airborne activity during the winter campaign of 1941–1942, airborne forces underwent another major reorganization the following summer. Responding to events in southern Russia, where German troops had opened a major offensive that would culminate in the Stalingrad battles, the ten airborne corps, as part of the *Stavka* strategic reserves, deployed southward, and reorganized into guards rifle divisions to bolster Soviet forces struggling in the Stalingrad region. Nine of these divisions participated in the battles around Stalingrad, and one took part in the defense of the northern Caucasus region. In addition, five airborne brigades and one airborne regiment, all at full TOE strength, reinforced Soviet defensive efforts in the Caucasus as ground units (see Figure 19).[27]

Former airborne units achieved considerable distinction in the bitter fighting of fall 1942, vindicating Stalin's decision to use airborne units in a ground role. Maj. Gen. V. G. Zholydev's 37th Guards Rifle Division fought tenaciously in defense of the Barricady and Tractor factories at Stalingrad and suffered 90 per cent casualties while exacting a heavy toll on the Germans.[28] Maj. Gen. S. S. Gur'ev's 39th Guards Rifle Division participated in the equally tenacious defense of the Red October plant.

FIGURE 19. CONVERSION OF AIRBORNE UNITS, SUMMER 1942

Old Airborne Designation	New Designation	Commander
Gds Abn Corps	Gds Rifle Div	
1st	37th	Maj. Gen. V. G. Zholydev
2d	32d	Col. M. F. Tikhonov
3d	33d	Col. A. I. Utvenko
4th	38th	Col. A. A. Onufriev
5th	39th	Maj. Gen. S. S. Gur'ev
6th	40th	Maj. Gen. A. I. Pastrevich
7th	34th	Maj. Gen. I. I. Gubarevich
8th	35th	Maj. Gen. V. A. Glazkov
9th	36th	Col. M. I. Denisenko
10th	41st	Col. N. P. Ivanov
Abn Bde	Rifle Bde	
1st	5th	
2d	6th	Names of commanders are
3d	7th	not available
4th	8th	
5th	9th	
4th Res Abn Regt	10th Rifle Bde	

Source: Sukhorukov, *Sovetskie vozdushno*, 146–79.

Likewise, Maj. Gen. A. I. Rodimtsev's 13th Guards Rifle Division won lasting fame in the street fighting for control of downtown Stalingrad.[29]

Although it had committed virtually all airborne forces to ground fighting in southern Russia, the *Stavka* still foresaw the necessity of conducting actual airborne operations later during the war. To maintain a force capable of fulfilling airborne missions, the *Stavka* created eight new airborne corps (1st, 4th, 5th, 6th, 7th, 8th, 9th, and 10th) in the fall of 1942. Beginning in December 1942, these corps were transformed into ten guards airborne divisions (two formed from the 1st Airborne Corps and the three existing separate maneuver airborne brigades). The new guards airborne divisions trained in airborne techniques, and all personnel jumped three to ten times during training. Training stressed rear area operations, mutual cooperation with *front* ground and air forces, antitank warfare, ground defensive techniques, and use of initiative.[30]

Sketchy German intelligence reports provide faint indicators of the process of reorganization (see Figure 20).[31]

In February 1943, as Soviet forces attempted to exploit German defeats in the winter battles of 1942–43, the *Stavka* dispatched all of these airborne divisions to the Northwestern Front where they fought at Staraia Russa and Demiansk as part of 1st Shock Army, 68th Army, and the Khozin Group. By April and May 1943, in response to prospects for renewed German offensive action in the Kursk region, the airborne divisions redeployed southward. Seven divisions (2d, 3d, 4th, 5th, 6th, 8th, and 9th) reinforced the Central Front by the end of May, and the remaining three (1st, 10th, and 7th) joined the 37th and 52d Armies at Khar'kov in August.[32] During the Kursk operation, airborne forces participated in heavy fighting, in particular 4th Guards Airborne Division, which defended successfully against German Ninth Army panzer forces at Ponyri, and the 9th Guards Airborne Division, which participated in the Soviet armored victory over German Fourth Panzer Army at Prokhorovka.

After the German defeat at Kursk, the bulk of the airborne divisions joined in the pursuit of German forces to the Dnepr River. Even as the original ten guards airborne divisions fought at the front, new airborne brigades formed in the rear areas. In April and May 1943 20 brigades formed and trained for future airborne operations. Although Soviet sources do not reveal the organization of the 1943 airborne brigades, German intelligence provides a fairly accurate picture. The new brigade consisted of two airborne battalions, one medical battalion, and one machine gun battalion designed to increase the brigade's firepower (see Figure 21). The machine gun battalion provided the firepower of two machine gun companies plus a reconnaissance company and intelligence company. Each airborne battalion fielded three airborne companies of

FIGURE 20.   SELECTED GERMAN INTELLIGENCE REPORTS ON SOVIET
AIRBORNE FORCES

Date of Report	Date of Information	Formation	Location
24.4.1944 (Security Police of SD)	Jan 42	7th Airborne (Airlanding) Corps	Engel's airfield, later at Saratov
		5th Airborne Corps	Besymjannaja (Beziminaia) Station
		8th Airborne Corps	"
		9th Airborne Corps	"
"	April 42	5th, 7th, 8th, 9th Airborne Corps	Moscow Region
21.10.43 (Abwehr)	1–15 July 43	10th Gds Airborne Bde	Ramenskoje (Ramenskoe)
	1 Oct 43	9th Gds Airborne Bde replaces 10th Airborne Bde	Ramenskoje
	4.7.43	4th Gds Airborne Bde	Ramenskoje
		7th Gds Airborne Bde	Teikowo (Ivanovo)
		? Airborne Bde	Svenigorod (60 km w of Moscow)
		3d Airborne Bde	Dmitrovsk (55 km north of Moscow)
		1st Airborne Bde	Ljuberzy (15 km sw of Moscow)
5.10.43 (1st Pz Army Radio Intercept)	30.4.43	6th Army Parachute Recon Detachment (70 men)	Sinel'nikovo
27.8.43 (Walli 1 Abwehr)	Aug 42	1st Gds Airborne Corps	Lyubertsy
		1st, 5th, 211th Gds Airborne Bde	
	Dec 42	1st Gds Airborne Corps converted into 9th Gds Airborne Division[31]	

150 men each, one mortar company, one machine gun company, and an antitank company for a total of 850 men. Each airborne company was equipped with two Maxim machine guns and two light mortars. Most of these brigades had become six new guards airborne divisions (11th through 16th) by September 1943.[33] The *Stavka*, however, earmarked three of these airborne brigades for use in an airborne operation to cross the Dnepr River.

As Soviet forces approached the new German defensive line on the Dnepr, the problem of securing bridgeheads for offensive operations across the river was paramount. Advanced elements of Soviet forces seized a number of small bridgeheads, but only light infantry formations were able to cross into these footholds. Larger bridgeheads, free from German interdiction, were necessary to build bridges across the Dnepr and to introduce heavy armored forces needed to continue the offensive. To gain a larger bridgehead, the *Stavka* ordered three airborne brigades to conduct a major airborne operation across the Dnepr River near Velikyi Bukrin. This third, and last, operational use of airborne forces failed because of inadequate preparations, poor reconnaissance, clumsy coordination of forces, and many of the same reasons that had caused the Viaz'ma operation to fail. The Soviets would conduct no further large-scale airborne operations. Instead, airborne forces continued to fight in a ground combat role.

After the failure of the Dnepr operation, the original ten guards airborne divisions participated in campaigns on the left and right banks of the Ukraine, in particular as part of 5th Army at Kirovograd, at Korsun'-Shevchenkovskii, and in the advance to the Dnestr River. In January

FIGURE 21.   AIRBORNE BRIGADE, 1943

1 machine gun battalion
  2 machine gun companies
  1 reconnaissance company
  1 intelligence company

2 parachute battalions (850 men each)
  3 parachute companies (150 men each)
    3 parachute platoons
    1 machine gun platoon (2 Maxim machine guns)
    1 mortar platoon (2 mortars)
  1 machine gun company
    3 machine gun platoons
  1 antitank company
    3 antitank platoons
  1 mortar company
    3 mortar platoons

1 medical battalion

Source: OKH, Fremde Heere Ost, *Vernehmingstelle des Ob. d. h.*

1944, the newer guards airborne divisions became rifle divisions within 37th Guards Rifle Corps, 7th Army, and fought to liberate Karelia.[34] In the summer and fall of 1944, seven guards airborne divisions, fighting as infantry and as part of 4th Guards Army, joined in the rout of German and Rumanian forces at Iassy-Kishinev and marched with Soviet forces into Hungary.

Attempts to revive large airborne units began in late summer 1944. In August the *Stavka* formed the 37th, 38th, and 39th Guards Airborne Corps. By October, the newly formed corps had combined into a separate airborne army under Maj. Gen. I. I. Zatevakhin (see Figure 22).[35] However, because of the growing need for well-trained ground units, the new army did not endure long as an airborne unit. In December the

FIGURE 22.   SEPARATE AIRBORNE ARMY, 1944

Separate Airborne Army, Maj. Gen. I. I. Zatevakhin

37th Guards Airborne Corps, Lt. Gen. P. V. Mironov
   13th Guards Airborne Division
   98th Guards Airborne Division
   99th Guards Airborne Division

38th Guards Airborne Corps, Lt. Gen. A. I. Utvenko
   11th Guards Airborne Division
   12th Guards Airborne Division
   16th Guards Airborne Division

39th Guards Airborne Corps, Lt. Gen. M. F. Tikhonov
   8th Guards Airborne Division
   14th Guards Airborne Division
   100th Guards Airborne Division

Source: Sukhorukov, *Sovetskie vozdushno*, 238.

Stavka reorganized the separate airborne army into the 9th Guards Army of Col. Gen. V. V. Glagolev, and all divisions were renumbered as guards rifle divisions. As testimony to the elite nature of airborne-trained units, the *Stavka* held the 9th Guards Army out of defensive actions, using it only for exploitation during offensives.[36] Other airborne divisions, separately or in groups, participated as elements of *Front* ground forces in the remaining campaigns of the war. Throughout the rest of the war, airborne operations were limited to low-level tactical or minor diversionary operations, usually conducted by air-landed ground force units. Of note were the numerous air-landings after the collapse of Japanese resistance in Manchuria in August 1945.

Although the bulk of the airborne force structure consisted of guards airborne divisions organized and fighting as guards rifle divisions, the *Stavka* continued to recognize the need for specialized airborne units. Consequently, it continued to organize separate airborne brigades similar to those of 1941 with 3,345 men, six 76-mm guns, eight 45-mm antitank guns, 28 37-mm antiaircraft guns, 24 antiaircraft machine guns, 36 heavy machine guns, and 81 antitank rifles.[37] At war's end, the guards airborne divisions and separate airborne brigades not demobilized would provide the nucleus of the Soviet postwar airborne force.

Thus, from 1942 on, wartime realities demanded that airborne forces be used repeatedly as infantry in ground fighting along the front. Earlier airborne operations on a grand scale had failed because of the light infantry nature of those forces, the paucity of aviation available to deliver units into battle, the absence of technology required to guarantee accurate delivery, and the inability of the light units to compete with the firepower of German formations. In 1944, transport aircraft capable of carrying the heavy equipment an airborne unit would require to survive and to fulfill its mission were still in short supply. Manpower shortage ruled out heavy expenditure of personnel on airborne operations whose chances of success the Soviets rated as only marginal. Thus, strategic and operational use of airborne forces faded into memory. On the other hand, Soviets still employed tactical assaults, particularly diversionary drops, because those types of airborne missions had proved successful earlier in the war.

In spite of the diminished use of large-scale airdrops, Soviet military theory still recognized the value of such airborne operations under proper circumstances. Declarations on the theoretical use of airborne forces changed remarkably little from the missions outlined in regulations of the mid-1930s. After the Soviet General Staff had thoroughly studied airborne experiences during the winter campaign of 1941–42, in early 1943 it published provisional *Instructions on the Combat Employment of Red Army Airborne Forces*. This comprehensive document surveyed the missions of airborne forces and provided detailed procedures to govern airborne operations at all levels of war. The instructions began by declaring:

1. *Red Army airborne forces are a means of the High Command and are usually handed over for the immediate operational use at the disposal of front commanders.*

By their organization, training, and armament, airborne forces are notable for high mobility, great saturation with automatic weapons of close battle, and availability to rapidly and by surprise appear and conduct battle in the enemy rear.[38]

The instructions designated the following missions for airborne forces:

– to cooperate with ground forces in encircling and destroying the enemy by actions against their withdrawal routes and by halting approaching reserves;

- to secure and hold important areas, boundaries, crossings, and points in the enemy rear;
- to cooperate with forces operating in the enemy's operational depths;
- to demolish important objectives in the enemy rear;
- to disrupt command and control and work in the enemy rear;
- to support the landing of naval assaults by securing coastal regions and isolating them from the approach of enemy forces; and
- to strengthen and broaden regions of partisan movements.[39]

At the same time, airborne forces were specifically *not to be employed* to penetrate fortified lines, seize well-defended strongpoints or to conduct prolonged firm defense. The instructions repeated types of employment listed in the 1930s regulations, specifically parachute delivery, air-landing (glider or aircraft), and mixed means.

The instructions offered a checklist of considerations before an air assault should be launched and minimal planning requirements necessary for an operation to achieve any success. Among the most important requirements were:

- effective reconnaissance
- secret preparations and surprise employment
- configuration of the force to match mission requirements
- timely planning and preparation of forces and supporting means
- cooperation with aviation, mobile forces, partisans, and forces operating along the front
- sufficient aircraft to initiate and support the mission
- proper and effective communications and command and control.

Clearly, articulation of these requirements was prompted by study of 1941 and 1942 experiences, when virtually all these requirements were not met. One notable condition absent from the list was the requirement for air superiority. This was the case probably because the Soviets planned to conduct virtually all airborne operations at night (and by 1943, they were able to achieve at least local air superiority).

The instructions went on to distinguish between tactical and operational airborne assaults. Accordingly tactical *desants* 'are used primarily in offensive battle to halt the approach of enemy tactical reserves, complete the encirclement of enemy forces, disrupt means of communications, destroy or disrupt command and control, and destroy ammunition and fuel in the tactical dispositions of the enemy.'[40] Specific objectives and regions of tactical airborne actions included enemy artillery positions, staff and command posts, tactical reserves, road junctions, commanding heights on approach or withdrawal routes, crossings and defiles, enemy rear installations and positions, ammunition and fuel warehouses and transport and transfer points, and bridgeheads for forced water crossings.

The instructions noted that tactical air assaults were designated to operate in the rear of high enemy force densities, 'Therefore the success of their actions as a whole depends on correct selection of the time and place of landing and the degree of coordination between the actions of the air assault force and the actions of other main ground forces, artillery, and aviation.'[41]

An operational airborne assault, according to the instructions, could be employed in all types and phases of an operation. Accordingly, 'Airborne assaults are used to greatest effect in a *front* offensive operation and at that stege of its development when, as a result of the penetration of our mobile formations, the enemy defense system is disrupted, and the possibility has been created for dismembering, enveloping, and encircling his grouping.'[42]

During the preparatory stage of an offensive operation, airborne assault forces performed such missions as destroying railroads and transportation routes, cutting lines of resupply and communications, destroying logistical warehouses, disrupting enemy command and control, and seizing enemy airfields. During the penetration of enemy tactical defenses, airborne assaults seized positions in the enemy rear, blocking movement of reserves and resupply and, in some instances, cooperated with ground forces effecting the penetration by attacking the enemy from the rear. In all subsequent phases of the offensive operation, the mission of airborne forces was to cooperate with mobile ground forces. When the operation was nearing completion, airborne forces were to cut enemy withdrawal routes to promote full encirclement and destruction of his forces.

During developing meeting engagements, airborne forces had the mission of landing (primarily by parachute) in the path of enemy main forces to seize obstacles to their movement and facilitate main friendly force maneuver plans. In addition, they were to conduct smaller assaults to disrupt the enemy rear area and block his withdrawal. In support of defensive operations, airborne forces had the mission of disrupting enemy command and control and logistical support, particularly in areas where the enemy main attack was developing. Airborne forces supported naval amphibious assaults by seizing beachheads and assisting landing operations of the amphibious forces' first echelon. Otherwise, they performed the usual mission of disrupting the enemy rear to prevent concentration of enemy forces to eradicate existing bridgeheads.

In short, 'disorganizing enemy command and control and rear service support in all types of operations is the constant mission of all airborne forces, irrespective of other missions they perform.'[43] In performing these missions, airborne forces would land and operate as a single unified body or in separate groups depending on the objectives.

Having specified airborne missions, the instructions elaborated on the organization and conduct of airborne operations, carefully delineating the responsibilities of each force headquarters involved and detailing preparatory measures and precise command and control measures. It then provided guidance on the conduct of ground operations after the landing and means for cooperation between the airborne force and forces they supported. The comprehensive nature of the instructions demonstrated the extent to which the General Staff had studied and exploited previous airborne experience. The fact that many of the provisions of the instructions have endured well into the postwar years testifies to their value. The paucity of airborne operations later in the war also underscored the complexity of these operations and the fact that the Soviets took the contents of the instructions seriously. These instructions were not the final written theoretical word on Soviet use of airborne forces. The General Staff incorporated many of its provisions into the next major series of Red Army regulations issued in 1944.

The *Field Regulation of 1944* echoed the *Field Regulation of 1936* and the 1943 *Instructions* by declaring in Article 34, 'Airborne troops are means at the disposal of the High Command. They are characterized by a high degree of mobility, powerful automatic armament, ability to appear quickly and suddenly and to conduct battle in the rear of the enemy.'[44] The regulation detailed the following airborne missions:

- Cooperate behind enemy lines with ground troops, jointly with partisan detachments, to encircle and utterly defeat the enemy and to combat approaching enemy reserves.
- Seize important enemy rear lines (boundaries) and crossings that protect enemy troops.
- Seize and destroy enemy air bases.
- Break up enemy rear command and control establishments.
- Protect seaborne troop landings by seizing coastal regions.

Having articulated the precise missions of airborne forces, the regulations added the important caveat that 'successful employment of airborne troops requires careful preparation and effective cooperation with aviation, partisan detachments, and mobile troops.'[45] As was the case with the 1943 *Instructions*, the combat experiences of Viaz'ma and Demiansk in the winter of 1941–42, as well as those of the Dnepr drop in 1943, were carefully woven into the new regulations. The regulations also pointed out that success in a *front* attack could be achieved, in part, by 'decisive actions in the rear of the enemy with airborne actions.' Paragraph 200 of the *Field Regulation of 1944* reiterated the airborne missions it had already listed and amplified what airborne forces could accomplish in a general offensive; paragraph 416, on pursuit operations, tasked airlandings to 'seize the defiles, crossings, road centers, and commanding heights and hold them until the approach of mobile units.'[46] Although airborne operations from 1944 to the war's end would be of extremely limited scope, the 1944 regulation captured the essence of war experiences and passed their legacy into the postwar years when peace and a restored economy would provide airborne forces the means to fulfill the missions for which they were most suited at the strategic, operational, and tactical levels.

CHAPTER 3

The Moscow Operation
(December 1941 – January 1942)

In late November 1941, the *Stavka*, having sensed the diminishing strength of the German drive on Moscow, began planning for a concerted counteroffensive in the Moscow region to drive German forces from the city's environs. This offensive, launched on 5 December, ended the long successive string of Soviet defensive operations, which extended back to the onset of war. Soviet planners of the Moscow operation were driven as much by desperation and circumstances as by a conscious well-planned effort to deceive and defeat German forces.

The Soviet counteroffensive, ordered by Stalin and planned by Zhukov, commander of the Western Front, envisioned the commitment of three new reserve armies to spearhead the offensive and penetrate German defenses. According to Vasilevsky, Deputy Chief of the General Staff:

> In essence, the plan envisaged defeating the enemy's flanking groups [Second and Third Panzer Groups] on the Moscow approaches; north of the capital by the 30th, the 1st Shock, the 20th and 16th Armies...south of the capital by the 50th and the 10th Armies....
>
> Neighboring armies were to provide active support to the Western Front. The Kalinin Front to the right of the Western Front was to make a thrust with the 31st Army... while to the left of the Western Front the Southwestern Front was to go into action with the 3d and 13th Armies.[1]

For the General Staff and Zhukov, the immediate task was the most formidable, namely penetrating German defenses and generating enough offensive momentum to drive the Germans back a comfortable distance from the close approaches to Moscow – that is perhaps 50–100

kilometers. At this stage Soviet commanders could not afford to antici-
pate major exploitation operations to greater depths. They understood
that one must walk before one could run, and the forces available to
Soviet commanders were not suited to deep exploitation. Mobile forces
were in short supply. The mechanized corps of June 1941 had long since
been destroyed or disbanded; their successor tank divisions had not fared
well, and most of them had likewise been decimated, disbanded, or
retained in smaller configuration. In fact, other than line foot infantry,
the only mobile forces available to the *Stavka* and *fronts* were small
separate tank brigades and agile, but fragile, cavalry divisions and corps.
In the circumstances of December 1941, these forces, of limited
sustainability and durability would have to suffice.

Airborne forces of the re-formed corps could add depth to the battlefield, but only in a well-orchestrated exploitation; and in December that
was only a dream. Airborne forces were, however, capable of conducting
diversionary and tactical assaults against the German rear, first to
weaken German defenses, second to assist in the penetration, and third,
and most important, to disrupt the German withdrawal and assist the
otherwise enfeebled exploitation operation. It was these missions that
airborne forces began to perform in December in a cascade of actions,
which intensified throughout the month and into the new year.

Archival documentation of the course of these operations is sketchy,
but existing accounts establish a well-articulated pattern. Elements of 1st,
4th, and 5th Airborne Corps and the Western Front's Special Airborne
Detachment participated. The most important tactical actions took place
at Teriaeva Sloboda in mid-December 1941 and at Medyn in early
January 1942, while other diversionary actions spread across the German
rear.

TERIAEVA SLOBODA, DECEMBER 1941

During the Soviet counteroffensive around Moscow in December 1941
and January 1942, the Soviets threw into combat virtually every resource
at their disposal to break the back of German Army Group Center. The
Soviets were particularly interested in employing those forces and techniques that facilitated deep battle and exploited tactical successes. They
sought to use mobile units of every variety, although such units were in
short supply at this stage of the war. Among those few mobile units that
could lend depth to the battlefield were airborne forces.

The Kalinin Front conducted the first of several tactical airborne
operations. Beginning on 5 December, it commenced the Klin operation,

an attempt by 30th Army and 1st Shock Army to drive German Third and Fourth Panzer Groups from the northern environs of Moscow and, if possible, destroy them. Pressured by the shock groups of the two Soviet armies, the Germans conducted a harrowing withdrawal through Klin to establish a new defensive line near Volokolamsk, along the Lama and Ruza Rivers.[2] The German retreat took place in subzero weather over snow-covered roads running through the town of Teriaeva Sloboda.

To disrupt the German withdrawal, on the night of 14–15 December, the Soviets dropped near the town of Lotoshchino a detachment of 415 paratroopers of the 214th Airborne Brigade, commanded by Capt. I. G. Starchak. A German situation map noted the airborne drop (see Figure 23).[3] Starchak's mission was to destroy bridges, interdict the road, and create general confusion among German forces withdrawing along the road from Klin (which fell to 30th Army on 15 December) through Teriaeva Sloboda. The paratroopers succeeded in cutting the Klin road near Teriaeva Sloboda. In fact they caused similar disruption of road traffic in the entire region from Lotoshchino eastward to Teriaeva in conjunction with other Soviet forces, which had penetrated German defenses, infiltrated into the rear area, and also threatened Teriaeva from the north (Teriaeva was held by German 14th Motorized Division elements, while 7th Panzer Division remnants concentrated east of Lotoshchino). The actions paralyzed German night road transport and forced the Germans to escort all daytime convoys with tanks.

For nine days, Starchak's command harassed the retreating German forces in a wide sector along the roads leading from Klin to Volokolamsk, from Klin to Novo Petrovskoe, and from Volokolamsk to Lotoshchino. From 15 to 25 December, Starchak's detachment repeatedly cut the rail line from Shakhovskaia to Novo Petrovskoe, interfering with the flow of German logistics.[4] After the Soviet occupation of Volokolamsk on 19 December, Starchak's unit moved west and continued harassing operations for six more days before being withdrawn for use in other operations. If subsequent operations were any indication, the Soviets were pleased with the achievement of Starchak's command. If he did half as well as they claimed, the Soviets should have been pleased.

Accounts by a former Soviet medical doctor in 1st Airborne Brigade, 1st Airborne Corps, describes the activities of several airborne diversionary groups, which operated in the region between Mozhaisk and Kaluga in late December 1941.[5] Although accounts of these actions, usually involving detachments of less than 100 men each, are replete with vivid descriptions of combat, the doctor records little regarding precise places and dates. This activity persisted until late January and was consistent with better-documented airborne activity, which took place in mid-January around Medyn. All of this activity was designed to disrupt the

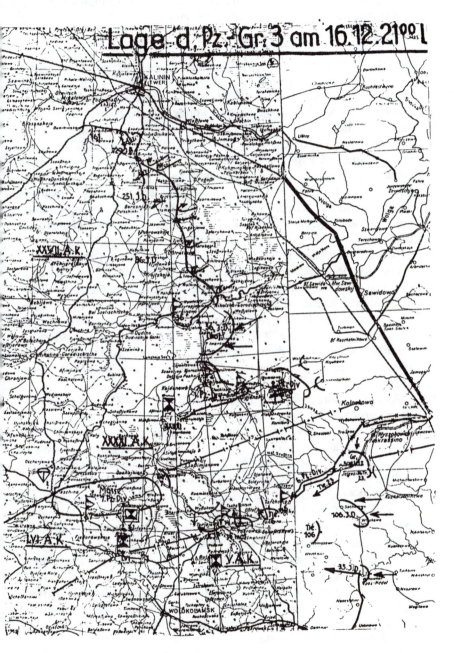

23. German Third Panzer Group Situation Map, 16 December 1941

immediate German rear area, and it continued until German forces were driven back through Medyn in late January.

MEDYN, JANUARY 1942

Apparently satisfied with the results of the earlier tactical airborne drop, *Stavka* and *front* planners decided to integrate similar airborne operations into the general Soviet offensive planned for early January 1942. Pleased with the progress of the December counteroffensive, the *Stavka* now entertained hopes of liquidating all the forces of German Army Group Center, pinned down by desperate fighting in the Rzhev, Viaz'ma, Briansk salient. In fact, it believed that all German forces forward of Smolensk were in jeopardy. Since the Germans had been unable to re-create a continuous front, numerous gaps existed, where attacking forces could exploit their success. The Germans clung stubbornly to the road network, using their superior mobility to capitalize on inner lines of communications and defend the threatened salient. To the Soviet High Command, it seemed that Viaz'ma was the critical node in the communications system. Seizure of Viaz'ma, it believed, would force utter German collapse. The approaches to Viaz'ma were dominated by the two vital centers of resistance at Gzhatsk and Iukhnov. The latter was already being threatened from the south and east and seemed most vulnerable. That town and Viaz'ma now became the immediate focus of new Soviet offensive planning.

A *Stavka* Directive of 7 January 1942 ordered Zhukov's Western Direction to encircle and destroy German Army Group Center.[6] This would be done by enveloping blows by the right wing of the Kalinin Front attacking toward Sychevka and Viaz'ma from the region northwest of Rzhev and by the left wing of the Western Front advancing from the Kaluga region toward Iukhnov and Viaz'ma. Simultaneously, the Western Front's right wing would continue their direct advance on Sychevka and Gzhatsk. During the initial phase of the operation, an airborne drop in the Medyn area was planned to facilitate the Western Front's advance. Subsequently, a larger-scale airborne assault would be launched against Viaz'ma proper, designed to coincide with the arrival in the region of *front* exploiting mobile forces.

These airborne operations were to play a significant role in the Soviets' operational plans. They were also designed to disrupt German command and control and logistical systems, block German withdrawal, and assist the advance of ground armies.

Pursuant to these aims, two associated drops were to take place to facilitate the advance of the Western Front. Western Front Directive

Number 269 of 9 January amplified earlier *Stavka* directives by ordering 43d, 49th, and 50th Armies and 1st Guards Cavalry Corps to attack from the Kaluga–Maloiaroslavets area against German forces in the Kondrovo, Iukhnov, and Medyn areas 'to surround and destroy the Kondrovo–Iukhnov–Medyn enemy group and develop the attack in a northwestern direction' (see Figure 24).[7] Two battalion-size airborne landings would occur along the axis of advance of Soviet 43d Army in the Medyn area. The parachute landing force consisted of Major I. G. Starchak's Western Front Parachute Assault Detachment, Captain I. A. Surzhik's 1st Battalion of the 201st Airborne Brigade (5th Airborne Corps), one battalion of the 250th Separate Rifle Regiment, and an air-landed group made up of the remainder of 250th Separate Rifle Regiment, commanded by Major N. L. Soldatov, who would command the entire operation.[8] The 250th Separate Rifle Regiment (Airborne) had been formed in mid-December 1941 from the 250th Rifle Regiment, 82d Rifle Division, recently arrived from the Trans-Baikal Military District. The regiment had three airborne infantry battalions, an artillery battery, a mortar company, and an anti-tank gun platoon. Its 1,425 men were trained for night combat in villages and in the use of explosives.

The planned airborne drop would occur in the German rear area along the boundary between XX and LVII Army Corps of German Fourth Army. On 29 December assaults by Soviet 33d and 43d Armies along the axis Maloiaroslavets–Borovsk–Medyn had split the two German corps from each other. XX Army Corps recoiled westward and northwestward of Borovsk where, on 4 January, it was attached to Fourth Panzer Army. The LVII Army Corps (34th Infantry, 98th Infantry, and 19th Panzer Divisions) and XII Army Corps of Fourth Army, by now fighting as intermingled *Kampfgruppen*, conducted a fighting retreat westward through deep snow and –30°C temperatures from Maloiaroslavets toward Medyn.[9] Soviet forces followed closely after, maintaining full pressure on the withdrawing German forces.

On 3 January, the Western Front directed Soldatov to drop his parachute forces in the vicinity of Medyn. First, he was to secure landing strips on which to land his regiment (see Figure 25). Then, his forces would cut all highways from Medyn to Gzhatsk and Kremenskoe, capture Miatlevo Station and temporarily cut the rail line, and block German Fourth Army withdrawal routes from Medyn to Iukhnov and from Polotnianyi Zavod to Detchina and disrupt movement of German rein-forcements to Medyn. Soldatov's forces were also expected to fight until the estimated 5 January approach of 43d Army into the area.[10]

Soldatov planned to conduct two parachute assaults. Starchak's detachment numbering 202 men was to secure the airfield at Bol'shoe Fat'ianovo and hold it until the arrival of TB-3 and PS-84 aircraft of

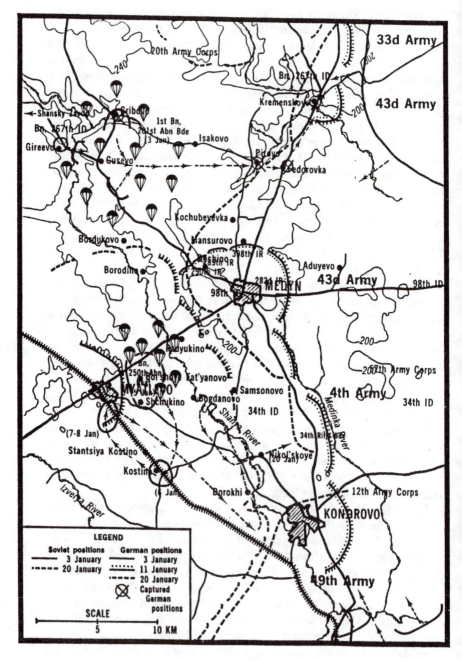

24. Medyn Area of Operations

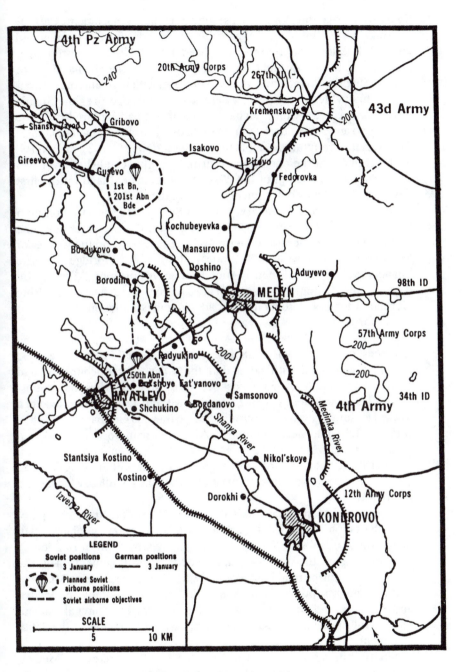

25. Medyn Operational Plan

Soldatov's air-landing force. The second parachute detachment, Capt. I. A. Surzhik's 1st Battalion, 201st Airborne Brigade with 384 men, would land 12–15 kilometers northwest of Medyn near Gusevo, Bordukovo, and Isakovo to capture and hold a bridge there over the Shania River, to occupy Shansky Zavod and Kremenskoe, and, with his main force, to cut the Iukhnov–Medyn highway, where a second bridge over the Shania River was located. After Starchak's detachment had captured Bol'shoe Fat'ianovo airfield, Soldatov's main force of 1,300 men was to land there. The scarcity of aircraft available for the operation (21 TB-3s and ten PS-84s) dictated that the operation occur in four lifts, conducted over two days. Surzhik's battalion of the 201st Airborne would land on the first day, with Starchak's detachment following the next day.[11]

On the night of 2–3 January, Captain Surzhik led his battalion on a paradrop into the Gusevo region (see Figure 26). After assembly, the battalion drove the surprised Germans out of Gusevo and the villages of Gribovo and Maslova as well. Soon it destroyed the bridge over the Shania River and established all-round defensive positions. After several days of interdicting the roads northwest from Medyn and repulsing German attempts to reopen the road, Surzhik's battalion prepared to move northeast.

At this time, Soviet 43d Army forces were approaching the Kremenskoe area. Two scouts [razvedchiki] from 43d Army reached Surzhik's command with news that the villages of Kochubeevo and Varverovka, south of Kremenskoe, were free of German troops. Surzhik's detachment occupied Pirovo without a fight and advanced toward Fedorovka, where reports indicated that 400 Germans of the 183d Infantry Division were stationed. After German forces abandoned Fedorovka, Surzhik's detachment cleared the town and moved on Kremenskoe, where, after a short engagement with withdrawing German forces, his detachment linked up after 11 January with advancing 43d Army forces.[12]

Meanwhile, Major Starchak's detachment, reinforced by one parachute battalion of the 250th Airborne Regiment, now numbering 416 men, attacked Bol'shoe Fat'ianovo and the nearby town of Miatlevo.[13] His force, plus the follow-on air-landed 250th Regiment, had the missions of securing road junctions in the Medyn region, seizing Miatlevo Station, and disrupting rail and road traffic between Iukhnov and Medyn and Iukhnov and Miatlevo Station. First, however, Starchak had to secure Bol'shaia Fat'ianovo airfield and assist the landing of the 250th Regiment.

Ninety minutes after a reconnaissance and air strikes on Medyn, Starchak's battalion was to land at the airfield in three lifts, using 21 TB-3 and 10 PS-84 aircraft. A securing group under Captain A. P.

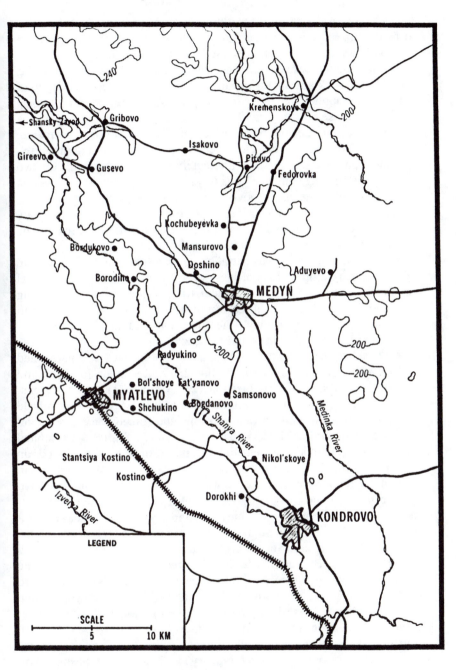

26. Medyn Operation, 3–20 January 1942

Kabachevsky was to jump into the area immediately adjacent to the airfield and secure runway facilities to allow aircraft from the starting command [*startovaia komanda*] to land its forces. A security group would then establish defensive positions two or three kilometers from the airfield and block any enemy advance. A platoon-size reserve, dropped with the battalion commander onto the airstrip, would respond to any threat that arose on the airfield.

The last element of the battalion to land was the starting command, equipped to prepare the airfield to receive aircraft. Thirty minutes after the initial parachute drop and immediately after the security group had landed, the starting command was to jump. After landing, they would establish landing signals, remove runway obstacles, and receive Major Soldatov's airlanding force. Meanwhile, the battalion would send out reconnaissance patrols in different directions to a distance of five to ten kilometers. If Starchak failed to take the airfield, he was to notify Soldatov and either move his battalion north to join Surzhik's forces or conduct separate operations of his own in the enemy rear. Before the operation each officer and individual trooper was given the plan of operations so each could still carry out his part, even if the plan was disrupted. Before the assault, the force engaged in map exercises, rehearsing how the airfield would be seized.

At 2100 hrs on the night of 3–4 January, Major Starchak's parachute detachment and the battalion of the 250th Regiment jumped into the airfield and immediately faced heavy resistance. Transport aircraft received heavy German antiaircraft fire throughout the drop, which caused excessive dispersion of the troops and forced some aircraft to return to base without dropping any paratroopers. Starchak assembled about 85 per cent of his men and attacked the German garrison, lodged in 12 fortified strongpoints, but was unable to overcome resistance there, or at Maloe Fat'ianovo or Shchukino. Consequently, at 0300 on 4 January, the starting command aircraft appeared over the airfield, but could not land because of continued enemy resistance below and heavy snow covering the landing strip. So, the starting command returned to its home airfield. On 4 January, Starchak continued to fight for the airfield and nearby villages. By nightfall he had secured it, and his battalion had established a perimeter defense around the field, as well as the villages of Bol'shoe and Maloe Fat'ianovo and Shchukino. The following day, *front* sent two MiG and one U-2 aircraft to establish communications with Starchak's unit, but this attempt failed. Although the U-2 did land, it quickly flew off when it mistook Starchak's men for Germans. Heavy snow and fog throughout 5 and 6 January also hindered establishment of communications and covered the runways. In such deteriorating conditions, *front* headquarters canceled Soldatov's landing and ordered

Starchak's force to operate independently. Meanwhile, Starchak's force continued to reduce German positions around the airfield.

On 5 January Major Starchak's battalion left Bol'shoe Fat'ianovo to conduct diversionary attacks against German installations. At Kostino, they destroyed a bridge, and then, on the night of 7–8 January, captured Miatlevo Station, destroying two trains and 28 German tanks. From 8 to 19 January, Starchak's force operated southward from Medyn to the Kondrovo area, ambushing German supply convoys and harassing withdrawing German forces. The battalion also destroyed bridges across the Shania River at Bogdanov, Samsonovo, and Iakubovsky. These bridges were critical to an orderly German withdrawal. Finally, on 20 January, the remnants of the force, 87 men, including the wounded Starchak, linked up with the advancing 34th Separate Rifle Brigade of 43d Army near Nikol'skoe on the Shania River.[14] The rest of Starchak's command had perished during the 17 days of combat.

Starchak had accomplished his basic mission and secured the airfield at Bol'shoe Fat'ianovo. Subsequently his detachment interdicted the rail line from Kondrovo to Miatlevo, destroyed many German fortifications and two trains, and disrupted work in the German rear area. All of this eased the task of 43d Army as it moved on Medyn and Miatlevo from the east. Despite this success, there were problems with the assault. Inadequate reconnaissance had not detected the actual size of the German garrison; and it took longer than planned to attain the objective. Moreover, better air cover might have improved the operation's success. Planners had also failed to consider weather conditions, predictably severe in January. Thus, Major Soldatov's larger operation failed. Though Major Starchak had shown flexibility and initiative in undertaking the diversionary tasks and his men had endured a long, difficult operation, the overall operation revealed deficiencies that would plague subsequent larger Soviet airborne operations.

Soviet airborne operations during December and January were of limited tactical significance. Since the Western Direction High Command was unsure of the degree of success its operations would achieve, it was difficult to articulate larger-scale missions for the airborne forces. Consequently, the assaults sought to add to the general confusion in the German rear area and further erode the capabilities of the Germans to resist. This mission the airborne assaults clearly accomplished, but in concert with other Soviet *front* forces, who often advanced parallel to or in the rear of withdrawing German forces.

Soviet critiques of the operations stated:

> While retreating after the defeat at Moscow in December 1941,
> the Germans tried to offer resistance along the line Volokolamsk,

Mozhaisk, Iukhnov, and Sukhinichi. The Western Front High Command, based on existing conditions, organized additional measures directed at completing the destruction of that German group. One of these measures was the insertion of airborne assaults in the rear of the withdrawing enemy.

At first, comparatively small airborne assaults were conducted in the beginning of January 1942 opposite the front of 43d Army with the mission of cooperating with the ground forces in the destruction of the Medyn-Miatlevo enemy grouping. Subsequently, the quantity and scale of airborne assaults increased. Already by the end of January, during the raid of General Belov's 1st Guards Cavalry Corps on Viaz'ma, the 250th Airborne Regiment and 8th Airborne Brigade cooperated with him.[15]

By late January, when the *Stavka* began realizing the fruits of its more ambitious plans, the potential role of airborne forces would become far more significant. The 250th Airborne Regiment and 8th Airborne initiated that new phase.

STRATEGIC CONTEXT, JANUARY 1942

The Soviets conducted three operational level airborne operations during the Great Patriotic War. The first and largest in scale and aim took place during the Soviet winter offensive of January–February 1942. It was preceded by a smaller-scale tactical airborne operation. These large-scale operations were undertaken as an adjunct to the Soviet winter strategic offensive, designed to push German Army Group Center away from Moscow and, if possible, destroy it. The first phase of the Soviet Moscow counteroffensive commenced on 5 December (see Figure 27). After a month of severe fighting in bitterly cold weather, Soviet forces drove German troops from the northern and southern approaches to Moscow, liberating the cities of Klin and Kalinin in the north and Tula and Kaluga in the south and threatening the flanks of German Army Group Center. During this first phase, the Soviets employed a tactical airborne operation west of Klin to facilitate the successful ground advance by dropping an airborne battalion in the German rear near Teriaeva Sloboda. In late December, as Soviet forces approached the Rzhev, Volokolamsk, Mozhaisk, Medyn, Iukhnov, and Kirov areas, the momentum of the Soviet offensive ebbed.

Despite the loss of momentum, the offensive had inflicted serious materiel and psychological damage on German forces. German personnel and equipment losses were heavy, and Soviet forces threatened to

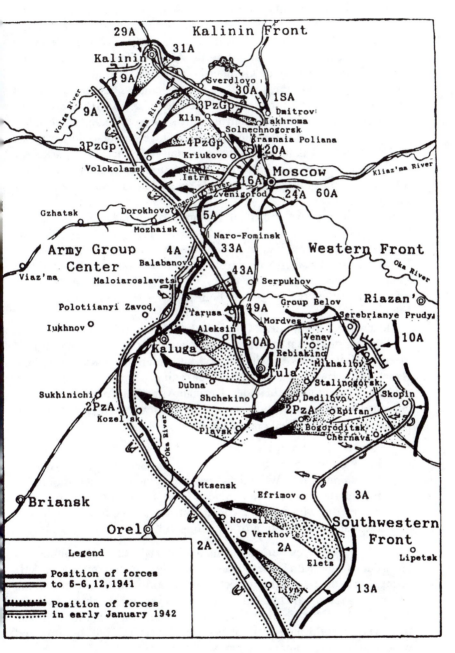

27. First Phase of Soviet Winter Offensive, 5 December–7 January 1942

break through the thinning German defense lines in three distinct sectors of Army Group Center. South of Kaluga, Soviet 50th and 10th Armies, spearheaded by 1st Guards Cavalry Corps, tore a major gap between German Second Panzer and Fourth Armies. The XII, XIII, and XXXXIII Army Corps of German Fourth Army withdrew westward toward Iukhnov in heavy snow and bitter cold under intense Soviet pressure. The Soviets threatened to encircle the XXXXIII Army Corps by turning both of its flanks. Fourth Army's rear service units and *ad hoc* lines of communication detachments pieced together loose defenses east and southeast of Iukhnov, and depleted units of Fourth Army's XXXX Panzer Corps (19th and 10th Motorized [Panzer Grenadier] Divisions) attempted to plug the yawning gap in German defenses between Iukhnov and Sukhinichi.[16]

At Maloiaroslavets, north of Kaluga, Soviet 33d and 5th Armies pressured Fourth Panzer Army and Fourth Army's left flank. By early January Soviet forces had breached Fourth Army's defenses on a 15-kilometer front between Maloiaroslavets and Borovsk. The Soviet thrust separated Fourth Army's left flank, XX Army Corps, from its parent unit; and neither the corps nor Fourth Army was able to repair the breach.[17]

Meanwhile, farther north, Col. Gen. I. S. Konev's Kalinin Front posed the third serious threat to Army Group Center. Konev's offensive forced German Ninth Army to withdraw 50 kilometers from Kalinin toward Rzhev and showed no evidence of weakening.

Colonel General Franz Halder, German Army Chief of Staff, recorded growing German desperation in his diary. Noting that 29 December was 'a very bad day,' Halder explained:

> ...in AGp. [Army Group] Center, however, the enemy's superiority on the fronts of Second Army and Second Panzer Army is beginning to tell. We did succeed in sealing the penetrations, but the situation on the overextended front, at which the enemy keeps hammering with ever new concentrations, is very difficult in view of the state of exhaustion of our troops...[18]

For Halder, 30 December was 'again a hard day' and 31 December was 'an arduous one,' with Soviet forces pressuring Fourth Army's XXXXIII Army Corps in the Iukhnov sector and Fourth Panzer Army in the Maloiaroslavets area. On 2 January, a 'day of vehement fighting,' Halder noted, 'In Fourth and Ninth Armies...the situation is taking a critical turn. The breakthrough north of Maloiaroslavets has split the front and we cannot at the moment see any way of restoring it again.'[19]

Soviet 33d Army's breakthrough between Maloiaroslavets and Borovsk, 50th Army's penetration south of Iukhnov, and the Kalinin

Front's thrust on German Ninth Army's left flank were major threats to the coherence of German Army Group Center's defenses. Faced with this crisis, Adolf Hitler became involved in operational and tactical decision-making and insisted that German forces either maintain their positions or counterattack. Hitler's actions led to the German decision to stand fast in a hedgehog defense throughout the winter and spring of 1942.[20] Hitler's orders forced local German commanders to improvise measures necessary to restore a coherent defense. Consequently Fourth Army's XXXXIII Army Corps conducted a tenacious, though harrowing, withdrawal toward Iukhnov, while XXXX Motorized Corps struggled to erect barriers to block the advance of Soviet 50th Army and 1st Guards Cavalry Corps southwest of Iukhnov. Cut off from Fourth Army and subsequently attached to Fourth Panzer Army, XX Army Corps failed on several occasions to repair the breached German defenses west of Maloiaroslavets. However, German counterattacks, the harsh weather and tenuous Soviet supply system combined to slow the momentum of the Soviet advance. The German situation remained critical, but not disastrous.

To restore momentum and to deliver the *coup de grâce* against the reeling German forces, Stalin and the *Stavka* marshaled the remaining strength of the Soviet forces in a final, desperate attempt to encircle German Army Group Center with both a shallow and a wide envelopment. The Kalinin and Western *fronts* would press German forces westward from Moscow, while the left wing of the Western Front and right wing of the Kalinin Front would attack from south and north to meet at Viaz'ma and encircle the bulk of German Army Group Center in a shallow envelopment. Together with these attacks, the reinforced Northwestern Front, on the Kalinin Front's right flank, would strike southward to seize Smolensk, deep in German Army Group Center's rear in an even wider envelopment. By capitalizing on growing German losses during the Moscow operations and the German distaste for winter battle, Soviet forces would achieve operational and, perhaps, strategic victory. Memories of Russia's destruction of Charles XII's Swedish army at Poltava more than two centuries before and Napoleon's army more than one century earlier mesmerized Soviet leaders. Yet, in those two earlier epochs, Russian armies had not been so seriously defeated as they were in the disastrous months after June 1941, when only the greatest of sacrifices had saved Moscow. Now, with scarcely any rest, those ragged survivors of the opening months of the campaign would be called on again to conduct deep, sustained operations against the foe that had already wrought such terrible havoc on them.

For his January offensive, Stalin massed his understrength rifle divisions, rifle brigades, and tank brigades on a broad front to strike against the entire German line. On main axes [direction or *napravlenie* in Russian], he assembled his dwindling mobile assets; a handful of tank brigades, cavalry corps and divisions, and ski battalions, which, with rifle division support, would form the shock and mobile groups necessary to convert tactical success into operational victory. Already weakened by the battles on the approaches to Moscow, these groups of men, tanks, and horses would carry the burden of leading the advance into the depths of the German defenses. The deep snow, subzero temperature, and fierce German resistance would test their mettle, and their staying power would dictate success or failure of the offensive. The *Stavka* threw its airborne forces into battle to assist them.

Rifle forces of the Soviet *fronts* had the task of attacking German forces and making initial penetrations through German defensive positions. To facilitate successful subsequent encirclement of German forces, mobile groups [*podvizhnie gruppy*] would advance into these penetrations to sow confusion in the German rear and to seize key objectives before the Germans could recover from the shock of initial breakthroughs. As required, airborne forces would go into combat either to assist rifle forces in making the initial penetrations or to reinforce the mobile groups once they had advanced deep behind German lines. With mobile forces successfully committed in the German rear, rifle forces would follow to isolate German units and destroy them piecemeal. To these ends, in the midst of one of the harshest winters in Moscow's history, Stalin ordered the unleashing of his forces.

Stavka orders issued on 7 January 1942 specified the missions of each force participating in the general offensive on the Western Direction.[21] The overall objective was to encircle and then destroy German Army Group Center. Soviet armies of the Kalinin Front's right wing, namely, 39th and 29th Armies, would attack from northwest of Rzhev toward Sychevka and Viaz'ma against the right flank of German Ninth Army. The 11th Cavalry Corps would exploit the Kalinin Front's successful penetration. The 10th, 50th, 49th, and 43d Armies (from south to north) of the Western Front's left wing would attack toward Iukhnov and Viaz'ma, led by a mobile group formed around the nucleus of 1st Guards Cavalry Corps. The attack would strike German Fourth Army and the junction between Fourth and Second Panzer Armies to the south. The remaining armies of the Western Front (from south to north – 33d, 5th, 16th, and 20th Armies), with 2d Guards Cavalry Corps as a mobile group, was to attack westward toward Sychevka, Gzhatsk, and Viaz'ma. The 33d Army thrust would strike the junction of Fourth Panzer and Fourth Armies. The 30th Army, 31st Army, and 1st Shock Army of the Kalinin Front's left wing would pressure German Ninth Army between Rzhev and Volokolamsk. Several tactical airborne drops in the rear of German forces on Soviet main attack axes would assist the initial Soviet advances. *Stavka* also planned a large operational airborne drop southwest of Viaz'ma, deep in the rear of German Fourth Panzer and Fourth Armies to complete the overall Viaz'ma encirclement. Precise objectives and timing of the airborne drop would depend on the progress of the main offensive.

On 8 January the Soviet offensive began in the Kalinin Front's sector and, during the next few days, spread to other sectors. That day, Soviet 39th Army of the Kalinin Front smashed through German Ninth Army defensive positions west of Rzhev and advanced 50 kilometers southward toward Viaz'ma. The 29th Army and 11th Cavalry Corps rushed to exploit the penetration. The latter raced southward 110 kilometers to the western outskirts of Viaz'ma, where it threatened the rear of German Ninth Army. The right wing of the Western Front joined the assault on 10 January, with 20th Army, 1st Shock Army, and 16th Army pushing German Ninth Army units westward through Shakhovskaia toward Gzhatsk. The same day, the Western Front's 5th and 33d Armies joined the attack and threatened German Fourth Panzer Army units at Mozhaisk and Vereia. Simultaneously with the advance of virtually all other Western Front armies, 43d, 49th, 50th, and 10th Armies (from north to south) penetrated German Fourth Army positions east of Iukhnov and Mosal'sk, moved on toward the critical Moscow–Warsaw highway near Iukhnov, and drove toward Kirov, thus encircling German forces at Sukhinichi. German Fourth Army, with its northern and southern flanks turned, withdrew toward Medyn. A 40-kilometer gap formed between German Fourth Army and Second Panzer Armies on Fourth Army's right flank. The 1st Guards Cavalry Corps entered this gap with the intention of exploiting across the Moscow–Warsaw highway into the German rear area south of Viaz'ma.

During the initial phases of the new offensive, the Soviets launched their two tactical airborne assaults to assist the advances of ground forces. On 3 and 4 January, battalion-size airborne assaults secured objectives in German Fourth Army's rear area at Bol'shoe Fat'ianovo, near Miatlevo, and in the Gusevo area north of Medyn. Both airborne forces eventually joined forces with advancing Soviet armies.

Despite initial successes, the advance had slowed by late January. Soviet formations were tired and at the end of their logistical tethers. Although mobile forces had penetrated into the German rear on at least three axes, they lacked the strength to secure their objectives. Compounding these difficulties, German counterattacks had delayed the advance of main frontal forces and cut off communications between these mobile forces and main *front* units. Originally threatened by strategic and operational encirclements, now the Germans threatened to encircle the exploiting Soviet mobile units. Marshal A. M. Vasilevsky, then a member of the *Stavka*, described the situation:

> At the beginning of 1942, having correctly assessed front conditions as favorable for a continuation of the offensive, the High Command inadequately took into account real Red Army capabilities. As a result, the nine armies at the disposal of the *Stavka* were almost evenly divided among all strategic directions. In the course of the winter offensive, Soviet forces expended all reserves created with such difficulty in the fall and the beginning of winter. Assigned missions could not be achieved.[22]

Vasilevsky referred to the deteriorating situation of January (see Figure 28). By then, the Germans had halted the main Soviet advance and launched violent counterattacks against forward Soviet positions. The Kalinin Front offensive ground to a halt short of Rzhev, Sychevka, and Viaz'ma. Renewed German counterattacks southwest of Rzhev threatened the overextended *front*'s shock group of 29th and 39th Armies. Northwest of Viaz'ma, 11th Cavalry Corps (18th, 24th, and 82d Cavalry divisions and 2d Guards Motorized Rifle Division) was capable of harassing German forces, but could not permanently cut the Smolensk, Viaz'ma, and Moscow highway. Armies of the Western Front's right wing and center took Mozhaisk and approached, but could not seize, Gzhatsk. Lead elements of Lt. Gen. M. G. Efremov's 33d Army penetrated between German Fourth Panzer and Fourth Armies' defenses north of Iukhnov and advanced toward Viaz'ma. The left wing of the Western Front swept south and west of Iukhnov against German Fourth Army but failed to take the city. Maj. Gen. P. A. Belov's 1st Guards Cavalry Corps advanced on Mosal'sk southwest of Iukhnov and south of the Moscow–Warsaw highway. To complicate matters further, the Germans, although encircled at Sukhinichi, stoutly resisted and soon mounted a relief effort that threatened the Western Front's left flank.

On 19 January, German Ninth, Fourth Panzer, and Fourth Armies occupied positions running from north of Rzhev, east of Zubtsov and Gzhatsk, to east and south of Iukhnov. Fourth Panzer Army's IX, VII, and XX Army Corps defended from northeast of Gzhatsk to 25 kilometers north of Medyn. Fourth Army's XII, XIII, LVII, and XXXXIII Army Corps defended along the Shania River west of Medyn in a semicircle facing east, southeast, and south of Iukhnov.[23] XX Army Corps' right flank divisions (167th and 255th Infantry Divisions) and the LVII Army Corps left flank divisions (98th and 52d Infantry Divisions) tried in vain to close the 20-kilometer breach in German defenses north of Medyn (a breach occupied by Soviet 33d Army).[24] Southwest of Iukhnov, overextended German XXXX Motorized Corps units and rear service

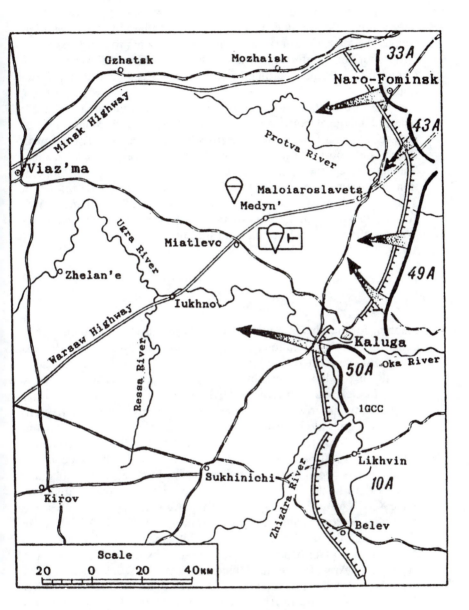

28. Western Front Situation, 2 January 1942

units of XXXXIII Army Corps desperately tried to halt the Soviet 50th Army advance toward the critical Moscow–Warsaw highway and the Viaz'ma–Briansk rail line. German control of that major *Rollbahn*, as well as the Moscow–Minsk *Rollbahn* (from Viaz'ma to Smolensk), was critical for the reinforcement and resupply of German Army Group Center forces. Hence, cutting the *Rollbahnen* became a primary Soviet objective.

In the face of these developments, the *Stavka* issued new orders. It believed a large airborne operation in the Viaz'ma area could reinforce advancing Soviet mobile forces, destroy the cohesion of German Fourth Panzer and Fourth Armies, and enable Soviet forces to seize Viaz'ma. Simultaneously, the main Soviet *fronts* would resume offensive operations to support the advancing mobile groups. The *Stavka* gave priority to 33d and 43d Armies attacking toward Viaz'ma from the east and to 50th Army attacking with 1st Guards Cavalry Corps toward the Moscow–Warsaw highway and Viaz'ma from the southeast.

THE ZHELAN'E OPERATION, JANUARY 1942

Planning

Planning for the Zhelan'e airborne operation occurred immediately after completion of the operation at Medyn. It was done by veterans who had planned or conducted the earlier operation. The operation coincided with the expanded Soviet January offensive into the flanks of Army Group Center and with growing Soviet hopes of enveloping the entire German strategic grouping. By mid-January, the left wing of the Western Front had penetrated German defenses south of Iukhnov with 50th and 10th Armies, spearheaded by Maj. Gen. P. A. Belov's 1st Guards Cavalry Corps. The attack hit German Fourth Army's left flank and tore a major gap between Fourth Army and Second Panzer Army. On Fourth Army's right flank, XXXXIII Army Corps fell back toward Iukhnov, while XXXX Motorized Corps, using small *Kampfgruppen*, tried to stave off Soviet forces driving into the Germans' rear on XXXXIII Army Corps' right flank.[25] Simultaneously, while the Soviet 43d and 49th Armies pressed German Fourth Army units back toward Iukhnov from the east, 33d Army threatened Iukhnov from the north. North and east of Iukhnov, a 20-kilometer gap formed between Fourth Panzer Army's XX Army Corps and Fourth Army's LVII Army Corps. LVII Army Corps divisions, with those of Fourth Army's XII and XIII Army Corps, were withdrawing into prepared positions along the Shania River west of Medyn. These positions covered the northern, eastern, and southern approaches to Iukhnov.

German Fourth Army's left flank, however, was suspended in midair. LVII Panzer Corps' 98th Infantry Division, reinforced by 52d Infantry Division, watched helplessly as Soviet 33d Army divisions marched through the deep snow westward past 98th Infantry Division's left flank in the Domashnevo area north of Miatlevo.[26] On 13 January Col. Gen. Franz Halder noted in his diary, 'The gap north of Medyn is as perturbing as ever.'[27]

The *Stavka* and Western Front wanted 33d Army to advance to Viaz'ma and link up there with Belov's 1st Guards Cavalry Corps, moving from the south, thus sealing the envelopment of a major portion of German Army Group Center. Before that linkup, however, Belov's cavalry corps had to penetrate newly established German defenses along the Moscow–Warsaw highway southwest of Iukhnov. The Western Front decided to conduct a tactical airborne operation north of the highway to assist Belov's crossing of that historic artery. The 250th Airborne Regiment and the 1st and 2d Battalions of the 201st Airborne Brigade were to land secretly 40 kilometers southeast of Viaz'ma near the villages of Znamenka, Zhelan'e, and Lugi, a region 35 to 40 kilometers behind the German front lines (see Figures 29 and 30).[28] Using skis for mobility after their landing, the Soviet forces could block German use of the Viaz'ma–Iukhnov and Lugi–Temkino highways and the Viaz'ma–Briansk railroad line, thereby disrupting German supply of its Iukhnov force. The airborne assault would also strike the German Iukhnov group from the rear, thus easing Belov's task.

Soviet aerial reconnaissance indicated that a German division headquarters, supply units, and up to an infantry battalion (300–400 men) were garrisoned at Znamenka. Another German battalion guarded an ammunition depot at nearby Godunovka and two platoons of infantry were located at Velikopol'e. A major German headquarters was at Podsosenki, with elements of other infantry battalions (300–500 men each) garrisoned at Klimov Zavod, Sidorovskoe, and Siniukovo. Further west, one battalion each garrisoned Debriansky and Ugra Station.[29] Deep snow isolated these garrison strongpoints from one another, for only the main roads remained open to traffic. Therefore, skillful operations by airborne forces could destroy each force separately.

The airborne force completed outfitting and training at Vnukovo airfield under supervision of the Air Force Administration of the Western Front. By 17 January, the forces and their aircraft had finished combat preparations. Twenty-one PS-84 (Douglas) aircraft of a 'special designation [*osobogo naznacheniia*] aviation unit of the Civil Air Fleet' were assigned to carry out the airborne operation. These civil air fleet aircraft were supported by several TB-3 bombers of the 23d Bomber Aviation Division, designated to transport 45-mm antitank guns.[30] All supporting

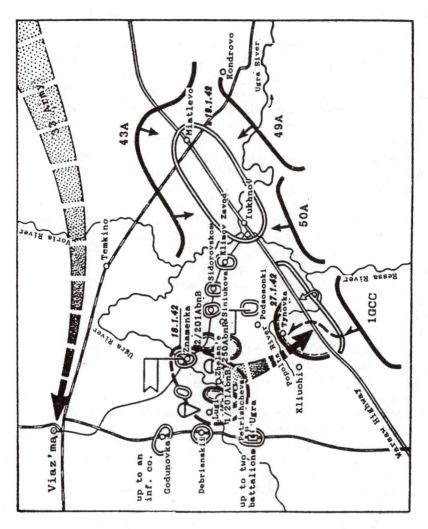

29. Zhelan'e Operational Plan: Overview

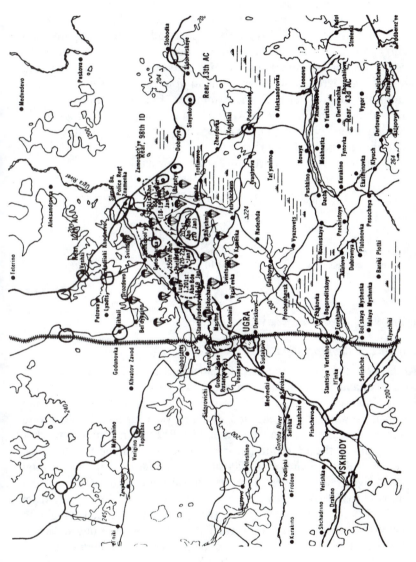

30. Zhelan'e Operational Plan: In Detail

aircraft were concentrated at Vnukovo airfield. Supporting aircraft crews were well-trained in night flight and the ability to land on relatively unprepared landing strips, even if snow-covered. The aircraft were also well-equipped and mounted heavy calibre machine guns.

The actual air assault was planned to take place in three phases. First, the 1st and 2d Battalions, 201st Airborne Brigade, would jump into and secure Znamenka airfield, organize all-round defense, and prepare to receive the starting command and air-landed group. Second, two and one-half hours later the starting command would arrive to set up a control area for the main landing. Third, 30 minutes after the starting command had landed, the main force of Major N. L. Soldatov's 250th Airborne Regiment would begin landing in groups of two to three aircraft to avoid congestion at the landing strip.[31]

The strength of the airborne forces was as follows:

	Parachute Assault Group	*Landing Group*
personnel	452	1200
rifles	263	300
machine pistols	142	646
sub-machine guns	28	40
heavy machine guns	10	28
mortars	11	0
antitank rifles	6	0
45mm guns	0	2

Source: Shaposhnikov, *Razgram, Vol. 3,* 115.

Conduct of the Operation

At 0335 on 18 January, the first 16 planeloads of paratroopers departed Vnukovo, and, by 0900, 452 men of Captain I. A. Surzhik's and Captain E. N. Kalashnikov's 1st and 2d Battalion, 201st Airborne Brigade had dropped between Znamenka and Zhelan'e (see Figure 31). A second group of ten aircraft flew in the next night at 0120 hours, but bad weather forced some of the aircraft to become disoriented and abort their drops. In the second group, only about 200 more men jumped, bringing the total to 642, lightly armed with mortars and antitank rifles. The starting command (65 men) landed between 1720 and 1750 on 18 January from four PS-84 aircraft. Guided in by partisans, the planes landed at night, in snow 50 to 60 centimeters deep, on an unfamiliar field, only one and a half to two kilometers south of enemy-occupied positions at Znamenka.[32] The aircraft lacked skis, so only one was able to take off after discharging its cargo. German troops destroyed the remaining aircraft the next day.

After landing, Captain Surzhik's 1st Battalion, 201st Airborne Brigade, assembled near Plesnovo, Mal. Lokhov and Zhelan'e and attacked the Znamenka airfield. Since they were unable to break through

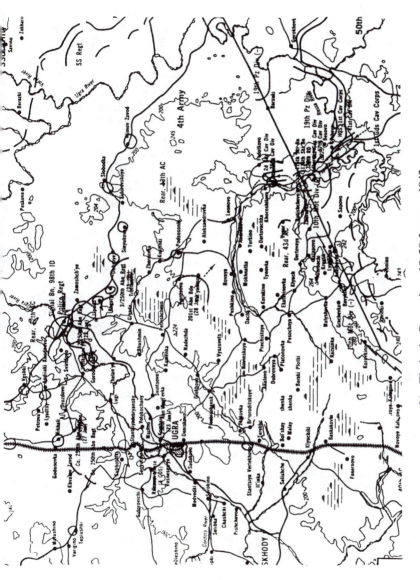

31. Zhelan'e Operation, 18–20 January 1942

the strong German defenses, Surzhik's paratroopers and the starting command disengaged and joined the main command at Zhelan'e after a march through knee-deep snow.

Throughout 19 January, Captain Surzhik's men, partisans, and local inhabitants prepared another landing strip northwest of Plesnovo for use by the 250th Regiment.[33] The following day Surzhik was able to radio headquarters, 'Landing on wheels is possible coordinates 38535; send [the remaining force] urgently. Surzhik.'[34] Despite unfavorable weather and heavy German artillery fire and bombing, an additional 1,100 troops of Major Soldatov's 250th Airborne Regiment landed in the Zhelan'e area, although the force had had to resort to only night landings from 20 to 22 January. These landings brought total airborne force strength at Zhelan'e up to 1,643. During the landings, the Germans shot down three Soviet aircraft, killed 27 paratroopers, and wounded nine others.[35]

The airborne main force began fighting within hours of landing. At 1700 19 January the Western Front staff sent the airborne force a radiogram which read, 'Zhukov has ordered: immediately occupy Bogatyri, Znamenka and Zarech'e to cut the withdrawal routes of the enemy Iukhnov group. Simultaneously advance security to Reitovo, to block the approach of enemy reserves from the Temkino region.'[36] One company of Kalashnikov's 2d Battalion, 201st Airborne Brigade, cut the Viaz'ma–Iukhnov highway near Zamosh'e and Murashovka and captured 54 German supply wagons. Two German companies with artillery support counterattacked the company during two days of heavy fighting.

Meanwhile, the Western Front's 43d, 49th, and 50th Armies battered German positions at and southwest of Iukhnov, and Belov's 1st Guards Cavalry Corps appeared ready to strike northward across the Moscow–Warsaw highway. On 20 January General of the Army G. K. Zhukov, the Western Front commander, radioed Major Soldatov, the 250th Airborne Regiment commander, to accomplish the following missions: 'By the morning of 21 January, with part of your force, secure square [kvadrat] 7530 (Kliuchi), establish communications with Belov, and cooperate with him by striking blows against the enemy in the direction of square 8145 (Liudinovo).' Zhukov soon expanded his original order:

> First – do not leave the regions 4746 (Znamenka), 5342 (Zhelan'e), 5338 (Lugi), at any cost hold the region, and occupy 4746 (Znamenka); second – our units [units of 33d Army] on 22 January enter area 2774 (Temkino) with the mission of establishing communication with you; third – give help to Belov with part of your force, for example, two battalions; fourth – at all costs halt enemy movement along the Iukhnov–Viaz'ma highroad.[37]

Major Soldatov sent the 1st and 2d Battalions, 201st Airborne Brigade, to attack Kliuchi and Liudinovo (see Figure 32). On 22 January Surzhik's force moved southward through the deep snow at an agonizingly slow pace and reached Petrishchevo at 1100. During the subsequent march, they eliminated small German garrisons at Tat'ianino, Borodino, Aleksandrovka, Andrianovka, and Novaia. Surzhik's force finally reached Tynovka on 28 January and met with elements of Belov's 1st Guards Cavalry Corps, which had cut the Warsaw–Moscow road only the day before.

While Surzhik's force operated to link up with Belov's cavalry, Soldatov's 250th Airborne Regiment and A. A. Petrukhin's local partisan detachment attacked Znamenka on the nights of 22 and 23 January. Strong Soviet attacks failed to dislodge the German garrison. Simultaneously, the 3d Battalion, 250th Regiment, and a company of the 1st Battalion, 201st Brigade, fought Germans on the Viaz'ma–Iukhnov road. To the west, the 1st Battalion, 250th Regiment, attacked German positions at Ugra Station and cut the Viaz'ma–Briansk rail line at two locations.[38]

On 24 January, *front* headquarters ordered Soldatov to 'reconnoiter [German positions] in the direction of Starosel'e, and Semlevo' (15 kilometers southwest of Viaz'ma), which added yet another mission to those his regiment was required to perform.[39] The next day, sub-units of the regiment captured Gorodianka and prepared an attack on Bogatyri and Lipniki along the Viaz'ma–Iukhnov road.

Between 25 and 29 January, the area of 250th Airborne Regiment's operations expanded, especially eastward along the Viaz'ma–Iukhnov road. Although the airborne forces severed several sections of the road, the important town of Znamenka remained under German control even after a heavy concerted attack by Soldatov's forces on the night of 29–30 January.

On 31 January Soldatov's regiment also linked up with Belov's cavalry forces, then en route to Viaz'ma and moved northward with them. When Belov's 1st Guards Cavalry Corps reached the southeastern approaches to Viaz'ma, where it joined newly arrived 8th Airborne Brigade on 2 February, the 250th Regiment moved northeast to join advanced elements of Soviet 33d Army, just then approaching Viaz'ma from the east. Two days later, the regiment joined with 33d Army's 329th Rifle Division, and both units cooperated in subsequent heavy fighting for possession of the approaches to Viaz'ma. Ultimately, both ended up threatened by destruction in the same German encirclement.

The operations of 250th Airborne Regiment and 1st and 2d Battalions, 201st Airborne Regiment, were a success. They secured a base area in the German rear, disrupted German logistics and communications, and

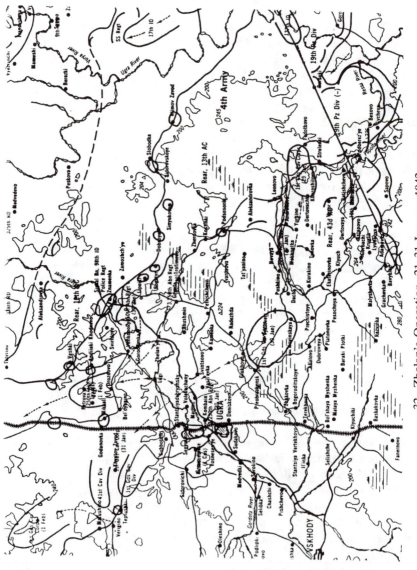

32. Zhelan'e Operation, 21–31 January 1942

assisted the advance of 1st Guards Cavalry Corps. The airdrop and air-landing went fairly well – most of the force landed – and, once on the ground, units performed their multiple missions well, despite organizational and equipment limitations.

Once again, operation problems the force experienced resulted from planners' mistakes. First, the operation was planned for too long a duration. Equipped with only light weapons and lacking armor and even medium artillery, the airborne force had to operate for 15 days isolated from the main force.[40] During that time the Western Front assigned them too many missions and thus fragmented airborne strength and tactical focus. *Front* had an exaggerated notion of what the small force could accomplish. The five-day landing period was too long, cost the unit the element of surprise, and permitted the Germans to organize their defenses and counterattacks accordingly. The landing operation suffered because the starting command landed at a different airfield from the parachute force and, even worse, less than two kilometers from German-held Znamenka. Furthermore, during the operation, troops had difficulty on skis, indicating a lack of adequate training for winter operations.

On the positive side, the regiment did accomplish its mission, and it proved the utility of operating with partisan detachments, which was mutually beneficial. This operation launched the long, complicated string of airborne operations collectively known as the Viaz'ma airborne operation.

CHAPTER 4

The Viaz'ma Operation, Phase 1
8th Airborne Brigade Operations,
(January–February 1942)

PLANNING

On 15 January 1942, the *Stavka* made the decision to insert Maj. Gen. A. F. Levashov's 4th Airborne Corps into the Ozerechnia area 30 kilometers southwest of Viaz'ma (see Figures 33 and 34). It was a bold decision because it involved a series of night parachute drops conducted in the harshest of winter conditions with temperatures well below zero. The 10,000-man 4th Airborne Corps, consisting of the 8th, 9th, and 214th Airborne Brigades, was then based at Ramenskoe, near Moscow. This corps was one of the most experienced – surviving – airborne units, and its commander, General Levashov, had previously operated for a long period in the enemy rear. Also, elements of its 214th Brigade had spent three months encircled in Belorussia. The projected airborne assaults would take off from Grabtsevo, Zhashkovo, Rzhavets, and Peremyshl' airfields, located some 30 to 40 kilometers behind the front, near Kaluga.[1]

Prior to 16 January, the staff of the airborne forces, in close coordination with the air force staff, had planned the operation with particular emphasis on operational objectives, unit missions, force composition, aviation and combat support, and logistical considerations. Unfortunately, they paid little attention to the conduct of ground operations, specifically to a coordinated linkup with *front* forces. Participating agencies shared responsibilities for the operation. The commander of airborne forces, Major General V. A. Glazunov, supervised preparation of the airborne drop, while the Western Front commander, General of the Army G. K. Zhukov, had operational control of the forces after landing. The air force commander had overall control of the operation from his Moscow headquarters, although he established a forward command post at Kaluga.[2]

On 17 January General Glazunov assigned specific missions to General Levashov of 4th Airborne Corps.[3] His corps was to cooperate with the Kalinin and Western Fronts to complete the encirclement of German Army Group Center and destroy it. The corps main body would land southwest of Viaz'ma to cut German communications between Viaz'ma and Smolensk, while a secondary force would interdict the withdrawal of German units from Viaz'ma to the west (see Figure 34). To confuse the Germans about the precise location of the main drop, the plan authorized several auxiliary reconnaissance-diversionary landings spread over wide areas of the German rear as well as several false air assaults.

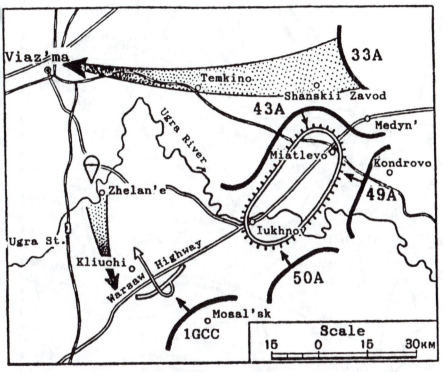

33. Western Front Situation, mid-January 1942

Only fragmented German forces were in the area west and southwest of Viaz'ma (see Figure 35). These forces sought shelter from the snow and bitter cold in villages along the Moscow–Minsk and Viaz'ma–Iukhnov roads. Garrisons of up to battalion-size defended populated points along major communications routes. Smaller units defended supply and maintenance installations in villages up to 20 kilometers off the highways. By mid-January, 11th Panzer Division had general responsibility for security of the *Rollbahn* west of Viaz'ma beyond the Dnepr River crossing. Although still committed to action farther east, 3d Motorized Division had units patrolling the highways east and south of

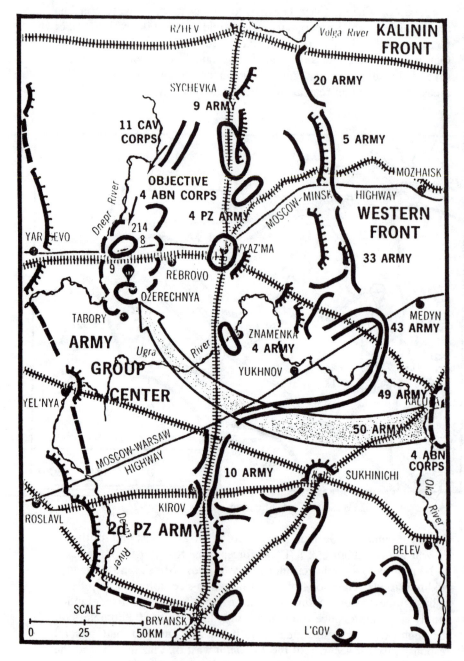

34. 4th Airborne Corps Operational Plan

35. Viaz'ma–Dorogobuzh Area of Operations

Viaz'ma. In late January the 208th Infantry Division's 309th Infantry Regiment garrisoned the *Rollbahn* west of Viaz'ma, and, after 30 January, 5th Panzer Division units moved into Viaz'ma and the region southwest of the city. These scattered forces would be the first to face the Soviet airborne assault.[4]

The Soviet airborne landing was scheduled to begin with a daylight drop of a battalion-size forward detachment. It would secure landing sites by the end of the first day for the corps' main force. The main drop would occur during darkness to minimize the risk of enemy attack. Originally, the operation was to begin on 21 January, but slow movement of the corps into the staging area had forced a postponement of the drop until 26–27 January. The corps moved to Kaluga over rail lines cut by the Germans, who had also destroyed the main bridge over the Oka River. Consequently, corps units had to ford the river, carrying their supplies with them. This entire movement to Kaluga had been poorly planned and was executed with almost complete disregard for secrecy or concealment. Supplies were left uncamouflaged, and personnel wore conspicuous new winter uniforms (other troops had not yet been issued them). Moreover, because winter weather had driven command posts into villages and towns, corps command posts were in populated areas recently evacuated by the Germans, who must certainly have left behind agents to report on Soviet movements.[5] Similar problems occurred in attempts to concentrate aircraft at the airfields. With this inauspicious beginning, 4th Airborne Corps paratroopers slowly arrived at their staging areas.

The 8th Airborne Brigade's movement typified the transfer to airfields. It loaded on trains beginning on 18 January, and troops had to detrain several days later at Aleksin to cross the frozen Oka River or, as the troops said, 'pass the train's contents over to the other side,' a process which took several days.[6] Finally, on the evening of 23 January, the brigade arrived in the Kaluga region, and the next day its subordinate battalions moved to separate airfields according to prearranged plans as follows: 1st Battalion–Grabtsevo; 2d Battalion–Zhashkovo; 3d Battalion–Zhashkovo; 4th Battalion–Peremyshl'. Soon the 9th Airborne Brigade, assigned to the corps to replace the less well-prepared 7th Brigade, also concentrated at Zhashkovo airfield. Meanwhile, the 214th Airborne Brigade completed its movement to an assembly at Rzhavets airfield permitting the starting date for the assault to be specified as the night of 26–27 January.[7]

By 25 January the Kalinin Front's 39th Army forces had penetrated German defenses west of Rzhev and driven southward west of Sychevka. The *front*'s spearhead mobile group, Colonel S. V. Sokolov's 11th Cavalry Corps was approaching the main Moscow–Minsk highway west of Viaz'ma. From the east Lieutenant General Efremov's 33d Army forces slowly advanced through forests south of the highway toward the eastern outskirts of Viaz'ma. Further south on 27 January Belov's 1st Guards Cavalry Corps had crossed the Moscow–Warsaw highway 35 km west of Iukhnov with his cavalry formations and linked up the next day with Soviet airborne forces operating from Zhelan'e (see Figure 36). However, the heavier units in Belov's corps (one rifle division and a tank brigade), as well as the follow-on forces of 50th Army, were stopped short of the highway by hastily assembled German forces (mostly from 10th Motorized Division). At this juncture, it seemed to the Western Direction High Command a propitious moment to commit an even larger airborne force to combat in the German rear.

On 24 January General Zhukov dispatched the following cryptic warning order to General Levashov: 'To comrade Levashov – Mission: 26–27 January, land corps and occupy positions in accordance with the map. Objective: Cut off withdrawal of the enemy to the west. Zhukov, 24 January 1942 1300H.' The order was posted on a 1:100,000 map indicating corps' jump and assembly areas and summarizing airborne force objectives.[8]

Having received his mission, Levashov reviewed the situation with his staff and at 1800 on 26 January issued orders to his corps. The corps' main force was to land southwest of Viaz'ma near Ozerechnia, Kurdiumovo, and Komovo. After landing, corps forces were to advance into the forested area west of Viaz'ma; secure the villages of Iamkovo, Mosolovo, Pleshkovo, and Azarovo; cut main German communications routes; and prevent both German withdrawal from and reinforcement of Viaz'ma. Cooperating with Kalinin and Western Front forces, the corps was to complete the encirclement and destruction of Army Group Center's Viaz'ma grouping. Seven smaller groups of 20 to 30 airborne troops each were to conduct reconnaissance-diversionary operations near the landing sites. They would establish contact with the 11th Cavalry Corps and Major N. L. Soldatov's airborne regiment, committed on 18 January in the Zhelan'e area.[9]

Levashov's orders specified the missions of his subordinate brigades. Lieutenant Colonel A. A. Onufriev's 8th Airborne Brigade, the corps' first echelon, preceded by its 2d Battalion operating as a forward detachment, would land near Ozerechnia to secure a line from Rebrovo through Gradino to Berezniki and block German movement along the Viaz'ma–Smolensk and Viaz'ma–Dorogobuzh roads. Onufriev's 2d Battalion would secure Ozerechnia and the landing area for the remainder of the brigade, while the brigade main force would secure the overall objectives. Colonel I. I. Kuryshev's 9th Airborne Brigade was to land near Goriainovo and secure a line from Goriainovo through Ivaniki to Popovo to prevent the approach of German reinforcements from the west.

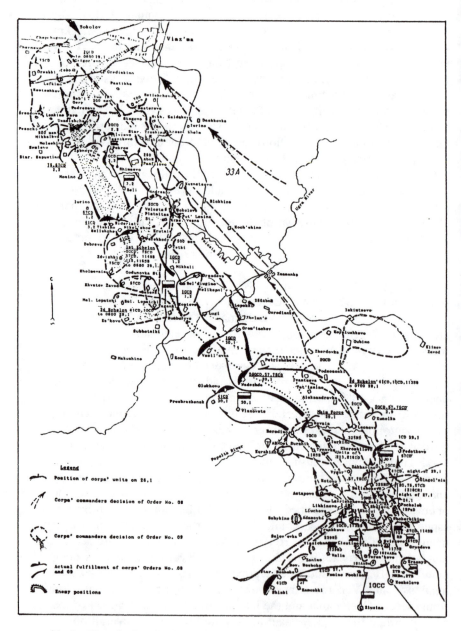

36. 1st Guards Cavalry Corps Operations, 28 January – 3 February 1942

Lieutenant Colonel N. E. Kolobovnikov's 214th Airborne Brigade, reinforced by the corps' separate antitank and artillery battalions, was to land and assemble in the Vekhotskoe, Pleshkovo, and Uvarovo areas and act as the corps reserve, prepared either to counterattack against German units should they penetrate airborne defensive lines or to reinforce the defense of the 8th and 9th Airborne Brigades.

The brigade's seven reconnaissance-diversionary teams were to block the approach of German forces to the landing site, while four smaller teams established communications with Sokolov's 11th Cavalry Corps. All these teams were to assault at the same time 8th Brigade's forward detachment was jumping.[10] Corresponding to missions assigned by General Zhukov, General Levashov's major consideration in decision making was to secure the designated objective by surprise and to hold it for two to three days until 11th Cavalry Corps, 33d Army, and 1st Guards Cavalry Corps had linked up with the airborne forces. On 15 January 4th Airborne Corps came under operational subordination to the Western Front.

After receiving Levashov's orders, commanders worked at assembling the airborne corps and supporting aircraft. Planning required the concentration at airfields around Kaluga of 40 PS-84 and 25 TB-3 aircraft to conduct the lift. These planes were insufficient for rapid movement of all airborne forces into the drop area, but severe shortages in military transport aviation had dictated using so few aircraft. In fact, when the tardy concentration of aircraft was complete, only 39 PS-84 and 22 TB-3 aircraft were available. Similar deficiencies plagued fighter cover for the operation. Originally, 30 fighters were expected to cover the concentration areas, and one fighter regiment (72 fighters) would protect landing sites. Only 19 fighters, however, were available to protect the operation.[11] Given these aircraft shortages, the plan necessitated each aircraft crew making two to three sorties a night to complete the movement in three or four days. Planners ignored the weather, potential aircraft combat losses, and the possibility of aircraft mechanical failures. In addition, the operation faced adverse aerial conditions because German aviation was especially active in the sector and was familiar with the Kaluga airfields, having recently used them.

Airborne units established liaison at the aviation commanders' command posts at each airfield and at the Western Front and air force headquarters to coordinate aviation support. Within the airborne force, commanders created signal operation instructions and special radio nets connecting brigades to the corps. No communications links, however, existed between the airborne force and combat aviation units. Transport aviation did coordinate well with the airborne forces throughout the planning phases.

The estimate of the situation did not, however, provide data on an important consideration, namely, information concerning enemy strengthin the drop area. There simply was no reliable information on such German forces. Neither partisan units (which proliferated in the area) nor Major Soldatov's paratroopers were close enough to Viaz'ma to provide such intelligence. Soviet reconnaissance flights also failed to detect precise locations of German units. *Front* headquarters optimistically reported a wholesale enemy withdrawal from the area when, in fact, none had occurred. On the contrary, considerable numbers of German troops were near the planned drop area.

On 26 January Lieutenant Colonel Onufriev assessed his mission and gathered with his chief of staff and subordinate commanders to discuss the mission and how it would be fulfilled. The aim was to land the brigade in one day so that it could protect the subsequent insertion of the corps. The brigade's 2d Battalion, operating as forward detachment, was to conduct the initial jump and secure other landing areas. The missions and instructions to other subordinate subunits were as follows:

- 3d Battalion – secure Rebrovo to prevent the approach of Germans along the railroad.
- 1st Battalion – seize Gradino and cut the Viaz'ma–Smolensk highway to block German movement into Viaz'ma from the west.
- 4th Battalion – cut the Viaz'ma–Dorogobuzh road to block enemy withdrawal from Viaz'ma.
- artillery battalion – receive initial missions after landing.
- brigade command post after landing to be located at Ozerechnia and, after seizure of the entire defense area, at Azarovo.
- Pass orders from battalion to companies and platoons today.
- By 1000 27 January accomplish the following measures:
  - coordinate more precisely with aviators the airborne landing sites and the loading of PDMM [parachute equipment and supply loads] on aircraft;
  - check the presence in the kit of every paratrooper all that is necessary for air-landing and also prepare weapons for combat and work in low temperature conditions;
  - verify the packing in the PDMM of daily rations, half load of ammunition for rifles, and one and one half loads of ammunition for mortars, antitank rifles and explosives and all required equipment according to estimates;
  - chief of parachute-landing services once more check the serviceability of all parachutes;
  - seat 15–18 paratroopers in every aircraft and load them with the PDMM and antitank rifles, mortars, machine guns, and ammunition;
  - define precisely lists of parachutists and inventories of cargo per

aircraft. Lists will be in three copies (one for aircraft commander, a second for the senior officer in the aircraft, and a third for the brigade staff);

- transmit combat missions to enlisted soldiers and NCOs within 2 hours before embarkation on aircraft;
- in all battalions and special subunits, conduct meetings with all personnel after they have received their orders.[12]

8TH AIRBORNE BRIGADE ASSAULT

From 24 to 27 January, the overall situation on the Western Front seemed to remain favorable for the airborne operation. The 11th Cavalry Corps of the Kalinin Front remained just northwest of Viaz'ma. The leading elements of 33d Army approached Viaz'ma from the east, and Belov's 1st Guards Cavalry Corps mounted persistent attempts to complete its crossing of the Moscow–Warsaw highway southwest of Iukhnov.

Imbued with optimism, at 0400 on 27 January the Western Front commander, Zhukov, sent the following message to 4th Airborne Corps at Kaluga: 'Tell Levashov that Sokolov's [11th Cavalry Corps] Cavalry Group has moved into the area that I marked on the map. Therefore, the situation has eased for Levashov. Think over the techniques of communications and give the men instructions so that there are no misunderstandings.'[13] Levashov quickly passed the orders to his brigade commanders and his forward detachment (see Figure 37). The forward detachment, consisting of the 2d Parachute Battalion under Captain M. Ia. Karnaukhov, was ordered to land at Ozerechnia and, by organizing all-round defenses, prepare the area for further landings of the brigade. At the same time, the reconnaissance-diversionary parties also received their orders.

Karnaukhov's battalion and the reconnaissance-diversionary force left Zhashkovo airfield at 1430 on 27 January aboard 39 PS-84 bombers. Because of poor pilot orientation over the drop area due to a heavy snow storm and 600 meter ceiling, the aircraft dropped the paratroopers at a higher altitude than desired and far south of the planned drop zone.[14] The paratroopers landed scattered over an area of 20 to 25 kilometers radius around the village of Tabory about 20 kilometers south of Ozerechnia. Fortunately there were no enemy in the immediate vicinity. The battalion commander landed with the first contingent and immediately sent a recce party into Tabory. At 1600, while the 2d Battalion was jumping into the Tabory region, other aircraft dropped the seven reconnaissance-diversionary groups, plus four other detachments to establish contact with the 11th Cavalry Corps and Soldatov's group, at various locations in the German rear.

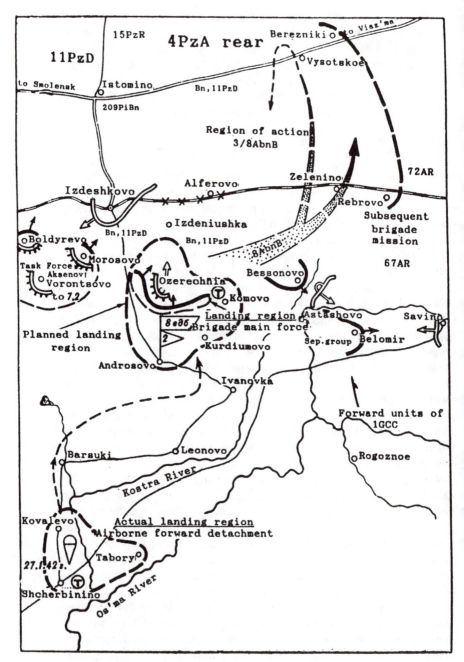

37. 8th Airborne Brigade Operations, 27 January – 2 February 1942

The German command was almost immediately aware of the airborne drop. Fourth Panzer Army received two reports. The first was that Soviet troops with machine guns and grenade launchers were operating along the Viaz'ma–Smolensk highway near Iakushino. The second, from 11th Panzer Division, was that, between 1600 and 1700 (after dusk) on 27 January, 20 transport aircraft had dropped about 400 paratroopers near Mitino station, west of Izdeshkovo (probably Soviet Group Aksenov). Subsequent reports spoke of Soviet attacks on an 11th Panzer Division battalion and a 309th Infantry Regiment battalion at Iziakovo and at several other points along the *Rollbahn*. Other reports said the airborne forces at Mitino had withdrawn south of the *Rollbahn*. Fourth Panzer Army alerted all of its forces in the region to the new danger.[15]

Meanwhile, Soviet airborne commanders continued the painstakingly slow assembly of their scattered forces. The 2d Battalion's reassembly around Tabory took considerable time. Of the original 648 men dropped, only 318 had assembled by evening on 27 January. The next morning, the total had risen to 476 men, but virtually all the unit's weapons, equipment, and supplies had been lost in the snow-covered fields and forests. Karnaukhov faced an immediate dilemma. Unable to establish contact with either 4th Airborne Corps or the other brigade commanders and able to contact 8th Airborne Brigade headquarters only long enough to report 'landed and operating' before communications failed, the commander could not notify headquarters of his new location. Nor could he make a drop zone visible from the air without confusing the main force, which expected him to be at Ozerechnia. Consequently, on the morning of 28 January, Captain Karnaukhov moved part of his force to Tabory and established a landing zone equipped with signals, in case other units of the 8th Airborne Brigade followed his battalion's course. With his main force, he moved to Ozerechnia to establish the prescribed landing strip. As he marched, he heard the roar of aircraft passing overhead and wondered where the paratroopers on board would be dropped. Karnaukhov's force arrived at Androsovo, three kilometers from Ozerechnia, on the evening of 28 January only to find Ozerechnia occupied by a small German force. He reconnoitered the German positions; and, during the night, was reinforced by elements of Major A. G. Kobets' 3d Battalion, which had jumped near Ozerechnia in daylight under heavy enemy fire.[16]

Meanwhile, at Kaluga, the commander of airborne forces, lacking information from the forward detachment, ordered the 8th Airborne Brigade main force to begin its assault on the night of 27–28 January. During the night two flights dropped Major A. G. Kobets' 3d Battalion, along with heavy equipment, ammunition, and supplies. As on the previous day, the drop was inaccurate, with half the units landing in the

Tabory area and the other half around Ozerechnia. The 3d Battalion could not establish communications with corps until late on 28 January.

Unfortunate events in the Soviet rear area further complicated the complex situation at the front. Throughout 28 January German aircraft, probably aware of the Soviet airborne operations, bombed the airfield at Zhashkovo. When the Soviets switched to Grabtsevo and Rzhavets airfields, German bombers followed suit. Ineffective Soviet air defenses at all three locations allowed German pilots to destroy seven precious TB-3 bombers, one fighter, and several fuel dumps. Consequently about 200 airborne troops were left 'without wings.'[17] Moreover, the availability of only 19 fighter aircraft meant that the transport aircraft traveled with their precious cargo over enemy territory with no armed escort. After the bombing of the airfields, the airstrip was repaired, and, by 2100 27 January, Major V. P. Drobyshevky's 1st Battalion took off in 15 aircraft. Soon the weather worsened as the snow storm turned into a blizzard. Large-scale flights were impossible, and thereafter only single flights took off at irregular intervals. Drobyshevsky's battalion was scattered throughout the Belomir region seven kilometers southeast of Ozerechnia. Ultimately, because of German air attacks and deteriorating weather, flights from all three airfields ceased.

Having received the radio message 'landed and operating' from its forward detachment, 8th Brigade had no way of knowing it had landed at Tabory rather than its assigned target Ozerechnia. Assuming that Ozerechnia was firmly under control of Karnaukhov's 2d Battalion, corps headquarters ordered Major Kobets' 3d Battalion to continue its assault into Ozerechnia during the day on 28 January. The air-landing occurred in a blinding snowstorm, but, despite the snow, the aircraft landed safely. As 4th Airborne Corps history related:

> None of the airborne troops anticipated what to expect over the landing area. All were prepared for the worst. Soldiers, staring out the aircraft's windows, did not know that their aircraft had already been fired at from the ground, and on the signal 'Let's go,' Major Kobets was the first to leap out of the open door. All was as if on an exercise; falling into emptiness, opening the cupola, deployment in the wind and transferring your automatic weapon into the landing position. All of this distracted the battalion commander from the ground. Having completed his preparations for landing, he once more looked up and was astonished – anti-aircraft rounds had pierced his percale cupola. Glancing toward a distant village, and it was Bessonovo, he saw the flashes of German automatic guns. Below was even worse, he was being carried toward Ozerechnia, where around 100 fascist soldiers poured from the houses. Some of

them had already fired on the descending parachutists. The battalion commander tried to side slip his chute to speed up the landing, but flopped in the snow 200 meters from Ozerechnia.[18]

Chaos broke out as battalion paratroops landed in and around the village frantically trying to land in the forest adjacent to it or otherwise avoid the Germans. Most made it – some did not. The battalion commander, after returning the German fire, made his way alone through the woods to the battalion assembly area at Androsovo, three kilometers from Ozerechnia. There, to his surprise, he met Captain Karnaukhov with 300 men plus 80 from his battalion and the machine gun company. The remainder of his 3d Battalion, due to a navigational error, were dropped in various places around Smolensk district. For example, his 7th Company had landed north of Viaz'ma in the dispositions of Kalinin Front's 39th Army. His 9th Company suffered the same fate. Major Kobets, as the senior officer present, assumed command of the two battalions and issued orders for a night attack on Ozerechnia.[19]

At 2300 28 January, Karnaukhov's and Kobets' battalions occupied jumping-off positions for the attack. The attack caught the Germans by surprise. Having seen the parachutists scatter all over the countryside during the day, they did not expect an organized attack through the deep snow and at night by a fairly well-organized force of almost 400 men. On the third assault, the German defenses gave way, and the company-size rear service unit was destroyed with heavy losses. Kobets' force captured six vehicles, an antiaircraft gun, documents, and 'a suitcase of a German general containing a parade uniform.'[20] During the early morning, Karnaukhov's men prepared a landing zone, organized all-round defenses, and sent out reconnaissance detachments to scout German approach routes into the area.

Unfortunately for this initial force, during the preceding night many aircraft full of paratroopers returned to base, their pilots reporting that landing markers in the Ozerechnia region were not visible. Despite their failure, two flights took place overnight, which dropped 1,500 troops, heavy weapons, ammunition, and supplies. These flights, however, were also inexact, and the brigade's subunits were scattered over the entire region.

After seizing Ozerechnia, Kobets' small 3d Battalion moved eastward on foot toward Rebrovo village on the main rail line running west from Viaz'ma. The battalion marched 20 kilometers through heavy snow, lamenting the loss of their skis in the initial drop. Meanwhile, the Airborne Command and 4th Airborne Corps commander were distraught over the lack of communication with 8th Brigade and the forward detachment. Repeated attempts to reach all of 8th Brigade's battalions had utterly failed.

To clarify the confused situation, on the morning of 28 January, General Levashov sent first one, and then a second aircraft to locate his missing forces. Neither aircraft returned. Then Levashov sent his assistant chief of reconnaissance, Senior Lieutenant A. P. Aksenov, in a PO-2 light aircraft to find the 2d Battalion's landing area and to determine its condition. The first attempt to find the battalion failed even after the aircraft had landed and subsequently had taken off under heavy German fire. In a second attempt, the aircraft was forced down by enemy fire seven kilometers from Iukhnov. In a third attempt, made on 29 January, Aksenov's aircraft, short of fuel, landed near Vorontsovo, 12 kilometers southwest of Alferovo. After a two-day search, Lieutenant Aksenov discovered small groups of Soviet troops near Vorontsovo, but not the airborne headquarters. Having reported to corps, he gathered 213 men and successfully attacked and destroyed small German garrisons at Vorontsovo, Morozovo, and Evdokimovo. On 1 February, using captured German fuel, Aksenov flew to 8th Airborne Brigade headquarters at Androsovo. His detachment remained in the area south of Izdeshkovo to harass German garrisons in the area.[21]

Although the VDV Military Council and corps commander gave considerable care to resupply of 8th Airborne Brigade, the brigade's position worsened. It had been decided, upon receipt of Karnaukhov's landing signal, to dispatch ten aircraft to him, each carrying supplies and two paratroopers. However, on 26 January only four of the necessary ten aircraft landed at Zhashkovo airfield. Consequently, Lieutenant Colonel Onufriev decided to fly on the first aircraft with his battalion commissar. Each of the other aircraft would carry two brigade command personnel. The fourth aircraft with the aviation unit commander would conduct a reconnaissance and be the first to land.

When Karnaukhov's signal 'landed and operating' had been received, Onufriev received permission of his corps commander to take off. At 2200 27 January, the aircraft took off into yet another snowstorm. After a four-hour flight, the pilot of one of the aircraft landed the aircraft along a road. The landing site was only three kilometers from its home base, Zhashkovo airfield. The other aircraft became similarly disoriented and landed near Maloiaroslavets and at other points equally far from their targets. Gathering again on 28 January at Zhashkovo airfield, the 8th Brigade commander and staff organized flights into the German rear, this time on a TB-3 bomber, from which they would jump along with an escort of 18 paratroopers. This attempt to join Karnaukhov's command also failed due to weather and German resistance. A third attempt at 0030 29 January, with a more experienced pilot, finally succeeded in unloading

Onufriev and his staff some 15 kilometers from Ozerechnia. After landing in the fog and snow, Onufriev's group engaged German soldiers, suffered some casualties, but finally reached the small village of Ivanovka, two kilometers from Androsovo, where it met a paratrooper patrol from Karnaukhov's battalion. By morning on 30 January, Onufriev had finally established radio contact with Karnaukhov's battalion.[22]

Thus, despite dwindling air transport, the landing of 8th Airborne Brigade continued. On the night of 28–29 January, aircraft dropped 500 skis, ammunition, and supplies at Ozerechnia. But of the original aircraft, only ten PS-84s and two TB-3s remained serviceable.[23] The *Stavka* ordered additional aircraft to continue the operation; and, by 2000 on 29 January, 540 more men had been airdropped. On the night of 29–30 January, however, German aircraft again bombed the Kaluga airfields. On 30 January the Germans struck again at both Zhashkovo and Rzhavets.

Bad weather (snow with temperatures of −40°C) and enemy aircraft activity had limited the total drop on 30 January to a mere 120 men. The following day 215 men jumped.[24] While parachute drops continued, at 0530 on 29 January, the 4th Airborne Corps commander ordered the aviation group to reconnoiter landing areas systematically to find his subordinate units.

After landing, Onufriev's group moved westward to Captain Karnaukhov's position. Assisted by the platoon sent out by 2d Battalion, the two forces merged on 31 January. That day corps finally received a fairly accurate report on airborne and enemy dispositions. Onufriev reported to both General Levashov and General Zhukov that the Germans held the nearby road junction of Ermolino–Bessonovo, perhaps in infantry battalion strength supported by tanks and armored cars. Smaller German units occupied the villages of Alferovo, Borovoi, and Ermolino; the German garrison at Izdeshkovo (units of 11th Panzer Division and Fourth Panzer Army rear service units) numbered about 400 men. He also reported that his brigade had been dropped over a wide area, and the location of many subunits was unknown. Out of radio contact, Onufriev's brigade was dispersed in the Ozerechnia, Androsovo, and Komovo areas, and some of his troops were operating along the Viaz'ma–Smolensk highway.[25]

While 8th Brigade commander Onufriev operated with Karnaukhov's 2d Battalion, Major Kobets' 3d Battalion, now numbering 131 men, moved on its objective, the rail line and road west of Viaz'ma. On 30 January his small band occupied Evdokimovo, where it organized all-round defense, began conducting recce toward its objectives, and planned for further action. That evening, they repulsed a small German force operating on sleighs, which, of course, gave away the location of Kobets' force. After remaining at Evdokimovo one more night to rest, early on 1 February his force trudged through the deep snow to the Smolensk–Viaz'ma rail line between Alferovo and Rebrovo Stations, an area from which they could also threaten the main road to the north. During the day they cut the rail line in four places and the road in one location. After establishing defensive positions and laying mines near each communications breech, Kobets' main force dug in on the south side of a copse of trees west of Es'kovo, a position which overlooked the railroad.

The Germans dispatched troops, supported by an armored train, to dislodge the Soviet force and restore rail communications. A first attempt on 2 February failed and the Germans withdrew to Alferovo. The next day a detachment sent out by Kobets destroyed a German rail repair party and returned to Es'kovo by evening. By this time Kobets' force fought from positions in the village itself. Another German attack on Kobets' position on 4 February failed as did yet another stronger attack on 7 and 8 February from German troops based in Rebrovo. These attacks, described by the Soviets as up to battalion in strength, were probably only half-hearted early attempts or reconnaissances in force for the larger, more decisive assault, which would soon take place. During these early attacks, Soviet casualties were reportedly eight killed and 25 wounded. Major Kobets was among the wounded (as he would be three times), and Senior Lieutenant Checherin took his place.[26]

Because of the heavy fighting on 8 February and the fact that the village was burning, late in the day Checherin moved his force westward into the woods to reoccupy old defenses and create new ones. Burdened by the casualties, running short of ammunition, and with no prospect of resupply from brigade, Checherin's position was increasingly desperate. Worst of all, German forces now concentrated against the paratroopers from three directions.

According to 4th Airborne Brigade's history:

> To restore the rail line, the enemy dispatched special detachments and infantry units supported by armored trains. The railroad sector between Rebrovo and Alferovo was put out of commission eight times, and the occupiers [Germans] were not capable of sending along it a single train. Vehicular travel along the highway was possible only when accompanied by tanks. When the Germans' venture to encircle the parachutists failed, they burned virtually every village in the region.[27]

For 21 days, Kobets' 3d Battalion continued to harass German forces, even after abandoning its positions close to Es'kovo (on about 9 February).

On 18 February Checherin dispatched recce elements to reestablish contact with brigade main forces, but the detachment did not return. Consequently, Checherin decided to move southeastward through Pustoshka to unite with brigade, which presumably was operating from the Izborovo region toward Bekasovo, which was seven kilometers east of Es'kovo. A detachment of wounded, escorted by 29 paratroopers led by Senior Lieutenant Fomenkov, led the way, followed by the main body. Early on about 20 February, Fomenkov's forces, with Kobets and the remaining wounded, reached the village of Berezki and linked up with the 41st Cavalry Division of Group Belov, which had just seized the village (as part of another attempt by Belov's 1st Guards Cavalry Corps and 8th Airborne Brigade to advance on Viaz'ma proper). Kobets and the other wounded were immediately evacuated by air to Glukhovo airfield in the Soviet rear area. Fomenkov's force rejoined 8th Airborne Brigade early on 22 February, just in time to participate in the brigade's assault on Bekasovo. The cruel fate of war caught up with Fomenkov as he died in heavy fighting for the town. Senior Lieutenant Checherin, with 3d Battalion's main force of about 100 men, fought his way forward over several days and finally succeeded in linking up with 1st Guards Cavalry Division elements. Soon his forces also reunited with 8th Brigade.[28]

Checherin brought back with him 85 men and the wounded Kobets. His detachment was absorbed into 2d Battalion, and the 3d Battalion ceased to exist. The 3d Battalion's more than three-week raid through the German rear area had failed to achieve major tactical objectives, but had considerable diversionary value. It cut the Viaz'ma–Smolensk road and rail line and forced German Fourth Panzer Army to commit valuable forces to reopen the army's lines of communications. Although Soviet sources describe its impact in hyperbole, German reports sufficiently attest to its value.

Major Kobets' battalion and other Soviet airborne and cavalry units cut the Viaz'ma–Smolensk *Rollbahn* repeatedly after 27 January, causing the German High Command considerable concern. On 31 January, Halder noted:

> In *Center*, …the situation remains tight. More heavy fighting on the supply road to Yukhnov. The enemy is moving new forces westward through the gap between Fourth Army and Fourth Panzer Army. The attack to seal the gap has been postponed to 3 Feb…. Enemy air landings continue. Highway and railroad lines between Smolensk–Vyaz'ma still not cleared. Condition of troops in Fourth Army is serious! Supply difficulties.[29]

Two days later, Halder revealed his impressions of the expanding battle:

The enemy elements that infiltrated behind our front are now being attacked by Fifth Armored [Panzer] Division. The scenes in this battle behind the front are absolutely grotesque and testify to the degree to which this war has degenerated into a sort of slugging bout that has no resemblance whatever to any form of warfare we have known.[30]

Fourth Panzer Army records confirm that the *Rollbahn* west of Viaz'ma was closed continuously for three days after 28 January.[31]

Meanwhile, despite the uncertain situation, Soviet landing operations continued. Throughout 31 January, another 389 men dropped into the area. Flights finally halted on 1 February, for the overall military situation indicated the hopelessness of continuing the effort. Over six days, from 27 January through 1 February, 2,081 of the 3,062 men of 8th Airborne Brigade landed equipped with 120 machine guns, 72 antitank rifles, 20 82-mm mortars, and 30 light 50mm mortars. Of those men, only 1,320 ultimately managed to join Lieutenant Colonel Onufriev's main force. In addition, 76 men of the 214th Airborne Brigade landed to establish communications with 11th Cavalry Corps north of the Viaz'ma–Smolensk road and to conduct diversionary operations.[32] With these few lightly equipped units, the 8th Airborne Brigade now had to cope with a new operational situation. On 1 February, to Onufriev's surprise, a PO-2 aircraft landed at Androsovo carrying Senior Lieutenant Aksenov. He reported that he had captured sufficient gasoline to make the flight, and that the 200 men he had collected were continuing operations around Izdeshkovo.

As the drops proceeded, conditions on the Western Front were changing. The 11th Cavalry Corps failed to cut the Smolensk–Viaz'ma highway, and German forces drove the cavalry units into the forests northwest of Viaz'ma. On 1 February 33d Army's 113th, 338th, and 160th Rifle Divisions under Lieutenant General M. G. Efremov pushed into the area immediately east of Viaz'ma, but German counterattacks threatened to cut these units off from the remainder of 33d Army. Farther south, Belov's 1st Guards Cavalry Corps forced its way across the Moscow–Warsaw highway southwest of Iukhnov and joined Major Soldatov's airborne force, only to find that the Germans had slammed the trapdoor shut, cutting off Belov's retreat and separating him from his two rifle divisions and his tanks and artillery, which remained south of the road.[33] With his own cavalry force of the 1st Guards and 2d Guards Cavalry Divisions, 57th and 75th Light Cavalry Divisions, and Major Soldatov's airborne force, Belov faced heavily armed German forces at Viaz'ma. In these circumstances and while heavy German air attacks pounded Soviet airfields, further drops of 4th Airborne Corps ceased. On 2 February brigade radiomen received the 'surprising' radiogram, 'Further corps airborne landings are suspended.' The remaining 4th Airborne Corps forces moved by rail from the Kaluga area to Ramenskoe, Liubertsy and Vnuknovo near airfields resting under the protective cover of the Moscow air defense sector. Now Onufriev understood why his 4th Battalion had not joined the air assault.[34]

8TH AIRBORNE BRIGADE OPERATIONS WITH 1ST GUARDS CAVALRY CORPS

Without reinforcements, Onufriev's 8th Airborne Brigade operated with the 746 men who had assembled by 1300 on 1 February. For seven days his forces attacked the small German garrisons south of Viaz'ma, spreading chaos in the German rear, but never seriously threatening any critical German installation (see Figure 38). Brigade operations did attract German attention, and even more German forces concentrated to eliminate the troublesome threat to their rear.

The landing of 8th Brigade forces throughout the region, although unintentional, had the added effect of revitalizing the partisan movement, and soon all of Smolensk district smoldered with partisan warfare. In fact, it was hard for the Germans to distinguish between the actions of the 8th Brigade itself, its reconnaissance-diversionary detachments and those of the 214th Brigade, and the many small bands of paratroopers separated from their main body.

Brigade Commissar, I. V. Raspopov understood, while meeting the local population,

> that if one announced a levy, one could completely outfit the battalions as well as form partisan detachments. And many responded to that call. A radiogram to the commander of airborne forces sought permission to call up military age youth in local regions to form partisan detachments and fill up brigades of up to 1,000 men from encircled commanders and men.'[35]

The following day a PO-2 arrived in the region carrying the message that General Glazunov approved of the brigade commander's request to draft from the local populace.

Onufriev dispatched the returning aircraft with a request for the Western Front and airborne commanders to replace lost brigade equipment and supplies (airborne soft cargo [*Parachutno-desantyi miagkii meshok* – PDMM]), in particular antitank rifles, battalion mortars (50mm), heavy machine guns, mines, ammunition, rations, and, most important, skis for troop mobility. Soon after, Onufriev reported that the airborne call-up measures and round-up of scattered troops had provided

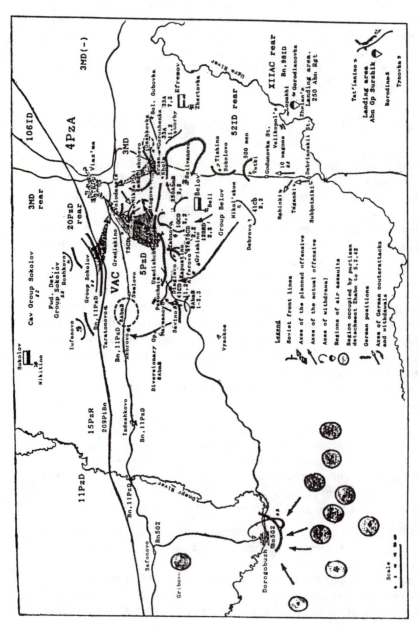

38. 8th Airborne Brigade Operations, 2–10 February 1942

enough men to form a 750-man partisan detachment and to bring the brigade to full strength. These forces also required supplies and equipment.[36] Within hours, all the required supplies began arriving except the skis. Without these the brigade had only 15–20 per cent of its force on skis, and this severely restricted its mobility across the snow-covered back country.

Onufriev understood that the brigade would likely have to operate in the German rear for longer than the required 2–3 days. Consequently, he issued orders for a prolonged operation. His chief of artillery organized uninterrupted supply of ammunition and distributed the existing weapons; the chief of rear services organized food resupply from existing and captured stocks, and the 1st Battalion doctor formed medical assembly and clearance points in the more secure Dorogobuzh region. Additional medical support also soon arrived from Western Front forces. Commissar Raspopov arranged for troop billeting and for the collection and housing of local recruits, many of whom arrived with rifles. Raspopov and other commissars and *politruks* [political workers] screened the new arrivals for political suitability to serve. Often the officers and NCOs who had recruited partisan bands provided testimony as to their reliability. By 5 February two such partisan bands under command of Soviet officers participated in the seizure of the village of Komovo from the Germans. Soon the partisan brigade strength rose to 900. From this brigade, Onufriev assigned 450 men to his 1st and 2d Battalions and, from the remainder, he formed a partisan detachment under Captain Zarubin.[37]

All Soviet units in the Viaz'ma area were in an equally uncomfortable situation. In reduced strength, 8th Airborne Brigade harassed German garrisons and dodged the blows of German 5th and 11th Panzer Divisions. Moving up from the south, Belov's 1st Guards Cavalry Corps encountered heavy German opposition 20 kilometers south of Viaz'ma near Tesnikovo, Moloshino, and Kapustino while, in the cavalry's rear, a strong German garrison held out at Semlevo.[38] On 4 February, the Western Front commander, Zhukov, ordered Belov to attack Viaz'ma from the south, in coordination with 33d Army, then operating just east of Viaz'ma, and 11th Cavalry Corps, located 15 kilometers west of Viaz'ma north of the Moscow–Minsk highway. The Germans repelled all of Belov's attacks and inflicted heavy casualties on the cavalry units. Only the village of Zabnovo fell to Belov's forces on 6 February.

Also on 6 February, German V Army Corps received from Fourth Panzer Army the missions of coordinating the defense of the Viaz'ma–Smolensk *Rollbahn* and of maintaining contact with Fourth Army along the Viaz'ma–Iukhnov road.[39] To this end, V Army Corps deployed 5th Panzer, 106th Infantry, and 11th Panzer Divisions north and south of the railroad and highway running west from Viaz'ma toward Smolensk. In addition, elements of 5th Panzer Division cooperated with the 3d Motorized Division in operations south and southeast of Viaz'ma against Soviet 33d Army forces bottled up in the region. Each of the German divisions fought against the enemy simultaneously in two directions. The 11th Panzer and 106th Infantry Divisions faced both north and south of the Viaz'ma–Smolensk road. The 5th Panzer Division engaged Soviet paratroopers southwest of Viaz'ma and 33d Army units southeast of Viaz'ma. Only by task organizing their units into several battalion-size *Kampfgruppen* (battle groups) could the German divisions successfully parry the numerous, although often uncoordinated and haphazard, Soviet attacks.[40]

By early February communications between 8th Brigade and 4th Airborne Corps headquarters were steady, and information passed easily between them. In response to Onufriev's message about formation of partisan forces, *front* responded, 'We are satisfied that you are personally involved with the formation of partisan detachments. Inform us regarding how you will proceed further in the matter. We will help with weapons. Zhukov, Khokhlov.'[41]

Despite the fact that corps had ceased landing new forces, Onufriev continued his attempts to gather scattered groups and subunits in the region, while the brigade's main force set about performing its original mission of cutting the main Viaz'ma–Smolensk railroad in the Semlevo–Alferovo sector where Major Kobets' 3d Battalion was already operating and in the highway sector between Iakushino and Barsukovo. As before, the battalion operated in deep snow without skis through partially wooded country.

As German defenses jelled, on 7 February Belov's 1st Guards Cavalry Corps lead units linked up with 8th Brigade forces. That same day Belov received a new order from Zhukov:

> Advance to the east with all forces of the 8th Brigade and take Grediakino, interdict the Viaz'ma–Izdeshkovo rail line and prevent the movement of enemy trains. Enter into communications with the 75th Cavalry Division advancing east of Grediakino and with Sokolov [11th Cavalry Corps] about which I wrote you previously.[42]

The day before, on 6 February, the 1,320 men of 8th Airborne Brigade, now located at Izborovo, were subordinated to General Belov's corps along with the 730-man partisan detachment; and he ordered them to attack east, secure Grediakino, and cut the rail line from Viaz'ma to Izdeshkovo in coordination with 11th Cavalry Corps. The 8th Airborne Brigade was to penetrate enemy defenses from Diagilevo to Savino and attack along the road to Dorogobuzh from Viaz'ma to secure Grediakino. Initially, on 8 February 8th Brigade's subunits had some success. Major V. P. Drobyshevsky's 1st Battalion left the Androsovo area and attacked and destroyed small German garrisons in Astashevo, Belomir, and Gvozdenkovo. Farther north battalion reconnaissance learned from local inhabitants that German unit staffs with numerous vehicles were headquartered in Savino and Diagilevo. Drobyshevsky reported this to brigade, and Onufriev ordered all of his available battalions and partisan detachments to concentrate and destroy German forces in the entire region around the villages of Semenovskoe, Gvozdenkovo, Marmonovo, Diagilevo, and Savino. To effect the envelopment, he ordered 1st Battalion with the partisans to seize Savino and Diagilevo, while Karnaukhov's 2d Battalion, with the brigade reconnaissance company and artillery battalion, attacked Marmonovo.

1st Battalion began fulfilling its new mission on 9 February, advancing northeast parallel to 2d Battalion, which operated to the south. In a skillful surprise assault early in the day, Drobyshevsky's reinforced battalion seized Savino and dispersed what Soviet authors have since claimed to have been German 5th Panzer Division headquarters at Diagilevo, along with its 13th Motorized Regiment, but which was actually a single battalion (2d) of the 116th Artillery Regiment, 5th Panzer Division. The Germans withdrew to Semlevo after losing one general and 1,500 men, 87 vehicles, 30 motorcycles, four radios, and considerable other equipment and documents.[43]

Meanwhile, Karnaukhov's 2d Battalion seized the villages of Gvozdenkovo and Semenovskoe and, after receiving news from its reconnaissance elements that German forces were defending Marmonovo, moved on that town. In early evening 9 February, Karnaukhov sent his main force, reconnaissance company, and artillery battalion to strike the village from the front, while the remainder of his battalion enveloped Marmonovo from the south and north. The combined assault forced the Germans to abandon the village, leaving behind 330 dead and many trophies. A captured banner identified the defending German units as the 8th Artillery Regiment.[44] Zhukov later recorded the achievements of 8th Brigade:

> On 10 February the 8th Airborne Brigade and partisan detachments raided the headquarters of the German 5th Panzer Division, capturing a considerable amount of equipment; and occupied the area of Morshanovo–Diagilevo. That same day, Generals Belov and Efrimov were informed of it and ordered to coordinate their actions with the commander of the 8th Airborne Brigade, whose headquarters was in Diagilevo.[45]

In an official order, the Western Front praised the brigade's action, stating 'I establish this assault brigade as an example to all forces.'[46]

The chief of the German General Staff, Halder, noted in his diary that day, 'The enemy continues to land airborne assaults (west of Viaz'ma). The road and railroad from Smolensk–Viaz'ma is still not cleared of enemy. The situation of 4th Army is very serious.'[47]

Other groups of parachutists, which landed in other locations distant from 8th Airborne Brigade between 27 January and early February, contributed to the growing confusion in the Germans' rear area. Over 200 parachutists attached themselves to Belov's 1st Guards Cavalry Corps and fought with that force just before it united with 8th Airborne Brigade southwest of Viaz'ma. Sixty-two troopers joined with the partisan detachment 'Dedushka' [Granddad] near Dorogobuzh. Under the command of 8th Brigade Doctor Iu. N. Pikulev and 1st Battalion Commissar I. G. Mazurkevich, on 15 February this detachment and detachment 'Uragan' [Hurricane] seized the large town of Dorogobuzh, which would remain a major partisan and airborne base for months. Three days later 8th Airborne Brigade received the radio report declaring, 'To Onufriev and Raspopov. Congratulations on the seizure of Dorogobuzh. Present the distinguished with awards. Zhukov, Khokhlov.'[48]

On 28 January the 8th Brigade's Chief of Staff, Major N. I. Sagaidachnyi, jumped northeast of Alferovo Station with a small group of parachutists. The next day he gathered four platoons of troops, which had landed in the area. Slowly moving north, gathering more men as he went, he finally established radio contact with brigade headquarters on 8 February. Acting on a reconnaissance report, on the same day his force seized Kurdiumovo in a surprise night attack. Sagaidachnyi dispatched a liaison element to brigade headquarters, and remained with 28 men to defend Kurdiumovo. Two days later, on 11 February, a German force dispatched to root out the group from the village attacked in strength and slaughtered the entire detachment, including the brigade chief of staff. Onufriev, on hearing the news, appointed Major P. M. Barkevich as his new chief of staff.[49]

The first phase of 8th Airborne Brigade's combined operations with Belov's 1st Guards Cavalry Corps, which had begun on 7 February, developed successfully until 10 February. By this time 8th Brigade had seized Marmonovo and Diagilevo, while the remainder of Belov's corps operated with equal success further eastward toward the Viaz'ma–Ugra road.

Belov's original instructions, received from Western Front on 3 February, had read:

Continue to fulfill your mission .... The enemy before you is numerous. A march to join with Sokolov [11th Cavalry Corps] will produce nothing but a loss of time and a strengthening of the enemy. Efremov [33d Army commander] fights for Viaz'ma in the Alekseevskoe area [southern limits of Viaz'ma]. His command post is in the Zeltovka region. Establish communications with him and cooperate with him; bypass enemy population centers .... Zhukov, Khokhtov.[50]

Since receipt of that order, Belov had oriented his advance on Viaz'ma itself and sought to coordinate his operations with those of 8th Airborne Brigade operating far forward on his left and with 33d Army, two of whose divisions (329th and 160th Rifle) had crossed the Viaz'ma–Ugra Station road and linked up with the 250th Airborne Regiment. Soldatov's airborne regiment now secured Belov's right flank, while 33d Army's main force operated in increasingly difficult conditions southwest of Viaz'ma, but short of the Viaz'ma–Ugra Station road. By 5 February Belov's lead 1st Guards Cavalry Division reached and seized Stogovo, 20 kilometers south of Viaz'ma and within the Germans' Viaz'ma defensive perimeter.[51] The next day 8th Airborne Brigade was subordinated to Belov and began to operate on Belov's left flank.

While 8th Airborne Brigade advanced and seized Diagilevo, Belov's 57th and 75th Light Cavalry Divisions joined battle in the Zabnovo region on 8th Airborne's right flank. Belov's main force fought in the Kaidakovo Station and Krasnyi Kholm sector along the Viaz'ma–Ugra Station rail line. Seeking to link up with 33d Army, Belov's forces drove virtually to the southern outskirts of Viaz'ma (at Mikhal'ki and Pastikhi) and attempted to seize Volodarets on the Viaz'ma–Dorogobuzh road (see Figure 39).

The classified record of Belov's activities noted the German response

> While considering the capabilities of our forces [against Viaz'ma], the German command intended, in the first instance, to destroy our cadre [provisional] units by separating them and then liquidating them and the partisan detachments. To that end they undertook a corresponding concentration of forces to the south of the Viaz'ma–Smolensk highway, chiefly in the Viaz'ma–Dorogobuzh sector. The delaying of the offensive of our force provided the enemy with the opportunity for organizing planned resistance.[52]

Heavy fighting ensued as Belov's force slowly and painfully fought its way toward Viaz'ma. German counterattacks on 9 February, however, finally convinced Belov of the futility of continuing a direct advance on the city. Classified after-action reports noted:

> It was insane to continue an offensive into the face of such a

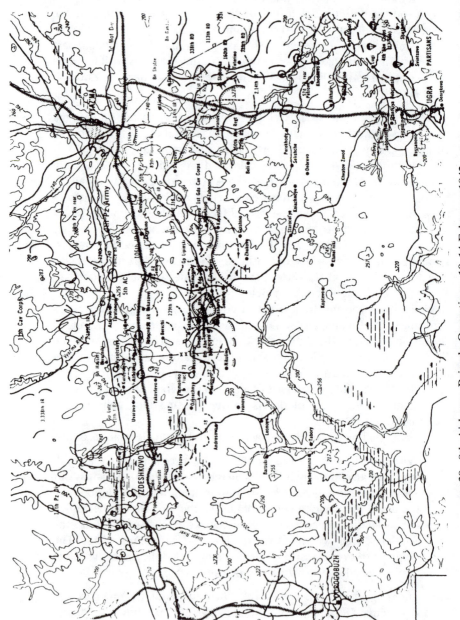

20. 8th Airborne Brigade Operations, 10-14 February 1942

grouping. Therefore General Belov sent a request to the *front* commander to change the direction of his offensive from Viaz'ma to Semlevo [west of Viaz'ma, along the Viaz'ma–Smolensk road] and, after securing Semlevo, continue the advance on Viaz'ma. The necessity of that decision was motivated by the strong German defense and the weakness of his units (there remained only 80 men and a command cadre in 57th Cavalry Division and 200 men in 2d Guards Cavalry Division; an analogous picture existed in other divisions). Besides, he had information that the Semlevo region had richer fodder for the horses. The corps commander intended to envelop the enemy right flank from Semlevo, unite with Sokolov, and, by joint operations, cut enemy withdrawal routes west from Viaz'ma.[53]

This decision was underscored by the increased German resistance to 8th Airborne Brigade's operations in the Diagilevo area. Again, classified reports recounted the action:

8th Airborne Brigade, fulfilling General Belov's order about an offensive against Grediakino, by this time had occupied Marmonov and Savino, where it concentrated its main force. Operating as an effective force, it hoped to secure the left flank of the corps (for the period of battle in the German rear from 1 to 8 February, it seized 72 vehicles, 4 tanks, 1 tractor, 19 motorcycles, 15 bicycles, 2 regimental flags, and various staff documents). While continuing the successful offensive, on 9 February it secured Diagilevo after heavy fighting, destroying there about 100 enemy soldiers and officers. However, it did not have success in its subsequent offensive – the Germans fiercely defended in the Pesochnia region, where they quickly committed reserves from Viaz'ma. At first light on 11 February, the Germans strengthened their counterattacks on the front of the brigade; while suffering losses [reportedly 140 men of Drobyshevsky's 1st Bn], it held on to its positions with difficulty. In these conditions the airborne brigade lost communications with corps and its detachments operating in the Rebrovo region. By day's end, having established contact with 41st Cavalry Division in the Diagilevo region, the brigade, together with it [41st Cav], advanced toward Pesochnia.[54]

Belov's change in operational plans did not forestall subsequent development of German counterattacks or improve the 8th Airborne Brigade's precarious position. After first light on 11 February, the Germans resumed strong attacks along a broad front south of Viaz'ma.

German 106th Infantry and 11th Panzer Divisions, attacking southward from Semlevo, struck 8th Brigade positions at Diagilevo, causing heavy losses to its 1st Battalion and forcing it to abandon temporarily the town. Although brigade had lost communications with corps, by day's end help from 41st Cavalry Division prevented further damage, and combined attacks by the two units again recaptured the town. The 8th Brigade commander, Lieutenant Colonel Onufriev, radioed Western Front head-quarters about the ten-hour battle for Diagilevo and his failure to make progress toward Staraia Polianovo and Pesochnia. Zhukov responded that Belov's 1st Guards Cavalry Corps was moving into the region to envelop the strongpoints, and that Viaz'ma was still the target.[55]

The following morning (12 February), Onufriev and his commissar, Raspopov, met with Belov at his headquarters. Onufriev related the past day's events and his increasingly perilous logistical situation. Belov, in turn, explained his new operational plan and issued the following mission based on Zhukov's instructions:

> While covering the front from Selivanovo–Stogovo–Zabnovo with the 329th Rifle Division and 250th Airborne Regiment, and with your remaining forces attack: 41st Cavalry Division, 8th Airborne Brigade and 1st Guards Cavalry Division – through Diagilevo, 75th Cavalry Division and 2d Guards Cavalry Division from Stanishche and Kaledino – to Astashevo, Gvozhenkovo, Levykino and Grigor'evo, while striking a blow against Viaz'ma from the west.[56]

Onufriev then outlined his plan of action, which involved operating from his bases at Diagilevo and Marmonovo against Semlevo Station west of Viaz'ma and supporting the operations of Kobets' 3d Battalion, then operating between Rebrovo and Alferovo. This clearly corresponded with Belov's plan. The northward thrust would unite Belov's combined force of cavalry and parachutists with 11th Cavalry Corps at Semlevo, where, after reprovisioning, the combined force could launch a subsequent attack on Viaz'ma from the west.

In a subsequent meeting with his staff and subordinate commanders, Onufriev explained his plan and issued specific orders. First, the brigade would turn over its positions at Diagilevo and Marmonovo to the 170th and 188th Cavalry Regiments of 41st Cavalry Division. While the 329th Rifle Division, 250th Airborne Regiment, and two battalions of the 201st Airborne Brigade covered the front south of Viaz'ma, the 8th Brigade and remainder of 1st Guards Cavalry Corps would concentrate for a surprise night assault on Semlevo Station. The assault was to be launched simultaneously by three Soviet columns: 8th Airborne Brigade against the northeast sector of Semlevo, 75th Cavalry Division with the 112th Ski Battalion against the eastern sector, and 1st Guards Cavalry Division and the 114th Ski Battalion against the southeastern sector. A short artillery and mortar preparation would precede the attack.[57]

In the days immediately preceding Belov's new offensive, the Germans had dispatched forces from Izdeshkovo southward to Ivanovka and Frolova and strengthened their forces north of Dorogobuzh. Because his forces were understrength, Belov asked Western Front permission to move the best of his cadre and partisan forces in the Dorozobuzh region eastward to join his corps. The new addition, approved by Zhukov, gave Belov an even stronger force to employ against Semlevo.[58]

At 0600 on 13 February, after an extensive night march through the snow, Belov's forces commenced their attack on German positions in Semlevo with a mortar barrage. Soon after, 8th Airborne Brigade attacked and secured a foothold in the northeast section of the town. Plunging deeper into the town, Onufriev's attack was finally halted with severe losses by heavy German artillery, mortar, and machine gun fire, punctuated by infantry counterattacks. Before dawn 1st Guards and 41st Cavalry Divisions and the ski battalions reached their lines of departure, late because of deep snow, which had delayed their march. They joined the attack propelling the combined force forward until it had occupied the entire eastern and northeastern half of the town. Heavy street fighting raged throughout the day. By evening heavy German resistance again halted the advance, inflicting even more severe casualties on Belov's dwindling force.

While fighting raged, Belov's signal company intercepted several reports of the German garrison commander, a Major Steinbach, to his superiors. One read, 'Position is difficult. Request immediate help – otherwise we will die or capitulate.'[59]

Meanwhile, Belov's position deteriorated as his forces outside of Semlevo came under even heavier German assault. On 13 February one battalion of Germans, supported by five tanks and APCs, drove the 188th Cavalry Regiment from Marmonovo and, by evening, seized Diagilevo from the 170th Cavalry Regiment as well, while killing or taking prisoner 200 wounded parachutists and the brigade surgeon. Further east the 329th Rifle Division was forced to abandon its forward defenses at Troshino Station south of Viaz'ma. Midday on 13 February two battalions of German infantry with five tanks from Viaz'ma advanced toward Semlevo supported by fighter aviation, but were halted at Belomir by elements of 75th Cavalry Division. 2d Guards Cavalry Division, recalled from providing left flank security, sought to dislodge German forces in Marmonovo, but failed. The only uncommitted force at Belov's disposal was his reserve 57th Cavalry Division, then at Nivki.

Combat raged at Semlevo all day on 14 February, but neither side could gain advantage (see Figure 40). The following day the scales tipped

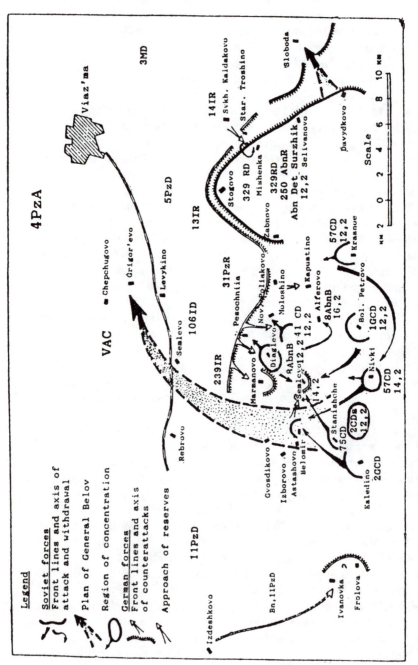

40. 8th Airborne Brigade Operations, 14–16 February 1942

in the Germans' favor. Early in the morning two battalions of infantry and eight tanks reinforced the German garrison. The garrison then launched a concerted counterattack, which drove in succession 75th Cavalry Division westward from the train and 8th Airborne Brigade to the north. Now 8th Brigade was encircled by the Semlevo garrison and the German force at Diagilevo to the north. 8th Brigade sought to break out eastward to 41st Cavalry Division positions south of Diagilevo but were blocked by Germans who attacked into the junction of the 8th Brigade and 41st Cavalry Division, driving the former westward and the latter eastward. No other units were available to assist Onufriev's force. 2d Guards and 75th Cavalry Divisions were heavily engaged attempting to seize Belomir, and 1st Guards Cavalry Division continued to cling to its foothold in the southeast section of Semlevo.[60]

Faced with an impossible situation, Belov had no choice but to abandon his plan to use Semlevo as a base for a new attack on Viaz'ma. His official report noted, 'Losses were so severe that 1st Guards Division Regiments again numbered 10–15 men, conducting combat on foot ... regimental artillery of the guards division was left behind (guns stuck in the snow and could only be moved by hand).'[61] Lack of artillery was a particularly vexing problem for both Belov and Onufriev, for

large losses, suffered by it during the initial period of the raid and in subsequent battles, forced Belov to resort to forming new batteries of trophy [captured] weapons, manned by artillerymen and partisans. However, even those measures met with difficulty in light of shortages of horses and harnesses. The material situation was better – during the corps' raid, more than 100 of our guns and ammunition warehouses for them were found in the Beli, Mishenka and Pokrov regions, left by our forces during the autumn 1941 withdrawal.[62]

As a consequence of the unsuccessful offensive against Semlevo, on 16 February General Belov requested and received permission from Zhukov to halt the offensive in order to refill his regiments from partisan ranks to the level of 100 men per regiment. That day 8th Airborne Brigade, having broken out of encirclement through the forests, concentrated in the Alferovo and Bol'shoe Petrovo region. Belov's corps' front lines now extended from Selivanovo, through Stogovo, Zabnovo, and Kapustino to Belomir. 8th Brigade and 1st Guards Cavalry Division, due to their heavy losses, were concentrated on the extreme left flank, where they could be reconstituted and used in future combat. Meanwhile, German forces continued to press Belov's forces in the Kaidakovo, Nestarovo, Moloshino, and Semlevo sectors.

On 17 February Belov gathered his subordinate commanders for a meeting to critique past operations and plan new options. At the session

Belov ordered his forces to return 200 former parachutists to 8th Brigade to improve their combat capabilities. He also resubordinated Captains Surzhik's and Kalashnikov's 1st and 2d Battalions, 201st Airborne Brigade to Onufriev's command.[63]

The same evening Belov received new orders from the Western Front. His corps' new mission was to continue to envelop Viaz'ma from the west, cut the Viaz'ma–Smolensk road, and link up with 11th Cavalry Corps, this time by an even wider envelopment. Belov then issued orders for his forces to attack northward on the evening of 18 February from Belomir and Nikulino to cut the rail line between Semlevo and Rebrovo Stations. Surprise, he thought, could be achieved, since the Germans would not expect such an advance after the defeat they had inflicted on Belov's forces during the past week.[64] Subsequent events would alter this plan as well, since the focus of the attack ultimately developed toward Iakovlevo, west of Rebrovo. This deviation from plans was forced by German forces, which continued to press Belov's right flank and extended their defenses along the rail line westward to block Belov's enveloping maneuver.

Throughout 17–18 February Belov's and Onufriev's forces regrouped for the new attack, which was now to begin at nightfall on 18 February (see Figure 41). During the day on 18 February, however, German pressure increased against Belov's right flank, driving the 250th Airborne Regiment from Stogovo and burning the town. To counter a growing German threat to Dorogobuzh on his left flank, Belov dispatched the 11th Guards Cavalry Regiment of 1st Guards Cavalry Division to reinforce the partisans, with orders to seize Dorogobuzh Station near Safonovo and block any German southward advance. Belov's latest intelligence confirmed German presence south of the Viaz'ma–Smolensk rail line and the fact that German armored trains were patrolling the rail segment between Viaz'ma and Alferovo.[65]

At 1900 18 February in the midst of yet another heavy snowstorm, Belov's forces commenced their offensive, and, by day's end, 2d Guards Cavalry Division, with 8th Airborne Brigade following and 57th Cavalry Division covering its left flank, had seized Izborovo and was preparing for a further advance the next day. That evening a surprise air assault near Izborovo brought reinforcements to Onufriev, 'To the surprise of the paratroopers, the snow-covered land was sprinkled with parachutes. It was the soldiers of Petr Pobortsev's battalion of the 214th Brigade.'[66] Of the 300 men in Pobortsev's battalion, 150 landed near Onufriev's forces, and, as usual, the others scattered across the region. These other groups replicated the experiences of earlier scattered forces. Many ultimately made it back to 8th Brigade.

With these new forces, on 19 February 8th Brigade, now operating on

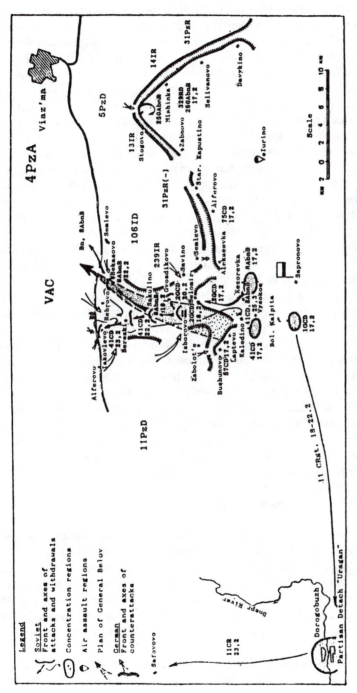

41. 8th Airborne Brigade Operations, 18–25 February 1942

2d Guards Cavalry Division's left flank, seized Sakulino. The Germans withdrew to the east and west, opening a virtual corridor for a subsequent Soviet advance to Iakovlevo on the rail line. Continuing the offensive, on 20 February 2d Guards Cavalry Division occupied Gvozdikovo on 8th Airborne's right flank. 8th Airborne, still concentrated at Sakulino, six to seven kilometers south of the rail line, was then suddenly struck on its left rear by a German infantry force supported by artillery and air strikes. Onufriev's troops stopped the German advance near Izborovo, but, in doing so, their 1st Battalion suffered heavy casualties. 8th Brigade's main forces continued forward through Bolotovo and, by 22 February, seized Bekasovo, just two kilometers south of the rail line and four kilometers west of Semlevo Station. Among the trophies seized by the brigade were several radio sets and German regimental mortars. Onufriev was heartened as, on 21 February, 25 men of his 4th Battalion jumped into the area to reinforce him.[67] Meanwhile, on 8th Brigade's left flank, 41st Cavalry Division secured Berezki, in so doing bringing the rail line under artillery and mortar fire. By evening cavalry forces fought for the southern outskirts of Iakovlevo.

8th Brigade reconnaissance elements and Kalashnikov's 2d Battalion, 201st Airborne Brigade crossed the rail line north of Bekasovo to link up with elements of 11th Cavalry Corps. When cavalry elements could not be found, after two days' fighting, Kalashnikov returned to Bekasovo. Although the brigade had technically fulfilled Zhukov's and Belov's missions, it was for naught. In the afternoon of 22 February, Onufriev's elation abated as German forces from Semlevo and Viaz'ma commenced heavy counterattacks on his positions, supported by devastating air strikes. The first attack struck Captain Surzhik's 1st Battalion, 201st Airborne Brigade, defending the eastern approaches to Bekasovo. In intense and often hand-to-hand fighting, Surzhik's battalion, as well as the reinforcing 2d Battalion, 8th Airborne Brigade, was finally forced to give ground with heavy losses.

After-action reports noted:

> On 22 February battle continued in existing positions and on 23 February the Germans counterattacked against 8th Airborne Brigade, occupied Bekasovo and again encircled that brigade, which was forced with heavy losses to punch through the road to Bekasovo. By day's end by repeated counterattacks, the position in that sector was restored, and Bekasovo was again occupied by corps units.[68]

While 8th Airborne clung tenaciously and at huge cost to Bekasovo, 41st Cavalry Division occupied Iakovlevo, driving the German defenders down the rail line. Other corps' attacks on Rebrovo, however, were repulsed. Further south German forces in Semlevo pressed hard against defending 75th Cavalry Division forces.

Belov personally noted the achievements of Onufriev's brigade. In a note dated 22 February, he said:

...in January 1942 thrown into territory occupied by the enemy in the Viaz'ma area [you have] performed your immediate mission excellently, having destroyed several hundred fascists. The Western Front's Military Council holds up the actions of the brigade as an example for others. Now [you have] successfully fulfilled the mission as first echelon of 1st Guards Cavalry Corps and approached Semlevo Station. You are deserving of the award of the Order of the Red Banner.[69]

That day brigade commissar Raspopov received the award on behalf of the brigade.

After-action reports accurately described the accomplishments of Belov's corps to date, as well as the problems Belov now faced:

Thus, in spite of German opposition, corps units succeeded in penetrating deep into their defensive dispositions between Rebrovo and Alferovo and presenting German forces with the fact of their arrival along the rail line. That region, however, was located almost 30 kilometers west of Viaz'ma, and the final objective of corps' operations was still far distant.[70]

Moreover, the Germans had no intention of permitting a further advance by Belov's forces. New German attacks materialized on 24 and 25 February by infantry with heavy air support. Three armored trains accompanied and supported the German thrust. Massive German assaults threw the 41st Cavalry Division out of Iakovlevo, and attacks from all sides smashed 8th Airborne forces in Bekasovo and other cavalry forces on Onufriev's flanks. The Germans seized Belomir, Bekasovo, and Sakulino, cutting the 8th Brigade and 41st Cavalry off from the remainder of Belov's corps and forcing them to withdraw to Izborovo. To assist the encircled forces, Belov ceased operations elsewhere and sent 1st Guards, 2d Guards, and 57th Cavalry Divisions to their assistance. With these reinforcements, Onufriev and 41st Cavalry Division broke the Germans' grip around them and withdrew to new positions near Kaledino and Vysokoe by nightfall on 25 February. The remainder of Belov's corps concentrated at Zabolot'e and Byshkovo on 8th Airborne's left flank. This final withdrawal, in essence, ended Belov's futile but persistent attempts to reach Viaz'ma.

Classified after-action reports noted dryly: 'Consequently, the third attempt of the cavalry to seize Viaz'ma by envelopment from the west also failed. However, the initiative of action in the German operational rear [still] was in the hands of the corps commander. Corps main forces regrouped and prepared for an offensive on Izdeshkovo.[71]

Belov's third offensive decimated Onufriev's 8th Airborne Brigade. Both Drobyshevsky's 1st Battalion, 8th Airborne Brigade, and Surzhik's 1st Battalion, 201st Airborne Brigade, ceased to exist, and Onufriev distributed their survivors to his other battalions, leaving the brigade with three weak battalions: Karnaukhov's 2d Battalion; P. V. Pobortsev's composite battalion; and Kalashnikov's 2d Battalion, 201st Airborne Brigade, plus Colonel Shmelev's partisan detachment. During the escape from encirclement, the brigade chief of staff, Major Barkevich, disappeared and was presumed dead. Major Drobyshevsky took his place.[72]

By now it was abundantly clear that Belov's force could not fulfill its mission, and larger forces were required if Viaz'ma was to be taken and the Western and Kalinin Fronts' offensives were to achieve their aims. While *front* pressed Belov to continue his operations against less ambitious objectives, Zhukov planned for expanded operations in the German rear, this time by inserting into the Viaz'ma region an even larger airborne force – the remainder of 4th Airborne Corps.

For more than a month longer, 8th Airborne Brigade operated with 1st Guards Cavalry Corps behind German lines, first attacking the rail line near Izdeshkovo west of Viaz'ma (see Figure 42) and then, on 7 March, swinging southeast in an attempt to relieve the 329th Rifle Division and 250th Airborne Regiment encircled by German forces east of Debrevo and Kniazhnoe at Perekhody (see Figure 43). From 7 to 13 March, Soviet attacks failed to break the German encirclement, although Major Soldatov's 250th Airborne Regiment did manage to penetrate the German cordon with 75 ski troopers. By 14 March, 250 to 300 men from the 329th Rifle Division finally broke out to join Belov, but no more.[73]

The 8th Airborne Brigade continued to operate with 1st Guards Cavalry Corps west of the rail line from Viaz'ma to Ugra station until 6 April. The next day the brigade rejoined its parent 4th Airborne Corps, then fighting in the German rear on the Iukhnov axis. Smaller groups of the 8th Airborne Brigade, including the original seven diversionary groups, continued operations in a wide area southwest of Viaz'ma. Elements of 3d Battalion and partisans operated near Dorogobuzh until they rejoined their brigade on 8 March. A 1st Battalion group was active in the Iurkino area. A larger group, supplemented by partisans near Dorogobuzh, which had attacked and captured the town on the night of 13–14 February, continued to make Dorogobuzh a major Soviet base in the German rear. A 1st Guards Cavalry Corps regiment reinforced these units to insure the town could be held.

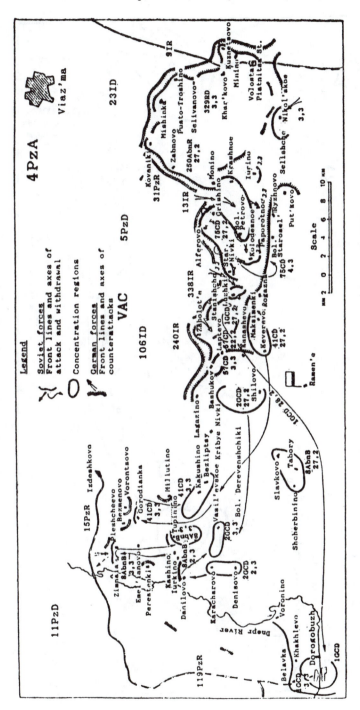

42. 8th Airborne Brigade Operations, 2–5 March 1942

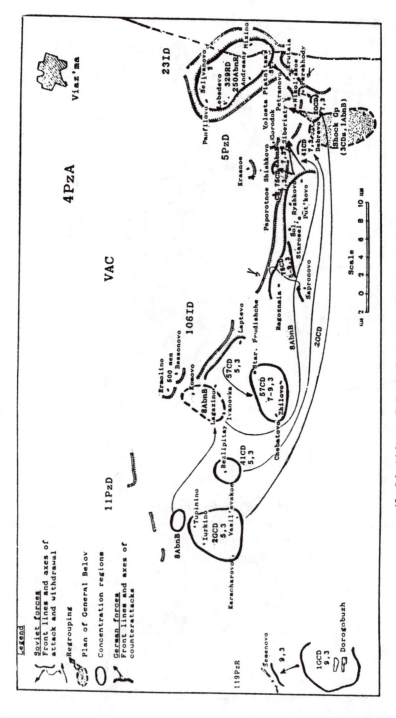

43. 8th Airborne Brigade Operations, 7–9 March 1942

CONCLUSIONS

For more than one month, 8th Airborne Brigade conducted a running fight with enemy units in the German rear area around Viaz'ma. What had begun as a major airborne operation to assist in the destruction of German Army Group Center quickly degenerated into a series of tactical drops with tactical consequences. Ultimately, airborne units sought to destroy small German installations, disrupt German supply routes, and avoid their own destruction. The initial drop failed for a variety of reasons, including poor reconnaissance, inadequate equipment and transportation, faulty initial coordination with ground forces, and chaotic delivery techniques. Because the drop lacked security, both ground and air forces suffered heavy losses.

Early on, it was evident that planning had been correct in outline, but weak in detail. Initial bottlenecks in the availability of transport aircraft forced the corps to issue fragmentary orders on the eve of each drop. The failure of disoriented aircrews to drop their cargoes of men and equipment in the correct zones disrupted planned deployment of forces forward and hindered staff officers in keeping track of force deployment. Piecemeal delivery only compounded dispersion and resulted in 'penny packet' employment of the force after landing. On the ground, troops fought as well as could have been expected, but their numbers and armament were simply not sufficient for the task, a deficiency planners should have foreseen. As a result, the full drop of 4th Airborne Corps aborted, and 8th Airborne Brigade, along with the units it was supposed to cooperate with (1st Guards Cavalry Corps and 33d Army), was, by the middle of February, essentially surrounded and fighting for survival.

Pragmatically, the Western Front ignored the desperate plight of Belov's and Onufriev's force or, more correctly stated, used them to its own operational advantage. Belov continued to receive real missions with real objectives. Even though the Western Front realized they were well beyond his means, it hoped that persistent action by his understrength, but dedicated, forces could still make a contribution to the Western Front's ultimate success.

Classified after-action reports provided an accurate assessment of what Belov's actions in January and February actually achieved, stating:

> The group did not fulfill its preeminent operational aim – the seizure of Viaz'ma. Technically, the weakly-equipped guards cavalry corps had to penetrate the enemy defensive sector with its force and, having penetrated into its deep operational rear, again overcome a rather durable enemy defense in the approaches to Viaz'ma.[74]

The 250th Airborne Regiment and the 8th Airborne Brigade (or according to the original plan, 4th Airborne Corps) were dropped into the region to assist Belov.

Despite the fact that Belov failed to accomplish his principal mission, the critique credited his force with significant contributions:

> In spite of not fulfilling its overall mission, the corps succeeded well in attracting to itself German forces, located in the Viaz'ma, Dorogobuzh, and Spas-Demensk region, having disrupted normal work in their rear for an extended period. The enemy was forced to spend February and March so as not to permit the expansion of territory occupied by the forces of Group Belov and retain in its deep rear a series of formations designated for strengthening the forward positions of the front.[75]

In addition, Belov's success created constant German concern for the situation in their rear area and provided considerable intelligence information about German force dispositions.

What classified after-action reports did not note, however, was that this diversion of German strength from their front lines did not contribute to what the Soviet High Command most wanted – penetration of the German front and destruction of Army Group Center.

The careful and extensive critiques of Belov's operations related principally to deep operations by mobile groups [*podvizhnye gruppi*] and only tangentially to airborne operations. It did underscore that, whereas in the first phase of the Viaz'ma operation the small airborne force had only limited tactical impact, in future operations larger and better-equipped airborne forces could have potential operational impact. That theory would be tested very soon, in late February 1942.

CHAPTER 5

The Viaz'ma Operation, Phase 2
4th Airborne Corps' Operations,
(February–March 1942)

STRATEGIC CONTEXT

Despite advancing up to 250 kilometers in some sectors and making temporary penetrations in others, the Soviet January offensive did not achieve its objectives. Operational gains came only at a prohibitive cost in men and equipment and never translated into strategic victory. The most articulate Soviet assessment reasoned that:

> the absence of large tank units, of powerful aviation, of sufficiently strong artillery, of a fresh flow of reserves, understrength forces, large deficiencies and difficulties in logistics (first and fore-most weapons and ammunition) – all that rendered impossible the decisive development of success to the depth of the defense after a penetration of the enemy front was realized–finally, the Western Front was capable of conducting operations only in separate sectors with limited means.[1]

The great, surging Soviet counteroffensive was over, but the *Stavka* renewed its efforts to liquidate the Germans in the Iukhnov salient and link up *front* forces with Soviet forces now trapped in the Viaz'ma encirclement, namely, 8th Airborne Brigade, 1st Guards Cavalry Corps, and four divisions of 33d Army. On 1 February, the *Stavka* appointed General Zhukov as supreme commander of forces on the Western Direction, with orders to coordinate more closely operations by the Kalinin and Western *Fronts*. Zhukov mustered his scarce reserves to resume the offensive in selected critical sectors. Following the *Stavka*'s orders, Zhukov focused his attention in general on the Viaz'ma salient and communications lines linking Viaz'ma with Rzhev, Briansk, and Smolensk, and, in particular, on the German Iukhnov Group (Fourth Army's XII, XIII, XXXXIII, and LVII Army Corps), whose destruction would facilitate the seizure of Viaz'ma. Whether the weary Soviet troops could muster enough strength to overcome the German force was in doubt. By now, the Germans were receiving a steady stream of reinforcements and building formidable hedgehog defenses woven into village strongpoints that dotted the area adjacent to main communication arteries.

The German situation had improved markedly by early February (see Figure 44). The Germans firmly held Viaz'ma, and the threat posed to the city by 11th Cavalry and 1st Guards Cavalry Corps had ebbed. The right wing of Fourth Panzer Army (XX Army Corps) had linked up with the left wing of Fourth Army (XII Army Corps), and German defenses now formed an unbroken front east of the Ugra River. Soviet 33d Army's impetuous thrust toward Viaz'ma had been cut off at its base, and the Germans had surrounded 33d Army's four leading divisions southeast of Viaz'ma, threatening the Soviet divisions with piecemeal destruction. The Gzhatsk–Iukhnov line remained firm, as did German positions facing westward from Rzhev toward Sychevka. The XII, XIII, and XXXXIII Army Corps of Fourth Army defended the northern, eastern, and southern approaches to Iukhnov, while LVII Army Corps and 10th Motorized Division of Fourth Army worked frantically to create a continuous defensive line to protect the Moscow–Warsaw *Rollbahn* southwest of Iukhnov. With the Moscow–Warsaw and Moscow–Minsk roads under firm German control, Soviet forces of the Western Front's left wing (10th, 50th, and 49th Armies) were contained south of the Moscow–Warsaw highway. The *Stavka* understood that if left unchanged, this situation doomed the encircled Soviet forces near Viaz'ma. If those encircled forces were crushed, the Germans could further strengthen their front with units presently tied down in reducing the encircled Soviet forces.

OPERATIONAL PLANNING

To remedy this situation, Western Direction forces planned and conducted several offensive operations aimed at the destruction of German Army Group Center. These operations, either by single *fronts* or by groups of *fronts*, represented the culminating phases of the Battle of Moscow. In the largest such operation, called the Rzhev–Viaz'ma operation, Kalinin and Western Front forces cooperated with forces of the Northwestern and Briansk Fronts in an attempt to encircle and destroy the main forces of Field Marshal G. Kluge's Army Group Center, which consisted of Ninth and Fourth Armies, Third and Fourth Panzer Armies, and the Second Air Fleet. After over one month of intense battle, it was clear to the *Stavka* and High Command of the Western Direction that initial offensive momentum had ebbed, and the attack had stalled. Moreover, not only had the large Soviet forces in the enemy rear (1st Guards and 11th Cavalry Corps, 8th Airborne Brigade, and half of 33d

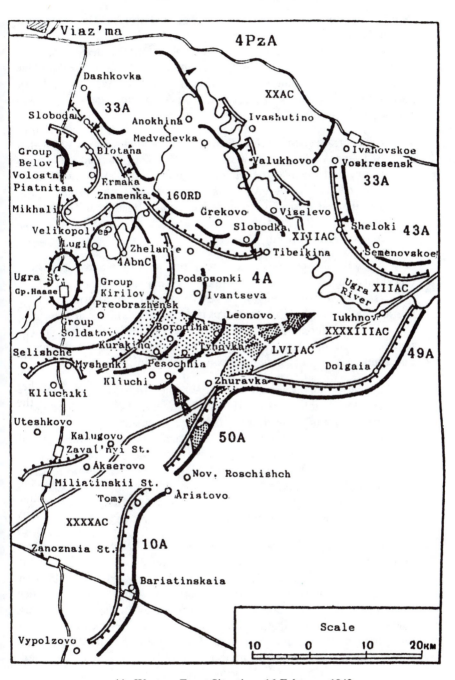

44. Western Front Situation, 16 February 1942

Army) failed to take Viaz'ma, but they were themselves threatened with destruction.

In these complex circumstances, the High Command decided to conduct the Iukhnov offensive operation, aimed specifically at breaking the German hold on Iukhnov, penetrating the Moscow–Warsaw highway and seizing Viaz'ma in concert with forces already operating in the region. The concept of the operation was:

> to penetrate enemy defenses in a 25–30 kilometer sector southwest of Iukhnov, direct a blow in the northeastern direction, and surround and destroy the enemy Iukhnov group with subsequent movement of Soviet forces into the operational region of 33d Army, 1st Guards Cavalry Corps and 8th Airborne Brigade and unite with Kalinin Front forces in the vicinity of Viaz'ma to encircle and destroy Army Group 'Center.'[2]

50th Army was to spearhead the penetration operation across the Moscow–Minsk highway southwest of Iukhnov. To assist 50th Army and the progress of the offensive in general, the Western Front decided to insert the remainder of 4th Airborne Corps into the German rear area west of Iukhnov (see Figure 45). On 10 February *Stavka* released the remaining two brigades of 4th Airborne Corps to Western Front control. That very day Zhukov gave Levashov's corps its combat mission:

> to conduct an air assault with the 9th and 214th Airborne Brigades and 4th Battalion, 8th Airborne Brigade, and corps subunits into the Velikopol'e, Shushmin, Zhelan'e region. After landing, strike a blow from the rear against the enemy defense in the general direction of Kliuchi, subsequently occupying the line Kurakino, Borodino, Podsosonki, and reaching the line Pesochnia, Kliuchi, Tynovka, and Leonovo (25–30 kilometers southwest of Iukhnov) where you will unite with 50th Army units for subsequent combined combat operations against the enemy Iukhnov group.[3]

Simultaneously, General I. V. Boldin's 50th Army was ordered to attack to penetrate German defenses along the Warsaw–Moscow road, linkup with 4th Airborne Corps at Batishchevo, Vygor', Kliuchi, and Pesochnia, and subsequently strike German forces at Iukhnov from the west. If 4th Airborne Corps could secure an extensive region in the enemy rear and link up with 50th Army, the combined force could not only complete the encirclement of the Iukhnov group, but also open the way for an advance into the region southwest of Viaz'ma, where 1st Guards Cavalry Corps, 8th Airborne Brigade, and 33d Army remnants were operating in encirclement.

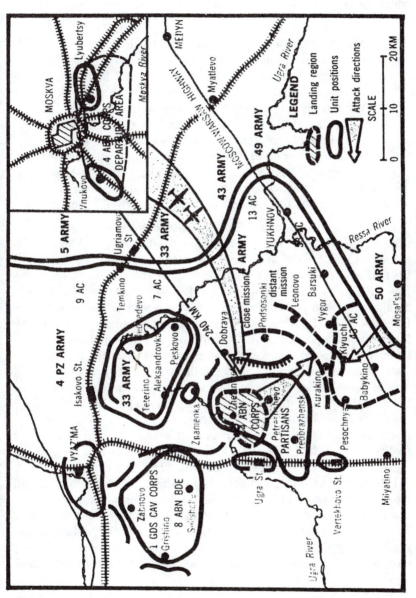

45. 4th Airborne Corps Operational Plan

Soviet after-action reports provide a succinct picture of the region in which 4th Airborne Corps was ordered to operate (see Figure 46):

> 4th Airborne Corps operated in the Viaz'ma–Iukhnov–El'nia–Dorogobuzh quadrilateral. Railroads and highways passed through the jump sector from the north and south, as well as the Viaz'ma–Kirov railroad, which ran along the front and had considerable operational significance.
>
> The terrain in the area of operations of the *desant* was sharply rugged with a great number of swamps. In the winter country tracks were impassable for vehicles. Movement of corps units without roads, through forested terrain, and without skis was very difficult.
>
> In population centers of the region where the corps operated, there were many refugees as well as the local inhabitants. A great majority of the population were sympathetic to the Red Army.[4]

The defenses the Germans had just finished erecting along the south side of the Moscow–Warsaw *Rollbahn* southwest of Iukhnov were tenuous at best. Fourth Army's XII and XIII Army Corps defended from the Iukhnov area southwest along the Moscow–Warsaw *Rollbahn* to the Ressa River. The LVII Panzer Corps defended the sector that Belov's cavalry corps had passed through two weeks earlier. The 19th Panzer Division, 137th Infantry Division, one regiment of the 52d Infantry Division, and a portion of the 10th Motorized Division defended a 20-kilometer stretch of the road southwest of the Ressa River, with other 10th Motorized Division elements deployed thinly southwestward toward Spas-Demensk. These forces struggled with lead elements of Soviet 50th Army as it pushed through the snows past Mosal'sk toward the *Rollbahn*.[5] Clearly, additional strength was necessary for the Germans to defend the highway. To provide this strength, Fourth Army, on 16 February, ordered the XXXXIII Army Corps to help defend the highway from the Ressa River to Fomino.[6] This Corps' 31st, 34th, and 131st Infantry Divisions, then defending Iukhnov, slowly disengaged and moved southwest. The XII and XIII Army Corps contracted their defensive lines north and east of Iukhnov and took over a portion of XXXXIII Army Corps' vacated positions south of the city. The continuing bitter temperatures ($-35°$ to $-40°C$) made the redeployment even more arduous, and knee-deep snow made even the *Rollbahn* difficult to use.

Also besieged by the cold and snow north of the Moscow–Warsaw *Rollbahn* and along the Viaz'ma–Iukhnov road were the rear service areas of Fourth Army's front-line divisions and scattered army security and support units. These units would be the first obstacles for the Soviet airborne force to overcome. South of the projected airborne landing area

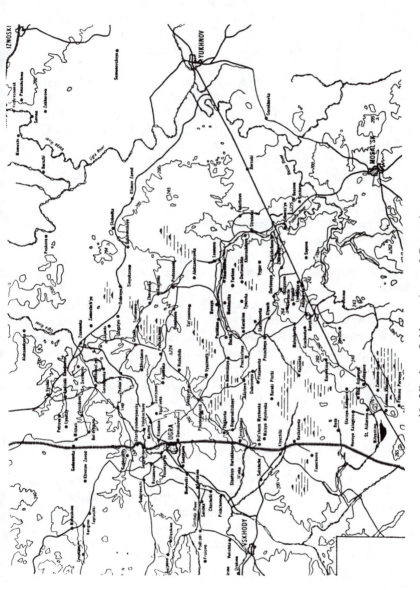

46. Viaz'ma–Iukhnov Area of Operations

were rear service elements of the 31st Infantry Division in the villages of Pesochnia, Dertovaia, and Kliuchi and in nearby hamlets.[7] East of the projected Soviet air-landing site, at and around Zherdovka and Podsosonki, were elements of the 131st Infantry Division. To the northeast, rear service elements of the 98th Infantry Division and a Fourth Army SS Police Regiment garrisoned the key Ugra River crossings at Znamenka. Other 98th Infantry Division units defended the Viaz'ma–Iukhnov road on both sides of Klimov Zavod. Farther north, at Ermaki, on the road from Znamenka to Viaz'ma, was Service Detachment 152 of the 52d Infantry Division. Finally, west of the airborne landing zone along the Viaz'ma–Kirov rail line, four companies of Group Haase protected the critical rail bridge across the Ugra River.[8] The 5th Panzer and 23d Infantry Divisions, which continued clearing airborne forces and Soviet 33d Army elements from either side of the Viaz'ma–Kirov rail line south of Viaz'ma, posed an even greater threat to the airborne force.

Alarmed by the earlier airborne operations of 250th Airborne Regiment and by Belov's recent cavalry operations, these small garrisons had erected all-round defenses centered on the stone houses of the villages. Where possible, the Germans had built breastworks and, often, snow and ice barricades and ramparts. Villages within artillery range of one another had prearranged mutual defensive fires. Scarce armored vehicles and transport vehicles had been formed into mobile detachments to patrol the snow-covered roads and to maintain tenuous communications, especially along the *Rollbahn* and Viaz'ma–Iukhnov supply arteries. In mid-February, with their attention riveted on the strained front lines, the Germans endured the cold isolation and awaited the Russians' next move, scarcely suspecting it would again come from the skies.

4TH AIRBORNE CORPS' ASSAULT

The 4th Airborne Corps staged out of Liubertsy, Vnukovo, and Ramenskoe airfields under cover of the Moscow Regional Air Defense System. Partisans of the 1st Partisan Regiment (Detachment Kirillov) operating in the Zhelan'e area were to assist the corps landing and assembly of forces and would thereafter fight as part of the airborne force. On 14 February the staffs of the airborne force and the air transport group worked out the assault plan, which called for 4th Airborne Corps to drop from two flights of aircraft on each of three nights. The plan took into account the fact that the airfields were located 240–250 kilometers from the assault landing area. An aviation-transport group of 41 PS-84s and 23 TB-3s would carry the paratroopers.[9]

No provision was made for fighter aircraft to escort the transport group. Although plans existed to drop three radio crews before the operation, none were actually dropped. Instead partisan units lit bonfires to guide the planes to their destinations. This tactic had limited success, however, for numerous fires existed anyway because of the cold and the fog, and the Germans had also lit diversionary fires. Moreover, German aircraft also guided on the fires and caused chaos in the planned landing area. Although the air drop was originally planned for the night of 16 February, the transport aircraft were late. Consequently the drop was delayed for two nights. Soviet critiques noted 'The decision of A. F. Levashov on the landing and subsequent operations of the corps fully corresponded with missions assigned by the Western Front commander, but, just as was the case in January, it was made without required information about the enemy in the landing and in the operational area of the corps.'[10]

On the night of 17–18 February, the 4th Battalion of 8th Airborne Brigade dropped into its jump zone (see Figures 47, 48, and 49). The first PS-84 aircraft carrying 18 paratroopers failed to find the assigned landing area and returned to Liubertsy. The second flight dropped its cargo of paratroopers 15 kilometers from Zhelan'e. Of the 18 men only nine were able to assemble at the required point. The operation was off to an inauspicious beginning. As in the earlier, January drop, instead of jumping from 600 meters, the paratroopers had to jump from 1,000 to 1,200 meters because of weather and fog.[11] The ensuing wide dispersion of men and supplies and the deep snow made reassembly difficult in the severe terrain of the forested, roadless region. Once again, many aircraft lost their way and returned with their human cargo rather than risk dropping them into enemy strongholds. Disrupted flight schedules prompted extra sorties and required more time for the actual drop.

By the morning of 18 February, 50 per cent of 4th Battalion personnel had found their way to the appointed assembly point. The same night elements of the 214th Airborne Brigade also took off from Liubertsy with similar mixed results. Captain P. V. Pobortsev's 2d Battalion jumped early on 18 February, well off target, in 8th Airborne Brigade's operational area. They subsequently fought with that brigade.[12] One hundred and fifty more fortunate souls of 2d Battalion landed in their proper area and assembled near Griada, just east of Zhelan'e. After suffering heavy casualties from German bombing, the remnants of the battalion took refuge in the nearby forests. Captain I.D. Polozkov's 1st Battalion aircraft failed to detect the signal lights near Zhelan'e and also returned to Vnukovo airfield. During a second attempt the same evening, because of a navigator's error, the battalion landed in dispersed fashion across the entire Ugra region. Finally, on the night of 22 February, the 214th

Brigade commander, together with his 3d and 4th Battalions, completed their landing in the designated location. That evening 300 parachutists of the brigade landed amidst the dispositions of encircled 33d Army forces just southeast of Viaz'ma. Thus, by early 23 February, the brigade finally assembled at its required location but minus 1,200 men.

9th Airborne Brigade's landing experiences resembled those of the 214th Brigade. The brigade began the landing operation on the night of 18–19 February. Its lead aircraft encountered heavy ground fire, and the first two aircraft crashed and burned while dropping their parachutists. One vivid account described the scene:

> A second TB-3 aircraft caught fire. From it through the tongues of flames fell black figures, over which opened parachute cupolas, several of them instantly burning up. Against the background of the sky...the parachutes stood out sharply. Laced across it were the fiery tracers of fascist fighter planes. The aircraft was engulfed in flames, as the first rushed at the ground to meet its destruction. The parachutists, who had not succeeded in abandoning it, shared its fate.[13]

In his report on the operation, Major P. M. Bazelev, 214th Airborne Brigade's chief of staff, provided a more optimistic view, stating:

> The landing of 9th Brigade basically occurred satisfactorily. Losses on the march route from the presence of fighter opposition were not great. There were greater losses due to the inaccuracy of the drop and the great dispersion of the parachutists, since, due to the opposition of fascist fighters, the height of the drop rose from 600 to 2,000 meters.[14]

Ultimately, many 9th Brigade troopers fell either into the dispositions of 1st Guards Cavalry Corps and 33d Army or on to enemy positions. As a consequence, more than 300 men of the brigade never reached their assembly area. Fortunately for the brigade, aircraft were able to deliver them four 45mm antitank guns.

Testifying to the inaccuracy of the drop, on 20 February 33d Army reported to Western Front that 110 parachutists of the 9th and 214th Brigades had landed near Dmitrovka. These forces were immediately formed into a detachment to operate under 33d Army command. At that point, 33d Army needed all the reinforcements it could obtain.[15]

Finally, on the evening of 22 February, the 4th Airborne Corps staff and specialized subunits left Liubertsy airfield with the remainder of the 214th Brigade. On board a single aircraft were the corps commander, Major General A. F. Levashov (just promoted to general), his chief of

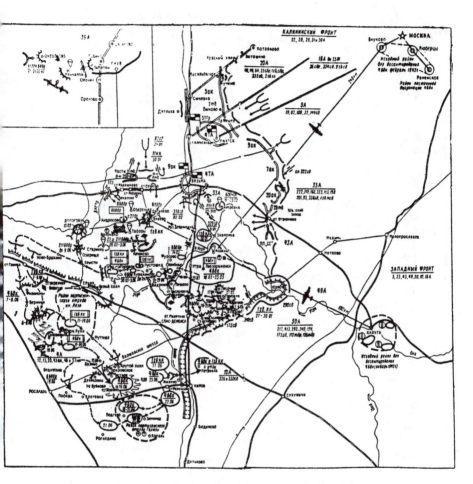

47. 4th Airborne Corps Operations, February–June 1942: Soviet View

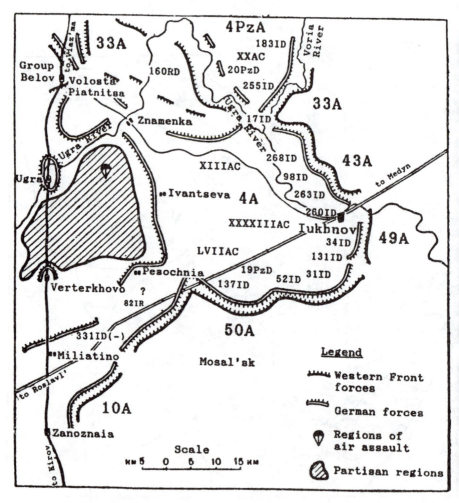

48. 4th Airborne Corps Operations: Overview

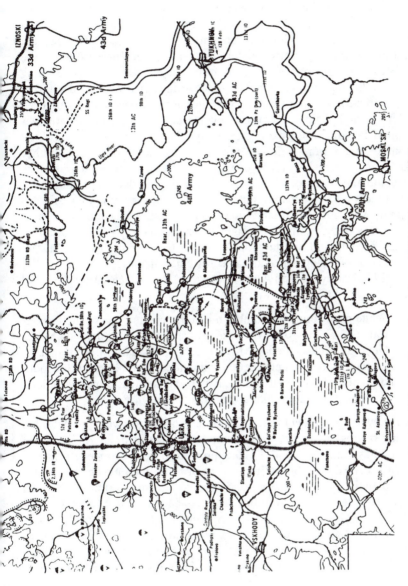

49. 4th Airborne Corps Operations, 17–24 February 1942

staff, Colonel A. F. Kazankin, and the entire command group and staff of the corps. As critiques later noted, 'It was fraught with serious consequences; the loss of but one aircraft would leave the corps without its command group and leading staff figures.'[16] Levashov's aircraft was preceded by one carrying the remainder of the corps staff. The first aircraft ran the gauntlet of enemy fire and landed successfully at the proper point southwest of Zhelan'e. Its passengers succeeded in reaching the corps headquarters assembly point in Griada. They watched in terror as, just to the north, the TB-3 carrying the corps commander encountered a German night fighter. Before the plane went down in flames, witnesses counted 24 parachutists exiting. Although the men and crew parachuted to safety, many were seriously burned during the descent. Yet another TB-3 appeared and was also engaged by enemy fighters. It was more fortunate and succeeded in landing, but with considerable damage. All but three of its occupants survived. The corps commander and his adjutant were not so fortunate and perished. As the parachutists returned Levashov's body on the next flight to Ramenskoe, Colonel Kazankin assumed command of the 4th Airborne Corps with Major M. M. Kozunko succeeding Kazankin as corps chief of staff.

On 27 February the Red Army newspaper, *Red Star* [*Krasnaia Zvezda*] memorialized Levashov, in part stating:

> While performing his combat mission, perished one of the famous warriors of the Red Army, a true son of the homeland, Major General Aleksei Fedorovich Levashov, a steadfast Bolshevik, a staunch fighter, an energetic commander, and a keen and responsive comrade. He enjoyed great love and authority among soldiers, commanders, and political workers.[17]

By the evening of 24 February, the landing operation was complete. No further troops or supplies crossed the front. By this time, 7,373 men of Kazankin's command and 1,525 supply loads had dropped from 612 aircraft sorties, but almost 30 per cent of those men never found their way to their corps, battalion, and brigade assembly points. Although some fell directly onto German positions and were lost, an estimated 1,800 men ultimately joined 33d Army units, 1st Guards Cavalry units, and partisan bands.[18] Obviously, the night drop had taken advantage of surprise, and thus few troops were lost to German ground fire. Night conditions and heavy snow, however, inhibited subsequent reorganization and assembly.

The Germans noted the drop but could do little to disrupt it beyond dispatching a few air sorties to intervene. Since the dramatic, large-scale landing of the Soviet 250th Airborne Regiment on 20 January, German Fourth Army had recorded numerous small airlandings at Lugi and

Velikopol'e. Suddenly, on the nights of 19 and 20 February, the Fourth Army war diary recorded a significant surge in activity when the 52d Infantry Division reported that 145 aircraft had landed without interference on brightly lit fields at Lugi and Velikopol'e.[19] Initially, the fatigue of overworked German aircrews had prevented effective *Luftwaffe* interference with the landings. Although air sorties were flown against the airborne forces, Fourth Army regarded the efforts of the German air force as unsuccessful. Ground reaction was similarly ineffective. Weather conditions and shortages of ammunition for artillery pieces precluded resistance or effective offensive counter-action. Moreover, Fourth Army lamented the inability of its units to prevent the airborne forces from cutting the Viaz'ma-Iukhnov road. Even the strongest German garrison could do little to thwart the airborne landings.[20]

Once they had recovered from the initial surprise, the Germans anxiously awaited the paratroopers' next move. The long period of airborne assembly and regrouping caused the Germans to underestimate the total enemy force and to wonder about Soviet intent. Russian inactivity caused subsequent critics to question Fourth Army and XXXXIII Army Corps estimates that 3,000 paratroopers had actually landed. In fact, more than 7,000 Soviet troops had made the jump, and about 5,000 had successfully assembled.

The assembly of this sizeable force was one positive product of careful planning. Before the operation commenced, while at the departure airfields, the force's mission had been explained to each soldier. Each well understand the ground signals system and where each subunit would gather. After the night assault, small groups of parachutists were to assemble on foot by battalion, and then by brigade. Terrain and weather difficulties hindered assembly of men and supplies. From 18 to 24 February, while the drop proceeded, the men slowly and tortuously assembled according to plan and hauled the heavy cargo through snow and frozen swampland into designated assembly areas. While doing so, they lost the advantage of surprise as German garrisons were alerted and strengthened their defenses.

While the Germans puzzled over Soviet intentions, Colonel Kazankin, by the evening of 23 February, had established communications with his 9th and 214th Airborne Brigades, which had reassembled at Svintsovo and Griada, respectively. He had also contacted 50th Army and learned that its units were locked in heavy fighting with the Germans at Sapovo and Savinki near the Warsaw road. But no breakthrough had yet been made. Kazankin now faced an advance southward of more than 30 kilometers across the rough, snow-covered country. The broken terrain, forests, and frozen swamps made any movement without skis difficult. The only consolation was that the few roads would not support German vehicles and the Germans were not skillful at winter operations in such terrain. Alerted by the drop, the Germans used the time the paratroopers were assembling to strengthen their network of village defenses. In villages, the Germans had shelter and warmth against bitterly cold weather; the Soviets had to fend for themselves in the open.

THE FEBRUARY OFFENSIVE

Colonel Kazankin ordered his airborne and partisan forces to make a two-pronged attack southward toward the Moscow–Warsaw road and 50th Army (see Figure 50).[21] 4th Airborne Corps was to conduct his main attack through Kurakino, Kliuchi, and Liudkovo to meet 50th Army forces, which had begun their attack on 23 February. 50th Army's mission was to penetrate enemy defenses along the Moscow–Warsaw road, secure Lavrishchevo, Vygor, Kliuchi, Pesochnia, and Kavkas and, after uniting with 4th Airborne Corps, attack toward Barsuki in the rear of the enemy Iukhnov group to effect its destruction. From its jumping-off points at Glukhovo and Novaia Dacha, which it reached on the evening of 23 February, 9th Airborne Brigade was supposed to advance through Viazovets, Kurakino, and Tynovka; occupy Preobrazhensk and Viazovets; then destroy the enemy in the Pesochnia and Kliuchi strong-points, and finally link up with 50th Army near Liudkovo. One battalion (4th), with partisan detachments of 1st Partisan Regiment attached, was to secure Ugra Station.

The 214th Airborne Brigade was supposed to seize Ivantsevo, Tat'ianino, Kostinki, and Zherdovka and, by evening 24 February, reach positions extending from Novaia, through Mokhnatka, to Leonovo. The 1st Partisan Regiment of Major V. V. Zhabo, which was subordinate to 4th Airborne Corps, would cover the airborne forces' rear along a line running through Gorodianka, Sviridovo, Andriiaki, and Bel'diugino against German attacks from the direction of Znamenka and Viaz'ma. Part of the force was to cooperate with the 4th Battalion, 9th Brigade, in an attack on Ugra Station. Three hundred men of the 4th Battalion, 8th Brigade, provided a reserve for 4th Airborne Corps. (The remaining 250 men of this battalion had jumped into the Iurkino area near Dorogobuzh to reinforce their parent unit.) Almost all Soviet movement and combat were to be conducted at night to capitalize on darkness and to avoid detection and attack by German air units. Darkness provided security, but it also meant slow movement through the deep snows of the rough terrain. Before the offensive, all troops were provided with signal tables to facilitate recognition and link-up with 50th Army forces. Kazankin

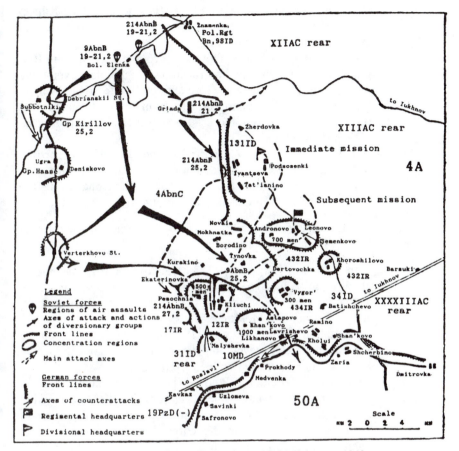

50. 4th Airborne Corps Operations, 25–28 February 1942

ordered the attack to begin on the night of 23–24 February and established the corps command post at Zhelan'e.

Having received orders from corps, the brigade commanders assigned missions to their subordinate battalions. Colonel Kuryshev's 9th Brigade order read:

- 2d Battalion [Captain M. Smirnov] capture the Prechistoe strong-point, and develop the offensive together with 4th Battalion against the Kliuchi strongpoint; subsequently, while covering the corps' right flank from an enemy attack from Malyshevka, simultaneously protect the offensive of 4th Battalion against Liudkovo.
- 4th Battalion [Captain D. Bibikov], destroy the enemy garrison

in Kurakino, cooperating with 2d Battalion, secure the Kliuchi strongpoint and develop the offensive to Liudkovo to meet with 50th Army forces.

- 1st Battalion [Captain A. Plotnikov], cooperating with 4th Battalion, seize the Tynovka and Iurkino strongpoints, develop the offensive to Dertovaia and Gorbachi, cover the brigade's main force from possible enemy attacks from the east, and, in cooperation with 4th Battalion, advance on Liudkovo to link up with 50th Army units.

- 3d Battalion [Major V. Sharov] cooperate with the partisan detachment in seizing Ugra Station. Subsequently turn over defense of the station to the partisans and concentrate the battalion in Prechistoe as brigade reserve.[22]

Lieutenant Colonel Kolobovnikov's 214th Airborne Brigade forces received the following missions:

- 4th Battalion [Captain A. Khoteenkov] destroy the enemy garrison in Ivantseva and subsequently seize the village of Tat'ianitsa. By day's end, in cooperation with 2d Battalion, secure Novaia and Mokhnatka.

- 3d Battalion [Senior Lieutenant P. Vasil'ev] destroy the enemy in Kostinki and, while developing the offensive, by day's end secure Leonova in cooperation with 1st Battalion.

- 1st Battalion [Captain I. Polozkov] destroy the enemy in Zherdovka stroingpoint and, while developing the offensive, by day's end in cooperation with 3d Battalion secure the village of Leonovo, while covering the corps' left flank from possible enemy attacks from the east.

- 2d Battalion in reserve.[23]

On the night of 23–24 February – which in peacetime would have marked the end of Red Army Day festivities celebrating the Soviet Army's birthday – Colonel Kazankin led his brigades southward. Despite the bitter cold and heavy snow, the advance initially fared well.

Kuryshev's 9th Brigade experienced initial success in its advance. His 1st Battalion cleared a platoon of Germans from Tynovka and left a platoon under the deputy battalion commander to defend the left flank against the approach of German forces from Iurkino. The 1st Battalion's 3d Company seized Khan'kova in a surprise assault. Meanwhile, the battalion's 1st Company and reconnaissance platoon drove a German company from Gorbachi without casualties to the Soviet force. 9th Brigade's 2d Battalion secured Prechistoe after midnight and, by morning, commenced attacks on German positions around Kliuchi, where the

4th Battalion joined in after seizing Kurakino during the night. The headlong attack found the Germans well-prepared, and, after suffering casualties from heavy machine gun and artillery fire, 2d and 4th Battalions fell back into the forests one kilometer north of Kliuchi.

Further west, 9th Brigade's 3d Battalion, operating with partisans, blockaded 800 Germans in Ugra Station, while one company raced south and, in a surprise attack, seized Verterkhovo Station, along with considerable supplies, ammunition, and foodstuffs.

Kolobovnikov's 214th Brigade made similar rapid progress southward during the night only to fail to seize its assigned objective in the early morning. The brigade marched south in columns of battalions, with 1st Battalion leading and 2d and 4th following. 3d Battalion remained in Zhelan'e while its reconnaissance units detected and reported to brigade about German garrisons in Prechistoe, Kurakino, Kliuchi, and Pesochnia. The main columns came under German air attack, which slowed their march and inflicted some casualties. Before dawn the three battalions struck at German defenses at Ivantseva, Kostinki, and Zherdovka, but were forced by heavy German return fire to return to their jumping-off positions to regroup. Insufficient Soviet artillery and mortar fire support spelled doom for 214th Brigade's initial attack. The heavy weapons could not be transported forward rapidly enough because of the heavy snow.

The lack of Soviet success on the night of 23–24 February, as it turned out, was a negative by-product of a reconnaissance the night before by elements of the 214th Brigade, which had alerted the Germans in Ivantseva, who, in turn, had warned German garrisons at Kostinki and Zherdovka. As a consequence, the two brigades suffered the loss of 280 men and failed to achieve their missions.[24] Once alerted, the German positions became an imposing obstacle to 4th Airborne Corps' advance.

German rear service units from five regiments of the 131st, 31st, and 34th Infantry Divisions were strongly entrenched in a thick network of villages, the strongest of which were Dubrovnia, Ekaterinovka, Kurakino, Dertovaia, Gorbachi, Zherdovka, Kostinki, Ivantseva, Pesochnia, and Kliuchi.[25] Each of the villages formed the nucleus of a company-size strongpoint organized for all-round defense, and a system of mutually supporting automatic weapons and artillery fires tied each village into a defensive network with nearby villages. Moreover, the Germans had been alerted to the presence of the airborne units, although they did not know the units' precise location.

Soviet after-action assessments characterized German defenses in this fashion:

Opposite the corps' right flank, the fortified regions of

Ekaterinovka and Pesochnia were the strongest; in the center, on the Dertovochka axis, German positions were weakly fortified; and, finally, against the left flank – the line Tat'ianino, Ivantseva and Zherdovka were fortified less strongly than the Pesochnia region.[26]

Desultory and inconclusive fighting went on throughout the day on 24 February as the paratroopers again endeavored to accomplish their missions. The 214th Brigade struck at German positions near Ivantseva, but was again repulsed. In addition to expected combat casualties, frostbite began exacting a cost on the Soviet soldiers. At a command and staff meeting that night, Lieutenant Colonel Kolobovnikov accepted that the Germans had known about the air drop since its beginning on 18 February and had prepared accordingly. Without mortars or artillery, it now seemed futile to continue the attacks. At this point, however, the corps commander reminded the officers that the mission had to be fulfilled by whatever means. Consequently, he ordered the brigade to leave their shelters and, on the night of 24–25 February, attack and seize Tat'ianino, then concentrate in Kurakino for an assault on the strongpoint at Pesochnia.

Senior Lieutenant P. Tereshchenko's 7th Company drove off German security forces and occupied Tat'ianino by midnight. Brigade commander Kolobovnikov still despaired, however, over prospects of seizing Pesochnia. His battalions numbered about 120 men each, and he had already dispersed the men of his 2d Battalion to reinforce the other brigade subunits. Meanwhile, 9th Airborne Brigade, whose mission had been to seize Pesochnia, failed in its attack and, instead, after enveloping the village, moved on toward Kliuchi, while the 214th Brigade continued its preparations for the assault on Pesochnia.

On the morning of 25 February, Polozkov's 1st Battalion, 214th Airborne Brigade dispatched toward Pesochnia a reconnaissance group under Junior Lieutenant F. Dolgov, which the Germans ambushed and destroyed. Dolgov, who had led his men out of the 214th Brigade's encirclement at Bobruisk in June–July 1941, perished outside Pesochnia. A second reconnaissance party determined Dolgov's fate and prompted the brigade commander to cease his direct attack on Pesochnia. Instead, his brigade blockaded the village and the nearby village of Ekaterinovka and waited to launch an assault timed to coincide with 9th Brigade's assault on Kliuchi. The simultaneous assaults were to commence after dark on 26 February.

In spite of heavy German opposition and German overall superiority in men and equipment, the airborne corps had advanced 20 to 25 kilometers on separate axes toward their junction with 50th Army, which was still fighting over a sector of the Moscow–Warsaw road. Elements of the 4th Airborne Corps and partisans along the rail line north of Ugra Station had succeeded in seizing Debriansky and Subbotniki from German Group Haase, in so doing capturing seven rail cars full of bombs, food, and weapons. Fighting farther south near Ugra Station and Verterkhovo revealed strong German garrisons at each station along the Viaz'ma–Kirov rail line, demonstrating the great importance the Germans attached to defense of the railroad.[27] Along the main line of advance, the major objectives at Pesochnia and Kliuchi, whose capture would open the way to Astapovo, Liudkova, and 50th Army had still to be overcome.

Kliuchi was the key. Located at a critical road junction on the crest of a ridge, its houses and buildings dominated the surrounding flat countryside.[28] Moreover, its defensive network interlocked with other villages, which, taken together, dominated the Moscow–Warsaw highway, three kilometers to the south. Its defenses consisted of ice walls, trenches, and strongpoints manned by some tanks and numerous infantry. Seizure of Kliuchi was a necessity if Kazankin's corps was to have any chance of piercing German defenses along the Moscow–Warsaw road. Soviet after-action reports characterized German defensive positions in the region as follows:

> Reconnaissance established that the Ekaterinovka, Pesochnia, and Kliuchi region was defended by up to 500 enemy officers and soldiers; in Khan'kovo and Astapovo, up to 1,000 men; in Vygor, up to 300 men (434th Infantry Regiment); and in Semenkovo, Leonovo, and Andronovo, up to 700 men. All these population points were German strongpoints, comprising the system of the Pesochnia, Leonovo, and Podsosonki center of resistance. In total, the corps had before it not less than two enemy infantry regiments. These regiments occupied well-prepared fortified positions, were reinforced by artillery, and supported by bomber aviation.[29]

On the evening of 26 February, the two brigades commenced almost simultaneous attacks on German positions at Pesochnia and Kliuchi. The first force to penetrate the defenses of Pesochnia was a ski platoon of the 214th Brigade, but, after heavy fighting, it was repulsed, and its commander killed. The brigade attack again faltered, and Pesochnia remained in German hands.

To the east 9th Airborne Brigade moved methodically against German defenses at Kliuchi. During daylight on 26 February, Plotnikov's 1st Battalion occupied the village of Dertovaia, Khan'kova, and Tynovka to secure the corps' left flank. It then reinforced Gorbachi, which the Germans had brought under heavy artillery and mortar fire the day before, and moved on Kliuchi from the southeast. Meanwhile, Captain

Smirnov's 2d and Captain Bibikov's 4th Battalions blocked approaches to Kliuchi from the north and west and Captain Polozkov's 1st Battalion, 214th Brigade, shifted from the besieged Pesochnia to attack Kliuchi from the west. After darkness fell, Captain Gor'kov's 4th Battalion, 9th Brigade, arrived with the corps artillery battalion, to be followed soon after by Major Sharov's 3d Battalion, 9th Brigade, which had been left in reserve. The combined attack by these forces was designated to begin on the evening of 26 February.

Throughout 26 February 4th Airborne Corps prepared to assault Kliuchi. The 214th Brigade's sapper company dispatched a platoon to envelop the town from the south and cut the communications of German forces in Kliuchi with those in Malyshevka and Kruglik. On the return route of its eight kilometer-deep mission, the platoon also mined the approaching roads to Kliuchi. As the time of the attack approached, the weather became more favorable. Heavy snow resumed, and visibility deteriorated, preventing the Germans from effectively coordinating their artillery fire.

After dark 4th Airborne Corps began the assault, and first the 2d Battalion, 9th Brigade, and then the 1st and 4th Battalions, 9th Brigade, reached and penetrated Kliuchi's ice wall defenses and seized several houses in the northern and northwestern sections of the town. Elements of 1st and 2d Battalions, 9th Brigade, soon encircled the town and penetrated the ice walls from the south. Heavy fighting raged all night. The inability of German troops in nearby Pesochnia and Ekaterinovka to provide fire support to the Kliuchi garrison assisted 9th Brigade's advance. After three hours of fighting, 9th Brigade forces reached the town square and Kuryshov committed his reserve 4th Battalion, 8th Brigade, to crush the last remnants of German resistance. By first light on 27 February, Kliuchi had been cleared of its German defenders, which the Soviets identified as staff units of the German 12th Infantry Regiment. Small groups of German survivors fled southwest to Malyshevka, another strongpoint just two kilometers north of the Moscow–Warsaw road.

Soviet accounts assessed German losses in Kliuchi as follows: 'The enemy lost in Kliuchi 600 dead soldiers and officers. Up to two infantry battalions and the staff of 12th Infantry Regiment were fully crushed, and many banners and trophies, including 50 horses, 200 vehicles and sleighs, and much other equipment was seized.'[30]

On the morning of 27 February, the 2d and 4th Battalions, 9th Airborne Brigade, followed on their flanks by the two battalions of 214th and 8th Brigades, struggled through the snow to engage German forces at Malyshevka and cut the Moscow–Warsaw road, which was almost in sight. Soon the Germans blasted the advancing battalions with artillery, air attacks, and ground attacks, supported by armor. German infantry and armor struggling against renewed 50th Army attacks to the south of the highway blunted the Soviet advance and quickly shifted forces northward to deal with the looming airborne threat. Far from its landing sites, the airborne force lacked adequate supplies as well as mobility and fire support. Conversely, the Germans' proximity to the Moscow–Warsaw road gave them the opportunity to use their superior mobility to bring up fresh reserve units.

Consequently, after suffering more casualties, the airborne forces gave ground and returned to Kliuchi in frustration, where they estabished all-round defenses. Kazankin pulled the 1st Battalion, 214th Brigade, and 4th Battalion, 8th Brigade, into reserve to regroup and refit. For two days German forces pounded the withdrawing paratroopers. All day on 27 February, German aircraft struck at Soviet positions around Kliuchi, but, despite the attack, Kazankin's forces repulsed German ground counter-attacks. Throughout 28 February groups of nine German aircraft con-tinually swooped down over the paratroopers defenses in Kliuchi, but the defenses continued to hold against German ground attacks and actions by small diversionary units. During the heavy fighting, Kazankin evacuated his wounded to the brigade medical point near Kurakino, while the lightly wounded continued to fight in the ranks.

As a result of the intense February battles, 4th Airborne Corps' forces were able to fulfill their initial mission from Western Front; that is, to occupy positions from which they could attack to link up with 50th Army. The corps, however, was unable to crack German resistance along the narrow bank of territory astride the Moscow–Warsaw road and link up with 50th Army forces. During operations to seize and defend Kliuchi, 4th Airborne Corps lost 1,200 men or 25 per cent of its combat strength.[31] The airborne failure, however, was not unique, for 50th Army experienced similar difficulties. After once again regrouping his forces, by late on 21 February General Boldin, 50th Army commander, assigned his army a new mission:

> to tie down the enemy on his right flank and strike the major blow with his left flank forces of the 413th, 290th, 344th, 173d, and 336th Rifle Divisions and the 2d and 32d Tank Brigades to penetrate enemy defenses in a 20 kilometer sector northeast of Mosal'sk, in order to subsequently advance into the rear of the enemy Iukhnov group in the direction of Barsuki.[32]

The 50th Army unit history succinctly relates the outcome of the failed operation:

> 4th Airborne Corps, cooperating with the army, while attacking

from the north, on 27 February secured several population points 25–27 kilometers northwest of Mosal'sk and developed the offensive with the mission of assisting 50th Army in the seizure of the sector of the Warsaw highway and destruction of the enemy Iukhnov group. However, all attempts to cut the Warsaw road from 23 February to 3 March had no success and, during the attempts, our forces suffered heavy casualties.[33]

Given these conditions, on 1 March Kazankin ordered his airborne corps to establish a temporary 35-kilometer defensive line running east and west of Kliuchi and anchored on the villages of Verterkhovo Station, Dubrovnia, Kliuchi, Gorbachi, Petrishchevo, Tynovka, Iurkino, Andronovo, and Novaia. Behind this line, corps headquarters hoped to take stock of its heavy losses, regroup, and replenish its dwindling supplies of ammunition and food.[34]

Perhaps the most vexing problem confronting Kazankin was that of logistical support. After-action reports record, 'To this time [26 February], corps units were aware of food and ammunition needs; their small reserves, stretched over eight days, were running out. The absence in the corps of ammunition and artillery did not facilitate the possibility of developing success.'[35]

Kazankin attempted to remedy the problem by providing extra support and encouragement to his corps chief of rear services, Colonel I. Morozov. Morozov created a special rear service organization for the corps by drawing upon 4th Airborne Corps' resources as well as those of Belov's 1st Guards Cavalry Corps, local inhabitants, partisans, and materiel sent by aircraft from behind the front itself. Special care was taken, whenever possible, to use captured German supplies and equipment, particularly those seized at Kliuchi.

Morozov's system included an improved landing strip at Zhelan'e, field hospitals at Zyki and Glukhov, and a series of supply points linking the rear near Zhelan'e with forward corps' positions near Kliuchi. Last, but not least, Kazankin notified Western Front and VDV headquarters of his logistical problems and makeshift supply system and asked for their support. Initially, higher headquarters limited their support to delivery of supplies and weapons. Later it would dispatch personnel reinforcements as well.

Soviet General Staff after-action critiques provided a balanced assessment of 4th Airborne Corps' operations from its landing around Zhelan'e to its withdrawal to Kliuchi. They identified the following shortcomings in the corps' operation:

1. The excessively long period spent in assembling 4th Airborne Corps after landing, caused by the great dispersion of personnel

during the landing (up to 40 kilometers), provided an opportunity for the enemy to prepare a defense, and to deprive our assault of surprise, having hampered their fulfillment of assigned missions.

2. Poorly organized ground reconnaissance on the eve of the corps [ground] offensive, as a consequence of which the enemy defense system and its weak points were detected only after the offensive began, which could not avoid having an influence on the grouping of corps' forces.

3. The absence of a sharply defined direction of main attack in corps' operations; the dispersion of forces along diverse axes (Kliuchi and Podsosinki), it being known that on the direction of main corps strength called for by the *front* combat order (Kliuchi) there was allotted less force (9th Airborne Brigade) than on the supporting axes (214th Airborne Brigade).

All of these shortcomings taken together could not avoid influencing the entire subsequent course of 4th Airborne Corps' operation. Besides the shortcomings in the combat operations and in the command and control of 4th Airborne Corps, a rather essential shortcoming was the absence of full cooperation and coordination of strength of 50th Army units with the assault.[36]

THE MARCH OFFENSIVE

The welcome respite from combat, however, was brief. Taking advantage of superior mobility and firepower, a German battalion of infantry supported by artillery and tanks began counterattacks north of the highway (see Figure 51). This time, however, the Soviet airborne force had the advantage of a village and forest-based defense, while German mobile forces, once they had left the road, found the going difficult in the forests north of the highway.

Beginning at 0930 on 1 March, German bombers struck two heavy blows at Soviet defensive positions. Shortly thereafter, the German ground troops commenced the counterattack. A battalion of infantry, supported by several tanks and artillery fire, struck Soviet positions south of Kliuchi. After losing several tanks to mines, antitank fire, and Molotov cocktails, the Germans withdrew. A second and even larger attack ensued against 9th Brigade positions, during which German aircraft bombed the brigade command post. Captain Smirov's 2d Battalion was forced to commit its reserve company to hold the battalion defensive positions, but hold them it did as the Germans again withdrew. The 9th

Airborne Brigade repulsed three German assaults on 1 March but at considerable cost.[37] Western Front headquarters against radioed congratulations to the force, 'To Kazankin, Olenino, Kuryshev, Shcherbin. Congratulations on your victory over Fascism and your seizure of Gorbachi and Kliuchi. Put the victors in for awards.'[38] While heartening Kazankin and his forces, this message scarcely made the situation less

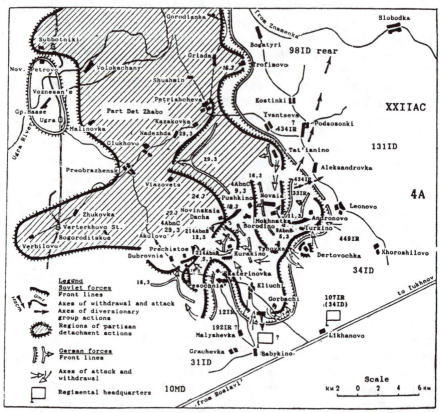

51. 4th Airborne Corps Operations, 1–20 March 1942

perilous. Official after-action reports recounted the situation in early March:

> During the first days of March, it was determined that the staff of German 131st Infantry Division was located in Podsosonki. That division, as it became clear later, had the mission of destroying our airborne forces, operating north of the Warsaw road. The offensive of that division on Kliuchi on 1 March was repulsed by 9th Airborne Brigade, and units of the 214th Airborne Brigade succeeded

in advancing westward somewhat, seizing Gorbachi, Tynovka, Iurkino, and Andronovo. The corps battled along that line until 4 March.[39]

German forces conducted reconnaissance and felt out the paratroopers' dispositions over the next few days. Meanwhile, 9th Brigade sent out reconnaissance elements and established ambushes along the road south of Kliuchi. While quiet reigned around Kliuchi, 3d and 4th Battalions, 214th Airborne Brigade, continued to seek ways to drive German forces from Pesochnia. Renewed attacks in early March cost the 3d Battalion its commander, Senior Lieutenant Vasil'ev, who died with many of his men under heavy German mortar fire. The remaining men of 2d Battalion were then assigned to the Brigade's remaining two under-strength battalions: Captain Khoteenkov's 4th Battalion and Captain Polozkov's 1st Battalion.

Between 3 and 5 March, 4th Airborne Corps received new stocks of ammunition and food, regrouped its units and subunits, and evacuated its burgeoning number of wounded to the rear. On 5 March the strength rolls of the corps showed 3,000 men present for duty, equipped with 30 AT rifles, 126 hand machine guns, seven 45mm guns, 16 82mm mortars, 707 automatic rifles, 1,300 rifles, and 15 radio sets. This dwindling force had to continue operating against elements of three German infantry divisions.[40]

On 4 March, changes in the military situation to the northeast resulted in new orders for the airborne corps. Soviet 43d and 49th Army pressure on Iukhnov had finally forced the Germans to abandon the city and the salient around it. German XXXXIII Army Corps withdrew its remaining divisions from the Iukhnov salient to the southwest where they joined the 137th Infantry Division and other Fourth Army units in defenses south of the Moscow–Warsaw *Rollbahn*. Each division occupied a sector for all-round defense (see Figure 52). The bulk of each division's strength faced southeast against Soviet 50th Army. Small battalion-size *Kampfgruppen*, often organized from division support units, occupied villages north of the *Rollbahn* to defend against Soviet airborne, cavalry, and partisan units. These divisions relied on the interlocking village defenses and *Rollbahn* communications to thwart Soviet attacks. Until the end of winter, XXXXIII Army Corps relied on occasional battalion-size forays north of the road to keep Soviet forces in the rear from mounting a successful, concerted drive southward to link up with 50th Army. On 7 March XXXXIII Army Corps assumed responsibility for the entire *Rollbahn* defense. While XXXXIII Army Corps moved southwest of Iukhnov, the XII and XIII Army corps of Fourth Army occupied prepared positions facing east along the Ugra and Ressa Rivers.[41]

In a flash of optimism generated by the German withdrawal on 4 March, the chief of staff of the Western Front sent the following orders to Kazankin's 4th Airborne Corps:

> To Comrade Boldin [50th Army] and Comrade Kazankin [4th Airborne]. Enemy is withdrawing from Iukhnov along the Viaz'ma highway.
>
> High Command Order:
> 1. Comrade Boldin, strengthen the tempo of the offensive, in every possible way cut the Warsaw highway and complete the encirclement of the enemy in that region.
> 2. Comrade Kazankin, while fulfilling the basic mission – strike against Malyshevka and Grachevka and send part of the force to cut the Viaz'ma highway near Slobodka. Organize ambushes along the Viaz'ma highway to destroy the enemy.[42]

On 3 March General Boldin dispatched his assistant chief of reconnaissance in a PO-2 aircraft to 4th Airborne Corps headquarters to coordinate the upcoming operations. Boldin passed word to Kazankin that, in view of Kazankin's failure to break the German front at Lavrishchevo and Adamovka, 50th Army would now attack toward hill 253.2. The following morning, Boldin specified that 50th Army's attack route to the hill would be through a three kilometer penetration sector between Solov'evka and Makarovka toward hill 253.2 and that the attack would occur on the night of 5–6 March against the German 31st, 34th, and 137th Infantry Divisions. He requested that 4th Airborne Corps cooperate, first by sending reconnaissance forces toward 50th Army and then by attacking to meet 50th Army units along two routes: Malyshevka–hill 253.2–Uzlovka and Kliuchi–Fedorovka–Chichkovo.[43]

Colonel Kazankin responded to Boldin's request by sending reconnaissance units along the first route to link up with 50th Army reconnaissance forces and to return by the second route. After-action critiques assessed that coordination measures were more than adequate. Kazankin then issued orders to his subordinate brigades. 9th Airborne Brigade, reinforced by the corps' artillery battalion and part of the 214th Airborne Brigade, was to secure Malyshevka and subsequently Babykino (800 meters north of the Moscow–Warsaw road), where 50th Army advance units had promised to meet the airborne force. The 9th Airborne Brigade intended to take Malyshevka by envelopment in a simultaneous surprise attack from both flanks and from the front. The 214th Airborne Brigade covered 9th Airborne Brigade's right flank by continuing to contain German forces in Pesochnia.

At 1800 5 March, in the woods north of Malyshevka, Colonel Kurys-

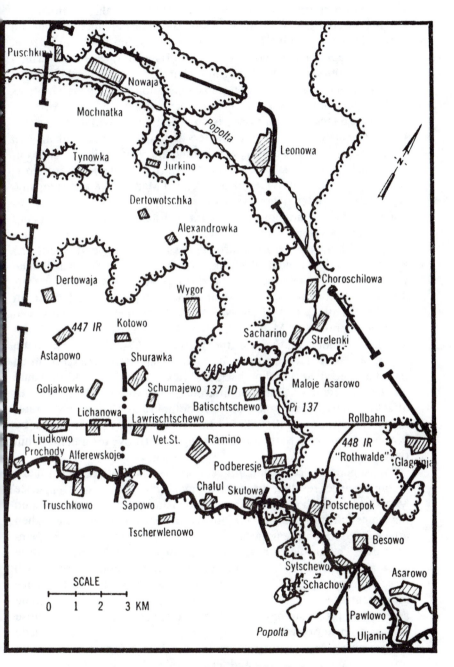

52. German 137th Infantry Division Defensive Area

chev of 9th Airborne Brigade issued orders to his battalion commanders and organized fire support. While his 1st Battalion defended Kliuchi and Gorbachi, his remaining battalions were to envelop Malyshevka from three sides and then develop the attack to Babykino, where they would unite with 50th Army. A short artillery barrage would precede the 0300 infantry attack. Kuryschev organized cooperation between his battalions on the spot, and Kazankin assigned specific orders to 214th Airborne Brigade to attack Pesochnia once again. The distance to Malyshevka (the immediate mission) was four kilometers and, to the planned link up with 50th Army, the distance was 8–9 kilometers. Both brigades sent out additional reconnaissance detachments, which confirmed earlier reports that up to a battalion of Germans defended Malyshevka and company-size forces defended nearby villages.

After dark the battalions began their painstaking movement forward into assault positions. Major Smirnov's 2d Battalion ran into problems early. At 2100, while moving through the northern edge of woods one kilometer south of Kliuchi, the force encountered heavy German fire and were driven back, with the loss of one company commander killed. The 3d and 4th Battalions continued their advance, expecting to take part in a coordinated attack on Malyshevka. At 0100 6 March Major Sharov's 3d Battalion approached Malyshevka from the northeast and, at first light, attacked without waiting for the arrival of Captain Bibikov's 4th Battalion. Heavy German resistance and a flank attack by a German ski battalion forced 3d Battalion back toward Gorbachi. With 3d Battalion already repulsed, 4th Battalion arrived late because of the deep snow, attacked Malyshevka, and secured footholds in the northwest and northeast portions of the village. Immediate German counterattacks, however, denied 4th Battalion time to dig in and drove the unit north out of the village.[44]

The supposedly concerted 9th Airborne Brigade attack failed. Poor reconnaissance resulted in underestimation of German strength in Malyshevka, which actually numbered two infantry battalions with anti-tank guns and mortars, later reinforced by a ski battalion. In addition, the attack failed to achieve requisite surprise to make up for the weakness of the force. The disjointed nature and slow progress of the attack in deep snow also doomed the operation. Finally, no diversionary or blocking forces equipped with AT guns or mines were employed to block the movement of German reserves. In the last analysis, Soviet critiques assessed that it would have been better to concentrate the entire corps against a single objective.[45]

German reserves counterattacking on 6 March forced the airborne force to conduct a grueling withdrawal through deep snow at agonizingly slow speeds (one kilometer an hour) back to its original assembly areas.

While Kazankin planned and conducted the attack toward Malyshevka, German forces became active on his left (eastern) flank. A German force of two companies attacked but was unable to occupy Tynovka, and other forces threatened Iurkino and Andronovo. After its unsuccessful offensive, 4th Airborne Corps, on 7 March, tried to consolidate its defensive area by capturing German positions at Pesochnia and Ekaterinovka, but both attempts failed.

50th Army had as little success in fulfilling its missions as 4th Airborne Corps. Boldin's army had received the mission of penetrating German defenses along the Moscow–Warsaw road in a 12-kilometer sector between Lavrishchevo and Adamovka and advancing 7–8 kilometers to the line Batishchevo, Vygor', Kliuchi, and Pesochnia to link up with 4th Airborne Corps and then wheel eastward to destroy the German Iukhnov group. 50th Army's offensive failed with heavy losses, including the death of a division commander (344th Rifle).[46]

Repeated 50th Army attacks in ever-narrowing sectors (first 12, then 10, and finally two kilometers) and to ever shorter depths (four kilometers) still failed to produce positive results. Soviet classified critiques attributed the failures to the following reasons:

Basic reasons:
1. Army forces for an extended period conducted uninterrupted attacks from Tula to Mosal'sk, in complex weather conditions and with understrength units. Sufficient force was not available to develop the offensive.
2. The army needed resupply of ammunition, but, while operating in difficult weather conditions, it had not a single road available to obtain it, as well as food, fuel, fodder, and the evacuation of wounded. The low supply of ammunition (0.1–0.2 combat loads) deprived the artillery and mortars of the capability of smashing the enemy defenses. There was not a single road construction or repair battalion in the army.
3. There was no airfield to accommodate army aviation, and it could not operate.
4. The direction of the main attack was poorly studied and reconnoitered.
5. Reconnaissance of the enemy was weak.
6. Cooperation of forces, organized at the beginning of the operation, was repeatedly violated during its conduct.
7. Radio communications between regiment and divisions was poor and wire communications worked unreliably in the bad weather conditions.
8. The enemy succeeded in fortifying his defenses north and south

of the Warsaw road, especially in an engineer sense. Having secured the Warsaw road, he could freely maneuver forces and reserves and rapidly build up the strength of forces in the army penetration sector.[47]

The 4th Airborne Corps' attempt to link up with 50th Army was condemned to failure in advance. The corps' 3,000 men, with their light weapons and meager supplies, were exhausted by more than two weeks of constant combat and were simply too weak to engage the heavy German defensive line.[48] The *front* commander, Zhukov, had clearly overestimated the capability of his forces. The 50th Army had proved earlier the futility of trying to break the formidable German defenses on the Moscow–Warsaw road. After the failed link-up, the situation again stabilized, and airborne forces continued conducting diversionary operations against the German rear from their base area near Zhelan'e.

As a consequence of the failed attempt to cut the Warsaw highway and unite with 50th Army, Kazankin's corps' strength dwindled further to the following level:

Manpower		*Weapons*	
Officers and NCOs –	843	Rifles –	1276
Enlisted –	1641	Machine pistols (PPSh) –	707
Total –	2484	Pistols –	376
		Machine guns –	126
		AT rifles –	39
		37mm mortars –	93
		50mm mortars –	22
		82mm mortars –	16
		Radios –	15[49]

This force now had to secure a 35-kilometer front, all the while conducting diversionary operations in the enemy rear. Moreover, the front was punctuated by German-controlled strongpoints such as Pesochnia. A Soviet after-action report recounted the corps' dilemma:

Prolonged combat along that line placed the corps in a difficult position; without the presence of a proper rear service, questions of supply and evacuation took on an acute character. Although, to that time, the supply of units and evacuation of wounded was arranged by means of transport aircraft, those methods, however, did not fully meet the corps' requirements. The corps command, as was the case with the commands of other units operating in the enemy rear, fell back on the help of partisans, one of the largest detachments of which, under the command of Zhabo, operated in the rear and along the left flank of the corps. Firm communications, which the corps established with that detachment, subsequently proved itself when the German offensive action in that sector became more widespread.[50]

Closer logistical links between 4th Airborne Corps and the partisans prompted closer tactical cooperation as well. Acting on Western Front orders, Kazankin sent corps engineers and two sapper squads from the 214th Airborne Brigade to Zhabo's headquarters in Shumilin. These engineers helped Zhabo's partisan forces lay mines and conduct diversionary operations and ambushes between Viaz'ma and Iukhnov, in particular along the Znamenka road. Joint airborne–partisan groups also operated at night in the Bogatyri, Znamenka, Slobodka sectors, seriously disrupting German transport between Viaz'ma and Iukhnov.

Concentrating up to four infantry divisions for operations along a number of diverse axes, the Germans sought to root out and crush the increasingly troublesome airborne force. The bulk of the 131st and elements of the 34th Infantry Divisions, reinforced by the 449th Infantry Regiment of 137th Infantry Division, massed near Kostinki, Ivantsevo, Leonovo, Dertovaia, and Andronovo to push westward toward Novaia, while elements of the 331st and 31st Infantry Divisions assembled south of 4th Airborne Corps positions and prepared to move north. These forces outnumbered the Soviet force tenfold in manpower and absolutely in weaponry.[51] The Germans also erected a strong defensive cordon around the airborne force with minefields, snow barriers, abatis, and pillboxes to restrict airborne force movement along the Slobodka–Znamenka road and toward the Moscow–Warsaw highway. Meanwhile, German task-organized mobile groups planned to penetrate the airborne defensive area from the southeast and south. Intensified German reconnaissance indicated an impending German effort.

German activity against Kazankin's force began across a broad front on 6 March, as the airborne troopers were withdrawing to their jumping-off positions after their last attempt to cut the Moscow–Warsaw road. A force of 200 Germans from Dertovochka struck 9th Airborne positions at Tynovka but were repelled with the loss of 50 men. Major G. I. Lebedev's battalion of the 214th Brigade, also defending near Tynovka, counted 35 more German dead.[52]

During this period an excellent example of counterintelligence operations occurred. Shortly before the German March offensive began, a U-2 aircraft landed during daytime near the village of Preobrazhensk. A staff officer on board carried an order from the Western Front command, which read, 'Since the units of Efremov's 33d Army are not having success in securing the city of Viaz'ma, corps units are to organize a withdrawal without delay.' The order then indicated the route of withdrawal. Kazankin issued preliminary orders for withdrawal, then consulted with corps Chief of the Special Department [*Osobyi otdel'*], Major I. A. Salov. Salov determined that the U-2 pilot did not know the whereabouts of airfields in the Moscow region. Subsequent queries to Western Front were answered with the succinct message, 'What are you talking about? Fulfill your assigned mission.' Soviet critiques commented, 'Thus, the alertness of a Chekist and other paratroopers saved from inevitable death hundreds of soldiers and commanders. I. A. Salov, having succeeded in uncovering the insidious fascist scheme, was awarded the Order of Red Banner.'[53]

On 11 March, after a thorough reconnaissance of the area, the German 131st Infantry Division attacked Andronovo and Iurkino after an artillery preparation. The Germans attacked from three sides at first light and forced two reinforced platoons of 4th Battalion, 214th Airborne Brigade, to withdraw into the woods west of Iurkino where the Soviets managed to hold desperately to their positions. German attacks against the center of the corps defense at Novaia Mokhnata and Tat'ianino also failed. Particularly heavy fighting occurred on the southern perimeter of the corps at Gorbachi, a key Soviet strongpoint within artillery range of the Moscow–Warsaw road. Kliuchi and Gorbachi also remained constant thorns in the Germans' side. Because their proximity to the Moscow–Warsaw road interfered with German communications, they became prime German targets.

By day's end on 12 March, having repulsed German attacks on Tynovka, Mokhnatka, and Tat'ianino, 4th Airborne Corps occupied the following positions: a mixed detachment of the 214th Airborne Brigade defended Dubrovnia, Prechistoe, and Kurakino and continued to block German forces in Ekaterinovka and Pesochnia with two companies (facing the German 12th Infantry Regiment); 9th Airborne Brigade defended Kliuchi, Gorbachi, and Tynovka and cut the Pesochnia–Malyshevka road with one company (facing 143d and 442d Infantry Regiments); and the 214th Airborne Brigade defended Mokhnatka and Novaia by all-round defenses against the German 434th and 33d Infantry Regiments.[54]

The main force of the German 131st Infantry Division was now concentrated in the Podsosonki, Kostinki, Ivantsevo, Leonovo, and Khoroshilovo area, intending to operate toward Novaia and Verterkhovo Station. Its companies were assessed at a strength of 40–50 men each. Because of its weakness, the 449th Regiment, located in Dertovochka and Aleksandrovka, was directed to cooperate with the 131st Infantry.

Additional German reinforcements continued to arrive. By 15 March prisoner of war reports identified the 107th Infantry Regiment, 34th Infantry Division, in Likhanovo and stated the regiment had relocated from Iukhnov to battle 4th Airborne Corps. This and other German forces tried to cordon off Kazankin's corps and destroy it. Soviet after-action reports lamented:

> While leaning against the Slobodka, Znamenka high road, at that time the Germans created along the corps' front a belt of obstacles and fortifications, consisting of minefields, snow barriers, ramparts, and pillboxes. In addition, they employed searchlights, anti-aircraft guns, field guns, tanks, etc.; all means which were denied to 4th Airborne Corps.[55]

To compound 4th Airborne Corps' difficulties, its strength steadily continued to fall. On 15 March its strength reports showed the following:

Manpower		*Weapons*	
Officers and NCOs –	665	Rifles –	1023
Enlisted –	1336	Machine pistols (PPSh) –	646
Total –	2001	Machine guns –	74
		AT rifles –	13
		45mm guns –	6
		37mm mortars –	8
		50mm mortars –	14
		82mm mortars –	18
		Radios –	31[56]

At dawn on 13 March, after an intense artillery preparation, two German infantry battalions from the 31st and 34th Infantry Divisions, supported by tanks, attacked Gorbachi from the northeast, west, and south. Repeated German assaults, taken under fire by the paratroopers at ranges of 50 to 70 meters, finally secured a foothold in the southeast portion of the airborne defense. Captain Plotnikov's 1st Battalion, 9th Airborne Brigade, was unable to dislodge the Germans, and, in the heavy fighting, Plotnikov was wounded. At 1700 the commander of 2d Battalion, Captain Smirnov was ordered by brigade to dispatch one of his companies from Kliuchi on skis to reinforce the 1st Battalion. Advancing rapidly through the forest, the ski battalion attacked the German left flank and forced a German withdrawal to Astapovo. By 1800 the two battalions, assisted by 45mm gun fire, had driven the last German troops from barns on the northern side of the village. Interrogation of German prisoners revealed the division had recently arrived from France and provided details of the dispositions and plans of German forces' attempt to encircle 4th Airborne Corps. The 2d Battalion commander's decisiveness and skillful maneuver had won the battle. German losses at Gorbachi included 200 men, 10 automatic weapons, 156 rifles, two mortars, two antitank guns, and one destroyed tank. A subsequent telegram from the Western Front Military Council lauded the efforts of the airborne force: 'The Corps operated in outstanding fashion, in spite of difficulties. Give to the units operating in the Gorbachi region my thanks. Recommend the distinguished for awards! Zhukov, Khokhlov.'[57]

Yet, despite the victory at Gorbachi and the subsequent respite offered by the arrival of a major snowstorm on 14 March, German pressure increased relentlessly as German reinforcements continued to arrive. Kazankin decided to attempt to steal the march on German forces, once and for all, by crushing the German garrison at Pesochnia. He ordered a night attack on 17 March by all available 9th and 214th Brigade forces, as well as 4th Battalion, 8th Brigade. The attack began at 2200 17 March, and, although one company penetrated the ice walls into the town proper, as had been the case earlier, German counterattacks drove the airborne troops from the town.

The following morning, elements of German 131st Infantry Division attacked airborne positions between Novaia and Mokhnatka, seized Pushkino from the 4th Battalion, 214th Airborne Brigade, and reduced that battalion to only 30 men. At 1300 the Germans attacked Borodino, Tynovka, Gorbachi, and Kliuchi and pushed back the corps' defensive lines east of Kurakino.[58] Repeated attacks cost the Germans heavily but killed 18 paratroopers in the process. Facing this heavy pressure and possible encirclement, the corps sought and received *front* permission to withdraw to a new defensive line running from Verterkhovo Station, through Zhukovka, Akulovo, Prechistoe, and Kurakino, to Novinskaia Dacha. The Soviet government recognized the paratroopers' efforts by awarding an honorific title to the 4th Airborne Corps.

Late on 18 March, Kazankin's corps began its planned withdrawal. The 214th Airborne Brigade secretly withdrew from its positions and occupied new defenses around Akulovo. Similarily, 9th Brigade battalions left the Pesochnia area, and 1st Battalion occupied new defenses at Novinskaia Dacha, the 2d Battalion at Prechistoe, and the 3d Battalion at Kurakino. Two days later, on 20 March, the Germans detected 4th Airborne Corps' withdrawal and moved forward into positions at Borodino and Dubrovnia, from which they could launch attacks on Kurakino and Prechistoe. Prechistoe was the most important German objective because through it ran the primary airborne east–west resupply route. Meanwhile, Major Zhabo's 1st Partisan Regiment repelled German attacks by the 52d Infantry Division from the Znamenka and Velikopol'e area against his defenses in the Andriiaki, Drozdogo, and Bel'diugino sectors. By evening 20 March, Kazankin's corps and Zhabo's partisans had, with Western Front permission, occupied a new defensive perimeter, running from Verterkhovo Station, through Bogoroditskoe, Akulovo, Prechistoe, and Kurakino to Novinskaia Dacha. The stage was set for an even fiercer defensive contest.

No sooner had 4th Airborne Corps settled in better defensive positions, than German attacks resumed (see Figure 53). At 0900 25 March German 131st Infantry Division units attacked and penetrated the positions of Capt. D. I. Bibikov's 4th Battalion, 9th Airborne Brigade, at Kurakino. In a street battle that lasted all day and the next night, Bibikov's Battalion suffered 38 killed and 91 wounded but was able to repulse the Germans. Although inflicting heavy casualties on the German force, the 4th Battalion, 9th Brigade, emerged with only 88 fit men.[59] The survivors transformed Kurakino into a fortress of small strongpoints, with the battalion command post at the center. Repeated small-scale German attacks on Kurakino culminated at 1200 on 31 March, when the Germans launched a major infantry and tank assault with three infantry battalions against the junction of 9th and 214th Airborne Brigade positions at Prechistoe, Dubrovnia, and Kurakino on the southern edge of Kazankin's defensive perimeter. German heavy artillery and aviation strikes preceded and accompanied the attack. Having both suffered and inflicted heavy losses, 4th Airborne Corps units abandoned, first, Dubrovnia and, several hours later, Prechistoe. By day's end and after heavy fighting, the Germans drove 9th Brigade from all three strongpoints. Kuryschev's men withdrew and established new defenses in the forests to the northwest. 9th Brigade troopers destroyed four German tanks but lost all of their antitank guns.[60]

While the airborne force tried in vain to join 50th Army, other encircled Soviet forces also fought for survival. By mid-April elements of 33d Army had been decimated by constant German counterattacks.[61] Remnants of the 329th Rifle Division, 33d Army, and the 250th Airborne Regiment managed to separate themselves from doomed 33d Army and joined Belov's 1st Guards Cavalry Corps, but only after the Germans had destroyed the bulk of 33d Army's four divisions in late March in a pocket north of Perekhody. Belov's 1st Guards Cavalry Corps, thwarted in its attempts either to free Viaz'ma or to rescue a major portion of 33d Army, withdrew its depleted forces westward toward Dorogobuzh where, supported by partisans, it reorganized and replenished its supplies in March.[62] Belov reconstituted the 329th Rifle Division by assigning to it the 250th Airborne Regiment and other small corps units. He appointed the 250th Airborne Regimental commander, Major N. L. Soldatov, to command the reconstituted division.

By 13 March Belov's forces had occupied positions extending from Dorogobuzh in the west southeastward through Starosel'e to Bel'diugino just east of Viaz'ma–Ugra road. He had long since given up efforts to seize Viaz'ma or cut the Viaz'ma–Smolensk road. 1st Guards Cavalry Division anchored Belov's left flank in the Dorogobuzh area flanked on the east by 57th Cavalry Division, 7th Guards Cavalry Regiment, 329th Rifle Division, 8th Airborne Brigade, and, finally, 2d Guards Cavalry Division, which linked up with Zhabo's 1st Partisan Regiment near the Viaz'ma–Ugra road. 41st Cavalry Division was in reserve.

Belov, appreciating his plight, and that of 4th Airborne Corps operating to the south, on 14 March decided to shift his forces southward to

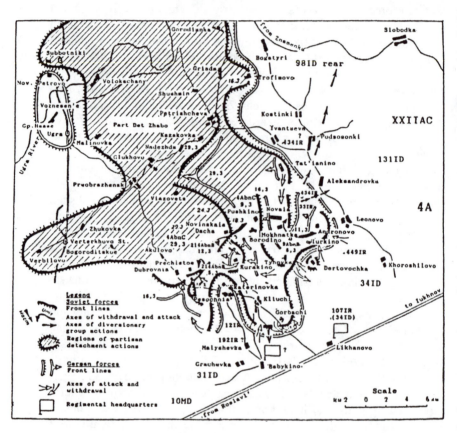

53.   4th Airborne Corps Operations, 21–31 March 1942

complete the seizure of key railroad stations along the Viaz'ma–Kirov rail line, particularly Ugra Station, where 800 Germans of Group Haase were encircled, and to join his dwindling forces to those of Kazankin's 4th Airborne Corps. At this point, Belov's corps numbered 6,252 men, equipped with 5,165 horses, 3,432 rifles, 128 machine guns, 1,047 automatic weapons, 43 heavy machine guns, 19 antitank rifles, 24 76mm guns, 11 45mm guns, two 37mm guns, and 61 mortars of various calibers.[63] This force, if united in a single effort with 4th Airborne's almost 1,500 men, could increase considerably the threat in the German rear.

After-action reports explained both Belov's problems and his opportunities:

> To this time, thanks to active operations of growing partisan detachments, German units in separate sectors began to find themselves in encirclement. Such a situation occurred in the region of Ugra Station, where an enemy group, made up of part of his forces operating along the Viaz'ma–Zanoznaia railroad, were encircled by the operations of Partisan Detachments Zhabo and Grachev.
>
> The presence of the enemy in the group's rear, guarded in fact only by partisans, who, as a rule, were not able to conduct prolonged combat with German regular units, was fraught with serious consequences. Therefore, the liquidation of the enemy encircled in the Ugra Station region became the next mission of the group.[64]

Ugra Station was a rich target. Not only was it strategically situated, but it was also a major supply point, with warehouses filled with ammunition, food, and other supplies.

Consequently, between 14 and 16 March, Belov regrouped his forces and coordinated his efforts with Kazankin (see Figure 54). Belov's orders required his forces to regroup by 16 March to the following locations:

- 41st Cavalry Division to the Sidorovichi region (eight kilometers northwest of Ugra Station);
- 2d Guards Cavalry Division to the Subbotniki–Godunovka region (6–10 kilometers north of Ugra Station) to defend against a German advance from Viaz'ma;
- 8th Airborne Brigade to the Lomy region (eight kilometers northwest of Ugra Station);
- 329th Rifle Division to the Mitrokhino, Debrevo area (12 kilometers northwest of Ugra Station) to defend against German attack from the north, assisted by 75th Cavalry Division to the west in the Starosel'e–Sapronovo sector and 57th Cavalry Division defending in the Staroe Prudishche region.[65]

Thus, while the bulk of Belov's forces still faced north, 2d Guards Cavalry Division and 41st Cavalry Division were available to assist the partisans in a concerted attack on enemy positions around Ugra Station. Shortly after the regrouping, the Western Front granted Belov permission to disband his understrength 41st, 57th, and 75th Cavalry Divisions and use their forces to reinforce 1st and 2d Guards Cavalry Divisions. This act strengthened both guards units and simplified Belov's command and control problems.

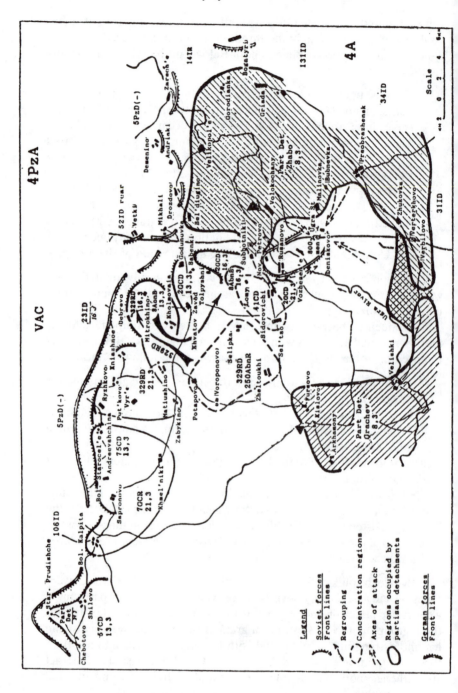

Lieutenant Colonel Onufriev's 8th Airborne Brigade had completed its movement southward by 15 March and thereafter spent five days replenishing its supplies and regrouping its subunits. The paratroopers were still outfitted for operations in winter conditions (in heavy felt shirts), and the beginning of the spring thaw required significant resupply efforts. Supplies were sent to them as well as to the cavalrymen by aircraft flying from Glukhovo airfield. Some tension existed between cavalrymen and paratroopers over who would receive which supplies; that required considerable negotiation and diplomacy.

Negotiations also took place between Belov, Kazankin, and *front* headquarters concerning the ultimate disposition of 8th Airborne Brigade. Kazankin asked that the brigade be returned to his control. Belov responded with a message to Western Front headquarters stating, '8th Airborne Brigade will advance on the main axis to Ugra Station. The brigade is the main shock force of the corps, and, in the event it cannot take part in the battle, we will have to give up seizing Ugra Station.'[66]

Western Front responded by continuing 8th Brigade's subordination to 1st Guards Cavalry Corps. Belov immediately implemented his offensive plans. At 0200 21 March, Captain Karnaukhov's 2d Battalion, 8th Airborne Brigade, penetrated German minefields and seized Deniskovo Station just south of Ugra. The following evening the 2d Battalion, with Pobortsev's composite battalion and Shmelev's partisans, in conjunction with 2d Guards Cavalry Division, struck at Ugra Station proper. Heavy fighting raged for three days, during which German aircraft pounded Soviet positions. Although 4th Airborne Corps' official history claimed that Ugra Station fell into Soviet hands, official Soviet records dispute this fact stating:

> The offensive [21 March] had no success; the uncoordinated actions of partisan detachments and their low combat capabilities did not permit them to occupy the strongly fortified region of Ugra Station with one spurt.
>
> The offensive continued on 22–23 March, but did not produce important results in light of the inability of enlisting other forces for that operation subsequent actions turned into an extended siege of the enemy Ugra grouping.[67]

The same report also summed up the subsequent role Group Belov would play in ensuing operations with 4th Airborne Corps, stating, 'Up to the end of March, the situation of the group remained without important changes. The subsequent struggle of Operational Group Belov took on the form of defensive combat, which continued during the period April to June 1942.'[68]

The operations around Ugra Station, while failing to reduce the

German garrison, did reestablish contact between 4th Airborne Corps and Group Belov, in general, and 8th Airborne Brigade, in particular. Finally, on 8 April, *front* orders resubordinated 8th Airborne Brigade to 4th Airborne Corps.

CONCLUSIONS

The 4th Airborne Corps' March defensive battles achieved limited success in holding off the attacks of elements of four German divisions. But the corps suffered greatly. By the end of March 2,000 paratroopers were sick or wounded, including 600 who required evacuation.[69] Supplies were short, antitank ammunition was gone, and rations were very low. Without reinforcement, there was little chance to resist continuing German attacks. Furthermore, the imminent spring thaw would make movement even more difficult than had the earlier heavy snow.

Soviet archival materials testify eloquently to the condition of 4th Airborne Corps at the end of March and candidly assess both its combat performance and that of the Germans. They describe 4th Airborne Corps' strength on 31 March as follows:

Manpower		*Weapons*	
Officers and NCOs –	535	Rifles –	718
Enlisted –	948	Antitank rifles –	15
Total –	1483	Machine guns/pistols –	577
		45mm guns –	4
		50mm mortars –	8
		82mm mortars –	10[70]

In short, the two weeks of fighting in late March had cost the corps over 500 men or 25 per cent of its strength. Without reinforcements, clearly the force would perish. Even with reinforcements, it was questionable whether it could succeed in breaking out of, what was by now, a firm encirclement.

Despite the perilous state of the corps, after-action reports credited it with achieving at least marginal success:

> The German command apparently decided to strike a last blow against our airborne forces...to gain for itself all territory occupied by 4th Airborne Corps and partisans for an unimpeded withdrawal of the main force of his Iukhnov grouping to the southwest (in the Iukhnov region at that time 43d and 49th Armies were conducting successful combat). However, the subsequent offensive of the Germans was halted by 4th Airborne Corps along the line Akulovo, Novinskaia Dacha.

Thus, in summary, the March persistent defensive battles of the corps ended in its favor. The units of two German divisions (34th and 131st) were unable to subdue the obstinacy of the parachutists, equal in numbers to a reinforced battalion, and were forced to be content with those small successes which they achieved in separate sectors. A month of combat was costly for the enemy; both of the divisions, while suffering casualties, failed to accomplish missions assigned by the German command. The airborne force continued to exist, as before inflicting heavy enemy losses. However, its situation with each day became more serious, the more so when the aim given the corps was still not fulfilled.[71]

4th Airborne Corps' official history echoed the judgement of the after-action reports, stating:

Thus, in February and March 1942, our forces were not able to destroy the German-Fascist grouping and liberate Rzhev, Gzhatsk, or Viaz'ma. The Western and Kalinin Fronts did not succeed in uniting in the region west of Viaz'ma and thus completing the encirclement and destruction of the main forces of Army Group 'Center.'[72]

Subsequent corps battles in April, May, and June would assume the aspect of an increasingly desperate fight for survival.

CHAPTER 6

The Viaz'ma Operation, Phase 3:
4th Airborne Corps' Operations,
(April–June 1942)

STRATEGIC CONTEXT

The decision to unite the forces of Belov and Kazankin reflected the realities of the situation at the beginning of April on the Eastern Front in general, and in the Moscow sector in particular. In fact, the power of the Soviet offensive had long since ebbed, and the frenetic headlong advance across the entire front had transformed itself into a nasty struggle for the initiative in specific sectors. Soviet forces had seized Iukhnov, but had failed to secure Rzhev, Gzhatsk, Viaz'ma, Kirov, and Sukhinichi. Wherever Soviet forces had penetrated deep into the German rear (39th Army, 33d Army, Group Belov, and 4th Airborne Corps), these forces were now subject to heavy German counterattacks and real or potential encirclement and destruction.

At first, the Soviet High Command had reinforced these forces, which were operating at the very end of tenuous logistical umbilicals. To this end, they relied primarily on additional airborne forces dropped into the German rear (near Viaz'ma, Rzhev, and Demiansk). By late March it became apparent that in doing so the High Command was simply reinforcing failure. Consequently, in April orders went to most of the encircled forces to conserve what men and resources they could by breaking through encircling German forces and reaching Soviet main frontal forces. To accomplish this mission, the High Command endeavored, whenever possible, to combine encircled forces in order to provide them with the requisite strength to break out. At the same time, the High Command continued issuing orders to *front* forces to continue offensive efforts in support of those forces encircled in the German rear.

Fighting in April took on an ever increasing air of desperation, as the High Command, as well as the ground forces, realized that breakout was no easy task. Nowhere was this realization clearer than in the ranks of Belov's and Kazankin's forces, and those of 50th Army as well.

THE APRIL OFFENSIVE

By late March it had become apparent that only joint efforts of the encircled units would ensure their survival as fighting entities. Consequently, Belov's cavalry corps had moved eastward to launch one last attempt to rescue the remnants of 33d Army or, failing in that, to reinforce 4th Airborne Corps' efforts to break out of German encirclement (see Figure 55).[1]

As 1st Guards Cavalry Corps moved east, German attacks on Kazankin's 4th Airborne Corps intensified. On 2 April the German 131st Infantry Division attacked from Dubrovnia and Maloe Prechistoe against 9th Airborne Brigade positions at Novinskaia Dacha and 214th Brigade defenses at Akulovo. Despite heavy losses, the Germans seized Novinskaia Dacha, further shrinking the restricted airborne defensive perimeter. Simultaneously, a small German force supported by tanks drove partisans from Bogoroditskoe. German employment of tanks and artillery made the task of defense even more difficult.

At this point Kazankin was left with two choices. Either he could abandon his positions and move his forces northwestward to the rail line in order to cooperate with Group Belov, or he could cling to his positions east of the rail line and wait for reinforcements. He chose the latter option despite the increasing German pressure. After dispatching part of his force to retake Bogoroditskoe, he extended his right flank to link up with Belov's force along the rail line and prepared to defend in place.

German forces continued their attacks on 214th Brigade positions at Akulovo on the morning of 3 April, this time throwing an even greater number of tanks into the action (see Figure 56). 214th Brigade troops used their dwindling supply of antitank rifles and destroyed two German tanks. While the fighting went on for Akulovo, on 3 April Onufriev's 8th Brigade troops linked up with Kazankin's corps near Preobrazhensk, eight kilometers southeast of Ugra Station. 8th Brigade brought with it 800 men, including 210 lightly wounded, organized into three battalions and commanded by Major Karnaukhov (2d Battalion), Captain Pobortsev (1st Battalion), and Captain Kalashnikov (3d Battalion). A fourth battalion, consisting of 400 men who had escaped from earlier encirclements, was commanded by Colonel Shmelev. In all, the brigade counted ten 82mm mortars, one 45mm antitank gun, and 16 antitank rifles. The exhausted force had virtually run out of food, ammunition, and other supplies.[2] Kazankin met with Onufriev and Raspopov and ordered their troops to occupy new defenses along the corps' right flank from Preobrazhensk to Zhukovka, thereby covering the rail line. This was the weakest portion of the airborne defense line, and any day one

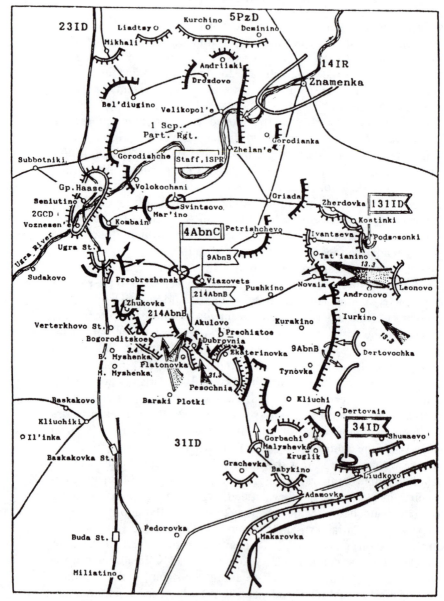

55. Situation, 31 March 1942

could expect a German attempt to advance north along the rail line and relieve its garrison at Ugra Station.

The only other Soviet force in the Ugra Station region was 2d Guards Cavalry Division. Belov had dispatched it south to help Kazankin after his latest attempt to rescue 33d Army had failed. The 2d Guards Cavalry Division, after securing Ugra Station, occupied positions in the Bas-

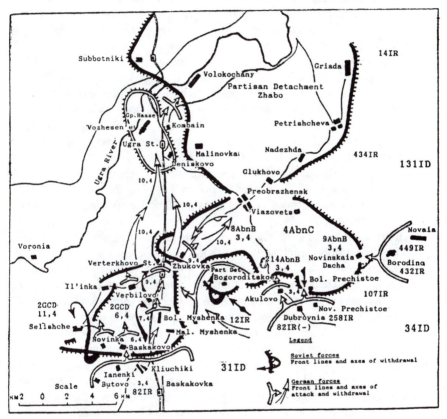

56. 4th Airborne and 1st Guards Cavalry Corps Operations, 3–10 April 1942

kakova area and, from 7 April, operated with 8th Airborne Brigade to repel German probes north along the rail line from Buda.[3] To further complicate matters for the Soviets, German Group Haase still held out at Voznesen'e and Seniutino in the rear of 2d Guards Cavalry Division.

Meanwhile, heavy fighting continued at Akulovo and around Prechistoe. Around midnight on 3 April, German forces, supported by six tanks and artillery, struck at 214th Brigade's positions at Akulovo. Despite losing a reported four tanks and 300 men, the Germans seized the town, inflicting 150 casualties on the airborne brigade. The same evening, 9th Airborne Brigade scored a rare success. In a night attack on a small German force in Prechistoe, the brigade cleared the town, killed 34 Germans, and captured one machine gun and a single damaged German tank.[4]

By early morning on 4 April, 214th Airborne Brigade dug-in in the forests just north and northwest of Akulovo, while 9th Airborne held firm to its positions around Prechistoe, Novinskaia Dacha, and Viazovets. Zhabo's partisans defended in the generally less-threatened area to the north.

A more serious situation was developing on Kazankin's right flank along the Viaz'ma–Kirov rail line south of Verterkhovo Station. There, 2d Guards Cavalry Division manned defensive positions, extending from Selishche through Baskakovo to Malaia Myshenka, as well as at Verterkhovo Station proper. Already, by day's end on 3 April, German forces had cleared cavalry outposts out of Kliuchiki, Ianenki, and Butovo. They then continued their northerly thrust along the rail line and seized Novinka, Baskakovo, and Bol'shaia Myshenka. The German assault struck directly at the boundary between 2d Guards Cavalry Division and 4th Airborne Corps and threatened to split the forces. Even worse, German forces operating further east near Bogoroditskoe were clearly coordinating their actions with the larger force along the rail line. The two efforts represented a concerted German effort to reach Verterkhovo Station and perhaps Ugra Station further north as well.

Kazankin's fears for his right flank were well founded. On 9 April, after conducting a systematic reconnaissance, German infantry with air, artillery, and armor support, struck northward against the junction between 2d Guards Cavalry Division and 4th Airborne Corps. Following heavy fighting, the Germans captured Verterkhovo Station and Zhukovka, driving 4th Airborne Corps eastward and 2d Guards Cavalry Division toward the west.[5] By nightfall 10 April, the German force had also seized Ugra Station and Kombain and lifted the Soviet siege of the German garrison at Voznesen'e.[6] Chief of the German General Staff, F. Halder, noted in his diary on 10 April, 'Relief forces have battled through to Combat Group Haase, which will be taken back.'[7] The slashing German attack continued on 11 April with other German forces advancing from the northeast. Most serious for Kazankin was the attack by one German column on Preobrazhensk and Marinovka, which threatened the integrity of 4th Airborne Corps' defensive perimeter.

Soviet after-action reports underscored the seriousness of the situation:

To allow enemy penetration still further north meant giving him the capability in the future of uniting with his Viaz'ma group. That threatened the full separation of 4th Airborne Corps and Partisan Detachment Zhabo from General Belov's group, which was operating northwest of Ugra Station. It was necessary to combine the actions of all units operating on that axis. With that aim, 4th Airborne Corps was operationally subordinated to General Belov, to whom the *front* commander gave the mission – by uniting the forces of all units to liquidate the penetrating enemy group, and, while attacking in the direction of Miliatino, unite with 50th Army, which had already attacked in the direction of that point.[8]

Given the rapidly deteriorating situation, Belov had fired off the following message to Zhukov's headquarters, asking for approval of the new plan:

I am reporting to you an assessment of conditions and proposals. The extent of the corps front in encirclement exceeds 300 kilometers. Enemy strength: On a line Miliatino–El'nia determined to be six infantry divisions. Toward El'nia are fortifications from Roslavl to Smolensk. West of the Dnepr an undetermined force defends. To the north – Iartsevo, Semlovo, Volosta Piatnitsa Station – mixed units, including the 35th and 23d Infantry Divisions, cover the approaches to the railroad.

Conclusion: The corps participates in the encirclement of the Viaz'ma–El'nia–Spas Demensk enemy group and in its turn is in operational encirclement.

The strength of the corps and extent of the front forces me to resort to defensive operations. The initiative is clearly in the hands of the enemy. There are no reserves. In such conditions, I suggest an offensive plan:

1. To break the encirclement ring to meet 50th Army in the general direction of Miliatino.
2. To this end concentrate in Vskhody a shock group made up of 1st and 2d Guards Cavalry Divisions, 4th Airborne Corps, and partisan detachment Zhabo.
3. Basic group of Colonel Moskalika's detachment to leave a small group to blockade El'nia and with the main force attack Spas Demensk.
4. Leave 'Dedushka' detachment to hold Dorogobuzh. Dnepr floods help that mission.
5. To secure the operation from north and northeast leave the 329th Rifle Division and small partisan detachments.
6. With 50th Army units and possibly 10th Army to seize the

Warsaw highway in the Zaitsev Heights section, Ersha, and also Miliatino. Thereafter to dig in on the road in the appointed sector.

7. After my link-up with Boldin in the Miliatino area to unite my corps with my trains including artillery, the tank brigade, the 2d Guards Cavalry Division and throw the corps either on Iartsevo to join with the Kalinin Front or for another assignment.

8. Preparations for the operation will involve 7–10 days and possibly will succeed in forestalling an enemy offensive.

No. 1596. Belov. Miloslavsky. Vashurin.[9]

On 11 April Zhukov approved Belov's proposal. By then, however, Belov's enthusiasm had waned because Zhukov had forbidden him to weaken his forces around Dorogobuzh and told him that 50th Army had exhausted itself again and was not yet ready to renew the attack.[10] Belov decided to attack anyway and, on 12 April, issued appropriate orders to his units, which now included 4th Airborne Corps (see Figure 57).

Belov's orders required 4th Airborne Corps to regroup and join 1st Guards Cavalry Corps in an advance southward along and east of the rail line to Miliatino. When ready, 50th Army would launch yet another attack (its fourth) northward to meet Belov's forces.[11] The distance from Belov's forces to those of 50th Army was only 25 kilometers, but between them were heavily entrenched German units lodged in all-round defensive positions.

The same day Colonel Kazankin developed his offensive plan.[12] While the 214th Airborne Brigade would continue to hold the airborne base area, the 8th and 9th Airborne Brigades would strike south in the direction of Buda, Novoe Askerovo, Staroe Askerovo, and Miliatino to cooperate with 50th Army and pierce the Moscow–Warsaw highway. The specific orders tasked 8th Airborne Brigade to attack on an axis of Bol'shaia Myshenka, Malaia Myshenka, western Buda, and Staroe Askerovo. The 9th Airborne Brigade was ordered to advance through eastern Buda to Novoe Askerovo, and 214th Airborne Brigade was to secure a defensive line from Akulovo to Plotki and cover the corps' left flank. On 4th Airborne Corps' right flank, the 2d Guards Cavalry Division was to bypass enemy strongpoints and reach Fanernovo Factory, three kilometers southwest of Baskakovka station. To protect the rear of 4th Airborne Corps, one battalion of the 1st Partisan Regiment and the 329th Rifle Division occupied former airborne defensive lines facing Viaz'ma.

Cooperative action by the two Soviet corps achieved immediate success, although the German forces along the rail line had accomplished their primary mission of relieving their encircled garrisons at Voznesen'e and Ugra Station and were then relatively content to withdraw. By day's

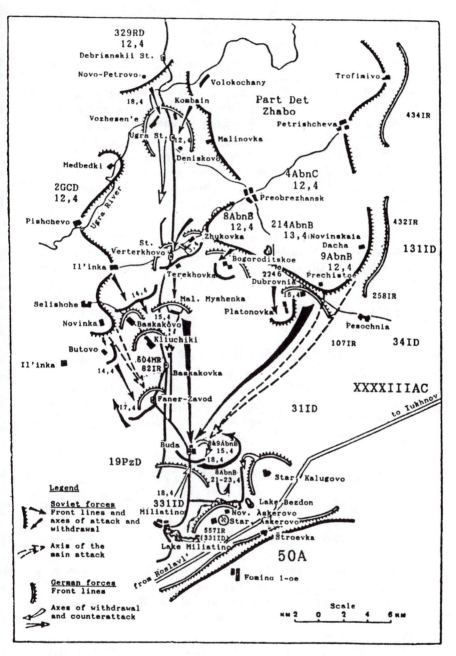

57. 4th Airborne and 1st Guards Cavalry Corps Operations, 11–20 April 1942

end on 11 April, 4th Airborne Corps had halted the German advance and commenced a counterattack. The following morning, the paratroopers reoccupied Kombain and Ugra Station, while the 329th Rifle Division recaptured Voznesen'e, and Zhabo's partisans the village of Deniskovo. By late evening 12 April, 8th Airborne Brigade secured Zhukovka and Verterkhovo Station. While elements of 8th Brigade provided security for corps headquarters at Preobrazhensk, the remainder of the brigade prepared to advance on Terekhovka, just south of Verterkhovo Station. Meanwhile, the 214th Airborne Brigade occupied Bogoroditskoe and Platonovka, and 8th Airborne defended around Prechistoe and Novinskaia Dacha.[13] German forces continued to defend from fixed positions from Malaia Myshenka on the rail line to Dubrovnia, while delivering heavy artillery fire on the regrouping Soviet corps.

The defensive battle and regrouping of corps' forces from 2–12 April succeeded in forestalling German attempts to destroy Belov's and Kazankin's corps piecemeal. Now the two forces faced an even tougher task of resuming the attack southward toward 50th Army. Much of their success would depend on how well Boldin's army accomplished its mission.

50th Army had already launched its third large offensive in late March. Its orders had been:

> To complete the penetration across the Warsaw road in a 12-kilometer sector between Fomino 1 and Kamenka, secure them, and unite with 4th Airborne Corps and 1st Guards Cavalry Corps .... Subsequently, while attacking in a northwest direction, accomplish the *front* mission by encircling and destroying the enemy Viaz'ma-Iukhnov group.[14]

At the time, 50th Army consisted of nine rifle divisions and one tank brigade for a strength of 54,634 men and 23 tanks operating on a 70-kilometer front. Prior to the 26 March attack, the army received two more reinforcing tank brigades with 2,267 men and 83 tanks. The shock group of this army had to traverse 25–30 kilometers of well-prepared German defenses to reach the encircled airborne and cavalry corps. During the preparatory period before the offensive (20–25 March), 50th Army still suffered from a lack of supply roads, ammunition shortages, and virtually no air support. The ill-defined and ill-reconnoitered penetration sector comprised a narrow three kilometer strip of land between a swamp and a forest, dominated by the strongpoints Fomino 1, hill 269.8, Fomino 2, and Zaitseva Gora [Zaitsev Heights].[15]

Boldin concentrated four rifle divisions and one tank brigade (112th) in first echelon and one rifle division (116th) and one tank brigade (11th) in second echelon. The second echelon forces were to commit between the

339th and 385th Rifle Divisions to secure Miliatino, while a reserve division (290th) would exploit behind the 336th Rifle Division. This force was opposed by the German 263d, 34th, 31st, and 331st Infantry and 19th Panzer Divisions dug in along the Warsaw road.

50th Army's main force swung into action on 26 March (16 hours after its secondary forces began diversionary attacks) in the midst of a spring snowstorm. Advancing at an agonizingly slow rate of 300–500 meters per hour, Boldin's forces finally penetrated enemy forward defenses. However, coordination between artillery fire, tanks, and infantry soon broke down, and ammunition shortages further curtailed fire support. Although the second echelon and reserve succeeded in entering combat, gains were minimal, and by 2 April the offensive faltered. On the night of 2–3 April, the army regrouped for a new attack, which began at 1200 on 5 April. This time Soviet forces seized Fomino 1 before the advance again faltered. In the ensuing ten days, Fomino 1 changed hands several times as each side threw in fresh forces. By evening 13 April, both Fomino 1 and Zaitseva Gora were under 50th Army's control, but that was as much as the army could achieve. Fresh attacks on 14 April against Fomino 2 failed as did subsequent 50th Army efforts to reach 4th Airborne Corps.[16] Meanwhile Kazankin set about launching his share of the operation in accordance with Western Front orders.

4th Airborne Corps' concerted offensive began on the night of 13–14 April, and, by dusk on 14 April, the 8th and 9th Brigades had surprised German forces and secured Terekhovka, Bol'shaia Myshenka, and Bogoroditskoe.[17] That evening Belov received heartening news from Western Front headquarters. It seemed that 50th Army had already secured the Zaitsev Heights and was but six kilometers from Miliatino – this after being unprepared to attack only three days before.[18] In any case, the *front* commander ordered Belov to accelerate his advance and rejected Belov's request to bring the 1st Guards Cavalry Division forward from Dorogobuzh.

Kazankin's forces pushed southward on the night of 14–15 April and occupied Platonovka, Baraki, and Plotki. On the left flank, the 214th Airborne Brigade took Akulovo, but heavy German fire from Dubrovnia halted further advance. Meanwhile, 2d Guards Cavalry Division reached within three kilometers of Baskakovka Station. Heavy German air attacks and ground resistance, however, made Belov rue the absence of his best cavalry division. Without a reserve, he could not sustain the advance much longer. On 15 April heavy German air attacks and ground counterattacks threw General Boldin's 50th Army forces off Zaitseva Gora and back from the Warsaw highway. That setback rendered Belov's and Kazankin's attacks futile. Nevertheless, they pushed their forces forward, hoping they could break the German lines by themselves. At

0600 15 April, Kazankin's forces approached Buda and thus were only three kilometers north of Miliatino. There the offensive stalled and soon recoiled under renewed German counterattacks. On 17 April, after two days of heavy battle, Pobortsev's and Karnaukhov's battalions of 8th Brigade entered northeastern Buda and seized the railroad station, while Smirnov's and Shuklin's 9th Brigade battalions struck southeastern Buda. By nightfall Buda fell to 4th Airborne Corps, together with considerable trophies. German casualties were 400 men, but Soviet losses were also considerable.[19]

Late that day General Kazankin notified Boldin of the fall of Buda and urged Boldin to speed up his offensive. The gap between the two forces was only eight kilometers, but 50th Army was still unable to seize strongpoints Fomino 2 and Zaitseva Gora. Zhukov, at Western Front headquarters, was impatient with both forces and demanded that 4th Airborne Corps seize Askerovo not later than 19 April.[20] Consequently, Onufriev of 8th Airborne Brigade left one company of Karnaukhov's 2d Battalion to defend Buda and sent the remainder of the 2d Battalion and Pobortsev's 1st Battalion to seize Askerovo. Kuryshev, of 9th Brigade, left Bibikov's 4th Battalion in Buda to cover the left flank and sent Smirnov's 2d Battalion and Shuklin's 1st Battalion against Kalugovo. While the Soviets had benefited from surprise in their seizure of Buda, surprise was now lost, and the Germans quickly reinforced their defenses at Miliatino, Novoe Askerova, and Kalugovo. Moreover, the Soviets left only a weak garrison in Buda.

Turning the tables on the Soviets, early on 18 April, a German force, supported by artillery, struck Soviet defenses around Buda. After a day-long battle which cost the Germans an estimated 400 killed and 600 wounded, by 1600 they secured the town. The cost to the defenders was likewise high, since Bibikov and most of his battalion perished as the town went up in flames. The remnants of the two battalions withdrew northward across frozen swamps to circle south and eventually rejoin their parent brigades.[21]

Belatedly, on 19 April, with airborne offensive strength expended, reinforcements arrived from the Western Front. The 4th Battalion, 23d Airborne Brigade, commanded by Senior Lieutenant S. D. Kreuts and numbering 645 men, had jumped during the previous three days into a drop zone west of Svintsovo.[22] With these meager reinforcements, the 4th Airborne Corps regrouped and again attacked toward Novoe Askerovo.

The 214th Airborne Brigade defended the eastern perimeter, and covering detachments from Malaia Myshenka to Baskakovka Station screened in the west. The corps' main force moved through the now completely thawed swamplands southward toward their objective. On the night of 20–21 April, the soaked and weary 8th Airborne Brigade attacked the heavily fortified and mined German-held village, only to be repulsed. In the attack, the commander of 1st Battalion, Pobortsev, was killed. At 0200 the brigade withdrew to the southern edge of the forest just north of Novoe Askerovo.

While 8th Airborne Brigade attacked, German units pounded airborne positions from Miliatino, Kalugovo, and Baskakovka with artillery and ground attacks. The Germans struck the 9th Airborne Brigade, defending 8th Airborne Brigade's flank and rear, and the 9th Brigade responded by using ambush tactics to exact a heavy toll of Germans. By morning, the Germans had given up their attacks in that sector.

The 1st Guards Cavalry Corps reconnaissance units identified elements of the German 331st Infantry Division (557th and 306th Infantry Regiments) and 504th Motorized Engineer Regiment in the Malaia Myshenka, Baskakovka, Buda, and Butovo regions and the 41st Motorized Regiment, 19th Panzer Division, supporting the 31st Infantry Division in the Novoie Askerovo and Kalugovo regions.[23] Thus, elements of at least one panzer and two infantry divisions held the narrow corridor between 4th Airborne Corps and 50th Army. Most of the German units held prepared fortifications established to defend the Moscow–Warsaw highway.

Once again, after yet another regrouping, 50th Army attacked on the night of 21–22 April with two fresh rifle divisions (58th and 60th). Once again the attempt to break the Germans' grip on Fomino 2 failed. In his report to *Stavka* and Western Front, Boldin highlighted the impact of the thaw on operations, 'The use of tanks was strongly hampered by ground conditions, stream flooding, and the accumulation of water in valleys.' In addition, 'Insufficiencies in ammunition supplies had a great influence on the tempo of operations. Low provisions of ammunition to units was a result of roads impassable for wheeled transport. As an extreme measure, in some units resupply of ammunition was by soldiers' hands.'[24] Clearly, 50th Army was reaching the limits of its capability.

Despite the long odds against success, 4th Airborne Corps made one final attempt to break the Germans' iron grip on the Moscow–Warsaw highway. On the night of 23–24 April, corps units struck at Novoe Askerovo three times; but heavy German machine gun and mortar fire from both Novoe Askerovo and Staroe and Novoe Kalugovo forced the paratroopers back to their starting position. Similar attempts by 2d Guards Cavalry Division to take the Farnerovo Factory also failed. The two-kilometer zone to the Moscow–Warsaw highway remained insurmountable. Halder noted in his diary on 22 April, 'In Fourth Army sector, the enemy attack at Fomino was repelled.'[25]

The next day the Germans struck back at Belov's and Kazankin's forces. With tank and air support, they attacked from Buda, Staroe and

Novoe Askerovo, and Kalugovo. German units pushed the airborne corps back into new defensive positions. The Western Front commander, General Zhukov, had no choice but to order 1st Guards Cavalry and 4th Airborne Corps to cease offensive actions. Such fruitless and costly attacks no longer served any useful purpose because 50th Army's attack on Miliatino at 0200 that day had been repulsed. On 26 April, 50th Army also went on the defense for the foreseeable future.[26]

Conditions facing 1st Guards Cavalry and 4th Airborne Corps could scarcely have been worse. The Germans had eliminated the 33d Army pocket by 17 April and driven Soviet Western and Kalinin Front forces onto the defense. German units could now regroup and, when the spring thaw had ended and the ground dried, they could thoroughly crush the last threat in their rear posed by the remnants of 1st Guards Cavalry Corps and 4th Airborne Corps. Now that the spring thaw was in progress, rivers were running high, swamps were unlocked, and terrain thus hindered movement of Soviet troops already facing a growing network of fortified positions and roads teeming with armed German convoys. In these conditions, resupply of the corps was impossible, except by risky direct-parachute delivery.

After the difficult April battles and the arrival of the additional battalion of 23d Airborne Brigade, 4th Airborne Corps' strength returns were as follows:

Unit	Officers and NCOs	Enlisted	Total
8th Airborne Brigade	132	619	751
9th Airborne Brigade	110	557	667
214th Airborne Brigade	65	110	175
Corps Headquarters and Support	62	372	434
Total	369	1658	2027[27]

Given the opposition it faced, this force was capable of erecting a strong defense of the region it occupied, but it could not undertake operations without severe risk, as the evidence of the stronger 50th Army operations indicated. To prove that point, the corps easily repulsed the few counter-attacks launched by the Germans over the remainder of the month.

The thaw which occurred in late April only complicated the corps' predicament. They faced the prospect of fighting in relatively open terrain against a stronger enemy, often ensconced in fortified positions. The paratroopers had to fight in open swamps, up to their waists in water, with very limited supplies of food and ammunition. All supply transport was by hand, since the few roads were seas of mud and impassable. Under these circumstances, the wounded suffered most of all. The corps supply base and medical points near Zhelan'e were more than 20 kilometers to the rear.

Faced with these conditions, Kazankin, with Western Front permission, began withdrawing his brigades northward to positions from which they had launched the offensive on Miliatino (see Figure 58). Noting the Soviet withdrawal, German forces also moved northward to occupy and fortify Malaia Myshenka, Dubrovnia, Trofimovo, and Novinskaia Dacha. Onufriev's 8th Airborne Brigade occupied defenses from Verterkhovo Station to Terekhovka; newly-promoted Captain Kreut's 4th Battalion, 23d Brigade defended Zhukovka; Kuryshev's 9th Brigade dug in at Bogoroditskoe; and Kolobovnikov's weaker 214th Airborne Brigade covered the corps' eastern flank from Prechistoe to Novinskaia Dacha. Corps dispatched diversionary groups along the roads from Baskakovka to Buda and from Dubrovnia to Pesochnia.[28] With the tension of two months' almost constant battle behind them, corps paratroopers enjoyed several weeks of respite before what they knew would be even greater trials ahead.

ENCIRCLEMENT AND BREAKOUT

The first half of May was quiet, as the effects of the spring thaw stifled coordinated action by either side. The 4th Airborne Corps used the lull to improve its defensive positions south and east of Ugra Station, extending from Verbulovo, through Bol'shaia Myshenka, Bogoroditskoe, and Platonovka to Akulovo, with a screen between Lager, Baraki, and Plotki. Sufficient supplies were dropped or flown to improvised airstrips to requip and resupply corps units. Returning aircraft also flew wounded back to *Bol'shaia zemlia* [the big world]. General Belov redeployed his 1st Guards Cavalry Corps into a wide area from Dorogobuzh to south of Viaz'ma and refitted his battleworn units. The 1,400-man 1st Partisan Regiment covered the broad north-northeastern flank of 4th Airborne Corps. Zhabo's force was especially ill-suited for heavy combat, so Kazankin assigned him a composite battalion made up of 33d Army men who had escaped from encirclement.

Augmented by the remnants of 8th Airborne Brigade, 250th Airborne Regiment, a battalion of 23d Airborne Brigade, and a composite battalion from 33d Army remnants, airborne corps forces by 1 May numbered 2,300 men, plus 2,000 wounded or ill and 1,700 partisans. Its weaponry consisted of seven guns, 37 antitank rifles, and 34 battalion mortars.[29] With this force, 4th Airborne Corps defended a perimeter of 35 kilometers anchored on a series of fortified strongpoints.

Belov and Kazankin still hoped to break out from the German encirclement. Their hopes rose even more when, on 9 May, the Western Front

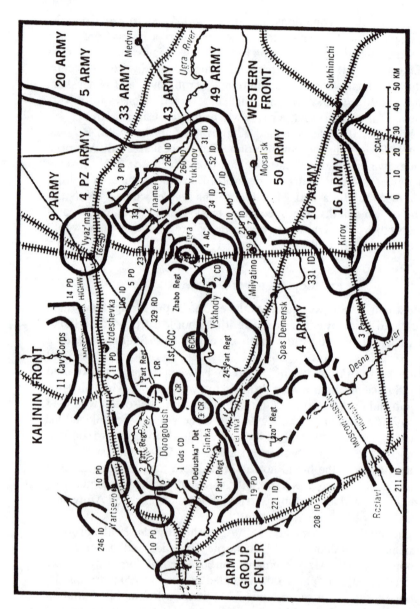

58. Situation, 20 April 1942

Chief of Operations, Maj. Gen. S. V. Golushkevich, flew into General Belov's headquarters with news of a future Soviet offensive.[30] The offensive would involve 50th Army, reinforced by new Soviet mechanized formations, and would occur no later than 5 June. But the nagging question remained, 'Would the Germans attack first?' Undeniable evidence suggested that as many as seven divisions of the German Fourth Panzer Army and XXXXIII Army Corps of Fourth Army were preparing to attack the encircled Soviet forces from both north and south. So, Belov and Kazankin prepared to meet the German blow.

Soviet intelligence sources reported that the Germans were continuing to reinforce and fortify their defenses at Ivantseva, Borodino, Kurakino, Maloe Prechistoe, Dubrovnia, and Malaia Myshenka. They also reinforced their garrisons north and south of airborne defensive positions to include concentrations at:

North
Mikhali (up to two regiments)
Veshki (up to 800 infantry)
Znamenka (up to 100 infantry and 12 tanks)
Bogotyr' (up to 200 infantry and 2 tanks)

South
Miliatino (up to two regiments).[31]

Soviet assessments also noted:

> By 21 May it was well known that the enemy were concentrating considerable forces in the Miliatino region, where up to 3,000 infantry, artillery and a large staff were detected. Thus, in the second half of May, two main enemy groups were formed: in the north in the Bogatyr', Znamenka, and Mikhali regions, and in the south in the Miliatino area. It was clear that both of these groups would attempt to strike a dual blow against the Corps.[32]

Prisoners of war seized by airborne forces revealed that the German command was preparing in the near future an operation codenamed 'Hannover' to liquidate Soviet forces encircled south of Viaz'ma. This information came from a German diversionary group dispatched from Miliatino, which the paratroopers intercepted and captured on 23 May. The members of the diversionary group wore Soviet uniforms, carried Soviet weapons, and had the mission to destroy airborne headquarters.[33]

Prisoners also revealed that Operation Hannover would involve seven divisions from two German army corps advancing from Znamenka (northwest), Miliatino (south), and Dorogobuzh Station (northwest).

The objective of the two- to three-day operation was to split Belov's 1st Guards Cavalry Corps from Kazankin's 4th Airborne Corps and destroy each force piecemeal.

Soviet critiques mildly faulted Kazankin for failing to respond to the threat posed by Operation Hannover. In particular, he did not undertake measures to prepare crossings over the Ugra River, which separated his forces from those of Belov. Nor did Kazankin negotiate a joint plan of action with 1st Guards Cavalry Corps.[34] This failure would have disastrous consequences on the outcome of ensuing operations.

At 0400 on 24 May, in pouring rain, Belov heard the distant rumble of guns announcing the opening of the German offensive (see Figures 59 and 60). Reports from all headquarters soon confirmed why the guns were sounding and, more ominously, revealed the coordinated nature of the impending German ground attack. The 6th Partisan Regiment at Vskhody soon reported to Belov that Germans had overrun their positions with scarcely a pause. The commander of the 6th Regiment was killed, and 2d Guards Cavalry Division's 8th Guards Cavalry Regiment was driven into and through Vskhody.[35] This German attack on Vskhody and a similar one north along the rail line from Ugra Station to Viaz'ma were indicative of the enemy's intent to separate the cavalry corps from 4th Airborne Corps units.

At the same time, Kazankin's airborne units were hard pressed on all sides. After the 0400 artillery preparation, elements of the German 23d Infantry, 5th Panzer, 197th Infantry, 131st Infantry, 31st Infantry, and 19th Panzer Divisions, with aviation and armor support (50 tanks), attacked airborne positions extending along a front from Mikhali and Znamenka to Miliatino. Vicious fighting ensued. Major Zhabo's 1st Partisan Regiment, by day's end, was forced to withdraw to the line Nadezhda, Kamenka, Anikanovo, Proskovo, and Kombain, thus abandoning a more that 10 kilometer wide sector of 4th Airborne Corps northeastern defensive perimeter. In doing so, Zhabo lost 60 per cent of his force. By nightfall pursuing Germans also occupied Vasil'evka and Kamenka, further fragmenting Zhabo's force.

From Miliatino in the south, 3,000 Germans with 20 tanks struck 8th Airborne Brigade positions at Bol'shaia Myshenka and quickly seized the town, driving 8th Brigade northward in disarray with losses of 15–20 per cent. A similar German force continued the rout of 2d Guards Cavalry Division's regiment, which had held Vskhody, and occupied Selishche, Pishchevo, Chashchi, and Selibka north of Vskhody and on the west bank of the Ugra River in 4th Airborne Corps rear area, threatening the corps with full encirclement.[36]

Unable to stop the concerted German advance and facing certain annihilation if he attempted to hold his ground, Colonel Kazankin, with

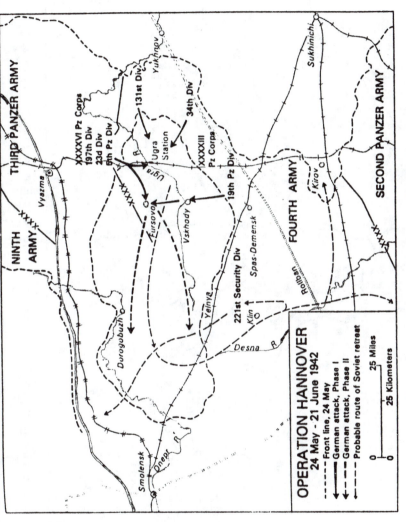

59. Operation Hannover: A German Perspective

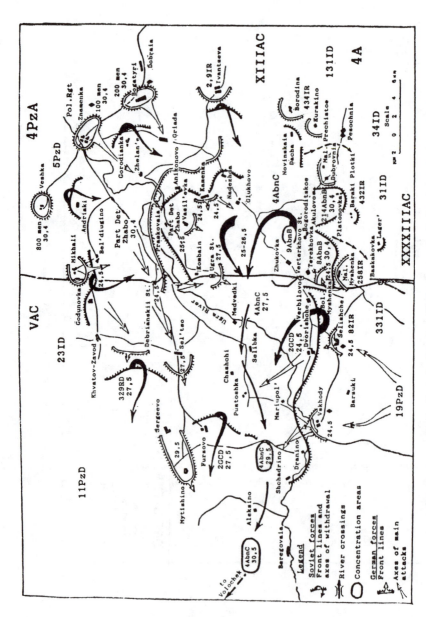

60. 4th Airborne and 1st Guards Cavalry Corps Operations, 30 April–30 May 1942

Western Front approval, designated covering units along his defensive lines to cover his withdrawal. On the night of 24–25 May, he moved his main forces westward toward the Ugra River at Selibka in hopes of crossing and rejoining Belov's force.[37] While on the night march, Kazankin designated the order of crossing by his forces over the Ugra River. 8th Airborne Brigade would proceed first, followed by 9th Brigade, corps headquarters, and, finally, the 214th Brigade, which would provide security for the crossing. Karnaukhov's 2d Battalion, 8th Brigade was to serve as forward detachment and seize the initial crossing site.

When 2d Battalion, 8th Airborne Brigade, reached the Ugra River on the morning of 25 May, it found that German forces in company strength had brushed aside partisan units on the far side and occupied Pishchevo, Selibka, and Sorokino. The corps lacked river-crossing equipment to traverse the 120-meter-wide water barrier – an obstacle compounded by strong, tricky river currents and open swamps on the far bank. Fortunately, 8th Airborne Brigade was able to conceal itself in the forests on the near bank of the river while it reconnoitered and searched for a means to cross the Ugra. By day's end, the brigade sapper company had cut down eight large pine trees and, by binding them together, built a narrow 70-meter floating footbridge. This attempt to cross, however, failed since the frail bridge repeatedly broke apart under pressure of the currents, and throughout 25 May the paratroopers sought in vain a new way to cross the river.

Almost miraculously, at 0200 26 May, the corps chief of reconniassance reported that he had located six boats at the nearby ferry site at Pishchevo.[38] All day on 26 and 27 May 8th Brigade personnel laboriously crossed the Ugra River in the small boats with the help of a telephone cable stretched across the river. Onufriev's brigade reconnaissance company reached the far side first and fanned out to a depth of six kilometers to reconnoiter the Pustoshka–Vskhody and Poldnevo–Vskhody roads. Karnaukhov's 2d Battalion, 8th Brigade, followed and established a two kilometer-deep by one-and-a-half kilometer-wide bridgehead on the west bank of the river opposite the villages of Selibka and Chashchi. The remainder of 8th Brigade and then the wounded and 9th and 214th Brigades followed and reinforced 8th Brigade forward detachment's positions. Fortunately for Kazankin's forces, bad weather prevented enemy aircraft interfering with his crossings. Less fortunately, the remnants of Zhabo's partisan regiment, also heading toward the Ugra River, were unable to link up with Kazankin's main force.

Kazankin's troubles were, however, just beginning. To his front strong German forces defended positions at Medvedki, Selibka, and Chashchi, blocking his withdrawal westward. During the latter stages of his movement across the Ugra River, the 4th Battalion, 214th Airborne Brigade, the last subunit to cross the river, came under heavy German fire, which killed its commander, Captain Khoteenkov, and many other officers and men. One company, unable to cross the river, withdrew southeastward into the swamps, where it dug in and hid. This company, with 42 survivors, finally made it back to 50th Army lines near Zaitseva Gora on 15 July. Another company of 214th Airborne Brigade, which was providing rear guard protection for the corps, was cut off and finally fought its way out of encirclement near Fursovo on 28–29 May to link up with the main force west of Podlipki. Another company, of 8th Airborne Brigade, trapped in the initial German assault on Bol'shaia Myshenka, perished to a man.[39]

General Kazankin, shortly after the harrowing Ugra River crossing, reestablished radio contact with Western Front and 1st Guards Cavalry Corps and reported on his new situation and location. By the evening of 29 May, his severely damaged force concentrated in the forests between Selibka and Chashchi. By this time he had been joined by Majors Shmelev and Zhabo, with the small remnants of their commands which had survived their run through the gauntlet of German fire. Soviet critiques later glibly noted that, 'The decision of General Kazankin to withdraw his corps' units from under the blows of strong enemy groups was timely and carried out successfully, in spite of extraordinarily complex conditions.'[40]

While the crossing proceeded, Belov launched several local counterattacks to relieve German pressure on 4th Airborne Corps. The 6th Guards Cavalry Regiment, supported by two T-26 light tanks, attacked German units crossing the Ugra River at Vskhody and forced them to withdraw. At great risk, the understrength 3d and 7th Guards Cavalry Regiments of 2d Guards Cavalry Division rushed to the Sorokino bridgehead of the 8th Airborne Brigade and assisted the remnants of the corps in their river crossing on the night of 26–27 May.[41]

Kazankin now addressed the more pressing problem of breaking out westward and linking up with the main force of Belov's 1st Guards Cavalry Corps, now being steadily forced southward by German forces attacking from Dorogobuzh, Izdeshkovo, and Viaz'ma. Reconnaissance indicated that the Germans held Selishche, Chashchi, and other nearby villages and were patrolling the Pustoshka–Vskhody road with tanks. At 2200 27 May, Kazankin consulted with his subordinate commanders, made his decision, and issued orders for the breakout.

Official archival sources recorded his decision:

> In light of the complete impossibility of penetrating in the direction
> of Fursovo, the corps commander decided: while exploiting the
> darkness on the night of 26–27 May to penetrate to the west

between the villages of Selibka and Chashchi, enter the forest masses and subsequently withdraw in the direction of Pustoshka.[42]

A detachment from 214th Airborne Brigade was to cover 4th Airborne Corps' movement from the north. After running the gauntlet between Selibka and Chashchi, the corps would concentrate in the forests one kilometer south of Podlipki, where it would regroup and then move westward through Podlipki, Frolovo, and Kurakino to unite with Belov's cavalry corps at Pustoshka.

At 0300 on 28 May, Kazankin's force began its breakout from encirclement. The forward detachment dispersed local German security forces, and 8th and 9th Brigades moved westward through the darkness, infiltrated around German strongpoints and headed for Podlipki. Enemy resistance stiffened toward daybreak, and the 214th Airborne Brigade, screening corps movement from the north, was forced to withdraw southward into the forests. At first light the corps concentrated in its appointed forest assembly site just south of Podlipki. At this point the rain stopped, and the weather began clearing, depriving the corps of its principal protection. Now, only stealth would offer the corps any security.

Up to this point, withdrawal had been accomplished in such secrecy that German forces commenced an artillery barrage at 0600 28 May from Selibka and Chashchi on presumed airborne camps, which, by then, were unoccupied. The artillery barrage was followed by heavy bombing from Junkers aircraft. German artillery fire did succeed in striking the 214th Brigade covering force, which dispersed in small groups toward the Gordota River pursued by German ground troops. Many died in the withdrawal, and, after a considerable chase, a group of 50 paratroopers under Brigade Chief of Staff, Major V. I. Spirin, were captured. Spirin spent the remainder of the war in German POW camps.[43] Remnants of 214th Brigade under Major Lebedev crossed the Gordota River, escaped from encirclement, and, on 29 May, reunited with Kazankin's corps near Fursovo.

Meanwhile, on 29 May, Kazankin contacted Western Front headquarters and requested air support for his continued withdrawal. That evening bombers struck German armor concentrations at Pustoshka and infantry and artillery positions north of Vskhody. This air activity made it possible for Kazankin's forces to cross the Vskhody–Pustoshka road unimpeded. On the night of 29–30 May, the airborne corps resumed its withdrawal through Shchadrino. During the passage Captain Smirnov, commander of 2d Battalion, 9th Brigade, was wounded and captured by the Germans due to the treachery of a certain former Major Bocharov, who subsequently provided the Germans with information about

Kazankin's plans.[44] As 4th Airborne's official history noted, 'Undoubtedly, he provided the enemy with information about the parachutists, and, from that day, tanks, infantry, artillery, and aviation uninterruptedly struck the corps throughout its 300-kilometer path of withdrawal.' Smirnov became a POW, but later escaped to join first Polish and then Belorussian partisans.[45]

Despite a diary entry by Chief of the German General Staff, F. Halder, that 'Fourth Army has closed the ring around the main body of Belov,' by 28 May, Belov's cavalry corps had escaped and reestablished a fairly firm front facing east on the north bank of the Ugra River near Vshkody.[46] His forces included 1st Guards Cavalry Division, 1st and 2d Partisan Divisions, and seven tanks, including a heavy *KV* (model *Klimenti Voroshilov*) and a medium T-34. Moreover, the 23d and 211th Airborne brigades, with 4,000 men, had begun landing to reinforce the corps and assist Belov in his withdrawal.[47] The 2d Guards Cavalry Division and 4th Airborne Corps soon joined Belov after their harrowing escape from German forces to the east. By 0400 on 30 May, Kazankin's 4th Airborne Corps had arrived west of Aleksino, where it united with Belov's cavalry corps. The 329th Rifle and 2d Guards Cavalry Divisions had preceded them. Belov's and Kazankin's combined forces now numbered about 17,000 thoroughly worn out men. These included 1,800 from the 4th Airborne Corps and 2d Guards Cavalry Division, 4,000 from the 23d and 211th Airborne Brigades, 2,000 from the 329th Rifle Division and Zhabo's partisan detachment, 4,500 from the 1st Guards Cavalry Division, and the remainder from partisan units with Belov.[48]

While 4th Airborne Corps was resting in assembly areas west of Aleksino, Kazankin sent his sick and wounded northward to Volochek airfield for evacuation to Western Front lines. With the wounded went the 8th Airborne Brigade Chief of Staff (and former 1st Battalion commander) Major Drobyshevsky, who was also wounded. On 2 June the corps itself moved 15 kilometers to Volochek to reinforce its defenses, but within 24 hours Belov ordered its return to 1st Guards Cavalry Corps' assembly area west of Aleksino.   Belov had anticipated the beginning of a new Soviet June offensive. Accordingly, he formed a shock group of 1st Guards Cavalry Division (4,500 men), 4th Airborne Corps (5,800 men), and a partisan regiment to cooperate yet again with an advance by reinforced 50th Army. Perhaps, he thought, Viaz'ma might yet be taken. But Belov's hopes were dashed when a major Soviet offensive conducted near Khar'kov in southern Russia resulted in a major defeat that negated any chance of a renewed Soviet offensive in the Moscow region. The die was finally cast for 1st Guards Cavalry and 4th Airborne Corps. German pressure continued to build up relentlessly. German 23d Infantry and 5th and 19th Panzer Divisions, advancing from the north and east, pushed back the 329th Rifle Division, secured Sergeevo and Mytishino, and occupied the best of Belov's aircraft landing strips (see Figure 61).

On 4 June Belov and Kazankin dispatched a message to *front* headquarters outlining the situation and requesting approval of their plan 'to penetrate west of El'nia in the region of the 5th Partisan Rifle Regiment, and subsequently to break through enemy lines by a blow to their rear northwest of Kirov to unite with *front* forces.'[49] The next day the Western Front recommended either a move north to link up with the Kalinin Front or a move east to Mosal'sk where Soviet forces were most active. Both moves were impossible, however, because the Dnepr River to the north was flooding, and main force German units prevented escape to the east. The Western Front command finally agreed that Belov should move southeast toward Kirov to rejoin 10th Army and stipulated he was to use partisan forces as stepping-stone bases for his march. Belov would leave major partisan units behind him to operate in small groups against the Germans to distract the German pursuit.

Belov's planned route of withdrawal passed through the forests south of El'nia, where Sergei Lazo's '24th Anniversary of the Red Army' Partisan Detachment operated, and then across the Warsaw highway into the forests west of Kirov, where Major Galiuga's partisan detachment could assist the airborne forces in rejoining 10th Army. The 4th Airborne Corps' mission was to penetrate German defenses west of El'nia and advance on the axis Khlysty, Glinka, Bel'yi Kholm, and Filimony. The 2d Guards Cavalry Division and 329th Rifle Division advanced on 4th Corps' left flank. The route required Belov's force to traverse 200 kilometers, penetrate at least three German defense lines, and run the gauntlet across the German-patrolled Moscow–Warsaw highway.[50]

Between 29 May and 3 June, Western Front dispatched forces to assist Belov and Kazankin in fighting their way through and out of the German rear area. The forces were the 23d and 211th Airborne Brigades, dropped in the region of Starintsa village 10 kilometers south of Dorogobuzh. Lieutenant Colonel A. G. Mil'sky's 23d Brigade of 10th Airborne Corps consisted of three battalions (the 4th battalion had joined 4th Airborne Corps in April). Mil'sky's force of about 1,900 men jumped into the area equipped with supplies for six days, and, unlike earlier air drops, they landed on or near the landing site.[51] Thus the brigade was fully combat ready. Shortly after Mil'sky's brigade had landed, with Major S. Gurin's 1st Battalion in the lead, German aircraft bombed the landing site. Fortunately, the deep mud reduced the effect of the bombing, and the brigade suffered few casualties.

After reporting to Belov to receive orders, the 23d Airborne Brigade had, by early 2 June, occupied defensive positions around Kriakovo,

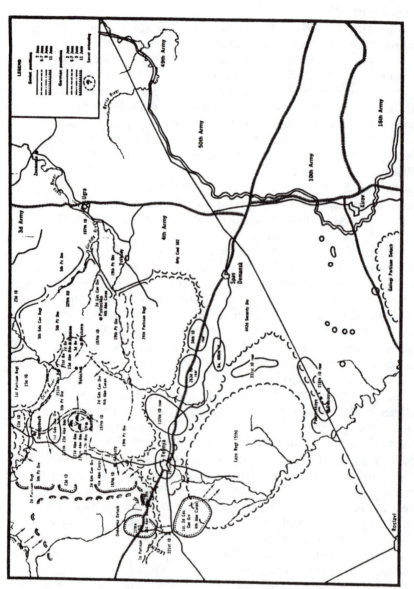

61. 4th Airborne and 1st Guards Cavalry Corps Operations, 1–11 June 1942

Afonino, and Gavrikovo, where they halted German forces advancing on Volochek air strip from the north. They were soon joined by 2,100 men of Lieutenant Colonel M. I. Shilin's 211th Airborne Brigade of 1st Airborne Corps, which landed soon after 23d Airborne Brigade's lead element had gone into action. So timely was their arrival that they had no time to dig in before German attacks commenced.[52] The combined airborne forces were deployed in broad defensive array covering the advance of German forces from Dorogobuzh and Izdeshkovo in the north to Volochek air strip to the northeast, which the German 5th Panzer Division was attempting to seize from Belov's forces.

Fighting raged for several days as the fresh airborne forces conducted a delaying action against 5th Panzer Division back through the Volochek region to Aleksino, south of Dorogobuzh. During the action, 1st Battalion, 23d Airborne Brigade, was encircled and had to fight its way through German lines. Finally, on 5 June and on Kazankin's orders, the force fought its way to the rear under heavy German ground fire and air attacks. By acting as rearguard for 4th Airborne Corps, the two brigades enabled the bulk of the airborne corps to withdraw in good order to the Khlysty area north of El'nia. Those airborne troopers bypassed by 5th Panzer Division's assault received orders to conduct diversionary operations in the German rear area.

On 6 June Belov subordinated all remaining airborne forces to Kazankin's 4th Airborne Corps. All operated under their former commanders except the 211th Brigade, which, during the fighting delay action, lost its commander to illness and its chief of staff to German fire. At 1300 Belov's combined force moved westward via Lopatino, Nikol'skoe State Farm, and Iakovlevichi toward Glinka Station on the El'nia rail line west of El'nia with 23d Airborne Brigade serving as rear guard. Reconnaissance elements determined that the rail line was defended by elements of the German 221st Security Division and two panzer grenadier battalions of 19th Panzer Division deployed in separate strongpoints strung out along the railroad.[53]

When Belov's advance guard reached the Ugra River 500 meters from the rail line, German outposts engaged the parachutists. In the subsequent heavy fighting, Glinka and Klokovo Station burned, and, after a sharp fight lasting several hours, the German outposts were crushed. Belov's force crossed the rail line and concentrated two kilometers south in the forests, leaving 2d Guards Cavalry and 329th Rifle Divisions in defensive positions just south of the rail line. On the night of 6–7 June, 23d Brigade caught up with the main force and, on Kazankin's orders, joined the 211th Airborne Brigade in the corps' advance guard. Without delay, Kazankin's force marched all night and the next day 25 kilometers southward, often through deep swamp toward its next objective,

Filimony, on the El'nia–Roslavl' road. As the force neared the road, it came under heavy artillery fire, but managed to cross the road and occupy Filimony. Once again, Kazankin's force had to drive off German battalion-size forces, which were advancing along the road from northeast and southwest, all the while under intermittent German air attack. All of these German attacks were repulsed by evening 8 June. Early on 9 June the force moved on, Belov's cavalry comprising a left column heading toward Byki from the north and 4th Airborne Corps four kilometers to the south, passing through Berniki and approaching Byki from the southwest.

At first light on 9 June, Belov's and Kazankin's forces reached the village of Byki, which was defended by a German company-size force. Major Gurin's 1st Battalion, 23d Airborne Brigade, skirted Byki from the south, cut a passage for itself and 1st Guards Cavalry Division through German defenses along the road, and escorted both 1st Guards Cavalry Division and 3d Battalion, 23d Brigade, through the German defenses. Meanwhile, Captain Deriugin's 2d Battalion, 23d Airborne, with the brigade staff, attacked the village proper and, before noon, overcame the German garrison, whose remnants withdrew northward along the road. The arrival of German aircraft finally forced 3d Battalion to abandon the town and move into the forests to the southeast.

Resuming their march southeastward on the night of 10–11 June, Belov's and Kazankin's forces hid in the forests occupied by Sergei Lazo's partisan detachment, where, for three days, they rested and replenished their food and ammunition (see Figure 62). During the night movement, 8th Airborne Brigade, Kazankin's right column, engaged and destroyed a small German force in Soloven'ki. After the attack German aircraft again struck 8th Brigade, seriously wounding its commissar, Raspopov. Attempts to evacuate him to the rear failed because German forces had seized nearby partisan air strips, including the principal one at Novyi Luki. Finally, he was evacuated to Moscow's Ramenskoe airfield via Lazo's reserve air strip at Mutishchi. During the ill-fated attempt to seize Novyi Luki airstrip, Lieutenant Colonel Shilin, commander of the 211th Brigade, was killed by German fire.[54]

Halder's diary entries continued to track Belov's progress. An entry for 9 June states, 'AGp Center reports break-out of Cav Corps Belov to the South.' The following day, Halder added, 'The escaped Cav Corps Belov is being pursued.' On 11 June, Halder sourly noted, 'Unluckily, the main body of Belov's Cav Corps and of Fourth Airborne Brig. have escaped south.'[55]

Belov's and Kazankin's corps finally approached the Moscow–Warsaw road in two columns late on 13 June. Belov's left column, facing the Krutoi Kholm sector of the highway, consisted of his corps headquarters,

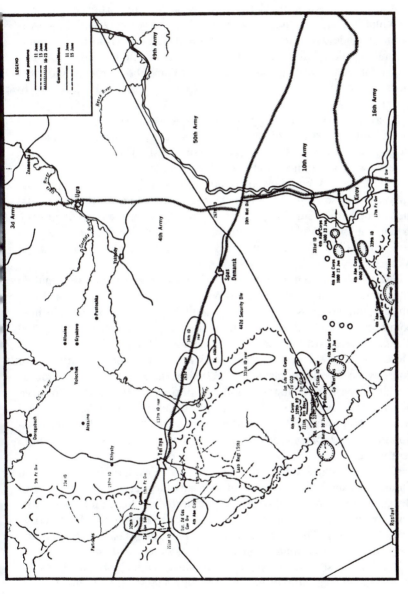

62. 4th Airborne and 1st Guards Cavalry Corps Operations, 11–23 June 1942

rear service units, the 329th Rifle Division, and 2d Guards Cavalry Division. Kazankin's right column, some four kilometers south near Lazino, consisted of 4th Airborne Corps staff, 23d and 211th Airborne Brigades, 1st Guards Cavalry Division with the sick and wounded, and 8th Airborne Brigade with the remnants of 9th and 214th Airborne Brigades. Kazankin ordered his forces to penetrate German highway defenses in a four-kilometer sector between Denisovka and Pokrovskoe and then assemble in the forests south of the highway east of Biukovo 1, 16 kilometers away.[56]

Reconnaissance indicated that German forces in the region consisted of one infantry regiment of the 211th Security Division dispersed in strongpoints along the road facing northwest. Their positions were covered with an extensive network of minefields, barbed wire, obstacles, and pillboxes. A company of tanks continuously patrolled along the highway, whose verge had been cleared of trees to a width of over 100 meters on either side. The extensive nature of the defenses and the exhaustion of Kazankin's force made envelopment of the German positions impossible. Only a surprise night attack would offer any chance of success.

The two Soviet columns began their night march across the final 20 kilometers toward the Moscow–Warsaw highway at 2200 14 June, through the darkness and rain, constantly harassed by random German bombing. At first light, the rain stopped, and Kazankin's column reached Lazino. There, 4th Airborne Corps deployed for its attack across the Moscow–Warsaw road near Denisovka, two kilometers southwest of Pokrovskoe. Kazankin placed his 23d Airborne Brigade and 1st Guards Cavalry Division in first echelon, supported by the 211th Airborne Brigade. 8th Airborne and the corps' wounded remained in second echelon. Meanwhile, Belov's left column, with 2d Guards Cavalry Division in the lead, prepared to cross the highway several kilometers to the northwest.

Kazankin's lead 23d Brigade and 1st Guards Cavalry Division attacked simultaneously before dawn without any artillery preparation. 23d Brigade had all of its battalions concentrated on line, and 1st Guards Cavalry led with its 1st and 3d Guards Cavalry Regiments, followed by the 5th and 6th. The units advanced in piecemeal fashion because the Germans took each unit under fire as they detected them.

Baranov's first-echelon cavalry regiments successfully broke across the road through a gauntlet of heavy German machine gun and mortar fire. Subsequently small groups crossed in dashes until German tanks arrived, firing down the highway. As daylight approached, Soviet second echelon cavalry groups balked at crossing the road under the withering fire. Maj. Gen. V. K. Baranov of 1st Guards Cavalry Division rallied the force of

3,000 cavalry and several thousand paratroopers who hurled themselves across the road in an unstoppable mass. German fire killed many, including the 6th Cavalry Regiment's commander, Lt. Col. A. V. Kniazev. Those who crossed the road successfully made a frantic dash southward. Those who followed ran a gauntlet of fire that stripped the trees of their leaves and took a frightful toll of casualties.

4th Airborne Corps' 23d Airborne Brigade cut a corrider across the highway and formed a barrier of its two flank battalions, which permitted the 211th Airborne Brigade and corps staff to follow across. Confused fighting ensued for over six hours, as the paratroopers cleared enemy strongpoints from along the south side of the highway. By noon 15 June, 4th Airborne had cleared the villages of Ashmarovo and Chetnoe and concentrated in the forests east of Bukovo 1.

Almost all of General Baranov's 1st Cavalry Division succeeded in crossing the deadly highway, as did about half of Kazankin's 4th Airborne Corps. However, the 2d Guards Cavalry Division, 8th Airborne Brigade, and stragglers from other airborne brigades could not cross nor could the 329th Rifle Division and the corps staff. Belov remained with these forces, trusting in Baranov's and Kazankin's ability to unite their forces with 10th Army. Halder's diary entries succinctly recount Belov's epic escape. On 16 June, Halder wrote, 'Cav Corps Belov has again broken out and is moving in the direction of Kirov. Nothing that we could brag about.' The following day he recorded his final diary entry on Belov, noting, with a touch of respect, 'Cav Corps Belov is now floating around the area west of Kirov. Quite a man, that we have to send no less than seven divisions after him.'[57]

Colonel Kazankin reorganized his truncated 4th Airborne Corps and, harried by German air attacks, moved southeast across the Kirov–Roslavl' rail line into the forests east of Podgerb. There the unit rested from 17 to 21 June, replenishing its ammunition and food under the protection of Galiuga's partisan detachment. Colonel Kazankin notified the 10th Army commander of his intentions to break through the German lines and requested artillery support and whatever other assistance 10th Army could provide. On 19 July wounded were evacuated to front hospitals by light aircraft operating from cleared forest landing strips near Kopol'; and the corps prepared to attack a German sector near Zhilino, just north of Kirov.[58]

As Kazankin planned the final stage of his operation, the bulk of Galiuga's partisans, including women, children, and old men, joined his force. On 22 July his force made its final dash northward and occupied positions early on 23 July in the forest northwest of Zhilino within 10 kilometers of the rear of German main defenses. Before them was an impressive German defense, albeit facing the other way, which had been in place since March 1942. Airborne forces reconnoitered those defenses and dispatched to the 326th Rifle Division of 10th Army, which operated in that sector, two liaison officers from 23d Airborne Brigade and one each from its cavalry and partisan units. Having established radio communications with 10th Army, Kazankin received the short message, 'Penetrate between hill 230.3 and the forester's house.'[59]

After dark on 23 July, Kazankin's forces occupied jumping-off positions and, at 2300, the 326th Rifle Division fired a short artillery preparation against German defenses. Into the battered sector rushed Kazankin's forces. The 1st and 2d Battalions, 23d Airborne Brigade, attacked first as a forward detachment supported by the bulk of the corps' remaining machine guns. The remainder of the corps followed, deployed in deep echelons with the wives and children of the partisans dispersed throughout the columns. All were greeted by heavy German small arms, machine guns, and mortar fire. 23d Brigade cleared several German strongpoints. After overcoming the first German defensive position, artillery fire intensified, wounding in the process both Kazankin and the 23d Airborne Brigade commander, Lieutenant Colonel Mil'sky. Major Gurin's 1st Battalion, 23d Brigade, finally pushed through to Soviet 10th Army lines, followed by the remainder of the 23d and 211th Brigades. After an intense four-hour fight during which it suffered 120 casualties, 4th Airborne Corps remnants finally reached 10th Army positions at Zhilino and safety.[60]

Belov's cavalry forces and those of 8th Airborne Brigade had a longer path to negotiate after their failure to break through German lines on the Moscow–Warsaw road on 15 June. After withdrawing north of the road, they united and moved southwestward through Vodneevka to a safer place to cross the road. On the night of 20–21 June, they successfully crossed the road north of Pobeda, and, marching through Ofanasovka and Krotovka, reached Rognedino on the evening of 21 June and the forests east of Kopol' on the morning of 22 June, where they linked up with Galiuga's remaining partisans. On 24 June Belov flew back to 10th Army headquarters in a U-2 aircraft, from Kopol' airfield together with wounded soldiers.[61]

Thereafter Major Karnaukhov, now commanding the entire force (and commander of the first 4th Airborne Corps' battalion to land in the German rear), followed the same trail blazed earlier by Kazankin's force. On the night of 28–29 June, his detachment, with minimal losses, penetrated German defenses and reached 326th Rifle Division positions at Zhilino. Shortly thereafter, trains carried 4th Airborne Corps' surviving forces back through Kaluga to its home base of Ramenskoe. After five months of bitter and harrowing combat, one of the longest and largest-scale airborne operations in history had ended.

Guenther Blumentritt, the former chief of staff of German Fourth Army, wrote a moving tribute to General Belov's accomplishments:

General Belov, who played a tragic-comic role and showed great daring in 1941–42, should be mentioned here. This Russian cavalry general crossed the Oka River in December near Farussa and Aleksin. By Christmas 1941 his cavalry troops and infantry on sleds had advanced as far as Yukhnov, deep in the rear of Fourth Army. It had been thought that he would cut the *Rollbahn*. However, for some reason he refrained from doing that. He crossed this road and disappeared in the swampy forests near Borodoritskoye. There he joined forces with partisans and airborne troops and constantly harassed the Fourth Army rear area. How he managed to obtain supplies was a mystery to us. He fought in this manner until May 1942. Only Russians and Russian horses can exist on absolutely 'nothing.' Nobody was able to catch him. German forces in the rear areas were too weak and not suited for that type of Indian warfare in the wintry forests. Only during May the entire forest area ... was crossed by combat patrols from all sides. Parts of several divisions, including some motorized units, were employed for this task. But Belov escaped with his forces time and again. In May 1942 he was finally cornered in the woods west of Spas-Demensk, but he broke through our lines with about 4,000 cavalry troops, galloped toward the south across the *Rollbahn*, and disappeared again in the forests east of Roslavl; from there he slowly moved eastward via Kirov and, avoiding the German security lines, escaped behind the Russian front lines. This episode caused many humorous remarks at the time and the motorized troops which had taken part in the operation became the butt of these jokes. I admired General Belov as a soldier and I was secretly glad that he had escaped. It was said that he was received with all honors in Moscow, and rightfully so.

The boundless endurance of Russian men and horses who led a Spartan existence for five months during a hard winter in those forests is typical. Orders to Belov were transmitted from Moscow by radio or liaison planes.[62]

CONCLUSIONS

Elements of 4th Airborne Corps had operated in the German rear for more than six months. In continuous combat, the paratroopers had freed 200 villages (many of which remained in partisan hands), traversed 600 kilometers, killed many Germans, and tied down seven divisions of four German army corps, thus limiting the Germans' counterattack potential.

German assessments, however, credited the Soviets with varying degrees of success. A German postwar critique of Soviet airborne operations around Moscow stated:

> The support given the partisans by parachutists considerably increased the latter's striking power and their threat in the rear of the German Armies. There is also no doubt that, in addition to mere reinforcement and supply by air, the systematic recruiting, equipment, and training of new troops was made possible by the Russians in the rear of the Germans.... However unpleasant it was for the Germans to have this danger in their rear and although it especially affected systematic supply of the front, at no time was there a direct, strategic effect. The Chief of Staff of the German Fourth Army stated in this connection that 'Although the whole matter was very annoying it had no strategic consequence.'
>
> According to the statements made by the Commander in Chief of the Fourth Panzer Army, the army estimated the breakthrough at the front to constitute a substantially greater danger than the parachute jumps in the zone of communications.[63]

General of Infantry Guenther Blumentritt wrote, 'Strategically, this commitment by the Russians had no detrimental effects in spite of the critical situation of the Fourth Army. From the tactical viewpoint, on the other hand, the "red louse in one's hide was unpleasant".'[64] Blumentritt, however, was impressed enough by the Soviet airborne operations to write a special postwar study concerning operations against rear lines of communication that focused on the Soviet airborne experience of 1941–42 and its applicability to modern battle.[65] The Germans did acknowledge limited Soviet airborne successes:

> The situation in Fourth Army was made far more serious by the appearance of the Russian airborne corps functioning as a compact unit. The war diary of this army almost daily mentions the fear that the *Rollbahn* will be threatened simultaneously from the north and south and the army cut off. The withdrawal of the army to the Ressa–Ugra line at the beginning of March 1942 may be regarded as a tactical result of this threat; that is to say that, in addition to other factors, it was due to the effects of the Russian airborne corps. It became necessary to release German forces (131st Infantry Division) to attack the airborne troops. Another direct result of the fighting for the *Rollbahn* was the abandonment of the plan to make a joint attack at the end of March with the German Second Panzer Army and the Fourth Army to retake Kirov. The forces set aside by the Fourth Army for this purpose were tied down by the violent

attacks of Russian Tenth [50th] Army on the *Rollbahn* from the south and the simultaneous threat to it from the north by the airborne corps and 1st Guards Cavalry Corps, combined into Group Belov. The effective share taken by the airlanding corps in this was relatively small.[66]

The assessment uncannily pinpointed the precise reasons for a lack of greater Soviet success:

The following may well have been the decisive reasons:

a. The lack of the element of surprise.
b. The lack of artillery and heavy weapons, although for the rest, the airborne troops were well equipped and trained. But this lack substantially diminished their striking power.
c. The difficulties of the terrain and of the weather, which undoubtedly decreased the mobility of the Russians also.
d. The lack of coordination in the measures taken by the two separate forces north and south of the *Rollbahn*, and the lack of synchronization in the date and hour of the attack (perhaps also influenced by road conditions); hesitation of the airborne troops between attacking and going on the defensive.

It is possible that there were also difficulties in the attempt to supply the troops exclusively by air and a rapid decrease of combat strength.

Not the least reason for the failure of the Russians was the steadfastness of German troops.[67]

That higher headquarters shared the concern of front-line commanders is evidenced by Halder's diary, which repeatedly mentions the airborne threat to Army Group Center.

For all their personal heroics and individual sacrifices, Soviet airborne units had failed in their primary mission – a failure for which the High Command was to blame. A mission with operational-strategic aims had achieved only tactical and diversionary objectives. The offensive it had supported also failed for reasons beyond the control of the individual airborne units.

Why did the offensive and airborne operation fail? The answers fall into three areas: first, High Command planning; second, execution and technical difficulties; and, third, bad weather. At the highest command level, official Soviet critiques of the winter offensive best summarized the failure:

When our offensive carried our forces deep into the depth of the position, there was unsatisfactory coordination between our forces which had broken into the enemy position and those which remained on the original front line. The initial [immediate] task given armies by *front* commands covered too long a phase of the operation, and flexibility was lacking in the change or correction of such initial missions in light of the subsequent development of the situation.... Mobile formations were given proper initial instructions [missions], but in the course of operations they often got cut off, and cavalry corps ended often by operating not in cooperation with the main force.[68]

Dizzy with success over the results of the December Moscow counteroffensive, the Soviet High Command expanded the scope and aim of the offensive in January with increasingly depleted forces. Mobile groups, consisting primarily of cavalry and small tank brigades, lacked the power to establish or sustain offensive momentum. They were able to achieve initial penetrations, but were seldom able to exploit them to great depths. Exploitation forces entered the narrow penetrations and advanced deep into the German rear only to find themselves exhausted, without proper support, and at the mercy of better equipped foes. Seldom did they achieve operational objectives. The Germans, ordered by Hitler to stand fast, used their heavier armament and greater mobility to close the penetrations and to trap the Soviet exploitation forces. While Soviet forces controlled the countryside, German forces clung tenaciously to the road network, rail lines, and population centers. Until the weather improved in June, neither could dislodge the other.

Furthermore, the High Command clung too long to original hopes and plans. It forbade its isolated forces from cooperating with other units until it was too late, and it required them to attack incessantly toward their original objectives until their combat strength was spent. Efremov's three divisions of Soviet 33d Army perished in overextended positions east of Viaz'ma. First forbidden to join Efremov, Belov was then forced to leave a major element of his force in Dorogobuzh. Only in April were the remnants of all encircled units permitted to join forces. By then, it was too late to conduct a serious offensive operation with any prospects of success. The Soviets themselves properly concluded that:

the launching of large-scale operations [in winter] impulsively, without regard to the available troops and resources, leads to a scattering of forces and a failure to achieve substantial results. [Moreover,] mobile formations [including airborne] in offensive operations under winter conditions are capable of carrying out independent operational missions. But the limitations imposed on them by winter conditions make it advisable for them to operate relatively near to the main body of the army and in close co-operation with it.[69]

Operational planning for the several airborne assaults was hasty and incomplete, and the Western Front staff did not participate in it. The poorly planned movement of aircraft and personnel to the launch air-fields disrupted the overall operational plan. Coordination between the airborne force and main *front* forces it was to link up with was nonexistent or limited. Aviation support of the operation, both combat and transport, was insufficient, and the Germans maintained air superiority throughout. Insufficient advanced reconnaissance of the landing sites resulted in unrealistically low estimates of enemy strength. Logistical support was inadequate in both weapons and amounts of supplies needed to overcome enemy forces. Lack of communications prevented efficient assembly and coordination of forces. A shortage of skis plagued the force throughout the operation.

Problems in assembling aircraft at Vnukovo airfield near Kaluga and subsqent German bombing of the airfield, delayed the operation for seven to ten days. The main drop itself then took seven instead of three days. Then, incredibly, the corps commander and most of his staff were transported in a single plane. His death doomed the corps to days of operations without proper command and control.

In addition to poor operational planning, technical difficulties further disrupted smooth operations. The lack of sufficient aircraft capable of carrying and accurately dropping paratroopers lengthened the dropping phase, made aircraft and airfields vulnerable to German attack, and guaranteed dispersal or outright loss of many of the combat troops and supplies in the drop area. Lack of navigational equipment on the ground and in the aircraft made accurate delivery almost impossible, and the corps landed over a 50-square-kilometer area. Scarce numbers of trained aircrews aggravated this problem, and shortages of good radios hampered communications throughout the operation.

The harsh weather conditions severely hindered the ground operations of both sides but had a particularly severe effect on the less mobile Soviet forces. Low temperatures (−30° to −45°C) and deep snow (to a depth of one meter) limited rapid assembly and movement of forces and robbed the airborne forces of their ability to capitalize fully on the initial surprise achieved. Only surprise produced by rapid movement could have com-pensated for the light armament of airborne units.

An official classified Soviet critique of 4th Airborne Corps operations, prepared by the General Staff prior to March 1943, summed up the lessons of the operation and candidly assessed what the corps did or failed to do. Its conclusion read:

The experience of three months of combat by 4th Airborne Corps permits the following conclusions to be reached:

1. Established views on the use of airborne units as a branch of forces designated to conduct active operations briefly with subsequent union of them with their own forces, are not always correct. In conditions of contemporary war it is necessary to consider that airborne forces will very often be forced to conduct protracted combat of various sorts – offensive, defensive, or in special conditions. This gives rise to the necessity for determining the nature of impending combat missions of the airborne assault ahead of time.

2. Insofar as an airborne assault will be designated for more or less extended combat work in the enemy rear, its equipment necessarily must correspond to the nature of its designated missions. In particular, the conduct of offensive battles will be associated with the necessity of having some quantity of artillery, although of small calibre; defensive combat must be supported with sufficient means of antitank defense and, even in a minimum scale, with special obstacles (portable in transports) and explosive substances. If there is a possibility to throw into the area of operations of an airborne assault even a small group of tanks (by means of executing a penetration in a most narrow sector of the enemy front), then the shock force of the assault will increase considerably. In all cases, one must take into account the necessity of saturating the airborne forces with as great a quantity as possible of shock means of combat, otherwise they will turn out too light and will not have the capability of performing active missions and will comparatively rapidly give way to the resistance of enemy ground forces.

3. The question of long-term resupply of airborne forces with ammunition and food is especially critical. One cannot count on uninterrupted efforts of his transport aviation in the presence of a strong enemy air defense.

Solutions of those questions of feeding and resupply depend directly on the nature of enemy operations. When operating in the presence of a weak enemy, in some cases it is inevitable to resupply at his expense, by means of organizing raids on warehouses, transport, or bases. The only real measure, as before, will be the use of transport aviation, in which the demand will be determined in each separate instance by the scale of the airborne operation.

When supplying by means of transport aviation, it is necessary to study the probability of losses of part of the supplies dropped by parachute, especially weapons, sometimes becoming worthless and the landing of aircraft on the ground is often impossible in light of unfavorable meteorological conditions.

Consequently, the techniques of delivery of cargo must be given special attention. Moreover, during delivery by air, one must study the additional inescapable losses of dropped cargo, otherwise by formal plan, the airborne force will receive all, but in reality this or that part of the cargo will not, in fact, reach them.

4. The landing of the airborne assault did not always occur successfully. Part of the personnel fell into enemy positions or those of neighboring units. Thus, more than 800 men of 4th Airborne Corps were dropped by mistake into 33d Army forces, as a result of which these people were not subsequently able to reunite with the corps, since 33d Army units were encircled. One must approach questions of organizing the drop of airborne units with exceptional accuracy and calculation. Otherwise, airborne units will find themselves in a hopeless situation.

5. The presence of partisan regions in the enemy rear is a mitigating condition for the work of airborne forces. When determining the landing regions, one must give preference to the region most thickly saturated by partisans in order to protect the productive work of both forces. It is also necessary to consider that in partisan regions questions of economic sustainment are considerably eased, and the necessity for evacuation of the lightly wounded in many cases decreases.

6. Airborne units are a comparatively dear type of force, which require great attention be paid to preparation and equipment; therefore the nature of their missions must be limited as far as possible to the shortest possible period of work. Prolonged commitment of these detachments in battle without their provision with artillery and tanks will not produce productive results and, as a rule, leads to the loss of combat quality of these detachments. In those cases when, according to existing conditions, airborne detachments are given a diversionary mission, they must not be drawn into prolonged battle with enemy ground units.

7. As the experience of the prolonged combat work of large airborne units shows, the most advantageous means of airborne assault is the immediate landing of forces on the ground. Dropping by parachute is extremely costly, for, in the presence of inexperienced navigators, it often occurs in very dispersed fashion. Hence, [there are] useless losses owing to the dropping of subunits

in enemy-occupied regions and excessive loss of time in assembling the formations.

Since the appearance of large airborne assaults in the enemy rear in the majority of cases can not go unnoticed, he [the enemy] always uses that delay in assembling units to organize corresponding countermeasures, directed at destroying the separate groups before their final assembly. Besides this fact, a majority of parachutists, representating great value, fell into the hands of the enemy or local population.

However, landing on the ground does not exclude the necessity for an advanced drop by parachute of 'securing groups' (as the basis, for example, of a battalion for a brigade) so that these groups secured projected landing areas from an enemy who happen to appear there prematurely.

This or other questions of airborne assaults will, in each separate case, depend on real front capabilities.[70]

Although this critique was compiled and written in late 1942, some aspects of its contents were well understood and taken into account as early as mid- and late February 1942, in particular during planning for the Demiansk operation.

Slow Soviet movement resulting from all these problems actually puzzled the Germans and confused them as to the actual Soviet airborne force mission. Postwar German critics claimed:

the operation [January–February] does not present the characteristics of an airlanding operation in the sense of an attack from the air. Rather, the fighting is solely a ground operation, only the assembly of forces takes place by air. This assembly, although taking place in the rear of the enemy, nevertheless occurred in an area which the enemy no longer controlled. The operation had sound prospects for success, but the Russians failed to take quick action and exploit the element of surprise. They let weeks pass between the first landings and the decisive thrust. As a result they lost the best chance they had for succeeding....The situation of German Fourth Army [would have been critical] if the Russians at the end of January 1942 had landed their brigade, which up till then had been landed in scattered units, as a compact force in the area southwest of Znamenka. If these airborne forces had then established communications between the Russian Thirty-Third and Tenth [50th] Armies, in cooperation with Cavalry Corps Belov, the German Fourth Army would have been completely encircled. It would have been doubtful whether this army could have broken out of encirclement, in view of the condition it was in at the time.

The reasons for the way the Russians behaved are not known. Perhaps, it was the temptation to achieve a greater objective, the encirclement of the German Fourth Panzer Army and Ninth Army. Perhaps it was impossible for them to undertake a landing synchronized in both time and space. It is useless to speculate without additional information on the subject from the Russians.[71]

Actual events, as revealed by the Soviets, confirmed the correctness of German speculation.

Mitigating these failures is the fact that this first Soviet airborne operation occurred during a desperate period under great pressures and extremely complex conditions. Unrealistically, the Soviet High Command threw all the forces at its disposal into a massive attempt to crush the Germans, who had recently wreaked havoc on the Soviet Union, but who now seemed vulnerable to a Soviet counterblow. Reflecting on the regulations of the 1930s and their prescription for modern successful deep battle, the High Command seized upon the panacea of airborne operations, keeping in mind what the regulations promised the use of such forces could produce, namely, confusion and ultimate defeat of the enemy.

The offensive of January 1942 was a bold, though flawed, attempt to follow the prescription of the 1930s for victory. To offensively-minded Soviet commanders, bold, imaginative resort to deep battle would produce victory. But, in 1942, it did not. Only later in the war, when forces and equipment matched doctrine and when leaders had educated themselves to the necessities and realities of battle, would the older concepts contribute to the achievement of victory.

Airborne forces paid the price of High Command failures. A total of about 14,000 men jumped into the cauldron of battle around Viaz'ma.[72] These men, under brave leaders, endured the subzero cold of January and February, and those who survived contended with the rotting moisture and mud of April and May. They fought daily battles with Germans, hunger, and the elements; and they reaped little of the euphoria of victory. About 4,000 Soviet paratroopers survived the four-month ordeal. Their only reward, save survival, was the knowledge that they had endured the longest airborne operation in history. Their personal sacrifice and endurance left a legacy of lessons, a step in the education of an army.

CHAPTER 7

Rzhev and Demiansk:
1st Airborne Corps Operations
(February–April 1942)

STRATEGIC CONTEXT

While throughout January and February 1942 the Soviet Western Front pounded German defenses along a front from south of Rzhev through Gzhatsk and Iukhnov to Sukhinichi, the Kalinin and Northwestern Fronts to the north struck at German positions from Lake I'lmen to Rzhev. Kalinin Front forces, operating in conjunction with the Western Front in the Rzhev–Viaz'ma operation, smashed German defenses west of Rzhev. On 8 January the Kalinin Front's 39th Army penetrated German defenses just west of Rzhev and, spearheaded by 11th Cavalry Corps, headed south through the German rear toward Viaz'ma and ultimate link-up with Western Front forces operating to the northwest out of the Mosal'sk area. The next day the Northwestern Front's left flank 3d and 4th Shock Armies, on the Kalinin Front's right flank, commenced the Toropets–Kholm operation by driving through German defenses in the Lake Seliger region heading through heavy forest into the German rear toward Toropets.

By the end of January, Kalinin Front forces had reached the approaches to Vitebsk, Smolensk, and Iartsevo, and threatened to sever German Army Group Center's lines of communication and envelop the army group from the northwest. At the same time, the Kalinin Front's 22d and 29th Armies threatened seven German divisions with encirclement in the Olenino region west of Rzhev. In mid-February, however, German Ninth Army mounted a relief operation west of Rzhev and, in so doing, encircled elements of Soviet 29th Army around Olenino.

Further north Northwestern Front armies developed the Toropets–Kholm operation. 3d Shock and 34th Armies penetrated toward Kholm, isolating German forces in the Demiansk region on their right flank. In February 1st Shock Army reinforced 11th Army on the Northwestern Front's right flank, and the combined force attacked toward Staraia Russa and southwestward toward Kholm in an attempt to unite with 3d

Shock Army and encircle major elements of German Sixteenth Army, which, on Hitler's orders, held firmly to its positions around Demiansk.

German operations against encircled Soviet 29th Army west of Rzhev and Soviet operations to liquidate German forces encircled at Demiansk provided additional opportunities for the Soviets to employ airborne forces to tip the scales of combat in their favor. In these two instances, the *Stavka* called on forces of 1st Airborne Corps to accomplish the complex missions assigned to the Northwestern Front. 1st Airborne Corps, originally largely destroyed in fighting around Kiev in September 1941, had been reconstituted in August and September in the Moscow region with its subordinate 1st, 204th, and 211th Airborne Brigades.

RZHEV, FEBRUARY 1942

Ongoing Soviet airborne operations in January and February 1942 aimed at encircling German forces on the approaches to Moscow, but one operation sought to do the reverse – assist Soviet forces trapped in a German encirclement. After the attack by the Kalinin Front in late January, 39th and 29th Armies, led by the 11th Cavalry Corps, pushed southward west of Rzhev toward Viaz'ma. In early February, however, German Ninth Army forces counterattacked and trapped seven divisions of 29th Army, which occupied a defensive perimeter of over 50 square kilometers around Olenino just west of Rzhev.[1] The Kalinin Front commander ordered 29th Army to break out of the trap and rejoin 39th Army forces, then operating to the southwest. He also mounted an airborne operation designed to reinforce encircled forces and help 29th Army break out.

The fully combat-ready 4th Battalion, 204th Airborne Brigade, of 1st Airborne Corps, commanded by Senior Lieutenant P. L. Belotserkovsky, took off from Liubertsy airfield to jump into the Monchalovo–Okorokovo area (see Figure 63). Signal fires arranged in the form of triangles and squares marked the drop zone in the middle of the 29th Army area. Officers acquainted all personnel with the names of villages in the drop zone and provided junior commanders sketches of the drop zone.

The 500-man battalion jumped from two flights of TB-3 aircraft on the night of 16–17 February.[2] But because the entire operational area – friendly as well as enemy – was ablaze with fires of one sort or another, the planned signal system failed. At least 100 men did not drop. Those who jumped did so from heights of 300 to 400 meters. In spite of heavy antiaircraft fire, no aircraft were lost. The entire seven-by-eight-kilometer encirclement area was subject to heavy German artillery fire. Moreover, German troops had penetrated into the encircled Soviets'

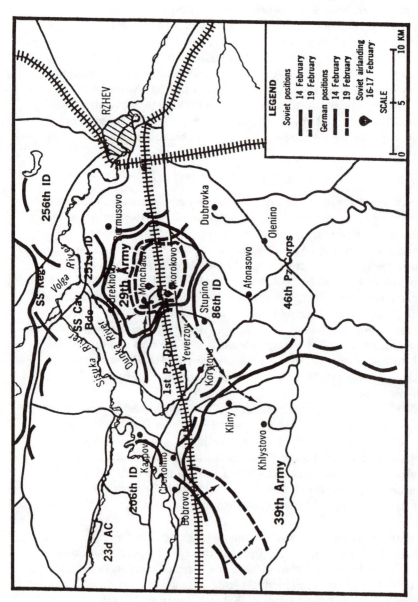

63. Rzhev Operation, February 1942

defensive perimeter. Paratroopers literally landed midst active fighting and had great difficulty assembling and finding the supplies and heavy weapons dropped in 'soft bags.'[3] German submachine gunners contested the landing, while a German infantry company with several tanks threatened Okorokovo from the northeast.

Lieutenant Borismansky's 3d Company landed at Okorokovo where it defended the northeast approaches to the town from the morning of 16 February until 1700 on 17 February. The 2d Company's assistant commander defended Monchalovo against repeated German infantry and tank attacks. Lieutenant Kovalevsky's 1st Company, along with a portion of Lieutenant Brusintsy's 2d Company, engaged in house-to-house, street-to-street fighting for possession of Everzovo.

On 16 February, the battalion commander, Senior Lieutenant Belotserkovsky, gathered 60 men south of Okorokovo and finally joined Lieutenant Borismansky's group northeast of the town. Only by nightfall on 17 February had the battalion commander finally succeeded in reassembling his command and establishing communications with the 29th Army commander, Lieutenant General S. V. Ivanovich.

For several days thereafter, the battalion supported 29th Army's breakout to the southwest by covering the flanks and rear of the withdrawing Soviet forces. Especially heavy fighting occurred at Zabrody where the battalion repulsed repeated German attacks. After suffering heavy casualties, on 22 February 100 men of the battalion followed remnants of 29th Army into 39th Army lines.

The operation at Rzhev differed from other airborne operations because its intent was simply to reinforce an encircled unit. Whether 29th Army could have broken free of German encirclement without airborne assistance is a moot point. Using such a small force for such a hazardous operation was indicative of the extremity of 29th Army's position. The actual drop experienced the same technical and coordination problems as previous drops. Repeatedly facing the same problems must have surely adversely affected unit capabilities and performance in battle.

DEMIANSK, FEBRUARY–APRIL 1942

Operational Context

In mid-January 1942 General P. A. Kurochkin's Northwestern Front engaged in heavy fighting for possession of his *front's* objectives, Staraia Russa and Kholm. In between his *front's* two main thrusts, German Sixteenth Army's II Army Corps was isolated and almost encircled. Anguishing over where his priorities should lie, Kurochkin reported on his dilemma to the *Stavka* and indicated he wished to give priority to destruction of the German Demiansk force.[4]

Kurochkin proposed shifting his 11th Army's axis of advance from Staraia Russa southward toward Kholm in the rear of the German Demiansk force, while his assigned 1st and 2d Guards Rifle Corps would press the attack on Staraia Russa. With these fresh forces, he hoped to fulfill his two most critical objectives: first, the seizure of Kholm and the encirclement and destruction of the German Demiansk group and, second, the seizure of Staraia Russa. The *Stavka* approved Kurochkin's proposal and, to facilitate better command and control, transferred 3d and 4th Shock Armies from his control to that of the Kalinin Front. In addition, *Stavka* assigned Kurochkin 1st Shock Army to spearhead an even more powerful drive on Kholm and beyond as part of *Stavka's* grand plan to conduct an ever-deepening envelopment of Army Group Center. Kurochkin later noted:

> But two such missions – the encirclement of the Demiansk grouping and conducting a deep penetration to the west – clearly did not correspond to the strength and capabilities of the Northwestern Front – And dividing our forces on two axes, the *front* could not achieve on either a decisive superiority of forces over the enemy.[5]

Kurochkin's mission and subsequent plan involved an attack by 1st Shock Army southward from just east of Staraia Russa toward Kholm. On 1st Shock Army's left flank, 34th Army would maintain pressure on and encircle German forces in Demiansk from the north (see Figure 64). The Kalinin Front's 3d Shock Army, positioned south of Demiansk, would attack toward Kholm in conjunction with 4th Shock Army and designate a portion of its force, Group Ksenefontov, to cooperate with 34th Army in liquidating the Demiansk pocket. One week later, on 24 January, *Stavka* permitted Kurochkin to also employ 1st and 2d Guards Rifle Corps in the encirclement and reduction of Demiansk – a force which Kurochkin described as an 'even greater force.'[6]

On 29 January 1st Guards Rifle Corps commenced its attack east of Staraia Russa, and, after several days of slow progress, on 3 February Kurochkin committed to combat his newly-arrived 2th Guards Rifle Corps. Together, by 15 February, the two corps smashed German defenses and linked up with 3d Shock Army forces at Kholm, loosely encircling the German Demiansk group. 1st Shock Army, committed days later, completed the isolation of the German force at Demiansk, but still had to devote considerable attention to large German forces stubbornly defending Staraia Russa. By late February 1st Guards Rifle Corps and Group Ksenefontov had linked up to form, with 34th and 3d Shock Armies, an internal encirclement line around the German Demiansk

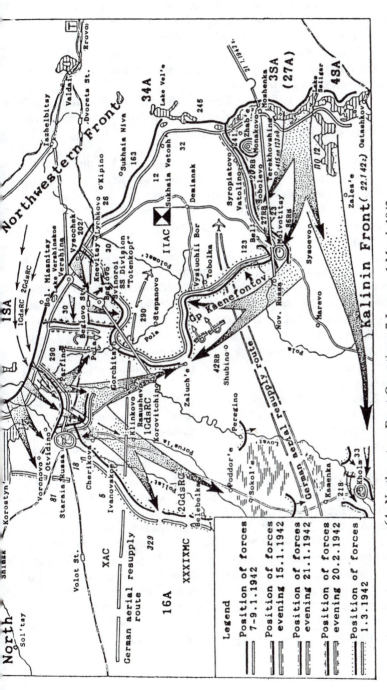

64. Northwestern Front Operations, 7 January–1 March 1942

Group. The encircled German force consisted of Sixteenth Army's II Army Corps and a portion of X Army Corps (12th, 30th, 32d, 123d, 290th Infantry Divisions, SS Motorized Division Totenkopf, and support units).[7] This was the first encirclement of German forces by the Soviets since the outbreak of war and, as such, had the full attention of the *Stavka*, which demanded its destruction.

On 25 February 1942, the Soviet Information Bureau (SOVIN-FORMBURO) declared, 'Our forces have encircled 16th German Army' (see Figure 65). The same day *Stavka* reported:

> Thanks to the weak coordinated action of the Kalinin Front's 3d Shock Army units with units of the Northwestern Front's 1st Guards Rifle Corps and 34th Army and because of the absence of a single command and control organization of these forces, the liquidation of the encircled Demiansk enemy group goes on very slowly.'[8]

To solve this problem, *Stavka* transferred Group Ksenefontov from Kalinin to Northwestern Front control and ordered it 'to compress continuously and persistently the ring of encirclement of the Demiansk enemy group and, not later than a four- to five-day period, finish with it.'[9] Kurochkin noted the impossibility of doing so, stating, 'We had insufficient forces. The absence of mobile formations did not permit us to inflict deep cutting blows. Having air superiority, the enemy utterly impeded our offensive.'[10]

On 22 February Hitler declared Demiansk to be a fortress pocket from which the Germans could launch a future offensive toward Moscow. He ordered that the pocket, which was separated from the main front at Staraia Russa by about 15 kilometers, be resupplied by air.[11] The resupply effort involved all of the aircraft available to Army Group Center and half of those stationed elsewhere on the Eastern Front.

To relieve German forces in the pocket, Sixteenth Army also planned Operation 'Brueckenschlag' [Bridging] to build a land bridge to the pocket. Approved by Hitler on 2 March, the plan involved a five-division attack eastward from south of Staraia Russa to link up with encircled II Corps. The commander of the relief force was Major General Walter von Seidlitz, and the attack was to commence on 21 March. In essence, both the Soviet Northwestern Front and German Sixteenth Army were now racing the clock.[12] Kurochkin had to crush German forces in the Demiansk pocket before the German relief operation succeeded, and von Seidlitz had to relieve the pocket before it was crushed.

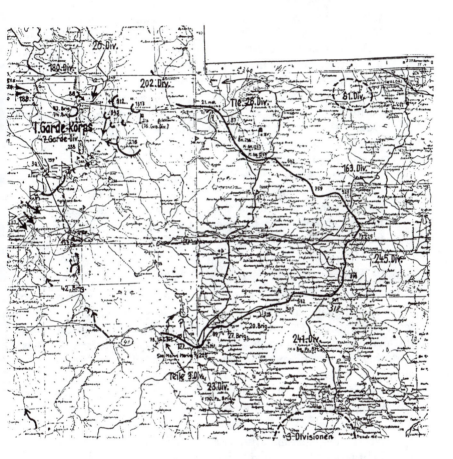

65. German Situation Map of the Demiansk Encirclement, 25 February 1942

Planning the Offensive

On 27 February Kurochkin advised 34th Army and 1st Guards Rifle Corps:

> Your assigned mission of quickly liquidating the enemy Demiansk Group demands above all an offensive tempo of not less than 10 kilometers per day. It is not possible to achieve that by usual methods of slow successive occupation of one population point after another. In this case, the enemy will achieve his aim of winning time and attracting to himself considerable strength.
>
> Experience indicates that the enemy fears deep envelopment of his forces by ours and the cutting of his supply lines. The encircled Demiansk enemy group is scattered in population points across a wide expanse and separated into isolated groups occupying a series of population points....
>
> In order to fulfill the encirclement mission and cut routes in the enemy rear, we need to use most decisively and skillfully entire formations, separate units, and especially ski battalions, capable of moving without roads. In this case, separate enemy garrisons can be fixed by small forces. On no account disperse main forces, but rather operate with them concentrated, for enveloping the enemy, or for destroying them on main directions.[13]

At this point for unknown reasons, Soviet sources become almost totally silent regarding the conduct of operations against the encircled German force at Demiansk. The only mention of the ensuing operation appears in the memoirs of a battalion surgeon in the 204th Airborne Brigade of 1st Airborne Corps. The memoir states, '...I recalled what Zhikarev said about the upcoming operation. We were expected to operate in the enemy deep rear in the Staraia Russa and Demiansk region, which forces advancing from the front would soon reach.'[14] The surgeon went on to note:

> No sooner had January passed than began a severe and snowy February of 1942. Conditions on the front intensified. One of the brigades of our corps was air-landed in the Staraia Russa and Demiansk region. We knew that it engaged in bitter combat with the enemy, and the command thought about providing it help, in particular communications and medical personnel. Thus, in the second half of February, it was decided to throw in a large group of sub-machine gunners and signalmen, with whom I was sent, to help doctors working in the region of concentrated wounded.
>
> I flew in together with the 5th Parachute Assault Company [2d Battalion], commanded by Senior Lieutenant N. V. Orekhov....[15]

The doctor described in general terms the heavy combat of the brigade, which he said was commanded initially by Major A. V. Grinev and, after he was wounded, by regimental commissar D. P. Nikitin. The doctor went on to relate:

Conditions in our sector worsened not only with each day, but also with each hour. The enemy pressed hard, having huge superiority in men and equipment. Our command undertook all measures to evacuate the heavily wounded, striving to do so with minimal losses. The enemy discovered the assembly area of the wounded and conducted uninterrupted mortar fire on them....

Battles with the enemy lasted several days, and all possibility for evacuating by air dried up. There remained one path – across the front lines....

That penetration to our forces was not easy....We traveled around for two weeks. It is difficult to describe the weariness, and difficult to describe what fell to our lot. Nevertheless, we handled our mission, delivered the wounded to the *front* medical department, and I returned to my brigade.[16]

Aside from these fragmentary recollections, virtually nothing about this airborne operation or the operational context in which it took place appears in Soviet sources. The general outline and many of the details of the operations can, however, be reconstructed from German sources, in particular intelligence reports, radio intercepts, operational summaries, and, most important, the reports of Soviet prisoners of war. What these reports describe is an air-land operation of considerable scope, which relied primarily on three airborne brigades to carry out the operation which *front* commander Kurochkin described in his explanation of what had to be done to destroy the German Demiansk force. Learning from the experience of earlier airborne operations, Kurochkin employed part of his airborne force to jump into the Demiansk pocket and prepare air strips and assembly points, while the major portion of the force advanced deep into the pocket by land, linked up with the air-dropped force and subsequently was resupplied by air as the combined force attacked German rear service installations.

Kurochkin's plan was simple in design but complex in execution. While main *frontal* forces pressured German forces in the Demiansk pocket, mobile forces would enter the pocket through a weakly defended sector in the north, penetrate southward through the frozen swampland and forests, and paralyze German command and control and logistical networks in the pocket. The exceedingly difficult terrain, then covered with deep snow, represented a formidable obstacle to achieving success. Of singular importance were the seizure and destruction of those key airfields near Demiansk, which were vital nodes in German efforts to resupply the encircled II Corps (see Figure 66).

The most critical planning factors were the selection of proper objectives, determination of the size of the force to be employed, and the development of methods for sustaining the force until it had secured its objectives. The principal airborne objectives were the Demiansk airfields, whose seizure would inevitably cause the German pocket to collapse. Of secondary importance were German defenses in the Knevitsy Station–Lychkovo sector along the northern extremity of the pocket. There German positions, in the form of a salient, blocked the main rail line from Valdai to Staraia Russa. If German forces abandoned these positions, the Northwestern Front would have unimpeded use of the rail line almost to Staraia Russa for its resupply efforts.

The strength of the Soviet force to be employed in the German rear area was determined by the estimated strength of German defenses. Seven German divisions (11th, 290th, 30th, SS Totenkopf, 32d, 12th, and 123d) defended the Demiansk encirclement. The Germans had 70,000 men, although Soviet planners originally estimated 50,000. Four of these divisions defended the eastern half of the pocket. Soviet planners reasoned that of these 50,000 troops, most would be tied down defending the extensive perimeter, and perhaps 5,000 were available to defend rear area installations. A Soviet force of about 10,000 men, if successfully inserted into the German rear, could therefore effectively disrupt German command and control and logistics.[17]

To accomplish these missions, Kurochkin earmarked three elite airborne brigades of 1st Airborne Corps, reinforced by at least one ski battalion, a total of about 10,000 men. Two airborne brigades were to attack Demiansk, and the third, German positions around and west of Lychkovo. The final plan called for two brigades (204th and 1st Airborne), advancing at night and in tandem through German lines from the Beglevo region via Pustynia, Solov'evo, and Maloe Opuevo to the Demiansk area (see Figure 67). After destroying the Demiansk airfields the two brigades were to continue their advance southward to Bel' and Vatolino respectively, if necessary driving completely through German lines. A third brigade (2d Airborne), reinforced by a ski battalion, was to follow the main force through Pustynia. Just short of the Polomet River, it was to turn northeast and strike the rear of German 30th Division defending Lychkovo and west of it.

The most difficult challenge was to sustain this airborne force throughout the duration of its operation. The initial plan called for the airborne force to carry three days' supply, enough to sustain the force in its penetration of German lines until it reached the Maloe Opuevo region. Thereafter, and while it operated against its main objectives (for an

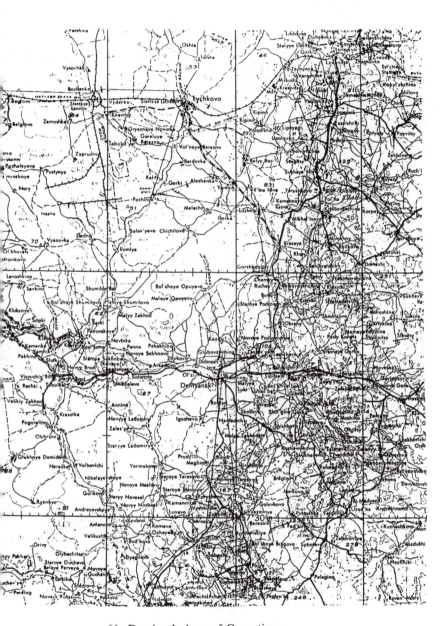

66. Demiansk Area of Operations

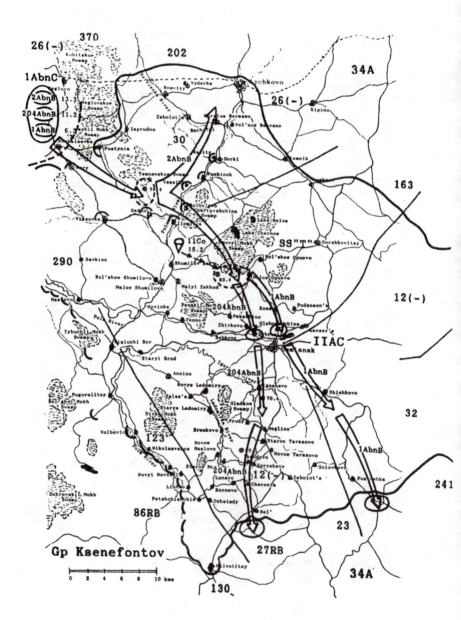

67. 1st Airborne Corps Plan of Operations

estimated 7–10 days), the force would be resupplied by airdrop and air-landing. To secure and prepare requisite landing strips and drop zones, the plan called for airborne forces from company to battalion strength to land in the German rear before the arrival of ground forces to seize key regions and prepare and secure landing sites. These airborne forward detachments would subsequently link up with and support the ground force. During the duration of the operation, additional air drops and air-landings, depending on the operational situation, would resupply and reinforce the ground forces. In addition, diversionary and reconnaissance air drops would occur prior to the ground operation.

The Soviet forces designated to conduct the operation were the newly subordinate brigades of 1st Airborne Corps (the 1st, 2d, and 204th Airborne Brigades), to operate in direct subordination to the Northwestern Front. After its initial battle around Kiev, the 1st Airborne Corps (2d formation) had been reformed during August and September 1941, north of Saratov on the Volga. Like other airborne corps in late 1941, its brigades were again reshuffled in December, and some were pulled from elements of other corps. After October 1st Airborne Corps were deployed to airfields near Moscow (Stupino and Liubertsy).[18]

Deployment

Lieutenant Colonel N. E. Tarasov's 1st Airborne Brigade deployed by air from Stupino airfield to Bologoe airfield in Kalinin District, 80 kilometers northwest of Moscow, on 2 March 1942 and traveled by rail to Vypolsovo Station, where it arrived on 4 March. After unloading, it traveled by light vehicle to an assembly area near Vereteika, where on 5 March, it prepared to cross the front on skis. The brigade numbered 3,000 men organized into four battalions of 600–620 men each plus supporting subunits.[19]

Lieutenant Colonel Vasilenko's 2d Airborne Brigade left Stupino airfield near Moscow on 6 March by rail and arrived in Vypolsovo Station on 11 March. After a 24-hour vehicle trip, it assembled near Vereteika on 11 March. It numbered approximately 2,000 men organized into four battalions of 450 men each.[20]

The 204th Airborne Brigade of Major A. V. Grinev, based in Liubertsy airfield southwest of Moscow, deployed its 4th Battalion in mid-February by parachute into the Demiansk and Iasski regions as a forward detachment for the 1st Airborne Corps and to perform reconnaissance and diversionary missions on the eve of operations. The remainder of the brigade, including a reformed 4th Battalion, left Liubertsy airfield on 7 March for rail transport through Romanushka to Liubnitsa. From Liubnitsa the brigade traveled by light vehicle to Vereteika assembly areas, where it arrived on about 10 March. Grinev's brigade numbered almost 3,000 men with about 750 men per battalion. After departure of the 4th Battalion in mid-February, brigade strength fell to under 2,000, with 400 men per battalion.[21] Additional corps reinforcements, including at least the 54th Ski Battalion with a strength of almost 500 men, brought the force up to an initial strength of just under 10,000 men.

After assembling in Vereteika, each brigade moved forward on skis to assembly areas near the front lines. This was done successively by brigade so as not to form too detectable a concentration. The timing of the passage of lines was as follows:

1st Airborne Brigade   6–8 March
204th Airborne Brigade   11–15 March
2d Airborne Brigade   13–16 March.

Planned march routes varied somewhat and were as follows:

lst Airborne Brigade – Vereteika–Pozhaleeva–Marker 56.4 (south of Temnenskoe Swamp)–Polomet River between Solov'evo and Iloml'ia–Maloe Opuevo;
2d Airborne Brigade – Vereteika–Pozhaleeva–Marker 56.4–Polomet River near Pochinok–Goreloe Beresino;
204th Airborne Brigade – same as 1st Airborne Brigade.[22]

Conduct of the Operation

The first stage of the operation commenced on 15 February 1942 when the 4th Battalion, 204th Airborne Brigade, jumped into two regions near and west of Demiansk to conduct reconnaissance, cooperate with partisan forces, and prepare base camps for the remainder of the brigade to use in later operations (see Figure 68). Over the course of four nights from 15 to 18 February, 100 TB-3 aircraft lifted the battalion to its requisite drop zones in conjunction with drops of elements of the same battalion near Olenino (Rzhev).[23]

The first flight, carrying men of the 11th Company, took off at 2200 15 February and, later that evening, dropped its cargo midway between Shumilov-Bor and Ilom'lia. After dropping from low altitude into the tree tops and deep snow, the company assembled and moved southeast toward Maloe Opuevo. The following night more aircraft transported the remainder of 4th Battalion and part of 1st Battalion to the same region and to a larger drop zone southeast of Iasski, just west of the Staraia Russa–Velikie Luki road.[24] This larger force had orders to link up with partisans operating in the region, particularly Partisan Brigade Vasilev, and cut German communications near Dedovitchi to the north and along

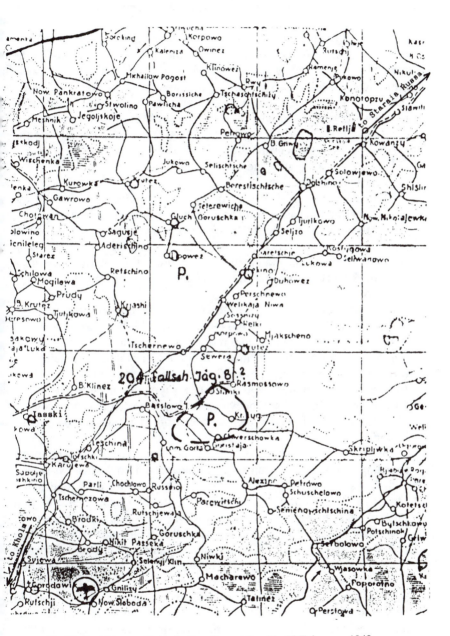

68. 204th Airborne Brigade Landing at Iasski, 15 February 1942

the Loknia–Kholm rail line, which was the principal resupply route for the encircled German garrison at Kholm.

Although Soviet sources say nothing about operations in the Iasski area, German reports speak of parachute-partisan operations in the region throughout March and April. Noting that the paratroopers wore German snowshoes and carried German weapons and equipment, German reports presumed 'the enemy had the obvious purpose of breaking through the road from Dedovitchi to the Loknia–Kholm rail line and creating a breach for part of 1st Shock Army,' then approaching the region.[25] Subsequent German reports in late February and early March recorded continuing airborne force ground operations in the region, but with no significant results.[26]

The airdrop in mid-February quickly alerted German forces to the impending threat against Demiansk. On 18 February German II Corps issued the following order to SS Totenkopf Division: 'An insertion of paratroopers against the Demiansk airfield is possible. SS "T" Division (Group Simon) immediately take over protection of the Demiansk airfield. Report at once the insertion of paratroopers to II AC headquarters.'[27]

Meanwhile, the company of 4th Battalion, 204th Airborne Brigade, which had jumped northwest of Demiansk, established base camps west of Maloe Opuevo and reconnoitered southward to the Demiansk region. On the night of 6–7 March, just as the ground advance of the airborne force was commencing, ten TB-3 bombers dropped supplies to 11th Company, 4th Battalion, with which to resupply the larger force once it had arrived in the Maloe Opuevo area. The Germans also detected the aircraft, and it reinforced their expectation of future combat in the region.[28]

On, 6 March, the day before the aerial resupply, the airborne force, traveling only at night, began its ground advance from Pozhaleeva on skis and showshoes (see Figure 69). Two nights later, on the evening of 8 March, 1st Airborne Brigade passed south of German positions at Pustynia into the region just south of the Temnenskoe Swamp. By early morning it had crossed the Polomet River between Solov'ev and Vessiki and established a concealed daylight encampment three kilometers beyond. On the evening of 9 March, the brigade passed Chernoe Lake and encamped two kilometers beyond on the edge of the Novyi Moch Swamp. Hastening to meet its schedule, the brigade moved out at 1300 on 10 March southward through the swamp toward Maloe Opuevo. At 1400 it made contact with a German patrol and suffered its first casualties (five wounded from 2d Battalion).[29]

The same day German forces at Pustynia and Pochinok lightly engaged flank detachments of 1st Airborne Brigade. Although the 1st Airborne

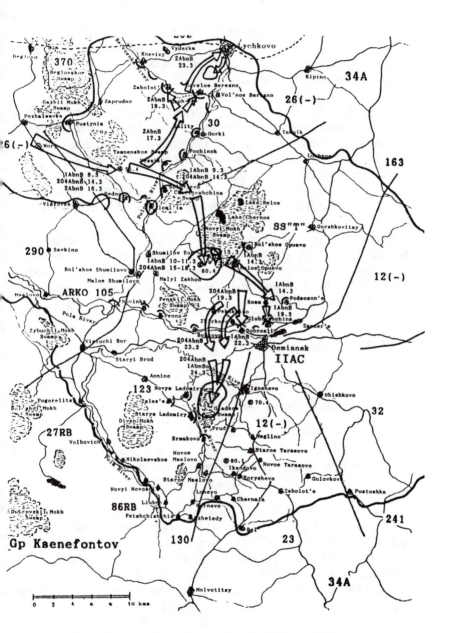

69. 1st Airborne Corps Operations, 6–23 March 1942

Brigade had run the gauntlet successfully and with few casualties, the Germans had now been alerted, and the follow-on brigades would not be so fortunate. By the evening of 11 March, 1st Airborne Brigade was safely lodged in base camps just west of Maloe Opuevo and was planning an attack on the small German garrison at Maloe Opuevo. Although the brigade's food supplies were exhausted by 12 March, resupply by air over the next three nights alleviated the situation.[30]

Grinev's 204th Airborne Brigade began its passage of lines through alerted German forces on the evening of 12–13 March after one night's march from Pozhaleeva. Almost immediately, its march evoked a response from the alerted Germans in the form of harassing fire, which slowed the brigade's night movement to a crawl and constantly forced the battalion to disperse in order to avoid suffering heavier casualties. The 1st and 2d Battalion led its march, followed by 3d Battalion and, finally, 4th Battalion bringing up the rear.[31]

After suffering some losses south of Pustynia, the 204th Brigade lead battalions received artillery fire from German positions at Dedno. Kurochkin's impatience with the slow advance soon became apparent. On 14 March the Northwestern Front staff radioed the following message to 204th Airborne Brigade:

> To Grinev:
> Flash! Immediately [report] the location you intend to occupy on 15.3
>
> Vatutin, Chief of Staff.[32]

204th Airborne Brigade responded:

> To Chief of Staff, Northwestern Front:
> The brigade at 0600 14.3 concentrated south of marker 56.4 [southern edge of Temnenskoe Swamp].
>
> Gubin, Chief of Staff, 204th Airborne Brigade.[33]

German resistance continued to intensify, requiring Grinev to rearrange his brigade's march order. 2d and 3d Battalions continued along a single axis, 1st Battalion split off to the north, and 4th Battalion did likewise somewhat south and to the rear. 4th Battalion took heavy casualties from German fire as it passed Pustynia, while 2d and 3d Battalions, on the night of 14–15 March reached the Polomet River between Solov'evo and Vessiki, where they met recurrent heavy German fire. German records reported the attacks on 4th Battalion from its Pustynia garrison, heavy enemy activity near Dedno [presumely 3d Battalion, 204th Airborne Brigade] and an enemy forcing of the Polomet River between Solov'evo and Vessiki. The same report noted the presence of 1st Airborne Brigade patrols southeast of Maloe Opuevo near Kosa and Podsoson'e on the northern approaches to Demiansk.[34]

The Germans engaged all of these Soviet troop concentrations with artillery fire and night bombers. Under heavy fire, Grinev slowed his movements once again, ordered a company of 3d Battalion to return to join 2d Airborne Brigade's advance toward Lychkovo, and soon did likewise with a company of 4th Battalion, after it had suffered additional heavy losses in its advance from Pustynia, through Dedno, to the Polomet River.

On the morning of 15 March, *front* again urged Grinev forward with the following message:

> From Northwestern Front Staff to 204th Airborne Brigade:
> Flash. What are the results of your mission? Before you in the area of Marker 60.4 [four kilometers west of Maloe Opuevo] is the 1st Airborne Brigade. Be certain to cooperate in your mission.
>
> Vatutin'[35]

Vatutin let Grinev know there would be fresh supplies in 1st Airborne's camp. The Soviet aerial resupply effort continued, with additional flights to drop zones west of Maloe Opuevo on the nights of 13 and 14 March. German reports recorded on 13 March, '20 inbound flights of Russian [TB-3] transport aircraft in direction of Novyi Moch Swamp. Red signal flares reported near the landing area in the swamp.'[36]

By late 14 March, the first forces of 204th Airborne Brigade reached the camps of Tarasov's 1st Brigade in the Maloe Opuevo area. That night, although the 204th Airborne Brigade had not fully assembled, Tarasov conducted a heavy attack on the German garrison defending Maloe Opuevo with his 4th Battalion and 204th Airborne Brigade's 2d Battalion and part of 3d Battalion, while other 1st Brigade battalions pushed on toward Demiansk through Kosa and Podsoson'e. The Germans reported an attack on Maloe Opuevo from three sides by 1,200–1,300 para-troopers.[37] After heavy fighting in which the paratroopers lost an es-timated 200 dead, the German garrison's remnants withdrew westward to Bol'shoe Opuevo. The same night German II Army Corps reported that at 2005 Soviet transports dropped additional paratroopers 'into the swamps north of Opuevo.'[38] By morning on 16 March, all German intelligence sources confirmed a likely Soviet advance on the Demiansk region via Maloe Opuevo, Kosa, and Podsoson'e.

Meanwhile, on the evening of 13 March, Lieutenant Colonel Vasilenko's 2d Airborne Brigade began its movement into the Demiansk pocket in the footsteps of 204th Airborne Brigade. The 1st Battalion led, followed in sequence by 2d Battalion, artillery detachment, 3d Battalion, and 4th Battalion. By the night of 16 March, the lead 1st and 2d Battalions had marched between Nory and Pustynia subject to the same harassing fire as experienced by 204th Brigade. As had been the case with the 204th Brigade, follow-on battalions suffered the most serious losses (3d Company, 4th Battalion, lost 25 men of its original 130).[39] By swinging northeast just short of the Polomet River, 2d Brigade avoided heavy losses, and, on late 17 March, concentrated south of Zabolot'e in German 30th Infantry Division's rear area. 4th Battalion remained to the rear along the Polomet River near Pochinok to care for wounded, while the 1st, 2d, and 3d Battalions prepared to attack German positions at Zabolot'e and Goreloe Berezno.

The Northwestern Front's attention now focused primarily on the main airborne force objective, the critical airfields around Demiansk. At 0940 16 March, *front* staff issued new instructions to 1st and 204th Airborne Brigades in a message which read:

> To Tarasov and Grinev:
> In connection with the approach march of Grinev into Tarasov's sector, I order: – the operation for the seizure of Demiansk, Dobrosli, and Globovshchina will be simultaneous with the re-supplied combined forces of the 1st and 204th Airborne Brigade, for the purposes of which 1. The 1st Airborne Brigade is placed under the operational direction of Grinev. 2. Comrade Grinev will energetically destroy the garrisons [above] by 18.3. Then it is possible for Tarasov to advance on Staroe Tarasovo and Bel' and Grinev to Shishkovo.
>
> Vatutin[40]

Later in the day, at 1830, in light of apparent complaints from the airborne forces about lack of provisions, Kurochkin dispatched yet another message:

> Northwestern Front Staff to 204th Airborne Brigade
> To Grinev
> You can receive ready provisions by means of aircraft landing. Protect the receipt of provisions. Tarasov can find them 1 kilometer south of Maloe Opuevo. Work out cooperation.
>
> Kurochkin[41]

The fact that lack of provisions and ammunition impeded the launch of airborne assaults on the Demiansk airfield was amply testified to by messages from Northwestern Front to the brigade and by the accounts of Soviet POWs picked up by the Germans, many of whom claimed they had not eaten for days. Due to these and other problems, the attacks originally scheduled for the night of 18 March had to be delayed until the next evening.

At 0135 17 March, *front* again radioed Grinev:

> To Grinev
> During the night the air force bombed Solov'evo, Ilom'lia and
> Vessiki. Get your provisions around the swamp 3 kilometers west
> northwest of Maloe Opuevo dropped by aircraft. On 15.3 at 1630
> provisions for your march were sent by dog [sled].
>
> Vatutin[42]

Apparently the bombing was intended to keep the ground supply route
open.

The next day at 1046 *front* dispatched yet another message:

> To Tarasov and Grinev:
> The provisions you have requested have been dropped one kilo-
> meter west of Marker 60.4 [east of Shumilov-Bor]. There is [also] a
> landing site for aircraft to pick up and evacuate wounded. From an
> intercepted radio report, [it is clear] the area has been cleared of
> enemy. Has the order for digging in been given yet? Organize
> speedy unloading and put out guard posts.
>
> Kurochkin[43]

Despite the reassurances, the attack preparations went slowly, prompt-
ing another *front* message at 0900 19 March:

> From Northwestern Front to 204th Airborne Brigade:
> Four companies of Tarasov's brigade have joined and are sub-
> ordinate to you. The provisions detachment is there for you to see in
> the region of Marker 60.4, four kilometers southwest of Maloe
> Opuevo. Tarasov has the mission to seize Dobrosli on 19.3 and if
> conditions are favorable, Demiansk. Further, you should [then]
> advance to Igoshevo and Bel'.
> I have sent back 1,000 unassigned reinforcements to Svinoroi.
> When they have broken through the Polomets River to the rest of
> the brigade, unite them with Tarasov. Otherwise turn them back to
> Svinoroi.
>
> Kurochkin, Vatutin[44]

Tarasov and Griev finally launched their attack on the German positions
around Demiansk on the night of 19 March. Paratroopers of 2d Battalion
and 4th Battalion, 1st Airborne Brigade struck Globovshchina airfield,
and 3,000 men of 1st and 3d Battalions, 1st Airborne Brigade, and
portions of 204th Airborne Brigade (1st and 3d Battalions) attacked

Dobrosli. The Germans deflected both attacks, killing 600 of the Soviet attacking forces at Dobrosli. Soviet 3d Battalion, 204th Airborne's 7th Company lost 50 of its 140 men.[45] Following the Soviet repulse, German artillery pounded airborne camps detected in the forest near Zhirkovo west of Dobrosli (see Figure 70).

On 22 March Grinev dispatched his wounded northward under armed escort to Maloe Opuevo and then moved westward to find a weak spot in enemy defenses along the road west of Demiansk, through which to pass southward toward his next objective, German 12th Infantry Division headquarters at Igoshevo. He found a weak spot in German defenses at Bobkovo west of Demiansk. On the night of 23 March, 3d Battalion, 204th Airborne launched its subordinate companies (7th, 8th, 9th) in an attack against Bobkovo. Although German defenses held, Grinev's Brigade succeeded in sweeping across the road and assembling the following evening in the swamps northwest of Igoshevo with a complement of 500 exhausted men of 1st, 2d, and 3d Battalions.[46]

Meanwhile Tarasov's 1st Airborne Brigade, after resupplying from the Maloe Opuevo base, moved south through German positions at Demiansk, unsuccessfully attacked Zhirkovo en route on 21 March, and assembled its four battalions of 2,000 men in camps along the eastern edge of Gladkoe Swamp southwest of Igoshevo by the evening of 24–25 March (see Figure 71). New instructions from *front* ordered Grinev's 204th Brigade to attack German 12th Infantry Division headquarters at Igoshevo, while Tarasov's 1st Brigade struck German positions further south at Tarasovo. This was a last desperate attempt to disrupt German defenses, this time along the southern portion of the German Demiansk pocket defensive perimeter, in conjunction with attacks by Soviet forces from outside the pocket.[47]

While Grinev and Tarasov's forces fought in vain to seize the Demiansk airfields, Vasilenko's 2d Airborne Brigade commenced operations in 30th Infantry Division's rear area southwest of Lychkovo. The brigade launched its first attack on the evening of 18 March when the 1st, 2d, and 3d Battalions assaulted German positions at Goreloe Berezino, Zabolot'e and westward in the Berezenka Valley. These attacks were coordinated with a major Soviet 34th Army attack on German positions east of Lychkovo. Both attacks failed. German reports stated:

> 18.3.42 1845 hours...east of Lychkovo an attack by a superior enemy force, supported by numerous artillery collapsed in front of the main defensive positions with bloody losses for the enemy. In Beresenka sector (Bach-Tal near Knevizy) there was a violent battle with 200 Russian dead counted near Zabolot'e.[48]

Other German reports identified enemy casualties near Zabolot'e as 230

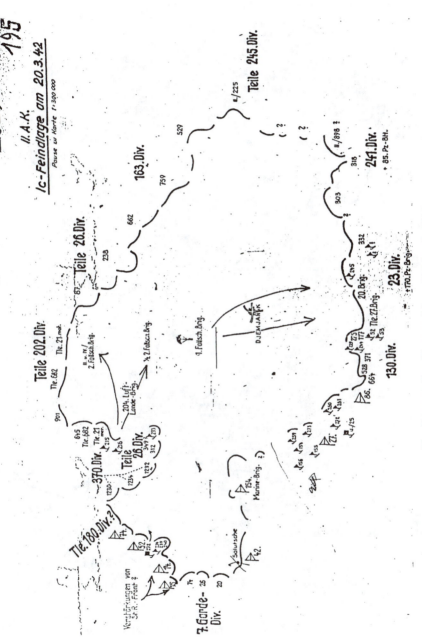

70. German Intelligence Map, 20 March 1942

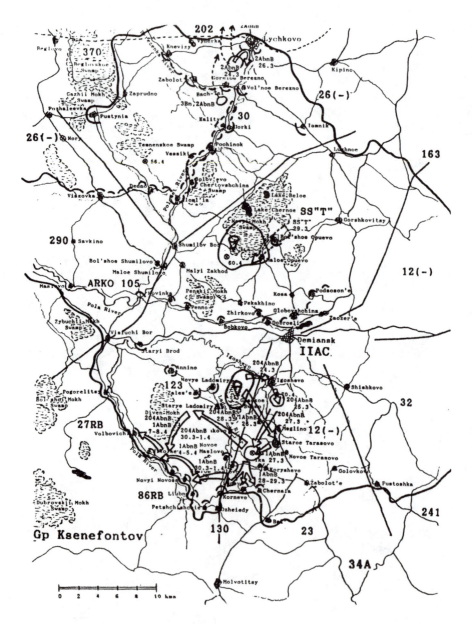

71. 1st Airborne Corps Operations, 23 March–9 April 1942

dead, 22 light machine guns and 15 antitank rifles captured, all from 2d Airborne Brigade.[49]

Vasilenko renewed his attacks several days later, on 23 March against the town of Lychkovo itself. In heavy fighting, paratroopers penetrated to the railroad station but were beaten back. In this attack the 2d Brigade was reinforced by two ski battalions (one of which was 54th Ski Battalion), sent forward on previous nights to reinforce his efforts, and by his 4th Battalion, held in reserve. The full day and evening of combat cost Vasilenko dearly. His 2d Battalion lost over 400 of its 580 men.[50] Losses of 1st Battalion and the ski battalions were somewhat less but still heavy. Early on the morning of 24 March, Vasilenko withdrew his forces to positions just south of the rail line. German reports tracked the movement, noting on 25 March:

> 2d Airborne Brigade continues to be positioned with parts of 1st Battalion, 2d Battalion and 4th Battalion in the forests south of Lytschkovo and Vyderka. Its strength is approximately 300 men. The mass of these battalions have broken out to the north and have, with the 54th Ski Battalion at Lytschkovo, become worn out. The 3d Battalion [in reserve during the attack on Lytschkovo] is still positioned south of the Goreloe Berezno road.[51]

Vasilenko launched his third attack on German positions on the night of 26–27 March. Again the Germans drove his force back with heavy losses. Now, in desperation, the force broke into small bands to infiltrate through German lines as best they could. German reports conceded that some of the 2d Brigade paratroopers made it out of the German rear, but not as an organized unit.

South of Demiansk Grinev's 204th and Tarasov's 1st Airborne Brigades launched their last desperate attempts to disrupt German defenses against the German garrisons at Igoshevo and Staroe Tarasovo. The 204th Airborne moved out of its camps north of Gladkoe Swamp in early evening of 24 March under constant German artillery fire and struck German positions at Igoshevo just before midnight. After an intense seven-hour battle, the German defenses held, and Grinev's brigade withdrew to hill 80.1, one-and-a-half kilometers south of Igoshevo. The battle cost Grinev 181 dead, including his 1st Battalion commander, 16 prisoners, and four radios. German losses were 33 killed and 37 wounded (including the 12th Infantry Division commander, who was wounded).[52] After the failed attack, Grinev dispatched reconnaissance groups to the south and west to Starye Ladomiry and Ermakovo to facilitate link-up with 1st Brigade by prior coordination at hill 80.1 west of Staroe Tarasovo, where the two brigades planned to institute a joint breakout westward. Meanwhile, while active German patrolling from Igoshevo picked up numerous Soviet POWs, 1st and 204th Brigade engineers prepared drop zones and a landing strip, which aircraft used to land supplies, in the Gladkoe Swamp between 20–25 March.[53]

Tarasov's stronger brigade, after regrouping and resupplying east of Gladkoe Swamp all day on 26 March, struck German positions at Meglino and Staroe Tarasovo shortly after dusk. Part of 1st Battalion cut roads leading from Starye Ladomiry in the west and Meglino and Staroe Tarasovo in the east, while the other three battalions attacked the German garrison at Staroe Tarasovo. About 2,000 parachutists participated in the operation, which was designed to link up with German forces attacking from Bel' in the south. After prolonged fighting, both Soviet attacks failed, again with heavy losses. While German reports listed 170 confirmed dead, Soviet POWs reported losses of 150 of 500 men in 4th Battalion, 200 of 300 men of 1st Battalion, and 86 men of 3d Battalion, and the 2d Battalion commander. The brigade withdrew with over 100 wounded in 3d Battalion alone. During the battle brigade commander Tarasov was also wounded.[54]

After the engagement 1st Airborne Brigade survivors withdrew westward to the prearranged assembly area near hill 80.1, where it linked up with the remnants of 204th Airborne Brigade. The new Soviet plan called for the brigade's forces to break out southward via Chernaia to Soviet front lines. By now, the 1st Brigade was encumbered with 300–400 wounded, and it sought to have them flown from the airstrip at Gladkoe Swamp. On 28 March a limited number of aircraft made it in and picked up wounded officers and commissars and a limited number of men. The rest would have to make it out of the pocket with the remaining combat force. Tarasov, for whatever reason, remained with his brigade.[55]

204th Brigade remnants planned to withdraw from the Gladkoe Swamp region and move southwest via Novye and Starye Ladomiry to the Nikolaevskoe area, where it hoped to break through German lines. 1st Airborne Brigade planned to move south and regroup its 1st, 3d, and 4th Battalions in the forests one-and-a-half kilometers northeast of Kornevo. Thereafter it would penetrate German lines and rejoin Group Ksenefontov forces operating south of the Demiansk pocket. Tarasov's brigade would advance in three groups via the Kornevo, Lunevo, and Chernaia axes to find a weak spot in German lines.

On the eve of the breakout attempt, at 2100 hours 27 March, Ksenefontov radioed 1st Airborne the following message:

> As soon as you are in motion, send a radio signal, after which I will open fire toward Ikandovo and Staroe Maslovo. Near the crossing

over line Staroe Maslovo–Ikandovo, send a radio signal, whereupon I will shift that fire towards Chernaia West and Lunevo. During the advance from Chernaia West, on receipt of another radio signal, I will strengthen the fire toward Chernaia East and Lunevo. Report your march route and recognition signal.

> Ksenefontov,
> Mavritshchev[56]

Again a German report anticipated the airborne troopers' actions. Issued at about 0700 28 March, it read, 'Mass of enemy paratroopers in the swamps three kilometers southwest of Igoshevo and forests south. Breakthrough to the south expected.'[57] 1st Airborne Brigade was about to run a fatal gauntlet of fire southward.

1st Airborne Brigade forces advanced at 0300 and, by 0430, were engaging German Group Simon of SS Totenkopf Division in a running fight, which lasted until well after daybreak. German 123d Infantry Division units engaged other paratrooper detachments south of Maslovo, as the Soviet force fractured into several distinct groups. A third Soviet column ran into German defenses just west of Chernaia and suffered a similar repulse. By afternoon, German forces counted 120 dead parachutists west of Chernaia, together with six machine guns and 100 abandoned skis. The 123d Infantry Division counted another eight dead south of Maslovo.[58]

Throughout the day Soviet headquarters radioed frantic instructions to the beleaguered force. At 1218 on 28 March, Ksenofontov sent another message to 1st Airborne:

> To Tarasov:
> I am advancing toward Chernaia West and Chernaia East. The 23d and 130th Rifle Divisions have not yet taken these towns. In cooperation we will push out toward Chernaia West and East and bypass them from the north and northwest. These directions must be marked by red and green AWK [signal] rockets.
>
> Ksenefontov,
> Mavritshchev.[59]

Less than one hour later at 1258, the next message arrived, stating:

> I am ready now to open artillery fire toward Staroe Maslovo, Novoe Maslovo, Ikandovo, Lunevo, Pen'kovo, Staroe Tarasovo and Novoe Tarasovo. During the march toward Lunevo and Ozcheiedy on order fire covering fires, those towns are strongpoints. In each case, radio requests for artillery fire.
>
> Ksenefontov,
> Mavritshchev.[60]

Just how close 1st Airborne Brigade came to escaping to the south was underscored by a 1606 hour order from Group Ksenefontov, which read:

> To Tarasov:
> The 23d Rifle Division is seizing and struggling around Chernaia East and finds itself 800 meters away from it....
> The 130th Rifle Division is advancing toward Chernaia West and is 300–400 meters distant from it. You advance with part of your force toward Lunevo.
> The 86th Rifle Brigade is advancing toward Ozcheiedy–Petshchishchie. Your order is to occupy either Lunevo or Chernaia West and then fortify the town. Report at once the seizure of either of these towns. Tonight 20 sacks of provisions will be air dropped in the area of Marker 80.1.
>
> > Ksenefontov,
> > Shchvamkin,
> > Mavritshchev.[61]

Despite these entreaties and careful coordination, 1st Brigade simply did not have the strength to break out.

Thwarted in their first attempt to move south, both 204th Airborne and 1st Airborne Brigades refocused their attention on the southern sector. After resting and regrouping south of the Gladkoe Swamp, 1st Airborne Brigade made yet another effort to break out on 29 March. This time the force thrust southward east of Kornevo, again into a curtain of fire, which chopped the force to pieces. The repulse at the hands of a 12th Infantry Division *Kampfgrupp* cost 1st Airborne Brigade another 50–60 dead. A third breakout attempt occurred at 0300 on 29 March near Lunevo when 200 paratroops tried to cross the highway south of Bel' 2, losing another 30–40 dead in the process.[62] Meanwhile 204th Airborne Brigade remnants consolidated in the Starye Ladomiry area and probed from the Zales'e area southwestward toward Nikolaevskoe, hounded by small German garrisons and pursuit detachments, one of which captured eight paratroopers near Zales'e.[63]

All thought of withdrawing the two brigades northward through Maloe Opuevo evaporated when, early on 29 March, forces of SS Totenkopf Division struck back at the Soviet basecamps at Maloe Opuevo and in the adjacent swamps. In a two-hour battle, SS Totenkopf troopers advanced from Bol'shoe Opuevo and overran Soviet positions at Maloe Opuevo, killing 180 paratroopers, capturing 27 prisoners and 50 civilians, three machine guns, and a sizeable stock of munitions; all at a cost of three dead and three wounded.[64] Other SS Totenkopf forces, with the help of air observation, shelled two Soviet base camps five kilometers northeast of Maloe Opuevo and destroyed yet another camp west of Bol'shoe Opuevo. In essence, the whole logistical structure for aerial resupply and support of the airborne force collapsed, leaving no recourse but flight through German lines out of encirclement.

As German II Army Corps reported at 1300 29 March:

> The 1st and 204th Airborne Brigades are being beaten to pieces through the 12th, 123d, and SS Totenkopf Divisions (Group Simon) so that the severe risk to Demiansk stronghold is reduced.
>
> 500 paratroopers have been driven into Novy Moch Swamp. The remainder of the brigades are moving south along the Visiuchii Bor–Demiansk road on both sides of the Ladomirka Valley. The mission of 12th, 123d, and SS Totenkopf Divisions is to overwatch these forces.[65]

After the ill-fated breakout attempts on 29 March, Tarasov's dwindling force moved westward from Chernaia and Lunevo toward the Ladomirka Valley south of Novoe Maslovo to regroup on 30 March and subsequently find a new exit from the shrinking trap it found itself in. By the evening of 30 March, the brigade continued westward toward Novyi Novosel, then under attack by Soviet *frontal* forces of Group Ksenefontov. 204th Brigade remnants moved southwest from Zales'e toward Nikolaevskoe to join forces with 1st Brigade. The following day, 31 March, they continued their movements, losing a steady stream of deserters and wounded along the way (123d Division reported taking 17 prisoners from 204th Brigade in the forest south of the Liubno–Maslovo road).[66]

On 1 April the German 123d Infantry Division reported numerous attempts by small groups to penetrate German defenses between Chernaia, Lunevo, and Novyi Novosel; but all failed, as the Soviet prisoner count mounted. The Soviet Northwestern Front continued radioing messages to the fugitive parachutists.[67] At 1715 1 April, Northwestern Front notified Group Ksenefontov:

> The *front* commander has directed the breakout of Tarasov through the front so as to keep losses down to as few as possible. If the execution of the order does not succeed, since the distance from Kornevo to Chernaia is too far, then execute the breakthrough through the front between Pogorelitsy and Nikolaevskoe! Execute reconnaissance at once.
>
> Vatutin.[68]

1st Airborne acknowleged receipt of this order. Less than one hour later, Northwestern Front dispatched another order to 1st Airborne Brigade, stating:

On the morning of 31.3 the 130th Rifle Division with support from three artillery regiments took Chernaia West.

The 86th Rifle Brigade has cut the road and holds it between Novyi Novosel and Nikolaevskoe. Petrovsky with his detachment was supposed to have cut the road between Nikolaevskoe and Pogorelitsy.[69]

By this time the remnants of both Grinev's and Tarasov's brigades were moving toward Novyi Novosel and Nikolaevskoe. From evening 1 April through 4 April, they searched in vain for exit routes through German lines, occasionally dispatching parties to test German defenses. While German patrols pressed against their rear from Zales'e southward to Novoe Maslovo, on three successive nights the 1st Airborne Brigade attempted to punch through German lines: on the night of 4–5 April northwest of Novyi Novosel; the next night near Nikolaevskoe; and on the night of 7–8 April near Volbovichi. German reports of the latter stated, 'On the Southwestern Front an attempt to break out by 600 men south of Volbovichi was prevented. The commander of 1st Airborne Brigade, Tarasov, was captured.'[70] Later in the day a subsequent report noted another breakout attempt, leaving 80 more dead, including the new brigade commander, Lieutenant Colonel Ustinov.[71]

The last recorded activity of 1st Airborne Brigade was noted in a German report dated 0845 9 April, which stated, 'The remainder of 1st Airborne Brigade with a strength of 400 men tried to break out yesterday 16 kilometers southwest of Demiansk while suffering heavy losses.'[72] Neither Soviet sources nor German reports relate the fate of 204th Airborne Brigade Commander Grinev. Several Soviet prisoners of war noted that he led the brigade attack at Igoshevo on 25 March, but disappeared during the fighting to be replaced in command by brigade commissar Nikitin.[73]

A 30 March 1942 report from Army Group North to OKH summarized the grizzly end of 1st and 204th Airborne Brigades. It read:

> During the period 21–29.3 the 204th Soviet Airlanding and the 1st Parachute Brigades, which had penetrated into the rear of the 123d and 12th Infantry Divisions, in bitter fighting with the brave troops of the front and rear services lost approximately 1,500 dead, over 70 prisoners, 73 machine guns, 18 grenade launchers, 174 machine pistols, 210 automatic weapons, 30 antitank rifles, countless other weapons, over 300 skis, and six radio sets. Over 500 wounded are supposedly still in the forest.[74]

German intelligence duly noted the destruction of the bulk of the three Soviet airborne brigades in their order of battle books and recorded new units into which their remnants were reorganized. According to these sources, by late April 1st and 2d Airborne Brigades became the 5th and 6th Separate Rifle Brigades, respectively.[75] At the same time, the re-formed 204th Airborne Brigade was detected in the Gridino region.

CONCLUSIONS

Within the larger context, Kurochkin's operations to gnaw away at the inner infrastructure of the Demiansk pocket and, by doing so, cause its collapse, utterly failed. German II Army Corps retained its coherence and parried Soviet blows from without and from within.

On the morning of 21 March, when the last of 1st Airborne Corps paratroopers completed their crossing of German lines and were assembling around Maloe Opuevo, German Operation 'Brueckenschlag' commenced. General von Seydlitz's five divisions moved slowly eastward from Staraia Russa to close the gap between Sixteenth Army and encircled II Army Corps. The painfully slow advance was complicated after 23 March, when the temperature rose above freezing and the water of the spring thaw began replacing the winter ice. The same mud and slush which had hampered airborne force operations during the last week of March brought the German relief thrust to a standstill. Resuming the advance on 4 April after a halt for regrouping, it would take almost a month for Sixteenth Army to reestablish a tenuous link with its II Army Corps. By that time the actions of 1st Airborne Corps brigades were only a memory.

At Demiansk, the Soviet command attempted to circumvent the problem that had plagued earlier airborne drops by inserting a force on the ground and supporting it by air. Initially, the Northwestern Front was able to push a sizeable force deep into the Demiansk pocket. Yet the preliminary drop of one advanced parachute battalion to prepare camps and airstrips was detected by the alert German forces, and the Soviets thereafter were deprived of the element of surprise. After 1st Airborne had advanced via Pustynia to Maloe Opuevo essentially unscathed, follow-on brigades were subject to unrelenting air and artillery bombardment, which inflicted heavy casualties and damaged unit cohesion. Despite all the difficulties, by 22 March a sizeable Soviet force was within striking distance of the German Demiansk airfields. Then poor Soviet radio security again alerted German forces to the threat as they intercepted messages ordering the subsequent Soviet advance, messages confirmed by documents taken off Soviet casualties. From this point on, the bravery of the parachutists was irrelevant. Their effort was doomed to defeat and they to destruction.

The Soviet *front* mustered a prodigious aerial resupply effort of food, ammunition, equipment, and, on occasion, reinforcements (such as the doctor of 204th Brigade, who flew in with a small force on about 23 March). Documented flights into Maloe Opuevo airstrips included at a minimum:

12–16 March – Nightly drops of equipment by TB-3 transports;
20–24 March – Drops of supplies and occasional aircraft landings;
25 March – 10 aircraft landed at Maloe Opuevo (3 TB-3, 7 U-2);
28–29 March – Evacuation of wounded from Maloe Opuevo and Gladkoe airstrips.

Despite this resupply effort, much of the supplies were lost, captured, or otherwise unavailable to the troops. After 23 March the spring thaw made resupply even more difficult. Only a fraction of the 500-plus wounded ultimately assembled near Maloe Opuevo were evacuated by air (even the wounded Tarasov remained with his forces until his capture).

Prisoner of war interrogations revealed chronic hunger among the parachutists, who had advanced into the pocket with only three days' provisions. A prisoner from 2d Battalion, 204th Airborne, captured on 19 March, reported he had eaten little for five days. Another 204th Brigade trooper, captured on 21 March, reported no reprovisioning for ten days. A prisoner of 4th Battalion, 1st Airborne Brigade, captured on 27 March, said food supplies ran out on 17 March. Another group of seven prisoners of 1st Airborne, captured on 28 March, confirmed no food had arrived to the units since 19 March.

Airborne losses were even more appalling. 1st Airborne Brigade began the operation with about 3,000 men. It lost 200 men from bombing and artillery strikes in the advance to Maloe Opuevo and suffered several hundred more casualties seizing Maloe Opuevo. By the time it reached Staroe Tarasovo, it could field less than 2,000 men, having lost 500 men alone in the assaults on Dobrosli. After the engagement at Tarasovo, only 800 men assembled at Marker 80.1 (3d Battalion alone with 86 men and 100 wounded). Many of the remainder split off in virtually suicidal attempts to rejoin the Soviet front on their own.

204th Airborne Brigade fared even worse. Of its original 2,000 men, it suffered up to 30 per cent casualties in the advance to Maloe Opuevo. By 19 March 1st Battalion strength had fallen from 600 men to only 90, and 3d Battalion to about 270. By 25 March the brigade mustered 500 men for the attack on Igoshevo and lost over 200 in that battle. Between 21–29 March, the Germans counted 1,500 dead paratroopers (of about 2,600). Additional casualties in the brigades prior to their last attempt to break out in early April claimed several hundred more lives. The two brigades probably brought out no more than 400 of their original 5,000 men.

2d Airborne Brigade probably fared little better. 2d Battalion strength fell from 680 initially to 120 men after the Lychkovo battle on 24 March. Its other battalions apparently suffered equally. 2d Brigade probably brought about 500 men out of the German rear area. The relative success of 2d Airborne was attested to by the fact that it continued to appear on German situation maps in the Lychkovo sector long after its last troops had crossed from the German rear.

Kurochkin's gambit was a magnificent attempt to succeed where others had failed with the use of the extraordinarily trained and motivated airborne force. That the operation was also a magnificent failure indicated the inherent weakness of these forces. They lacked the firepower and staying power of conventional ground forces, however well they were led. The Demiansk case was all the more depressing, for, in the future, no Soviet historians or military theorists recorded or as much as mentioned the sacrifice of the 7,000-plus paratroopers.

CHAPTER 8

Across the Dnepr
(September 1943)

STRATEGIC CONTEXT

The Soviets conducted their last major operational level airborne assault in September 1943 during the general Soviet advance to the Dnepr River. After repulsing the last major German offensive of the war, at Kursk in July 1943, Soviet forces launched a strategic counteroffensive in mid-July and August. The counteroffensive ultimately developed into the summer–fall campaign, which engulfed the Eastern Front in flame from the Smolensk region to the Black Sea coast. Operation Kutuzov, launched in mid-July against German forces in the Orel salient, by mid-August had reduced that strategic salient. The second offensive, Operation Rumiantsev, which commenced in early August against German forces defending Belgorod and Khar'kov, smashed German Fourth Panzer Army and Operational Group Kempf, and severely mauled critical German mobile operational reserves.[1] By late August, the Soviets had captured Khar'kov. In early September the Soviet Central Front pierced German defenses north of Sumy and plunged deep into the German rear toward Chernigov, precipitating a German decision to withdraw to the Dnepr River line. There the Germans hoped to erect an impenetrable 'Eastern Wall.'

Although as yet largely unfortified, the Dnepr River posed a significant physical obstacle to further Soviet advances. The German command believed that it could establish a stable defensive line along this formidable water obstacle. On the other hand, Soviet planners strove to secure quickly strategic or operational bridgeheads over the Dnepr River before the Germans could restore a stable defense along the front. In particular, the *Stavka* sought to seize a strategic bridgehead in the vicinity of Kiev, out of which it could conduct major new offensive operations deep into the Ukraine.

During the second half of September, the Soviet Central Front advanced westward toward the river on a general axis from Chernigov to the Dnepr north of Kiev (see Figure 72). Soon, as the Germans withdrew slowly from the Poltava region, *Stavka* resubordinated Central Front's 3d

Guards Tank Army to General N. F. Vatutin's Voronezh Front and ordered the tank army to lead the drive toward the Dnepr River. Lieutenant General P. S. Rybalko's tank army lunged in head-long fashion at the Dnepr River in the sector extending from Kiev to south of Cherkassy. To counter the accelerated Soviet advance, German Army Group South frantically sought to conduct an orderly withdrawal to the Dnepr River in what, by the last two weeks of September, had become a race to the bank of the Dnepr.

OPERATIONAL PLANNING

Confronted by weakening German resistance and spurred on by *Stavka* orders, on 19 September General Vatutin ordered his Voronezh Front to accelerate its advance. His order read:

> To the commanders, 3d Guards Tank Army, 38th Army, and 40th Army. The enemy, while withdrawing, tries to burn all the bread [crops]. Conditions demand maximum offensive tempo. I order:
> 1. Comrade Rybalko [3d Guards Tank Army] move with care at a speed of 100 kilometers per day to the Pereiaslavl area by means of your best mobile units and tanks, to arrive not later than 22-9-43.
> 2. Commanders of 40th and 38th Armies, speed the tempo of the offensive, first of all with mobile forces, to arrive at the Dnepr River also on 22-9-43.
> 3. Report measures undertaken
>
> Vatutin.[2]

The Voronezh Front's mobile group [*podvizhnyi grupp*], 3d Guards Tank Army with 1st Guards Cavalry Corps attached, raced forward, with four corps abreast, across a front of seventy kilometers. Corps' forward detachments, advancing far in advance of their parent corps, reached the Dnepr River on the night of 21–22 September. The next day, these detachments secured small and fragile bridgeheads across the Dnepr at Rzhishchev and Velikyi Bukrin.[3] The same day lead elements of adjacent Soviet 40th Army reached the river and also secured a small bridgehead.[4] All of these bridgeheads were secured by infantry forces, which had crossed the river on makeshift rafts or by swimming. Once lodged on the far bank, they ferried across light artillery and antitank weapons, but were unable to reinforce the bridgeheads with heavy artillery, tanks, or self-propelled guns. The survival of these bridgeheads depended on protective artillery fire delivered from the northern bank of the river. Until larger bridgeheads had formed and heavy weaponry could cross the river, infantry on the south bank of the river had to stay within range of

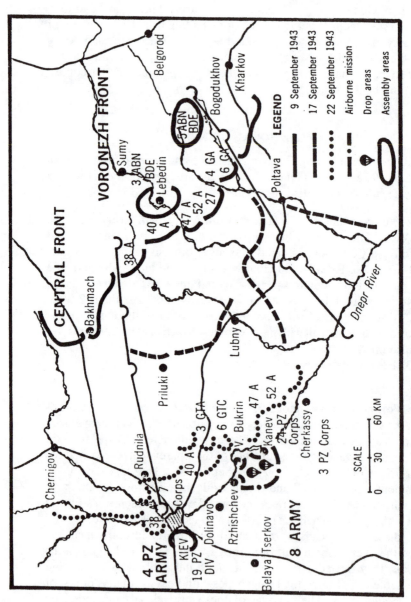

72. Voronezh Front Advance to the Dnepr River

Soviet artillery. Ensuing heavy German air attacks and the Soviets' inability to move tanks across the river (due to shortage of bridging equipment) subjected the fragile bridgeheads to potential destruction by German counterattacks. At this critical juncture, the *Stavka* decided to use an airborne assault to increase the size of the bridgehead near Velikyi Bukrin (see Figure 73).

The Soviet High Command had already anticipated the need to employ airborne forces in Dnepr River crossing operations. During August and September, the *Stavka* ordered Major General A. G. Kapitkochin, commander of airborne forces, to train airborne forces intensively for use in such missions in the near future. The 3d Guards Airborne Brigade conducted training exercises near Moscow; and the 1st, 5th, and other guards airborne brigades underwent similar training.[5] As the Soviet offensive continued to develop favorably, the *Stavka*, in early September, detached the 1st, 3d, and 5th Guards Airborne Brigades from the Airborne Administration and assigned them to the Voronezh Front commander to use in the event an airborne operation was required. To ensure unity of command, *Stavka* appointed Major General I. I. Zatevakhin, deputy commander of airborne forces, to command the new 'provisional' airborne corps and provided him with staff officers from the Airborne Administration. The new 10,000-man corps consisted of Colonel P. I. Krasovsky's 1st Guards Airborne Brigade, Colonel P. A. Goncharov's 3d Guards Airborne Brigade, and Lieutenant Colonel P. M. Sidorchuk's 5th Guards Airborne Brigade.[6]

The airborne forces commander and the long-range aviation commander jointly prepared contingency plans for an airborne operation (see Figure 74). By 16 September, airborne force headquarters had developed detailed plans for objectives, force composition and unit missions, requisite phasing of preparations, and the conduct of each phase of the operation. The airborne forces' commander was responsible for preparing the overall plan and all stages until the actual loading of the force onto aircraft. The aviation commander was then responsible for the plan's in-flight phase. Vatutin, Voronezh Front commander, exercised control of the operation after landing. To facilitate joint planning, the airborne force staff deployed an operational group to Lebedin airfield northwest of Khar'kov, where it worked with an aviation operational group, and the 2d Air Army command post, which supported the Voronezh Front. The new airborne corps staff joined the operational groups at Lebedin; but, as the time for the operation neared, the operational groups moved nearer to the front lines at 40th Army's command post.

On 23 September the communications network linking all units and headquarters involved in the operation became operational. The airborne force operational group established communications with

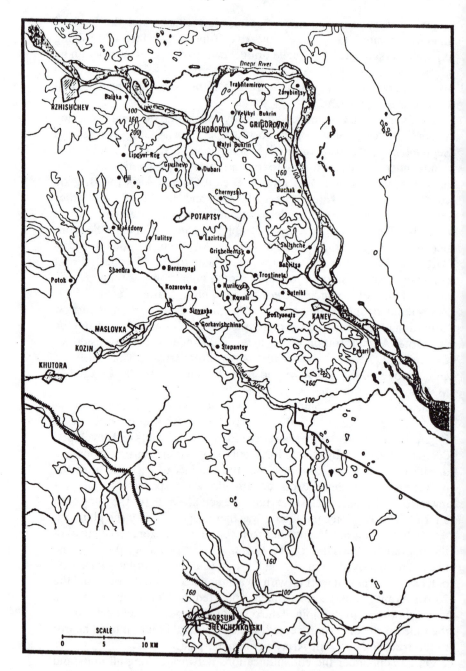

73. Rzhishchev–Kanev Area of Operations

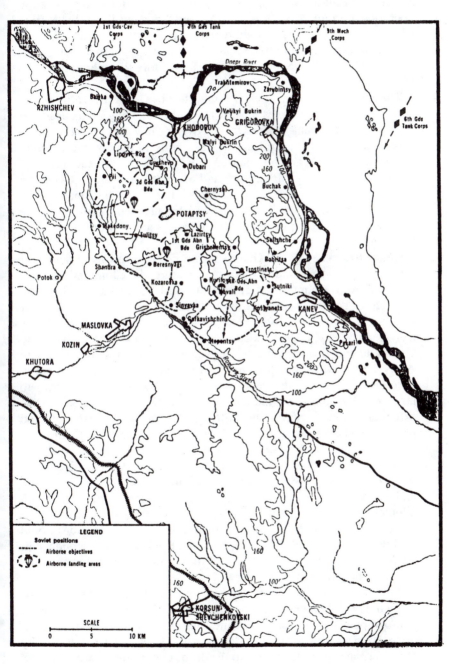

74. Dnepr Airborne Operational Plan, 20 September 1943

Voronezh Front headquarters, 40th Army, and the long-range aviation operational group, as well as with 2d Air Army and the airfields from which the airborne corps would depart. Concentration of the airborne corps and its equipment at these airfields was supposed to be completed on the night of 23–24 September, two days before the operation was to commence.

The airborne corps' mission, as established by General Vatutin, was to cooperate with *front* forces in securing and reinforcing bridgeheads on the right (south) bank of the Dnepr River near Velikyi Bukrin and to expand and fortify the bridgehead sufficiently to deploy into it forces sufficient to conduct another major offensive.[7] Specifically, the corps was to seize Lipovyi Rog, Makedony, and Stepantsy and prevent German counterattacks from penetrating to the south bank of the Dnepr in the sector from Kanev to Traktomirov. The planned corps defensive perimeter embraced a depth of 30 kilometers and a width of 15 to 20 kilometers.

Colonel Krasovsky's 1st Guards Airborne Brigade was to land near Lazurtsy, Beresniagi, and Grishentsy to capture Makedony and Siniavka and to prevent enemy counterattacks toward Kurilovka and Bobritsa. Colonel Goncharov's 3d Guards Airborne Brigade was to land near Grushevo, Makedony, and Tulitsy to secure a defensive line running from Lipovyi Rog to Makedony, and to prevent a German advance to Chernyshi and Buchak. The 3d Brigade would hold the line until 40th Army units had moved forward from Traktomirov and Zarubentsy. Lieutenant Colonel Sidorchuk's 5th Guards Airborne Brigade was to land near Trostinets, Kovali, and Kostianets to secure a defensive line extending from Gorkavshchina through Stepantsy to Kostianets and prevent an enemy advance to the Dnepr from the south and southwest.[8]

The landing, which would be conducted over a period of two nights, would require 50 PS-84, 150 IL-4 and B-25 aircraft, 10 towed gliders, and 35 A-7 and G-11 gliders. Aircraft would lift the force from Smorodino and Bogodukhov airfields near Lebedin, a distance of from 175 to 220 kilometers from the drop sites. Each aircraft would have to make two to three sorties a night.[9] The 1st and 5th Guards Airborne brigades would land the first night, and 3d Guards Airborne Brigade on the second night. Gliders carrying artillery would land during the intervals between the drops of the parachute echelons.

Aircraft equipped with cameras were to conduct continuous reconnaissance over the drop area for three days before the operations to provide photographic support and other information on enemy troop dispositions. *Front* aviation forces would then strike German targets detected by reconnaissance in and adjacent to the drop zone. Bombers would follow to attack the area immediately prior to the paratroopers' assault.

Immediately after the parachute drop and at first light, *front* assault and bomber aviation aircraft were to provide close air support as directed by the airborne corps commander. Communications units dropped into the landing area would provide for close coordination between air and land forces. In addition, artillery observers were to accompany the force to ensure timely artillery support, and a squadron of artillery adjustment (spotting) aircraft would help control and shift artillery fires. Thirty-five aircraft (25 LI-2, 10 PO-2) were dispatched to carry supplies to the airborne force and evacuate casualties on return trips from the bridgehead. The paratroopers were to carry with them into the drop zones two days' rations and two or three basic loads of ammunition.[10] Finally, the Voronezh Front commander provided 100 vehicles for movement of men and materiel to the departure airfield.

The actual landings were to occur in several phases. First, small detachments were to parachute into the region to clear landing sites and establish contact with local partisan units. The brigades would follow, landing according to a schedule [air assault table] worked out jointly by the corps staff and the military transport aviation staff. Radio communications would link the brigades to the corps and the Voronezh Front command post. Two radio channels were reserved for communications between the Voronezh Front and airborne corps and four between *front* and the brigades. The Voronezh Front's auxiliary command post and the 40th Army command post also had stations in the communications net. Elaborate communications security measures included a strict regime of radio silence observed during the preparatory phase and false call signs for airborne units designating them as so-called replacement units in order to mask their true identity.[11]

On 19 September Marshal G. K. Zhukov, *Stavka* representative who coordinated the strategic advance, approved the plan. He stressed that the missions of the Voronezh Front and the airborne corps had to match one another right up to the time of actual landing. Zhukov ordered Vatutin to update continuously all subsequent brigade missions.[12]

Meanwhile, the pace of the Soviet counteroffensive had quickened; and, on 21–22 September, lead ground elements reached and crossed the Dnepr River near Rzhishchev and Velikyi Bukrin. Then, a series of unforeseen events disrupted the carefully laid plans for conducting the airborne assault. Airborne forces were unable to concentrate at the airfields in the required two-day period because of insufficient railroad cars to transport the corps. Furthermore, the railroad tracks were in disrepair, so the requisite supplies and equipment for the forces did not arrive on time. In addition, bad weather prevented military transport aviation from assembling the necessary aircraft at the proper airfields. Only eight planes had arrived at the airfields by the appointed time.[13]

Consequently, General Vatutin, who arrived at 40th Army headquarters late in the morning of 23 September, altered the airborne mission and issued amended orders (see Figure 75). He delayed the drop by one day, to the night of 24–25 September, and, instead of committing three brigades over two nights, he decided to dispatch the two brigades that could fully complete their movement to departure airfields. Vatutin ordered the 3d Guards Airborne Brigade to jump southeast of Rzhishchev near Tulitsy, Beresniagi, Lazurtsy, and Potaptsy. The 3d Brigade would secure a defensive line from Kipovyi Rog through Makedony and Siniavka to Kozarovka and hold it until the approach of 40th Army, while blocking German movement from the west and southwest. The 5th Guards Airborne Brigade was to land west of Kanev near Kovali, Kostianets, and Trostinets; secure positions extending from Gorkovshchina through Stepantsy to Sutniki; and hold those positions until Soviet ground forces had advanced from Buchak, Selishche, and Kanev to link up with them. The 5th Brigade was also tasked with blocking a German advance from the south and southwest.[14] The 1st Guards Airborne Brigade was initially designated as reserve, scheduled to join the other brigades on the second or third night of the operation, as soon as the brigade could fully concentrate at the departure airfields.

The delay in the operation and the last-minute changes in plans caused near chaos in command channels. The airborne command and airborne landing forces received the changes on 23 September at 40th Army headquarters. The commander of airborne forces and the corps commander needed the entire day to clarify missions, evaluate the situation, and make decisions in response to the alterations. Orders to subordinate units went out on 24 September. Brigade commanders, in turn, studied the changes, made their decisions, and issued their orders a mere one and one-half hours before the troops loaded onto the aircraft. This ripple effect resulting from changed orders most seriously affected battalion and company commanders and their men. Company commanders had only 15 minutes before takeoff to brief their subordinates. Platoon leaders passed the information to their men during the flight to the drop zone. As a consequence:

> the lateness in mission assignment to units and subunits of the landing force deprived the commanders of the opportunity to clarify problems of coordination within the landing force and with other combat arms, to check on how subordinates understood the mission, and to map out a battle plan after landing in the enemy rear.
> Preflight drills were not conducted with personnel or officers,

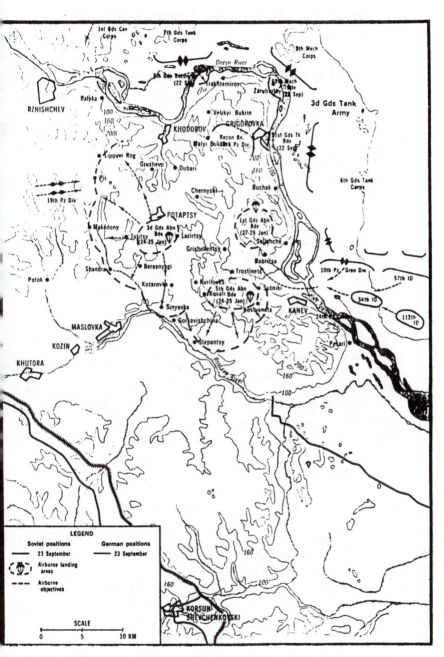

75. Revised Dnepr Airborne Operational Plan, 23 September 1943

either on maps or on mock-ups of the terrain, in connection with the forthcoming mission.[15]

This shortage of time forced brigade and battalion commanders to limit their briefings to basic information about drop zones, assembly areas, objectives, and defensive zones. Nor did they have time to address questions of supplying the troops with adequate weaponry. On the assumption that *front* units would quickly relieve the paratrooper force, parachute units lacked both shovels to dig entrenchments and antitank mines with which to establish an effective defense. Troops did not even carry ponchos for protection against the autumn night frosts.[16]

Moreover, Soviet commanders had virtually no intelligence on enemy dispositions in their drop area. Bad weather had prevented aerial reconnaissance and aerial photography, but commanders operated on the assumption that German forces were weak, as indeed they had been up to a week before the operation. Unknown to the Soviets, however, the situation was dramatically changing. In essence, a race to the Dnepr River in the Rzhishchev–Kanev area was in progress. What was at stake was the possiblility that the Soviets could seize a major foothold on the south bank. Before 22 September there had been virtually no German troops defending the south bank in this critical sector. The Fourth Panzer Army was withdrawing to and across the Dnepr River at Kiev. The Eighth Army, responsible for defense of the Dnepr River from south of Kiev to south of Cherkassy, still had the bulk of its forces on the river's north bank. XXIV Panzer Corps (34th, 57th, 112th Infantry, and 10th Motorized Divisions) was supposed to anchor Eighth Army's left flank. But until the XXIV Panzer Corps could disengage from heavy fighting with advancing Soviet forces on the north bank of the Dnepr, a large gap would continue to exist in the German Dnepr defenses north of Kanev.[17]

It was this gap that lead elements of Soviet 3d Guards Tank Army approached. When small groups of Soviet troops crossed the river on the morning of 22 September, few German troops were on the south bank. That day, 120 noncommissioned officer candidates from the flak combat school at Cherkassy and the reconnaissance battalion of 19th Panzer Division manned scattered picket defenses along the river. The remainder of 19th Panzer Division was still crossing the Dnepr 60 kilometers to the north at Kiev. On the evening of 21 September Eighth Army ordered XXIV Panzer Corps to move its most mobile elements across the river and secure the undefended sector. XXIV Panzer Corps began disengaging from combat on 22 September and moved its lead elements to the river's south bank at 1500 on 23 September, just as Soviet infantrymen, who had crossed the river at Zarubentsy and Grigorovka, attacked and pierced the thin German defensive screen.

The same afternoon, Fourth Panzer Army, fearing for its open right flank, sent an urgent message to Eighth Army to hasten reinforcement of the German defenses in the Bukrin bend of the Dnepr River. Eighth Army responded, and, at 2010 on 23 September, it ordered the main body of 19th Panzer Division and the truck-mounted 72d Infantry Division to reinforce 19th Panzer Division's hard-pressed reconnaissance battalion in the Dnepr bend. But that reinforcement would take precious time. The best hope for successful reinforcement still lay with the XXIV Panzer Corps, which, by the evening of 23 September, had succeeded in moving the bulk of its forces across the Dnepr further south at Kanev. By 2115 23 September, 57th Infantry Division had crossed the Dnepr and was occupying positions east and west of Kanev. Its sister 112th Infantry Division was in the process of crossing the river to reinforce German units in the threatened Dnepr bend. The 34th Infantry and 10th Motorized Divisions crossed later in the evening. The former deployed adjacent to XXIV Panzer Corps' left flank, west of Rzhishchev and the latter to positions just east of Rzhishchev. By 0500 24 September, movement of the entire panzer corps across the river had been completed, so the Germans demolished the bridge at Kanev. Motorized elements of all XXIV Panzer Corps divisions had moved to their new defensive sections, and the foot-bound divisional main bodies would do so during the day. Completing the German defensive picture, 19th Panzer Division continued its movement southward from Kiev toward the threatened Dnepr River bend.[18]

German redeployments occurred just in time to contain Soviet forces in the Dnepr bend. By noon on 24 September, Soviet ground troops had secured Traktomirov, Zarubentsy, and Grigorovka, but they lacked the strength to push farther south to unite those bridgeheads into a more formidable lodgment. By late afternoon on 24 September, the German 57th and 112th Infantry Divisions had arrived in their defensive positions, and 19th Panzer and 10th Motorized Divisions were en route to their new positions – positions that, unfortunately for the Soviets, traversed the precise regions where Soviet airborne forces would land. All this movement occurred unknown to Soviet intelligence.

DNEPR ASSAULT

Throughout 24 September, men of the airborne brigades, supplies, and supporting aircraft slowly assembled at the departure airfields. Despite the one-day delay, the full complement of aircraft never did arrive on time. By the time 5th Guards Airborne Brigade had assembled, for instance, only 48 of the required 65 LI-2 aircraft had arrived; bad weather had halted the remainder. In addition, for safety reasons, aircraft commanders insisted on loading 15 to 18 units (men and cargo) instead of the planned 20 on each aircraft.[19] Because these changes disrupted planning calculations, commanders reallocated men and cargo just before takeoff, which resulted in a significant quantity of supplies left sitting on the runway.

Landing preparations were also careless. Many battalion and brigade commanders did not carry radio crews with them, but Colonel Goncharov had the entire command group of 3d Guards Airborne Brigade with him on his plane. The same bad weather that contributed to general ignorance concerning enemy dispositions also prevented planned advanced marking of drop zones with bonfires and colored squares.

At 1830 on 24 September, 3d Guards Airborne Brigade began departing the airfields. Although lead elements of 5th Brigade were to take off two hours later, the schedule immediately went awry (see Figure 76). The capacity of fuel trucks supporting the aircraft was less than expected, so the support organs could not fuel the planned number of aircraft on time. The first wave of aircraft, due to takeoff ten minutes before the second wave, could not complete its launch on time. Subsequently, as soon as each aircraft had received a full load of fuel, it took off. Thus all waves ultimately took off intermingled with one another. Refueling of subsequent waves was equally confused, and often airborne troops shifted from one plane to another in search of an earlier departing flight. Fuel shortages naturally developed. Because of the fuel shortage, 5th Brigade operations from Bogodukhov had to be halted at 0100 on 25 September, although all the men had not yet been lifted into action.[20]

Nevertheless, a total of 298 sorties (instead of the planned 500) departed the airfields and dropped 4,575 paratroopers (3,050 from 3d Brigade and 1,525 from 5th Brigade) and 660 light parachute bags with ammunition and supplies. However, 2,017 men, or 30 per cent of the planned drop, most of them from 5th Brigade, were left behind at the airfields. By first light on 25 September the drop of 3d Brigade from aircraft flying from Lebedin airfield was complete. Unfortunately, aircraft flying from Smogodino airfield carrying 3d Brigade's 45-mm antitank guns were not ready on time due to bad weather and thus failed to join the flight.[21]

Just as had occurred in the Viaz'ma operation, inaccurate drop techniques scattered the airborne forces far and wide. One aircraft dropped its men into the Dnepr River, and another plane-load fell into friendly positions on the near side. Two aircraft dropped their men in what turned out to be an even safer area deep in the enemy rear. Indicative of the

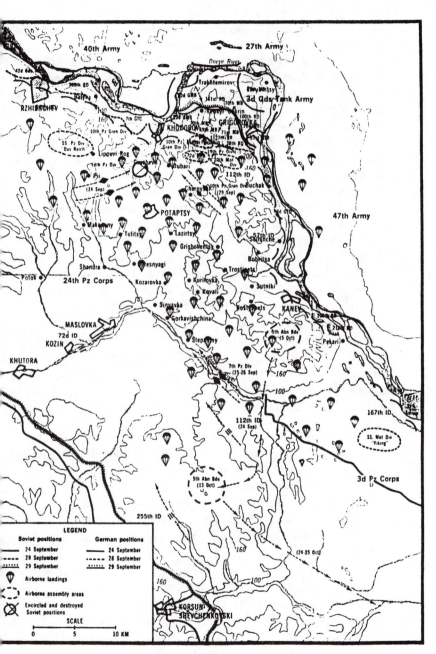

76. Dnepr Airborne Operation, 24 September–13 October 1943

turmoil, 13 aircraft simply returned without dropping their men, which further complicated the already confused flight schedule.[22]

The aircraft flying over the intended drop zone ran into dense hostile antiaircraft fire. The pilots' subsequent evasive action did not improve the accuracy of the drop. Most paratroopers jumped from aircraft flying 200 kilometers an hour at altitudes of from 600 to 2,000 meters and taking evasive action to avoid the antiaircraft fire. But even greater shocks awaited the paratroopers. Instead of landing in the planned, relatively compact 10-by-14-kilometer area, they found themselves scattered over the 30-by-90-kilometer area. The area was also infested with German defensive positions.[23] In short, from the very beginning, the airborne assault was a disaster.

The amazement of German troops on the ground, viewing the armada of aircraft spewing forth long strings of paratroopers, was surpassed only by the horror of Soviet paratroopers quickly aware of what awaited them. Lead Soviet airborne forces jumped into the Dubari-Grushevo area 'just as the first troops of the main body of the 19th Panzer Division reached this locality by way of Pii and Potaptsy. As a result, the parachutists and their transport planes immediately came under accurate defensive fire. The approaching aircraft were dispersed while the parachutists, who had in the meantime jumped, were scattered on the ground.'[24] German accounts describe the reaction of German troops as the paratroopers descended onto their positions. Some Germans fired small arms and machine guns at the paratroopers as they descended, while others turned their heavier weapons on the falling host of parachutes. Col. E. Binder of 19th Panzer Division recorded a vivid picture of the events.

> The 19th Panzer Reconnaissance Battalion was fighting west of Zarubentsy. The armored personnel carrier battalion of the 73d Panzer Grenadier Regiment, with elements of the division staff of the 19th Panzer Division, was advancing by way of Pii–Potaptsy–Dudari[Dubari]–Kolesishche; it was followed by the main body of the 73d Panzer Grenadier Regiment, and the 74th Panzer Grenadier Regiment. Behind these forces came the rest of the division, including the 19th Panzer Regiment. After the Germans had reached Dudari [Dubari], the first Russian parachutists jumped from a transport plane flying at an altitude of 600 to 700 meters directly above the little village. While these parachutists were still in the air they were taken under fire by machine guns and a 20-mm four-barreled flak gun. A half minute or a minute later, the second plane came over and thereafter, at like intervals, other planes

followed, flying in single file; only seldom did two craft fly side by side.

The parachutists were fired on while they were still in the air with all available weapons, including rifles and the flak guns which had in the meantime been set up. As a result the fourteenth or fifteenth plane turned off in a northerly direction and dropped its parachutists in the area of Romashki. These parachutists were immediately taken under fire by men of the supply trains, repair teams, and maintenance sections of the 19th Panzer Reconnaissance Battalion.

The jumps, which continued for one to one and a half hours, steadily became more irregular, one of the reasons being the swift German counteraction and another the signal lights going aloft on all sides. The parachutists were dropped without any plan. Wherever they landed they were immediately attacked. Those who could took cover in the numerous clefts in the ground.

With the parachutists split up in small groups, the fate of the undertaking was sealed. During the night great numbers of prisoners were brought in. The rest of the parachutists were destroyed the next day.[25]

Throughout the night, German troops, using the white parachutes as beacons, hunted down and killed disorganized groups of Soviet paratroopers. The backdrop of bonfires, glowing embers, and German and Soviet flares illuminated the bizarre and macabre battle.

As they fell to earth, individual paratroopers fired on German positions, returning the deadly fire directed at them. On the ground the troops frantically attempted to reassemble to survive in the midst of the enemy. The dispersed landing of the paratroopers and the darkness itself offered some succor to the attackers, but only partial compensation for the huge initial losses they suffered. Between Dubari and Rossava, the Germans counted 1,500 parachutes in the first 24 hours, as well as 692 Soviet dead and 209 prisoners. Near Grushevo, the 3d Company, 73d Panzer Grenadier Regiment, suffered heavy losses while annihilating an estimated 150 Soviet paratroopers in what was really a microcosm of the bigger battle.[26] Well into daylight on 25 September, fragmented skirmishes raged as small groups of Soviet paratroopers waged unequal struggles with German forces. Succinctly put, 'a series of fatal mistakes during preparation and during the landing placed the airborne troops in a very difficult position in the first hours after landing. All attempts of subunit commanders to gather their subordinates and establish command and control in the course of the night had no success.'[27]

To survive, paratroopers from different units formed *ad hoc* groups. All hopes of accomplishing the brigade's primary missions faded. The landing problems forced higher headquarters to postpone indefinitely further drops of the 1st and 5th Airborne Brigades.

5TH GUARDS AIRBORNE BRIGADE OPERATIONS

After the disastrous landing, the scattered parachute units and soldiers first sought to survive and then to inflict whatever damage they could on the Germans. As units struggled frantically to assemble, serious communications problems compounded the effects of German resistance. Radios and radiomen had been widely scattered during the drop. Only five of 26 radios were operative; the remainder had been either destroyed or buried by their operators to keep them from German hands.

Lieutenant Colonel Sidorchuk was the first to establish contact with Soviet forces on the left bank of the Dnepr. He passed a message in the clear to friendly forces.[28] Airborne force headquarters and Voronezh Front headquarters sent additional radios across the river to establish communications. Three groups of men with radios dropped on the night of 27–28 September, but nothing more was heard of them. The next night a PO-2 aircraft sent out with radios was shot down.[29] Not until 6 October did the *front* finally manage to establish even sporadic radio communications with elements of the landing force.

Surviving paratroopers reassembled slowly. Planned assembly areas were obviously too dangerous, so each man or knot of men had to improvise. On 25 September, the Germans systematically began to scour the countryside with mobile detachments of various sizes. German records indicate no great concern over the airborne drops. Soviet airborne forces were too fragmented and had sustained such heavy casualties that they posed no real tactical threat to German defenses. While the almost casual cleanup of airborne remnants progressed, the Germans focused their attention on the dangerous bridgeheads to their front. On the right flank of XXIV Panzer Corps, SS Motorized Division 'Viking' of the III Panzer Corps cleaned up airborne forces dropped south and southwest of Pekari. Meanwhile, Army Group South dispatched reinforcements to XXIV Panzer Corps to assist in containing and reducing the Soviet bridgeheads. On the morning of 25 September, 20th Panzer Division was ordered forward to reinforce XXIV Panzer Corps. The 72d Infantry Division also continued its march forward. The XXIV Panzer Corps postponed an attack on the Bukrin bridgeheads planned for 26 September and, instead, scheduled the attack for 28 September, by which time the reinforcements would have arrived. By then, 7th Panzer Division would also be available.

The planned attack finally occurred on 29 September; and, although it did not eliminate the bridgeheads, it did truncate them and remove the threat of a future major Soviet breakout in the region. While the Germans prepared to deal with the bridgeheads, they paid only scant attention to the airborne force. By 2100 on 26 September, the Germans considered action against the parachutists to have been completed. By then, only remnants of the airborne force still resisted in the forests south of Kanev, north of Buchak, and south of Dubari.[30]

For the Soviets, the task now was to salvage whatever benefits they could from the abortive drop. From 25 September to 5 October in the area between Rzhishchev and Cherkassy, 43 separate Soviet groups assembled, totaling 2,300 men of the 3d and 5th Brigades' original 4,575-man landing force.[31] Many others had been killed or captured, while others managed to join with the nine partisan groups operating in the vicinity. A small group of 230 men who had survived drops into the Dnepr or behind Soviet lines rejoined main *front* forces.

Initially, the largest groups of assembled paratroopers gathered in three regions: 600 in the Kanev and Cherkassy forests; 200 around Chernyshi; and four groups totaling 300 near Iablonovo.[32] These groups conducted diversionary attacks against German targets of opportunity. Much of their time, however, was spent searching for equipment, ammunition, and supplies dropped into the region. Without these items, they could not operate. Because German patrols had gathered and destroyed the scattered Soviet supplies, ammunition shortages quickly limited the effectiveness of these units. Still, a few small groups experienced a modicum of success. On the night of 29–30 September, a group of 150 men under Senior Lieutenant S. Petrosian successfully attacked a German police headquarters in Potok village and later ambushed a German artillery column south of the village. Petrosian's detachment made its way south through Maslovka to Kanev where, on 5 October, it joined a larger group commanded by the 5th Guards Airborne Brigade commander, Lieutenant Colonel Sidorchuk.[33]

By early October surviving Soviet airborne groups were in the northern area from Rzhishchev to Kanev and farther south from Kanev to Cherkassy. In the north, where the terrain was relatively open and the Germans had extensive defensive positions, more than 1,000 paratroopers were forced to operate in small bands to escape detection. Consequently, their operations had limited effectiveness. In the south, however, the terrain was rough and heavily forested, and the sparsely populated region had few German defenses. Here, growing concentrations of paratrooper groups harassed the Germans for more than a month. Organized in at least five large detachments, more than 1,200 men operated in this region.

Typical of the chaotic action after the disastrous air drop was the case of Major A. Bluvshtein, assistant commander (commissar) of 2d Battalion,

3d Guards Airborne Brigade.[34] After landing near hill 200.1 just north-west of Tulitsy, he gathered a group of nine paratroopers and, at the appointed assembly time (1800 hours), reached the designated battalion assembly point, a grove of trees codenamed 'Chapli.' When his commander and most of the battalion's men failed to arrive, he decided to assemble what men he could and operate independently. For the next several days, Bluvshtein's group moved south almost 100 kilometers, dodging German patrols and increasing in size to almost a full battalion as other scattered bands of paratroopers joined him.

After finally establishing radio control with 5th Guards Airborne Brigade in early October, Bluvshtein received orders to attack a German reserve battalion garrisoned in Bovany just north of the Kanev Forest. His attack on the night of 8–9 October scattered the garrison and produced a cache of documents, weapons, ammunition, and other supplies. German counterattacks immediately recaptured the town and, by the evening of 11 October, also threatened Bluvshtein's sanctuary in the Kanev Forest. At 2200 11 October, leaving a small force to cover its withdrawal, Bluvshtein's 2d Battalion withdrew southwestward to the Tagancha Forest, where it linked up with a larger parachute force under the 5th Airborne Brigade commander, Lieutenant Colonel P. M. Sidorchuk.

Meanwhile, 3d Guards Airborne Brigade chief of staff, Major V. F. Fofanov, experienced a similar hegira.[35] Landing west of Rzhishchev, by evening 25 September, he had assembled 29 men, established a defensive perimeter, and sent out reconnaissance patrols. The following evening, after receiving reports of German activity from his reconnaissance, he attacked and destroyed a small German outpost in Medvedovka. Failing to establish communications with his brigade or other units, on 28 September he moved his detachment to the Veselaia Dubrava region, where his brigade was originally supposed to create a defensive perimeter. After several engagements with enemy patrols, at nightfall on 28 September, Fofanov's force reached the designated assembly area, where, like Bluvshtein before him, he spent two days assembling other small groups of paratroopers around his band. Still unable to locate the bulk of the brigade, his force attacked small German outposts at Tulitsy and Shandra, destroying one German tank, three vehicles, and killing several Germans.

Fofanov's force then headed south, arriving on 1 October in the forests just northeast of Potashnia, striking a series of German outposts as they marched. Near Maslovka they engaged a battalion of German infantry and at night had to fight their way out of impending encirclement. On 21 October Fofanov's detachment finally joined Sidorchuk's larger force in the Tagancha Forests.

The largest and most effective of the groups of paratroopers who survived the drop was the 600-man force commanded by Lieutenant Colonel Sidorchuk, which had come together by 5 October in the Kanev Forest. Unlike other groups, Sidorchuk's unit had sufficient manpower and equipment to organize an effective fighting force. Sidorchuk organized his force into a brigade with three rifle battalions and sapper, antitank, reconnaissance, and communications platoons. On 6 October, by a stroke of luck, a radio crew joined the brigade and established communications with 40th Army headquarters and, through it, *front* headquarters.[36] From 8 to 11 October, *front* delivered supplies and ammunition to the brigade in the Kanev area. After concerted German attempts to smash Sidorchuk's brigade, the force, with authorization of the *front* commander, moved southward on 19 October into the more remote and, hence, more secure Tagancha Forest. There it joined other scattered groups, totaling about 300 men, operating under Senior Lieutenant E. G. Tkachev, Major Bluvshtein, Major Fofanov, and others. This combined force of more than 1,000 men under 5th Airborne Brigade control established defensive positions in the forest and conducted forays and raids against small German garrisons and supply points near the periphery of the area.

The first successful Soviet attack occurred on 22 October when Sidorchuk's unit blew up the rail line between Korsun' and Tagancha Station, destroying a train in the process. That evening his force assaulted the village of Buda-Vorobievska, scattering the staff of the German 157th Reserve Battalion and burning warehouses in nearby Potashnia. The attacks, however, did not go unanswered. The next day, heavy German attacks on Sidorchuk's forest position took a heavy toll. Consequently, the brigade withdrew under cover of darkness southward through Baibuz into the Cherkassy Forest northeast of Bol'shoe Starosel'e. By then, the brigade had picked up additional personnel and numbered about 1,700 men, despite earlier losses. Sidorchuk added one more battalion to his force and armed it with weapons dropped by *front* aircraft.[37]

The 5th Guards Airborne Brigade established a defensive base in the Cherkassy Forest and raided German installations and communications routes in the region from 28 October to 11 November. Aside from conducting diversionary raids, the unit also passed intelligence information to the 2d Ukrainian Front (by messenger), in whose sector it operated. Throughout its operations the brigade was able to establish only intermittent communications with 52d Army, which was preparing to cross the Dnepr River in the Cherkassy sector.[38] On 11 November 1943, 40 days after landing in the German rear, the paratroopers received orders to participate in a new operation intended to achieve what the

September operation had failed to achieve, namely, the advance of Soviet main forces across the Dnepr (see Figure 77).

A *Stavka* directive of 5 November 1943 ordered 2d Ukrainian Front to 'strongly fortify occupied positions and attack with the forces of 37th, 57th, and 5th Guards Tank Armies in the general direction of ... and secure Krivoi Rog.'[39] The attack was to take place on 12–14 November in concert with an advance by 3d Ukrainian Front. While the bulk of Marshal I. S. Konev's 2d Ukrainian Front struck toward Krivoi Rog, 52d Army, on the *front's* right flank, was to force the Dnepr River north of Cherkasssy, secure a bridgehead, and thereafter seize Cherkassy.

52d Army's attack order No. 0021 of 11 November 1943 required its

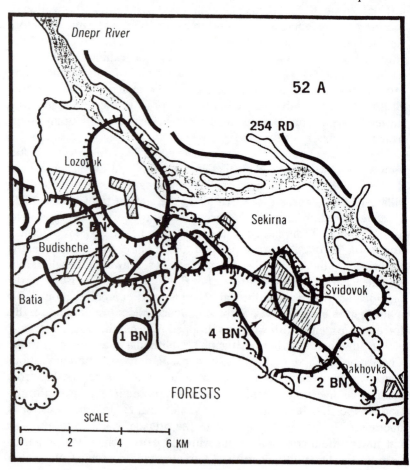

77.   5th Guards Airborne Brigade Operations, November 1943

73d Rifle Corps to make the army main attack in the eight kilometer-wide Elizavetovka–Svidovok sector to force the Dnepr River and create a bridgehead on its south bank. The 73d Rifle Corps

> must, with the forces of 254th Rifle Division, strike a blow in the direction of Svidovok and Russkaia Poliana with the immediate mission of forcing the Dnepr River north of Svidovok on the night of 13 November. In cooperation with the air assault group and partisan detachments, secure a bridgehead around Elizavetovka, Budishche, and Svidovok and, while firmly securing the attacking group's right flank, secure Russkaia Polianaia.'[40]

Subsequently, the force was to assault and seize Cherkassy. Thus, the airborne force was to play a distinct and important role in the operation.

52d Army ordered Sidorchuk's brigade to attack and capture the villages of Lozovok, Sekirna, and Svidovok, on the left bank of the Dnepr River, thereby assisting the river crossing by 52d Army units. The attack was scheduled for 12–13 November. On the morning of 12 November, a 52d Army liaison officer flew to Sidorchuk's headquarters to coordinate army missions, order of attack, and the mission the brigade was to perform.[41] The 5th Guards Airborne Brigade's attack would coincide with an attack by the 254th Rifle Division from across the Dnepr River. The 254th Rifle Division commander's mission was as follows:

> The 929th Rifle Regiment had to force the Dnepr River at crossing point No. 1 west of Sekirna and secure a bridgehead in the Elizavetovka, Sekirna region. Subsequently, the regiment was to seize Budishche, while protecting the main force of the division from Moshny in the west. The 933d Rifle Regiment received the mission to force the Dnepr north of Svidovok (crossing point No. 2) and secure Svidovok. The 936th Rifle Regiment was in division second echelon. It was designated for use in securing Russkaia Polianaia.[42]

Division operations were closely coordinated with those of Lieutenant Colonel Sidorchuk's airborne brigade and partisans. This was a difficult task, for reliable and constant communications between these forces was not established until the morning of 12 November, only hours before the attack. At that time, the air assault force received orders to attack and seize strongpoints in Svidovok and Elizavetovka. The attack was to begin at 2400 12 November, simultaneously with the commencement of the river crossing by 254th Rifle Division's first echelon battalions. To provide for closer coordination, 52d Army staff dispatched a representative with a radio set and signals recognition table to Sidorchuk's headquarters in the forests south of Svidovok.[43]

The Germans in Lozovok had one infantry battalion with engineer units. At the nearby village of Elizavetovka were two companies from the 266th Infantry Regiment, 72d Infantry Division, while an infantry battalion and five tanks defended Svidovok. Sidorchuk assigned 1st Battalion to take Sekirna by surprise, while the 3d Battalion would attack Lozovok. The 2d Battalion had the difficult job of reducing the Svidovok strongpoint. In reserve, 4th Battalion would assist the 2d Battalion. Two attached partisan detachments would occupy Budishche, halt German movement from Moshny to Lozovok, and assist 3d Battalion should the need arise. All of the night attacks would occur simultaneously.[44]

At 0100 on 13 November, brigade units in attack positions waited for Sidorchuk's signal to move through the darkness to attack. Major Bluvshtein's 2d Battalion (4th, 5th, and 6th Companies) faced a German battalion entrenched in several strongpoints, but lacking anchored flanks. The five German tanks at Svidovok posed a considerable problem for the lightly armed paratroopers.

Bluvshtein's plan of attack took maximum advantage of surprise and darknesss. Advancing without artillery preparations, two assault groups would tie down the defenders and, if possible, secure the strongpoints on the south fringe of Svidovok. Following the assault groups, two rifle companies would attack along the main street and, in coordination with units operating on the left, overcome the strongpoints in the town center. One company would advance on the town from the east toward the church in the town center. While the three companies drove into Svidovok, one squad with machine pistols would deploy on the southeast side of the town to cover any German relief from Dakhnovka. After the battalion had secured the town and emerged on the northeast side, two companies were to secure islands in the Dnepr, while the third company blocked enemy approach routes from Dakhnovka. Major Bluvshtein established a small reserve of a platoon armed with automatic weapons, one machine pistol, and an antitank rifle.

At 0400 the assault groups attacked, employing hand grenades and small-arms fire.[45] Hard on the heels of the assault groups, the 4th and 5th Companies, followed by the reserve, moved down the darkened streets toward the center of town and secured the nearest strongpoints before the surprised German garrison could react. From the east, the 6th Company attacked German outposts on hill 73.8, but heavy German automatic fire halted their attack. Approaching the center of town, the 4th and 5th Companies ran into machine gun and tank fire that stopped their advance. The 6th Company, unable either to take or to envelop hill 73.8, retreated under intense German fire.

The 4th Battalion, itself facing heavy enemy fire on 2d Battalion's left, detached one platoon to cover its advance. The remainder of the battalion entered Svidovok from the west to envelop German strongpoints in the center of town. Bluvshtein maneuvered his reserves to the east to attack the strongpoints from the right flank. An automatic weapons platoon attacked the strongpoints frontally, using the houses for cover; and the antitank riflemen engaged the five tanks, destroying one.

For the final push, a company of 4th Battalion joined the 4th and 5th Companies and the automatic weapons platoon in overcoming German resistance. Having lost two more tanks in the battle, the Germans withdrew to northeast of the town where they joined the force which, in the meantime, had retreated from hill 73.8. Meanwhile, other Soviet units took Lozovok and Sekirna and established defenses along the Ol'shanka and Dnepr Rivers.

Despite its success, 2d Battalion now faced a bigger threat. A German relief battalion with seven tanks rushed down the road from Dakhnovka, broke through 2d Battalion's covering force, and attacked Svidovok from the flank and rear. Unfortunately for Bluvshtein and Sidorchuk, the 254th Rifle Division of the 2d Ukrainian Front was unable to mount its attack across the Dnepr on the night of 12–13 November. German forces attacking from south and east then ejected the 2d and 4th Battalions from their newly won prize. To avoid German encirclement in Svidovok, the two battalions withdrew into the forests southwest of the town. It was a fitting denouement for the frustrating, tragic operation.

To close the tale of the 5th Airborne Brigade, on the night of 13–14 November, advanced elements of 254th Rifle Division captured a foothold on the south bank of the Dnepr. A company of 933d Rifle Regiment finally linked up with Sidorchuk's forces in the afternoon of 13 November northwest of Svidovok. Official Soviet accounts recorded:

> The air assault group, operating together with the partisan detachments, by day's end [14 November] again occupied Budishche, and part of its force fought for Svidovok. Part of the air assault and partisan forces fought in the forests northwest of Svidovok, with the mission of cooperating with the 929th Regiment in the seizure of Sekirna, whose garrison consisted of up to a regiment of infantry, 20 tanks and up to two artillery battalions....
>
> In the course of the first half of 15 November, the enemy undertook continuous attempts to drive the 254th Rifle Division from Svidovok, but our forces firmly held on to the village.[46]

By 15 November, that division, followed by 52d Army, had cleared the river towns and linked up with 5th Guards Airborne Brigade. After 13 more days of combat, 5th Brigade was evacuated to the rear. It had endured two months of harrowing combat under the most adverse conditions. Lieutenant Colonel Sidorchuk, commander of 5th Guards

Airborne Brigade; Major Bluvshtein; and others received the title 'Hero of the Soviet Union' for their feats, not the least of which was simple survival. More than 60 per cent of the force never returned.[47] Other survivors received mention in orders and medals, small consolation for the thousands who had perished in the poorly coordinated operation.

CONCLUSIONS

It is understandable that the Dnepr operation was the last major airborne operation Soviet forces conducted. Even compared with the Viaz'ma and Demiansk ordeals of 1942, the Dnepr operation is a classic case of how not to conduct an airborne operation. As in the earlier cases, the men of the parachute units were not at fault, for they were victims of circumstances, the worst of which were higher command planning failures of major proportions. As a result, a major drop, which could have had strategic significance, utterly failed.

Stavka staff officer and future chief of the General Staff, S. M. Shtemenko, remarked on the operation, but only addressed the most basic failure: 'The launching of a massive airborne assault at night time bears witness to the ignorance of the organizers of the affair, since experience indicates that the launching of a massive night assault, even on one's own territory, was associated with major difficulties.'[48]

The choice of a night operation, however, was deliberate, and those who made the decision were well aware of the risks that a night drop entailed. The Viaz'ma experience with such drops was available. Beyond that, planning deficiencies for the Dnepr operation would have condemned even a daytime drop to abject failure. A Soviet critique of the operation surfaced the basic requirements for any successful airborne operation:

> Experience has affirmed that the conduct of airborne operations demands from commanders and staff a high degree of foresight, an ability to define optimum missions and timing for the landing, sober assessment of combat capabilities of forces designated for the operation, and sharp agreement [coordination] on their actions.[49]

On all of these counts, the Dnepr operation was a distinct failure. German critiques echoed this assessment:

> The Russian command lacked the necessary sensitivity for the timing, the area, and the feasibility, as well as a correct evaluation of the German forces in the organization of the joint operation. The whole action carries the stamp of dilettantism. Fundamentally the

reasoning was sound, but apparently an expert was lacking to implement the plans. The operation was accordingly a failure.[50]

In their haste to cross the Dnepr River, the Soviets committed the airborne corps without adequate preparation time.[51] Personnel and aircraft were hastily gathered and poorly coordinated. Responsible headquarters planners did not provide proper equipment and support. They committed the corps into an area where intelligence data on the enemy was virtually lacking, thus feeding the unit to waiting German guns. In his 19 September review of plans, Zhukov warned planners to proceed with prudence. They did not, and the operation failed. In the words of one Soviet critic, 'In this regard, the commander of the Airborne Forces deserved a reprimand because he did not draw the appropriate conclusions from the experience of 4th Airborne Corps, which had landed [at Viaz'ma] in the winter of 1942.'[52]

German critics pointed out that both the timing and the location of the airborne drop were ill-advised. An operation conducted against the key Dnepr River bridge at Kanev even as late as 23 September could have resulted in the destruction or Soviet possession of the bridge, the isolation of XXIV Panzer Corps on the north bank of the river, and a possible major Soviet bridgehead over the river.[53] The Germans, however, praised the capability of individual airborne unit officers and soldiers:

> There were individual cases...where tenacious and fanatic resistance was put up by the Russian soldier. The officers did try to reach the rendezvous according to the sketches captured by the Germans. [However,] captured sketches of the enemy rendezvous areas facilitated the German measures. Whenever Russians were encountered, the German officers took the pertinent measures without needing to consult their superiors.
>
> This explains why there was no long drawn out fighting in the rear of the corps.[54]

Amid the chaos of battle, the Germans did underestimate the strength of the Soviet forces and, hence, the damage inflicted on the Soviet force. According to German records,

> of the 1,500 parachutists counted ... in the area west of the Dnepr line and west of Cherkassy–Rzhishchev it is safe to say the total strength was at least 1,500 to 2,000 men, since it is certain that a considerable number of parachutes were never found or were not seen from the air. During the first two days about two-thirds of the minumum strength had been put out of action.[55]

In fact, more than 4,500 Soviet parachutists had dropped into the region.

Even the Viaz'ma operation had achieved certain tactical and diversionary results. The Viaz'ma force survived insertion into the German rear and conducted operations for about four months, while tying up precious German troops. Not so on the Dnepr; the Dnepr force was spent within a matter of hours of takeoff, and all hope of tactical gain was lost. The few diversionary operations carried out by Sidorchuk's command and the host of other tiny groups scarcely justified the tragic losses the airborne corps endured.

German assessments credited the Soviet airborne drop with having only an extremely limited impact. Thus, 'because of the lack of German forces, this area [Kanev region] could never quite be cleared of enemy forces. As a result, it constituted a latent threat to German rear communications and occasionally had unpleasant effects.'[56]

The final irony, symbolic of the wasted efforts of the paratroopers, was that in early 1944, when Soviet armies had crossed the Dnepr at virtually every point and pushed deep into the German rear, the only portion of the river still in German hands was that area around Kanev, the September 1943 objective of the airborne corps.

The Dnepr operation was the last example of Soviet operational use of airborne forces. The experiences at Viaz'ma, Demiansk, and on the Dnepr revealed the weaknesses of airborne forces: dependence on weather conditions, great vulnerability, technical deficiencies, and fragile support systems. 'In large airborne operations, serious mistakes occurred that reduced the effectiveness of the airborne force. That created in the High Command a hesitation to believe in the use of such airborne forces.'[57] For the remainder of the war, major airborne units, whose men had proven their courage and endurance, would serve in a role that the Soviet army was more accustomed and better trained to play, namely, infantry conducting ground operations. Only once would the *Stavka* again consider use of a large airborne force, around Polotsk in June 1944.

CHAPTER 9

To War's End

INTRODUCTION

Soviet experiences with the combat employment of airborne forces at Viaz'ma, Demiansk, and along the Dnepr River had a sobering effect on the High Command's view of the utility of parachute troops. While it was clear that VDV forces were perhaps the best motivated and most highly trained soldiers in the Red Army, it was equally clear that their employment by parachute was equivalent to their sacrifice, if not outright slaughter. By 1944 the prerequisites for their successful use were well established, at least in theory. First, it would be beneficial if they were employed only where a viable and competent military force was already operating. Only then could they survive the critical period of assembly and reorganization on the ground. Second, some means had to be found to provide for their self defense against better-equipped enemy forces. This meant adequate heavy equipment had to be inserted with them, and, if they operated in isolation, a steady supply of this equipment had to be assured. Third, it was imperative that they operate within range of *frontal* ground forces, so that link up could be effected in a reasonable period of time.

If these preconditions for success were clear, they were also difficult to insure. In all previous operations, planning staffs well understood the necessity to meet these prerequisites. Still, they had not been met, and the airborne force suffered the inevitable negative consequences. This legacy of limited success or outright failure produced caution on the part of the High Command and *front* headquarters, which had airborne forces at their disposal. Henceforth, while the bulk of airborne forces operated in a ground role, the Soviet High Command held the nucleus of an airborne force under its tight control in case an eventuality arose suited to its use. The High Command and *fronts* continued intense use of these forces in a diversionary role, but only seldom contemplated their employment in an operational or tactical role. The first of these even rarer cases occurred in late 1943, after the failure along the Dnepr, when the Soviet High Command planned to employ a sizeable airborne force to help smash German defenses in the Vitebsk sector.

THE POLOTSK OPERATION, NOVEMBER 1943

With the Kursk and Smolensk strategic operations at an end and the Russian Republic largely free of German forces, in September and October 1943, the *Stavka* made plans to commence the liberation of Belorussia and the Ukraine. Although it placed greatest strategic priority on the latter, it planned for operations into Belorussia as well.

In early October the *Stavka* developed a detailed plan to overcome German defenses across the central sector of the Eastern Front from Vitebsk to Gomel' (see Figure 78). From the north the Kalinin and Baltic Fronts were to cooperate in an offensive along the Vitebsk axis to envelop German Army Group Center from the north. Meanwhile, the Soviet Western and Central Fronts would strike from the east and south against Mogilov and Bobruisk respectively.

The Kalinin Front commenced its offensive on 2 October, when its 3d and 4th Shock Armies struck by surprise in the Nevel' sector (see Figure 79).[1] Five days later, on 7 October Soviet forces stormed and seized Nevel', creating a sizeable salient in the German defenses and new opportunities for offensive action.

> The liberation of Nevel' completed the destruction of the triangle of German defences based on the strong center of resistance Novosokol'niki, Velikie Luiki, and Nevel', which served as an original shield, covering the main Dno–Novosokol'niki–Nevel' rail line. This railroad linked German Army Groups North and Center and provided the Hitlerite command free maneuver of forces along the entire left wing of the Soviet–German front. Now before the Kalinin Front opened a path from the north to Vitebsk and also Polotsk – the larger rail center, across which enemy 3d Panzer and 4th Armies were supplied.[2]

Moreover, seizure of Polotsk and Vitebsk would open the way for a Soviet advance into the Baltic region and possibly for subsequent isolation of Army Group North. The German command faced the prospect of a Soviet advance on Polotsk, 'where they could enter into the large Polotsk–Lepel' partisan region and, together with the Rossonsk and Lepel' partisans create a threat to the rear of Army Groups North and Center.'[3] In a message to the High Command, German Major General Heidkamper wrote:

> The Third Panzer Army command considers that from the Nevel' salient, having established communications with large partisan regions of Lepel and Rossony, the enemy can begin to develop a winter operation, the consequences of which for Army Groups

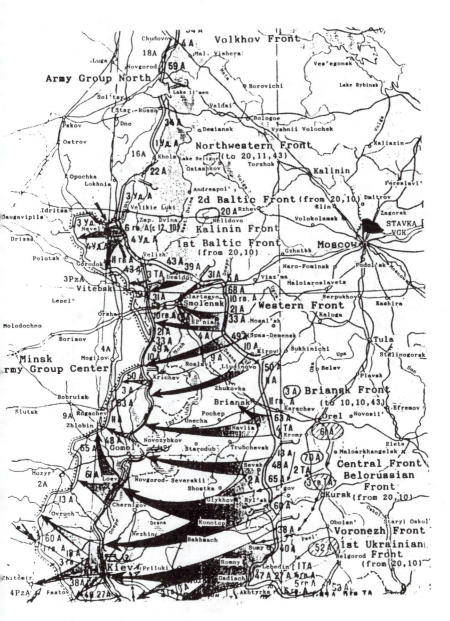

78. Operations in the Vitebsk–Gomel' Sector through October 1943

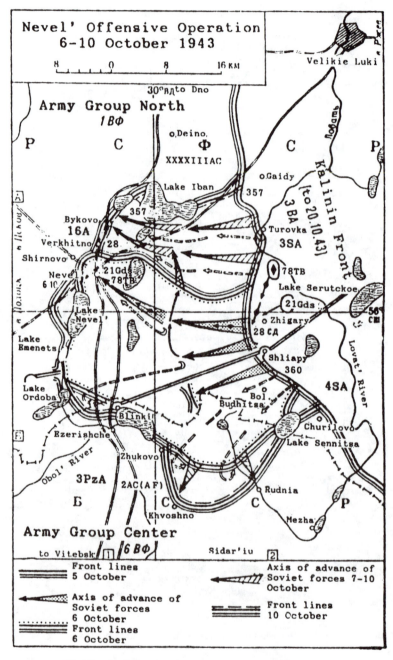

79. Nevel' Offensive Operation, 6–10 October 1943

North and Center cannot even be supposed and which can have decisive importance for the entire Eastern Front.[4]

After completion of the Nevel' operation, the *Stavka* showed its appreciation for the opportunities offered by an even larger offensive by directing a further advance from the Nevel' salient by the newly renamed 1st and 2d Baltic Fronts (on 20 October the Baltic Front was renamed 2d Baltic, the Kalinin Front became 1st Baltic, and the Central Front became the Belorussian Front).

On 28–29 October, the 1st and 2d Baltic Fronts, egged on by the *Stavka*, approved plans for the further advance. 2d Baltic Front's 3d Shock Army was to drive westward from Nevel' in early November to cut the Nevel'–Polotsk rail line, penetrate deep, and envelop German forces defending west of Nevel' from the south and west. 1st Baltic Front's 4th Shock Army was to penetrate westward and then southwestward along the rail line through Dretun' toward Polotsk on the Northern Dvina River. According to General K. N. Galitsky, commander of 11th Guards Army, 'The arrival of 3d and 4th Shock Army units in the Pustoshka and Dretun' regions and their link up with partisan detachments seriously worried the German-Fascist command.'[5]

The operation began in early November, assisted mightily by unusually warm and dry weather, which kept the forest roads dry and trafficable. By 10 November Soviet forces had reached the outskirts of Pustoshka and Dretun', and, if the good weather held, there was every prospect for further success.

At this juncture, the *Stavka* released an airborne corps to 1st Baltic Front to facilitate further development of the operation. As recorded in Soviet accounts:

> With the aim of accelerating the destruction of the enemy Vitebsk-Gorodok group, in November 1943 the 1st Baltic Front command, together with the air force and airborne commands and the staff of the Belorussian partisan movement, worked out an operational plan to encircle and destroy enemy forces in the Polotsk region. By the combined action of an airborne corps, partisan brigades, and 4th Shock Army forces, it planned to encircle the enemy and, having secured Polotsk, to prevent the approaches from the west and southwest of enemy reserves to Vitebsk and thus isolate the Vitebsk-Gorodok enemy grouping.[6]

The plan called for the landing of a composite airborne corps in the Begoml'–Ushiachi partisan regions and its cooperation with over 19,000 partisans operating in the area (see Figures 80 and 81). The guards airborne corps consisted of three guards airborne brigades (1st, 2d, and 11th Guards Airborne Brigades), based around Moscow and numbering

11,681 men, 92 guns, and 192 mortars.[7] The partisan region covered an area of 60 kilometers from east to west and 15–20 kilometers from north to south, south and southwest of Polotsk, and the region was relatively free of German troops. The airborne assault was to be both by parachute drop and aircraft landing into six designated landing zones.

After the airborne assault and the commencement of 4th Shock Army's offensive toward Polotsk, the airborne corps' three brigades would deploy with partisan detachments and attack Polotsk from the south. The 2d and 11th Guards Airborne Brigades and partisans were to attack Polotsk from the southeast and west, while partisan forces secured bridges and crossing sites over the Western Dvina River and, with airborne support, covered the flanks and rear of the airborne corps. The actual air assault was to take place over the course of three nights. On the first night, the 4th Battalion, 2d Guards Airborne Brigade, and special brigade subunits were to parachute into the region southwest of Novosel'e to assist partisans in preparing subsequent landing sites. On the second and third nights, the 11th Guards Airborne Brigade and 1st Guards Airborne Brigade were to parachute into landing areas west and south of Starniki. Subsequently, heavy equipment and supplies were to be landed by aircraft at several preplanned airstrips.

An elaborate signal system was emplaced and employed by partisan forces to control the night airborne drop and landing. Light signals designated landing sites, and, to prevent interference by the Germans, 'stop' and 'go' designations were used each night in each landing region. Partisans were to encircle completely and defend each parachute landing and assembly area. All aspects of partisan support were thoroughly worked out in advance. Two specially trained partisan commands were formed to unload aircraft, one to handle damaged aircraft, and one to light necessary signal bonfires and torches.

The Belorussian partisan staff participated in all stages of planning, and key figures flew between the front and rear to coordinate fully all planned measures. The final plans were also approved by the Central Staff of the Partisan Movement in a formal 'Plan of Cooperation of Partisan Formations Operating in the Northern Regions of Belorussia with Airborne Forces of the Red Army.'[8]

The partisan brigades of the Begoml'-Ushiachi region had the responsibility for securing the region and the specific airborne drop zones, landing sites, and airborne assembly areas. They were also required to operate along the periphery of the partisan-occupied region to block the approach of German forces, gather intelligence, and disrupt enemy communications. Once the airborne operation had begun, an operational group formed from representatives of the Central Partisan Staff and the Belorussian Partisan Staff would deploy into the region, equipped with

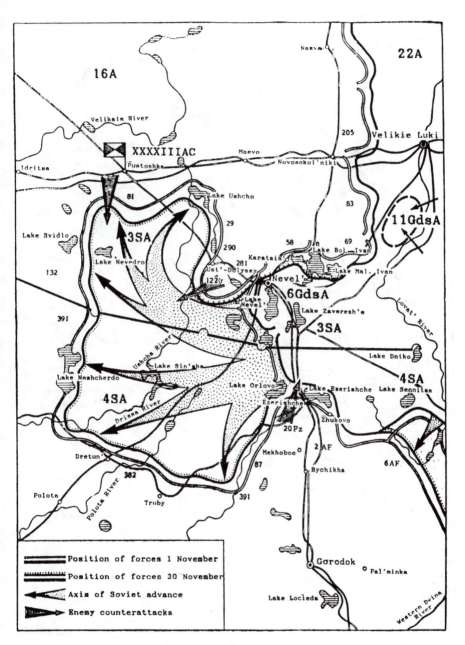

80. Situation, 10 November 1943

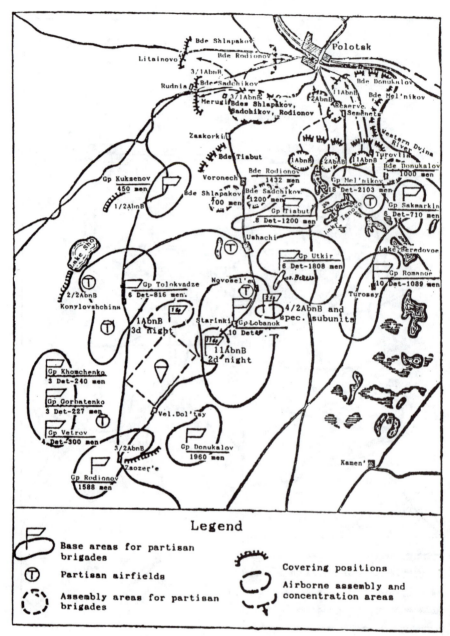

81. Begoml'–Ushiachi Operational Plan, November 1943

requisite communications equipment to coordinate partisan brigade operations.

Individual partisan brigades received specific redeployment orders, missions to conduct reconnaissance and diversionary operations and security mission involving the establishment of picket lines around airborne landing and assembly sites. Finally, the brigades developed plans to resist any last-minute attempt by the Germans to penetrate and occupy the partisan region. Each brigade prepared its own set of plans, coordinated it with adjacent brigades, and sent it to the partisan staff operational group for approval. The operational group had overall responsibility for organizing cooperation among the brigades and between partisan and airborne forces.

The subsequent ground operation to secure Polotsk required that the following tasks be accomplished in sequence:

– movement of partisan brigades to designated regions;
– covering of the landing of airborne forces;
– disruption of enemy railroad resupply;
– preparation and deployment of diversionary and reconnaissance elements to Polotsk;
– receipt and distribution among the brigades of supplies from the 'big land' [the Soviet rear area];
– preparation of diversionary groups and assault detachments to launch repeated attacks on rail lines on the night of the main attack on Polotsk.[9]

Partisan forces were also tasked to provide materiel and individual support to the airborne forces, including:

– 800 horses and 350 sleighs;
– guides from partisan forces or local inhabitants on the basis of one per airborne platoon;
– unarmed partisan manpower to replace losses in airborne units;
– work groups from partisans or local inhabitants to repair roads and airborne force advance routes;
– food for airborne forces.[10]

Finally, each partisan brigade received a specific combat mission to perform alongside airborne forces during the final assault on Polotsk.

As the time of the assault neared, adjacent partisan units intensified operations in coordination with 4th Shock Army's continued advance.

The Rossonsk 'Stalin' Partisan Brigade, operating near Polotsk, destroyed 17 German railroad trains. Partisans north of Vitebsk secured river crossing sites, bridgeheads, strongpoints, and liberated several villages. At the same time, partisan brigades sent out reconnaissance parties, which met the forward elements of 4th Shock Army's 219th Rifle Division near Dudchino.[11]

After 10 November 4th Shock Army forces occupied Trudy, southeast of Dretun', and drove south through the forests toward the Polotsk–Vitebsk rail line and the Western Dvina River just beyond. At this critical juncture, when the final order for the airborne operation was about to be given, the weather sharply worsened. Galitsky recalled, 'Beginning from 15 November, the weather, having been favorable in the first days of the month, deteriorated – torrential rains began and a thaw struck. The supply of food and, more importantly, ammunition practically ceased.'[12] In essence, all movement ground to a halt, and the airborne operation was cancelled.

Galitsky reminisced in his memoirs about the lost opportunity:

> The most favorable conditions [for the above]...occurred in the first half of October, immediately after the successful conclusion of the Nevel' operation, when it was apparently possible for the reinforced 3d and 4th Shock Armies to widen the penetration to the northwest to Idritsa or to the southwest in the Polotsk direction.[13]

By trying to do both, the Soviet advance slowed. Then, after 15 November, all hopes of reaching Polotsk were dashed by the rainy weather and thaw. The well-prepared and potentially spectacular airborne operation was cancelled, and it would be another eight months before Polotsk finally fell to Soviet forces. According to one Soviet source, however, the planning experiences from November 1943 'were utilized in the future, in particular during the movement of 2d Czechoslovakian Parachute-Assault Brigade to the area of the Slovak popular uprising in September 1944.'[14]

THE SLOVAK OPERATION, SEPTEMBER 1944

The last large-scale Soviet planned and ordered airborne operation occurred in September 1944 within the context of Soviet support for the Slovak uprising (see Figure 82). In August 1944 elements of the Slovak National Council and army, supported by the Soviet government, launched an uprising against the Slovakian government and its formal ally, Germany. Soviet support for the Slovak partisans had begun earlier, on 26 July, when a group of 11 Soviet-trained partisans parachuted into Slovakia to set up base areas.[15] Over the ensuing month, Soviet aircraft dropped more partisans, supplies, arms, and ammunition in operations coordinated by the Ukrainian Partisan Staff. The 25 August national uprising was led by three Slovak Army colonels, who had conducted

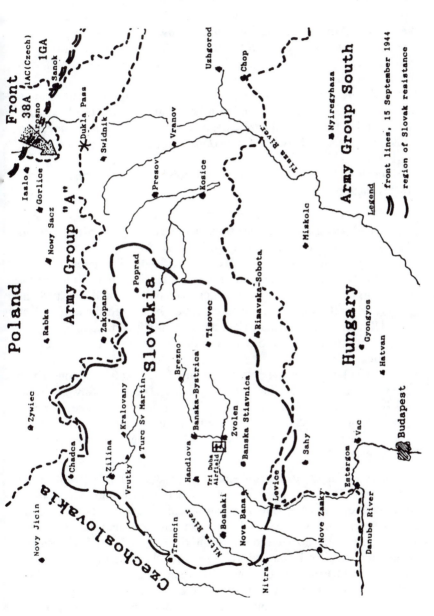

82. Slovak Uprising Area of Operations, August–September 1944

complex negotiations for support from both the London-based Czech government-in-exile and the Soviet government. The initial uprising secured several key Slovak cities, particularly in eastern Slovakia. The key Slovak Army force was the Eastern Slovakian Army Corps of two divisions, which was, early in the revolt, designated to cooperate with Soviet forces then massed east of the Carpathian Mountains, poised for a future drive into Slovakia.

On 31 August the deputy corps commander, Colonel V. Talsky, and a delegation of Slovak officers landed at 1st Ukrainian Front headquarters. The next day Talsky met the *front* commander, Marshal I. S. Konev, who talked by phone with Stalin about cooperation of Soviet forces with the uprising.

Konev's written report summed up the points of cooperation and asked for instructions:

> Colonel Talsky has said that in the event of a Soviet westward drive, the Slovak 1st and 2nd divisions deployed on the border ... could advance eastward to link up with the Red Army.
>
> Our units in the area of Krosno are 30–40 kilometres from the Slovak border. Should you decide that we link up with the Slovak units and the partisan movement in Slovakia, it would be expedient to carry through a combined operation by the left flank of the 1st Ukrainian Front and the right flank of the 4th Ukrainian Front and enter the territory of Slovakia in the Stropkov–Medzilaborce sector.
>
> The 1st Ukrainian Front can commit four infantry divisions of the 38th Army and a Guards cavalry corps. The main blow could be delivered at Krosno, Dukla and Tyliava. It would be desirable to commit the Czechoslovak 1st Corps in this sector, too. The operation can be launched in seven days. Awaiting your orders on this question.[16]

Stalin responded by ordering Konev to organize an offensive to assist the Slovaks. The newly-created 4th Ukrainian Front would also organize an offensive, and commanders of all Soviet partisan units in Czechoslovakia were ordered to assist the Slovak uprising. Almost immediately, on 4 September, Soviet aircraft from the 4th and 5th Long-Range Aviation Divisions began delivering supplies and equipment to the insurgent-held airfield at Tri Duba. Between 5 and 17 September, they airlifted to the Slovaks 603 submachine guns, 329 machine guns, 174 antitank rifles, 1.3 million rounds of ammunition, and 1,096 kilograms of dynamite.[17]

1st Ukrainian Front's mission from the *Stavka* clearly reflected the intent to assist the Slovaks. It read:

Moscow 2 September 1944

In connection with the activation of the partisan movement in
Slovakia and the development of armed struggle of separate-
regular units and formations of the Slovak Army against the German usurpers, the *Stavka* orders:

1. Prepare and conduct an operation at the junction of the 1st and
    4th Ukrainian Fronts, and with a blow from the Krosno, Samok
    regions in the general direction of Pressov reach the Slovak
    border and unite with Slovak forces.
2. To conduct the operation [you are] allowed to enlist the
    Czechoslovakian Corps and use Slovak forces located northeast
    of Pressov, about which you must agree in timely fashion.

Antonov.[18]

The subsequent 1st Ukrainian Front and 38th Army orders issued on
4 and 8 September, respectively, laid out the plans of advance and
mandated use of Czech ground forces and cooperation with Slovak forces
in the Pressov region (see Figure 83). Konev's forces were to reach the
Slovak border in three days and secure Pressov in five.

German operations against the Slovak uprising in late August and early
September regained considerable territory and drove Slovak units into
eastern Slovakia. More important, on 1–2 September, the Germans
disarmed the two divisions of the Eastern Slovakian Corps, which had
been designated to seize the Dukla and Lupkow Passes and link up with
advancing Soviet forces. The Soviet offensive began nonetheless. To
reinforce the partisans, on 6–7 September Soviet aircraft delivered more
partisan units from Ukrainian bases, raising the number of Soviet forces
to 3,000 men. Another 600 men of V. J. Prokopyuk's Partisan Brigade
soon joined them.[19]

The Soviet ground offensive begun on 8 September quickly bogged
down by 10 September on the distant approaches to the Dukla Pass, as
the German High Command shifted forces to this sector from Poland
and Hungary. Now the Soviet command was faced with a race to
penetrate into Slovakia before the Germans had crushed the Slovak
uprising.

A major role in the ground fighting for the Dukla region was played by
Czech forces. The 1st Czech Corps of three brigades fought with 38th
Army, and two of its brigades soon spearheaded the main army thrust
toward the Dukla Pass. Its 2d (Parachute) Brigade cooperated with the
Soviet 242d Tank Brigade in fighting on 38th Army's left flank.[20] The
Czech Corps, commanded after 10 September by General A. Svoboda,
had evolved from the Separate Czech Battalion, which had been fighting

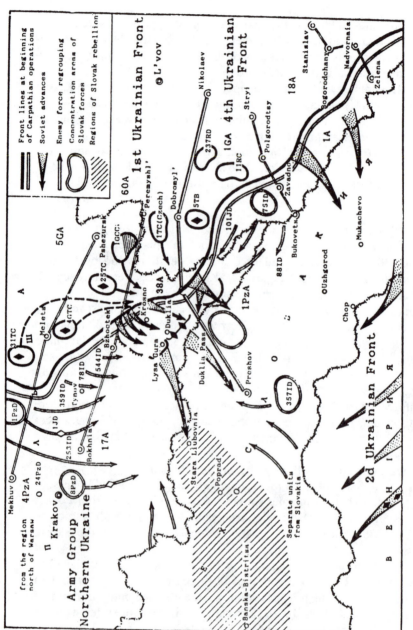

83. Dukla Operation, September 1944

as a part of the Soviet command since early 1943.[21] The 2d Brigade (Airborne) had been formed on 1 February 1944 at Efremov, near Tula, as the Separate Czechoslovak Airborne Brigade. The brigade consisted of headquarters, 4 parachute assault battalions, antitank, antiaircraft, artillery, and armored battalions, and reconnaissance, signal, and sapper companies, for a strength of 4,282 men.[22] It was made up of prisoners of Czech nationality, Czechs who had emigrated abroad earlier, and senior Czech officers who had managed to flee to the Soviet Union.

By 19 September the Czech airborne brigade and its supporting Soviet forces, fighting in a ground role, had seized a mountain pass near Roztoki and captured Pulavy on 38th Army's right flank. On orders of 38th Army, 4th Guards Tank Corps shifted westward through the pass to join 38th Army mobile forces, already struggling in vain to penetrate through Dukla Pass into Slovakia. By 20 September 4th Guards Tank Corps, with 1st Czech Army Corps, had seized the town of Dukla and was fighting for possession of the pass beyond.

At this juncture, the *Stavka* and Konev sought to reinforce the fading Slovak resistance movement, in hopes of easing 38th Army's advance. On 13 September the *Stavka* authorized release of 1st Czechoslovak Fighter Regiment to Slovakia via the Tri Duba airfield. These fighter planes (20 La-5s), together with supplies, ammunition, fuel, and radios, flew into Slovakia on 17 and 18 September. Also on 13 September, *Stavka* released 2d Czech Airborne Brigade and ordered 5th Long-Range Air Transport Corps to air-land the unit and its equipment in Tri Duba.[23]

The first airborne contingent, an advance party consisting of 12 paratroopers and two radio sets, parachuted into Tri Duba on 17 September. Ten days later, the first combat units landed. Thereafter, during the first week of October, 700 men of the brigade's main body arrived with 104 tons of equipment. These forces deployed immediately to the west and southwest in the Banska Stiavnica region. By 25 October Soviet transports had landed 1,855 men of the brigade, together with 360 tons of supplies, and had flown out 784 wounded partisans and soldiers.[24] These joined the three partisan divisions, six brigades, and 20 separate detachments, totalling 15,845 men fighting in Slovakia.[25]

The optimism generated by the arrival of Moskalenko's 38th Army at the Dukla Pass and the reinforcement of the Slovak uprising faded in mid-October. On 18 October German troops, concentrated to crush the rebellion, finally struck, seizing Brezno, Zvolen, and, on 27 October Banska Bystrica, the capital of free Slovakia. Just before Tri Duba airfield fell, the 1st Czech Fighter Regiment flew back to Soviet soil. By late October the remainder of the Slovak Army, together with Colonel Prokryl's 2d Czech Airborne Brigade, fled into the mountains to continue resistance through the winter. The Czechs paid a high price for the

Stavka and Konev's gambit. 1st Czech Corps lost 6,500 men, half of its strength, including the 1st Brigade commander, in the failed operation.[26]

The transport of the 2d Czech Airborne Brigade to Tri Duba airfield did not involve a combat assault, but rather was almost administrative. In this sense, the operation, as well as earlier insertions of partisans and equipment was similar to other operations taking place across the breadth of the Eastern front, but particularly in Poland. By late 1944 the *Stavka* was, to an increasing degree, employing airborne forces for diversionary operations, reconnaissance, and to reinforce partisan efforts. The *Stavka* had concluded that large-scale insertion of airborne forces into an active combat arena was far too costly and could not be adequately supported.

CHAPTER 10

Reconnaissance and Diversionary Operations

GENERAL

Reconnaissance and diversionary operations were the most numerous and, perhaps, the most successful type of airborne operation the Soviets conducted during the Second World War. These operations varied widely in mission and scale. Small landing parties routinely conducted reconnaissance and struck at objectives deep in the enemy rear. Others simply established contact with organized partisan forces to raid German rear areas. Larger reconnaissance or sabotage groups reported on enemy dispositions and troop movements or attacked important enemy installations.

Reconnaissance and diversionary operations were conducted by special purpose [*spetsial'noe naznachenie*] forces under NKVD, GRU (*front* intelligence directorate), *front* and sometimes army control and by regular airborne forces serving the same masters. These operations were either separate or associated closely with major operations conducted by either *front* or airborne forces. They took place, with ever increasing frequency, throughout the entire duration of the war.[1] Reconnaissance and diversionary operations by these diverse groups kept the German rear in turmoil and tied down in a security role German forces that could have been better used at the front (such as numerous security divisions). At the other extreme, small organized groups conducted diversionary raids in support of operations by other ground elements. Often, diversionary operations sought to achieve political, as well as military aims. The following examples illustrate their diversity.

ODESSA, SEPTEMBER 1941

In early July 1941, German forces drove deep into the Ukraine. The 204th Airborne Brigade (1st Airborne Corps) organized more than ten landings in the enemy rear, usually at night, to attack German lines of communication and logistical facilities.[2] Airborne forces bypassed or encircled in the initial German offensive also routinely undertook reconnaissance and diversionary operations in the enemy rear areas. These operations were the earliest manifestations of the significant partisan network that in later years grew throughout all German-occupied territory, but particularly in Belorussia, the RSFSR (the Russian Republic), and Ukraine.

A well-organized diversionary operation with direct tactical implications occurred during the defense of Odessa in early fall 1941.[3] In September the siege of Odessa reached its decisive stage (see Figure 84).

After a month's battle, German and Rumanian forces had pushed back Soviet defenders of the port and threatened the Soviet sea lines of communication. On the city's eastern defense sector, Rumanian forces were within 8–15 kilometers of the harbor and able to subject Soviet ships to artillery fire. To further defend the city and to prepare and conduct an evacuation, if necessary, it was essential to drive Rumanian forces back out of artillery range. To do so, the Soviet command planned a joint air, land, and sea operation against Rumanian forces pressing against Odessa's eastern defenses.

The ground force designated to launch the counteroffensive consisted of the 421st and newly arrived (from the Crimea) 157th Rifle Divisions. These divisions were to attack eastward and then northward, and, in cooperation with flank units, would collapse and drive back Rumanian defenders. At the same time, the 3d Naval Infantry Regiment was to conduct an amphibious assault near Grigor'evka and thereafter attack to the northwest in concert with the advancing rifle divisions. A small parachute assault into the region just north of Chebanka had the mission of 'disorganizing the work of the rear and disrupting enemy communications.'[4] The overall aim of the counterattack was to encircle and destroy enemy forces located between the Adzhalyk and Bol'shoe Adzhalyk estuaries. The assault, originally planned for 17 September, was postponed until 22 September to permit adequate preparation of the landing force. To preserve secrecy the missions and planning table for the operation, worked out by the Coastal Army staff, were passed to subordinate units on 21 September, the day before the attack. It contained the following sequence of operations:

21 September – personal reconnaissance of jumping-off positions and the forward edge of the enemy defensive sector; organization of cooperation and combat command and control; selection and preparation of command and observation points; and the organization of communications.

22 September – 0130 – commencement of the parachute assault;

0300 – landing of the 3d Naval Infantry Regiment;

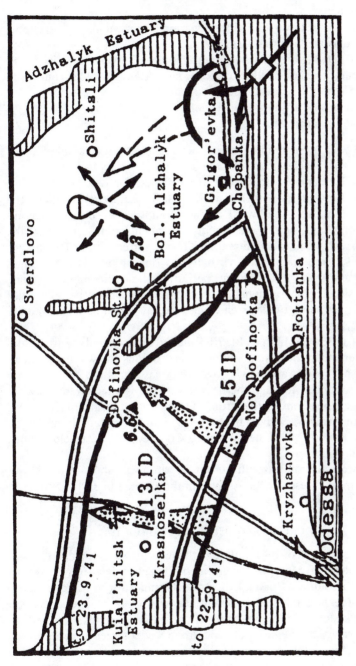

84. Odessa Operation, September 1941

0400 – air attacks on enemy reserves in the Sverdlovo and Kubanka regions;

0600 – attack by 69th Fighter Aviation Regiment aircraft on enemy airfields at Baden and Zel'tsy;

0700 – strikes by Black Sea Fleet aviation (63d Aviation Brigade) on enemy second echelon dispositions: Aleksandrovka, hill 58.0, Sverkhnaia Il'ichevka and Gil'dendorf;

0730–0800 – artillery preparation;

0800 – infantry attack.[5]

At 0114 on 22 September, ahead of schedule, the naval amphibious force hit the beaches east of Odessa, and by 0230 had cleared the surprised Rumanian forces from Grigor'evka. Simultaneously, TB-3 bombers dropped 23 parachutists near hill 57.3. After landing, the parachutists moved southward in two groups. They destroyed communications lines, seized one enemy command point, and, by 0500, linked up with the naval infantry force. Their drop caught the Rumanians by surprise, and they faced virtually no opposition. The combined airborne and naval assault force 'permitted the overcoming of strong enemy resistance in the Chebanka region, where an enemy battalion staff was destroyed, and, by day's end, the force had fulfilled its immediate mission.'[6]

At 0800 the Soviet 421st and 157th Rifle Divisions joined the attack and forced Rumanian forces to abandon their positions and withdraw northward and northwestward, leaving over 1,000 casualties and 200 prisoners. Combat continued through the next day as the Rumanian forces withdrew to new positions further from the Odessa harbor. Ultimately, 4th Rumanian Army was driven back five to eight kilometers, losing in the action 6,000 men (2,000 killed and prisoners), 39 guns, 127 machine guns, and 15 mortars.[7]

The successful joint assault permitted safe evacuation of the Soviet garrison from Odessa to Sevastopol' in the Crimea in early October.

KERCH–FEODOSIIA, DECEMBER 1941

Throughout the fall of 1941, although the focus of war remained fixed on the approaches to Moscow, the German offensive tide also swept across the plains of southern Russia. By October German armies had conquered the Ukraine and reached the Don Basin. Colonel General E. von Manstein's Eleventh German Army surged into the Crimea, besieged the Soviet naval base at Sevastopol', and drove Soviet forces from the Kerch peninsula, the eastern extremity of the Crimea. In early December, while Manstein was reducing the Sevastopol' fortress, the *Stavka* ordered its Transcaucasus Front to prepare an operation to recapture the Kerch peninsula, raise the siege of Sevastopol', and expel Manstein's forces from the Crimea.

The operation was an overly ambitious one. On 13 December the *Stavka* ordered two armies and elements of the Black Sea Fleet to conduct a joint amphibious, airborne, and ground operation.[8] They confronted an estimated German force of two divisions and two cavalry brigades at the eastern end of the peninsula and two infantry regiments at Feodosiia.[9] The Transcaucasus Front ordered 51st Army and the Black Sea Fleet to force the Kerch Straits, occupy Kerch and the Turkish wall fortifications, and subsequently attack toward Ak Monai at the base of the peninsula. The 44th Army would attack Marfovka and, with 51st Army, destroy all German forces on the Kerch peninsula preparatory to a subsequent drive to relieve the siege of Sevastopol'.[10]

The airborne forces' role was to support the amphibious assault with a parachute company drop near Baragova Station west of Kerch (see Figure 85). The paratroopers were to capture a base of operations to support a future naval force landing at Cape Ziuk. An airborne unit from 2d Airborne Corps had the mission of capturing the Vladislavovka airfield for Transcaucasus Front aviation units to use. After the landings, the parachute units would become subordinate to 44th Army. At the last moment, however, high seas and floating ice forced cancellation of the Ak Monai landing. The airborne units then received a new mission from *front*: to land near Arabat and block either a German advance down the Arabat spit from Genichesk or a German withdrawal along the same route. The commander of airborne forces planned and was to conduct the operation.

While Major Niashin's airborne battalion at Krasnodar airfield prepared for the drop, small reconnaissance groups of naval paratroopers carrying radios were inserted into the German rear to collect and transmit intelligence to the assault force. On 31 December, during extremely poor weather conditions, the small, but elite force took off in TB-3 bombers. Heavy cloud cover forced the aircraft to fly in single column at substantial intervals. Thick clouds forced the aircraft to fly at 75 meters, too low for a safe drop. After the aircraft navigator had threatened Major Niashin with aborting the mission because of the low altitude, the two agreed to ascend to 450 meters in the clouds just before the jump.[11]

In those harrowing conditions, the paratroopers finally exited the aircraft. As they fell, German troops escorting an ammunition convoy fired machine guns at the helpless troops, and heavy winds dispersed them. Assembly was difficult, but the dispersion also created the impression among the Germans that a much larger Soviet force was landing. Heavy but fragmented fighting followed the drop. Small groups of

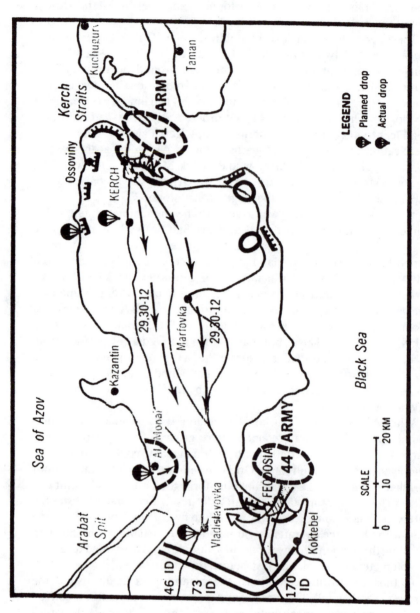

85. Kerch–Feodosiia Operation, December 1941–January 1942

paratroopers painstakingly infiltrated past German strongpoints and advanced on Ak Monai. When the battalion had assembled enough men, it attacked and captured a German artillery position on the north flank of the Ak Monai defenses. Early on 1 January 1942, the battalion had occupied German defenses at Ak Monai and across the base of the Arabat spit.

Meanwhile, 44th Army had occupied Feodosiia and then advanced 15 kilometers inland to Vladislavovka, but there the Germans stood fast and prevented Soviet encirclement of their forces. As the Germans withdrew westward, the Soviet airborne force split up into diversionary groups and harassed retreating German forces. The paratroopers were later replaced by a naval infantry unit. The *front* commander's decision to cancel the airborne drop designed to secure Vladislavovka airfield for Soviet fighters meant that Soviet forces lacked effective air cover during the entire offensive.[12]

Although the Kerch–Feodosiia airborne landing was a relatively small operation, less than battalion size, it suffered from the same ills as the larger operations. Its size was insufficient to achieve its assigned mission. Bad weather hindered landing operations, and reconnaissance had failed to detect enemy strength and dispositions. At the command level, planners vacillated over determining what objectives to seize and were thus unable to tailor a force suited to the mission. As was the case in other operations, the airborne force landed in dangerous conditions, but, once on the ground, the men acted resolutely. The battalion commander displayed initiative when conditions seemed appropriate for him to change the unit's mission. In essence, the operation was a microcosm of other unsuccessful Soviet operations by larger airborne units.

MAIKOP, OCTOBER 1942

During the critical months of the fall of 1942, German forces advanced to Stalingrad and into the Caucasus. German aircraft operating from Maikop raised havoc with Soviet installations along the Black Sea.[13] The Soviet Trans-Caucasus Front planned and carried out an airborne, diversionary operation to neutralize the critical German air base (see Figure 86). For this purpose, *front* formed a specially trained detachment of 42 men commanded by Captain M. Orlov and his deputy Captain P. Desiatnikov. The detachment was further subdivided into 'destruction,' 'covering,' and 'command' groups, each under a responsible officer or non-commissioned officer.

Before the operation commenced, *front* air forces concentrated on knocking out German antiaircraft defenses and ground strongpoints and also inserted special teams to mark the location of the drop. During the

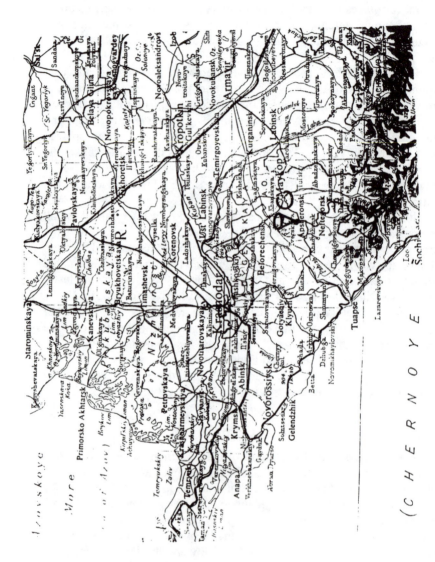

86. Maikop Operation, October 1942

assault ground attack aircraft units were assigned the mission of blocking all approach routes to the air base from north and southwest, of flying diversionary missions to attract the fire of remaining German air defense forces, and of supporting the extraction of the force after it had completed its mission. Intense air reconnaissance preceded the assault to determine objectives and German defensive dispositions.

The detachment itself worked out an intricate plan of operations. The 'command' group, after landing, was to establish a command and control center in the center of the airfield, from which it could effectively control all subsequent action by the other two groups. The 'covering' group was to overcome German security forces and establish defenses along the roads approaching the airfield from the northwest and southeast. The 'destruction' group, after landing and without prior assembly, was to operate in small groups against specific pre-planned targets in specific airfield sectors. This principally involved the blowing up of aircraft and airfield support facilities.

The three small groups of the detachment were armed and equipped with special weapons, explosives, and equipment suited to their precise mission. Each soldier in the 'destruction' group had an automatic weapon with two full magazines, three incendiary devices [grenades], two gasoline-filled bottles, five concussion grenades, an axe, a dagger, a compass, a lantern, and food for two days. Each member of the 'covering' group had two sub-machine guns and an automatic pistol.

After completing its mission and upon the signal of the commander, the detachment was to gather its 'command' and 'destruction' groups. Once assembled for departure, the 'covering' group would return from its covering positions and unite with the main body of the detachment. Subsequently the detachment was to 'operate in accordance with the situation and try to reach the [nearby] partisan region.' If they failed to reach partisan sanctuaries, arrangements were made for further resupply of the detachment at specific points.

To maintain security for the operation, only a few key officers participated in the planning phase, and detachment personnel learned of the plan and their specific missions only four days before the assault. Preparations also included intense training for each detachment member on German aircraft recognition and study of mock-ups of the target area, and the characteristics of each of their weapons. Twenty days before the assault, the Black Sea Fleet air staff, on the basis of constant reconnaissance, recorded every possible detail of Maikop airfield flight activities. They also enlisted the support of Maikop partisans in the reconnaissance effort.

On the night of 24 October, the 42 paratroopers, transported in TB-3 and PS-84 aircraft and covered by bombers, raided the Maikop airfield.

Roughly one-half of the force landed on the airfield proper, and the others landed slightly to the west. Partisan guides led the way as the paratroopers dropped on and near the airfield. After an hour-long intense struggle, the Germans finally drove off the airborne force, which in the meantime had destroyed 22 of the Germans' 54 aircraft and damaged another 20. Fourteen paratroopers were killed in the operation.

This operation typified many others, as the Soviets by 1942 had an acute understanding of the role that small, well-trained, but unfortunately expendable, airborne diversionary groups could play in the vast scheme of operations on the Eastern Front.

NOVOROSSIISK, FEBRUARY 1943

During the winter of 1943, while Soviet forces were reducing encircled German Sixth Army at Stalingrad and pushing German Army Group Don westward toward Khar'kov and the Dnepr River, Soviet forces strove to clear the northern Caucasus region of German forces. By early February German forces were defending forward (east) of the Taman Peninsula and on the eastern outskirts of the Black Sea port of Novorossiisk.

To accelerate the liberation of the Taman Peninsula and Novorossiisk, the *Stavka* ordered the Black Sea Fleet and Black Sea Group of Forces to mount a joint land and sea drive on the Novorossiisk region. The 1 February order from the Black Sea Group to 47th Army read:

> Continue to attack in the direction of Krymskaia, with the left flank penetrate enemy defenses in the Mount Dolgaia–cement factory sector, after which develop the offensive along the [mountain] crests across Mount Sakharnaia Golova [Sugar Head], to secure the Markotkh Pass and subsequently attack toward the northeastern region of Novorossiisk – the Mefodievskii suburb. Thereafter, together with an amphibious assault, 56th Army and 47th Army must, by 9 February, fully liberate Novorossiisk.[14]

The Soviet frontal attack on German positions northeast of Novorossiisk failed, as did an attack by 56th Army in the Krasnodor sector on 2 February. To break the deadlock in the region, the North Caucasus Front decided to implement a contingency plan, developed as early as November 1942, to conduct an amphibious assault directly against Novorossiisk. As a part of the complex amphibious operation, planned and commanded by Vice-Admiral F. S. Oktiabr'sky, a diversionary airborne assault was planned to divert German attention from the amphibious actions and disrupt German command and control (see Figure 87).

The amphibious operation was to occur on the night of 3–4 February, with the main force landing near Iuzhnaia Ozereika and an auxiliary force striking the sea coast near Stanichka. The simultaneous assaults were co-ordinated with overall 47th Army ground operations aimed at seizing Novorossiisk. Black Sea Fleet ships and aircraft were to support the assault.

An airborne diversionary detachment of 80 men from the 31st Parachute Landing Regiment (made up of remnants of former 2d Airborne Corps) was ordered to land in the vicinity of Vasil'evka and Glebovka, the supposed location of German 10th Infantry Division headquarters, with the mission of attacking division headquarters to disrupt troop control, blow up nearby bridges, delay the forward movement of enemy reserves, and prevent withdrawal of enemy forces from Iuzhnaia Ozereika.[15] Organized into four combat groups, the detachment was to be transported to its designated landing site by an air transport detachment of PS-84 aircraft. Additional bombers and fighters were assigned to support the landing and provide cover for the diversionary operations.

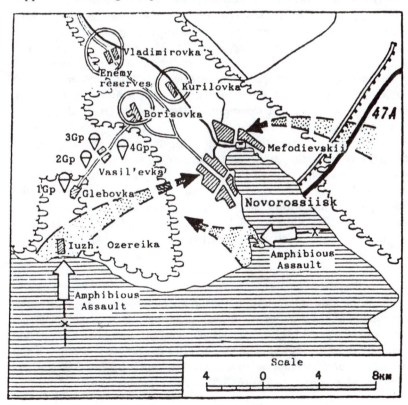

87. Novorossiisk Operation, February 1943

The transport aircraft were based in a Trans-Caucasus airfield and assembled two days prior to the assault.

According to the plan, the detachment was to drop into its assault sector at 0100 hour on 4 February, 45 minutes before the beginning of the artillery preparation for the naval assault. Each of the four combat groups received a specific drop zone near Glebovka and Vasil'evka. Two minutes before the drop Soviet bombers were to attack and set fire to both towns to cover the subsequent airborne assault. While the parachutists were landing, fleet bombers were to strike Iuzhnaia Ozereika to set it afire as a 'lighted checkpoint' for the ships of the naval landing force. If the naval assault failed, the paratroopers had orders to withdraw in small groups to Abrau Diurso Sovkhoz (state farm) by day three of the operation and thereafter link up with ground forces or operate independently.

The airborne assault occurred as planned at 0100 4 February. The detachment attacked Vasil'evka and destroyed the garrison, but the reported infantry division headquarters was not located there. For three days the airborne detachment operated in the German rear, reportedly killing more than 100 enemy soldiers, disrupting communications, and destroying several enemy firing positions. Meanwhile, the main naval landing at Iuzhnaia Ozereika was unsuccessful due to the late arrival of ships and heavy enemy fire. The auxiliary landing at Stanichka was successful despite heavy enemy resistance, and a foothold was established as a base for future operations. (The foothold received the name Malaia Zemlia [Little Land].)

During the operation the 80-man detachment lost 15 men, but the remnants rejoined the amphibious landing force at Stanichka. One Soviet source assessed the role of the airborne force as follows, 'The small airborne landing force could not provide substantial assistance in the landing of the naval forces near Iuzhnaia Ozereika, but was able to pin down a large part of the enemy force in this area, which indirectly aided the landing of naval forces at Stanichka.'[16]

MANCHURIA, AUGUST 1945

Perhaps the most interesting, but often misunderstood, Soviet airborne operations of the war were conducted during the Soviet Manchurian offensive of August 1945.[17] Late in that operation, after Soviet troops had penetrated deeply into Manchuria and after the Japanese command had decided to surrender, a series of airborne landings brought Soviet soldiers to major Manchurian and Korean cities and Japanese command installations.

Between 18 and 24 August, the Soviet 54th Transport and 21st Guards

Transport Aviation Divisions, escorted by combat aviation forces of 9th and 12th Air Armies, carried out over 15 hastily planned and organized air-landing operations, most at the behest of the Far Eastern High Command and *front* headquarters (see Figure 88).[18] All of these landing operations were designed to accelerate the surrender of Japanese units, and, since the imperial order for surrender was neither universally received nor always accepted, a considerable degree of risk attached to each operation.

The earliest of these landings was planned and conducted by the 1st Far Eastern Front commander, Marshal K. A. Meretskov. On 16 August the *front*'s 1st Red Banner and 5th Armies seized the Japanese stronghold at Mutanchiang, and General A. P. Beloborodov's 1st Red Banner Army and General N. I. Krylov's 5th Army began a rapid advance toward Harbin and Kirin, respective headquarters of the Japanese First Area

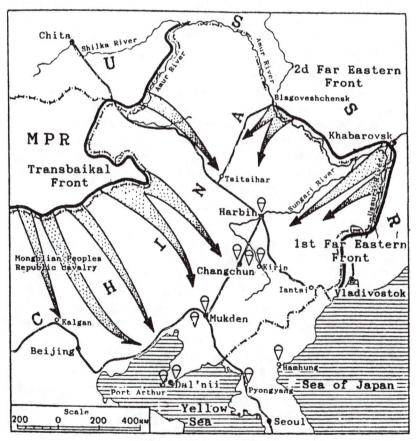

88. Air-landings in Manchuria, August 1945

Army and the Kwantung Army. Two days earlier, the Japanese government had ordered its forces to surrender, but the order had not been distributed to all units, and, in some cases, it was being ignored. On 17 August Soviet Far Eastern TVD [Theater of Military Operation] commander, Marshal A. M. Vasilevsky, radioed the following message to General O. Yamada, commander of the Kwantung Army:

> I propose ... that at 1200 hours on 20 August you cease all military actions against Soviet forces along the entire front, lay down your arms, and surrender.... As soon as Japanese forces begin to surrender their weapons, Soviet forces will cease their military operations.[19]

To underscore the seriousness of the proposal, with Vasilevsky's approval, 1st Far Eastern Front implemented 'Operation Bridge,' ostensibly designed to secure bridges across the Sungari River at Harbin and Kirin, but also to pressure the Japanese command into prompt surrender.[20] Vasilevsky mandated this and other air-landing operations with an 18 August order to all of his *fronts*, which read:

> In connection with the fact that Japanese resistance is crumbling, and deteriorating road conditions strongly hinder rapid movement of our main forces, it is necessary without delay for the seizure of the cities of Chanchun' [Changchun], Girin [Kirin], and Kharbin [Harbin] and to employ specially formed, extremely mobile, and well-equipped detachments. These detachments or like forces are to be used to resolve subsequent missions, without fear of being sharply separated from their main forces.[21]

By virtue of this order, all *front* and army commanders organized and dispatched special, highly mobile ground forward detachments to co-operate with the air-landed forces.

1st Far Eastern Front organized two assault forces of 150 men each, selected from the 20th Motorized Assault Engineer Brigade. Members of the assault force were hand-picked, battle-hardened veterans of earlier combat against particularly strong Japanese prepared defensive positions in eastern Manchuria. These detachments were equipped with automatic weapons, machine guns, flame throwers, grenades, explosives, and radios. Each man was given a city map marked with all routes and objectives, and each had practiced his mission in advance.[22]

At 1700 18 August, the first detachment under Lieutenant Colonel I. N. Zabelin left a Soviet airfield headed for Harbin. With him was Major General G. A. Shelakhov, 1st Far Eastern Front Military Commissar, who was authorized to negotiate for the Japanese surrender. Shortly thereafter, the second detachment, commanded by Lieutenant Colonel

D. A. Krutskikh, with *front* War Council representative, Colonel V. I. Lebedev in tow, assembled for departure for Kirin the following day. After being escorted to its destination by fighter aircraft, the first detachment landed at its objective at about 1900.

Japanese security at Harbin airfield scattered when faced with the surprise Soviet landing. Within minutes, Soviet troops had seized all airfield facilities, and soon Lieutenant General Hata, Kwantung Army Chief of Staff, arrived at the airfield with a group of officers. Shelakhov took Hata to the Soviet consulate, where he presented him with the surrender ultimatum.[23] By 2300 on 18 August, the air-landed assault force had seized the key bridges over the Sungari River, the railroad station, telegraph office, police station, postal facilities, and other key objectives. The surrender of Japanese forces progressed peacefully, and the following day senior Japanese officers were flown to Vasilevsky's headquarters for formal surrender. Soviet ground forces reached Harbin on 20 August. Early on 19 August the detachment of Lieutenant Colonel Krutskikh and Colonel Lebedev flew into Kirin and seized the airfield and key facilities against virtually no opposition.[24] On 20 August the forward detachment of 10th Mechanized Corps reached the city, and together they received the surrender of Japanese units in the region.

Further south on 18 August, General I. M. Chistiakov, 25th Army commander, flew with a small security detachment and an operational group of his staff to Iantsi, headquarters of Japanese 3d Army. There he linked up with his army's 72d Tank Brigade and received the surrender of Lieutenant General Murakami Keisaku, 3d Army Commander.[25] Less than one week later, 25th Army conducted yet another air landing at Pyongyang, Korea, in conjunction with a ground advance into the region by 10th Mechanized Corps. Two other landings occurred virtually simultaneously at Wongson and Kanko [Hamhung] on the Korean east coast in conjunction with operations by Soviet naval forces.

The Transbaikal Front responded to Vasilevsky's orders by organizing air-landings of its own, first against the cities of Changchun, Mukden, and Tupliao, and then against Darien and Port Arthur. The landing forces designated for operations against Changchun and Mukden were selected from 6th Guards Tank Army. The Changchun force consisted of 200 men from the 30th Guards Mechanized Brigade, 9th Guards Mechanized Corps, commanded by Colonel P. N. Avremenko. The *desant* itself was supervised by the assistant chief of intelligence for 6th Guards Tank Army, Lieutenant Colonel M. I. Mel'nichenko.[26]

At first light on 19 August, Colonel I. T. Artemenko, special representative of the Transbaikal Front commander, escorted by five fighters, landed at Changchun airfield, accompanied by five officers and six men. Upon his safe arrival, Artemenko signaled for the rest of the detachment to follow. Artemenko proceeded to Kwantung Army headquarters, where he presented General Yamada Otozo with a surrender ultimatum. Shortly thereafter, at 1100 hours, the reconnaissance aircraft of the main airborne force arrived at the airfield, manned by Lieutenant Colonel Mel'nichenko and 18 men. Mel'nichenko landed and radioed for the main force to land and for an element of the force to divert to Tupliao airfield, site of another Japanese headquarters. By 1315 the Soviet force had fully assembled and secured all important objectives in the city. By day's end 40,000 Japanese soldiers had surrendered, including 17 general officers. The following morning forward detachments of 6th Guards Tank Army entered the city.

Also on 19 August, at 1315 hours a force of 225 men from 2d Battalion, 6th Guards Motorized Rifle Brigade, 5th Guards Tank Corps, commanded by Major P. E. Chelyshev, landed at Mukden airfield. With them was Major General A. D. Pritula, special representative of the Transbaikal Front's staff (political department). The force seized the city, took prisoner the Emperor of Manchuria, Pu Li, and freed a large number of U.S. and British prisoners of war.[27] Almost simultaneously, other aircraft landed a reconnaissance company from 5th Guards Tank Corps at Liaoyuan airfield, where it received the surrender of the Japanese garrison. 6th Guards Tank Army commander, General A. G. Kravchenko, flew into Mukden later in the day and formally received the surrender of Japanese 3d Army.[28] The next morning a forward detachment of 5th Guards Tank Corps also reached the city.

The air-landing operations continued in subsequent days as Soviet air assault forces leap-frogged southward in advance of the ground forces to occupy key cities and force the surrender of Japanese garrisons. Early on 22 August, 200 men from 9th Guards Mechanized Corps, 6th Guards Tank Army under Major N. K. Beloded, assistant chief of operations for the corps, landed at Port Arthur airfield. With him was Lieutenant General V. D. Ivanov, deputy *front* commander. After initially receiving Japanese ground fire, fighters struck the airfield, the firing ceased, and the air-landing progressed uneventfully.[29] Shortly before the Port Arthur assault took place, another 250 troopers under Lieutenant Colonel B. S. Likhachev, with *front* representative Major General A. A. Iamanov, had secured Dairen airfield and city.[30] Soon they also linked up with Soviet ground forces of 6th Guards Tank Army.

In addition to these air landings, the Soviets used air-landed forces in their conquest of southern Sakhalin Island. Three groups of 35 men each landed on 23 August on Japanese airfields, also to hasten Japanese capitulation. As was the case elsewhere, they suffered no casualties.[31]

In Manchuria Soviet air-landing detachments ranged in size from 150 to 500 men. All forces were air-landed without extensive prior reconnaissance and sometimes in an atmosphere of uncertainty concerning Japanese reactions. The landings were as much political as military in their aims, for they sought to reinforce Japanese intentions to surrender, hasten disarmament of the sometimes recalcitrant Japanese troops, and establish an immediate Soviet presence in Manchuria.[32] In this sense, the Manchurian airborne assaults were forerunners of Soviet paratrooper landings in Czechoslovakia in 1968 and Afghanistan in 1980.

Soviet diversionary operations were more successful than most larger tactical and operational operations. They were more economical in terms of manpower, and they could be mounted by limited means and with more primitive techniques. Although their direct dividends were sometimes not readily apparent, their long-term importance mounted. They were also a useful adjunct to the successful partisan warfare of 1943 and 1944. Since the war, the Soviets have viewed diversionary operations with ever intensifying interest.

CHAPTER 11

The First Postwar Years (1946–1953)

CONTEXT

During the inevitable force demobilization of the immediate postwar years, the Soviet Union concentrated its analytical energies on building an armed force of sufficient size to guarantee its security, to protect its emerging sphere of influence, and to advance Soviet interests whenever feasible. If a single slogan personified Soviet attitudes since the almost messianic seizure of Berlin in May 1945, it was the words so often seen in print, on walls, and on placards in the Soviet Union. '*Nikto ne zabyt, nichto ne zabyto* [No one will forget, nothing will be forgotten].' Accordingly, the Soviet Union examined the historical lessons of the recent past and proceeded to build for the future.

The military was no exception. The historical lessons of the late war loomed large. For the Soviets, it had been the ultimate struggle (equivalent in Stalin's view to nuclear war) out of which would emerge ultimate truths. Never before in history had such a titanic struggle been waged – a twentieth century *Kulturkampf* [war of culture] – in which only one culture could emerge supreme. The Soviet Union had won, but at tremendous cost and sacrifice and after suffering catastrophic initial defeats. The victory confirmed for the Soviets the validity not only of their military theory but also of their political ideology, and it proved that the Soviet military could absorb the shock of major defeats, learn from those defeats, and prevail. Thus, original Soviet military theory, the events and lessons of war, and the postwar theory that emerged victorious had an aura of truth, tried and tested in the heat of war as it was. Security for future generations demanded that those truths be transmitted to younger military officers as accurately and in as much detail as possible. The historical study of war experience and technique was the essential base from which to derive and validate subsequent military theory. By extension, without such a historical basis, present and future theory could not be understood. Obviously, as a counterpoint, or antithesis, to the thesis of that emerging theory stood the technological changes after 1945. Since that time a process of synthesis of those enduring elements has existed: the tried and true techniques and theory of the past juxtaposed against and modified by the often momentous technological changes since the profound experiences of the Great Patriotic War.

The Soviet Union reformed its military establishment in 1946, and theories, practices, and organizations judged to have contributed most to victory were emphasized. Taken from the experiences of 1944–45, the preeminent offensive model stressed deep operations; maneuver; and judicious use of massed armor, artillery, and airpower to achieve success on the battlefield. Combined arms armies remained the numerically most important element of the Soviet ground force structure. These armies were organized into rifle corps and rifle divisions, just as in the late war years; but now they also contained integrated tank and mechanized elements. Mechanized armies of mechanized and tank divisions, as the heirs to the wartime tank armies, mechanized corps, and tank corps, emerged as the Soviet Army's powerful mobile force and, as such, received the most attention and resources. The Soviet Union also maintained as many as ten airborne divisions in the immediate postwar years as an adjunct to its large, increasingly mechanized army. But the real emphasis remained on mechanized ground warfare, and airborne forces played only an auxiliary role. Stalin's view of war, in general (reflected in his 'Permanent Operating Factors'), plus his skeptical view of the utility of airborne operations, based on wartime experience, in particular, and the absence of a sufficient technological base to sustain airborne operations relegated large airborne forces and their projected operations to the realm of theory rather than practice.[1]

Theoretical study of airborne warfare, however, continued. Soviet military theorists intensely studied war experiences to refine the precise missions airborne forces could realistically perform. Theoretical missions were extensive, reaching into the strategic realm.[2] Theorists also investigated airborne organizations, planning, equipment, delivery techniques, and methods of ground operations. Despite this intellectual activity, there remained severe reservations about the real utility and survivability of airborne forces in modern mechanized combat. The ghosts of Viaz'ma, Demiansk, and the Dnepr operations were too vivid and too unpleasant. While Stalin lived, guards airborne divisions did exist, but those divisions were copies of the ground-oriented guards airborne divisions of the late war years. A model for the Soviet army, they were elite divisions, well trained and well equipped. Prospects for these show troops being used in actual airborne warfare would remain remote until Stalinist doubts as to their effectiveness had faded and airborne forces had an efficient airborne transport to the battlefield and equipment to ensure their survival in battle. Sophisticated theory, elaboration of missions, and organizational adjustments would develop in tandem with technological changes – changes that would soon occur and result in a rejuvenation of airborne warfare theory and practice.

POSTWAR AIRBORNE REORGANIZATION

The general postwar reorganization of the armed forces also affected airborne units. At the highest command levels, the air force lost control of airborne forces when, in June 1946, they became directly subordinate to the Ministry of Defense. The position of commander of airborne forces was reestablished, and Colonel General V. V. Glagolev was appointed the first postwar airborne commander in April 1946.[3]

During the demobilization, new airborne divisions emerged from

FIGURE 89. AIRBORNE DIVISION ORGANIZATION, 1946

Guards airborne rifle division (about 7,000 men):
1 parachute regiment
   3 parachute battalions
2 parachute-glider regiments
   1 parachute battalion
   2 glider battalions
1 gun artillery regiment (24×76-mm guns)
1 mortar regiment (24×120-mm mortars)
1 antitank battery (12×45-mm, 57-mm guns)
1 reconnaissance company
1 signal company
1 engineer company
1 medical company
1 motor transport company

wartime rifle divisions and guards airborne brigades. The new guards airborne divisions were organized under airborne corps headquarters control and paralleled the organizational structure of rifle divisions. They lacked, however, the heavy weapons that augmented rifle division equipment tables in the postwar years (that is, the medium tank and self-propelled gun regiment). The postwar airborne division consisted of six or seven battalions of 960 men each, organized into one paratroop and two air-transportable regiments, for a total strength of from 6,000 to 7,000 men. Its principal weaponry was a battalion of six 76-mm guns, 57-mm antitank guns, mortars, many antitank weapons (bazookas), and machine guns. In addition to standard airborne divisions, the VDV fielded units 'tailored to specific missions, with units down to battalion – or in some cases company and even platoon level – being prepared for independent action.'[4] The airborne division organization was probably as shown in Figure 89.[5]

Controlled by the aviation of airborne troops branch of the air force, air transport divisions consisted of transport and glider regiments and provided lift capability for the new airborne corps. An airborne corps consisted of from two to three guards airborne divisions and an air transport division.[6] Soviet stocks of IL-12 and LI-2 transport aircraft were assessed by U.S. intelligence as sufficient 'to conduct a single lift of several well-equipped airborne divisions without impairing other essential military air transport services.'[7]

The weaponry available to the units and the air-delivery means provided by the air force determined both the potential combat role of these airborne divisions and unit training, which was rather limited at first. Until basic technological changes had occurred, training and combat use had to be patterned after Second World War operation and were therefore limited in scope. Thus, 'in the first postwar years, real changes in the means of fulfilling military missions by airborne forces did not occur. It is fully understandable because there were changes in neither the techniques nor means of landing.'[8] Airborne divisions were combined arms operational-tactical divisions that operated in close concert with tank and mechanized forces and aviation units during *front* offensive operations.

THEORETICAL WRITINGS

While Soviet sources, even closed ones, were reticent over describing the organization of airborne forces, they thoroughly analyzed the combat roles airborne forces could perform. Major General Iu. Kostin, writing in 1946 in the General Staff journal *Military Thought* [*Voennaia mysl'*], reviewed wartime operations of Western airborne forces, scarcely mentioning the unfortunate Soviet experiences. He highlighted the most prominent future mission for airborne forces:

> One finds that first of all, the kind of mission given an air-landing operation was one which necessitated the overcoming of a substantial obstacle, which would have presented great difficulties for ground troops; natural or man-made obstacles such as wide rivers, stretches of ocean or difficult mountainous terrain, fortified areas, etc.... In many cases this was the only possible way in which the objective could have been achieved.[9]

Recognizing the limitations on the use of these forces (primarily aircraft limitations) and the fact that they had not reached their full potential, Kostin predicted much more widespread use and success of airborne operations in the future:

> But the progress which has been begun in air-landings cannot be

halted now, on the one hand because they represent the very
embodiment of the efforts of present-day military art to increase the
depth of penetration into the enemy rear and to increase the
rapidity of maneuver, and on the other hand, because air-landings
are the means by which both depth of penetration and rapidity of
maneuver can be achieved with surprise, with sizeable forces, and
over long distances.[10]

Kostin concluded that airpower in conjunction with air-landing operations was capable of striking strong blows against the enemy rear area and
seizing and holding objectives in the depth of the enemy defenses.
Specifically:

> Large tank formations, carrying out actions in the enemy opera-
> tional rear, can move with increased speed and can acquire greater
> shock power if they are aided by air-landings set down either ahead
> of them or on their flanks.
>
> Thus, the most important mission of present-day operational art
> – striking the enemy a blow in depth by means of cooperation
> between aviation, motor-mechanized forces, and the main body of
> the force – can be carried out in a more decisive and complete
> manner with the help of air-landings. Air-landings prevent the
> possible breach in coordination between the air attack and the
> advance of mobile formations, and convert a deep blow into the
> enemy's position into a continuous action in the enemy depth,
> beginning with an attack from the air and ending with the attack on
> land.[11]

Kostin went on to assess the improving capabilities of transport aviation, which could now operate to depths of 400–500 kilometers in support
of advancing ground forces, and he provided a rationale for creation of
special directorates to control and coordinate the use of these valuable
assets. Based on his analysis of U.S. island-hopping operations in the
Pacific, Kostin concluded that air-landings could play a critical role in
future strategic operations:

> In these operations, large groupings of land troops will be used;
> forces of army size will be entirely transported by air to strategically
> important regions deep in the enemy's rear in order to seize them,
> or to establish new fronts there from which to attack the vital
> centers from the most unexpected (and close) directions.[12]

This potential expanded use of air transport, in Kostin's view, completely
eclipsed the former limited use of airborne drops and required formation
of a special branch of service encompassing air-landing forces and their

delivery means. The judgment contained the rationale for direct subordination of VDV forces to the Ministry of Defense, which also controlled strategic air assets.

Kostin then described in detail a wide range of tactical, operational, and strategic missions for air-landing forces, including disruption of enemy mobilization and strategic concentration in the initial period of war, seizure of industrial regions, creation of new theaters of operations, and seizure of islands and beachheads. In a more practical vein, he articulated specific requirements which had to be met for future air-landing operations to be successful. These included:

- secrecy and careful preparation (reconnaissance) and surprise execution;
- thorough and full support of combat and transport aviation, including the achievement of air superiority and firm antiaircraft defense;
- enough air transport to lift the entire force in a short period;
- close cooperation of air-landed and *frontal* forces and timely link up between the forces;
- close correlation of mission with air-landing force strength;
- a reserve of air-landing troops and air transport aircraft.[13]

Kostin's optimistic view of the future combat role of air-landings made no mention at all of Soviet wartime experiences, establishing a trend which would last until 1960. Despite this silence, he concluded:

> The possibilities of further growth of air transport equipment and long-range bomber aviation provide a firm basis for the employment of air-landing troops on such a scale that quite possibly further changes in the form of present-day military operations may be necessary.[14]

The following year, in the same journal, Lieutenant General D. Grendal' examined in greater detail the purposes and techniques of air-landings. He reinforced Kostin's conclusions regarding the increased importance of air transport and the vertical dimension of operational and strategic maneuver by detailing strengths and capabilities of contemporary and future air transport. In a detailed analysis of weight and load factors, Grendal' estimated that a 15,000-man infantry division with full armament (including medium tanks and armored transporters) could be air transported in a single lift by 715 transport aircraft and 478 gliders or in a double lift by 358 aircraft and 239 gliders.[15]

He then listed necessary conditions for such an operation to succeed, including:

1. The presence of an airfield (or several airfields) in the region, seized and firmly held by large air-landing forces;

2. The presence of a necessary quantity of air transport means (aircraft and gliders) having sufficient lift capacity for transporting the formations;

3. The achievement of air superiority over the regions in the enemy rear, secured by air assault forces for the period of landing of transported forces;

4. Reliable protection of the assault echelon by accompanying fighter aviation to defend them from attack by enemy fighters;

5. Detailed clarification of conditions in which the air-landed formations will carry out their assigned missions. Maintenance of security in preparing the operation to achieve surprise use of maneuver from the air. An obligatory condition for success of such an operation is accuracy of coordination of the landed force with *front* aviation and with the air assault occupying the landing region;

6. Regular resupply of landed forces with all types of supplies, combat equipment and evacuation by means of air transport. The duration of reliance on air transport will depend on the course of the developing operation and the time it takes for air-landed forces to link up with attacking ground forces.[16]

Grendal' proceeded to provide a wealth of planning details for air-landing operations and detailed analysis of each phase of the developing operation. He concluded by reemphasizing the potential importance of such operations, insisting:

> Maneuver, accomplished in the air by combined-arms formations, has many pecularities and overall distinguishing features associated with the preparation, planning, and conduct of assaults of specialized airborne forces. Knowledge of these pecularities, careful training and preparation of ground forces for delivery by air in transport aircraft and gliders, and study of the specific organization and control in the period of loading, transport, and landing of planes provides full guarantee of successful conduct of maneuver of combined-arms formations by air into the enemy rear area.[17]

A series of articles in the late 1940s and early 1950s further developed the theme of air transport by citing specific wartime examples when ground forces were resupplied by air (Khalkhin-Gol, Stalingrad, Ukraine, 1944, etc.) and fueled the Soviet belief that air transport could solve the major problems experienced by airborne forces during the war and expand the horizons of air-landing operations.[18] This theoretical work seemed to reinforce the validity of Soviet VDV policies to emphasize air-delivered combat arms forces at the expense of traditional parachute-delivered airborne forces. Based upon these writings, a new series of airborne and air-landing missions emerged within the context of conventional *front* offensive operations.

AIRBORNE FORCE EMPLOYMENT

Front operations in the first postwar period sought to overcome enemy army group defenses to a depth of 150 to 200 kilometers by means of successive army operations. The *front*'s operational formation consisted of a first echelon of combined arms armies, a *front* mobile group of a mechanized army and a second echelon, plus *front* aviation, airborne forces (one to two divisions), a *front* antiaircraft group, and a reserve. An army organized itself into a first echelon of several rifle corps; a second echelon of a rifle corps or several rifle divisions; an army artillery group; an army antiaircraft group; and combined arms, antitank, tank, engineer, and chemical reserves. Sometimes, an army employed a mobile group of a separate mechanized or tank division.[19]

Front operations had the immediate mission of first penetrating the enemy army group defense and then encircling and destroying the enemy force. First-echelon combined arms armies performed this mission. The *front*'s subsequent mission was to develop the offensive with mechanized armies to destroy enemy operational and strategic reserves.[20] The *front*'s and army's operational frontage and depth of mission increased, compared with norms of the third period of the Great Patriotic War. The Soviets expected the duration of *front* and army operations to be shorter than had been the case during the war years.

In *front* operations, airborne and air-landed forces operated to operational depths (100 kilometers) to assist mechanized armies in exploiting the initial breakthrough. These operations were an integral part of *front* offensive operations or were conducted in conjunction with amphibious operations.[21] Furthermore, after 1950, Soviet theorists envisioned potential use of airborne and air-landed forces in separate sectors, assisting other ground, naval, and air forces to achieve strategic offensive missions. Specially prepared rifle forces, military transport, *front* aviation, and antiaircraft forces (*PVO Strany*) would be attached to the airborne force on such occasions.[22]

Because of the light nature of airborne forces and the limited availability of transport aviation assets, the guiding operating principles for the use of airborne forces were the same as during the Great Patriotic War. Airborne forces, consisting of air-assault and air-landed elements would be:

landing in limited regions, securing and holding objectives until the arrival of main *front* forces. Missions were thus passive. The depth of landings did not exceed 20 to 100 kilometers, and the length of independent combat action was comparatively short. Air transport of that time, the IL-12 and IL-14 aircraft were able to land only personnel with light weapons, including 82-mm mortars.[23]

Even more modern aircraft were in relatively short supply. The official *50 Years of the Soviet Armed Forces* stated, 'however, in the airborne forces there remained not a few of the obsolete aircraft (IL-2) with low speed and cargo capacity. Therefore, for towing gliders and transport of heavy equipment TU-2 and TU-4 [bombers] supplied by the air force were used.'[24] This limitation changed after 1950, when larger numbers of modern aircraft became available.

Foreign assessments recognized the overall Soviet airborne employment concepts and the emphasis on surprise, deception, and use of darkness. A 1951 U.S. intelligence assessment traced the history of Soviet airborne forces and focused on their postwar training, organization, and prospective employment. It noted the existence of an extensive network of training centers, including specialized facilities at Klin, Tula, and Vladivostok, and cited Kostin's article in describing potential wartime airborne missions. The assessment recognized that, 'Although present Soviet capabilities make such strategic operations [as described by Kostin] largely hypothetical, present trends – particularly in the field of unconventional warfare – may indicate that the Soviets are seeking to translate theory into practice.'

In particular, the report judged that Soviet airborne capabilities were adequate to '(1) Affect greatly the conduct of a future war in the sphere that the Soviets term "operational"; and (2) have strategic implications as well.' It went on to judge that:

> The use of large-scale airborne operations, enabling the Soviets to exploit more fully the speed, mobility, and firepower of their mechanized ground forces, therefore represents a logical extension of conventional doctrine rather than a reduced deviation from it.... In the future, greater dependence on air movement of both troops and supplies will enable the Soviets to increase the mobility of their mechanized ground forces and to make possible the projection of operations in greater depth.[25]

Another U.S. assessment, prepared in 1958, noted:

> the Soviets believe that airborne troops should be used as a surprise element and should be employed in sufficient strength to insure successful operation against the selected objective. The enemy rear and flanks are probable areas of employment. Darkness and decep-

tion are used in order to strike the enemy when and where he least expects it. The airborne troops transported by either helicopter or cargo aircraft or both. Although gliders may be used, helicopters and assault-type aircraft are expected to play the primary role.[26]

Although the materiel status of airborne forces still limited the scope and range of operations, it was improving. The assessment added:

> Support weapons that can be airlifted include both towed and self-propelled antitank guns, antiaircraft guns, mortars up to 120-mm, recoilless rifles, and lightweight vehicles. The previous Soviet dependence upon captured enemy equipment and supplies has now been somewhat reduced. The lack of armor and heavy caliber artillery in the airhead, however, must still be compensated for by close support ground attack aircraft and early linkup with friendly ground forces.[27]

Operational techniques and field exercises shaped specific missions airborne forces were to perform.[28] The paramount mission was to secure crossing sites (bridges or fords) over major water obstacles on the main axis of the ground force attack. Securing such crossings would preempt enemy defenses. If airborne forces faced a defended crossing, they would maneuver around the enemy flank and rear while the main force attacked from the front. Another high-priority mission was to seize important objectives or key terrain in the operational depths of the enemy defense to assist main forces in encircling and destroying the enemy or blocking enemy withdrawal or reinforcement. In airborne operations, key terrain included water obstacles, mountain passes, and defiles between lakes. In other instances, an airborne force could land over a wide area to disrupt enemy withdrawal plans by conducting harassing attacks on his columns or by destroying roads and communications routes. At the lower end of the combat spectrum, smaller airborne forces (groups, detachments) could attack small, but important, objectives, such as airfields, enemy command posts, key road junctions, bridges, warehouses, and enemy bases. Complementing amphibious operations, airborne forces could make surprise landings to secure beachheads where amphibious naval forces could land. In amphibious operations, airborne forces could block the advance of enemy reserves to a beachhead or prevent enemy withdrawal from the beachhead. In certain cases, paratroops could seize a port or naval base facilities.

With such assigned missions, airborne forces trained using tactical techniques derived from the study of wartime experiences. Most airborne training involved close coordination of airborne units with mechanized mobile forces operating in realistic simulation of wartime conditions, to include all-weather and all-season exercises. Training emphasized refining of parachuting techniques, orientation of units on the ground, rapid assembly of units, timely seizure of objectives, and the establishment of defenses on the ground, which were capable of holding terrain until the arrival of mobile ground forces.[29] Airborne operations took place in distinct phases: first, landing in a limited geographical area; second, securing objectives; and, third, holding those objectives until the main force arrived. Missions were passive because, after landing, paratroopers lacked mobility and heavy mobile firepower.

Soviet theorists and foreign analysts alike recognized the potential value of airborne operations at all levels of war and, like their predecessors, postulated three types of airborne operations: strategic, operational, and tactical. Scope and significance of the action distinguished the three types. Strategic operations were large-scale and carried out deep in the enemy rear. The objective was 'to impair the enemy's war making capabilities by seizing or neutralizing industrial, administrative, and other strategic targets.'[30] To be successful, strategic operations required continuous maintenance of air superiority to secure air delivery and supply routes and to protect the airborne force before, during, and after landing.

Operational level airborne assaults were 'effected deep in the enemy's rear defensive area in conjunction with frontal operations by ground forces of at least army size.'[31] Time-phased operational assaults began with small airborne forces dropping to secure airfields and landing areas. A main body of varied size and composition then air-landed on the captured airfield, performed its combat mission, and linked up with advancing ground forces. Tactical airborne actions were smaller assaults by paratroopers or by aircraft- and helicopter-transported units operating at shallower tactical depths in the enemy defense. Such forces usually operated on main attack axes:

> to facilitate the breakthrough of the main zone of resistance; to delay the forward movement of enemy reserves and divert their commitment from the point of the main effort; to complete the encirclement of enemy forces and take control of commanding heights; to seize enemy antitank, artillery, and atomic delivery systems and simultaneously disrupt his communications lines; to disrupt enemy rear area activities and destroy stocks of ammunition and fuel; to seize tactical airfields, bridges, and other tactical objectives; and to assist in river crossing operations and support amphibious landings.[32]

When discussing these missions, Soviet theorists constantly focused on two major concerns. The first was the necessity for reducing airborne force drop time to improve surprise, unit concentration, and firepower once on the ground. The second was the need to attain air superiority over the drop area to protect the transport aircraft from enemy anti-aircraft fire and aviation and to provide air support for airborne units on the ground in order to compensate for their inherent weakness in fire support.[33] Constant field exercises provided solutions for both problems. Larger aircraft and improved drop techniques reduced the existing two- to three-day war years' drop time to one to two days. This speed produced greater tactical surprise and led to more effective ground operations.

To reduce drop time even more and to capitalize on surprise, the Soviets emphasized the importance of reconnaissance and a time-phased rapid assault on or near the objective. Reconnaissance determined the suitability of the landing sites, enemy dispositions, and weather conditions that could affect the assault. Actual landings occurred in three distinct waves. The first wave of paratroopers secured and marked landing areas for gliders, helicopters, and transport aircraft. The second wave of gliders and/or helicopters carried troops and light equipment into the secured landing area. A third wave of transport aircraft lifted additional troops and heavier equipment into the landing area.[34] Clearly, these procedures incorporated the experiences and lessons of Second World War operations.

While airborne forces trained on the basis of Second World War experiences, the materiel standards of airborne units improved, thus increasing their combat capabilities. The Soviets launched a concerted effort to improve airborne troop weaponry and sustainability in combat. Units received more automatic weapons, modern artillery, mortars, antitank, and antiaircraft guns. To supplement the wartime 45-mm guns and 50-mm and 82-mm mortars, airborne forces received the self-propelled ASU-57 guns and later the SU-85 (1962), 85-mm antitank guns, 120-mm mortars, and 122-mm (M-30) howitzers.[35] These weapons sharply increased unit firepower, provided better antitank protection, and improved existing limited force mobility. New GAZ-67 trucks and tractors could move guns, and the ASU-57 was mobile. However, personnel could not move so readily. Parachute battalions and companies still advanced to combat on foot and also attacked on foot in combat formation, supported by ASU-57 guns, recoilless guns, and 82-mm mortars. When attacking the enemy flank and rear, airborne forces rode on the self-propelled guns.[36]

Another primary Soviet concern during the first postwar period was the limited availability of delivery aircraft. Without adequate numbers of aircraft configured to carry airborne units and their equipment and to drop them accurately, airborne operations would remain largely theoretical. The Soviets had lacked such aircraft during the war. After 1945 they developed and fielded new aircraft better equipped to land airborne forces more accurately. The IL-12 and IL-14 aircraft of the late 1940s had improved carrying capabilities and guidance systems; but, because of their side cargo doors, they lacked the capacity to deliver large, bulky items to the battlefield. A new generation of gliders, towed by the TU-2 and TU-4 bombers, could carry men and equipment more effectively. New aircraft and improved guidance systems also increased the depth at which airborne forces could operate. Similar experimental work produced safer parachutes capable of carrying larger equipment payloads. Improved parachutes also permitted dropping equipment from aircraft flying at speeds of 280 to 300 kilometers per hour rather than the standard 160 to 180 kilometers per hour.[37]

Beyond these developments, work also proceeded on helicopters. By the end of the first postwar period, the Soviets had produced the MI-1 and MI-4 helicopters. Though Soviet theorists certainly considered the use of helicopters for air-landing operations, real progress in this regard would not be made until later.

CONCLUSIONS

Airborne concepts and forces during the first postwar period were afflicted by the dark shadow of wartime experiences. The disastrous or near disastrous consequences of large-scale airborne operations left a legacy of skepticism over the prospects for survivability of airborne forces in modern combat and a deafening historical silence, so characteristic of the Stalin years, about the real historical record. Stalin simply did not permit open discussion of failures. He was, however, impressed enough by those failures to deemphasize the parachute-delivered role of airborne forces. The airborne force remained in the force structure with theoretical missions, training bases, and doctrinal literature governing their use. In reality, the airborne force remained as it had in the later war years, an elite segment of Soviet ground forces.

Soviet military theoreticians continued to speculate over future air assault, but in the absence of large numbers of modern air transport and equipment which would enable an airborne force to survive in intense ground combat, it remained speculation. After Stalin's death, it was the realization of the potential of atomic weapons for transforming ground combat that began the process of liberating airborne forces and concepts from their state of enforced hibernation. When that occurred, it was the theoretical work of Kostin and other writers of the 1940s and early 1950s which propelled airborne forces forward to new utility and, ultimately, a renaissance in the importance of the force.

Airborne operations in the first postwar period were an integral part of

Soviet offensive theory. Training of airborne forces continued apace with that theory. Materiel limitations, however, inhibited prospects for full implementation of the theory. The subsequent introduction into the force of modern equipment gradually improved airborne forces' capabilities and brought them closer to realizing in combat the conceptual framework governing their wartime use. Although there was progress in the first postwar period, the status of airborne forces did not improve, and the Soviets did not begin recognizing their important contemporary role until the mid-1950s.

CHAPTER 12

The Revolution in Military Affairs (1953–1970)

CONTEXT

In the mid-1950s, several important factors combined to produce a renaissance in the stature and importance of airborne forces. First and foremost, Stalin's death in 1953 removed a major obstacle in the path to reform. In the broadest sense, Soviet military thought after Stalin began to cast off the shibboleths harbored since the end of the Great Patriotic War and began judging military affairs with more emphasis on contemporary and future realities, but without abandoning faith in the lessons derived from the war. In addition, a growing recognition of the importance of nuclear weapons and the increased possibility and significance of surprise engendered by initial wartime use of those weapons triggered a basic revision of Soviet military theory and also a fundamental force reorganization. The ensuing period, usually identified as the period of the Zhukov reforms, was characterized by intense reinvestigation of all areas of military science in the light of recent technological changes. This reappraisal resulted in a wholesale reorganization of the armed forces, a redefinition of the role and capabilities of the various arms and services within a new concept of conducting military operations, and accelerated development and fielding of new weaponry. A second wave of change began in the early 1960s, keynoted by Nikita S. Khrushchev's January 1960 speech announcing Soviet recognition that a 'revolution' had taken place in military affairs.[1] The second wave represented a full maturation of concepts developed during the first, or Zhukov, phase.

The emergence of a new view on war, in general, and offensive operations, in particular, was fundamental to the changes after 1953. The new view ultimately held that general war would likely begin with a nuclear exchange. Ground operations would occur against this nuclear backdrop, and the premier ground mission would be to mop up enemy resistance in the theater of operations after a devastating nuclear exchange. Ground operations would involve the action of mobile tank and motorized rifle formations, supported by rocket forces conducting high-speed deep operations, often along multiple axes, to exploit the effects of nuclear strikes, defeat enemy forces, and conquer and occupy territory.[2] In this nuclear environment, ground forces would play a distinctly secondary role to the newly-formed strategic rocket forces.

Such new doctrine and altered strategic and operational concepts required a major reorganization of the armed forces. The subsequent force reorganization created smaller, more mobile forces better capable of fighting and surviving on first, an atomic, and later a nuclear battlefield. Marshal G. K. Zhukov began the first wave of structural changes in 1954 and 1955, and his successors (principally Marshal R. Ia. Malinovsky) continued them after his ouster in 1957.[3] The ponderous mechanized armies and mechanized divisions were abolished, as were weaker rifle corps, rifle divisions, and cavalry divisions. A new stream-lined tank army replaced the mechanized army, and a more flexible motorized rifle division replaced both the mechanized division and the rifle division.[4] The combined arms army emerged as a balanced force of tank and motorized rifle divisions, and the tank division was reduced in size as well.[5] Units were fully motorized, and new equipment, rocket artillery, new tanks (T-55), tactical missiles, armored personnel carriers (BTR series), and early model surface-to-air missiles were incorporated into the force structure.

The second wave of change occurred after 1960, when the Soviets further streamlined both motorized rifle and tank divisions and tailored them to the fully nuclear battlefield.[6] Equipment modernization continued with the introduction of the T-62 tank, antitank guided missiles (ATGMs), infantry combat vehicles (BMP and BMD), and tactical missiles at division level. This 'Khrushchev period' placed even greater emphasis on the predominance of nuclear weapons on the battlefield. The ground forces became a mobile, useful adjunct to strategic rocket forces, capable of flexible, semi-independent operations on an increasingly nuclear battlefield.

Fundamental doctrinal changes also affected the strategic, operational, and tactical role of airborne forces in contemporary operations. Airborne forces were tailored to perform more realistic combat missions on the nuclear battlefield. Symbolizing the closer integration of airborne operations with ground operations was the reintegration of airborne forces into the ground forces in 1956.[7] New weaponry also made airborne units more mobile, hence more capable of surviving in nuclear war. Military theorists could now postulate new, more realistic and extensive missions for airborne forces.

THEORETICAL WRITINGS

Soviet theoretical writings on the use of airborne and air-landing forces evolved in consonance with developing theories for ground combat in future war. This encompassed two distinct stages: the first, between 1954 and 1960, involving Soviet recognition of the realities of combat in an increasingly atomic age; and the second, after 1960, reflecting Soviet recognition that a full-blown nuclear revolution was occurring in military affairs. While the former required relatively minor adjustments in combat techniques, the latter seemed to demand more fundamental changes.

Writing in *Military Thought* in 1956, Colonel I. Lisov, himself a veteran of wartime airborne operations, first recognized the import of the atomic age. While claiming that, 'The experience of the past war and postwar development of military technology and military art with all persuasiveness confirms the growing importance of air assaults in operations of various scales,' he acknowledged that, 'The employment of air assaults in combination with the use of means of mass destruction opens broad possibilities in the realization of deep offensive operations, in the increase in their tempo, and in organizing the encirclement of modern highly mobile forces.'[8]

Air assaults, according to Lisov, could be used to cooperate with ground forces in encircling enemy forces, to secure key regions and objectives in the path of advancing enemy forces (crossings, mountain passes, road junctions, etc.), in cooperation with ground forces to preempt or quickly overcome hasty enemy defenses, and generally to facilitate the rapid movement of advancing ground forces. Most important, he claimed, 'will be small air assaults, the actions of which, in conjunction with atomic strikes on the enemy, could play an important role in the securing of the unceasing movement of advancing forces.'[9]

Lisov reiterated the requirements for success in airborne operations spelled out by earlier theorists and reviewed the successes and failures of Allied wartime operations, although he remained silent about specific Soviet experiences. He placed particular emphasis on thorough planning, reduced time constraints on organizing and carrying out the operations, and the importance of surprise because of the looming atomic threat to all forces. After examining required technical characteristics of aircraft and landing sites, he summed up the impact of atomic warfare on airborne operations of various scales, writing:

> The appearance of atomic weapons does not exclude the condition that the main prerequisite for the successful realization of airborne operations is the presence of air superiority; tactical – for operations counting on the link up of the air assault with advancing forces in a short period; and operational – for airborne operations, when, in

the course of several days, regular supply and reinforcement of the *desant* and continued air support of it must be realized.[10]

In the absence of air superiority, air assaults to lesser depths could be conducted if temporary air protection was provided during the assault or if the assault occurred at night.

Lisov emphasized that contemporary airborne operations could be performed by both air assault and conventional combined-arms forces similar to mixtures of forces employed in the 1930s. This required specialized training for officers and men from all types of forces in the basic techniques of air delivery and air assault. Lisov reiterated the basic requirement that airborne and air delivered forces be equipped with sufficient supplies to operate for two to three days before link-up with main force units. These forces had to be ready for 'repeated employment' within the realm of the modern *front* operation.[11] Rapidly developing operations required constant readiness of all forces trained in air assault, both parachute and air delivered, for immediate and often repeated employment in air assaults.

The following year, in the same journal, Colonel V. Schensnovich focused on tactical air assaults in atomic warfare. He began with the premise that:

> The employment of atomic weapons in armed combat has, as is well known, a great influence on the nature of contemporary battle and operations. Atomic attacks, in combination with other means of struggle, provides requisite neutralization of the enemy, rapid penetration of his defensive belt, and the achievement of great tactical and operational success in a shorter period of time.[12]

In short, the use of atomic weapons had unleashed maneuver war to an even greater degree than before. Rapid, skillful maneuver was necessary to exploit atomic strikes, further disrupt the enemy, and destroy him in piecemeal fashion. Because of the threat of atomic weapons, attacking forces had to move continuously at high tempo to exploit success and also neutralize enemy atomic delivery means to the entire depth of the enemy's defense. 'In these conditions,' wrote Schensnovich, 'during the course of an offensive, great importance is attached to force subunits and units, which, by air-landing, attack from the air in the enemy rear for immediate cooperation with forces attacking from the front.'[13] These air assaults could, by virtue of their size, scale, depth, and mission, be rated as tactical or operational. Tactical assaults were normally conducted by force subunits [battalions] or units [regiments] to perform missions in the interests of divisions or armies, and, in each case, depth of operations permitted link up with main forces in a relatively short time. Operational assaults, serving the interest of *fronts*, were conducted at greater depths with larger forces, in pursuit of more ambitious missions. Whereas, since the end of the Great Patriotic War, tactical air assaults had been avoided because they were too dangerous and vulnerable to defensive fires, the introduction of atomic weaponry had restored the combat utility of such assaults:

> It [atomic warfare] is opening new possibilities for successful employment of tactical air assaults. Airborne forces, landed after atomic strikes earlier than any other forces, can exploit the effects of the actions of these weapons and prevent the enemy from undertaking measures to counter the effects of the atomic explosion.[14]

Schensnovich then detailed the methods, requirements, and difficulties encountered in airborne operations. He catalogued potential airborne missions to include the following:

– seizure of sectors of positions in the region of the atomic strike to deny the enemy the chance to restore defenses in the breach;
– seizure and destruction of atomic, rocket, or other means of mass destruction, located within the limits of the tactical defense zone or in its close operational depths;
– seizure and holding for a short time sectors of positions on the direction of attack of the main group of advancing forces to prevent the arrival of reserves in the defense in that direction;
– seizure of crossings and bridgeheads over river obstacles in the enemy rear;
– seizure of forward airfields and the destruction of aviation means based on them;
– cooperation with forces advancing from the front in repelling counterattacks and in destroying counterattacking groupings;
– disruption of command and control of forces and disorganization of rear service work of defending forces.[15]

Air assaults, according to Schensnovich, were applicable to pursuit operations, meeting engagements, and defensive battles and operations as well. In this sense, air assaults performed many of the same missions as envisoned by Soviet theorists in the 1930s and during the Great Patriotic War. Moreover, airborne forces now functioned like classic ground forward detachments, which understandably also reemerged as an important tactical feature in the late 1950s.

Schensnovich and Lisov postulated new uses for air assaults which would, by the early 1960s, restore the former significance of airborne forces as a useful combat force at both the tactical and operational levels of war. Their theoretical work, and that of other theorists writing in the 1960s, would pave the way for and accompany the reemergence of a viable and expanded airborne force structure which possessed real wartime capabilities and missions.

In 1960 the Soviet leadership openly embraced the concept that a revolution had occurred in military affairs, characterized by the appearance and dominance on the battlefield of nuclear weaponry. Recognition of the reality of nuclear war accelerated theoretical trends of the late 1950s, established a new mileu for the conduct of battles and operations and further increased the utility and, hence, stature, of Soviet airborne forces. While V. D. Sokolovsky articulated the influence that nuclear weapons were having on military strategy and future war, a host of writers formulated new roles and missions for airborne forces on the nuclear battlefield.

Writing in 1961, I. Lisov built upon his earlier description of the nature of atomic warfare to form a more coherent picture of combat in the nuclear arena. He noted that 'huge technical progress in the realm of military matters and the arming of modern armies with nuclear-rocket weaponry has inescapably led to changes in the means and form of conducting war, and in the organization and use of armed force.'[16] Citing Western sources, Lisov focused on the new concept of 'vertical envelopment' as an essential aspect of modern warfare. Airborne forces would now perform two basic missions: first, to exploit success achieved as a result of the use of nuclear weapons, and, second, to perform regular missions after nuclear weapons had suppressed enemy air defenses and blocked the movement of reserves. Airborne forces would now operate for two to three days or even longer, while separated from main forces to depths of from 20–100 kilometers behind the front.[17] Lisov cited foreign sources to expand the scope and depth of potential airborne missions. Among these expanded missions were the following:

- exploitation of the effect achieved by massive bombing (nuclear or conventional) and seizure of vital important enemy centers (military, administrative-political, or economic);
- creation of bridgeheads, securing the movement into the enemy rear by landing means of additional forces, sufficient for seizure and occupation of entire zones of enemy territory;
- incursions on a continent in cooperation with forces landing by sea;
- conduct of special operations in various types of raids in the enemy rear, for cooperation with amphibious assaults or to assist these assaults, as well as actions in the interests of forces attacking from the front;

– destruction of strategically important objectives, which cannot be neutralized by other means.[18]

These new, broader tasks, noted Lisov:

> ... embraced missions of operational-strategic, tactical, and reconnaissance-diversionary nature. Consequently, airborne assaults, depending on the scale of their employment, constitute a distinctive forward echelon, operating to the entire depth of the enemy defenses and securing a strengthening of forces during an operation and are looked upon by military specialists of many countries as an important means of contemporary armed struggle.[19]

By citing foreign sources, Lisov postulated for Soviet military theorists, planners, and force designers a vastly expanded realm of operations for future Soviet airborne forces.

The following year Colonel Ia. Samoilenko, also citing foreign views, built upon Lisov's analysis to contemplate the expanded role of airborne forces in future nuclear war. Accepting Lisov's premise of the increased importance and expanding combat role of airborne forces, he articulated the fundamental change that had occurred as follows:

> Great changes have occurred in the nature of combat actions of airborne force formations and units in the enemy rear. In the period of the past war, the actions of airborne assaults consisted of the following. As a rule, they secured this or that region of terrain in the enemy rear, and then strove to hold it until the arrival of advancing forces. The only exception were actions of a reconnaissance-diversionary nature.
>
> Today the combat actions of airborne forces have a maneuver character. Airborne assault forces, after landing in the enemy rear area and fulfilling their initial missions, along with defending seized regions, will often move to new regions and fulfill new missions. Undoubtedly, such a nature of combat operations has established new demands on the organization and armament of formations, units, and subunits of airborne forces.[20]

Samoilenko went on to describe the airborne force organization in foreign armies, stressing the foreign upgrading of airborne weaponry to include the integration into airborne forces of heavier artillery (often nuclear), antitank weapons, and tanks. His description provided the basis for Soviet theorists to work out analogous Soviet organizations.

Lisov again entered the debate in 1963 with an article on airborne training. He opened with a succinct description of contemporary combat by writing:

The study of the experiences of the past and the direction of development of means and methods of armed struggle in the postwar years demonstrates that combat actions of ground forces in conditions of nuclear war can vividly acquire a pronounced spatial air-ground character. Therefore, actions with the use of the air sphere will become still greater in scope and considerably varied by virtue of content, than was the case before.[21]

Lisov again reviewed the work of foreign specialists to focus on new facets of the air-ground problem, specifically the use of heavy lift in the form of mobilized civilian air fleets and the emergence of special designation forces, which were specially trained to accomplish reconnaissance-diversionary missions. Lisov noted a speech by Soviet Minister of Defense R. Ia. Malinovsky, which declared 'that the Soviet Army can count on not only military-transport aviation, but also the numerous part of Civil Air Fleet [*Grazhadnskyi vozdushnyi flot* – GVF] for carrying out air-landing and movement of forces.'[22] Lisov then surveyed in detail Civil Air Fleet assets and their heavy lift capabilities.

In addition, Lisov focused on Western (particularly U.S.) programs designed to prepare officers in 'airborne and reconnaissance-diversionary training.'[23] This he juxtaposed against U.S. mobilization of airborne assets for possible action in Cuba during the missile crisis to demonstrate growing Western capabilities for conducting extensive airborne operations.

A new dimension in airborne warfare surfaced in Soviet theoretical writings in 1965, in part in response to increased Soviet appreciation of the nature of U.S. combat actions in Vietnam. For the first time, a Soviet theorist pondered the impact of the helicopter's use in the realm of air assault operations. Major General G. Kublanov, in an article in *Military Thought*, surveyed airborne operations in modern war. Beginning with a, by now, familiar picture of combat in the context of nuclear war, Kublanov immediately identified the helicopter as an important new vehicle for air assault. He wrote:

Equipment of the armed forces of the leading countries of the world with atomic weapons and the development of aviation, including heavy lift helicopters, provides a basis for military-theoretical thought to reach the conclusion that exceptionally wide use of airborne assaults will occur in nuclear war. They can be landed in subunit, unit, and formation strength in the immediate and deep rear, on the flanks, in the intervals, and in front of operating forces, at any time and along any direction. Depending on the aim of their use and the nature of assigned missions, *desants* can be strategic, operational, tactical, and special. Strategic *desants*, landed in the deep rear, can be designated to develop the success of a strategic offensive in a theater of military operations, for securing and holding large bridgeheads on sea or ocean coasts, or for occupying important military, administrative-political and economic regions. Operational *desants* are employed chiefly in the interest of operations of forces in ground theaters. Exploiting the results of nuclear strikes, they can seize and, together with forward units of attacking forces, hold operationally and tactically important sectors, regions, and objectives until the approach of their main forces, secure and destroy warehouses and bases for nuclear weapons, and disrupt force command and control and the work of enemy rear services. Tactical air assaults will be employed basically in the interest of actions of separate formations. Large operational and strategic *desants* are called upon to play a special role, to land with missions of cooperating with advancing operational large formations in the destruction of nuclear rocket weaponry and important enemy ground forces and aviation groupings.[24]

Moreover, 'Tactical *desants* are becoming the most important means of maintaining high offensive tempos of ground forces.'[25]

Kublanov again cited American sources to argue for careful selection of dispersed assembly, jumping-off, and landing areas, and he subsequently analyzed specific missions suited for resolution by airborne forces at every level of combat. He devoted special attention to defensive measures suited to repelling enemy airborne operations, a measure of the seriousness with which Soviet theorists approached U.S. airborne capabilities.

Another article published in 1966 and written by Colonels N. Andrukhov and B. Bulatnikov, which reviewed the history of air assault, echoed Kublanov's arguments for the future ubiquitousness of 'vertical envelopment' and focused attention on several new issues. While discussing lift characteristics of transport aviation, the authors underscored Western (U.S.) development of an air assault division equipped with 428 helicopters and six aircraft, which they cited to show the growing utility in air assault of large, well-equipped helicopter-delivered combined-arms forces.[26] They went on to emphasize new facets of successful airborne operations, including the necessity for comprehensive detailed planning, the criticality of antiair defense for the airborne force, the importance of pre-assault intelligence [*razvedka*], and the growing role played by radio-electronic combat (REC) in air assault.

A follow-on article, published in 1969 by Lieutenant General A. Sopil'nik filled in many of the voids in Soviet assessments of airborne experiences and claimed for the Soviets a leading prewar role in the development of theory and forces for vertical envelopment.[27] He then thoroughly reviewed the parameters of airborne operations (mission, size and composition of force, duration of action, and course and outcome of operation) and finally the prerequisites for success adjusted to operations in modern war. He again emphasized that, in a contemporary sense, strategic missions for airborne forces were becoming likely within the context of a strategic offensive within a theater of military operations during nuclear war.

AIRBORNE FORCE EMPLOYMENT

On the basis of these extensive theoretical writings, more recent Soviet military theorists have looked back in an attempt to describe, retrospectively, the proper context for airborne operations in the period of the 1960s. General V. Margelov, Chief of Airborne Forces, writing in 1977 described the context for airborne operations during the 1960s as follows:

> Nuclear rocket weapons are able to strike enemy forces located at any distance from the front lines. However, considerable gaps in time between nuclear strikes on objectives in the deep rear of the enemy and the entering of that region by ground forces do not permit to a full measure exploitation of the results of those strikes. The problem of shortening that gap can be resolved by landing airborne forces in the region struck by rocket forces in order to secure key enemy positions. Airborne units came to be considered a combat means able to exploit effectively and quickly the results of nuclear strikes and completely destroy the enemy. Moreover, airborne forces could undertake new missions, such as destroying enemy nuclear delivery means, bases, and warehouses for nuclear weapons, etc.
>
> They retained the missions of cooperating with the ground forces in securing administrative and industrial centers of the enemy, seizing crossings and bridgeheads on wide water obstacles, mountain passes and any difficult area to access.[28]

Airborne unit capabilities improved as well, so 'the basic tendency of the development of tactics in that period became a rejection of the passive defense of limited regions (objectives) and a transition to maneuver combat in a wider region.'[29] Improved airborne unit mobility and broadened combat uses occurred with the appearance of nuclear weapons because

> the possibility of suppressing the enemy improved, especially in enemy antiaircraft systems in the landing region. Favorable con-

ditions were created for landing large airborne assaults. Use of nuclear weapons created high tempos for offensive action of ground forces and shortened the period of time they took to arrive in the landing region. This permitted increasing the depth of regiment and division drops.[30]

The introduction of nuclear weapons greatly expanded the overall range of airborne missions, and the fielding of new weaponry and airborne delivery systems also increased the variety of missions airborne forces could perform. New antitank weapons (PTURS), self-propelled artillery (ASU-85), light armored vehicles (PT-76), and the prospective development of new airborne combat vehicles (BMD in 1973) improved airborne force survivability in combat, as well as sustainability while

FIGURE 90. AIRBORNE DIVISION ORGANIZATION, 1968

> 3 parachute regiments
>   3 parachute battalions
> 1 artillery regiment
> 1 antiaircraft battalion (ASU-57/85)
> 1 reconnaissance battalion
> 1 engineer battalion
> 1 signal battalion
> 1 medical battalion (assumed)
> 1 transportation battalion
> 1 chemical defense company.

engaged in longer duration operations. Furthermore, new transport aircraft, including the AN-8 (1956), the AN-12 (early 1960s), and ultimately the AN-22, enabled airborne forces to deploy with more versatile combat weaponry at longer ranges.[31]

By 1968 a new airborne division organization had emerged, which would set the form for the parachute-delivered force in the future. Numbering about 6,500 men, the division was organized as shown in Figure 90.[32]

Theorists could also articulate more precise tactical and operational missions, such as the use of air assaults to reinforce the actions of forward detachments on the offensive. 'The role of forward detachments in rapidly exploiting the results of nuclear strikes and securing high rates of advance has also increased. Tactical air-landings – a new element of the combat formation in divisions – could perform such missions as destruction of enemy nuclear delivery means and closing gaps created as a result of their use.'[33] Airborne forces also came to play a greater role in meeting engagements. By operating deep in the enemy's rear, tactical air-landings and ground forward detachments could, in a meeting engagement, forestall enemy use of nuclear conventional fire and block deployment of the enemy main forces.[34]

Army exercises reflected this extensive expansion in airborne missions within the Soviet Union and outside the nation's borders. A major innovation, which appeared in exercises of the late 1950s, was the use of maneuverable airborne forces in the enemy's rear area. Exercises in the late 1950s and early 1960s routinely included airborne elements. By 1963, Soviet airborne forces were participating in such exercises abroad. During Warsaw Pact Exercise Quartet held in East Germany that year, at least one airborne regiment with heavy equipment dropped from AN-12 aircraft. An advanced assault reconnaissance group of reinforced company size landed initially, secured the landing site, and prepared for further drops. The main body dropped by parachute with heavy equipment and secured the airfield for a subsequent large air-landing operation.[35] Quartet initiated a series of similar exercises in the late 1960s using the same general scenario, each involving larger forces.

Perhaps the clearest statement concerning the employment of Soviet airborne forces, and one that best described the function of airborne forces within the realm of the revolution in military affairs, appeared in V. D. Sokolovsky's classic work on military strategy:

> During the operation [the offensive], wide use will be made of tactical and operational airborne landings. These will have the task of solving problems of the most effective use of the results attained by massing nuclear strikes ... [such as] capture of the regions where nuclear weapons are located, important objectives, river crossings, bridgeheads, mountain passes, defiles and the annihilation of strategic objectives which cannot be put out of commission in any other way. Helicopters will be used as the main means of dropping tactical airborne troops. Transport planes can be used for operational landings. To assure the landing of a large airdrop at a great depth, the enemy air defense must be neutralized by ECM [electronic countermeasures], air operations, and rocket strikes.[36]

Sokolovsky's work not only captured the expanded role of airborne forces, but also marked the emergence of new concepts of air delivery using the helicopter.

Official U.S. assessments of Soviet airborne force missions changed little from the 1950s to the 1960s. Assessments categorized Soviet airborne operations as strategic, operational, and tactical and described the nature of these missions in the same language as was used in 1958.[37] One subtle change was the mention of a new *front* special purpose mission. A special purpose mission was classified as 'a highly specialized, small-size operation conducted by a well-trained unit generally of company size or smaller. These operations are designed to harass and disrupt lines of communications, to conduct sabotage, or to support partisan activities.'[38]

The assessment also noted the emergence of Soviet concern for helicopter operations as a vital means for facilitating rapid ground advance.
Specifically, 'helicopter assaults usually involve forward detachments
and are used to assist the attacking forces to maintain a high tempo of
attack. This is accomplished by using a helicopter assault to surmount
obstacles and large areas of contamination.'[39]

Conducted in the Ukraine from 24 September to 3 October 1967,
Exercise Dnepr amply demonstrated the expanded role of airborne
forces. Elements of two guards airborne divisions participated and
engaged in both operational and tactical landings. At the operational
level, a reinforced airborne division landed to secure an objective deep in
the enemy rear. In the phased landing, first a lead battalion parachuted
as an airborne reconnaissance force. Heavy transports followed and
dropped a forward detachment and then the main force. A novelty of the
drop was the use of rockets to break the fall of parachute-landed heavy
equipment. At the tactical level, a helicopter-borne battalion-size force
secured a bridgehead across the Dnepr for ground forces to exploit.[40] This
symbolic replay of the unsuccessful 1943 Dnepr operation signaled Soviet
commitment to the expanded role of airborne forces and became a model
for future exercises.

CONCLUSIONS

Despite the extravagant use of airborne divisions in major showpiece
operations, a full renaissance in Soviet faith in the utility of airborne
forces had yet to emerge. Prior to 1960, discussion of the use of these
forces was largely theoretical because of their persistent fragility on the
battlefield when faced with devastating modern weaponry. While articles
still provided theoretical missions for these elite forces, operational and
tactical manuals and studies gave short shrift to airborne operations. The
major series of operational and tactical studies published by the Ministry
of Defense in 1958 made little or no mention of airborne forces, nor did
the numerous case studies used to illustrate virtually every type of combat
include examples of airborne operations, in part because of these operations' singular lack of success.[41] It took the advent of the nuclear era and a
healthy dose of historical candor (early *glasnost'*) to revive the fortunes of
airborne forces. Beginning in 1960, during the Khrushchev thaw, Soviet
writers were encouraged to address failure as well as success. Thus, the
first book on airborne experiences appeared in 1962.[42]

Nuclear combat offered new horizons for the employment of airborne
forces and encouraged greater historical candor. The two trends merged
to place once again the public spotlight on the potential uses of airborne
forces. Even with this renewed attention, serious consideration for the

use of airborne forces in combat would remain minimal until Soviet theorists fully recognized the role and utility of a new battlefield weapon – the helicopter and its associated concepts of air assault. This new recognition, spurred on by intense observation and assessment of what U.S. forces were doing with air assault in Vietnam, grew by the 1970s into a real renaissance for air assault forces in terms of force organization and the combat functions these forces were expected to perform.

CHAPTER 13

On the Threshold of a New Technological Revolution (1971–1985)

CONTEXT

After Khrushchev's fall from power, a lengthy debate began over Soviet military policy and doctrine. It culminated in significant changes by the early 1970s. The Soviets reassessed Khrushchev's single-option war-fighting strategy and reached a consensus that conventional war was possible. Theorists initially treated techniques for conducting conventional war within a nuclear context. By the 1970s, however, that context had eroded, so theorists wrote about nuclear and conventional war, often as separate topics. Historical and theoretical military writings showed such a shift in emphasis and seemed to indicate a basic change in the Soviet view of war.[1] The Soviets still considered nuclear war a real possibility, but they increasingly indicated an acceptance of, and perhaps a desire for, a nonnuclear initial phase of operations if war occurred.

They concluded that the existence of a strategic and tactical nuclear balance (or superiority for the Soviets) could generate reluctance on both sides to use nuclear weapons, a form of mutual deterrence that increased the likelihood that initial conventional operations would remain conventional. At a minimum, the Soviets prepared themselves to fight either a nuclear war or a conventional war in a 'nuclear-scared' posture. This Soviet version of 'flexible response' emphasized the necessity for expanding and perfecting combined-arms strategic, operational, and tactical concepts.

These revisions in concepts for waging modern war had a major impact on Soviet force structuring and military theory. Lighter combat units of the Khrushchev era (in particular, the motorized rifle division) now received significantly heavier weaponry and, to some extent, increased manpower. A new emphasis on *front* operations and tactics and the study of such previous operations required development and fielding of new weapons in greater numbers in line units, a process that continued throughout the 1970s.[2] These changes in military policy, of course, affected airborne forces and concepts for their combat use.

Initially, Soviet articulation of tactical, operational, and strategic airborne missions did not change significantly from the early 1960s. The new caveat, however, that such missions could be performed in either a nuclear or a conventional environment was important.[3] For theorists, the primary concern was the issue of airborne force survivability in a more lethal tactical and operational environment, especially without benefit of early use of the devastating striking power of nuclear weapons. The problems of Soviet airborne units in the Great Patriotic War once again became an intense focus of study and concern.[4] The major objective was to determine what missions the airborne force should perform in such an intense combat environment and, more important, how it should perform such missions. The most important by-product of this study was the investigation of the most suitable delivery means – helicopter or aircraft – for an airborne force. Soviet study of U.S. experiences in Vietnam, in part, intensified this concern over helicopter-borne airmobile operations.[5]

Study and experience again proved the vulnerability of forces parachuted into combat or air-landed from aircraft. An alternate delivery means had emerged in the 1950s when the MI-4 helicopter appeared in the Soviet aircraft inventory. The MI-4, a helicopter capable of carrying troops, light vehicles, and artillery, was used in the first experimental helicopter-lift operations in the mid and late 1950s. Other helicopters, the Vak-24 and MI-6, appeared in the late 1950s and added the much-needed lift capacity to the helicopter force. The MI-6 could transport heavier weapons and about 65 men into combat.[6] Helicopter development ultimately dovetailed with the new theoretical requirements to wage war on the nuclear battlefield. Helicopters, rather than aircraft, seemed better suited to perform many of the newly articulated missions. Therefore, exercises involving helicopter-lifted forces increased, reaching a peak during the 1967 Dnepr exercise. The addition of two new helicopter models to the inventory in the 1970s fueled the more and more convincing arguments for helicopter superiority. The MI-8 troop transport heli-copter provided improved troop transport capability, and the MI-24 attack helicopter afforded accompanying fire support for helicopter-landed operations.[7]

THEORY AND PRACTICE TO 1975

As lift equipment improved, theorists intensified their discussion of the utility of helicopters in operational and tactical level actions. Shortly before Exercise Dnepr, an article in the General Staff journal *Military*

Thought [*Voennaia mysl'*] had assessed the role of airborne forces in modern combat. Although accepting the validity of airborne operations in general, it again raised the helicopter issue:

> The creation of the helicopter has increased the possibilities for landing airlifted troops from the personnel of regular ground troops which have not been trained in airborne landing. And this, in turn, has helped to resolve certain serious problems. While in the parachute method of landing, the troops were greatly dispersed after their landing and their combat efficiency remained low for a certain period of time, the troops delivered to the landing region in helicopters are ready to enter battle immediately.[8]

This article's uniqueness rested in its emphasis on using other than airborne forces for air assault operations and on the technical and tactical advantages of helicopter-landed forces over parachute or air-landed forces.

By 1969, the Soviet investigation of a variety of air assault methods had produced detailed conclusions.[9] Although recognizing that airborne (parachute) forces could still operate successfully, Soviet theorists highlighted the conditions that made their use difficult. Parachute forces required special training and equipment to perform their mission, a mission, moreover, that depended on favorable weather conditions for success. Also, to land an airborne force of sufficient size, parachute troops had to secure a suitable landing area. Because of the special landing requirements of modern aircraft, such areas were often scarce. Since existing means of parachute delivery usually dispersed airborne forces over a considerable area during landing, assembling men and equipment before beginning combat missions took a long time. Past experiences continually illustrated these difficulties, and exercises indicated the persistence of this problem.

The helicopter, however, seemed to solve part of the problem and provided greater flexibility to operational planners. Helicopters had better maneuverability in combat, carried heavier loads of men and equipment than before (although less than aircraft), and, by using vertical takeoff and landing, placed forces in precise combat order at a specific location, ready to commence ground operations. Because helicopters were able to land in a wide variety of locations, forces could more readily secure their objectives. Helicopters could also operate at considerable ranges and at high speeds, thus making them less vulnerable to enemy ground fire and detection than aircraft operating at low altitudes. During landing, helicopter firepower could suppress enemy fire as effectively as fighter aircraft escorting a landing force if not more so. Perhaps more important, however, was the fact that troop training for helicopter assault required less time, thus reducing preparation time for an operation. Furthermore, helicopters could carry any type of force into combat, including motorized rifle forces with their weapons and various types of support units. In short, helicopters could deliver a true combined-arms force.

As articulated in 1969, the ideal tactical air assault unit was the reinforced motorized rifle battalion, able to conduct long-term combat in the enemy rear, independently, if necessary, and free from the require-ments of fire support from *front* units.

> Thus, a contemporary motorized rifle battalion could successfully conduct battle with its TOE weapons against large numbers of enemy tanks; every motorized rifle company could defend a strong-point extending to one kilometer of front (sometimes more), having created in its sector high densities of automatic weapons fire. It is clear that in a tactical landing the battalion, on many occasions, must be reinforced by mortars and artillery, engineer subunits, radiation and chemical reconnaissance and other means to increase its combat capabilities.[10]

Besides motorized rifle battalions performing the usual helicopter air assaults, task-organized companies and even platoons could conduct such missions as seizing enemy nuclear delivery means, destroying command facilities, and disorganizing the enemy rear. As with airborne operations, helicopter assaults involved landing in enemy territory and confronting enemy fighter aircraft, and antiaircraft, infantry, artillery, and rocket fire. The Second World War had taught that successful completion of all prospective missions required thorough preparation, uninterrupted reconnaissance, firm command and control, effective suppressive fire, adequate supply, and exact landing in the designated area.

Writing in *Military Thought* in 1969, Colonel Ia. Samoilenko also focused on the utility of helicopter operations, stating, 'The appearance of helicopters widens even more the sphere of using airborne assaults, in the capacity of which it has become possible to employ conventional motorized infantry units and subunits.'[11] He added, 'Changing conditions of the conduct of war, summoned forth by the revolution in military affairs, requires a fundamental re-examination of the role and mission of airborne assaults as well as the organization of their use and conduct of combat actions in the enemy rear.'[12] Drawing again on foreign experi-ences, Samoilenko examined the nature and uses of airborne forces in future war. Reassessing strategic, operational, tactical, and special missions, he concluded that:

> In future war, the airborne assault will not be merely an episode in

the operations of general forces (as it was before), but will become a constant element of their operational formation. In light of this, it has become insightful to consider simultaneous landing of strategic, operational, tactical and special airborne *desants* in operations as an *offensive by air* [*nastuplenie po vozdukhu*] [author's italics]. The essence of that offensive consists in the use of a considerable quantity of air assaults, coordinated in time and location with nuclear strikes and accomplished according to a single concept for the development of ground combat actions to the entire depth of the formation of enemy forces.[13]

The supplementing of regular airborne forces with conventional motorized rifle units employing helicopters made the 'offensive by air' possible. While admitting and detailing the complexities involved in conducting and coordinating such an operation, Samoilenko charted a new, expanded role for air assault in the future.

A year later Samoilenko expanded his views to embrace the factor of terrain. In an article on the use of airborne forces in special conditions, he argued that modern helicopter air assaults could solve many of the classic problems of conducting relatively high speed operations in difficult terrain, in particular in 'special theaters' such as mountainous or desert regions. He said:

One can propose that in the mountains the main aim of the use of air assaults is cooperation with ground forces in the achievement of high offensive tempos and in the rapid overcoming by them of mountain summits and other inaccessible terrain sectors. While penetrating into the depth of the defense by air, air assaults can preempt enemy occupation of mountain passes and passages, dominating heights, rail and road sectors, crossings and bridgeheads over water obstacles and defiles and hold them until the approach of main forces; prohibit the withdrawal of his forces from the front to new positions; halt the forward movement of reserves from the depths; and cooperate with attacking forces in the encirclement and rapid destruction of enemy groupings.[14]

By virtue of Samoilenko's and others' work, by 1970, the concept of helicopter assault had become firmly entrenched in the Soviet lexicon of suitable airborne techniques. In the wide range of missions allocated to airborne forces, all that remained to be decided was which precise functions aircraft and helicopters would perform across the spectrum of airborne combat. In 1970, Colonel A. A. Sidorenko's *The Offensive* articulated the tasks each type of force would perform. Writing in the context of nuclear war, Sidorenko outlined the by now classic portrayal of the stages of nuclear war, adhering to Sokolovsky's general concepts. General airborne troops, using modern transport aviation and equipped with new weaponry, could perform the following basic missions in the enemy rear: destroy enemy nuclear delivery means; secure important areas and objectives; complete the utter defeat of enemy forces subjected to nuclear strikes; assist the attacking troops in overcoming water obstacles, mountain passes, and passages from the march; prevent the approach of enemy reserves and enemy withdrawal; and disrupt the operation of the rear area and troop control.[15]

Echoing the views contained in V. G. Reznichenko's 1966 book, *Tactics* [*Taktika*], Sidorenko emphasized the combat utility of airborne parties working in tandem with ground forward detachments. To penetrate an enemy defense:

> airborne forces landed from helicopters in the depth of the enemy's defense right after nuclear strikes can make more rapid use of their results than ground troops and can capture important areas, junctions of lines of communication, and crossings over water obstacles. They can hinder the approach of reserves and, thus, facilitate an increased rate of the attack.[16]

Similarly, helicopter-lifted forces could conduct pursuit operations to secure river crossings.

> In addition to forward detachments, tactical airborne landing forces can also be employed. Usually they are landed from helicopters on axes of operations of forward detachments, advanced guards and tank battalions, and regiments. The area for the airborne landing is chosen to ensure a rapid seizure of crossings and other important objectives and the assault crossing of the waterbarrier at high rate.[17]

Having dealt with tactical and operational missions, Sidorenko surveyed the range of diversionary missions airborne forces could conduct at all levels of combat. Accordingly,

> The outfitting of modern tactical airborne landing forces with powerful weaponry and combat equipment permits them to perform various missions by raid methods, to make surprise assaults on withdrawing and approaching enemy columns, control points, and rear service areas, and to cause panic in the enemy disposition.[18]

In addition, he pointed out that Second World War experiences had shown that darkness favored successful employment of tactical airborne landings, in spite of the inherent difficulties encountered in conducting night operations.

Samoilenko's and Sidorenko's ground-breaking work on the expanded role of air assault unleashed a continuing barrage of theoretical works on air assault published over the ensuing four years. These works drew heavily on Western experiences, for example those of the U.S. in Vietnam, and proposed a wide array of new missions within the general rubics of 'vertical envelopment' and the 'offensive by air.' Colonel N. Andrukhov, in a 1971 *Military Thought* article, thoroughly reviewed Western experiences with helicopter assaults in Indochina, Korea, Algeria, the Middle East, and elsewhere, and focused also on the emergence of the helicopter as a weapons platform (such as the U.S. AN-56A Cheyenne).[19] Also attracting Andrukhov's attention was the creation and operations in Vietnam of the U.S. airmobile division and the ensuing development of the concept of the 'airmobile operation.' He then catalogued the offensive and defensive missions helicopter delivered and supported forces could perform, including assault, fire support, resupply, and *razvedka* [reconnaissance].

The following year Samoilenko again weighed into the discussion by fitting Andrukhov's observations into the overall context of air assault operations. He keynoted his article with the acknowledgement that:

> The development of air-assault forces proceeds along the path of increasing their firepower, shock force, mobility on the field of battle, and combat autonomy, as well as decreasing the weight and size of armaments and combat equipment. The latter circumstance is considered especially important for moving forces by air and delivering them by parachute.[20]

Samoilenko argued that newer, more powerful, but lighter, weaponry (artillery, tanks, antitank, and antiair weapons) had also reinvigorated the potential use of parachute forces at the same time that helicopter forces were receiving wider attention. All of this made it possible to revive thought about the use of air armies (a 1943 U.S. concept) under the cloak of concepts for air mobility. Within this context, he reviewed the missions of airborne forces at all levels of war, concluding that:

> Airborne operations can be part of a *front* offensive or amphibious operation, as well as being carried out independently in the interest of a strategic offensive operation. We can foresee enlisting for their conduct air assault forces; specially prepared motorized rifle forces, military transport and *frontal* aviation, as well as forces and means of other types of armed forces...as demonstrated in exercises 'Dnepr,' 'Iug,' and the 'Dvina' maneuvers.[21]

Shortly thereafter, in 1973 Colonel A. Bykov devoted an entire article to the employment of airborne forces in combined amphibious assault operations. His detailed analysis concluded with the judgement:

> It follows to emphasize that the use of air assaults in combined operations facilitates the increased tempo of landing of amphibious assaults and considerably increases the effectiveness of all amphibious operations overall, in spite of the great complexity of its organization and conduct. Air assault units (formations) in such an operation usually comprise a forward (assault) echelon of *desant* forces either landed earlier or simultaneous with the landing of the amphibious assault for destroying objectives of the amphibious defense and means of nuclear strikes; for seizing important terrain positions (regions); and for isolating regions of combat actions from approaching enemy reserves. Their actual operations in general protect the fulfillment of combat missions and the achievement of the aims of a combined *desant* operation.[22]

The chief of Soviet VDV, General V. Margelov, followed in 1974 with a comprehensive survey of the state of airborne operations in contemporary war. Noting the historical linkage between airborne and deep offensive operations, Margelov reviewed postwar developments and the array of contemporary missions airborne forces could perform, stating that 'The role of air assaults in contemporary conditions has grown, first of all as a result of the increase in their significance in the achievement of the overall aims of operations (battles).'[23] He recognized the fact that, 'Now, in operations of ground forces, air assaults are no longer episodic, as they were before, but rather represent a relatively constant element of their combat (operational) formation.'[24] As a consequence of the growing radius of transport and combat aircraft, 'In practice, air assaults can be landed throughout the entire depth of the TVD [theater of military operations].'[25] Margelov went on to underscore the importance of mass use of air assaults and their achievement of surprise. To reinforce Margelov's view, Lieutenant General K. Kurochkin, in the same year and journal issue, reviewed in detail the employment of air assaults in local wars, concluding that airborne forces could perform the same diverse missions in a variety of regional and terrain circumstances, either in the initial or subsequent phases of war.[26]

To cap this thorough analysis, Colonel Samoilenko, in a 1975 issue of *Military Thought*, synthesized the five years of debate in an article which focused on the roots, nature, and contemporary variants of the so-called 'air-assault operation' during the initial and subsequent stages of war. Samoilenko concluded that,

> In contemporary conditions the air-assault operation, while

remaining the basic and, in some cases, the sole form of fulfilling combat missions in the deep enemy rear, is becoming an objective requirement, for example, a component part of operational and stategic operations of the armed forces of opposing sides.[27]

With these and other postulations on the theoretical employment of airborne forces, Soviet military theorists and planners continued throughout the 1970s to reform theory, reorganize airborne forces, and to test their theories in frequent exercises and field training. The issue of airborne operations in a conventional environment, as well as in a nuclear environment, posed a particular challenge: specifically, a means to suppress enemy fire in the absence of nuclear strikes on enemy positions.

FIGURE 91. AIRBORNE DIVISION ORGANIZATION, 1975

1975 airborne division (7,200 men):

3 parachute regiments
   3 parachute battalions
1 artillery regiment
   1 artillery battalion (18×122-mm)
   1 rocket launcher battalion (140-mm)
   1 antitank battalion (85-mm)
   1 assault gun battalion (ASU-57/85)
1 antiaircraft battalion (18×ZU-23)
1 reconnaissance battalion
1 engineer battalion
1 signal battalion
1 transportation battalion
1 maintenance battalion
1 medical battalion
1 chemical defense company
1 parachute rigging company

1975 parachute regiment:

3 parachute battalions (450 men)
1 mortar battery (6×120-mm)
1 antiaircraft battery (6×ZU-23)
1 antitank battery (6×85-mm)
1 engineer company
1 signal company
1 medical company
1 maintenance company
1 chemical defense platoon

The airborne forces also required greater firepower and protection in combat. Ultimately, the fielding of the MI-24 helicopter gunship, the BMD airborne combat vehicle, the BRDM reconnaissance vehicle, the 140-mm multiple rocket launcher, the ASU-85 assault gun, new ATGMs, and new antiaircraft guns and missiles solved these problems. The IL-76 jet transport aircraft substantially improved Soviet air transport lift capacity.

By 1975 the Soviet parachute-delivered airborne division had expanded somewhat in size over its 1968 predecessor. More important, it, and its subordinate regiments, possessed even greater firepower and, hence, staying power in combat. Western estimates of its organization were as shown in Figure 91.[28]

Foreign assessments detected the changing emphasis of Soviet airborne concepts, particularly the growing flexibility of those forces in a potential nuclear or conventional environment. Foreign military analysts presumed Soviet airborne forces would perform the primary missions of 'helping ground forces maintain momentum in the attack by dropping to the rear of enemy defenses, possibly in independent operations in overseas areas, possibly in conjunction with amphibious landings by naval infantry.'[29] Aircraft-landed paratroopers along with helicopter- or aircraft-landed motorized rifle troops trained within a 'nuclear battle-field' context in large-scale operations as part of a general advance or in small-scale drops to conduct reconnaissance, capture or destroy limited objectives, or inflict sabotage. This assessment concluded that battalion-size groups could operate up to 160 kilometers in the enemy rear area, regimental-size units up to 320 kilometers deep. It ascribed to airborne forces the mission 'to facilitate the movement of the ground strike force by seizing bridges and fords, capturing airfields for follow-up landings of airborne troops and heavy equipment, and carrying out sabotage missions against enemy nuclear launching and communications facilities.'[30] This mission had the intent of disrupting the enemy's offensive and defensive capabilities.

Soviet exercises throughout the 1970s were indicative of the more sophisticated use of airborne forces. The largest exercise occurred in March 1970 in Belorussia along the Dvina River. Under the direction of the airborne troops' chief of staff, Lieutenant General P. Pavlenko, AN-12 aircraft (and one AN-22) dropped an entire airborne division (7,000 men) within 22 minutes. Its mission was to secure key terrain in the enemy rear and prevent the advance of enemy reserves after a friendly nuclear strike. In June 1971, another airborne division participated in Exercise 'Iug.' In 1974–75 exercises, the new IL-76 and AN-22 aircraft dropped an airborne force after a drop of BMD vehicles. The IL-76 appeared again in February 1978 in Exercise 'Berezina' in Belorussia. There, two battalions of an airborne regiment secured an airstrip for the landing of main force elements in IL-76 aircraft, which also carried SU-85 guns.[31] The decade-long series of exercises clearly demonstrated to Soviet military theorists the validity of their airborne concepts, and, with the new IL-76 with its 5,000-kilometer range, those concepts included operations in the strategic realm.

THEORY AND PRACTICE, 1975–1985

After 1976 the projected scale of wartime aircraft-delivered airborne operations diminished, attesting not only to Soviet reluctance to advertise such a clearly offensive weapon, but also to a growing Soviet interest in helicopter-landed forces in both the operational and tactical context. The proliferation of Soviet articles on helicopter assault forces in the 1980s, paralleled by changes in Soviet force structure and weaponry, documented the growing belief in the utility of such forces.[32] The missions performed by helicopter-landed forces were virtually the same as those expressed in 1969, but more often without mention of nuclear warfare. In place of nuclear fires, the airborne landing force supported itself with its own organic fires and ultimately with fire from the force advancing to link up from the front (a standard Second World War procedure). Another mission often mentioned and once performed by parachute landing forces was to support amphibious landings by seizing a beachhead in advance of main force landings or in conjunction with advanced naval amphibious landing elements.

Soviet faith in the concept of airmobility by use of helicopter-delivered forces continued to mature after 1975, although Soviet theorists retained significant missions for the more classic parachute-delivered airborne forces. Theoretical writings, although diminished in frequency, bore out these trends, as did a proliferating number of more practical articles on the operational and tactical employment of helicopter- and parachute-delivered forces.

While articles in the journals *Military Thought* and *Military-historical journal* continued to describe the strategic and operational utility of air assault operations, the tactical level journal *Military Herald* [*Voennyi vestnik*] explored the nuts and bolts of tactical air assault actions. A 1975 article investigated techniques employed by a parachute battalion, which, after its *desant*, was forced to engage enemy assault helicopters.[33] The battalion repelled the attack, supported by its ASU-57 battery, a battery of 122-mm howitzers, and its organic antiaircraft guns, and proceeded to carry out its principal mission of cutting and securing a main enemy supply artery. The same year another article described the use of a parachute assault battalion to seize and hold a key river crossing.[34] Using its organic BMD combat vehicles and an attached SU-85 assault gun battery, the battalion seized its objective with the help of thorough reconnaissance and skillful maneuver.

A 1976 article featured the positive characteristics of the BMD as a means by which parachute assault forces could solve the problems of their less fortunate world war forebears by resort to rapid maneuver with more than adequate fire support. According to the article, 'The combat vehicle *desant* [BMD] substantially raised the tactical capabilities of the subunit; its firepower and maneuverability was increased, allowing them to deliver a decisive surprise attack, completing the destruction of the enemy before he was able to render organized opposition.'[35] Once on the objective (in this case, an airfield and river crossing), the BMD also enabled the battalion to conduct a credible defense.

The following year three articles in *Military Herald* featured widely diverse aspects of air assault operations. In the first a parachute assault company seized a mountain objective in concert with ground operations by its parent battalion.[36] In the second a parachute assault battalion conducted a successful night surprise *desant* to secure an enemy airfield.[37] The last focused on operations of a parachute assault battalion to seize a river crossing and hold it until the main force arrived.[38] All three articles detailed necessary preparatory measures such as planning, force organization, missions, and timing of the assault, and provided a detailed step-by-step account of the ensuing actions. Finally, all critiqued the successes and failures of each operation. Five similar articles in the same journal in 1979 and 1980 focused on night mountain operations, an attack to seize a river crossing, seizure and destruction of an enemy command and control point, and an incident from exercise 'Brothers in Arms 1980,' when a parachute battalion secured an airfield in the enemy rear area.[39]

Hard on the heels of this long series of theoretical writings on tactical airborne assaults, in 1980 Major General I. A. Skorodumov wrote a major article in *Military Thought* on airmobile forces and operations. Surveying in detail past Western experiences, he noted that:

> At the present time, foreign military experts look upon helicopters as a most dynamic means, which permit a sharp rise in the mobility of units and formations in the zone of combat operations, remove the lack of balance between repeatedly growing combat capabilities of attack means (especially with the appearance of nuclear weapons) and mobility of forces, and materially raise the effectiveness of hitting important targets and objectives on the field of battle. They [Westerners] think that the creation and development of helicopters is an important step in the improving of ground forces, which by its importance, can compare with transition to a motorized army.[40]

After reviewing the record of the American 101st Air Assault Division and 173d Airborne Brigade, Skorodumov cited American sources to relate how an airmobile operation was planned and conducted. He concluded by sketching out American views on the utility of helicopter air assaults in the future, which, by virtue of Skorodumov's work, interested Soviet theorists as well. As if to measure that concern, most Soviet articles on tactical air assault thereafter focused on helicopter assault operations.

During each of the following two years, the newly-appointed Soviet Chief of VDV, Colonel General D. S. Sukhorukov, wrote articles for *Military Thought* on air assault operations. In the first, he extracted from his major 1980 work on the history of Soviet airborne forces to survey the history and future prospects for airborne and air assault forces. His survey detailed the evolution of airborne missions and forces from 1946 to

1980 in more detail than any previous article, ending with the declaration:

> Thus, along with the equipping of airborne forces with new weapons and military technology, the organization of their formations and units have improved. As a result, their combat capability, as well as their mobility on the field of battle, have considerably improved. The role and specific influence has grown and the missions of airborne forces have changed considerably, right up to the solution of independent operational missions in the deep enemy rear, in great isolation from advancing forces. They have become one of the means for the simultaneous hitting of enemy groupings to the entire depth of their formation.[41]

In his second article, Sukhorukov surveyed the most important problems confronting contemporary airborne forces, through the prism of combat experience. As context, he identified the two most notable trends in warfare as, first, an increase in armed forces mobility and in the sophistication of equipment, weaponry, and command and control; and, second, more widespread use of airborne forces of all types in all circumstances. Among the principal problems (or more properly, issues) he addressed were:

- airborne missions at the strategic, operational, and tactical levels;
- the overall 'system of airborne assault,' including diverse aspects of integration into overall operations and support;
- insertion of forces into the enemy rear area;
- increased importance of surprise;
- basic principals of employment;
- repeated use of specific air assault units and formations.[42]

He concluded by assessing that:

> It is logical to suppose that the further widening of the scale of transporting forces by air may call forth new means of conducting combat operations. It will not simply be envelopment of the enemy force from the air, but rather its own type of 'offensive by air.' From that point of view, as a first step, an offensive by air, a principally new form of type of combat action, can replace the contemporary system of enveloping the enemy from the air.[43]

Sukhorukov's declaration of the importance of an 'offensive by air' would, in the future, be reinforced and further developed by theorists of the mid-1980s who talked of 'land-air combat' and the concept of an 'air echelon' in future combat and operational formations.

By 1983 most Soviet tactical articles were focusing on the utility of tactical air assaults by helicopter-delivered forces. Not only did they laud the capabilities of helicopter assault forces, but they also broadened the range of missions those forces could perform. A 1983 article in *Military Herald* described a helicopter air assault designed to move critical sapper (engineer) forces into a mountainous region to clear obstacles from the path of advancing forces.[44] The following year another article portrayed a helicopter air assault by a reinforced motorized rifle battalion, which performed in the role of forward detachment in coordination with advancing ground forces.[45] Within the next two years, Soviet theorists routinely wrote about helicopter assault battalions performing in the role of forward detachment in their own right.

This theoretical work in air assault operations paralleled more general trends in prospective ground forces employment. During the 1970s, when theorists were stressing the growing importance of operational maneuver, parachute-delivered tactical- and operational-level forces seemed to fit well with ground maneuver schemes. In the early 1980s, as Soviet theorists wrestled with the potential impact of high-precision weaponry on ground combat, the solution they reached was to place greater emphasis on tactical maneuver by agile tailored combined-arms forces, which could close quickly with the enemy and render his use of high-precision weapons less effective. In this case, maneuverable helicopter assault companies and battalions, operating once or repeatedly, could further 'loosen up' the battlefield and contribute to successful widespread tactical maneuver. Of course, all of these theoretical concepts required considerable force structure changes if they were to be fully realized in combat.

Force structure changes quite naturally reflected the expanded mission being articulated for parachute- and helicopter-landed forces. Large numbers of helicopters were to deploy with potential wartime *fronts*, and virtually all motorized rifle battalions were trained to perform in an air assault role. The air assault brigade, an operational-level helicopter assault force introduced at front level, was a unique organization combining parachute elements with helicopter-lift units.[46] The brigade's combat elements consisted of two BMD-equipped battalions, two parachute battalions, and an artillery battalion organized as shown in Figure 92.[47]

This organization accorded to Soviet commanders the capability of operating with heavy BMD-equipped forces deep in the enemy's rear or with lighter parachute troops closer to the front lines. The air assault brigade provided the *front* commander with a means for supporting either a penetration of enemy defenses or an exploitation into the operational depth of the defense (up to 100 kilometers). So, although helicopter assault forces claimed a wider role in performing airborne missions, that role was commensurate with the Soviets' reassessment of potential wartime combat requirements within their current concept of war. And helicopter assault forces shared that role with more traditional airborne forces.

FIGURE 92.   AIR ASSAULT BRIGADE ORGANIZATION, 1982

1982 air assault brigade (2,000 men):

2 assault battalions (BMD)
2 parachute battalions
1 reconnaissance company
1 antiaircraft battery (6×ZU-23)
1 artillery battalion
1 antitank battery (6×85-mm)
1 engineer company
1 signal company
1 parachute rigging and resupply company
1 transport and maintenance company
1 medical platoon/company
1 supply company
1 chemical defense platoon

As helicopter operations expanded in the 1970s and additional helicopters and helicopter air assault units appeared in the Soviet force structure, the classic airborne division also improved its force structure and capabilities. The basic airborne division structure had changed little since the early 1960s. While retaining its basic triangular configuration (three regiments, each with three battalions), the division's size diminished slightly. The introduction of new equipment, however, markedly improved its firepower and mobility. From a strength of more than 7,500, the division decreased in 1982 to about 6,500. Airborne division and regimental organization from 1978–82 evolved as shown in Figure 93. Commensurate decreases in manpower occurred at regimental, battalion, and company levels as the Soviets introduced combat-fighting vehicles and rationalized the division support structure.

Although official Western sources often disagreed about the exact size and configuration of divisional subunits, some general trends were distinguishable. The gradual equipping of the airborne regiments after 1973 with the BMD airborne combat vehicle not only reduced the regiment's size but also drastically increased its capability for maneuvering to its combat objective. The BMD's 73-mm smoothbore gun and ATGM improved the regiment's and battalion's firepower and the new ATGM battery equipped with AT-3 Saggers, which replaced the older gun antitank battery, further augmented battalion and regimental firepower. The BRDM reconnaissance vehicle and new GAZ-69 trucks contributed to greater divisional mobility.

Similar improvements occurred in airborne individual weapons and automatic weapons. What emerged from this modernization program

FIGURE 93. AIRBORNE FORCES ORGANIZATION, 1978–1982

1978 airborne division (7,673 men):

3 airborne regiments (126 BMDs)
  3 airborne battalions
1 artillery regiment
  1 howitzer battalion (18×122-mm)
  1 rocket launcher battalion (18×140-mm)
1 assault gun battalion (18×ASU-85)
1 antiaircraft battalion (18×ZU-23)
1 reconnaissance battalion
1 engineer battalion
1 signal battalion
1 transportation battalion
1 maintenance battalion
1 medical battalion
1 chemical defense company
1 parachute rigging company

1978 airborne regiment (1,837 men, 40 BMDs):

3 airborne battalions (350 men)
1 assault gun battery/battalion (9×ASU-57)
1 antitank battery (6×85-mm)
1 antiaircraft battery (6×ZU-23)
1 mortar battery (6×12-mm)
1 ATGM battery (6×AT-3)
  support units

Source: U.S. Army, Combined Arms Combat Developments Activity, Concepts, Doctrine, and Literature Directorate, Threats Division, HB 550-2, *Organization and Equipment of the Soviet Army* (Fort Leavenworth, KS, 31 July 1978), 2–12, 2–13.

1980 airborne division (7,151 men, 127 BMDs, 13 BRDM/BRDM-2s):

3 airborne regiments (1 BMD, 2 non-BMD)
  3 airborne battalions
1 artillery regiment
  1 howitzer battalion (18×122-mm)
  1 rocket launcher battalion (18×140-mm)
1 assault gun battalion (18×ASU-85)
1 antiaircraft battalion (18×ZU-23)
1 reconnaissance battalion
1 engineer battalion
1 signal battalion
1 transportation battalion
1 maintenance battalion
1 medical battalion
1 chemical defense company
1 parachute rigging company

1980 airborne regiment (BMD) (1,322 men, 107 BMDs, 3 BRDMs):

3 airborne battalions (270 men)
1 ATGM battery (9×AT-3)
1 air defense battery (6×ZU-23)
1 mortar battery (6×120-mm)
  support units

1980 airborne regiment (non-BMD) (1,564 men, 10 BMDs):

3 airborne battalions (326 men)
1 BMD company (10×BMD)
1 mortar battery (6×120-mm)
1 antitank battery (6×85-mm)
1 air defense battery (6×ZU-23)
  support units

Source: U.S. Army, Combined Arms Combat Developments Activity, Concepts, Doctrine and Literature Directorate, Threats Division, HB 550-2, *Organization and Equipment of the Soviet Army* (Fort Leavenworth, KS, 15 July 1980), 2–15, 2–19.

1982 airborne division (6,500 men, 330 BMDs):

3 airborne regiments (13 BRDM/BRDM-2s)
   3 airborne battalions
1 artillery regiment
   1 howitzer battalion (18×122-mm)
   1 composite artillery battalion (12×122-mm, 6×140-mm)
1 assault gun battalion (31×ASU-85)
1 antiaircraft battalion (18×ZU-23)
1 reconnaissance battalion
1 engineer battalion
1 signal battalion
1 transport and maintenance battalion
1 medical battalion
1 chemical defense company
1 parachute rigging, resupply company

1982 airborne regiment (1,455 men, 109 BMDs, 4 BRDMs):

3 airborne battalions (310 men)
1 mortar battery (6×120-mm)
1 antitank guided missile battery (8×AT-3)
1 air defense battery (6×ZU-23)
   support units

Source: FM 100-2-3 (Draft), 1982, 4-188, 4-195.

was a more compact, powerful airborne formation that could more flexibly execute missions assigned to it by recently articulated doctrine. The modern airborne division, side by side with air assault battalions and brigades, posed a significantly greater battlefield threat than the older classic parachute division.

The Soviets constructed airborne forces that could be transported into combat both by aircraft and helicopter. These forces were tailored flexibly to perform a wide spectrum of potential tactical, operational, and strategic missions, which had been articulated since the early 1960s, in both a nuclear and a conventional environment. Airborne forces either performed strategic missions in support of the theater-strategic operation or performed a variety of independent strategic missions. During either day or night, they were tasked with conducting operational or diversionary missions to support a *front* offensive in close coordination with other *front* forces, and were to carry out a variety of tactical missions to support army offensive operations.

Strategic forces (*strategicheskii desant* [strategic landing force]) were composed of aircraft-delivered units of up to division size, destined for employment at considerable depths in the enemy rear. Because of the relative weakness of airborne divisions, without reinforcement by heavier forces, they were to be employed only in the waning stages of hostilities, after enemy resistance in the theater operations had crumbled. Then they were to secure key administrative, logistical, or communications regions. In addition, strategic airborne forces were used as a political tool to 'show the flag,' demonstrate support for a government, or exhibit a 'presence' in a region. Smaller airborne groups (*desant spetsial'nogo naznacheniya* [special purpose landing force]) were to perform a lower level strategic mission, such as conducting reconnaissance and diversionary operations deep in the theater rear under KGB or GRU control. They were to attack such key targets as enemy nuclear delivery or storage sites, command and control facilities, communication centers, transportation control centers, and possible wartime seats of government.

Operational airborne forces (*operativnyi desant* [operational landing force]) were tasked with supporting *front* operations. They operated in close coordination with other *front* forces to facilitate achievement of *front* missions, specifically penetration, exploitation, and destruction of enemy army group forces. Airborne and air assault forces were organized to operate at depths of 100 to 300 kilometers against enemy nuclear delivery means, command and control facilities, reserves, logistical facilities, and the rear of enemy army group forward defenses. *Front* air assault brigades operated in tandem with the lead elements of the main attack army or the *front* operational maneuver group at depths of up to 100 kilometers to assist in penetration of the army group defensive zone or in exploitation operations deep into the army group rear.[48] Once Soviet forces had penetrated enemy army group defenses, regimental or multi-regimental airborne assaults were to be conducted at depths of up to 300 kilometers to secure major terrain features, such as river crossings, to disrupt enemy attempts to regroup and reestablish new defensive lines, and to block movement of enemy reserves. Such drops occurred only if warranted by the progress of the *front* offensive and if link-up with advanced ground force elements was anticipated within two or three days of the drop. Elements of airborne divisions could also deploy numerous small diversionary teams in support of *front* operations. These teams attacked enemy nuclear delivery means and storage areas, command and control installations, and other targets, the engagement of which would disrupt command and control and logistical support of enemy army group operations.

Tactical airborne forces (*takticheskii desant* [tactical landing force]), primarily helicopter assault units, supported army operations. Reinforced motorized rifle battalion-size helicopter assault forces cooperated with the advance of army and division forward detachments. Helicopter-landed forces, operating primarily at night, sought to destroy enemy covering forces by landing in their rear, preempt the establishment of forward defenses or penetrate those defenses by landing within or to the rear of them, and block movement of enemy reserves dispatched to reinforce or reestablish the forward defense by securing key terrain or road junctions in the enemy rear.[49] Platoon- or company-size helicopter assault units also attacked enemy nuclear delivery means and command

and control installations at tactical depths (from 20 to 100 kilometers) in the army offensive sector. Operational or tactical airborne units also supported operations by amphibious forces by securing beachheads or by blocking enemy movements to contain or crush an amphibious assault.

CONCLUSIONS

The 1970s and 1980s saw Soviet airborne forces mature into what the visionaries of the 1930s anticipated they could become, namely, a full-fledged vertical dimension of deep battle. They were a credible, diverse, and more survivable force whose capabilities added yet another facet to the concept of deep combined-arms operations. Their existence was the result of years of careful study. Evolving technology enabled military theorists and practitioners to realize the fruits of that study and to overcome many of the problems that had previously plagued airborne forces. A nation whose experience should have made it skeptical of prospects for waging successful airborne combat, by 1985 had overcome that skepticism. The Soviets displayed new confidence in the capabilities of their expanded airborne force and were even more optimistic about what they could accomplish in the future.

CHAPTER 14

On the Eve of the Twenty-First Century

GROWING PROBLEMS – TENTATIVE SOLUTIONS

By the end of 1985, a date which the Soviet tactical specialist V. K. Reznichenko identified as the end of an old and the beginning of a new period of military development, Soviet military analysts were facing acute military dilemmas, which accompanied ongoing serious economic problems.[1] The prospective quickening pace of combat resulting from enhanced force mobility and the burgeoning lethality and accuracy of weaponry called into question long-held assumptions regarding the nature of future ground combat. The Soviets still adhered to the general concept of the theater-strategic operation, and Soviet theoretical writings still evidenced an all-abiding faith in the offensive as the best guarantor of victory in future war. There were, however, some major problems to be addressed.

The first problem was the appearance in battle of high-precision weapons [*vysoko-tochnye oruzhiya*], the more lethal and sophisticated descendants of older ATGMs of the 1970s.[2] The new weapons exploited miniaturization and computer technology, fields in which the Soviets woefully lagged behind the West. The increased range of these weapons and their incredible accuracy made possible long-range stand-off fires against military targets. When combined with equally sophisticated target acquisitions means, they posed a significant problem to attacker and defender alike. As a result, older concepts of maneuver and, in particular, mass and concentration had to be reassessed. Forces which massed too early and lingered in concentration areas courted disaster.[3]

The traditional ways of preparing for and conducting a penetration operation were clearly obsolete, and new methods had to be found to propel forces through enemy tactical defenses into the operational depths.

Compounding the adverse effects this technological revolution had on traditional offensive concepts was Western development of new maneuver and combat concepts. The U.S. concept of Airland Battle and the NATO concept of Follow-on-Forces Attack (FOFA) sought to capitalize on the characteristics of new weaponry by conducting deep battle to strike enemy forces to the depth of their formation. These concepts placed second echelons, operational maneuver groups, and rear area facilities in increased jeopardy. In short, the new weaponry and imaginative Western force employment concepts forced the Soviets to abandon, or at least seriously alter, traditional concepts of echelonment.

In the early 1970s, the Soviets had developed the concept of anti-nuclear maneuver [*protivoiadernyi manevr*], which their maneuver specialist, F. D. Sverdlov, defined as 'the organized shifting of subunits with the aim of withdrawing them out from under the possible blows of enemy nuclear means, to protect their survival and subsequent freedom of action to strike a blow on the enemy. Therefore, anti-nuclear maneuver is also one of the forms of maneuver.'[4] The defensive aspect of antinuclear maneuver was complemented by offensive measures 'to rapidly disperse subunits or change the direction of their offensive, and to conduct other measures related to defense against weapons of mass destruction.'[5]

The work of Sverdlov and other Soviet military theorists throughout the 1970s led them to conclude that the most effective manner in which to conduct anti-nuclear maneuver was through expanded reliance upon operational and tactical maneuver. These concepts provided the basis for Soviet concepts of operational maneuver (by maneuver groups – the OMG) and tactical maneuver (by forward detachments), which had reached full articulation by 1980. Since the mid-1980s, the Soviets have generalized that concept and applied it to all forces (perhaps also reinforced by experiences in Afghanistan).

By the late 1970s, under threat of tactical and theater nuclear weapons, Soviet military theorists had recommended use of shallower strategic and operational echelonment, in essence a single echelon of *fronts*, each with the preponderance of its armies also arrayed in single echelon. The operational maneuver group (OMG) concept represented a solution to the problem by replacing cumbersome second echelons with more dynamic, flexible, and rapidly moving exploitation forces in the form of OMGs, which would impart a non-linear nature to combat at the operational level of war.

The Soviet solution to the dilemma of countering the high-precision weaponry of the 1980s involved their wholesale abandonment of linear concepts of warfare. Soviet military theorists advanced new concepts of non-linear [*ochagovyi*] warfare, characterized by the adoption of new echelonment concepts, the formation and employment of tailored combined-arms forces down to the lowest tactical levels, increased frequency of independent actions by tactical subunits, and a proliferation of air assault forces at every level of combat.

The tone and tenor of this new Soviet attitude toward warfare found expression in a host of forward-looking theoretical monographs, each addressing but one aspect critical to the achievement of success in non-linear combat. M. M. Kir'ian's book, *Surprise in Offensive Operations of the Great Patriotic War*, published in 1986, detailed imaginative ways to achieve this essential factor in future combat.[6] V. N. Lobov's *Military Strategem in the History of War*, published in 1988, exceeded the level of sophistication of Kir'ian's work by focusing on the art of the commander in achieving surprise.[7] These works were not isolated phenomena, for they were accompanied by a flood of articles on the same subject in a variety of Soviet military journals. Iu. K. Kuznetsov's 1989 work, *Movement and Meeting Battle* sketched out vividly and in detail the basic requirements for fighting on the non-linear battlefield.[8] And F. D. Sverdlov's 1989 work, *The Forward Detachment in Battle*, featured the operations of forward detachments as a microcosm of how tactical maneuver would have to be conducted by all future forces. This work devoted an entire chapter to forward detachment cooperation with tactical air assaults.[9] Finally, V. G. Rezhichenko's *Tactics* of 1984 identified the technological dilemma of the early 1980s, while his 1987 edition of *Tactics* provided tentative answers to many of the ensuing problems by sketching out the parameters and characteristics of non-linear combat.[10]

As recently as 1987, the concept of anti-nuclear maneuver still provided a cornerstone for Soviet operational and tactical techniques designed to preempt, preclude, or inhibit enemy resort to nuclear warfare. As articulated in 1987 by V. G. Reznichenko, 'The continuous conduct of battle at a high tempo creates unfavorable conditions for enemy use of weapons of mass destruction. He cannot determine targets for nuclear strikes precisely and, besides, will be forced to shift his nuclear delivery means often.'[11] In addition, by the mid-1980s, Soviet analysts had concluded that high-precision weapons essentially posed the same sort of threat to attacking forces as had tactical nuclear weapons. In addition, these new weapons promised a capability of more flexible engagement of attacking forces before such forces made actual contact with the enemy. The Soviets tentatively decided that even greater emphasis on operational and tactical maneuver was also a partial remedy to countering enemy use of high-precision weaponry.[12] To capitalize fully on the effects of maneuver, the Soviets believed that they had to reduce planning time and execute command and control more precisely. This required increased emphasis on the use of cybernetic tools, including automation of command and expanded reliance on tactical and operational calculations (nomograms, etc.).

The Soviets also realized that advantage accrued to that force which could quickly close with the enemy, thus rendering high-precision weapons less effective. This judgement, in turn, increased the operational and tactical significance of first echelons. Thus, by 1987, in the tactical realm, Soviet writers were able to argue, 'There arises the problem of defining the optimal structure for the first and second echelons at the tactical level. With the enemy using high-precision weapons, the role of the first echelon has to grow. It must be capable of achieving a mission without the second echelon (reserve).'[13]

In the Soviet view, operational and tactical combat embraced 'simultaneously, the entire depth of the combat formations of both contending sides.'[14] As a result, combat missions were no longer solely described in linear fashion by the seizure of lines. The new approach, according to Reznichenko in the 1987 edition of his book *Taktika*, was, 'to determine them not by line, as was done before, but rather by important area (objective), the seizure of which will secure the undermining of the tactical stability of the enemy defense.'[15]

Reznichenko and others suggested that tactical missions required the seizure of objectives, whose loss would fragment the enemy forward defense and render it untenable, along multiple axes throughout the depth of the enemy's defense. At the tactical level, specifically designated and tailored maneuver forces (usually forward detachments) had earlier performed this function, while tailored operational maneuver forces did the same at the operational level.[16] In the future, theorists argued, all tactical units and subunits were likely to operate in this fashion.

This description of operational and tactical combat in future war significantly altered traditional Soviet concepts of echelonment, not only by reducing the number of ground echelons, but also by supplementing the ground echelon with a vertical (air assault) echelon, which added greater depth to battle. According to Reznichenko:

> One can propose that, under the influence of modern weapons and the great saturation of ground forces with aviation means, the combat formation of forces on the offensive is destined to consist of two echelons – a ground echelon, whose mission will be to complete the penetration of the enemy defense and develop the success into the depths, and an air echelon created to envelop defending forces from the air and strike blows against his rear area.[17]

A 1988 article rounded out these vivid descriptions of non-linear combat by adding: 'Modern combined-arms battle is fought throughout the entire depth of the enemy combat formation, both on the side's contact line [FLOT] and in the depth, on the ground and in the air.'[18] As a consequence, the fragmented [*ochagovyi*] nature of battle would result in 'mutual wedging [overlap] of units and subunits, which will have to operate independently for a long time.'[19] In essence, what emerged by 1988 was a Soviet concept of land-air battle juxtaposed against the U.S. concept of Airland Battle, equally applicable to offensive and defensive operations.

New Soviet concept for waging non-linear war portended greater Soviet task-organization of forces and the fielding of combined-arms forces at ever lower level (for example, brigades and battalions). This program had already been in progress for several years as the Soviets experimented with and then fielded corps-type operational maneuver formations, first, within the Soviet Union and, then, in the forward groups of forces. They also experimented with the creation of combined-arms battalions (whose theoretical basis was thoroughly covered in Soviet published works) and with new air assault forces at *front* (air assault brigade), army (air assault battalion), and probably divisional level.[20] Within the Warsaw Pact forces, the Hungarian Army converted its entire force structure to a corps and brigade configuration, possibly indicating that the Soviets intended to do so as well.

THE ROLE OF AIRBORNE AND AIR ASSAULT FORCES IN NON-LINEAR BATTLE

Within this context of non-linear war, it seemed that air assault forces were finally about to realize that ambitious vision set forth by those who originally created airborne forces in the 1930s. From being mere participants in deep battle, air assault forces now seemed on the verge of forming their own distinct air echelon, working as coequals to the long-dominant ground echelons, as a virtual partner in land-air battle.

Soviet tactical articles continued to stress the utility of tactical air assaults in modern combat, in support of ground forces and performing more and more independent missions in their own right. A March 1987 article described the actions of a parachute battalion functioning as a forward detachment for an advancing main force.[21] Incorporated in the assault were, by now, common raiding missions designed to disrupt enemy command, control, and communications. By late 1987 either the airborne or the helicopter assault battalion could perform a variety of critical missions at the tactical level, while the air assault brigade normally cooperated with operational maneuver forces and larger airborne forces in support of *front* operations as a whole.

Lending impetus to airborne and helicopter operations were Soviet combat experiences in the Afghan War, where airborne and air assault forces played a crucial role, details of which began to emerge after 1985.

Although details are still sketchy, airborne forces participated in the initial Soviet invasion of Afghanistan, cooperating with Brigades of Special Designation, *front-* and GRU-level reconnaissance-diversionary forces, to seize key political, military, and economic installations. Subsequently, airborne forces took part in security operations and also saw some service in the field. Air assault forces were especially useful and active in Afghanistan. Two experimental motorized rifle brigades – the 66th and 70th – located at Jalalabad and Kandahar, each fielded an air assault battalion, in addition to their three organic motorized rifle battalions, one tank battalion, and support subunits. The best information on their organization and employment states:

> According to reports from Afghan resistance personnel, both the motorized rifle and air assault battalions took part in numerous heliborne assault actions, supported by helicopter resources from nearby airfields. The 66th Motorized Rifle Brigade – whose personnel were highly decorated – was one of the first units to withdraw from Afghanistan in May 1988.[22]

These units, in Afghanistan since May 1979, were equipped with BTR armored personnel carriers. Numerous fragmentary accounts in the Soviet press related to air assault actions carried out by these two units or special bands of reconnaissance-diversionary personnel. It is clear that these brigades, largely because of their flexible air assault elements, were better able to deal with counterinsurgency, security, and local combat operations than their counterpart regiments which lacked the logistical support and mobility to engage in significant independent combat operations. It is also likely that Soviet experiences with these brigades prompted Soviet fielding in the mid-1980s of air assault brigades throughout their force.

As late as 1987 and 1988, Soviet-inspired writings continued to laud the future importance of land-air battle. A series of candid Polish articles, in customary manner, addressed the subject in more open and explicit fashion than those of their Soviet counterparts. Referring to the more familar Western concept of air-land combat, the leading Polish theorist, Colonel S. Koziej, writing in Polish *Military Thought* [*Mysl wojskowa*] thoroughly traced the development and contents of air-land combat. Linking the concept with 1920s advocates of air theory, Koziej traced development to the present, noting that:

> The quantitative and qualitative development of aviation and the emergence of air assaults [*powietrzno desantowy*] troops are factors which resulted in the appearance of the concept of joining air and

land actions at the operational scale. This idea was expressed in the Soviet theory of deep operations, the essence of which was co-operation between aviation, air assault troops, and ground troops.[23]

The concept of deep operations amounted to a prototype of the air-land operation. However, claimed Koziej, until the development of the helicopter, the air dimension fell short of playing its full role. He attributed credit to the U.S. Army for developing the concept of air assault by air cavalry forces, principally in Vietnam.[24] Finally, the U.S. 1982 concept of Airland Battle 2000 gave full impression to the concept of air-land operations. Koziej pointed out that, since the late 1960s, Soviet theorists had worked on similar concepts to develop assault-storm [*desan-towoszturmowy*] groups and units, distinct from airborne and air assault [*powietrznoszturmowy*] troops. Assault-storm forces relied on the MI-29 helicopter, which, in addition to transporting troops, performed a variety of fire missions (like a flying BMP).[25] Transport and storm helicopters combined to form assault-storm groups. Koziej predicted:

At the beginning of the twenty-first century, there will be three fundamental types of combined-arms configurations (mechanized and armored or mechanized-armored; helicopter-armored; air-mechanized) in ground (air-land) forces, and six possible variants (levels, degrees, forms) of air-land combat action which may evolve in this period can be distinguished. However, most probably, the basic and most widespread of these will be the one which ensues during an encounter of helicopter-armored configurations with one another, and their battle against air-mechanized and mechanized-armored configurations.[26]

Regarding traditional relationships between offense and defense, Koziej stated:

It can be forecast that the difference between methods for attaining offensive and defensive objectives will be eradicated to an increas-ing degree. Therefore, the differentiation between offense and defense (this mainly concerns battle of air-mechanized groupings) will not be precise. The primary types of actions will be raids, which include closing with the enemy (approach), sudden encounter of a meeting nature, and withdrawal in order to 'gather' forces for the next missions (next raid action). Losing their raison d'être, such categories as the penetration, for example, will expressly change....[27]

Koziej was clearly defining a battlefield environment which had not yet been fully realized. Nevertheless, the tendencies he identified closely echoed Soviet concerns. Other Polish articles published in 1987 described in even greater detail than Soviet sources the functions, organization, and employment technique of air-assault forces.[28]

DILEMMAS OF THE 1990S

Despite Soviet fixation on the offensive and the nature of non-linear combat, sharp changes were occurring, which halted this long-term evolution of Soviet military theory and force structure. In all likelihood, the changes were prompted by the worsening Soviet economic and political situation and not by military necessity. In fact, military-theoretical writings remained remarkably evolutionary and consistent right up to 1987, when the Soviet political and military leadership announced a fundamental shift to a defensive military doctrine. Understandably, the General Staff journal *Military Thought* was the first to reflect the altered military doctrine. Whereas prior to 1987 the journal had consistently published two to four times as many articles on offensive themes as on defensive ones, in 1987 the ratio began shifting the other way. By 1990 defensive articles outnumbered offensive ones by a ratio of three to one.

Other journals embraced defensiveness more slowly. *Military-historical Journal* made the shift in 1988. Prior to that year, the journal published three to five times more articles on offensive themes (and had done so every year since 1963). In 1988 almost half of the journal's articles were defensive in orientation. The tactical level journal *Military Herald* was the last to make the shift, which occurred in mid-1988. Prior to 1989 the ratio of offensive articles to defensive ones varied from ten to one in 1980 to over two to one in 1988. In 1989 the ratio shifted abruptly to two to one in favor of defense.

Beginning in 1986, Soviet theorists began shifting their attention to defensive themes, first strategically, then operationally, and finally tactically. Articles had already appeared, interspersed with normal articles on offensive themes, which probably indicated high-level concern over defensive matters. For example, in 1984 Marshal S. F. Akhromeev had himself written an article on Kursk as the fundamental turning point in the Second World War, which stressed the international ramifications of that titanic battle.[29] During the same year, Major General I. N. Vorob'ev wrote a two-part article on the influence of high-precision weaponry on the conduct of contemporary warfare.[30] Perhaps even more indicative of things to come was a debate which commenced in October 1985 in *Military-historical Journal* on the nature and classification of strategic operations.[31] As this debate unfolded during 1986, two articles dealt specifically with strategic defense, and, in so doing, lamented the lack of attention hitherto devoted by the Soviet military press to this critical topic.[32]

During 1986 Soviet theorists addressed a growing number of defensive themes, among the most important of which were the following: defense against weapons of mass destruction; the effects of weapons of mass destruction on operational and tactical defenses; defense in the initial period of war; the nature of strategic operations (including strategic defense); and the utility of studying the experience of past wars.[33]

In 1987 Soviet examination of the defense expanded further. An article in January of that year began a re-examination of Soviet defensive thought in the inter-war years, a trend which would culminate the following year in the rehabilitation of A. Svechin, the predominant, but long-discredited defensive theorist of the 1920s.[34] By 1989, Soviet authors were treating Svechin as the virtual patron saint of new defensive doctrine. Two other major articles published in 1987 accorded further prestige and respectability to the theme of defense. General D. T. Iazov wrote on the question of 'durability' and 'activeness' [*aktivnost'*] of the modern defense and A. Kokoshin and V. Larionov assessed the Kursk operation 'in the light of contemporary defensive doctrine.'[35] The latter paved the way for the two authors' June 1988 article, which posited the existence of a range of enduring paradigms governing military-strategic relationships in peace and war.[36] Other defensive themes of 1987 included: the nature of 'first operations' in the initial period of war; the durability of operational defense; and continued examination of the relevance of the study of war experience.[37]

Soviet focus on defense exploded in scope and scale in 1988, and continued to accelerate after Gorbachev's December 1988 speech on defensiveness at the United Nations, in which he outlined specific force reductions to underscore the seriousness of defensive doctrine. Throughout 1988 Soviet theorists examined the dialectical relationship between offense and defense, and concluded that modern weaponry had blurred the distinction between the two.[38] Other authors investigated the nature of army defensive operations and the fundamental bases of defensive battle at the operational and tactical levels.[39] V. Larionov built upon his (and Kokoshin's) earlier article on the battle of Kursk to postulate that the Kursk operation had been a classic model of 'premeditated defense'; moreover, one suited to provide a model for Soviet 'post-Cold War' strategic defensive posture.[40] V. N. Lobov traced the evolution and utility of defensiveness in the Soviet search for what he described as a 'strategy of victory.'[41] Finally, Soviet authors began investigating in more detail topics which had been touched upon in the past, but never fully developed. These included the role of maneuver in the defense, the problem of making the transition from defense to the counteroffensive, and the role of counterstrokes in defensive operations.[42]

Subsequently, as the defense grew to predominance in Soviet military thought, a wide range of defensive topics became the subject of extensive and intense analysis, which is still going on today. Among the most prominent topics which Soviet analysts are currently examining are the following:

– requirements for 'defensive sufficiency';
– the influence of modern weaponry on warfare;
– the nature of land-air operations and battle;
– protecting force deployment;
– the creation, preparation, and employment of reserves;
– first operations in initial periods of war;
– strategic and operational regrouping;
– deception [*maskirovka*] and strategem [*khitrost'*] in war;
– surprise in war and while on the defense;
– maneuver in modern defense (positional vs maneuver);
– structuring the tactical defense;
– use of fires on the defense;
– antitank defense;
– defense of cities and key economic regions;
– meeting engagements in defensive operations;
– counterattacks and counterstrokes in defensive battles and operations;
– force survivability in battle;
– radio-electronic combat (and the influence of the cosmos on operations;
– command, control, and cooperation in modern combat;
– operations of forces in encirclement; and
– the experiences of recent wars (in particular, the Gulf War).

Parallel to these writings, and particularly after Gorbachev's 1988 speech, Soviet political and military authorities announced and began implementing a vigorous and public program to reduce and restructure the armed forces in accordance with the parameters of defensiveness. This included an announced reduction of armed forces' strength by 500,000 men, the future reduction in the strength of Soviet forward groups of forces, and the abolition or reduction of certain classes of nuclear weapons. Moreover, the Soviets pledged to restructure their combat forces to reduce their offensive capability. This involved a reduction in the quantity of tanks in line divisions, abolition of separate tank regiments in the forward groups of forces, disbanding of air assault forces (brigades and battalions) in the forward groups, reduction in assault bridging capabilities in the forward groups, and an overall reduction in the size, and offensive potential, of the Soviet armed forces as a whole.

This program for defensiveness initially included Soviet adoption of a strategic posture of 'forward defense' in Europe. Subsequent events, particularly the 'velvet revolution' in eastern Europe, destroyed this initial 'post-Cold War' Soviet military strategy, hastened political change and discord within the Soviet Union, and, at least initially, accelerated the move toward defensiveness and Soviet force reductions overall. As an immediate consequence, the Soviets agreed to withdraw, and subsequently withdrew their forces from Czechoslovakia and Hungary, and pledged to do so from Germany (which was soon unified) and Poland.

The ensuing August 1991 revolution in the Soviet Union and the December 1991 creation of a Commonwealth of Independent States accelerated these changes and resulted in the dissolution of the Soviet Union. Although the Union institution of the former Soviet military endured as a focus of controversy between Russia and other Commonwealth states, classic Soviet military doctrine, strategy, and operational and tactical concepts remain in doubt. While defensiveness suited the aims of the post-1988 Soviet leadership, it remains to be seen whether it will accord with the strategic needs of the new Commonwealth (if it survives), Russia, or the other former Soviet republics. If offensiveness reemerges in response to future Russian strategic needs, without a doubt, the offensive theories so abruptly relegated to the waste bin of history in 1987 in the name of defensiveness will reappear. If so, the airborne forces, in their varied forms, will be heard from in the future.

DEFENSIVENESS AND AIR ASSAULT CONCEPTS AND FORCES

The Soviet shift to a defensive military doctrine affected both air assault concepts and air assault forces. The most noticeable effect was a diminution in the number of articles on air assault published in Soviet journals. It must be noted, however, that this phenomenon occurred relatively late, and few, if any, articles have since appeared on the defensive employment of air assault forces. The Soviets continued to publish articles on offensive air assault through March 1987 (and Polish articles of their offensive use continued through fall 1988). One major article has since appeared in Soviet journals on air assault. The March 1989 article discussed the organization of fires against enemy defenses during an assault by a parachute-assault battalion.[43]

A debate did occur in summer and fall 1988 in the Polish press over the utility of air-delivered forces in defensive circumstances. The first article

(July) argued that, unlike airborne (parachute) *desants*, helicopter assaults could be employed in a defensive context principally in the form of raids to disrupt the regrouping and maneuver of an approaching enemy main force.[44] Air assaults were also useful in engaging and defeating enemy air assault forces operating in the defenders' rear area. An October article took issue with this point of view, claiming that the only useful means of air assault in the defense was through employment of *desant* assault operations. These the author described as rapid, raid-type operations of heavily armored helicopters and infantry into the enemy rear, which he described as follows:

> *Desant*-assault operations are based on rapidly and covertly trans-ferring *desant*-assault subunits by helicopters to the enemy's rear areas, striking from the air and land against any objective, destroy-ing it, rapidly advancing (maneuvering) to a new area without becoming engaged in a long battle, and eventually returning to one's own troop grouping. An operation according to such a variant makes it possible to accelerate the realization of the combat mission and to react rapidly and effectively to unexpected changes in the situation.[45]

In addition, a November 1988 article investigated the employment of helicopters for fire support and troop transport in a defensive environ-ment. It concluded that, 'They [helicopters] will become one of the main maneuver assets in battle, which will transform present-day combat operations; they will play no less a role in combat activities than tanks in World War II.'[46]

Another article by Colonel S. Koziej, this time in summer 1990, stressed the utility of operational and tactical raids in defensive battle, in part by 'raid actions of units and land and air-land groupings especially created for this purpose.'[47] Koziej identified so-called assault-storm troops [*desantoszturmowe wojska*] as best suited to perform the mission. Raid groups of this type could perform a wide range of operational and tactical missions in a variety of conditions, 'Among raids executed during ground forces combat activities (operation, battle), helicopter and heli-copter-tank raids can play a particular role,' although, 'Providing suitable conditions for carrying out helicopter raids requires, above all, the neutralization (disruption) of the air defense system.'[48]

Koziej then became more specific, stating:

> Helicopter-tank raids must be analyzed only at the operational scale as the action of a separate operational unit in the air-land dimen-sion. At the tactical scale this problem must be examined in the aspect of cooperation between infantry and tank subunits (units) with helicopters, and not their integration into a single combat

organism. A separate operational unit equipped with helicopters should use them, above all, for organizing a helicopter raid unit designated for assault-storm raids. The use of helicopters to land classical assaults is less economical, although it is justified if it is necessary to capture and hold a particularly important objective.[49]

Presumably, although Koziej was writing this commentary for the military establishment of a free Polish state, his views clearly reflected those of his Soviet counterparts. The revolution in air assault employment concepts continued, albeit in a defensive context.

The shift to defensiveness has also had an effect on the structure and quantity of air assault forces. The most radical changes occurred first in forward area forces, where the Soviets announced, as a matter of defensive principal, deemphasis of air assault and abolition or removal of air assault brigades (although helicopter transport forces were not affected). Subsequent changes in airborne and air assault forces within the Soviet Union are less clear.

Understandably, traditional parachute-delivered forces should feel the effects of defensiveness to a considerable degree because they are of lesser utility in conducting defensive operations. Despite this fact, airborne forces have gradually begun to assume a new role by operating to perform security missions. Because of their high state of training and morale, as political, economic, and ethnic unrest has spread throughout the union republics, the Soviet leadership has called upon airborne divisions to restore order (such as in Lithuania, Moldova, and the Trans-Caucasus republics). At least one airborne division has been resubordinated to the KGB for this purpose, and further such resubordination of airborne forces to either KGB or MVD (Ministry of Internal Affairs) may occur. This trend is likely to continue and limit reductions in the overall size of the airborne force. In early 1991 airborne forces in the ATTU region (areas west of the Urals subject to constraints of CFE arms control agreements) consisted of the formations shown in Figure 94. At least one additional division is likely located outside the ATTU region in the Far East or Central Asia.

In addition, the Soviets list seven separate air-landing or parachute assault brigades in the ATTU region equipped with helicopters and disposed as shown in Figure 95.

The current airborne division, according to Soviet statements, is organized similar to its earlier variants as shown in Figure 96. While no definite information is available on any recent reorganization of helicopter-lifted air assault formations, presumably the same support structure exists in these forces as in the airborne division (a materiel support battalion).

FIGURE 94. AIRBORNE FORCES IN THE ATTU REGION, 1991

VDV (airborne force) Headquarters	Moscow
7th Guards Airborne Division	Kaunas
97th Guards Parachute Assault Regiment	Alytus
108th Guards Parachute Assault Regiment	Kaunas
119th Guards Parachute Assault Regiment	Mariampol'e
76th Guards Airborne Division	Pskov
104th Guards Parachute Assault Regiment	Pskov
234th Guards Parachute Assault Regiment	Pskov
237th Guards Parachute Assault Regiment	Pskov
98th Guards Airborne Division	Bolgrad
217th Guards Parachute Assault Regiment	Bolgrad
299th Guards Parachute Assault Regiment	Bolgrad
300th Guards Parachute Assault Regiment	Kishinev
104th Guards Airborne Division	Giandzha
328th Guards Parachute Assault Regiment	Giandzha
337th Guards Parachute Assault Regiment	Giandzha
345th Guards Parachute Assault Regiment	Giandzha
106th Guards Airborne Division	Tula
51st Guards Parachute Assault Regiment	Tula
137th Guards Parachute Assault Regiment	Riazan'
331st Guards Parachute Assault Regiment	Kostroma
103d Guards Airborne Division	Vitebsk (recently transferred to MVD [internal security force] control)

INTO THE FUTURE

The immense political and military changes now occurring in the Soviet military realm, so staggering in their magnitude and consequences, seemed to guarantee that future Soviet military strategy, operational art, and tactics would, of necessity, be defensive. In recent months, however, voices have been raised in the ranks of military analysts which question the wisdom and validity of too great a dependance on defensiveness and express concern that planners err on the side of prudence when attempting to define what future force will satisfy the requirements of defensive sufficiency.[50]

In the light of these expressed reservations, some of which are probably officially sanctioned, it is reasonable to presume, and in fact discernible from Soviet writings, that Soviet theorists will, while addressing defensive topics, also incorporate elements from their offensive military

FIGURE 95. AIR ASSAULT FORCES IN THE ATTU REGION, 1991

21st Separate Air-landing Brigade	Kutaisi
38th Separate Air-landing Brigade	Brest
23d Separate Air-landing Brigade	Kremenchug
36th Separate Air-landing Brigade	Garbolovo
37th Separate Air-landing Brigade	Cherniakhovsk
40th Separate Air-landing Brigade	Nikolaev
35th Separate Air Assault Brigade	Cottbus

The precise organization of these forces is, as yet, unclear. The forces are supported by the following lift and training units:

58th Separate Military Transport Aviation Squadron	Riazan'
242d Training Center	Gaizhenai
224th Training Center	Khyrov
Airborne School (Academy)	Riazan'

FIGURE 96. AIRBORNE DIVISION, 1991

Airborne (Air-landing) Division
  3 parachute-landing regiments
  1 artillery regiment
  1 separate antiaircraft missile battalion
  1 separate signal battalion
  1 separate materiel support battalion
  1 separate engineer sapper battalion
  1 separate airborne support battalion
  1 separate repair-reconstruction battalion
  1 separate medical battalion
  1 separate military transport aviation squadron
  1 separate chemical defense company

Strength:

7,134 men	6 122-mm guns/howitzers
312 BMD-1(2)	72 120-mm mortars/howitzers
123 BTR-D	

analysis, which dominated their attention through 1985, and persisted in some forums well into 1987. This synthesis of old and new should prompt Soviet analysis of at least the following topics (for obvious political reasons, probably in closed forum):

– the employment of operational maneuver groups in the defense and, in particular, in the counteroffensive, counterstroke, and counterattack;
– the use of airborne and air assault forces in defensive battles and operation and in offensive counteractions (counteroffensive, counterstrokes, and counterattacks);
– raid tactics in defensive combat;
– the future evolution of land-air battle and development of the air echelon;

– the future development of non-linear warfare; and
– the future employment of firepower (artillery and air).

Most of these subjects are inexorably interrelated with the question of air assault, and it is likely airborne and helicopter-delivered forces will play a key role in their resolution. In fact, recent critiques by Polish military analysts of Poland's future military force structure may provide a hint regarding the direction their Soviet counterparts will follow. One recent critique listed as but one force structuring option, 'to go over from tank and mechanized reserve units to air-assault (with helicopters) and air-armored units (divisions, brigades), first at the central and then at the military district level.'[51] If this is the case, then the concepts of non-linear warfare, air-land battle, and the increased importance of the air echelon, indeed, have a place in the future.

CHAPTER 15

Conclusions

Soviet experimentation with airborne and air assault operations has spanned half a century. That the Soviets would consider adopting such a revolutionary military concept was understandable. Airborne operations were a natural outgrowth of a greater attempt to free battle from the fetters of positional warfare. Those who developed the concept of deep battle to restore the primacy of the offensive to the battlefield viewed airborne operations as yet another dimension of mobile, fluid war. Vertical envelopment by airborne forces emerged as an adjunct to high-speed mechanized operations intended to strike deeply into enemy rear areas. Tanks, mechanized infantry, and airborne forces became the means of effecting deep battle. Under the guidance of Marshal Tukhachevsky, the twin theories of deep battle and deep operations matured; and a force structure evolved to translate those theories into practice. But, although the members of the Soviet High Command accepted the utility of the new doctrinal concepts, reality weighed against full realization of their dreams.

Lagging technology, underdeveloped resources, and an unsophisticated populace were the sobering, and often frustrating, realities Soviet leaders faced. In the 1930s, equipment was scarce, levels of technological sophistication were low, and Soviet manpower was still rooted in its peasant past. Research, industrial development, and education would overcome those problems, but only at a cost of precious time. Even if the developers of deep battle and deep operations theory had survived to test and improve their theories in war, they might not have fully mastered the problems of translating advanced theory into practice. Perhaps, at best, their imagination might have better adjusted Soviet forces and doctrine to those realities. But the purges of the innovators settled the issue and sounded the death knell for an effective prewar Red Army.

The ambitious plans of the Soviet High Command for successfully employing their massive and varied forces in battle foundered on the rocks of incompetent leadership, inadequate weaponry, and lack of equipment as sophisticated as the Soviet force structure. Concepts for integrating the combat power of infantry, mechanized, and airborne forces were useless in the absence of a sound command and control system. Without modern communications (radios), a refined logistics system, or leaders capable of orchestrating the actions of large forces, Soviet military concepts became mere dreams. In June 1941, the more rehearsed and technically competent German Army, with its own concepts of deep battle and better means to realize those concepts, turned Soviet dreams into nightmares.

Soviet airborne forces escaped the worst effects of those nightmares. While Soviet mechanized forces perished and the Soviet ground force structure was shaken to its very foundations, airborne forces maintained their cohesion and survived the harsh first months of war. The opening phases of war sucked airborne forces into the cauldron of ground combat. The fact that the Soviet High Command used these forces as fire brigades to stem the German tide where it rose highest testified to the High Command's high esteem of airborne units. Well trained, highly motivated, and relatively well equipped, the airborne forces paid a high price for their military competence. By late 1941, when few Soviet units qualified as elite, airborne forces still warranted that distinction. So, when the High Command mustered its forces to strike back at the Germans on the approaches to Moscow, airborne forces were thrown into action. The desperate battle of December 1941 and January 1942 drew airborne forces center stage. In a threadbare and imperfect attempt to realize the goals of offensive deep battle, the High Command committed airborne forces to combat in tandem with cavalry units, seasoned divisions from Soviet Asia, and exhausted survivors of the summer and autumn campaigns.

The airborne operations in the winter of 1942 were an adjunct to the surging efforts of the Soviet High Command to crush an overextended and exhausted German *Wehrmacht*. Over a four-month period, lightly equipped airborne units, from detachment to corps size, conducted numerous airborne and ground assaults supported from the air in the German rear area in a vain attempt to disrupt German defenses, link up with Soviet ground forces, and destroy large chunks of German Army Groups Center and North. Plagued by poor planning; inadequate quantities of transport aircraft; faulty coordination of air, ground, and airborne units; deficient weaponry; and the paralyzing cold of a severe winter, the airborne forces failed to achieve operational success. The high morale and endurance of the lightly armed units could not compensate for the loss of surprise, an element so critical for success. As a result, airborne operations became an endurance test. At stake was the survival of those forces. Despite heavy costs in lives, airborne forces generally passed the test and survived.

Clearly, the paratroopers had a disconcerting effect on the Germans and made German defensive efforts more difficult. But however difficult it was for the Germans, their defenses held, and Soviet airborne operations failed to achieve their primary missions. Again in 1943 on the Dnepr River, a hasty Soviet attempt to capitalize on the capabilities of airborne forces failed for many of the same reasons that 1942 operations had failed. This failure produced reluctance on the part of the High Command to use, and possibly waste, these valuable units throughout the remainder of the war.

From the outset during the war, the Soviet High Command maintained a healthy respect for what airborne forces could accomplish strategically. Writing in November 1941, Major General G. D'iakov thoroughly examined German use of airborne forces in the initial period of the Second World War, particularly in France, Yugoslavia, and Crete, and noted the positive role these forces played in the subsequent Allied strategic collapse on the European continent.[1] As late as November 1942 Soviet theorists continued to stress the potential strategic impact of airborne operations. Examining both Western and Soviet experiences, Major General M. Spirin wrote, 'They can be used to accomplish missions of an operational-strategic nature,' such as seizing enemy air bases and airfields or assisting in the conduct of a major sea landing.[2] In addition, he credited Soviet airborne forces with contributing to the growth of the strategically important partisan movement in the German rear area. His concluding judgement was that, 'The airborne forces of the Red Army are a means of the High Command. With the help of airborne forces, missions of an operational-tactical or operational-strategic nature can be accomplished.'[3] By 1945, however, similar writers were limiting their assessments of the significance of airborne forces to the operational-tactical realm.[4]

Despite these contemporary writings, experience indicated that airborne forces were not yet capable, either technically or organizationally, of accomplishing strategic missions. Classified Soviet analysis of their 1942 experiences bore out this fact. The ambitious strategic operations aimed at destroying German Army Group Center and elements of German Sixteenth Army near Viaz'ma and Demiansk in 1942, which depended for success in large measure on the proper functioning of airborne forces, failed miserably for a variety of reasons. Large-scale use of airborne forces by the Allies in Normandy and later in Holland only reinforced the fact that airborne forces were too slender a reed to depend upon for resolving critical strategic missions. (Apparently Soviet analysts consider the Allied Rhine air-drops in 1945 as only operational in scale.) Having reached this conclusion, Soviet theorists could only muse about strategic roles and missions of airborne forces in a future context.

Operationally, Soviet hopes and expectations also fell short. At best, the impact of Soviet airborne operations throughout the war could be termed operational, but here again only in intent and potential outcome. Writing in 1942, one theorist stated:

> Combat experience on the Soviet–German front prompts a whole series of missions, which airborne forces can carry out. With the help of airborne forces, it is possible to ease considerably the withdrawal of separate groups of our forces from encirclement. Sometimes, as experience shows, the use of airborne forces can be the sole means of supporting the activity [*aktivnost'*] of units located in encirclement. And conversely, air assaults, landed in territory occupied by an encircled enemy, can considerably lighten the mission of destroying these encircled forces. Finally, in the past war, there were occasions when the landing of large formations of our airborne forces interfered with the movement of large enemy force groupings penetrating into our territory.[5]

In the winter of 1942, Soviet airborne operations clearly had some operational significance, but at high cost in lives to the elite airborne force. The operations of 4th Airborne Corps, in conjunction with Cavalry Group Belov, did disrupt the German rear area and attracted the attention of numerous German forces whose strength could have had greater impact elsewhere along the front. The operational drop across the Dnepr River in September 1943 was a bold stroke, which could have had considerable operational significance if its preparation had been more effective and if bad luck had not intervened in the form of German forces who happened to arrive in the region just as the drop was taking place. Aside from these tangential effects and musings about 'what ifs,' Soviet airborne operations achieved little of operational significance. They did, however, clearly indicate what could be achieved operationally if forces were better prepared and equipped in the future.

Soviet experiences with tactical airborne operations were more pro-ductive than their operational experiences. Because tactical operations involved smaller units (up to a battalion or a regiment) employed at more limited depths (20 to 30 kilometers) than operational landings, they were better suited to the Soviets' level of expertise and technology during the war years. High-level command controlled such operations more closely, and the shallow depth of employment allowed better coordination between airborne and ground forces.

The missions of units conducting tactical operations were limited in nature and, hence, more easily attainable. Tactical operations usually involved missions that facilitated the ground advance in an army sector, such as engagement of enemy fire delivery systems, disruption of enemy command and control, dislocation of the enemy supply system, and attacks on critical junctions and bridges on the enemy lines of communication. These tactical operations involved relatively small forces in support of a specific unit's advance, so they were of shorter duration. The short duration alone reduced logistical problems, increased the chances of airborne unit survivability, and produced better chances of tactical success. In addition, small groups of men were better able to escape enemy detection during landing and operation. They could avoid the twin threats of enemy ground and air attacks.

Tactical airborne operations, by virtue of their small size and limited duration, often resembled diversionary operations. The primary difference between the two was in the intent and, to a degree, the depth of each. Tactical operations occurred close to the front, but small-unit (usually less than a battalion) diversionary operations extended well into the enemy rear. Airborne units performing tactical missions operated in close coordination with forces (usually armies) advancing on a precise axis, and usually linkup was envisioned within a matter of days. Diversionary units usually engaged German objectives deep in the rear along enemy lines of communication or attacked targets whose destruction would weaken the German war effort in general. Diversionary forces also conducted special reconnaissance and sabotage missions at varying depths in the enemy rear. Of course, some operations, such as that at Odessa in 1941, did not fit neatly into either category.

Overall, however, the Soviets were more satisfied with their tactical and diversionary operations and believed that those types of operations provided greater returns for manpower expended than did the large-scale airborne operations. Thus, after the 1943 disaster along the Dnepr, the Soviets restricted themselves to small-scale airdrops. One Soviet theorist writing in 1945 accurately summed up wartime experiences:

> In the conditions of the Soviet–German front, in the presence of a deeply echeloned enemy defense, mobile reserves, and a considerable quantity of combat aviation, the actions of airborne forces, if they continued more than three to seven days, usually proceeding in close cooperation with units advancing from the front, developed into ordinary partisan operations. With the transitioning of the Red Army into a general offensive, after the defeat of German forces at Stalingrad, and especially after the battle of Kursk, the activities of partisan forces in the enemy rear became more active and took on a more organized nature, as a consequence of which the necessity for throwing airborne forces into the enemy rear sharply decreased.[6]

The author qualified his limited assessment of the impact of airborne forces during the war by adding:

Combat experience demonstrated that airborne assaults are a means of the High Command and *front* commands, which are able fully and effectively to maintain cooperation with ground forces and combat aviation and realize their [ground force] success in the interests of decisive operations.

The negative side of the use of airborne assaults, which appeared in the Second World War, in no way belittles the strong conclusion that well-organized and properly secured use of them in accordance with operational-tactical conditions has fully justified itself.[7]

On the surface, major Soviet Second World War airborne operations projected an image of abject failure. Operational experiences did achieve only limited success, and so small was the success that the Soviets abandoned ideas of using large airborne forces later in the war. However, at the same time the Soviets were experiencing failure with large-scale operations, they were achieving success with tactical and diversionary airborne operations. Experience, whether good or bad, has been, and still is, for the Soviets a vehicle for education and improvement. The bitter airborne force experiences of 1942–43 were not merely noted and forgotten. The Soviets studied and evaluated them just as they did the other combat failures of 1941–42. That study rendered failure useful as an analytical tool to build a force and a doctrine that could succeed in battle. Soviet study of Second World War airborne experiences focused on the major operational failures around Moscow and on the Dnepr. It also surveyed the other tactical and diversionary operations conducted throughout the war as well as German and Allied operations. That study paved the way for sounder theory and practice in the future.

The war pointed out those elements necessary for successful operational airborne assaults and created in the Soviets a resolve to address those necessities in the future. Study of war experience also evidenced the success of airborne forces in the tactical and diversionary realm, and, to this day, the Soviets have capitalized on building forces to exploit that dimension of battle.

In the immediate postwar period, the Soviets built a formidable airborne force and refined their airborne doctrine in light of wartime experiences. Although airborne forces had a distinct place in the operational and tactical scheme, that place was a modest one. The complexity of airborne operations, the vulnerability of airborne forces in high-intensity mechanized warfare, the limited delivery capability of transport aircraft, and the restricted mobility of airborne forces dictated that airborne units perform only modest missions in close coordination with ground forces.

The 'revolution in military affairs' and improved Soviet technology resulted in a reemphasis on airborne warfare in the 1960s. The projection of nuclear firepower onto the battlefield spelled an end to dense combat formations, tight multiple echelons, and contiguous defenses arrayed in great depth. Nuclear weapons fragmented combat and forced potential combatants to disperse their forces and to resort to mobility and speed to achieve operational and tactical success. If nuclear strikes could rupture and fragment defenses, then airborne forces could again operate at great depth with less fear of inevitable destruction. Airborne forces became a useful adjunct to high-speed armored and mechanized forces exploiting the effects of nuclear fires deep into enemy defenses.

Advances in technology increased the firepower and mobility of airborne forces and their survivability in battle, whether nuclear or conventional. The development of adequate transport means, helicopters for transport and fire support, air-transportable assault guns, airborne combat vehicles, light surface-to-air missiles, and improved communications equipment unfettered airborne forces. New types of airborne forces evolved, and the helicopter emerged as a versatile means of projecting airborne combat power within new concepts of air mobility and air mechanization.

Soviet airborne forces of the 1970s were structured to perform a multitude of missions in support of offensive operations at every level of combat. They were designed to be a flexible element of the Soviet combined arms structure. The Soviets intensely studied the historical employment of such forces in combat and well understand the strengths and limitations of those forces. In practical terms, the Soviets placed the greatest faith in the use of airborne troops at the tactical and operational levels. In the words of General of the Army V. Margelov:

> Now airborne forces are equipped with the most perfect means of waging combat. Perhaps in no other type of force is there concentrated such a variety of arms and equipment. Soviet airborne forces can appear in the enemy rear, having at their disposal all that is essential for the conduct of battle (operations); they are also able to perform large strategic missions in contemporary combat.[8]

By the 1980s traditional parachute-delivered forces were supplemented with experimental types of helicopter-delivered formations. Their potential wartime use was fully integrated into concepts for rapid and deep operational and tactical maneuver, all fitting into the general concept of the theater-strategic operation. By 1987 airborne and air assault units and formations were the nucleus of a newly emerging air echelon, cooperating on an equal basis with traditional ground echelons to conduct warfare in a new high-techology conventional warfare environment. In short, these forces were the most critical element of forces structured and trained to wage non-linear war.

The abrupt Soviet doctrinal shift to defensiveness in 1987, and particularly after Gorbachev's December 1988 speech to the United Nations, halted Soviet fixation on the offensive and muted subsequent discussions on the use of airborne and air assault forces in their traditional offensive role. The intensity and frequency of Soviet writings on airborne or air assault matters has diminished in consonance with Soviet public announcements of their deemphasis of these forces in their 'post Cold War' force structure. Since that time, only articles published in the press of former Warsaw Pact armies provide an indication of the sincerity and intensity of the now unvoiced view of the role of air assault in future war.

Although defensiveness now predominates in Soviet public writings on operational art and tactics, and airborne and air assault forces are now accorded a growing role within the parameters of defense, it is highly unlikely that the strictly military rationale for their use developed so carefully in the 1980s has now entirely faded. In the theoretical realm, airborne and air assault forces, as the air echelon in future non-linear warfare, will continue to receive their deserved attention. In fact, the Soviet theoretical approach developed in the 1980s may be of use and guidance for foreign theorists who are themselves trying to master the dilemmas of future war. In an optimistic view, one must hope that traditional and new theories of warfare and the role of airborne and air assault forces in modern battle will remain theoretical as political and economic changes produce a new global order based on democratization, peace, and mutual security. In the event this optimism is misplaced, one would do well to understand where theory of warfare now resides and what direction it is likely to take in the future. For, should a less peaceful world emerge, there is surely a growing role for the vertical dimension of battle – airborne and air assault forces.

Notes

CHAPTER 1

1. For a brief survey of Frunze's work and thought, see *Sovetskaia voennaia entsiklopediia* [Soviet military encyclopedia], 8:342–45 (hereafter cited as *SVE*). A selection of his writings can be found in *Voprosy strategii i operativnogo iskusstva v sovetskikh voennykh trudakh 1917–1940gg* [Questions of strategy and operational art in Soviet military works, 1917–1940], (Moscow: Voenizdat, 1965).
2. V. Matsulenko, 'Razvitie taktiki nastupatel'nogo boia' [The development of tactics of offensive battle], *Voenno-istoricheskii zhurnal* [Military-historical journal], No. 2 (February 1968), 28–9 (hereafter cited as *VIZh*).
3. D. S. Sukhorukov, ed., *Sovetskie vozdushno-desantnye* [Soviet air-landing forces] (Moscow: Voenizdat, 1980), 9–10.
4. N. Ramanichev, 'Razvitie teorii i praktiki boevogo primeneniia vozdushno-desantnykh voisk v mezhvoennyi period' [The development of the theory and practice of the combat use of air-landing forces in the interwar period], *VIZh*, No. 10 (October 1982), 72–7.
5. *Voprosy strategii*, 348.
6. Ibid., 352.
7. I. I. Lisov, *Desantniki – vozdushnye desanty* [Air-landing troops – air-landings] (Moscow: Voenizdat, 1968), 8–12.
8. Ibid., 11.
9. Ramanichev, 'Razvitie teorii,' 73.
10. Sukhorukov, *Sovetskie vozdushno*, 11; Lisov, *Desantniki*, 14–15.
11. Sukhorukov, *Sovetskie vozdushno*, 12.
12. Lisov, *Desantniki*, 20.
13. Sukhorukov, *Sovetskie vozhushno*, 13.
14. Lisov, *Desantniki*, 20–22.
15. Sukhorukov, *Sovetskie vozdushno*, 13–14; Ramanichev, 'Razvitie teorii,' 73.
16. Sukhorukov, *Sovetskie vozdushno*, 14.
17. I. Korotkov, 'Voprosy obshchei taktiki v sovetskoi voennoi istoriografii (1918–1941gg)' [Questions of general tactics in Soviet military historiography], *VIZh*, No. 12 (December 1977), 88; Ramanichev, 'Razvitie teorii,' 73.
18. Ramanichev, 'Razvitie teorii,' 73.
19. Sukhorukov, *Sovetskie vozdushno*, 15.
20. *Voprosy strategii*, 122.
21. Ibid., 355.
22. 'Transport of Troops by Air,' *Soviet Russia (Aviation), G-2 Report No. 8777-5110/6720* (Washington, D.C.: Military Intelligence Division, War Department, July 14, 1934). Secret, now declassified.
23. Ibid.
24. Ibid.
25. 'Transport of M. G. Units by Air,' *Soviet Russia (Aviation), G-2 Report No. 8924-5110/6720* (Washington, D.C.: Military Intelligence Division, War Department, November 23, 1934). Secret, now declassified.
26. Sukhorukov, *Sovetskie vozdushno*, 34; Lisov, *Desantniki*, 22. In 1935, the brigade

received the honorific name Kirov Brigade in memory of the Leningrad Communist party chief murdered in 1934.

27. Ramanichev, 'Razvitie teorii,' 75.
28. Ibid., 74. The course stressed such topics as parachute training, landing techniques, and combined operations after landing, including regrouping for combat, maneuvers, raids on objectives, and techniques for accomplishing typical missions.
29. 'Air Units in the Leningrad Military District,' *Soviet Russia (Aviation-Military), G-2 Report No. 9334-9180* (Washington, D.C.: Military Intelligence Division, War Department, October 19, 1935), 2. Secret, now declassified.
30. I. I. Lisov, *Soviet Airborne Forces* (Moscow: DOSAAF, 1967), 5–10, translated from the Russian title, *Sovetskie vozdushno-desantnye voiska*, by the Techtran Corporation in 1969. Today, *DOSAAF* (All Union Voluntary Society for Assistance to the Army, Air Force, and Navy) performs the same function.
31. 'Activities of the OSOAVIAKHIM,' *Soviet Russia (Combat), G-2 Report No. 9059-6790* (Washington, D.C.: Military Intelligence Division, War Department, April 10, 1935). Secret, now declassified.
32. Ramanichev, 'Razvitie teorii,' 74–5.
33. Sukhorukov, *Sovetskie vozdushno*, 39.
34. Ramanichev, 'Razvitie teorii,' 75–6.
35. Sukhorukov, *Sovetskie vozdushno*, 40–41; M. A. Gareev, *Obshche voiskovye ucheniia* [Combined-arms exercises] (Moscow: Voenizdat, 1983), 97–100.
36. 'Recent Maneuvers in the Kiev Military District,' *Soviet Russia (Combat-Army), G-2 Report No. 9374-6760* (Washington, D.C.: Military Intelligence Division, War Department, November 27, 1935), 2. Secret, now declassified.
37. Ramanichev, 'Razvitie teorii,' 76; Sukhorukov, *Sovetskie vozdushno*, 40. The parachute regiments were created from airborne troops of airborne brigades and airborne battalions. The two rifle regiments were the 43d and 90th of the 59th Rifle Division. A detailed English language description of the exercise is in A. Eremenko, *The Arduous Beginning* (Moscow: Progress Publishers, 1966), 8–10.
38. John Weeks, *The Airborne Soldier* (Poole, Dorset, England: Blandford Press, 1982), 19.
39. 'Red Army Maneuvers: Kiev Military District,' *USSR (Combat-Army), G-2 Report No. 333-6760* (Washington, D.C.: Military Intelligence Division, War Department, September 18, 1935). Secret, now declassified.
40. Ibid.
41. 'Order of the People's Commissar of Defense on Kiev Maneuvers,' *USSR (Combat-Army), G-2 Report No. 348-6760* (Washington, D.C.: Military Intelligence Division, War Department, September 27, 1935), 2. Secret, now declassified.
42. 'Comments of Foreign Military Missions on Soviet Maneuvers,' *USSR (Combat-Army), G-2 Report No. 345-6030* (Washington, D.C.: Military Intelligence Division, War Department, September 25, 1935), 2. Secret, now declassified.
43. Ibid., 3.
44. 'Recent Maneuvers in the Kiev Military District,' *Soviet Russia (Combat-Army), G-2 Report No. 9374-6760* (Washington, D.C.: Military Intelligence Division, War Department, November 27, 1935), 3. Secret, now declassified.
45. Ibid., 4.
46. 'Air Maneuvers Red Army,' *USSR (Combat-Army), G-2 Report No. 6760* (Washington, D.C.: Military Intelligence Division, War Department, January 8, 1936). Secret, now declassified.
47. Sukhorukov, *Sovetskie vozdushno*, 41–2.
48. 'Fall Maneuvers of the Red Army in 1936,' *Soviet Russia (Combat-Army), G-2 Report No. 9675-6720/9720* (Washington, D.C.: Military Intelligence Division, War Department, January 23, 1937). Secret, now declassified.
49. 'Fall Maneuvers in the White Russian Military District,' *Soviet Russia (Combat-Army), G-2 Report 9695-6720* (Washington, D.C.: Military Intelligence Division, War Department, February 25, 1937), 3. Secret, now declassified.
50. Ibid.

51. 'Fall Maneuvers of the Red Army in 1936,' *G-2 Report No. 9675.*
52. Ibid., 1–2.
53. Ibid., 4.
54. Ibid., Enclosure.
55. Ibid.
56. Sukhorukov, *Sovetskie vozdushno*, 41–2.
57. 'Tactics of Mass Parachute Descents,' *Aviation (Military), G-2 Report No. 626-9120* (Washington, D.C.: Military Intelligence Division, War Department, September 28, 1936). Secret, now declassified.
58. 'Increase of Soviet Aviation and Parachute Jumping,' *Aviation (Military), G-2 Report No. 9609* (Washington, D.C.: Military Intelligence Division, War Department, November 23, 1936), Enclosure No. 1. Secret, now declassified.
59. 'White Russian Maneuvers, September 1937,' *USSR (Combat-General), G-2 Report No. 985-6760* (Washington, D.C.: Military Intelligence Division, War Department, October 2, 1937). Secret, now declassified.
60. Ramanichev, 'Razvitie teorii,' 77.
61. Korotkov, 'Voprosy obshchei,' 89.
62. V. Daines, 'Razvitie taktiki obshchevoiskovogo nastupatel'nogo boia v 1929–1941gg' [The development of tactics of combined-arms offensive battle in 1929–1941] *VIZh*, No. 10 (October 1978), 96.
63. Ibid.
64. *Vremennyi polevoi ustav RKKA (PU-36)* [Temporary field regulation of the Red Army], (Moscow: Voenizdat, 1936), para. 7.
65. A. Volpe, 'Vnezapnost'' [Surprise], *Voennaia mysl'* [Military thought], No. 3 (March 1937), 17 (hereafter cited as VM).
66. A. Ia. Ianovsky, 'Vozdushnyi desant v sovremennoi voine' [Air assault in contemporary war], VM, No. 5 (May 1938), quoted by *Voprosy strategii*, 360.
67. Ibid., 361.
68. Ibid.
69. Ibid., 362.
70. *Voprosy taktiki v sovetskikh voennykh trudakh (1917–1940gg)* [Questions of tactics in Soviet military works (1917–1940)] (Moscow: Voenizdat, 1970), 347.
71. I. A. Kovalev, 'Reconnaissance by Aviation,' *VM*, No. 9 (September 1938), quoted in 'Strategical and Tactical Doctrines,' *USSR (Combat-Army), G-2 Report No. 1460-6020* (Washington, D.C.: Military Intelligence Division, War Department, February 27, 1939), 4-5. Secret, now declassified.
72. Sukhorukov, *Sovetskie vozdushno*, 35–6.
73. Ibid.
74. Eremenko, *Arduous Beginning*, 24–39. For a more thorough coverage of the discussion, see M. V. Zakharov, *General'nyi shtab v predvoennye gody* [The General Staff in the prewar years] (Moscow: Voenizdat, 1989), 192–211. Full text of the conference is now available from the Soviet Ministry of Defense archives.
75. Weeks, *Airborne Soldier*, 18–26.
76. Ibid., 20.
77. Sukhorukov, *Sovetskie vozdushno*, 47–8. For details on Khalkhin-Gol action, see G. Shelakhov and G. Plotnikov, 'Razgrom Iaponskikh zakhvatchikov no reke Khalkhin-Gol' [Destruction of Japanese invaders on the Khalkhin-Gol River], *VIZh*, No. 8 (August 1969), 31–41; P. A. Zhilin, ed., *Pobeda na reke Khalkhin-Gol* [Victory on the Khalkhin-Gol River] (Moscow: 'Nauka,' 1981); Edward J. Drea, *Nomonhan: Japanese–Soviet Tactical Combat 1939*, Leavenworth Papers No. 2 (Fort Leavenworth, KS: Combat Studies Institute, U.S. Army Command and General Staff College, January 1981).
78. Sukhorukov, *Sovetskie vozdushno*, 49–50; Lisov, *Desantniki*, 31–2.
79. 'Parachute Troops in the Finno-Soviet War and Finnish Countermeasures,' *USSR (Aviation-Military), G-2 Report No. 0132-9920-18* (Washington, D.C.: Military Intelligence Division, War Department, May 21, 1940), 1. Secret, now declassified.
80. Ibid., 2.

81. V. Kostylev, 'Stanovlenie i razvitie vozdushno-desantnykh voisk' [The growth and development of airborne forces], *VIZh*, No. 9 (September 1975), 82.
82. A. I. Starunin, 'Operativnaia vnezapnost" [Operational surprise], *VM*, No. 3 (March 1941), 27.
83. A. Kononenko, 'Boi vo flandrii' [Battle in Flanders], *VIZh*, No. 3 (March 1941), 22–5.
84. S. K. Timoshenko, *Zakliuchitel'naia rech' narodnogo komissara oborony soiuza SSR geroia i marshala Sovetskogo Soiuza S. K. Timoshenko na voennom soveshchanii, 31 dekabria 1940g.* [Concluding speech of the People's Commissar of Defense of the USSR, Hero and Marshal of the Soviet Union S. K. Timoshenko at a military conference, 31 December 1940] (Moscow: Voenizdat, 1941), 5.
85. Ibid.
86. Lisov, Desantniki, 37–8.
87. 'Distribution of Parachute Units,' *Military Attache Report USSR No. 258-9115* (Washington, D.C.: Military Intelligence Division, War Department, December 30, 1940). Secret, now declassified.
88. The 201st, 204th, and 214th Airborne Brigades were stationed in European Russia; the 202d, 211th, and 212th Airborne Brigades in the Far East. In 1940, the 211th and 212th Brigades moved to the Ukraine. The 202d Airborne Brigade remained at Khabarovsk until March 1944, when it moved to Moscow. Lisov, *Desantniki*, 38.
89. V. A. Anfilov, *Proval 'Blitskriga'* [The failure of blitzkrieg], (Moscow: 'Nauka,' 1971), 123; Lisov, *Desantniki*, 38–9.
90. Kostylev, 'Stanovlenie,' 82. The airborne corps consisted of the following brigades:

Location	Airborne Corps	Airborne Brigades
Pre-Baltic MD	5th	9th, 10th, 201st
Western Special MD	4th	7th, 8th, 214th
Kiev Special MD	1st	1st, 204th, 211th
Kharkov MD	2d	2d, 3d, 4th
Odessa MD	3d	5th, 6th, 212th

The 3d Airborne Corps moved from the Odessa Military District to the Kiev region sometime before or after 22 June 1941.
91. 'Separate Information About the Red Army,' *Enclosure No. 7 to Army Group 'B' Document No. 500/41 of 13.2.40 classified Top Secret*, cited in *Sbornik voenno-istoricheskikh materialov Velikoi Otechestvennoi voiny*, vypusk 18 [Collection of military-historical materials of the Great Patriotic War, issue 18] (Moscow: Voenizdat, 1960), 86–8, 134–5, 139, classified secret, declassified 1964.
92. Kostylev, 82.
93. Sukhorukov, *Sovetskie vozdushno*, 51. An airborne variant of the PS-84 would have permitted dropping 25 men from side doors and dropping equipment through a cargo door of the aircraft.

CHAPTER 2

1. For a candid view of Soviet military readiness in 1941, see S. P. Ivanov, ed., *Nachal'nyi period voiny* [The initial period of war] (Moscow: Voenizdat, 1974); and especially V. Petrov, *June 22, 1941: Soviet Historians and the German Invasion* (Columbia, SC: University of South Carolina Press, 1968), with its translation of and commentary on A. M. Nekrich's *1941–1942 iiunia* [June 1941–1942] (Moscow: 'Nauka,' 1965). Recently released Soviet archival materials provide even more detail about Soviet intelligence collection and combat in the initial period of war. See also David M. Glantz, *Soviet Military Intelligence in War* (London: Frank Cass, 1990).
2. General I. S. Bezugly, commander, 5th Airborne Corps; General A. I. Rodimtsev, commander, 5th Airborne Brigade; General A. S. Zhadov, commander, 4th Airborne Corps. For Rodimtsev's and Zhadov's airborne experiences, see A. I. Rodimtsev, *Tvoi otechestvo, syny* [Your fatherland, sons] (Kiev: Izdatel'stvo politicheskoi literatury, 1974); and A. S. Zhadov, *Chetyre goda voiny* [Four years of war] (Moscow: Voenizdat,

1978).
3. Kostylev, 'Stanovlenie,' 82.
4. Sukhorukov, *Sovetskie vozdushno*, 53–4.
5. 'Boevoe rasporiazhenie komanduiushchego voiskami zapadnogo fronta ot 28 iiunia 1941g. komandiru 4-go vozdushno desantnogo korpusa i komanduiushchemy voenno-vozdushnymi silami fronta na desantirovanie 214-i vozdushno desantnoi brigady v raion Slutsk' [Combat order of the commander of Western Front forces of 28 June 1941 to the commander of 4th Airborne Corps and the commander of *front* airborne forces on the desant of the 214th Airborne Brigade in the Slutsk region], *Sbornik boevykh dokumentov Velikoi Otechestvennoi voiny, vypusk 35* [Collection of combat documents of the Great Patriotic War, issue 35] (Moscow: Voenizdat, 1958), 56, classified secret, declassified 1964 (hereafter cited as *SBDVOV*, with appropriate document title, issue, and page).
6. 'Boevoe rasporiazhenie komanduiushchego voiskami zapadnogo fronta ot 28 iiunia 1941g komandiru 20-go mekhanizirovannogo korpusa na nastuplenie 210-i motorizovannoi divizii v napravlenii Slutsk' [Combat order of the commander of Western Front forces of 28 June 1941 to the commander of 20th Mechanized Corps on the offensive of the 210th Mechanized Division in the Slutsk direction], *SBDVOV*, issue 35, 57–8.
7. 'Chastnyi boevoi prikaz komanduiushchego voiskami zapadnogo fronta No. 012 ot 29 iinia 1941g komandiru 4-go vozdushnodesantnogo korpusa na vydvizhenie 214-i vozdushnodesantnoi brigady na slutskoe napravlenie i na perekhod k oborone os-tal'nymi voiskami korpusa' [Particular combat order No. 012 of 29 June 1941 of the commander of Western Front forces to the commander of 4th Airborne Corps on the movement of the 214th Airborne Brigade on the Slutsk direction and on the transition of remaining corps forces to the defense], *SBDVOV*, issue 35, 63.
8. I. I. Gromov, V. N. Pigunov, *Chetvertyi vozdushno-desantnyi: voenno-istoricheskii ocherk o boevom puti 4-go vozdushno-desantnogo korpusa* [Fourth airborne: a military-historical sketch concerning the combat path of 4th Airborne Corps] (Moscow: Voenizdat, 1990), 61–64, (hereafter cited as *4th Airborne*). For details on 214th Brigade operations, see I. I. Gromov, V. N. Pigunov, *V boi ukhodili desantniki* [Into battle went air-landing troops] (Minsk: Belarus', 1989).
9. Ibid., 67–9. The second formation of 4th Airborne Corps assembled in September 1941 near Engel's Airfield in the Moscow region.
10. Ibid., 70–1.
11. Ibid., 73–90; see also Zhadov, *Chetyre*, 14–18. By 7 July, the 7th and 8th Airborne Brigades had shrunk to 1,000 or 1,100 men each and 15 45-mm guns.
12. 'Die Luftlandetruppen der Roten Armee,' *Generalkommando V. AK. Abt.ia/ic K.Gel.St. den 25 Marz 1942*, National Archives Microfilm (hereafter cited as NAM) T314, roll 252.
13. Sukhorukov, *Sovetskie vozdushno*, 54–69; Rodimtsev, *Tvoi otechestvo*, 25–167. By late September, Rodimtsev's 5th Airborne Brigade had only about 500 men, 20 heavy machine guns, and 25 light machine guns. See also I. Samchuk, *Trinadtsataia gvardeis-kaia* [Thirteenth Guards] (Moscow: Voenizdat, 1971), 3–24.
14. Gromov, Pigunov, *4th Airborne*, 92–100.
15. M. F. Gliakin, *Budet zhit'* [He will live] (Moscow: Voenizdat, 1989), 10–11.
16. Ibid., 12–16.
17. P. Sukhorukov, *Sovetskie vozdushno*, 70–6; see also the account of 1st Guards Rifle Corps commander in D. D. Leliushenko, *Moskva–Stalingrad–Berlin–Praga* [Moscow–Stalingrad–Berlin–Prague] (Moscow: 'Nauka,' 1985), 32–53.
18. Sukhorukov, *Sovetskie vozdushno*, 71.
19. Ibid., 73–4.
20. Ibid., 76–7.
21. Ibid., 83.
22. Lisov, *Desantniki*, 39.
23. Kostylev, *Stanovlenie*, 82.
24. 'Die Luftlandetruppen der Roten Armee,' 3–4.

25. Ibid., 4–5.
26. Ibid., 6–12.
27. Sukhorukov, *Sovetskie vozdushno*, 146–79. A. V. Morozov, *39-ia Barvenkovskaia* [39th Barvenkovo] (Moscow: Voenizdat, 1971), 3–5, relates the experiences of one of those divisions.
28. Ibid., 161.
29. See also Rodimtsev, *Tvoi otechestvo*, 337–48; and Vasilii Chuikov, *The Battle for Stalingrad* (New York: Holt, Rinehart, and Winston, 1964).
30. Sukhorukov, Sovetskie vozdushno, 180–1.
31. See documents including 'Luftlandetruppen' *Auszugsweise Abschrift Akte:27A, Quelle: Chef der Sicherheitspolizei und des SD vom 24.4.1944; Auszugsweise Abschrift, Akte:27A, Quelle: Abwehrtrupp 'Bill' vom 21.20.43; Auszugsweise Abschrift aus Fernschreiben v.5.10.43, Pz. AOK1*; 'Russ-Luftandetruppen' *Dienststelle Walli I-Lages, Tgb. No. 2200/43 geh. Quelle: V-Mann 'Tumanow,' fruher Lt. und Komp. – Fu[umlaut]her im 28. Luftlande-Regt*, all issued by Oberkommando des Heeres [OKH], Generalstab des Heeres, Abt. Fremde Heere Ost (II z/a').
32. Sukhorukov, *Sovetskie vozdushno*, 181–4.
33. Lisov, *Desantniki*, 183.
34. Sukhorukov, *Sovetskie vozdushno*, 226.
35. Ibid., 238.
36. Ibid., 238–9.
37. G. P. Sofronov, *Vozdushnyi desanty vo vtoroi mirovoi voine* [Airlandings in the Second World War] (Moscow: Voenizdat, 1962), 12.
38. 'Instruktsiia po boevomu primeneniiu vozdushno-desantnykh voisk krasnoi armii (proekt)' [Instruments on the combat use of airborne forces of the Red Army (project)], *Sbornik materialov po izucheniiu opyta voiny, No. 5, mart 1943g.* [Collection of materials for the study of war experience, No. 5, March 1943] (Moscow: Voenizdat, 1943), 131. Prepared by the General Staff of the Red Army and classified secret, declassified in 1964 (hereafter cited as *VMPIOV* with appropriate title, volume, and pagination).
39. Ibid., 131–2.
40. Ibid., 133.
41. Ibid.
42. Ibid.
43. Ibid., 134.
44. *Polevoi ustav krasnoi armii (PU-44)* [Field regulations of the Red Army] (Moscow: Voenizdat, 1944), 20–1.
45. Ibid., 21.
46. Ibid., 84–5, 157.

CHAPTER 3

1. A. M. Vasilevsky, *A Lifelong Cause* (Moscow: Progress Publishers, 1978), 122–3. A translation of *Delo vsei zhizni* (Moscow: Izdatel'stvo politicheskoi literatury, 1973).
2. V. D. Sokolovsky, *Razgrom nemetsko-fashistskikh voisk pod moskvoi* [The defeat of German-Fascist forces at Moscow] (Moscow: Voenizdat, 1964), 206–12, 250–4, provides context for but does not mention the airborne operations.
3. The operational account is from Lisov, *Desantniki*, 75–6; and Sukhorukov, *Sovetskie vozdushno*, 78–9.
4. Franz Halder, *The Halder Diaries: The Private War Journals of Colonel General Franz Halder* (Boulder, CO: Westview Press, 1976), 235, entry for 19 December notes the growing rear area problem: 'The Russians attack during the night and turn up behind our positions at the break of daylight.'
5. Gliakin, 19.
6. Sokolovsky, *Razgrom*, 307–10; Georgii Konstantinovich Zhukov, *The Memoirs of Marshal Zhukov* (New York, Delacorte Press, 1971), 352–3.

7. See Sokolovsky, *Razgrom*, 317–20; and Lisov, *Desantniki*, 77. The precise order is found in B. M. Shaposhnikov, ed., *Razgrom nemetskikh voisk pod Moskvoi III* [The defeat of German forces at Moscow, Vol. III] (Moscow: Voenizdat, 1943), 109. These volumes prepared by the General Staff were classified secret [*Sekretnyi*] and declassified in 1964.

8. N. Soldatov, A. Korol'chenko, 'Znamenskii desant' [The Znamenka air assault], *VIZh*, No. 12 (December 1972), 72. The remainder of Soviet 5th Airborne Corps took part in the ground operations under 43d Army command.

9. Charles de Beaulieu, et al., 'Die Operationen der 4. Panzerarmee im Feldzug gegen die Sowjetunion' [The Operations of 4th Panzer Army in the campaign against the Soviet Union], *Foreign Military Studies MS No. P-206, Phase C, Vol. 1*, 80–90, reproduced by U.S. Army, Europe, 1959 (hereafter cited as *MS No. P-206*); Albert Seaton, *The Battle for Moscow*, (Rockville, NY: Playboy Press, 1980), 243; M. Gareis, *Kampf und Ende der Frankisch-Sudeten Deutschen 98.Division* [The combat and end of the Frankish-Sudeten German 98th Division] (Tegesnsee, FRG: Garev, 1956), 191–4.

10. Sofronov, *Vozdushnye desanty*, 14.

11. Lisov, *Desantniki*, 77.

12. Sofronov, *Vozdushnye desanty*, 14; Lisov, *Desantniki*, 78–81; *MS No. P-206, Phase D, vol. 1*, 82–9. The 4th Panzer Army noted on 6 January that Soviet airborne forces, identified as the 201st Airborne Brigade, cut the Medyn–Shansky Zavod road east of Gireevo. Unfortunately, the overextended right flank division of 20th Army Corps (267th Infantry) was unable to deal with this threat and to reestablish links with 4th Army's 98th Infantry Division, then conducting an agonizingly slow fighting withdrawal to Medyn.

13. Lisov, *Desantniki*, 77, cites the planned figure. Sofronov, *Vozdushnye desanty*, 16, gives actual landed strength. Subsequent action of Captain Starchak's battalion is covered in Sukhorukov, *Sovetskie vozdushno*, 137–9; and Lisov, *Desantniki*, 77–86.

14. Lisov, *Desantniki*, 86; Shaposhnikov, *Razgrom*, 113.

15. 'Deistviia 4 vozdushno-desantnogo korpusa v operativnom tylu protivnika' [The actions of 4th Airborne Corps in the enemy operational rear], *SMPIOV*, No. 5, 43.

16. Seaton, 240–56.

17. *MS No. p-206, Phase C, vol. 2*, 68–90.

18. Halder, 243.

19. Ibid., 244–6.

20. Seaton, 209–11.

21. V. D. Sokolovsky, *Razgrom*, 307–10.

22. Vasilevsky, *Life's Work*, 201.

23. K. Reinhardt, *Die Wende vor Moskau* [The turning point at Moscow] (Stuttgart: Deutsche Verlags-Anstalt, 1972), 243–55, Skizze [Map] 6.

24. *MS No. P-206*, 104–23; Gareis, *Kampf und Ende*, 1199–201; Walter Friedrich Poppe, 'Winter Campaign West of Temkino, Mid-December 1941 to April 1942,' *Foreign Military Studies MS No. D-184*, 1–12, reproduced by the Historical Division, U.S. Army, Europe, 1947.

25. Seaton, 248–50; W. Meyer-Detring, *Die 137. Infanterie division im Mittelabsschnitt der Ostfront* [The 137th Infantry Division in the Central Sector of the Eastern Front] (Ansbach, FRG: Georg Gebhardt, 1962), 111–5.

26. Gareis, *Kampf und Ende*, 200–2; Lothar Rendulic, 'Combat in Deep Snow,' Foreign Military Studies *MS No. D-106*, 6–10, reproduced by the Historical Division, U.S. Army, Europe, 1947. Rendulic commanded the 52d Infantry Division.

27. Halder, 253.

28. For context and details, see Shaposhnikov, *Razgrom*, V. III, 112–24; Sokolovsky, *Razgrom*, 345–50. On 349, he includes a short account of the airborne operation.

29. Lisov, *Desantniki*, 87; Gareis, *Kampf und Ende*, 208; Seaton, 260. German records confirm that 4th Army rear service, security, and police units occupied these locations. A 4th Army police regiment and a 98th Infantry Division signal battalion garrisoned Znamenka. Other 98th Infantry Division service units garrisoned towns along the

Znamenka–Iukhnov road, including Klimov Zavod. The 52d Infantry Division rear service units occupied towns along the road from Znamenka to Viaz'ma.

30. Lisov, *Desantniki*, 87.
31. Sukhorukov, *Sovetskie vozdushno*, 140; Soldatov and Korol'chenko, 'Znamenskii desant,' 71–2.
32. Lisov, *Desantniki*, 88–89. Sofronov, *Vozdushnye desanty*, 16, says 452 men landed the first day.
33. Soldatov and Korol'chenko, 'Znamenskii desant,' 72. About 1,000 partisans co-operated with the paratroopers, but only 800 were armed.
34. Sukhorukov, *Sovetskie vozdushno*, 141.
35. Sofronov, *Vozdushnye desanty*, 16–17; Gareis, *Kampf und Ende*, 208; 98. Infanterie Division/Ia, *Kriegstagebuch 4*, 15 January–5 March 1942. On the night of 20–21 January, 98th Infantry Division antitank and signal units observed a portion of the airlanding operation. They reported parachute jumps on 20 January near Klimov Zavod and larger airlandings on the night of 20–21 January near Voronovo (not shown on maps but presumed to be south of Znamenka). In the latter instance, 162 twin-engine aircraft landed on 'brilliantly illuminated' landing strips.
36. Shaposhnikov, *Razgrom, Vol. III*, 117.
37. Soldatov and Korol'chenko, 'Znamenskii desant,' 73. Shaposhnikov, *Razgrom, Vol. III*, 117, provides coordinates of the action.
38. Gareis, *Kampf und Ende*, 208–10; Seaton, 261; H. Reinhardt, 'Russian Air Landings in the Area of German Army Group Center,' in 'Russian Airborne Operations,' *Foreign Military Studies MS No. P-116*, 7, reproduced by the Historical Division, U.S. Army, Europe, 1953. The 98th Infantry Division reported combat with the airborne force near Znamenka on 29 January and, later, further north at Chodnevo (Khod-nevo), Petrovo, and Mikaeli (Mikhali). Only by 2 February had the division succeeded in relieving the surrounded garrisons in its rear service area.
39. Soldatov and Korol'chenko, 'Znamenskii desant,' 74.
40. Ibid., 74. Soldatov's force was equipped with two 45-mm antitank guns, 34 mortars (including ineffective 50-mm), and 11 antitank rifles.

CHAPTER 4

1. Sukhorukov, *Sovetskie vozdushno*, 85-6. Much of the operational and tactical detail of 8th Airborne Brigade operations and subsequent 4th Airborne Corps operations is in Sukhorukov's and Lisov's work and in A. Lukashenko, *Dorogami vozdushnogo desanta* [The paths of airborne forces] (Moscow: Moskovskii Rabochii, 1971). For a general outline of the Viaz'ma airborne operations in their operational context, see SVE, 2:445–6. The partisan role in the operations is covered in N. F. Iudin, *Pervaia partizanskaia* [The First Partisan (Regiment)] (Moscow: Moskovskii Rabochii, 1983).
2. For details on coordination of air and airborne forces, see A. Fedorov, *Aviatsiia v bitve pod Moskvoi* [Aviation in the battle of Moscow] (Moscow: 'Nauka,' 1971), 230–44.
3. Lisov, *Desantniki*, 95.
4. *MS No. P-206, Phase D, vol, 1*, 32–48; Panzer-Armee oberkommando 4/Ia, *Karten-lagen zum Kriegstagebuch, Nr 7–8 (Moskau)*, 24–29 January 1942, NAM T313, roll 348. Subsequent 4th Panzer Army unit positions shown on maps in the text are from this source, which covers the period 7 December 1941–26 April 1942.
5. Lisov, *Desantniki*, 96.
6. Gromov, Pigunov, *4th Airborne*, 104–5.
7. Ibid., 105–6.
8. D. Sukhorukov, 'Vozdushno-desantnye voiska' [Air-landing forces], *VIZh*, No. 1 (January 1982), 40.
9. Sofronov, *Vozdushnye desanty*, 20.
10. Sukhorukov, *Sovetskie vozdushno*, 86–7; Gromov, Pigunov, *4th Airborne*, 106–7.
11. Sofronov, *Vozdushnye desanty*, 19. A single lift of the airborne force would have taken 550 to 600 aircraft. See Lisov, *Desantniki*, 100.

12. Gromov, Pigunov, *4th Airborne*, 108–9.
13. Sukhorukov, *Sovetskie vozdushno*, 87; Gromov, Pigunov, *4th Airborne*, 111.
14. Gromov, Pigunov, *4th Airborne*, 111–12.
15. *MS No. P-206, Phase D, Vol. 1*, 40–2. German after-action reports confirmed the Soviet accounts. See Generalkommando V AK Abt Ia/Ic, *Die Luftlandetruppen der Roten Armee*, 25 March 1942, 12–16, NAM T314, roll 252. See also 5. Panzer Division/Ic, *Tatigskeitsberichte mit Anlagen, 26–30 January 1942*, NAM T315, roll 2311; and 11. Panzer Division/Ic, *Tatigskeitsberichte zum Kriegstagebuch 3*, 26–30 January 1942, NAM T315, roll 589.
16. Sukhorukov, *Sovetskie vozdushno*, 88. For details on Captain Karnaukhov's initial operations, see Lisov, *Desantniki*, 103–6; Gromov, Pirugov, *4th Airborne*, 112–13.
17. Sofronov, *Vozdushnye desanty*, 20; Gromov, Pigunov, *4th Airborne*, 112.
18. Gromov, Pirugov, *4th Airborne*, 114.
19. Ibid., 115.
20. Ibid.
21. Ibid., 118–19.
22. Ibid., 119–23.
23. Sukhorukov, *Sovetskie vozdushno*, 89–90. Twelve aircraft were damaged by anti-aircraft fire, two were shot down, seven required repairs, and one disappeared while on a mission.
24. Ibid., 90. Onufriev brought with him 174 rifles, 129 automatic weapons, nine antitank rifles, 22 machine pistols, 20 82-mm mortars, five 50-mm mortars, and one radio station.
25. Gromov, Pigunov, *4th Airborne*, 122–3.
26. Ibid., 133–4.
27. Ibid., 135.
28. Ibid., 135–6; see also Sukhorukov, *Sovetskie vozdushno*, 92–3.
29. Halder, 262.
30. Ibid., 263.
31. *MS No. P-206, Phase D, Vol. 1*, 41.
32. Sukhorukov, *Sovetskie vozdushno*, 91. Sofronov, *Vozdushnye desanty*, 20, claims that 2,328 men of 8th Brigade landed.
33. For Belov's operation during this time, see P. A. Belov, *Za nami Moskva* [Behind us Moscow] (Moscow: Voenizdat, 1963), 177–219; and P. A. Belov, 'Piatimesiachnaia bor'ba v tylu vraga' [A five-month struggle in the enemy rear area], *VIZh*, No. 8 (August 1962), 55–75. For operations of Soldatov's 250th Regiment, see N. Soldatov and A. Korol'chenko, 72–4.
34. Gromov, Pigunov, *4th Airborne*, 124.
35. Ibid., 126.
36. Ibid.
37. Ibid., 128–9.
38. Belov, *Za nami Moskva*, 204–7.
39. Reinhardt, 71.
40. *MS No. P-106, Phase D, Vol, 1*, 120–31.
41. Gromov, Pigunov, *4th Airborne*, 129.
42. Lisov, *Desantniki*, 109.
43. Gromov, Pigunov, *4th Airborne*, 130.
44. Ibid., 130–1; Belov cited 100 German losses.
45. Zhukov, *Memoirs*, 357.
46. Gromov, Pigunov, *4th Airborne*, 131.
47. Halder, 264; *MS No. P-106, Phase D, Vol. 1*, 120–8. German Fourth Panzer Army estimated Soviet strength in the German rear area at 12,000 men and German strength in the same area at only 7,000.
48. Gromov, Pigunov, *4th Airborne*, 131–2.
49. Ibid., 132–3.
50. 'Deistviia gruppy generala Belova v operativnom tylu Nemtsev' [Actions of Group General Belov in the German operational rear], *SMPIOV, No. 5*, 28, cites Western

Front order No. 055/Op of 3.2.42.

51. Ibid.
52. Ibid., 29.
53. Ibid., 30. The critique assesses German strength, stating:

> The enemy grouping opposing the corps at that time consisted of the following: garrisons of a strength of from 100 to 300 men, equipped with machine guns, mortars, and artillery, occupied the Krasnyi Kholm, Svkh. Kaidakovo, Batish-chevo, Mikhal'ki, Volodarets, Paldino, Podrezovo, Il'ino, and Moloshino. An estimated overall [force] of up to 5000 rifles with 20 tanks and armored vehicles were in these regions.

54. Ibid.
55. Gromov, Pigunov, *4th Airborne*, 138.
56. 'Deistviia gruppy generala Belova,' 30.
57. Gromov, Pigunov, *4th Airborne*, 138–41.
58. 'Deistviia gruppy generala Belova,' 30; Belov, *Za nami Moskva*, 209–10.
59. Gromov, Pigunov, *4th Airborne*, 141.
60. 'Deistviia gruppy generala Belova,' 32; *MS No. P-106, Phase D, Vol. 1*, 136.
61. Ibid.
62. Ibid.
63. Gromov, Pigunov, *4th Airborne*, 142.
64. Ibid.
65. 'Deistviia gruppy generala Belova,' 33.
66. Gromov, Pigunov, *4th Airborne*, 142–3.
67. Ibid., 143–4.
68. 'Deistviia gruppy generala Belova,' 34.
69. Gromov, Pigunov, *4th Airborne*, 145.
70. 'Deistviia gruppy generala Belova,' 34.
71. Ibid.
72. Gromov, Pigunov, *4th Airborne*, 146.
73. Belov, *Za nami Moskva*, 217–19; *MS No. P-106, Phase D, Vol. 1*, 152–7. The Germans referred to this encirclement operation as the *Andrejany Kessel* [Andrejany Cauldron]. The 5th Panzer Division and 23d Infantry Division (that arrived 24 January) reduced the pocket. The 4th Panzer Army claimed 2,380 Soviet soldiers killed and 1,762 prisoners. *MS No. P-116* states that Soviet losses were 5,000 killed and 700 prisoners.
74. 'Deistviia gruppy generala Belova,' 39.
75. Ibid.

CHAPTER 5

1. Sokolovsky, *Razgrom*, 361.
2. Gromov, Pigunov, *4th Airborne*, 151.
3. Ibid., 152.
4. 'Deistviia 4 vozdushno-desantnogo korpusa,' 45.
5. Meyer-Detring, *137. Infanterie*, 129–31, 139. For unit dispositions before and after 15 February, see Heeresgruppe Mitte/1a, *Anlagen zum Kriegstagebuch: Lagekarten, eigene und Feindlage, 1 January–31 March 1942*, NAM T311, roll 225. An account of 4th Army's battles is in Armeeoberkommando 4/1a, *Sonderbeilage zum Kriegstage-buch, Nr 14, Die Kampfe der 4. Armee im ersten Kriegsjahr gegen die Sowjets*, June 1941–June 1942, NAM T312, roll 186.
6. Meyer-Detring, *137. Infanterie*, 266; F. Hossbach, *Infanterie im Ostfeldzug 1941–42* [Infantry in the eastern campaign] (Osterode, Harz, FRG: Verlag Giebel-Oehls-chlagel, 1951), 206.
7. Ibid., 204.
8. Seaton, 260–1; Meyer-Detring, *137. Infanterie*, 134; Gareis, *Kampf und Ende*, 208–13; Reinhardt, 'Russian Air Landings,' 9. Detailed German order of battle and unit

dispositions are in Generalkommando V Ak/1a, *Lagenkarten zum Kriegstagebuch 2*, 7 February–29 April 1942, NAM T314, roll 252.

9. Sofronov, *Vozdushnye desanty*, 22.
10. Gromov, Pigunov, *4th Airborne*, 154.
11. Sukhorukov, *Sovetskie vozdushno*, 101.
12. Gromov, Pigunov, *4th Airborne*, 155.
13. Ibid., 156.
14. Ibid., 156–7.
15. Ibid., 157. The 4th Airborne history notes:

> The deputy chief of the operations department of the corps staff Major Antroshchenko also landed in 33d Army's area of combat operations. He requested permission from General Efremov to gather all airborne troops and return to his corps. He was permitted to take 30 commanders with him. With these commanders Antroshchenko arrived in the corps region of operations. This was all of the 600 paratroopers that the commander of 33d Army could return to 4th Airborne Corps.

16. Ibid., 158.
17. Ibid., 161.
18. Sofronov, *Vozdushnye desanty*, 23, claims that 6,988 men had landed by 20 February. Sukhorukov, *Sovetskie vozdushno*, 102, says the total was 7,373 by 23 February. Lisov, *Desantniki*, 114, cites the figure of 1,800 men who joined other units.
19. Reinhardt, 'Russian Air Landings,' 11; *MS No. P-206*, 138, states that the 52d Infantry Division reported that 130 aircraft landed 3,000 paratroopers on 19 and 20 February. Halder, 272, entry for 20 February notes, 'A. Gp. Center reports increasing number of paratroopers put down behind its lines.' The 52d and 98th Infantry Divisions also confirmed the landing in 52. Infanterie Division/1a, *Kriegstagebuch 5 mit Anlagenband B Operationsakten*, 20 February 1942, NAM T315, roll 958; and 98. Infanterie Division/1a, *Kriegstagebuch 4*, 20 February 1942, NAM T315, roll 1203.
20. Reinhardt, 'Russian Air Landings,' 11–13.
21. Sukhorukov, *Sovetskie vozdushno*, 103.
22. Gromov, Pigunov, 4th Airborne, 167.
23. Ibid., 167–8.
24. 'Deistviia 4 vozdushno-desantnogo korpusa,' 46.
25. Reinhardt, 'Russian Air Landings,' 13. See also 31. Infanterie Division/1a, *Kriegstagebuch 6, Bande I u. II mit Anlagenbande 1, 2, 4a, 4b, 4c, und 5*, 1 January–31 May 1942, NAM T315, rolls 865–6; and 34. Infanterie Division/1a, *Anlagenband 3 zum Kriegstagebuch 4*, 1 January–28 February 1942, NAM T315, roll 877; Lisov, *Desantniki*, 118. For a thorough treatment of the nature of German winter defenses, see 'Operativno-takticheskie uroki zimnoi kampanii 1941/42 g' [Operational-tactical lessons of the winter campaign 1941/42], *SMPIOV* No. 2, September–October 1942, 3–7. Secret, declassified 1964.
26. 'Deistviia 4 vozdushno-desantnogo korpusa,' 46-7.
27. Hossbach, *Infanterie*, 104. Rear service elements of the 31st Infantry Division's 17th, 12th, and 82d Infantry Regiments held Pesochnia, Kliuchi, and Dertovaia, respectively.
28. Lisov, *Desantniki*, 119.
29. 'Deistviia 4 vozdushno-desantnogo korpusa,' 47.
30. Gromov, Pigunov, *4th Airborne*, 78; Sukhorukov, *Sovetskie vozdushno*, 107, claims that the Germans lost 600 men of two infantry battalions and a regimental headquarters, as well as 50 horses and 200 sleighs. German accounts of the Kliuchi battle are in 31. Infanterie Division/1a, *Kriegstagebuch 6, Bande I u. II*, report of I/AR67, 2 March 1942, NAM T315, roll 865. German strength is given as 435 men. German losses are reported as 14 killed, 34 wounded, 2 missing, and 559 horses lost. The Germans suffered additional losses at Malyshevka and during the retreat from Kliuchi, but nowhere near the 600 claimed by the Soviets. The Germans reported 83 Soviets dead. On the other hand, formerly classified Soviet records substantiate the Soviet claim. See 'Deistviia 4 vozdushno-desantnogo korpusa,' 47.

31. 'Deistviia 4 vozdushno-desantnogo korpusa,' 48.
32. F. D. Pankov, *Ognennye rubezhi: boevoi put' 50-i armii v Velikoi Otechestvennoi voine* [Firing lines: combat path of 50th Army in the Great Patriotic War] (Moscow: Voenizdat, 1984), 114–15.
33. Ibid., 115.
34. Sukhorukov, *Sovetskie vozdushno*, 107.
35. 'Deistviia 4 vozdushno-desantnogo korpusa,' 47.
36. Ibid., 48.
37. Gromov, Pigunov, *4th Airborne*, 183, states, 'The fascists, on the approaches to the village [Kliuchi], lost in killed alone 500 soldiers and officers and 13 tanks. But our losses were also considerable.'
38. Ibid.
39. 'Deistviia 4 vozdushno-desantnogo korpusa,' 48.
40. Gromov, Pigunov, *4th Airborne*, 184.
41. Reinhardt, 'Russian Air Landings,' 15.
42. Sukhorukov, *Sovetskie vozdushno*, 108.
43. Ibid., 108–10, covers subsequent operations against Malyshevka. The German garrison unit was identified as the 82 Infantry Regiment, 31st Infantry Division.
44. Ibid., 14. See also Generalkommando XLIII AK, *Korpsbefehl Nr 121*, 8 March 1942; and *Korpsbefehl Nr. 122*, 9 March 1942, NAM T315, roll 1381.
45. Gromov, Pigunov, *4th Airborne*, 187.
46. Pankov, 115.
47. Gromov, Pigunov, *4th Airborne*, 187–188.
48. Sukhorukov, *Sovetskie vozdushno*, 108–10; Reinhardt, 'Russian Air Landings,' 15. Reinhardt confirms 4th Airborne problems:

> The behavior of the airborne troops itself seemed obscure and changeable. Sometimes the prisoners stated that the captured villages were merely to be held until the Tenth Army [50th Army] crossed the *Rollbahn* from the south, and sometimes that a breakthrough across the *Rollbahn* was planned. It appeared that the airborne force did not have any artillery or heavy weapons, and that its striking power was limited.

49. 'Deistviia 4 vozdushno-desantnogo korpusa,' 49.
50. Ibid.
51. Lisov, *Desantniki*, 126–7. The Germans committed two regiments of the 131st Infantry Division (1,100 men). The remaining regiment was committed farther north against Soviet 33d Army's Group Efremov. Reinhardt, 'Russian Air Landings,' 16. Details on 131st Infantry Division/1a, *Kriegstagebuch 6 mit Anlagen*, 6 March–16 June 1942, NAM T315, roll 1381.
52. 'Deistviia 4 vozdushno-desantnogo korpusa,' 49. The formerly classified critique states:

> The Germans, in an answer to our offensives, in a group of 200 men undertook a counteroffensive against Dertovochka and attacked Tynovka. But by a combined counterattack by units of both brigades, they were repulsed, having lost 52 men killed, 9 submachine guns, 7 automatic weapons, 43 rifles, 4 pistols, and 7,000 rounds of rifle ammunition (of these 50 per cent exploded).

53. Gromov, Pigunov, *4th Airborne*, 189–90.
54. 'Deistviia 4 vozdushno-desantnogo korpusa,' 50.
55. Ibid.
56. Ibid.
57. Sukhorukov, *Sovetskie vozdushno*, 111–12. See also 34. Infanterie Division/1a, *Anlagenband 1 zum Kriegstagebuch 5, Til 1*, 1 March–31 July 1942, NAM T315, roll 877.
58. Reinhardt, 'Russian Air Landings,' 16, comments on the airborne defenses:

> With difficulty, it [131st Infantry Division] plowed a way through the snow and attacked one village after the other. There were reverses; the air landing forces were composed of the very best type of Russian infantry. They had ample machine guns, mortars, and automatic rifles. The German reports laid parti-

cular stress on the fact that these forces were trained marksmen. Installed in trenches made up of banked-up snow, they defended tenaciously the villages they had captured.

59. Lisov, *Desantniki*, 127–8. Soviet losses according to Gromov and Pigunov, *4th Airborne*, 196, were 38 killed and 91 wounded. They claimed German losses of 500.
60. 'Deistviia 4 vozdushno-desantnogo korpusa,' 51; Gromov, Pigunov, *4th Airborne*, 196–8.
61. The Germans called the operation against encircled 33d Army the *Droshino Kessel* [Droshino Cauldron]. Reduction of the cauldron is described in *MS No. P-206, Phase D, vol. 1*, 170–8, 198–201; and Reinhardt, 'Russian Air Landings,' 21. In Halder, 21, the entry for 16 April reads, 'Russian Thirty-third Army has been liquidated.' For descriptions of Soviet attempts to relieve 33d Army, see Belov, *Za nami Moskva*, 225–9; A. P. Beloborodov, *Vsegda v boiu* [Always in battle] (Moscow: Voenizdat, 1962), 163–71; and P. A. Kuznetsov, *Gvardeitsy – Moskvichi* [Guardsmen – Muscovites] (Moscow: Voenizdat, 1962), 163–71.
62. Belov, *Za nami Moskva*, 222–3.
63. 'Deistviia gruppy generala Belova,' 38.
64. Ibid.
65. Ibid.
66. Gromov, Pigunov, *4th Airborne*, 149.
67. 'Deistviia gruppy generala Belova,' 38–9.
68. Ibid.
69. Lisov, *Desantniki*, 131.
70. 'Deistviia 4 vozdushno-desantnogo korpusa,' 51.
71. Ibid.
72. Gromov, Pigunov, *4th Airborne*, 150.

CHAPTER 6

1. Reinhardt, 'Russian Air Landings,' 18–19, confirms Belov's position on 18 March:

Under this [German] pressure Cavalry Corps Belov again drew south and apparently tried to establish contact with the airborne corps. In doing so it encountered the small German Group Haase at the railroad bridge over the Ugra. This group had been cut off since the end of February and was being supplied from the air. On 18 March the main body of the Russian Cavalry Corps was situated on both sides of the Viazma–Kiev road and directly north of the Ugra. On this day for the first time radio communications between the Russian cavalry corps and the airborne corps were intercepted.

Belov's attempt to rescue 33d Army began on the night of 27 March, but, by 14 April, it had failed. Belov, *Za nami Moskva*, 226–7; Reinhardt, 'Russian Air Landings,' 20–1, notes Belov's attempted rescue.
2. Gromov, Pigunov, *4th Airborne*, 201–2.
3. Sukhorukov, *Sovetskie vozdushno*, 116; Belov, *Za nami Moskva*, 228–9.
4. 'Deistviia 4 vozdushno-desantnogo korpusa,' 52.
5. Lisov, *Desantniki*, 132.
6. For details on the relief of Group Haase, see 131. Infanterie Division/1a, *Kriegstagebuch 6*, 6–10 March 1942, NAM T315, roll 1281. The 82d Infantry Regiment effected the relief.
7. Halder, 296.
8. 'Deistviia 4 vozdushno-desantnogo korpusa,' 53.
9. Belov, *Za nami Moskva*, 229–31.
10. Zhukov smoothed over his relations with Belov. See Zhukov, *Memoirs*, 356–8.
11. Halder, 297–8, entry for 12 April notes 50th Army attack preparations, 'On XXXX Corps front apparently preparations for an attack (two new divs.; tanks brought up).' The entry for the next day mentions, 'Heavy attacks against Fourth Army and XXXX Corps and XII Corps.' Some details concerning 50th Army's attack plan are in A. A.

Andreev, *Po voennym dorogam* [Along military roads] (Moscow: Voenizdat, 1971), 13.
12. Sukhorukov, *Sovetskie vozdushno*, 118–19.
13. Gromov, Pigunov, *4th Airborne*, 206–8.
14. Ibid., 208.
15. Pankov, 116–18.
16. Ibid., 118–21.
17. Lisov, *Desantniki*, 134. Details on the German defense are in 131. Infanterie Division, *Kriegstagebuch 6*, 13–25 April 1942.
18. Belov, *Za nami Moskva*, 231–2.
19. Halder, 298–9, notes the heavy Soviet attacks on XXXX Corps in the Milyatino sector and the return of 'quiet' by the 18th. See also Reinhardt, 'Russian Air Landings,' 22.
20. Gromov, Pigunov, *4th Airborne*, 213.
21. Ibid., 214.
22. Sukhorukov, *Sovetskie vozdushno*, 119; A. A. Iaroshenko, *V boi shla 41-ia gvardeiskaia* [Into battle went the 41st Guards] (Moscow: Voenizdat, 1982), 4.
23. Sukhorukov, *Sovetskie vozdushno*, 119.
24. 'Boevoe donesenie shtaba 50-i armii No. 25 ot 22.4.1942g o resul'tatakh nastupleniia voisk armii v noch' na 22.4.1942 g' [Combat report of 50th Army staff No. 25 of 22.4.1942 about the results of the offensive of army forces on the night of 22.4.42], SBDVOV, issue 25, 31. Classified Secret, declassified 1964.
25. Halder, 301. Halder mentions no heavy activity in his entries for 23–24 April.
26. Sukhorukov, *Sovetskie vozdushno*, 120; also noted by Halder, *Diaries*, 301.
27. 'Deistviia 4 vozdushno-desantnogo korpusa,' 55.
28. Gromov, Pigunov, *4th Airborne*, 217.
29. Lisov, *Desantniki*, 137.
30. Belov, *Za nami Moskva*, 283.
31. Gromov, Pigunov, *4th Airborne*, 225.
32. 'Deistviia 4 vozdushno-desantnogo korpusa,' 56.
33. Sukhorukov, *Sovetskie vozdushno*, 121. For details on Operation Hannover, see Reinhardt, 'Russian Air Landings,' 22; Armeeoberkommando 4/1a, *Lagekarten, Anlagen zum Kriegstagebuch, Nr 12*, April–May 1942, NAM T312, roll 183; and 131. Infanterie Division/1a (Reports, orders, and messages], 24 May–1 June 1942, NAM T315, roll 1381. Halder, 318–20, mentions the operation often, particularly the bad weather and stubborn resistance of Belov's force.
34. Gromov, Pigunov, *4th Airborne*, 225–6.
35. Belov, *Za nami Moskva*, 294–5.
36. 'Deistviia 4 vozdushno-desantnogo korpusa,' 57; Gromov, Pigunov, *4th Airborne*, 226.
37. Lisov, *Desantniki*, 138–9.
38. Gromov, Pigunov, *4th Airborne*, 228–9.
39. Lisov, *Desantniki*, 139–40.
40. Gromov, Pigunov, *4th Airborne*, 230.
41. Belov, *Za nami Moskva*, 297.
42. 'Deistviia 4 vozdushno-desantnogo korpusa,' 57.
43. Gromov, Pigunov, *4th Airborne*, 233. Spirin survived POW life in camps at Krichev, Bremen, Neustadt, and elsewhere, was later freed, and in 1958 received the Order of Red Banner.
44. Ibid., 231–3.
45. Ibid., 231.
46. Halder, 319.
47. Sukhorukov, *Sovetskie vozdushno*, 123. The two airborne brigades also brought with them 131 antitank rifles, 48 50-mm mortars, and 184 machine pistols.
48. Belov, *Za nami Moskva*, 299.
49. Ibid., 301.
50. Ibid., 302.
51. Iaroshenko, 6–8; Gromov, Pigunov, *4th Airborne*, 237.

52. Gromov, Pigunov, *4th Airborne*, 238–9.
53. Ibid.
54. Iaroshenko, 14–16; Gromov, Pigunov, *4th Airborne*, 239–44.
55. Halder, 323.
56. Gromov, Pigunov, *4th Airborne*, 243–4; Iaroshenko, 19–23. The attack across the Warsaw highway is most vividly described in Belov, *Za nami Moskva*, 308–10. Both Lisov, *Desantniki*, 143, and Sukhorukov, *Sovetskie vozdushno*, 125, play down Soviet difficulty in crossing the highway.
57. Gromov, Pigunov, *4th Airborne*, 244, 245; Halder, 327–8.
58. Gromov, Pigunov, *4th Airborne*, 246.
59. Ibid., 249.
60. Sukhorukov, *Sovetskie vozdushno*, 126–7; Gromov, Pigunov, *4th Airborne*, 248–53.
61. Belov, *Za nami Moskva*, 320.
62. Guenther Blumentritt, 'Operations Against Rear Lines of Communications,' *Foreign Military Studies MS No. B-684*, 6–7, reproduced by the Historical Division, U.S. Army, Europe, 1947.
63. Reinhardt, *Russian Air Landings*, 26–7.
64. Ibid.
65. *MS No. B-684*, 5–8. Although Blumentritt uses the Soviet example to point out that 'war against rear lines of communications can be very effective even on the ground,' he believes 'it will be the air force and armored units who are likely to attack the rear area of a modern army successfully in any future war.'
66. Reinhardt, *Russian Air Landings*, 27–8.
67. Ibid., 28–9.
68. 'Operativno-Takticheskie uroki zimnoi kampanii,' 5.
69. Ibid., 6, 8.
70. 'Deistviia 4 vozdushno-desantnogo korpusa,' 58–9.
71. Reinhardt, 'Russian Air Landings,' 25–6.
72. Ibid., 30. The Germans estimated that between 15,000 and 20,000 Soviet airborne forces operated at one time in the rear of German Fourth and Fourth Panzer Armies, which was close to the actual number.

CHAPTER 7

1. Sokolovsky, *Razgrom*, 335–8; see also Seaton, 270; and Panzer-Armeeoberkommando 4/1a, *Kartenlagen zum Kriegstagebuch, Nr 7–8 (Moskau)*, 12–28 February 1942.
2. Sukhorukov, *Sovetskie vozdushno*, 143.
3. Ibid.; and Lisov, *Desantniki*, 91, claim that 400 men made the drop. Sofronov, *Vozdushnye desanty*, 26–7, states that 75 men returned to the airdrome, 312 were dropped, and 38 fell into Soviet lines. Only 166 men of the 312 dropped reached the 29th Army area. The details of combat are in Sukhorukov, *Sovetskie vozdushno*, 143–4.
4. V. Zhelanov, 'Iz opyta pervoi operatsii na okruzhenie' [From the experience of the first encirclement operation], *VIZh*, No. 12 (December 1964), 26.
5. P. A. Kurochkin, 'My srazhalis' na Severo-Zapadnom fronte' [We struggled on the Northwestern Front], *Na severo-zapadnom fronte 1941–1943* [On the Northwestern Front 1941–1943] (Moscow: 'Nauka,' 1969), 35.
6. Ibid., 37.
7. Ibid., 38; E. F. Ziemke, M. E. Bauer, *Moscow to Stalingrad: Decision in the East* (Washington, D.C.: Center of Military History, United States Army, 1987), 154, claims 95,000 Germans were encircled at Demiansk. Zhelanov, 30, supports the German figure. Ziemke and Bauer provide a clear account of the action from the German viewpoint and, unlike Soviet sources, mention Soviet use of airborne forces.
8. Kurochkin, 39–40.
9. Ibid., 40; Zhelanov, 30.
10. Kurochkin, 40.

11. Ziemke, Bauer, 154.
12. Ibid., 155–6.
13. Kurochkin, 40.
14. M. F. Gliakin, 38.
15. Ibid., 45–6.
16. Ibid., 48. The only other Soviet source which mentions airborne force participation in operations around Demiansk is G. I. Berdnikov, *Pervaia udarnaia: boevoi put' 1-i udarnoi armii v Velikoi Otechestvennoi Voine* [First shock: the combat path of 1st Shock Army in the Great Patriotic War] (Moscow: Voenizdat, 1985), 85, which states, 'On 29 March according to his [Kurochkin's] order, 1st Shock Army had subordinated to it: ... from *front* reserve the 204th Airborne Brigade was successfully transferred.' The author uses the verb 'to jump' for transfer, thus the sentence has double meaning.
17. Based on a variety of prisoner of war interrogations and the author's reasoning.
18. Gliakin, 13–39. After its initial battles around Kiev, the 1st Airborne Corps (2d formation) had been re-formed during August and September 1941 north of Saratov on the Volga. It consisted of 1st, 3d, and 204th Airborne Brigades, which were transferred after October to airfields near Moscow. POW interrogations and German assessments indicate that the airborne troopers were well-trained and highly motivated.
19. 'Betr. Gefangenenaussagen Dem A.O.K. 16-1c-' *Generalkommando II. A.K. Abt. Ic Az.19a*, K. Gef. St., 17 Marz 1942, NAM T-314, roll 141, contains two prisoner-of-war interrogations, also 'Betr. Gefangenenaussagen Dem A.O.K.-1c' *Generalkommando II. A. K. Abt.Ic* Az-19a, K. Gef. St., 25 Marz 1942. One POW interrogation of an airborne sergeant, NAM T-314, Roll 141.
20. 'Betr.: Gefangenenaussagen Dem A. O. K. 16-1c' *Generalkommando II A. K. Abt. Ic Az.19a*, K. Gef. St., 21 Marz 1942, NAM T-314, roll 141; 'Betr: Gefangenenvernehmung An Generalkommando II. A. K. - Abt.1c' *30 Division Abt.1c*, Div. Gef. St., den 19. Marz 1942, 3, NAM T-314, roll 141 Prisoner report provides airborne brigade strength, commander, and chronology of action to 17 March.
21. Among many POW reports, see 'Gefangenen-Vernehmung' *SS-Totenkopf Division-Abschnitt Simon*, Gef-St., den 22.2.1942, NAM T-314, roll 141; 'Betr.: Gefangenaussagen Dem A. O. K. 16-1c' *Generalkommando II. A. K., Abt. 1c Az. 19a*, K. Gef. St. 20. Marz 1942, NAM T-314, roll 141.
22. March routes are based on over 40 prisoner-of-war interrogations, German radio intercepts of Soviet communications traffic, and German combat reports.
23. 'Gefangenen-Vernehmung,' *SS-Totenkopf*, 22.3.1942, 2. Each TB-3 bomber could carry a maximum of 40 parachutists, but, since considerable cargo also had to be transported, troop capacity of each aircraft was considerably less.
24. Among numerous reports about the airborne drop, see 'Feindbeurteilung, Stand 22.2.1942' *Anlagenband zum Tätigkeitsbericht, AOK 16, 1c/A.O* AOK 16, 23468/39 1 January–31 March 1942 and subsequent reports in the series NAM T-312, roll 567; '1c-Abendmeldung 25.2.42.' *Anlagenband zum Tätigkeitsbericht, AOK 16, 1c/A.O.*, dated 23 Dec 1941–31 Mar 1942 AOK 16, 23468/40, NAM T-312, roll 567; 'Betr: Partisanenbekampfung und Sicherung des ruckw. Armee-Gebiets,' *A. O. K. 16 Ia. Nr. 190/42 g. Kdos*. A. H. Qu., den 28.2.1941. Filed under Anlagenband zum Kriegstagebuch Nr. 5, AOK 16, 1a, dated 16–27 Mar 1942, AOK 16, 23468/35. NAM T-314, roll 566.
25. 'Feindbeurteilung, Stand 22.2.1942' *AOK 16, 1c/A.O.*, NAM T-312, roll 565.
26. See subsequent II Army Corps and Sixteenth Army records which mention airborne and partisan activity in the region into early April.
27. 'Korpsbefehl' *Generalkommando II. Armeekorps Abteilung 1a*, K. Gef. Std., den 18. II. 1942 NAM T-314, roll 140.
28. 'Fernspruch den Gen. Kdo. II. A.K.' *30 I.D. und Arko 105, 7.3.1942 Unterlagen Ostfeldzug, Meldungun Band 34*, 7–11 Mar 1942, AKII. 29088/10. NAM T-314, roll 111.
29. 'Betr.: Gefangenenaussagen Dem A.O.K. 16-1c-'*Generalkommando II. A.K. Abt 1c, Az 19a.*, K. Gef. St., 17 Marz 1942, NAM T-314, roll 141.
30. 'Betr.: Gefangenenaussagen Dem A.O.K. 16-1c-'*Generalkommando II. A.K. Abt 1c, Az19a*, K. Gef. St., 25 Marz 1942. NAM T-314, roll 141.

31. 'Betr.: Gefangenenvernehmung vom 16.3.1942 'An Generalkommando II. A.K., Abt 1c' *30. Division Abt 1a*, Div. Gef. Stand, den 16.3.42. NAM T-314, roll 141.
32. 'Auszug aus Funklagemeldung vom 26.3.42' *Anlagenband zum Tätigskeitsbericht, AOK 16, 1c/A.O., 2*, in series dated 15 Jan–30 Mar 1942. AOK 16, 23468/41, NAM T-312, roll 567.
33. Ibid.
34. 'Tagesmeldung SS-T Div. (Gruppe Simon) den 18. Marz 1942' *Unterlagen Ostfeldzug, Meldungen Band 36*, series dated 18–23 Mar 1942, AK II, 20085/12, NAM T-314, roll 112; see also '1a-Zwischenmeldung vom 15.3.1942 An Heeresgruppe Nord' *Anlagenband zum Kriegstagebuch Nr. 5, AOK 16, 1a* in series dated 16 Mar–27 Mar 1942, AOK 16, 23468/35, NAM T-314, roll 566.
35. 'Auszug aus Funklagemeldung vom 26. Marz 1942,' 3.
36. 'Morgenmeldung der SS-T Div. (Gr. Simon), 13. Marz 1942' *Unterlagen Ostfeldzug, Meldungen Band 25*, series dated 12–17 Mar 1942, AK II, 20085/11, NAM T-314, roll 112.
37. 'Morgenmeldung vom 15.3.1942, AOK. 16, 1a' *Tätigkeitsbericht 1c H. Gr. Nord* in series dated 16 Dec 41–25 Mar 1942, H. Gr. Nord, 75131/10 Box 95, NAM T-311, roll 86; '1a-Zwischenmeldung vom 15.3.1942 An Heeresgruppe Nord' *Morgen-, Zwischen- und Tagesmeldungen an Heeresgruppe Nord (Nr. 1-137). AOK 16,1a* in series dated 1 Apr–15 May 1942, AOK 16, 32647/10, NAM T-314, roll 566.
38. 'Noch 15.3.42' *Kriegstagebuch H. Gr. Nord* in series dated 1–30 Apr 1942, H. Gr. Nord, 75128/9, Box 34 NAM T-311, roll 54; 'Nochtrag zur Abendmeldung AOK 16, 1c, 15.3.1942' *Tätigkeitsbericht 1c H. Gr. Nord* in series dated 16 Dec 41–25 Mar 1942, N. Gr. Nord, 75131/10. NAM T-311, roll 86.
39. Among several POW reports, see 'Betr.: Gefangenenvernehmung An Generalkommando II A.K.-Abt 1c.'
40. 'Auszug aus Funklagemeldung vom 26. Marz 1942,' 2.
41. Ibid.
42. Ibid., 3–4.
43. Ibid., 4.
44. Ibid.
45. Many POW reports recount the attacks on German garrisons around Demiansk and provide outlines of future airborne force plans. See 'Fernschreiben oder II. A. K.-1c-1915, 21.3.1942' *Meldungen der Truppe, AKII*, in series dated 1 Feb–31 Mar 1942, AKII, 35947/15 NAM T-314, roll 141; 'Abteilung 1c, Div. Gef. St., am 23 Marz 1942' *Meldung der Truppe, AKII* in series dated 1 Feb–31 Mar 1942, AKII, 35947/15, NAM T-314, roll 141.
46. 'Betr.: Gefangenenaussagen A. O. K.-16-1c-' *Generalkommando II. A.K., Abt. 1c, Az 19a* K Gef. St., 25 Marz 1942, NAM T-314, roll 141; 'Abteilung 1c, Div. Gef. St., am 23 Marz 1942.'
47. Ibid. By this time all German reports assessed that the Soviet airborne forces would attempt a breakout to the south in conjunction with Soviet ground attacks launched along the main front in that sector.
48. 'Abendmeldung AOK 16, 1c, 18.3.1942, 1845 uhr' *Tätigkeitsbericht 1c H. Gr. Nord* in series dated 16 Dec 41–25 Mar 1942, H. Gr. Nord, 75131/10, Box 95, NAM T-311, roll 86.
49. 'Tagesmeldung II A. K.' *Generalkommando II. Armeekorps, Abt. 1a*, K. Gef. Std., den 22 Marz 1942, NAM T-314, roll 111.
50. 'Betr.: Gefangenenvernehmung vom 24.3.42 An Generalkommando II. A. K., Abt, 1c' *30 Division Abt 1c*, Div. Gef. Stand, den 24.3.42, NAM T-314, roll 141. Reports from two prisoners from 4th Company, 2d Battalion, 2d Airborne Brigade and one prisoner from 3d Company, 54th Ski Battalion.
51. 'Angaben unter die hinter der inneren Linie aufgetretenen 3 Luftlande-bzw. Fall-schirm-Brigaden' *Generalkommando II. A. K. Abt 1c, Az. 7 Nr. 753/42 geh*, K. Gef. St., 25 Marz, 1942, NAM T-314, roll 140.
52. Good accounts of the battle for Igoshovo provided by two POW reports, 'Abteilung 1c Div. Gef. St. am 28. Marz 1942' *Meldungen der Truppe AKII* in series dated 1 Feb–31

Mar 1942, AK II, 35947/5, NAM T-314, roll 141; 'Betr.: Gefangenenaussagen Dem A. O. K. 16-1c-' *Generalkommando II. A. K., Abt 1c, Az 19a* K. Gef. St., 30 Marz 1942 NAM T-314, roll 141. German account and losses in 'Angeben uber die hinter'; '1a-Tagesmeldung vom 25.3.1942 An Heeresgruppe Nord.' *Morgen-, Zwischen- und Tagesmeldungen an Heeresgruppe Nord (Nr. 1-137) AOK 16, Ia,* in series dated 1 Apr– 15 May 1942, AOK, 32647/10 NAM, T-314, roll 566.

53. 'Gefangenenvernehmung vom 30.3.1942, 123 Inf. Division, Abt. 1c' *Meldungen der Truppe AKII* in series dated 1 Feb–31 May 1942, AKII, 35947/5, NAM T-314, roll 141 and other POW reports contained in the document.

54. Ibid.; 'Zwischenmeldung II. A. K. 1a' *Unterlagen Ostfeldzug, Meldungen Band 34 AK. II* in series dated 7–11 May 1942, AKII, 29085/10, NAM T-314, roll 111.

55. 'Gefangenenvernehmung vom 30.3.1942, 123 Inf. Division, Abt. 1c.'

56. 'Auszug aus Funklagemeldung vom 28.3.42' 12, *Anlageband zum Tätigkeitsbericht, AOK 16, 1c/AO* series dated 15 Jan–30 Mar 1942, AOK 16, 23468/41 NAM T-312, roll 567.

57. 'Morgenmeldung vom 29.3.1942 II AK' *Tätigkeitsbericht 1c H. Gr. Nord* series dated 16 Dec 41–25 Mar 1942 H. Gr. Nord, 75131/10 Box 95, NAM T-311, roll 86.

58. 'Zwischenmeldung 123, I.D. den 28 Marz 1942' *Unterlagen Ostfeldzug, Meldungen Band 34* and associated reports contained under this title. See also 'Tagesmeldung II A. K. 28 Marz 1942' *Generalkommando II., Armeekorps Abt. 1a.*

59. 'Auszug aus Funklagenmeldung vom 28.3.42', 2.

60. Ibid.

61. Ibid.

62. 'Zwischenmeldung 12. I. D, den 29. Marz 1942,' 'Zwischenmeldung II. A. K. den 29 Marz 1942' *Unterlagen Ostfeldzug, Meldungen Band 24.*

63. 'Betr.: Tagesmeldung An Generalkommando II. A. K.' *123. Inf. Division Abt. 1c,* Div. Gef. St., den 31.3.1942 series dated 1 Feb–31 Mar 1942 AKII, 39547/15.

64. 'Tagesmeldung Gruppe Simon den 29. Marz 1942' *Unterlagen Ostfeldzug, Meldungen Band 34.*

65. 'Korpsbefehl Nr. 119' *Generalkommando II. Armeekorps, Abt 1a Nr. 803/42 geh K.* Gef. St., den 29 Marz 1942 (in *Unterlagen Ostfeldzug, Meldungen Band 34*).

66. '31.3.1942' *Kriegstagebuch H. Gr. Nord.*, contains running count of Soviet losses in previous days as well.

67. Ibid.

68. 'Auszug aus Funklagen meldung vom 1.4.1942', 2, *Tätigkeitsbericht 1.4.42–30.6.42 Auszuge aus Funklagenmeldungen. Anlagenband VI, AOK 16, AO* series of reports dated 1 Apr–30 Jun 42, AOK 16, 32647/42. NAM T-312, roll 572.

69. Ibid.

70. 'Abendmeldung AOK 16, AOK 16, Abt 1c (S) Gef. St. 8.4.1942 1840 uhr' *Tätigskeitsbericht 1c, H. Gr. Nord.*

71. 'Ia-Tagesmeldung vom 8.4.1942 An Heeresgruppe Nord' (A. O. K. 16) *Morgen-, Zwischen- und Tagesmeldungen am Heeresgruppe Nord (Nr. 1.137).*

72. 'Morgenmeldung AOK 16, AOK 116, Abt 1c (S)' Gef. St. 9.4.1942 8.45' *Tätigskeitsbericht 1c, H. Gr. Nord.*

73. Gliakin, 47, claims that Grinev was wounded but later flown out to safety. Prisoner reports all state that Grinev disappeared after heavy fighting.

74. 'Des Feldzug gegen Sowjiet-Union der Heeresgruppe Nord, Kriegjahr 1942,' *Fuhrungsabteilung des Oberkommandos der Heeresgruppe Nord,* 1942, H. Gr. Nord. 75884/1, NAM T-311, roll 136.

75. *Truppen-Uebersicht und Kriegsgliederungen Rote Armee Stand August 1944.* Fremde-Heere Ost, Merkblatt. geh. 11/6 Pruf No. 0157, 252,253 (Secret), NAM T-78, roll 459.

CHAPTER 8

1. For operational context, see David M. Glantz, *From the Don to the Dnepr: Soviet Offensive Operations, December 1942–August 1943,* (London: Frank Cass, 1990), 215– 365.

2. K. S. Moskalenko, *Na iugozapadnom napravlenii* [In the southwest direction] (Moscow: Voenizdat, 1972), 122.
3. *Istoriia vtoroi mirovoi voiny 1939–1945* [History of the Second World War, 1939–1945], (Moscow: Voenizdat, 1976), 7:212–13 (hereafter cited as *IVMV*). This volume devotes but four lines to the subsequent airborne landing. Elements of 51st Guards Tank Brigade, 6th Guards Tank Corps, 3d Guards Tank Army seized a small bridgehead at Grigorovka. See A. M. Zvartsev, ed., *3-ia gvardeiskaia tankovaia* [3d Guards Tank Army] (Moscow: Voenizdat, 1982), 95. See a brief synopsis of the operation in Ia. P. Samoilenko, 'Dneprovskaia vozdushno-desantnaia operatsiia 1942' [The Dnepr airlanding operation, 1943], *SVE*, 3:206–7.
4. Sofronov, *Vozdushnye desanty*, 27.
5. E. Binder, 'Employment of a Russian Parachute Brigade in Bend of the Dnepr Northwest of Kanev,' in 'Russian Airborne Operations,' *Foreign Military Studies MS No. P-116*, 72, reproduced by the Historical Division, U.S. Army, Europe, 1953, confirms this:

> A Russian parachute brigade was used in the operations. It had been organized and trained about a year previously in the area south of Moscow. Approximately half of the men in the brigade were trained parachutists who had on the average made seven to ten jumps. The rest of the brigade was composed of men from seven regiments all mixed up together. These men had not received any parachute training.

Binder was chief of operations, 19th Panzer Division, at the time of the operation.
6. Ibid., 29; Sukhorukov, Sovetskie vozdushno, 195–196.
7. Ibid., 195.
8. Lisov, *Desantniki*, 158.
9. Sofronov, *Vozdushnye desanty*, 28. According to Lisov, *Desantniki*, 159, each airplane would carry 20 men.
10. Ibid., 160. Each man carried one and one-half units of fire. One unit was in a container.
11. Ibid.
12. Sukhorukov, *Sovetskie vozdushno*, 197. Zhukov's memoirs do not mention the disastrous airdrop.
13. Lisov, *Desantniki*, 157.
14. Sukhorukov, *Sovetskie vozdushno*, 198.
15. Lisov, *Desantniki*, 158.
16. Ibid., 159.
17. W. K. Nehring, 'Employment of Russian Parachute Forces in Cherkassy–Kiev Area (24–25 September 1943),' in 'Russian Airborne Operations,' *Foreign Military Studies MS No. P-116*, 35–55, reproduced by the Historical Division, U.S. Army Europe, 1952. Nehring was commanding general of XXIV Panzer Corps at the time of the Soviet airborne drop. Paul Carell [Schmidt], *Scorched Earth: The Russian–German War, 1943–1944* (New York: Ballantine, 1971), 401–4, confirms Nehring's account. Sukhorukov, *Sovetskie vozdushno*, 198, portrays slightly more rapid German deployment.
18. Ibid; Binder, 68–70.
19. Lisov, *Desantniki*, 162.
20. Sukhorukov, *Sovetskie vozdushno*, 199. Germans cite 1730 as the time the drop began. Nehring, 46.
21. Lisov, *Desantniki*, 162–3; Sukhorukov, *Sovetskie vozdushno*, 199; Sofronov, *Vozdushnye desanty*, 31.
22. Ibid.
23. Sukhorukov, *Sovetskie vozdushno*, 199.
24. Nehring, 46.
25. Binder, 70–1. Binder's account refers primarily to actions of the 19th Panzer Division reconnaissance battalion because the division's main body did not reach the area until 25 September.
26. Carell, 407. Nehring, 47, 59, states that the bulk of Soviet casualties occurred from 24–

26 September. He noted Soviet parachute drops at Dudari-Gruschevo (200 parachutes), at Shandra (300 parachutes), at Beresniagi (400 parachutes), and in the region west of Pekari.

27. Sukhorukov, *Sovetskie vozdushno*, 199.
28. Lisov, *Desantniki*, 166.
29. Sukhorukov, *Sovetskie vozdushno*, 200.
30. Nehring, 51–8.
31. Sofronov, *Vozdushnye desanty*, 32.
32. Lisov, *Desantniki*, 167–8.
33. Sukhorukov, *Sovetskie vozdushno*, 200–3.
34. Ia. Samoilenko, 'V tylu vraga' [In the enemy rear], *Voennyi Vestnik* [Military Herald], No. 1 (January 1973), 38–39.
35. Sukhorukov, *Sovetskie vozdushno*, 217–18.
36. Lisov, *Desantniki*, 171–2.
37. Sukhorukov, *Sovetskie vozdushno*, 203.
38. 'Forsirovanie Dnepra 52-i armiei v raione Cherkass (Noiabr'-dekabr' 1943g)' [The forcing of the Dnepr by 52d Army in the Cherkassy region (November–December 1983)], *Sbornik voenno-istoricheskikh materialov Velikoi Otechestvennoi voiny, vypusk, 12* [Collection of military-historical materials of the Great Patriotic War, issue 12] (hereafter cited as *SVIMVOV*), (Moscow: Voenizdat, 1953), secret, declassified 1964, 61–2, states:

> Partisan detachments and Major Sidorchuk's airborne group from subunits of 5th Guards Airborne Brigade operated in the enemy rear, in the forests northwest of Cherkassy. Subunits of that brigade were airdropped on the night of 24 September 1943 west of the Bukrin bend of the Dnepr. After the unsuccessful airborne landing, brigade subunits fought a fighting withdrawal into the forests west of Cherkassy. Here, together with local partisans, they operated against enemy communications. The overall strength of airborne troops and partisans operating in the enemy rear reached 1,600–1,700 men. Of that number, the airborne group of Major Sidorchuk made up about half. The group had 12 heavy machine guns, 6 antitank rifles, as well as rifles and automatic weapons for each man. Local partisans, numbering in all 800–900 men operated in separate detachments. The strength of the detachments varied from 60 to 300 men. The strongest of these detachments counted 300 men and was headed by the secretary of underground party organization of the Cherkassy region G. A. Ivashchenko. Partisan detachments had arms for about half of their personnel. The staff of 52d Army did not have communications with the airborne group and partisans. 52d Army staff received its last information about the airborne group and partisans on 27 October from 1st Ukrainian Front staff. According to this information, the airborne group and partisans were located in two groups: one in the region of marker 173.9 (4 km south of Moshny) and the other in the groves of Vasil'evka. 52d Army staff succeeded in establishing radio communications with these groups only on 12 November.

39. Ibid., 65.
40. Ibid., 66.
41. Lisov, *Desantniki*, 175.
42. 'Forsirovanie Dnepra 52-i armiei,' 67.
43. Ibid., 73.
44. Sukhorukov, *Sovetskie vozdushno*, 204–6; and Lisov, *Desantniki*, 175–6, cover details of fighting, 11–15 November.
45. Ibid. See also Samoilenko, 40–2.
46. 'Forsirovanie Dnepra 52-i armiei,' 84, 87.
47. Lisov, *Desantniki*, 178.
48. S. M. Shtemenko, *General'nyi shtab v gody voiny* [General staff in the war years] (Moscow: Voenizdat, 1981), 1:248.
49. Sukhorukov, *Sovetskie vozdushno*, 210.

50. Nehring, 56.
51. Ibid., 58, testifies to Soviet haste, 'The Russians had not thought over the presumable course of events carefully enough; ... [they] did not brief the main body of their troops on the mission, so that the men are said to have believed that they were going on a training flight.' Binder, 72, states that 'the jumps came as a surprise. There was no advanced information. The Germans did not expect an operation of this sort.'
52. Lisov, *Desantniki*, 177.
53. Nehring, 58.
54. Ibid., 58–9.
55. Ibid., 60.
56. Ibid.
57. Sukhorukov, Sovetskie vozdushno, 209–10.

CHAPTER 9

1. P. N. Pospelov, et al., eds, *Istoriia Velikoi Otechestvennoi voiny Sovetskogo Soiuza, 1941–1945 T3* [History of the Great Patriotic War of the Soviet Union, V.3] (Moscow: Voenizdat, 1962), 371–6 (hereafter cited as *IVOVSS*, with appropriate volume and page); N. A. Svetlishin, 'Nevel'skaia operatsiia 1943' [The Nevel Operation of 1943], *SVE*, 5:560–1.
2. *IVOVSS*, 374.
3. Ibid.
4. K. N. Galitsky, *Gody surovykh ispytanii 1941–1944* [Years of rigorous education 1941–1944] (Moscow: 'Nauka,' 1973), 347.
5. Ibid.
6. M. Absaliamov, V. Andrianov, 'Iz opyta vzaimodeistviia vozdushnykh desantov s partizanami v Velikoi Otechestvennoi voine' [From the experience of the cooperation of airborne forces with partisans in the Great Patriotic War], *VIZh*, No. 11 (November 1964), 104.
7. Ibid.
8. Ibid., 106.
9. Ibid.
10. Ibid.
11. *IVOVSS*, 374.
12. Galitsky, 347–8.
13. Ibid., 357.
14. Absaliamov, Andrianov, 106–7.
15. For the most thorough English language account of the Slovak rising, see J. Erickson, *The Road to Berlin* (Boulder, CO: Westview Press, 1983), 292–307.
16. A. A. Grechko, ed., *Liberation Mission of the Soviet Armed Forces in the Second World War* (Moscow: Progress, 1975), 302.
17. Ibid., 303.
18. *Osvoboditel'naia Missiia Sovetskikh Vooruzhennykh Sil v Evrope vo vtoroi mirovoi voine: dokumenty i materialy* [The liberating mission of the Soviet armed forces in Europe during the Second World War: Documents and materials] (Moscow: Voenizdat, 1985), 376–7.
19. Erickson, 300.
20. I. Ia. Vyrodov, et al., eds., *V srazheniiakh za Pobedy* [In battle for victory] (Moscow: 'Nauka,' 1974), 442.
21. For Svoboda's story, see L. Svoboka, *Ot Buzuluka do Pragi* [From Buzuluk to Prague] (Moscow: Voenizdat, 1984). The former Czech corps' commander had been relieved during the Carpathian–Duklin operation.
22. Osvoboditel'naia missiia, 426–7.
23. K. S. Moskalenko, *Na Iugo-zapadnom napravlenii: 1943–1945 K. 2* [On the South-western Direction: 1943–1945 Book 2] (Moscow: 'Nauka,' 1973), 469, 472, provided orders dispatching the forces.

24. Erickson, 304.
25. Grechko, 307.
26. Erickson, 307.

CHAPTER 10

1. For an account of Soviet reconnaissance-diversionary activity in service of Soviet intelligence, see D. M. Glantz, *Soviet Intelligence in War* (London: Frank Cass, 1990).
2. See chapter 2 and Sukhorukov, *Sovetskie vozdushno*, 59.
3. For detailed accounts of the Odessa operation, see N. Krylov, *Glory Eternal* (Moscow: Progress, 1972), 237–67; I. I. Azarov, *Osazhdennaia Odessa* [Besieged Odessa] (Odessa: 'Maiak,' 1975).
4. 'Oborona Odessy v 1941 gody,' *SVIMVOV*, Issue 14 (1954), 54, secret, declassified 1964.
5. Ibid., 55.
6. Ibid., 56–7.
7. Ibid., 58; see also Halder, 116–23, entry for 22 September reads, 'At Odessa, the Romanians are making no headway.' The entry for the following day notes that 'Romanian reverses before Odessa are inconvenient.' On 26 September, General Hauffe of the German Army Mission to Rumania reported 'The Romanians cannot get Odessa by themselves' and passed to Halder a request for German assistance.
8. For details on the Kerch–Feodosiia operation, see A. A. Grechko, et al., ed., *Istoriia vtoroi mirovoi voiny 1939–1945* T, 4 [History of the Second World War, 1939–1945, Vol. 4], (Moscow: Voenizdat, 1975), 295–9.
9. Sukhorukov, *Sovetskie vozdushno*, 81. Erich von Manstein, *Lost Victories* (Chicago: Henry Regnery, 1958), 227, claims that only the 46th Infantry Division, a regiment of the 73d Infantry Division, and elements of the Rumanian Mountain Corps were available to resist the Soviets the first two days. D. D. Kodola, 'Kerchensko–Feodosiiskaia desantnaia operatsiia 1941–42' [Kerch–Feodosiia landing operation, 1941–42], *SVE*, 4:145–7, states that German strength on the peninsula included the 46th Infantry Division, a Rumanian cavalry brigade, two tank battalions, two artillery regiments, and five antiaircraft battalions.
10. Sofronov, *Vozdushnye desanty*, 37.
11. Lisov, *Desantniki*, 184.
12. Ibid., 189.
13. Ibid., 187–9.
14. I. S. Shiian, *Na maloi zemle* [At the little land] (Moscow: Voenizdat, 1974), 8. See also I. S. Shiian, *Ratnyi podvig Novorossiiska* [Feat of arms at Novorossiisk] (Moscow: Voenizdat, 1977).
15. Sukhorukov, *Sovetskie vozdushno*, 188; Sofronov, *Vozdushnye desanty*, 41.
16. Sukhorukov, *Sovetskie vozdushno*, 189.
17. For full account of the operations, see D. M. Glantz, *August Storm: The Soviet Strategic Offensive in Manchuria*, Leavenworth Papers No. 7, and *August Storm: Soviet Tactical and Operational Combat in Manchuria*, 1945, Leavenworth Papers No. 8 (Fort Leavenworth, KS: Combat Studies Institute, U.S. Command and General Staff College, February 1983 and June 1983, respectively). See also L. N. Vnotchenko, *Pobeda na dal'nem vostoke* [Victory in the Far East] (Moscow: Voenizdat, 1971).
18. M. N. Kozhevnikov, *Komandovanie i shtab VVS Sovetskoi Armii v Velikoi Otechestvennoi voine, 1941–1945 gg* [The command and staff of the Soviet Army Air Force in the Great Patriotic War, 1941–1945] (Moscow: 'Nauka,' 1977), 236.
19. A. Khrenov, 'Engineer Operations in the Far East,' *Znamia* [Banner], No. 8 (August 1980), 172–3. Translated by JPRS.
20. Ibid., 173.
21. N. I. Krylov, I. I. Alekseev, I. G. Dragan, *Navstrechu podede: boevoi put' 5-i armii oktiabr' 1940 g- avgust 1945 g* [Meeting victory: the combat path of 5th Army, October 1940–August 1945] (Moscow: 'Nauka,' 1970, 450–1.

22. Khrenov, 173–4.
23. Sukhorukov, *Sovetskie vozdushno*, 296; G. Shelakhov, 'S vozdushnym desantom v Kharbin' [With the airborne assault on Harbin], *VIZh*, No. 8 (August 1970), 67–9.
24. Sukhorukov, *Sovtskie vozdushno*, 297.
25. I. M. Chistiakov, *Sluzhim otchizne* [We served the fatherland] (Moscow: Voenizdat, 1975), 295–9.
26. G. T. Zavizion, P. A. Korniushin, *I na Tikham okeane* [To the Pacific Ocean] (Moscow: Voenizdat, 1967), 230–1.
27. Ibid., 231; Sukhorukov, *Sovetskie vozdushno*, 297.
28. Zavizion, Korniushin, 232–3.
29. Ibid., 233–4.
30. Ibid., 233.
31. Sukhorukov, *Sovetskie vozdushno*, 299.
32. Lisov, *Desantniki*, 187–9.

CHAPTER 11

1. Stalin defined the 'Permanent Operating Factors' as stability of the home front, morale of the armed forces, quantity and quality of divisions, armaments, and the ability of commanders.
2. Iu. Kostin, 'Vozdushnyi desanty v sovremennykh operatsiiakh' [Airborne assaults in contemporary operations], *VM*, No. 8 (August 1946). The author cites a wide range of tactical, operational, and strategic missions, including disruption of enemy mobilization and strategic concentrations at the beginning of war, seizure of industrial regions, creation of new theaters of operations, and seizure of islands and beachheads. He concludes, 'The possibilities of further growth of air transport equipment and long-range bomber aviation provided a firm basis for the employment of air-landing troops on such a scale, that quite possibly further changes in the form of present-day military operations may be necessary.'
3. Sukhorukov, *Sovetskie vozdushno*, 263. Subsequent airborne VDV commanders have been as follows:

April 1946–October 1947 – Colonel General V. V. Glagolev
October 1947–December 1948 – Lieutenant General A. F. Kazankin
December 1948–March 1950 – Colonel General S. I. Rudenko
March 1950–May 1954 – Colonel General A. V. Gorbatov
June 1954–March 1959 – Lieutenant General V. F. Margelov
March 1959–July 1961 – Lieutenant General I. V. Tutarinov
July 1961–December 1978 – General V. F. Margelov
January 1979–July 1987 – General D. S. Sukhorukov
July 1987–1989 – Colonel General N. V. Kalinin
1989–December 1990 – Colonel General V. A. Achalov
December 1990–August 1991 – Colonel General P. S. Grachev
August 1991–Present – Lieutenant General Ie. N. Podkolzin

4. 'Soviet Airborne Forces,' *Military Intelligence Review*, No. 186, (Washington, D.C.: War Department, General Staff G-2, November 1951), 7–13, formerly classified secret, now declassified.
5. See U.S. Department of the Army, Assistant Chief of Staff for Intelligence, *Soviet Airborne and Aerial Supply Operations*, Intelligence Research Project No. 9845 (Washington, D.C., 1 October 1956), 10, declassified October 1982.
6. Ibid. The airborne corps probably consisted of two or three guards airborne divisions and an air transport division comprising three transport aircraft regiments (each with 32 aircraft) and one glider regiment of 32 gliders.
7. 'Soviet Airborne Forces,' 10.
8. P. Pavlenko, 'Razvitie taktiki vozdushno-desantnykh voisk v poslevoennyi period' [The development of airlanding force tactics in the postwar period], *VIZh* (January 1980), 27.

9. Kostin, 30.
10. Ibid., 30–1.
11. Ibid., 31.
12. Ibid., 33.
13. Ibid., 36–8.
14. Ibid., 39.
15. D. Grendal', 'Perebroska voisk dlia deistvii v tylu protivnike' [Transporting of forces for actions in the enemy rear], *VM*, No. 8 (August 1947), 19–21.
16. Ibid., 21–2.
17. Ibid., 26.
18. N. Lovtsov, N. Budnikov, 'Vozdushnyi transport v sovremennoi voine' [Air transport in contemporary war], VM, No. 9 (September 1950), 32–41.
19. Changing operational formations are addressed in David M. Glantz, 'Soviet Operational Formation for Battle,' *Military Review*, 63 (February 1983),2–12. A combined-arms army contained three rifle corps, a heavy self-propelled gun regiment, and support units. A mechanized army had two tank divisions, two mechanized divisions, and support units. The rifle corps comprised three rifle divisions, or two rifle divisions and one mechanized division, and support units. The tank division, with 3 medium tank regiments, a heavy tank self-propelled gun regiment, a motorized rifle regiment, and support units, had 10,659 men, 252 tanks, and 63 self-propelled guns. A mechanized division consisted of 3 mechanized regiments, a medium tank regiment, a heavy tank self-propelled gun regiment, and support units, for a strength of 12,500 men, 197 tanks, and 63 self-propelled guns. The rifle division consisted of 3 rifle regiments, a medium tank self-propelled gun regiment, and support units, for a strength of 11,013 men, 52 tanks, and 34 self-propelled guns.
20. For details, see I. Kh. Bagramian, ed., *Istoriia voin i voennogo iskusstva* [History of war and military art] (Moscow: Voenizdat, 1970), 478–87.
21. Ibid., 481; L. N. Vnotchenko, 'Nekotorye voprosy teorii nastupatel'nykh i oboronitel'nykh operatsii (1945–1954 gg)' [Some questions on the theory of offensive and defensive operations (1945–1953), *VIZh* (August 1970), 34.
22. Ibid., 37.
23. Pavlenko, 'Razvitie taktiki,' 27.
24. M. V. Zakharov et al., eds, *50 let vooruzhennykh sil SSSP* [50 years of the Soviet Armed Forces] (Moscow: Voenizdat, 1968), 489, (hereafter cited as 50 Let).
25. 'Soviet Airborne Forces,' 13.
26. U.S. Department of the Army, Pamphlet no. 30-50-1, *Handbook on the Soviet Army* (Washington, D.C., 1958), 33 (hereafter cited as DA Pam 30-50-1).
27. Ibid.
28. Sukhorukov, *Sovetskie vozdushno*, 265.
29. Ibid., 260.
30. DA Pam 30-50-1, 33.
31. Ibid.
32. Ibid., 34. Subsequent U.S. assessments continued to categorize Soviet airborne operations as strategic, operational, and tactical. A 1969 assessment incorporated the same verbiage as the 1958 assessment.
33. Sukhorukov, *Sovetskie vozdushno*, 266; Kostin, 15–17.
34. Lisov, *Desantniki*, 240, 250–1, 263–4; DA Pam 30-50-1, 36.
35. S. A. Tiushkevich et al., eds, *Sovetskie vooruzhennye sily* [The Soviet armed forces] (Moscow: Voenizdat, 1978), 384–8.
36. Pavlenko, 'Razvitie taktiki,' 28.
37. Sukhorukov, *Sovetskie vozdushno*, 264.

CHAPTER 12

1. For a clear definition of the nature of the 'revolution in military affairs,' see R. Ia. Malinovsky, 'Revoliutsiia v voennom dele i zadachi voennoi pechati' [The revolution in military affairs and the tasks of military writers], *Problemy revoliutsii v voennom dele*

[The problems of the revolution in military affairs] (Moscow: Voenizdat, 1965), 3–7 (hereafter cited as *Problemy*).

2. For an excellent statement of Soviet attitudes toward nuclear war in the 1954–1960 period, see V. A. Semenov, *Kratkii ocherk razvitiia sovetskogo operativnogo iskusstva* [A short outline of the development of Soviet operational art] (Moscow: Voenizdat, 1960), 289–97. For the post-1960 view, see I. S. Glebov, 'Razvitie operativnogo iskusstva' [The development of operational art], in *Problemy*, 133–9.

3. In March 1953 G. K. Zhukov became first deputy minister of defense. He was minister of defense from February 1955 to October 1957, after which R. Ia. Malinovsky replaced him. For details of his career, see 'Zhukov,' *SVE*, 3:345–6.

4. The new tank army consisted of four tank divisions and support units. The motorized rifle division had three motorized rifle regiments, a medium tank regiment, and support units, for a strength of 13,150 men and 210 tanks.

5. The combined-arms army comprised three or four motorized rifle divisions, one tank division, and support units. The tank division consisted of two medium tank regiments, a heavy tank regiment, a motorized rifle regiment, and support units, for a strength of 10,630 men, 368 tanks, and 52 self-propelled guns.

6. By 1968 the motorized rifle division had shrunk to 10,500 men and 188 medium tanks. The tank division's heavy tank regiment had become a third medium tank regiment, and the division strength had decreased to 9,000 men and 316 medium tanks.

7. V. Margelov, 'Razvitie teorii primeneniia vozdushno-desantnykh voisk v poslevoennyi period' [The development of the theory of the use of airlanding forces in the postwar period], *VIZh*, (January 1977), 54.

8. I. Lisov, 'Nekotorye voprosy podgotovki i obespecheniia vozdushnykh desantov' [Some questions on the preparation and securing of airborne landings], *VM*, No. 9 (September 1956), 19.

9. Ibid.

10. Ibid., 25.

11. Ibid., 29.

12. V. Schensnovich, 'Takticheskie vozdushnye desanty v boiu i operatsii' [Tactical airborne landings in battles and operations], *VM*, No. 10 (October 1957), 42.

13. Ibid.

14. Ibid., 43.

15. Ibid., 44.

16. I. Lisov, 'Vozdushnye desanty – vazhnoe sredstvo sovremennoi vooruzhennoi bor'by' [Airborne landings – an important means of contemporary armed struggle], *VM*, No. 2 (February 1961), 46.

17. Ibid., 49.

18. Ibid., 53.

19. Ibid.

20. Ia. Samoilenko, 'Nekotorye tendentsii razvitiia vozdushno desantnikh voisk' [Some tendencies in the development of airborne landing forces], *VM*, No. 8 (August 1962), 56.

21. I. Lisov, 'Vozdushnodesantnaia podgotovka voisk' [Airborne landing training of forces], *VM*, No. 3 (March 1963), 15.

22. Ibid., 17.

23. Ibid., 20.

24. G. Kublanov, 'Vozdushnye desanty i bor'ba s nimi v sovremennoi voine' [Airborne landings and combat with them in contemporary war], *VM*, No. 8 (August 1965), 46.

25. Ibid., 49.

26. I. Andrukhov, V. Bulatnikov, 'Vozrastaiushchaia rol' vozdushnikh desantov v sovremennykh voennykh deistviiakh' [The growing role of airborne landings in contemporary military actions], *VM*, No. 7 (July 1966), 24.

27. A. Sopil'nik, 'Vozdushnye desanty vo vtoroi mirovoi voine' [Airborne landings in the Second World War], *VM*, No. 8 (August 1968), 60–70.

28. Margelov, 'Razvitiia,' 58.

29. Pavlenko, 'Razvitie taktiki,' 28.

30. Ibid., 27–8.
31. Margelov, 'Razvitiia,' 59.
32. *Handbook on the Soviet Armed Forces* (Washington, D.C.: U.S. Department of Defense, Defense Intelligence Agency, July 1969), 30.
33. V. G. Reznichenko, 'Osnovnye napravleniia razvitiia sovetskoi taktiki v poslevoennye gody' [The basic direction of the development of Soviet tactics in the postwar years], *VIZh*, No. 8 (August 1971), 35.
34. Ibid., 36. For details on such use of airborne forces, see V. G. Reznichenko, *Taktika* [Tactics] (Moscow: Voenizdat, 1966), 239–313.
35. Sukhorukov, *Sovetskie vozdushno*, 296. For a good survey of exercises, see R. Oden and F. Steinert, 'The Soviet Airborne Troops,' *Review of the Soviet Ground Forces* (March 1980), 5–12.
36. V. D. Sokolovsky, *Voennaia strategiia* [Military strategy] (Moscow: Voenizdat, 1968), 339, translated by the Foreign Technology Division.
37. *Handbook on the Soviet Armed Forces*, (1969).
38. Ibid., 46.
39. Ibid., 47.
40. Sukhorukov, *Sovetskie vozdushno*, 270–2.
41. For example, see K. S. Kolganov, ed., *Razvitie taktiki sovetskoi armii v gody Velikoi Otechestvennoi voiny (1941–1945 gg.)* [The development of tactics of the Soviet Army in the years of the Great Patriotic War (1941–1945)] (Moscow: Voenizdat, 1958), and companion books published in the same year on rifle corps, division, and regiment tactics. See also V. D. Semenov, *Kratkii ocherk razvitiia sovetskogo operativnogo iskusstva* [A short survey of the development of Soviet operational art] (Moscow: Voenizdat, 1960).
42. Sofronov, *Vozdushnye desanty*.

CHAPTER 13

1. For a sample of the changing views, see M. M. Kir'ian, 'Armeiskaia nastupatel'naia operatsiia' [Army offensive operations], *SVE*, 1:239–44; N. Kireev, 'Primenenie tankovykh podrazdelenii i chastei pri proryve oborony protivnika' [The use of tank subunits (battalions) and units (regiments) during the penetration of an enemy defense], *VIZh*, No. 2 (February 1982), 38–40.
2. The motorized rifle division added a separate tank battalion, and its strength increased to 12,510 men and about 250 tanks. Tank division strength increased to 10,000 men and 325 tanks.
3. Kir'ian, 'Armeiskaia,' 239–44.
4. It is perhaps not by accident that these experiences were first revealed in detail in 1968 with virtually nothing said about them before that date. The first general survey of Soviet and foreign airborne operations during the Second World War was written by Sofronov in 1962. Lisov's detailed work appeared in 1968, following the more general Lisov account, *Sovetskie vozdushno-desantnye voiska*, published in 1962. Sukhorukov's detailed work followed in 1980. Few articles of substance on airborne experiences appeared before Lisov's work was published.
5. Articles on the U.S. experience include P. Maslennikov, 'Nekotorye osobennosti taktiki sukhoputnykh voisk SShA vo V'etname' [Some characteristics of the tactics of U.S. ground forces in Vietnam], *VIZh*, No. 8 (August 1970), 105–10; V. Matsulenko, 'Voina v Iuzhnom V'etname' [The war in South Vietnam], *VIZh*, No. 1 (January 1971), 37–49; A. Sinitsky, 'Agressiia SShA v Kambodzhe i Laose' [The aggression of the U.S.A. in Cambodia and Laos], *VIZh*, No. 7 (July 1971), 47–52; N. Nikitin, 'Nekotorye operativno-takicheskie uroki lokal'nykh voin imperialisma' [Some operational-tactical lessons of the local wars of imperialism], *VIZh* (December 1978), 60–6; V. Matsulenko, 'Lokal'nye voiny imperializma (1946–1968gg)' [Local wars of imperialism, 1946–1968], *VIZh*, No. 9 (September 1968), 36–51.
6. For information on specific helicopter types and capabilities, see G. H. Turbiville,

'Soviet Airborne Forces: Increasingly Powerful Factor in the Equalization,' *Army* 26 (April 1976), 18–27; and G. H. Turbiville, 'A Soviet View of the Heliborne Assault Operations,' *Military Review* 55 (October 1975), 3–15.
7. Ibid.
8. Andrukhov, Bulatnikov, 'The growing role.''
9. An extensive analysis of tactical airborne (helicopter) landings appeared in I. S. Liutov and P. T. Sagaidak, *Motostrelkovyi batal'on v takticheskom vozdushnom desante* [The motorized rifle battalion in tactical airlandings] (Moscow: Voenizdat, 1969). In addition to theoretical, organizational, and operational details, it gives detailed instructions on how to engage specific missile systems (U.S. Corporal and Sergeant missiles).
10. Ibid., 12–13.
11. Ia. Samoilenko, 'Vozdushnye desanty v sovremennykh operatsiiakh' [Airborne landings in contemporary operations], *VM*, No. 10 (October 1969), 15.
12. Ibid.
13. Ibid., 19.
14. Ia. Samoilenko, 'Primenenie vozdushnykh desantov v osobykh usloviiakh' [The use of airborne landings in special conditions], *VM*, No. 12 (December 1970), 32.
15. A. A. Sidorenko, *The Offensive (A Soviet View)*, Soviet Military Thought, No. 1 (Washington, D.C.: U.S. Government Printing Office, 1983), 50, translated by the U.S. Air Force from the Soviet work, *Nastuplenie* (Moscow: Voenizdat, 1970).
16. Ibid., 149–50.
17. Ibid., 193.
18. Ibid., 173.
19. I. Andrukhov, 'Primenenie vertoletov v boevykh deistviiakh sukhoputnykh voisk' [The use of helicopters in ground force combat actions], *VM*, No. 10 (October 1971), 50–8.
20. Ia. Samoilenko, 'Tendentsii razvitiia i primeneniia vozdushno desantnykh voisk' [Tendencies in the development and use of airborne landing forces], *VM*, No. 2 (February 1972), 57.
21. Ibid., 66.
22. A. Bykov, 'Vozdushnye desanty v sovmestnykh desantnykh operatsiiakh' [Airborne landings in contemporary assault operations], *VM*, No. 3 (March 1973), 38.
23. V. Margelov, 'Tendentsii razvitiia primeneniia vozdushnykh voisk' [Tendencies in the development of the use of airborne landings], *VM*, No. 12 (December 1974), 8.
24. Ibid.
25. Ibid., 9.
26. K. Kurochkin, 'Vozdushnodesantnye voiska v lokal'noi voine' [Airborne landing forces in local war], *VM*, No. 2 (February 1974), 42, where he states: 'In the first phase of a local war, the role of airborne forces consists in realizing a surprise blow on selected objectives (regions) with the aim of seizing the initiative in the very beginning of military actions and rapidly concluding the war or strengthening forces located in the region of armed conflict.''
27. Ia. P. Samoilenko, 'Razvitie vzgliadov na provedenie vozdushno-desantnykh operatsii' [The development of views on the conduct of airborne-landing operations], *VM*, No. 11 (November 1975), 55.
28. U.S. Department of the Army, FM 30–40, *Handbook on Soviet Ground Forces*, (Washington, D.C.: 30 June 1975), A-14, A-15.
29. Ibid., 6–33.
30. Ibid., 6–36, 6–37.
31. Sukhorukov, *Sovetskie vozdushno*, 278–92; Oden and Steinert, 'Soviet Airborne Troops,' 5–12.
32. For example, see V. Kokhanov, 'By Joint Efforts,' *Soviet Military Review* (December 1974), 20–1, which discusses coordination of ground and airborne forward detachments; and M. Belov, 'Airlanding Forces,' *Soviet Military Review*, (January 1979), 22–3, which surveys airborne missions and conditions necessary for achieving success.
33. A. Gorbachev, 'Desant otrazhaet udary vertoletov' [Airborne landing repels helicop-

ter attacks,' *Voennyi vestnik* [Military herald], No. 10 (October 1975), 62–8 (hereafter cited as *VV*).

34. M. Muslimov, V. Saprunov, 'Forsorovanie reki s khodu' [Forcing a river from the march], *VV*, No. 12 (December 1975), 59–61.

35. I. Zuev, 'Manevr obespechivaet BMD' [The BMD protects maneuver], *VV*, No. 2 (February 1976), 85.

36. V. Dregval', 'Parashutno-desantnaia rota zakhvatyvaet ob'ekt v gorakh' [A parachute-landing company seizes objectives in the mountains], *VV*, No. 4 (April 1977), 74–7.

37. R. Salikhov, 'Parashiutno-desantnyi batal'on deistvuet noch'iu' [A parachute-landing battalion operates in the night], *VV*, No. 6 (June 1977), 64–7.

38. V. Grechnev, 'Sovershenstvuia takticheskuiu vyuchku' [While improving tactical training], *VV*, No. 12 (December 1977), 74–77.

39. M. Muslimov, 'Batal'on zakhvatyvaet gornyi prokhod noch'iu' [A battalion seizes a mountain passage at night], *VV*, No. 5 (May 1979), 39–43; A. Fedotov, 'Zakhvat perepravy' [Securing a crossing], *VV*, No. 10 (October 1979), 25–7; B. Koziulin, 'Rota zakhvatyvaet punkt upravleniia' [A company seizes a command and control point], *VV*, No. 2 (February 1980), 39–41; V. Syromiatnikov, 'Rota forsiruet reku s khodu' [A company forces a river from the march], *VV*, No. 9 (September 1980), 34–6; Iu. Protasov, 'V atake desantniki' [Airborne troops in the attack], *VV*, No. 11 (November 1980), 48–50.

40. I. A. Skorodumov, 'Aeromobil'nye voiska i ikh operatsii' [Airmobile forces and their operations], *VM*, No. 5 (May 1980), 30.

41. D. S. Sukhorukov, 'Razvitie sovetskikh vozdushno-desantnykh voisk' [The development of Soviet airborne landing forces], *VM*, No. 8 (August 1980), 23.

42. D. S. Sukhorukov, 'Problemy primeneniia vozdushnykh desantov' [Problems in the use of airborne landings], *VM*, No. 11 (November 1980), 34–41.

43. Ibid., 41.

44. N. Zavitnevich, V. Sokolov, 'Sapery na vertoletakh' [Sappers in helicopters], *VV*, No. 12 (December 1983), 81–3.

45. A. Ul'ianskii, Iu. Borodin, 'V takticheskom vzaimodeistvii' [In tactical cooperation], *VV*, No. 7 (July 1984), 22–4.

46. U.S. Department of Defense, *Soviet Military Power* (Washington, D.C., 1982), 29.

47. U.S. Department of the Army, FM 100-2-3 (Draft), *Soviet Army Troop Organization and Equipment* (Fort Leavenworth, KS: Threats Directorate, Combined Army Combat Developments Activity, Combined Arms Center, U.S. Army Training and Doctrine Command, 1982), 4–108. See also 'Sowjetische Luftlande-Sturmbrigaden' [Soviet airlanding brigades], *Soldat und Technik* [Soldier and technology], December 1978:634.

48. For parameters of operations in the period 1971–85, see David. M. Glantz, *Soviet Military Operational Art: In Pursuit of Deep Battle*, (London: Frank Cass, 1990), 205–43.

49. Army forward detachments would be of reinforced tank regiment size; division forward detachments of reinforced tank battalion size. See Kireev, 'Primenenie,' 38–9. For the origins of the concept and current applicability, see N. Kireev and N. Dovbenko, 'Iz opyta boevogo primeneniia peredovykh otriadov tankovykh (mekhonizirovannykh) korpusov' [From the experiences of the combat use of forward detachment of tank (mechanized) corps], *VIZh*, No. 9 (September 1982), 20–7. For details on the employment of forward detachments, see David. M. Glantz, *Soviet Conduct of Tactical Maneuver: Spearhead of the Offensive* (London: Frank Cass, 1991).

CHAPTER 14

1. V. Reznichenko, 'Sovetskie voorushennye sily v poslevoennyi period' [The Soviet armed forces in the postwar period], *Kommunist voorushennykh sil* [Communists of the armed forces], No. 1 (January 1988), 86–8.

2. For example, see I. N. Vorob'ev, 'Novoe oruzhie – novaia taktika' [New weapons – new tactics], *VM*, No. 2 (February 1984), 34–5 and No. 6 (June 1984), 48–59; E. G. Korotchenko, 'Novye sredstva vooruzhennoi bor'by i kharakter sovremennykh nastupatel'nykh operatsii' [New means of armed struggle and the nature of contemporary offensive operations], *VM*, No. 11 (November 1984), 48–58.
3. For example, see V. V. Krysanov, 'Massirovanie sil i sredstv na glavnykh napravleniiakh – iskusstvo i raschet' [Massing of forces and means on main directions – art and calculation], *VM*, No. 5 (May 1984), 27–33; N. K. Shishkin, 'Proryv oborony' [Penetration of a defense], *VM*, No. 3 (March 1986), 36–43.
4. Among the many articles, see F. Sverdlov, 'K voprosu o manevre v boiu' [Concerning the question of maneuver in combat], *VV*, No. 8 (August 1982), 31. For antecedents of the concept of antinuclear maneuver, see also V. Savkin, 'Manevr v boiu' [Maneuver in battle], *VV*, No. 4 (April 1972), 23.
5. Sverdlov, 'K voprosu,' 31.
6. M. M. Kir'ian, ed., *Vnezapnost' v nastupatel'nykh operatsiiakh Velikoi Otechestvennoi voiny* [Surprise in offensive operations of the Great Patriotic War] (Moscow: 'Nauka,' 1986).
7. V. N. Lobov, *Voennaia khitrost'* [Military cunning] (Moscow: Voenizdat, 1988).
8. Iu. K. Kuznetsov, *Peredvizhenie i vstrechnyi boi* [Movement and meeting battle] (Moscow: Voenizdat, 1989).
9. F. D. Sverdlov, *Peredovye otriady v boi* [Forward detachments in battle] (Moscow: Voenizdat, 1986).
10. V. K. Reznichenko, *Taktika* [Tactics] (Moscow: Voenizdat, 1984); and, by the same author, *Taktika* (Moscow: Voenizdat, 1987).
11. Reznichenko, *Taktika* (1987), 72.
12. See, for example, I. Vorob'ev, 'Novoe oruzhie i printsipy taktiki' [New weapons and tactical principles], *Sovetskoe voennoe obozrenie* [Soviet military review], No. 2 (February 1987), 18.
13. Iu. Molostov, A. Novikov, 'High precision weapons against tanks,' *Soviet Military Review*, No. 1 (January 1988), 13.
14. Reznichenko, *Taktika*, (1987), 200.
15. Ibid. For additional analysis of this change, see L. W. Grau, *Changing Objective Depths: A Reflection of Changing Combat Circumstances* (Fort Leavenworth, KS: Soviet Army Studies Office, 1989) and L. W. Grau, *Soviet Non-Linear Combat: The Challenge of the 90s* (Fort Leavenworth, KS: Soviet Army Studies Office, 1990).
16. David M. Glantz, *Soviet Conduct of Tactical Maneuver: Spearhead of the Offensive* (London: Frank Cass, 1991).
17. Reznichenko, *Taktika*, (1987), 206.
18. Molostov, Novikov, 13.
19. Ibid.
20. See L. W. Grau, *Soviet Combined Arms Battalion: Reorganization for Tactical Flexibility* (Fort Leavenworth, KS: Soviet Army Studies Office, 1989) and an interesting Soviet piece, M. N. Golovnin, 'O primenenii korpusov sukhoputnykh voisk' [Concerning the use of the corps of ground forces], *VM*, No. 10 (October 1981), 37–44.
21. R. Salikhov, 'V peredovom otriade' [In a forward detachment], VV, No. 3 (March 1987), 33–6.
22. G. H. Turbiville, Jr., *Soviet Airborne Troops (1987–1989)* (Fort Leavenworth, KS: Soviet Army Studies Office, 1989), 4.
23. Stanislaw Koziej, 'The development of the concept of air-land combat actions,' *Mysl Wojskowa* [Military thought], No. 7 (July 1987), 19, translated by Dr Harold Orenstein.
24. Koziej also cites use of air assault forces in Grenada.
25. Ibid., 22–3.
26. Ibid., 26–7.
27. Ibid., 29–30.
28. See, for example, W. Skrzypczak, 'Assault-Landing Operations,' *Mysl Wojskowa*, No. 2 (February 1987), 17–22; S. Koziej, 'Some Concepts Concerning Air-Land Opera-

tions,' *Mysl Wojskowa*, No. 4 (April 1987), 17–23.
29. S. Akhromeev, 'Rol' Sovetskogo Soiuza i ego Vooruzhennykh Sil v dostizhenii korennogo pereloma vo vtopoi mirovoi voine i ego mezhdunarodnoe zhachenie' [The role of the Soviet Union and its armed forces in the achievement of a fundamental turning point in the Second World War and its international significance], *VIZh*, No. 2 (February 1984), 11–26.
30. See Note 2, this chapter.
31. The articles in this Soviet-designated '*Diskussiia*' [Debate or discussion] included: V. V. Gurkin, M. I. Golovnin, 'K voprosu o strategicheskikh operatsiiakh Velikoi Otechestvennoi voiny 1941–1945 gg.' [On the question of strategic operations in the Great Patriotic War 1941–1945], *VIZh*, No. 10 (October 1985), 10–23); N. K. Glazunov, B. I. Pavlov, V. S. Shlomin, 'K voprosu o strategicheskikh operatsiiakh Velikoi Otechestvennoi voiny' [On the question of strategic operations in the Great Patriotic War], *VIZh*, No. 4 (April 1986), 48–55; A. I. Mikhailov, V. I. Kudriashov, 'K voprosu o strategicheskikh operatsiiakh Velikoi Otechestvennoi voiny 1941–1945 gg.' *VIZh*, No. 5 (May 1986), 48–50; Kh. Dzhelauknov, B. N. Petrov, 'K voprosu o strategicheskikh operatsiiakh Velikoi Otechestvennoi voiny 1941–1945 gg.' *VIZh*, No. 7 (July 1986), 46–8; A. P. Maryshev, 'Nekotorye voprosy strategicheskoi oborony v Velikoi Otechestvennoi voine' [Some questions about strategic defense in the Great Patriotic War], *VIZh*, No. 6 (June 1986), 9–16; P. T. Kunitskiy, 'O vybore napravleniia glavnogo udara v kampaniiakh i strategicheskikh operatsiiakh' [About the selection of the direction of the main attack in campaigns and strategic operations], *VIZh*, No. 7 (July 1986), 29–40; P. T. Kunitsky, 'Sposoby razgrom protivnika v strategicheskikh nastupatel'nykh operatsiiakh' [Means of destroying the enemy in strategic offensive operations], *VIZh*, No. 10 (October 1987), 25–31; 'Itogi diskussii o strategicheskikh operatsiiakh Velikoi Otechestvennoi voiny 1941–1945 gg.' [Results of the discussions on strategic operations of the Great Patriotic War], *VIZh*, No. 10 (October 1987), 8–24; V. V. Gurkin, M. I. Golovnin, 'Operatsii v bitvakh (K voprosu o strategicheskikh i frontovykh operatsiiakh provedennykh v khode bitv Velikoi Otechestvennoi voiny)' [Operations in battles (Concerning the question of strategic and front operations conducted during battles of the Great Patriotic War)], *VIZh*, No. 9 (September 1988), 3–8.
32. Ibid., see Mikhailov, Kudriashov, Maryshev.
33. For example, see Korotchenko, 'K voprosu'; A. F. Bulatov, 'Ob ustoichivosti takticheskoi oborony' [About the stability of the tactical defense], *VM*, No. 1 (January 1986), 32–41; A. G. Khor'kov, 'K voprosu ob ugrozhaemom periode' [Concerning the question of the threatening period], *VM*, No. 3 (March 1986), 18–25; M. I. Cherednichenko, 'O metodakh issledovaniia istoricheskogo opyta v tseliakh razvitiia sovremennogo voennogo iskusstva' [Concerning the methods of investigating historical experience with the aim of developing contemporary military art], *VM*, No. 3 (March 1986), 44–51; and Note 2 this chapter.
34. R. A. Savushkin, 'Evoliutsiia vzgliadov na oboronu v mezhvoennye gody' [The evolution of defensive views during the inter-war years], *VIZh*, No. 1 (January 1987), 37–42. Svechin was next referred to in V. N. Lobov, 'Strategiia pobedy' [Strategy of victory], *VIZh*, No. 5 (May 1988), 3–11. A fuller coverage of Svechin's work appeared in V. N. Lobov, 'Aktual'nye voprosy razvitiia teorii sovetskoi voennoi strategii 20-kh-serediny 30-kh godov' [Real questions concerning the development of Soviet military strategy in the 1920s and mid-1930s], *VIZh*, No. 2 (February 1989).
35. D. T. Iazov, 'K voprosu ob ustoichivosti i aktivnosti oborony' [Concerning the question of the stability and activeness of the defense], *VM*, No. 2 (February 1987), 23–33; A. Kokoshin, V. Larionov,'Kurskaia bitva v svete sovremennoi oboronitel'noi doktriny' [The Kursk battle in light of contemporary defensive doctrine], *Mirovaia ekonomika i mezhdunarodnye otnosheniia* [World economics and international relations], No. 8 (August 1987), 32–40 (hereafter cited as *MEMO*).
36. A. Kokoshin, V. Larionov, 'Protivostoianiia sil obshchego naznacheniia v kontekste obespecheniia strategicheskoi stabil'nosti' [The counterposition of general purpose forces in the context of strategic stability], *MEMO*, No. 6 (June 1988), 23–31.

37. N. G. Popov, 'Kharakternye cherty pervykh operatsii agressora v nachal'nyi period voiny' [The nature of first operations of the aggressor in the initial period of war], *VM*, No. 3 (March 1987), 13–23; A. I. Bazhenov, 'Puti povysheniia ustoichivosti operativnoi oborony' [Ways of increasing the stability of the operational defense], *VIZh*, No. 5 (May 1987), 16–24; V. F. Shul'gin, 'Nekotorye problemy povysheniia ustoichivostu operativnoi oborony' [Some problems in increasing the stability of the operational defense], *VM*, No. 7 (July 1987), 14–23; I. E. Krupchenko, 'Ob izuchenii i ispol'zovanii opyta voin v sovremennykh usloviiakh' [Concerning the study and use of war experience in contemporary conditions], *VM*, No. 10 (October 1987), 72–9.

38. For example, see E. D. Grebish, 'O dialekticheskikh vzaimosviaziakh v razvitii voennogo dela' [Concerning dialectical relationships in the development of military affairs], *VM*, No. 1 (January 1988), 60–7.

39. Among many such articles, see V. P. Krikunov, V. G. Matveev, 'Iz opyta armeiskihk oboronitel'nykh operatsii' [From the experience of army defensive operations], *VIZh*, No. 2 (February 1988), 67–75; G. Ionin, 'Osnovy sovremennogo oboronitel'nogo boia' [The bases of contemporary defensive battle], *VV*, No. 3 (March 1988), 18–21.

40. V. V. Larionov, 'Triumf prednamerennoi oborony' [The triumph of premeditated defense], *VM*, No. 7 (July 1988), 12–21.

41. Lobov, 'Strategii.'

42. N. K. Shishkin, 'Manevr v sovremennom oboronitel'nom boiu' [Maneuver in contemporary battle], *VM*, No. 8 (August 1988), 45–53; V. N. Andrienko, 'Ot oborony k kontrnastupleniiu' [From defense to counteroffensive], *VM*, No. 12 (December 1988), 23–32; A. G. Khor'kov, 'Kontrnastupleniie: opyt podgotovki i vedeniia' [The counteroffensive: experience of preparing and conducting], *VM*, No. 10 (October 1988), 12–27.

43. A. Grekhnev, 'Organizatsiia ognevogo porazheniia protivnika pri nastuplenii parashiutno-desantnogo batal'one' [The organization of fire strikes on the enemy during the attack of a parachute-landing battalion], *VV*, No. 3 (March 1989), 40–1.

44. Z. Scibiorek, 'Desants on the Defense,' *Zolnierz Wolnosci* [Soldier of freedom], 26 July 1988, 3.

45. C. Marcinkowski, 'Desants – or desant-assault operations,' *Zolnierz Wolnosci*, 18 October 1988, 3.

46. S. Suchora, 'The helicopter – an effective fire asset,' *Zolnierz Wolnosci*, 30 November 1988, 3.

47. S. Koziej, 'Operational and tactical raids,' *Mysl Wojskowa*, No. 4 (July–August 1990), 17. This article is particularly rich in details of how raids can be conducted in future war.

48. Ibid., 17, 24.

49. Ibid., 26.

50. Timothy L. Thomas, 'The Soviet Military on "Desert Storm": Redefining Doctrine,' *The Journal of Soviet Military Studies*, Vol. 4, No. 4 (December 1991), 594–620.

51. A. Madejski, 'Procedures when undertaking armed forces restructuring,' *Mysl Wojskowa*, No. 1 (January–February 1991), 21–32.

CHAPTER 15

1. G. D'iakov, 'Vozdushnye desanty i bor'ba s nimi' [Airborne landings and combat against them], *VM*, No. 10–11 (October–November 1941), 63–73.

2. M. Spirin, 'Vozdushye desanty' [Airborne landings], *VM*, No. 8 (August 1942), 49.

3. Ibid.

4. Ibid.

5. N. Vlasov, 'Vozdushno-desantnye voiska vo vtoroi mirovoi voine' [Airborne landing forces in the Second World War], *VM*, No. 11–12 (November–December 1945), 70.

6. Ibid., 72.

7. Ibid.

8. Margelov, 'Razvitie teorii,' 59.

Appendix 1

LOGISTICAL SUPPORT OF THE VIAZ'MA OPERATION

Rear service support for the airborne force, because of the prolonged nature of its operations, was chiefly the responsibility of brigade and battalion rear service organizations. The original VDV plan for the Viaz'ma airborne operation provided for corps units to operate initially with two to three days of supplies, enough to support operations up to link-up with 33d Army forces. Thereafter, the corps would receive all logistical support through 33d Army channels. When 33d Army forces were themselves encircled, the plan went awry.

Initially airborne forces were well-equipped with airborne jump suits, felt boots, warm clothing, winter camouflage dress, dry rations for three days, individual toiletry packs, unlimited ammunition for personal weapons, two hand grenades and one antitank grenade, a knife, a machine pistol, self-loading rifles, and submachine guns. Heavy machine guns, one battalion mortar, antitank guns, knives, one combat load of ammunition, two daily loads of rations, medical supplies and medicine in PDMM, and skis were rigged and dropped by parachute. In addition, several 45mm guns were delivered by TB-3 aircraft.

During the initial two to three day parachute drop, because of deep snow and enemy resistance, the force gathered only 30–50 per cent of the supplies, and most of the skis were broken. Only 15–20 per cent of the paratroopers were thereafter equipped with skis. Very quickly, the logistics problem became critical for the corps. Consequently, within two weeks, the Western Front Directorate of Rear Services, the VDV command, and agencies of the People's Commissariat of Defense created an improvised system of resupply for 4th Airborne Corps.

In March and April, an average of 15–17 tons of materiel supply per day was delivered to the airborne corps in lieu of its minimum requirement of 85–100 tons. Because of problems in the rear services, poor weather, or limited transport aircraft, air resupply was intermittent, but it still played an important role in sustaining airborne units.

The VDV administration created warehouses and an airborne evacuation and reception center near Ramenskoe airfield, where a small team of paratroopers packed and loaded equipment for airdrop in response to requests received from brigades or corps. The evacuation points distributed sick and wounded to military or civilian hospitals and clinics. Otherwise the airborne force itself cooperated with cavalry and partisan forces and the local population to make up shortfalls in supplies. In addition, troopers exploited warehouses and stocks left in the region from autumn 1941 operations and, whenever possible, used captured equipment.

The care and evacuation of medical casualties was especially complex. Lightly wounded soldiers tended to remain with their parent force and were often used in security missions or to defend medical points. After their recovery, they formed a reserve with which to refill depleted units and subunits. In the area of operations of 4th Airborne Corps were a total of 13 hospitals, staffed by corps medical staff, personnel left in the rear during 1941 operations, airborne medics, and local inhabitants which some medical training.

Epidemic conditions threatened the rear area, especially in the spring. Typhus became the most frequent illness in general and among the paratroopers. A strict epidemic regime was introduced, an infectious disease section was formed in each hospital, and finally a separate hospital administered to the numerous typhus patients.

In March a large supply of medicine and medical supplies became available. Over the course of five months, 60 tons were shipped forward. The *front* chief of medical services, at the request of corps, sent several qualified medical specialists forward, who advised corps medical staff and performed operations. On 12 May the 4th Airborne Corps Chief of Rear Services, Colonel I. Z. Morozov, reported the following to the Western Front Medical Directorate:

> Through 12 May 900 men have been evacuated. There remain 3,400 wounded in the entire group. Of these there are 1,193 in the airborne corps, 84 in Zhabo's regiment, 109 in 33d Army, 400 in Lazo's detachment, and 1,623 in 1st Guards Cavalry Corps. Of this total, 400 men are bed-ridden. Am organizing an advanced section field evacuation and reception point (GOPEP) with hospitals: surgical – 300 beds; for light wounded and convalescents – 300 beds; infectious – 100 beds; and five military-field hospitals. In order to concentrate wounded and sick in the landing area, am gathering all hospital and part of corps transport and state farm vehicles. Registration and medical help is concentrated at the GOPEP. Ill with typhus – 304 cases. Of these, 93 are in the airborne corps and 39 in other units. The remainder are cavalrymen. Request you, send antigangrene and antitetanus serum.

Of the 3,024 wounded lying in corps hospitals and battalion and brigade medical points, 2,136 (70 per cent) eventually returned to duty.

Source: Gromov, Pigunov, *4th Airborne*, 253–4.

Appendix 2

June–September 1941

4th Airborne Corps

Commander – Major General A. S. Zhadov (29 June – 2 August)
    Colonel I. T. Grishin (2–8 August)
    Colonel A. F. Levashov (after 8 August)
Chief of Staff – Colonel A. F. Kazankin
Commissar – V. M. Olenin

214th Airborne Brigade

Commander – Colonel A. F. Levashov (to 8 August)
    Colonel N. E. Kolobovnikov
Chief of Staff – ?
Commissar – ? Tugunov
    I. V. Kudriavtsov
Reconnaissance Company – Lieutenant P. V. Pobortsev
lst Battalion – Major G. I. Lebedev
2d Battalion – Captain F. N. Antroshchenkov
3d Battalion – Captain N. V. Solntsev (POW in July)
4th Battalion – Captain I. D. Polozkov
Identified Company Commanders
    1st Company – Lieutenant A. Tsatskin
    2d Company – Senior Lieutenant S. Vinogradov
    4th Company – Lieutenant M. Soldatenko
    8th Company – Lieutenant A. Mart'ianov/Senior Lieutenant A. Khoteenkov
    10th Company – Senior Lieutenant N. Romanenko
    ? Company – Lieutenant G. Iakovlev
    ? Company – Lieutenant N. Drozd
    ? Company – Lieutenant I. Tkachenko/Lieutenant V. Prokof'ev

8th Airborne Brigade

Commander – Lieutenant Colonel A. A. Onufriev
Chief of Staff – Lieutenant Colonel V. I. Spirin
Commissar – V. A. Nikitin
Chief of Operations – Captain N. I. Sagaidachnyi

lst Battalion – Captain V. P. Drobyshevsky (wounded 16 July),
Captain A. G. Kobets
2d Battalion – Major N. I. Samarin (wounded 28 July),
Captain D. F. Gavrish
3d Battalion – Captain Bortkevich (wounded 19 July)
4th Battalion – Major I. Zhurko
Identified Company Commanders
5th Company – Lieutenant G. Machkov
7th Company – Lieutenant P. V. Tereshchenko
? Company – Lieutenant P. M. Revy (wounded 28 July)
? Company – Lieutenant Kulitsky

7th Airborne Brigade
Commander – Colonel M. F. Tikhanov (killed June),
Major V. A. Leshchinin
Chief of Staff – Major A. J. Evgrafov (killed 20 August)
Commissar – N. I. Gorokhov
1st Battalion – Captain I. Chepurny

January – June 1942

4th Airborne Corps
Commander – Colonel A. F. Levashov (killed 23 February)
Colonel A. F. Kazankin
Chief of Staff – Colonel A. F. Kazankin, Major M. M. Kozunko
Commissar – V. M. Olenin
Chief of Reconnaissance – Captain A. P. Aksenov

214th Airborne Brigade
Commander – Colonel N. F. Kolobovnikov
Chief of Staff – Major V. I. Spirin (POW 28 May)
Commissar – ?
1st Battalion – Captain I. D. Polozkov (wounded 4 March)
2d Battalion – Captain P. V. Pobortsev (killed 18 April)
3d Battalion – Senior Lieutenant P. Vasilev (killed 4 March)
4th Battalion – Captain A. Khoteenkov (killed 26 May)
Identified Company Commanders
None

8th Airborne Brigade
Commander – Lieutenant Colonel A. A. Onufriev
Chief of Staff – Major N. I. Sagaidachnyi (killed 11 February)
Major P. M. Barkevich (killed May)
Major V. P. Drobyshevsky
Commissar – I. V. Raspopov (wounded 10 June and evacuated)
1st Battalion – Major V. P. Drobyshevsky
2d Battalion – Captain M. Ia. Karnaukov
3d Battalion – Major A. G. Kobets (wounded 7 February)

4th Battalion – Captain A. I. Gor'kov
Identified Company Commanders
    9th Company – Senior Lieutenant D. V. Fomenkov (killed 22 February)
    7th Company – Senior Lieutenant P. V. Tereshchenko (wounded 26 February, rejoined 50th Army on 15 July)

9th Airborne Brigade

Commander – Colonel I. I. Kuryshev
Chief of Staff – Major P. M. Bazelev
Commissar – P. V. Shcherbin (killed 31 March)
1st Battalion – Captain A. Plotnikov (wounded 13 March)
              Captain A. D. Shukin
2d Battalion – Captain M. Smirnov (wounded 20 May, joined partisans)
3d Battalion – Major V. N. Sharov
4th Battalion – Captain D. I. Bibikov (killed 18 April)
Identified Company Commanders
    1st Company – Lieutenant I. Batenko (killed 21 April)
    3d Company – Lieutenant V. Il'na

250th Airborne Regiment

Major N. L. Soldatov (13 March Commander of 329th Rifle Division)

Western Front Airborne Detachment

Major I. G. Starchak

201st Airborne Brigade

1st Battalion – Captain I. A. Surzhik
2d Battalion – E. N. Kalashnikov

23d Airborne Brigade

Commander – Lieutenant Colonel A. G. Mil'sky (wounded 23 June)
1st Battalion – Major S. Gurin
2d Battalion – Captain Deriugin
? Battalion – Captain S. D. Kreuts

211th Airborne Brigade

Commander – Lieutenant Colonel M. I. Shilin (killed 6 June)

Post-1942 Known Data on Key Personnel

I. I. Lisov – 1934 – Belorussian airborne maneuvers
            1936 – Junior officer 47th Air-landing Detachment/Brigade
            1938 – Commander 1st Light Machine Gun Battalion, 214th Airborne Brigade
            1939 – General Staff School in Moscow
            1941 – Airborne Administration (VDV)

1943 – Major, Chief of Staff, 99th Guards Rifle Division in Svir
   River operation
1960s – Lieutenant General, Deputy Commander of Airborne
   Forces

2 August 1942

4th Airborne Corps (3d formation) became 38th Guards Rifle Division

38th Guards Rifle Division

Commander – Colonel A. A. Onufriev (Major General 27 November 1942 –
   killed 23 February 1943 at Barvenkovo)
Commissar – V. M. Olenin
Staff Officers – Major V. P. Drobyshevsky, Captain A. P. Aksenov (wounded at
   Chuguev, April 1943)
110th Guards Rifle Regiment – Major A. G. Kobets (wounded, left division
   May 1943)
113th Guards Rifle Regiment – Major A. I. Plotnikov (killed 3 September at
   Stalingrad)
115th Guards Rifle Regiment – Major G. I. Lebedev (wounded in September at
   Stalingrad)
   Major V. P. Drobyshevsky (May 1943, Chief of
   Staff 267th Rifle Division)
Assistant Regimental Commander – Major M. Ia. Karnaukhov
Regimental Chief of Staff – Major N. I. Samarin
Regimental Commissar – D. F. Gavrish
Battalion Commanders – Captain P. M. Revy (wounded August 1942)
   Captain I. P. Zarubin
Company Commander – Senior Lieutenant N. Romanenko (killed in September
   at Stalingrad)

September 1942 – 4th Airborne Corps (4th Formation)

Commander – Major General A. F. Kazankin (left division November 1943)
Converted to 1st Guards Airborne Division, December 1942

Survived the War

Major General A. F. Kazankin – buried Novodevichyi Cemetary
J. D. Polozkov – retired in 1953, 80 years old in 1987
V. I. Spirin – released as POW 1946
A. G. Mil'sky – (Commander, 23d Airborne Brigade)
I. V. Raspopov – (Commissar, 8th Airborne Brigade)
P. M. Bazelev – (Chief of Staff, 9th Airborne Brigade)
P. V. Tereshchenko – wounded at Stalingrad, in Parade of Victory 1945
D. F. Gavrish
N. F. Kolobnikov

INDEX

Abrau Diurso Sovkhoz (State Farm), 316
Achalov, Colonel General V. A., 415 n.3
Adamovka, 172, 175
Adzhalyk Estuary, 306
Afghan War, 373–374
Afghanistan, 321, 370, 374
Afonino, 213
Air Armies, Soviet
  2d, 265, 268
  9th, 317
  12th, 317
Air Fleet, German
  Second, 146
air echelon, Soviet concept of, 362–364,
  372–373, 383, 391
Airland battle, U.S. concept of, 369–370,
  375
Akhromeev, Marshal S. F., 376
Ak Monai, 309–311
Aksenov, Captain A. P., 118, 122, 427,
  429
Akulovo, 180, 186, 189, 191–192, 194,
  197, 201
Aleksandrovka, 101, 178
Aleksandrovka (Odessa), 308
Alekseevskoe, 129
Aleksin, 108
Aleksino, 210, 213, 219
Alferovo, 118–120, 126, 128, 132, 135–
  136, 139
Algeria, 356
Alytus, 302
Andrejany Kessel (Cauldron), 402 n.73
Andrianovka, 101
Andriiaki, 160, 180
Andronovo, 165, 168, 171, 175, 177–178
Androsovo, 115, 117–119, 122, 127
Andrukhov, Colonel N., 344, 356
Anikanovo, 204
antinuclear maneuver, Soviet concept of,
  370–371
Antonov, Colonel General A. I., 301
Antroshchenko, Major F. N., 403 n.15,
  426
Apanasenko, I. R., 21
Apisovka, 56
Arabat, 309, 311
Area Army, Japanese
  First, 317–318

Armies, German
  Second, 88
  Second Panzer, 88, 90–91, 94, 220
  Third Panzer, 146, 290
  Fourth, 79, 88–92, 94–95, 121, 128, 145–
    146, 150, 152, 158–159, 171, 199, 203,
    210, 219–220, 226, 399 n.12, 399 n.29,
    405 n.11, 407 n.72
  Fourth Panzer, 65, 79, 89–92, 94, 115,
    119, 121–122, 125, 146, 203, 220, 227,
    263, 272–273, 290, 399 n.12, 400 n.4,
    401 n.47, 402 n.73, 407 n.72
  Sixth, 314
  Eighth, 272–273
  Ninth, 65, 88–92, 146, 227–229
  Eleventh, 308
  Sixteenth, 229, 231, 234–261, 387, 408
    n.26
Armies, Japanese
  3d, 319–320
  Kwantung, 318–321
Armies, Soviet
  1st Red Banner, 317
  lst Separate Far Eastern, 44
  1st Shock, 65, 74, 76, 90–91, 232, 244,
    408 n.16
  2d Separate Far Eastern, 44
  3d, 55, 74
  3d Guards Tank, 263, 272, 411 n.3
  3d Shock, 228–229, 232, 234, 290, 293,
    298
  4th, 51
  4th Guards, 68
  4th Shock, 228, 232, 290, 293–294, 297–
    298
  5th, 56, 67, 90–91, 317
  5th Guards Tank, 282
  6th, 56
  6th Guards Tank, 319–320
  7th, 68
  9th Guards, 68
  10th, 74, 90–91, 94, 146, 193, 211, 217–
    218, 220, 226
  11th, 228, 232
  11th Guards, 293
  13th, 52, 74
  15th, 38
  16th, 74, 90–91
  20th, 74, 90–91

22d, 228
25th, 319
27th, 49
29th, 90–92, 228–229, 407 n.3
30th, 74, 76, 90
31st, 90
33d, 79, 88, 90–92, 94–95, 101, 108, 111,
  113, 122, 125–126, 129, 143, 145–146,
  148, 152, 154, 158, 177, 181, 188–189,
  191, 200–201, 222, 225–226, 403 n.15,
  403 n.51, 405 n.61, 424
34th, 228, 232, 234, 236, 250
37th, 65, 282
38th, 263, 300, 301, 303
39th, 90–92, 108, 117, 188, 228–229
40th, 263, 265, 268–270, 281
43d, 79, 82, 85–86, 90–91, 94, 100, 171,
  186, 399 n.8
44th, 309, 311
47th, 314–315
49th, 79, 90–91, 94, 100, 146, 171, 186
50th, 59, 74, 79, 88–91, 94, 108, 146,
  148, 150, 159–188, 193–194, 196–200,
  208, 210, 220, 226, 404 n.48, 405 n.11
51st, 309
52d, 65, 281–283, 285, 411 n.38
56th, 314
57th, 282
68th, 65
Airborne (Separate), 68
Coastal, 306
Army Groups, German
  Center, 44, 49, 63, 75, 78, 86, 88–90,
    94–95, 104, 109, 143–144, 146, 148,
    187, 214, 220, 228, 232, 234, 290, 293,
    386–387, 403 n.19
  South, 56, 263, 278
  North, 258, 290, 293, 386
Artemenko, Colonel I. T., 319–320
Ashmanovo, 218
Astapovo, 165, 179
Astashevo, 127, 132
August 1991 Revolution (Soviet Union),
  379
Avremenko, 319
Azarovo, 109, 112

Babykino, 172, 174
Bach-tal, 250
Baden, 308
Baibuz, 281
Banska Bystriea, 303
Banska Stiavnica, 303
Baragovo Station, 309
Baraki, 197, 201
Baranov, Lieutenant General V. K., 216–
  217

Baranovichi, 44, 50–51
Barkevich, Major P. M., 128, 140, 427
Barricady Factory, 64
Barsuki, 160, 167
Barvenkovo, 429
Baskakovo, 191–193
Baskakovka Station, 194, 197–199, 201
Basmach, 4, 10
Batenko, Lieutenant I., 428
Batishchevo, 148, 195, 402 n.53
Battalions, German
  19th Panzer Reconnaissance, 276–277
  157th Reserve, 281
Battalions, Soviet
  54th Ski, 242, 253, 409 n.50
  112th Ski, 132
  114th Ski, 133
Bazelev, Major P. M., 154, 428–429
Beglevo, 238
Begoml', 293–204
Bekasova, 121, 138–139
Bel', 238, 248–249, 254
Belgium, 40
Belgorod, 262
Bel'guidino, 160, 180–181
Beli, 135
Beloborodov, Lieutenant General A. P.,
  317
Beloded, Major N. K., 320
Belomir, 116, 127, 133, 135–136, 139
Belorussia, 104, 290, 294, 306, 359
Belorussian maneuvers of 1936, 20–21
Belorussian maneuvers of 1937, 29–30
Belotserkovsky, Senior Lieutenant P. L.,
  229–230
Belov, I. P., 6
Belov, Lieutenant General P. A., 86, 92,
  94–95, 100–101, 108, 113, 121–122,
  125–144, 150, 152, 168, 181–227, 388,
  401 n.1, 406 n.33
Bel'yi Kholm, 211
Berezenka Valley, 250
'Berezina,' Exercise (1980), 361
Berezina River, 49, 51–52
Berezino, 49, 51
Berezki, 121, 138
Berezniagy, 268, 270, 411 n.26
Berezniki, 109
Berlin, 10, 322
Berniki, 214
Bessarabian operation (June 1940), 38–39,
  47
Bessonovo, 116, 119
Bezugly, Lieutenant General I. S., 36, 49,
  396 n.2
Bibikov, Captain D. I., 161, 166, 174, 181,
  198, 428

Binder, Colonel E., 276
Black Sea, 263, 311, 314
Blumentritt, Lieutenant General
   Guenther, 219–220
Bluvstein, Major A., 279–280, 284–286
Bobkovo, 250
Bobritsa, 268
Bobruisk, 50–52, 164–290
Bogatyri, 100–101, 177, 203
Bogdanov, 85
Bogodukhov, 268, 274
Bogoroditskoe, 180, 189, 192, 196–197,
   201, 219
Boitsev, M. V., 7, 11
Boldin, Colonel General I. V., 148, 167,
   172, 175, 194, 196, 198–199
Bolgrad, 38, 382
Bologoe Airfield, 241
Bolotovo, 138
Bol'shaia Adzhalyk Estuary, 306
Bol'shaia Myshenka, 192, 194, 197, 201,
   204, 208
Bol'shoe Fat'ianovo, 79, 82, 84–85, 91
Bol'shoe Opuevo, 247, 256–257
Bol'shoe Petrovo, 135
Bol'shoe Starosel'e, 281
Bordukov, 82
Borismansky, Lieutenant, 230
Borodino, 101, 148, 180, 203
Borovoi, 119
Borovsk, 79, 88, 101
Bortkevich, Captain, 427
Bovany, 280
Bremen, 406 n.93
Brest, 383
Brezno, 303
Briansk, 78, 94–95, 145
Brigades, Czech
   2d Czechoslovak Parachute Assault,
      298, 301, 303–304
Brigades of Special Designation
   (SPETSNAZ), 374
Brigades, Soviet
   airborne, general, 36, 43, 61–62, 65, 68–
      69
   1st Airborne, 45, 48, 56–57, 62, 64, 66,
      76, 229, 238–261, 396 n.90
   1st Guards Airborne, 265, 268, 270–293,
      298
   2d Airborne, 45, 48, 64, 238–261, 396
      n.90, 409 n.50
   2d Guards Airborne, 293–298
   2d Tank, 167
   3d Airborne, 45, 48, 64, 66, 296 n.90,
      408 n.18
   3d Airlanding (Special Purpose-
      Airborne), 11, 13, 36

3d Guards Airborne, 265, 268, 270, 274,
   280
4th Airborne, 45, 48, 64, 396 n.90
4th Tank, 59
5th Airborne, 45, 48, 56, 64, 66, 396
   n.90, 397 n.13
5th Guards Airborne, 265, 268, 270,
   274, 278–288, 411 n.38
5th Rifle, 64, 259
6th Airborne, 45, 48, 62, 396 n.90
6th Guards Motorized Rifle, 320
6th Rifle, 64, 259
7th Airborne, 45, 48, 55, 60, 62, 108,
   396 n.90, 397 n.11
7th Rifle, 64
8th Airborne, 48, 55, 62, 86, 101, 104–
   145, 148, 153, 187–227, 396 n.90, 397
   n.11, 400 n.1, 401 n.32, 426–427
8th Rifle, 64
9th Airborne, 45, 48, 60, 62, 66, 104,
   108–109, 111, 148–227, 396 n.90, 428
9th Rifle, 64
10th Airborne, 45, 48, 57, 59, 62, 66,
   396 n.90
10th Rifle, 64
11th Guards Airborne, 293–298
11th Tank, 196
13th Air Assault (Airborne), 36
20th Motorized Assault Engineer, 318
21st Separate Air-landing, 383
23d Airborne, 62, 198, 200–201, 210–
   211, 213–214, 216–218, 428
23d Separate Air-landing, 383
30th Guards Mechanized, 319
32d Tank, 167
34th Separate Rifle, 85
35th Separate Air-landing, 383
36th Separate Air-landing, 383
37th Separate Air-landing, 383
38th Separate Air-landing, 383
40th Separate Air-landing, 383
47th Air Assault (Special Purpose-
   Airborne), 20, 36
51st Guards Tank, 411 n.3
63d Aviation, 308
66th Motorized Rifle, 374
70th Motorized Rifle, 374
72d Tank, 319
86th Rifle, 256
201st Airborne, 36, 38, 43, 45, 48, 54,
   57–60, 62, 79, 82, 95, 98, 100–101,
   132–136, 138, 140, 396 n.88, 396 n.90,
   399 n.12, 428
202d Airborne, 36, 43–44, 396 n.88
204th Airborne, 36, 38, 43, 45, 48, 51,
   56, 62, 229, 236, 238–261, 305, 396
   n.88, 396 n.90, 408 n.16, 408 n.18

208th Airborne, 44
211th Airborne, 36, 43–45, 48, 56, 66, 210–211, 213, 216–219, 229, 396 n.88, 396 n.90, 428
212th Airborne, 36, 38, 43–45, 48, 396 n.88, 396 n.90
214th Airborne, 36, 38, 43, 45, 48–56, 60, 76, 104, 111, 122–123, 148–227, 396 n.88, 396 n.90, 426
242d Tank, 301
Rossonsk 'Stalin' Partisan, 297
Vasilev Partisan, 242
Brigades, U.S.
173d Airborne, 361
'Brother in Arms', Exercise (February 1978), 359
Brovary, 17
Brueckenschlag, operation (Bridging), 234–261
Brusinsky, Lieutenant, 230
Buchak, 268, 270, 279
Buda, 191, 194, 198–199, 201
Buda-Vorobievska, 281
Budenny, S. M., 14, 20
Budishche, 283, 285
Buikovo 1, 216–217
Bulatnikov, Colonel B., 344
Butovo, 192, 199
Byki, 214
Bykov, Colonel A., 356
Byshkovo, 139

Cape Ziuk, 309
Carpathian–Duklin operation (September–October 1944), 413 n.21
Carpathian Mountains, 300–304
Caucasus (Mountains), 311, 314
Central Asia, 381
Central Staff of the Partisan Movement (TsSPD), 294
Changchun, 318–319
Charles XII (Sweden), 89
Chashchi, 204, 207–209
Chebanka, 306, 308
Checherin, Senior Lieutenant, 120–121
Chelyshev, Major P. E., 320
Chepurny, Captain I., 427
Cherkassy, 263, 272, 279, 281–283, 287, 411 n.38
Chernaia, 254–258
Cherniakhovsk, 383
Chernigov, 262
Chernoe Lake, 244
Chernyshi, 268, 279
Chetnoe, 217
Chichkovo, 172
Chistiakov, Colonel General I. M., 319

Chita, 44
Chodnovo, 400 n. 38
Chugarev, 429
Civil Air Fleet (Soviet), 343
Civil War, Russian, 1
Cold War, 379, 392
Commonwealth of Independent States, 379
Conventional Forces in Europe (CFE) Agreement, 381
Corps, Czechoslovakian
1st Rifle, 300–304
Corps, German
II Army, 231–261, 408 n.26
III Panzer, 278
V Army, 125
VII Army, 92
IX Army, 92
X Army, 234
XII Army, 79, 88, 92, 94, 145–146, 150, 171, 405 n.11
XIII Army, 88, 92, 94, 145–146, 150, 171
XX Army, 79, 89, 92, 94, 146, 399 n.12
XXIV Panzer, 57, 59, 272–273, 278, 287, 411 n.17
XXXX Panzer, 88–89, 92, 94, 405 n.11, 406 n.19
XXXXIII Army, 88–89, 92, 94, 145–146, 150, 159
LVII Army, 79, 92, 94–95, 145–146, 150
Corps, Slovak
Eastern Slovakian Army, 300–304
Corps, Soviet
airborne, general, 45, 48, 61
1st Airborne, 44–45, 48, 56–57, 60–63, 75–76, 213, 231–261, 305, 396 n.90, 408 n.18
1st Airborne (2d Formation), 64
1st Guards Cavalry, 79, 86, 88–92, 94–95, 100–101, 103, 108, 111, 113, 121–146, 148, 154, 158, 168, 181–227, 263, 425
1st Guards Rifle, 57–60, 231, 234, 236
2d Airborne, 44–45, 48, 56, 61, 309, 315, 396 n.90
2d Airborne (2d Formation), 64
2d Cavalry, 14
2d Guards Cavalry, 90
2d Guards Rifle, 232, 234
3d Airborne, 44–45, 48, 56, 61, 396 n.90
3d Airborne (2d Formation), 64
4th Airborne, 44–45, 48–52, 54–56, 60–62, 75, 104–227, 287, 388, 396 n.90, 400 n.1, 403 n.15, 424–427
4th Airborne (2d Formation), 64
4th Guards Tank, 303

5th Airborne, 44–45, 48–49, 54–57, 60–
  62, 75, 79, 396 n.90, 399 n.8
5th Airborne (2d Formation), 64, 66
5th Guards Tank, 320
5th Long Range Air Transport, 303
6th Airborne, 64
6th Guards Tank, 411 n.3
7th Airborne, 64, 66
8th Airborne, 64, 66
8th Rifle, 14
9th Airborne, 64, 66
9th Guards Mechanized, 319–320
10th Airborne, 62, 64, 211
10th Mechanized, 319
11th Cavalry, 90–92, 108–109, 111, 113,
  122, 125–126, 129, 132, 136, 138, 146,
  228–229
17th Rifle, 14
20th Mechanized, 49–50
21st Mechanized, 49
37th Guards Rifle, 68
38th Guards Rifle, 68
39th Guards Rifle, 68
45th Mechanized, 14
73d Rifle, 283
Cottbus, 383
Crete, 37, 387
Crimea, 13, 19, 63, 308–309
Cuba, 343
Czechoslovakia, 300, 321, 379

Dakhnovka, 284–285
Danube River, 38
Darien, 319–320
Daugavpils, 48–49
Debrevo, 140, 183
Debriansky, 95, 165
Dedno, 246–247
Dedovitchi, 242
deep battle, concept of, xv, 3–4, 7, 14, 30,
  35–36, 368, 373, 385–386
deep operations, concept of the, xv, 32,
  144, 375, 385
Demiansk, 188, 228–229, 231–261
Demiansk operation (February–April
  1942), xv, 63–65, 72, 226, 231–
  261, 286, 288–289, 387, 407 n.7,
  408 n.16
Demidov, 54
Denisenko, Colonel M. I., 36, 64
Deniskovo Station, 185, 196
Denisovka, 216
Deriugin, Captain, 214, 428
Dertovaia, 152, 162, 165, 177, 403 n.27
Dertovochka, 164, 177–178, 404 n.52
Desiatnikov, Captain P., 311
Detachments, German

Service, 152
Detachments, Soviet
  1st Airlanding (Special Purpose), 11
  2d Airlanding (Special Purpose), 11
  3d Airlanding (Special Purpose), 11
  3d Motorized Airborne Landing, 7–8,
    11
  4th Airlanding (Special Purpose), 11
  47th Airlanding, 428
  Partisan '24th Anniversary of the Red
    Army', 211
  Partisan 'Dedushka', 193
  Partisan 'Grachev', 183
  Partisan 'Lazo', 214
  Partisan 'Moskalika', 193
  Partisan 'Uragan', 128
  Western Front Parachute-Assault, 54,
    75, 79
Detchina, 79
Detskoe Solo, 7, 12
Diagilevo, 126–129, 131–132, 135
D'iakov, Major General G., 387
Directions (Strategic), Soviet
  Western, 78, 85, 90, 108, 145–146
Divisions, German
  3d Motorized, 105, 126
  5th Panzer, 108, 122, 125–127, 132, 152,
    204, 210, 213, 402 n.73
  7th Air, 37
  7th Panzer, 76, 278
  10th Infantry, 315
  10th Motorized, 88, 108, 146, 150, 272–
    273
  11th Infantry, 238
  11th Panzer, 105, 115, 119, 125–126
  12th Infantry, 234–261
  14th Motorized, 76
  19th Panzer, 79, 150, 199, 204, 210, 213,
    272–273, 276, 411 n.5, 411 n.25
  20th Panzer, 278
  23d Infantry, 152, 193, 204, 210, 402
    n.73
  30th Infantry, 234, 238, 248, 250
  31st Infantry, 150, 152, 163, 172, 177,
    179, 199, 204, 403 n.27, 403 n.43
  32d Infantry, 234, 238
  34th Infantry, 79, 150, 163, 172, 177–
    179, 187, 197, 272–273
  35th Infantry, 193
  46th Infantry, 414 n.9
  52d Infantry, 92, 95, 150, 152, 159, 180,
    399 n.26
  57th Infantry, 272–273
  72d Infantry, 273, 278, 284
  73d Infantry, 414 n.9
  98th Infantry, 79, 92, 95, 152, 399 n.12,
    399 n.29, 400 n.35, 400 n.38, 403 n.19

106th Infantry, 125–126, 132
112th Infantry, 272–273
123d Infantry, 234, 238, 255, 257–258
131st Infantry, 150, 152, 163, 170, 177–
   178, 180–181, 187, 189, 197, 204, 220,
   404 n.58
137th Infantry, 150, 171–172, 177
167th Infantry, 92
183d Infantry, 82, 88
197th Infantry, 204
208th Infantry, 108
211th Security, 216
221st Security, 213
255th Infantry, 92
263d Infantry, 197
267th Infantry, 399 n.12
290th Infantry, 234, 238
331st Infantry, 177, 189, 197, 199
SS Motorized 'Totenkopf', 234–261
SS Motorized 'Viking', 278
Divisions, Slovak
   1st Infantry, 300
   2d Infantry, 300
Divisions, Soviet
   airborne, general, 324–325, 346, 358–
      359, 364–366, 381–383
   1st Guards Airborne, 65, 429
   1st Guards Cavalry, 122, 129, 132–133,
      135–136, 139, 193, 197, 210, 214, 216
   2d Guards Airborne, 65
   2d Guards Cavalry, 123, 131–133, 135–
      136, 138–139, 182–183, 185, 191–194,
      197, 199, 204, 208, 210–211, 213, 216–
      217
   2d Guards Motorized Rifle, 92
   3d Guards Airborne, 65
   4th Guards Airborne, 65
   4th Long Range Aviation, 300
   5th Guards Airborne, 65
   5th Long Range Aviation, 300
   6th Guards Airborne, 65, 382
   7th Guards Airborne, 65
   8th Guards Airborne, 65, 68
   9th Cavalry, 14
   9th Guards Airborne, 65–66
   10th Guards Airborne, 65
   11th Guards Airborne, 68
   12th Guards Airborne, 68
   13th Guards Rifle, 56, 65, 68
   14th Guards Airborne, 68
   16th Guards Airborne, 68
   18th Cavalry, 92
   21st Guards Transport Aviation, 317
   21st Mountain Cavalry, 49
   23d Bomber Aviation, 95
   23d Rifle, 255–256
   24th Cavalry, 92

   32d Guards Rifle, 64
   33d Guards Rifle, 64
   34th Guards Rifle, 64
   35th Guards Rifle, 64
   36th Guards Rifle, 64
   37th Guards Rifle, 64
   38th Guards Rifle, 64
   39th Guards Rifle, 64
   40th Guards Rifle, 64
   41st Cavalry, 121, 131–133, 135, 138–
      139, 182–183
   41st Guards Rifle, 64
   43d Rifle, 394 n.37
   50th Cavalry, 54
   53d Cavalry, 54
   54th Transport Aviation, 316
   57th Light Cavalry, 122, 129, 131, 133,
      136, 139, 182–183
   58th Rifle, 199
   59th Rifle, 394 n.37
   60th Rifle, 199
   75th Light Cavalry, 122, 126, 129, 132–
      133, 135, 139, 183
   76th Guards Airborne, 382
   82d Cavalry, 92
   82d Rifle, 79
   84th Rifle, 22
   87th Rifle, 56
   90th Rifle, 394 n.37
   98th Guards Airborne, 68, 382
   99th Guards Airborne, 68
   99th Guards Rifle, 428
   100th Guards Airborne, 68
   103d Guards Airborne, 382
   104th Guards Airborne, 382
   106th Guards Airborne, 382
   113th Rifle, 122
   116th Rifle, 196
   130th Rifle, 255–256, 258
   157th Rifle, 306, 308
   160th Rifle, 122, 129
   173d Rifle, 167
   210th Motorized, 50–52
   219th Rifle, 298
   254th Rifle, 283, 285
   290th Rifle, 167, 197
   326th Rifle, 218
   329th Rifle, 101, 129, 132–133, 140,
      181–183, 193–194, 196, 210–211, 213,
      216–217, 428
   336th Rifle, 167, 197
   338th Rifle, 122
   339th Rifle, 197
   344th Rifle, 167, 175
   385th Rifle, 197
   421st Rifle, 306, 308
Divisions, United States

101st Air Assault, 361
Dmitrovka, 154
'Dnepr' Exercise (September–October 1967), 348, 351, 356
Dnepr operation (September 1943), xiv, 263–288, 323, 348, 386, 388–390
Dnepr River, xiii 117, 52, 65, 67, 105, 193, 211, 263–289, 314, 323, 348
Dnestr River, 67
Dno, 290
Dobrosli, 248–250, 260
Dolgov, Junior Lieutenant F., 164
Domashnevo, 95
Don Basin, 308
Dorugobuzh, 109, 112, 125, 127–129, 133, 136, 140, 144, 150, 160, 181, 193–194, 197, 201, 203, 208, 211, 213, 222
Dovator, Major General L. M., 54
Dretun', 293, 298
Drobyshevsky, Major V. P., 116, 127, 131, 140, 210, 427, 429
Droshino Kessel (Cauldron), 405 n.61
Drozd, Lieutenant N., 426
Drozdovo, 180
Dubari, 276–277, 279, 412 n.27
Dubrovnia, 163, 168, 178, 181, 189, 196–201, 203
Dudchino, 298
Dukhovshchina, 54–55
Dukla, 300
Dukla Pass, 301, 303
'Dvina' Exercise (March 1970), 356, 359
Dvinsk, 44
Dzherzhinsky, 57

'Eastern Wall,' German defense line, 262
East Germany, 347
Efremov, 303
Efremov, Lieutenant General M. G., 92, 108, 122, 127, 129, 177, 222, 403 n.15, 403 n.51
Egorov, Marshal A. I., 14, 23, 26, 29
Ekaterinovka, 163–166, 175, 178
Elizavetovka, 283–284
El'nia, 150, 193, 211, 213–214
Engel's Airfield, 54–56, 66
Eponek, General, 41
Eremenko, Lieutenant General A., 36
Ermaki, 152
Ermakovo, 253
Ermolino, 119
Ersha, 194
Es'kovo, 120–121
Estonia, 29
Evdakimovo, 118–120
Everzovo, 230
Evgrafov, Major A. I., 427

Far East, 381, 396 n.88
Farnerovo Factory, 194, 199
Farussa, 219
Faymonville, Major P. R., 17, 19, 28–29
Fedorovka, 82, 172
Feodosiia, 309, 311
Field Regulations of the Red Army
  1929, 3
  1936, 30, 36
  1940, 37
  1941, 37, 39–40, 44
  1944, 72–73
Filimony, 211, 214
Five Year Plan, 3
Fleets, Soviet
  Baltic, 10
  Black Sea, 308–309, 313–315
Fofanov, Major V. F., 280
Follow-On Forces Attack (FOFA), NATO concept of, 369–370
Fomenkov, Senior Lieutenant D. V., 121, 427
Fominikh, General, 50–51
Fomino 1, 150, 196–197
Fomino 2, 196–199
France, 40, 387
Frolovo, 133, 209
Fronts, Soviet
  1st Baltic, 293
  1st Far Eastern, 317–318
  1st Ukrainian, 300, 381, 412 n.38
  2d Baltic, 293
  2d Ukrainian, 281–282, 285
  3d Ukrainian, 282
  4th Ukrainian, 300, 301
  Baltic, 290, 293
  Belorussian, 293
  Briansk, 57, 59, 146
  Central, 55, 65, 263, 290, 293
  Kalinin, 54, 74–75, 78, 88–92, 104, 109, 113, 117, 140, 145–146, 148, 187, 194, 200, 211, 228–229, 232, 234, 290, 293
  North Caucasus, 314
  Northwestern, 49, 63, 65, 89, 146, 228–229, 231, 233–234, 238, 241, 246–249, 257, 259
  Southwestern, 55–56, 74
  Transbaikal, 319–321
  Transcaucasus, 309, 311
  Voronezh, 263, 265, 268–269, 278
  Western, 49–52, 57, 59–60, 74–75, 78, 86, 89–92, 94–95, 100, 103–104, 109, 111, 113, 122, 125, 128, 132–133, 136, 139–140, 143, 145–146, 148, 153–154, 167–168, 170, 172, 177–179, 183, 185, 187, 197–201, 207–211, 223, 228, 290

Frunze, M. V., 3, 393 n.1
Fursovo, 208–209

Gaizhenai, 383
Galitsky, Lieutenant General K. N., 293, 298
Galiuga, Major, 211, 217–218
Gamarnik, Ia. B., 14
Garbolovo, 383
Garm, 4
Gavrilovka, 213
Gavrish, Captain D. F., 427, 429
Genichesk, 309
Germany, 379
Giandzha, 382
Gil'dendorf, 308
Gireevo, 399 n.12
Gladkoe Swamp, 250, 253–254, 256, 260
Glagolov, Colonel General V. V., 68, 324, 415 n.3
Glazkov, Major General V. A., 64
Glazunov, Major General V. A., 36, 61, 104, 123
Glebovka, 315–316
Glinka, 211
Glinka Station, 213
Globovshchina, 248–249
Glukhovo (airfield) (also spelled Glukhov), 121, 160, 168, 185
Godunovka, 95, 183
Golushkevich, Major General S. V., 203
Gomel', 290
Goncharov, Colonel P. A., 265, 268, 274
Gorbachev, M. S., 377–378, 391
Gorbachevo, 57
Gorbachi, 162–163, 165, 168, 170–171, 174, 178–180
Gorbatov, Colonel General A. V., 415 n.3
Gordota River, 209
Goreloe Beresino, 242, 248, 250, 253
Goriainovo, 109
Gorkavshchina, 268, 270
Gorki, 22, 52
Gor'kov, Captain A. I., 166, 428
Gorochowez, 23
Gorodianka, 101, 160
Gorodok, 293
Gorokhov, N. I., 427
Gorokhovets, 22
Grabtsevo (airfield), 104, 108, 116
Grachev, Colonel General P. S., 415 n.3
Grachevka, 172
Gradino, 109, 112
Great Britain, 37
Grediakino, 126–127, 131
Grendal', Lieutenant General D., 327–328
Griada, 153, 158–159

Gribovo, 82
Gridino, 259
Grigor'evka, 306, 308
Grigor'evo, 132
Grigorovka, 273, 411 n.3
Grinev, Major A. V., 237–261, 410 n.73
Grishentsy, 268
Grishin, Colonel I. T., 426
Group of Forces, Soviet
  Black Sea, 314
Groups, German
  Haase, 152, 165, 182, 191–192, 405 n.1
  Simon, 244, 255, 257
Groups, Soviet
  Aksenov, 115
  Khozin, 65
  Ksenefontov, 232–261
GRU (Main Intelligence Directorate, Soviet General Staff), 305, 374
Grusha, 51
Grushevo, 268, 276–277, 412 n.26
Gubarevich, Major General I. I., 64, 66
Gubin, Major, 246
Guderian, General H., 52, 57, 59
Guenther, Major G. B., 20–23, 26, 29
Gur'ev, Colonel S. S., 57, 64
Gurin, Major S., 211, 214, 218, 428
Guron, 49
Gusevo, 82, 91
Gvozdinkovo (also spelled Gvozdikovo), 127, 132, 138
Gzhatsk, 78–79, 90–92, 146, 187–188, 228

Halder, Colonel General Franz, 88, 95, 121, 128, 192, 199, 210, 214, 217, 220
Hannover, operation (May–June 1942), 203–227
Harbin, 317–319
Hata, Lieutenant General, 319
Heidkamper, Major General, 290
Helsinki, 43
High Commands, Soviet
  Far Eastern, 317
Hill 57.3, 308
Hill 58.0, 308
Hill 73.8, 284–285
Hill 80.1, 253, 254
Hill 200.1, 280
Hill 230.3, 218
Hill 253.2, 172
Hill 269.8, 196
Hitler, Adolf, 89, 222, 234
Holland, 40, 387
Hungary, 68, 301, 378

Iablonovo, 279
Iakir, I. K. (also spelled Yakir), 6, 14, 19

Iakovlev, Lieutenant G., 426
Iakovlevichi, 213
Iakovlevo, 136, 138–139
Iakubovsky, 85
Iakushino, 115, 126
Iamkovo, 109
Iamonov, Major General A. A., 320
Ianenki, 192
Ianovsky, A. Ia., 33–34
Iantsi, 319
Iartsevo, 52, 193–194, 228
Iasski, 242, 244
Iassy–Kishinev operation (August 1944), 68
Iazov, General D., 377
Idritsa, 298
Igoshevo, 249–250, 253–255, 258
Ikandovo, 254–255
Il'ino, 402 n.53
I'lmen, Lake, 228
Il'na, Lieutenant V., 428
Iloml'ia, 242, 249
Indochina, 356
Indzer, A. O., 36
Isserson, G., 1
'Iug', Exercise (June 1971), 356, 359
Iukhnov (also spelled Yukhnov), 54, 60, 78–79, 82, 86, 88–92, 94–95, 100–101, 104, 108, 113, 118, 121–122, 125, 140, 145–146, 148, 150, 152, 159, 160–188, 196, 228, 400 n.29
Iurkino, 140, 160, 162, 168, 171, 175, 178
Iuzhnaia Ozereika, 315–316
Ivaniki, 109
Ivanov, Colonel N. P., 4, 64
Ivanov, Lieutenant General V. D., 320
Ivanovich, Lieutenant General S. V., 230
Ivanovka, 119, 133
Ivanovskaia, 59
Ivantsevo (also spelled Ivantseva), 160, 162–164, 177–178, 203
Ivashchenko, G. A., 412 n.38
Izborovo, 121, 126, 136, 138–139
Izdeshkovo, 115, 118–119, 122, 126, 133, 140, 208, 213
Iziakovo, 115
Izmail, 38

Jalalabad, 374
Japan, 38
Japanese Army, 317–321

Kabachevsky, Captain A. P., 84
Kagul, 38
Kaidakovo Station, 129, 135
Kalashnikov, Captain E. N., 98, 100, 136, 138, 140, 189, 428

Kaledino, 132, 139
Kalinkovichi, 55
Kalinin, 54, 86
Kalinin, Colonel General N. V., 415 n.3
Kaluga, 76, 78–79, 86, 88, 104, 108, 111, 113, 115, 119, 123, 218, 223
Kalugovo, 198–200
Kamenka, 196, 204
Kandahar, 374
Kanev, 268, 270, 272–273, 279–281, 287–288
Kanko, 319
Kapitochkin, Major General A. G., 265
Kapotna, 57
Kapustino, 125, 135
Karelia, 68
Karmeliuk, Brigade Commander, 21
Karnaukhov, Captain N. Ia., 113, 115, 117–119, 127, 140, 189, 198, 207, 427, 429
Katukov, Colonel M. E., 59
Kaunas, 382
Kavkas, 160
Kazankin, Lieutenant General A. F., 49, 51–52, 158–227, 415 n.3, 426, 427, 429
Keisiku, Lieutenant General Murakami, 319
Kerch, 63, 308–311
Kerch–Feodosiia operation (December 1941), 308–311
Khabarovsk, 43–44, 396 n.88
Khalkin-Gol, 38, 328
Khan'kova, 162, 165
Khar'kov, 48, 65, 210, 262, 265, 314
Kholm, 228, 231–232, 242, 244
Khoroshilov, 178
Khoteenkov, Captain A., 162, 171, 208, 426–427
Khlysty, 211, 213
Khmost'e River, 54
Khrushchev, Nikita S., 336–337, 348, 350
Khyrov, 383
Kiev, 15, 17, 48, 52, 55–56, 229, 241, 262–263, 272, 405 n.1, 408 n.18
Kiev, maneuvers of 1935, 14–19, 28
Kipovyi Rog, 270
Kir'ian, M. M., 371
Kirin, 317–319
Kishinev, 44, 382
Kirov, 86, 91, 150, 152, 165, 188, 192, 211–212, 217, 219–220
Kirovograd, 67
Klimov Zavod, 95, 152, 400 n.29, 400 n.35
Klimovskikh, Major General V. E., 50–51
Klin, 86, 330
Klin operation (December 1941), 75–76
Kliuchi, 100–101, 148, 152, 160–187, 403

n.27, 403 n.37
Kliuchiki, 192
Kljasma (also spelled Kliasma) River, 26
Klokovo Station, 213
Kluge, Marshal G. von, 146
Knevitsy Station, 238, 250
Kniazev, Lieutenant Colonel A. V., 217
Kniazhnoe, 140
Kobets, Major A. G., 115, 117, 119, 121, 126, 132, 427, 429
Kochubeevo, 82
Kokhansky, I. S., 36
Kokoshin, A., 377
Koktebel, 13
Kolesishche, 276
Kolobovnikov, Lieutenant Colonel N. E., 56, 111, 162–164, 201, 426–427, 429
Kolumna, 57
Kombain, 192, 196, 204
Komitet gosudarstvennoi besopostnosti (KGB) [Committee of State Security], 381
Komovo, 109, 119, 125
Komsomol (Communist Union of Youth), 12, 39, 49, 60
Kondrovo, 79, 85
Konev, Marshal I. S., 88, 282, 300, 301, 303–304
Kononenko, Colonel A., 40–41
Konotop, 56
Kopol', 217–218
Korea, 319–320, 356
Kork, A. I., 6
Korneva, 254, 256–257
Korsun', 281
Korsun'-Shevchenkovskii, 67
Kosa, 247
Kostianets, 268, 270
Kostin, Major General Iu., 325–327, 330, 334
Kostinki, 160, 162–163, 177–178
Kostino, 85
Kostroma, 282
Kovalev, Lieutenant Colonel S. M., 59–60
Kovalevsky, Lieutenant, 230
Kovali, 268, 270
Kovrovo, 22
Kovtyukh, Army Commander E. I., 21
Kozarovka, 270
Koziej, Colonel S., 374–376, 380–381
Kozunko, Major M. M., 158, 427
Krasnoarmeiskyi, 10
Kransnodar, 309
Krasnoe Selo, 6
Krasnogvardeisk, 6, 8
Krasnyi Kholm, 129, 402 n.53
Krasovsky, Colonel P. I., 265, 268
Kravchenko, Colonel General A. G., 320

Kreichi, General, 19
Kremenchug, 383
Kremenskoe, 79, 82
Kreuts, Captain S. D., 198, 201, 428
Kriakovo, 211
Krichev, 52, 406 n.43
Krivoi Rog, 282
Krosno, 300, 301
Krotovka, 218
Kruglik, 166
Krutoi Kholm, 214
Krutskikh, Lieutenant Colonel D. A., 319
Krylov, Lieutenant General N. I., 317
Krymskaia, 314
Kubanka, 308
Kublanov, Major General G., 343–344
Kudriavtsov, I. V., 426
Kuibyshev, 44
Kulitsky, Senior Lieutenant, 54, 427
Kupanna, 62
Kurakino, 148, 160, 162–164, 167, 178, 180–181, 203, 209
Kurdiumovo, 109, 128
Kurilovka, 268
Kurochkin, Lieutenant General K., 357
Kurochkin, Colonel General P. A., 230–232, 234, 236–237, 246, 248–249, 259, 261, 408 n.16
Kursk, 65, 263
Kursk operation (July–August 1943), 290, 376–377, 389
Kuryshev, Colonel I. I., 109, 161–162, 166, 170, 172, 174, 181, 198, 201, 428
Kutaisi, 383
'Kutuzov,' operation (Orel) (July–August 1943), 262
Kuznetsov, Iu. K., 371

Ladomirka Valley, 257
Lager, 201
Lama River, 76
land-air combat, concept of, 362–364, 373, 378
Lapchinsky, A. N., 4–5
Larianov, V., 377
Latvia, 29
Lavrishchevo, 160, 172, 175
Lazino, 216
Lazo, Sergei, 211, 214, 425
Lazurtsy (airfield), 268, 270
Lebedev, Major G. I., 177, 209, 426, 429
Lebedev, Colonel V. I., 319
Lebedin, 55, 265, 268, 274
Leliushenko, Colonel General D. D., 57
Leningrad, 6, 12
Leonovo, 148, 160, 162, 165, 177–178
Lepel', 290
Leshchinin, Major V. A., 427

Levashov, Major General A. F., 36, 49,
   55–56, 104, 109, 111, 113, 118–119,
   148, 153–154, 158, 426–427
Levykino, 132
Liaoyuan, 320
Likhachev, Lieutenant Colonel B. S., 320
Likhanovo, 176
Lipniki, 101
Lipovyi Rog, 268
Lisov, Lieutenant General I. I., xiv, 43,
   338–343, 428
Lithuania, 29, 381
Liubertsy (airfield), 57, 66, 123, 152–154,
   229, 241
Liubnitsa, 241
Liubno, 257
Liudinovo, 100–101
Lobov, Colonel General V. N., 371, 377
L'Oiseau, General, 18
Loknia, 242, 244
Lomy, 183
Lotoshchino, 76
Lozovok, 283–285
Lubnishche, 50
Luga, 10–12
Lugi, 95, 100, 158–159
Luidkovo, 160–162, 165
Lukin, Ia. D., 6
Lunevo, 254–257
Lupkow Pass, 301
Lychkovo, 238, 247, 250, 253, 261

Maas River, 40
Machkov, Lieutenant G., 427
Maikop, 311–314
Maikop operation (October 1942), 311–
   314
Makarovka, 172
Makedony, 268–270
Malaia Myshenka, 192, 194, 196, 198–199,
   201, 203
Malaia Zemlia, 316
Malakhovki, 57
Malinovsky, Marshal R. Ia., 237, 343, 417
   n.3
Maloe Fat'ianovo, 84
Maloe Opuevo, 238, 242, 246–250, 256–
   257, 259–260
Maloe Prechistoe, 189, 203
Maloiaroslavets, 60, 79, 88–89, 118
Maloshino, 125, 135
Malyi Lokhov, 98
Malyshevka, 161–187, 403 n.30, 403 n.43
Manchuria, 68, 316–321
Manchurian operation (August 1945),
   316–321
Manstein, Colonel General E. von, 308–
   309

Marfovka, 309
Margelov, Lieutenant General V., 345–
   346, 357, 391, 415 n.3
Mariampol'e, 382
Marina Gorka, 48–49
Marinovka, 192
Markotkh Pass, 314
Marmonovo, 127–128, 131–133
Mart'ianov, Lieutenant A., 426
Maslovka, 279–280
Maslovo, 82, 255, 259
Mazheninov, S. A., 13
Mazurkevich, Battalion Commissar I. G.,
   128
Medvedki, 207
Medvedovka, 280
Medzilaborce, 300
Medyn, 79, 82, 85–86, 91–92, 94, 399 n.12
Medyn operation (January 1942), 60, 63,
   75–76, 78–86, 94
Mefodievskii, 314
Meglino, 254
Mel'nichenko, Lieutenant Colonel M. I.,
   319–320
Meretskov, Marshal K. A., 317
Miatlevo Station, 79, 82, 85–86, 91, 95
Middle East, 356
Mikhali, 203–204, 400 n.38
Mikhal'ki, 129, 402 n.53
Miliatino, 193–194, 197–201, 203–204, 406
   n.19
Military Districts, Soviet
   Belorussian, 7, 11, 13, 23, 35–36
   Central Asian, 49
   Khar'kov, 23, 44–45, 48, 396 n.90
   Kiev (Special), 6, 14, 35–36, 43, 45, 48,
      55, 396 n.90
   Leningrad, 4, 6–7, 9, 11–13, 36
   Moscow, 5, 7, 11, 22–23, 26, 28, 35, 49
   Odessa, 36, 44–45, 48, 396 n.90
   Pre-Baltic, 44–45, 48–49, 57, 396 n.90
   Siberian, 44
   Transbaikal, 35, 44, 79
   Transcaucasian, 44
   Ukrainian, 7, 11
   Ural, 23
   Volga, 11, 35, 56
Mil'sky, Lieutenant Colonel A. G., 211,
   218, 428–429
Minino Station, 115
Ministerstvo vnutrennikh del (MVD)
   [Ministry of Internal Affairs], 381
Minov, L. G., 5–6
Minsk, 13–14, 21, 50, 94, 105, 108, 125,
   146
Mironov, Lieutenant General P. V., 68
Mishenka, 135
Mitrokhino, 183

Mogilev, 50, 52, 55, 290
Mogilevka, 6
Mokhnatka, 160, 162, 177–178, 180
Moldova, 381
Moloshino, 402 n.53
Monchalovo, 229–230
Mongolia, 38
Monino, 44
Morozov, Colonel I. Z., 168, 425
Morozovo, 118
Morshanovo, 127
Mosal'sk, 91–92, 150, 167–168, 175, 211, 228
Moscow, 17, 36, 43, 54, 56–57, 60, 63, 89, 105, 108, 210, 219–220, 229, 234, 241, 265, 293, 308, 382, 385, 396 n.88
Moscow operation (5 December 1941–April 1942), xiv, 63, 74–103, 222, 390
Moscow, maneuvers of 1936, 22–28
Moshkovsky, Ia. D., 5–6
Moshny, 284, 412 n.38
Moskalenko, Colonel General K. S., 303
Moskalika, Colonel, 193
Mosolovo, 109
Mount Dolgaia, 314
Mount Fui, 38
Mount Sakharnaia Golova, 314
Mozhaisk, 76, 86, 91–92
Mtsensk, 57
Mtsensk operation (October 1941), 57–60
Muchnaia, 44
Mukden, 319–320
Murashovka, 100
Murom, 22
Mutanchiang, 317
Mutishchi, 214
Mytishino, 211

Nadezhda, 204
Napoleon, 3, 89
Nara River, 60
Narodnyi komissariat oborony (NKO) [Peoples' Commissariat of Defense], 8
Narodnyi komissariat vnutrennikh del (NKVD) [Peoples' Commissariat of Internal Affairs], 305
Navtlug, 44
Nestarovo, 135
Neustadt, 406 n.43
Nevel', 290
Nevel' operation (October 1943), 293–294
Niashin, Major, 309
Nikishev, D. N., 6
Nikitin, Regimental Commissar D. P., 237, 258
Nikitin, V. A., 426
Nikolaev, 383

Nikolaevskoe, 254, 256–258
Nikol'skoe, 85
Nikol'skoe State Farm, 213
Nikulino, 136
Nikvi, 133
non-linear war, Soviet concept of, 370–376, 384, 391–392
Normandy operation (June 1944), 387
Northern Dvina River, 293
Nory, 248
Novaia, 101
Novaia Askerovo, 194, 198–200
Novaia Dacha (also referred to as Novaia), 160, 162, 168, 177–178, 180
Novaia Kalugovo, 199
Novaia Mokhnata, 178
Novinka, 192
Novinskaia Dacha, 178–180, 186, 189, 192, 196, 201
Novo Petrovskoe, 76
Novoe Maslovo, 255, 257–258
Novorossiisk, 314–316
Novorossiisk operation (February 1943), 314, 316
Novosel'e, 294
Novosokol'niki, 290
Novye Ladomiry, 254
Novyi Luki, 214
Novyi Moch Swamp, 244, 247, 257
Novyi Novosel, 257–258

Odessa, 306, 414 n.7
Odessa operation (September 1941), 305–308, 389
Ofanasovka, 218
Oka River, 108, 219
Okorokovo, 229, 231, 242
Oktiabr'sky, Vice Admiral F. S., 314
Olenin, V. M., 426–427, 429
Olenino, 228–231
Ol'shanka River, 285
Onufriev, Colonel A. A., 64, 109, 112, 118–119, 122–144, 185, 189–227, 401 n.24, 426–427, 429
Operational Group Kempf, 262
operational maneuver groups, Soviet concept of, 370, 372, 383
Operation Barbarossa, 44
Optukha, 59
Orekhov, Senior Lieutenant N. V., 236
Orel, 57–60, 263
Orlov, Captain M., 311
OSOAVIAKHIN (Society for the Promotion of Defense and the Furthering of Aviation and of the Chemical Industry of the USSR), 12–13
Otozo, General Yamada, 318, 320

Ozcheiedy, 255–256
Ozerechnia, 104, 109, 122–113, 115–117, 119

Pacific Ocean, 326
Paldino, 402 n.53
Panzer Groups, German
  Second, 52, 57, 59, 74
  Third, 74, 76–77
  Fourth, 76
Parichi, 51
Pastikhi, 129
Pastrevich, Major General A. I., 64
Pavlenko, Lieutenant General P., 359
Pavlov, General D. K., 49–51
Pekari, 278, 411 n.26
Penkovo, 255
Pereiaslavl, 263
Perekhody, 140, 181
Peremyshl', 104–108
Permanent Operating Factors (of Stalin), 323, 415 n.1
Pesochnia, 131–132, 148, 152, 160–187, 201, 403 n.27
Petrishchevo, 101, 168
Petrosian, Senior Lieutenant S., 279
Petrovo, 400 n.38
Petrukhin, A. A., 101
Petshchishchie, 256
Pii, 276
Pikulev, Dr Iu. N., 128
Pirovo, 82
Pishchevo, 204, 207
Platonovka, 196–197, 201
Pleshkovo, 109, 111
Plesnovo, 98, 100
Plitsch (also spelled Ptich) River, 21
Plotki, 194, 197, 201
Plotnikov, Captain A. I., 162, 179, 428–429
Pobeda, 218
Pobortsev, Lieutenant P. V., 136, 140, 153, 185, 189, 198–199, 426–427
Pochinok, 242, 244, 248
Podgerb, 217
Podkolzin, Lieutenant General Ie. N., 415 n.3
Podlipki, 208–209
Podol'sk, 60
Podrezovo, 402 n.53
Podsosenki (also spelled Podsosonki), 95, 148, 152, 165, 169–170, 178
Podsoson'e, 247
Pogorelitsy, 257–258
Pokrovskoe, 216
Poland, 40, 301, 304, 379, 381, 384
Poldnevo, 207
Polish Army, 40

Polomet River, 238, 242, 244, 246–249
Polotnianyi Zavod, 79
Polotsk, 288
Polotsk operation, 290–298
Polozkov, Captain I. D., 153, 162, 164, 166, 171, 426–427, 429
Poltava, 89, 262
Ponyri, 65
Popovo, 109
Port Arthur, 319–320
Potashnia, 280–281
Potok, 279
Potoptsy, 270, 276
Pozhaleeva, 242, 244, 246
Pravda, 18
Prechistoe, 161–187, 191–192, 201
Preobrazhensk, 160, 177, 189, 192, 196
Pressov, 301
Pritula, Major General A. D., 320
Prokhorovka, 65
Prokof'ev, Lieutenant V., 426
Prokopyuk, V. G., 301
Prokryl, Colonel, 303
Proskovo, 204
Pskov, 10, 135, 382
Pu Li, Emperor of Manchukuo, 320
Pulavy, 303
Pushkino, 49, 180
Pustoshka, 121, 207–209, 293
Pustynia, 238, 244, 246–249

'Quartet,' Warsaw Pact exercise (1963), 347

Ramenskoe (airfield), 56, 66, 104, 123, 152, 158, 214, 218, 424
Raspopov, Brigade Commissar I. V., 123, 125, 128, 132, 139, 189, 214, 427, 429
Rebrovo, 109, 112, 117, 120, 131–132, 136, 139
Red Army (Raboche-Krest'ianskaia Krasnaia Armiia–RKKA), 1, 7–9, 12, 18, 26–27, 38–39, 289
Red Army Air Force (Voenno-vozdushnyi sil'–VVS), 4, 44
Regiments, Czech
  1st Fighter Aviation, 303
Regiments, German
  8th Artillery, 127
  12th Infantry, 166, 178, 403 n.27
  15th Motorized, 127
  17th Infantry, 403 n.27
  33d Infantry, 178
  41st Motorized, 191
  73d Panzer Grenadier, 276–277
  74th Panzer Grenadier, 276
  82d Infantry, 403 n.27, 403 n.43, 405 n.6
  107th Infantry, 178

116th Artillery, 127
143d Infantry, 178
266th Infantry, 284
306th Infantry, 199
309th Infantry, 108, 115
434th Infantry, 165, 178
442d Infantry, 178
449th Infantry, 177–178
504th Motorized Engineer, 199
557th Infantry, 199
Regiments, Soviet
1st Airborne, 36, 44
1st Guards Cavalry, 216
1st Partisan, 152, 160, 182, 194, 201, 204, 210
1st Rostov, 36
2d Airborne, 36, 44
2d Gorokhovets, 36
2d Partisan, 210
3d Airborne, 44
3d Guards Cavalry, 208, 216
3d Naval Infantry, 306
3d Voronezh, 36
4th Reserve Airborne, 64
5th Airborne, 36
5th Guards Cavalry, 216
5th Partisan, 211
6th Guards Cavalry, 208, 216, 217
6th Partisan, 204
7th Airborne, 44
7th Guards Cavalry, 182, 208
8th Guards Cavalry, 204
11th Guards Cavalry, 136
31st Parachute Landing, 315
51st Guards Parachute Assault, 382
69th Fighter Aviation, 308
97th Guards Parachute Assault, 382
104th Guards Parachute Assault, 382
108th Guards Parachute Assault, 382
110th Guards Rifle, 429
113th Guards Rifle, 429
115th Guards Rifle, 429
119th Guards Parachute Assault, 382
137th Artillery, 14
137th Guards Parachute Assault, 382
170th Cavalry, 132–133
188th Cavalry, 132–133
217th Guards Parachute Assault, 382
234th Guards Parachute Assault, 382
237th Guards Parachute Assault, 382
250th Airborne (Separate Rifle), 60, 62, 79, 82, 84, 86, 95, 98, 100–101, 129, 132, 136, 140, 144, 152, 158, 181, 201, 401 n.33, 428
299th Guards Parachute Assault, 382
300th Guards Parachute Assault, 382
328th Guards Parachute Assault, 382
331st Guards Parachute Assault, 382

337th Guards Parachute Assault, 382
345th Guards Parachute Assault, 382
929th Rifle, 283, 285
933d Rifle, 283, 285
936th Rifle, 283
Reitovo, 100
Ressa River, 150, 171, 220
Revolutionary Military Soviet (*Revoensovet–RVS*), 4, 6–8, 11–12, 35
Revolution in Military Affairs, 336–349, 390, 416 n.1
Revy, Lieutenant P. M., 427, 429
Reznichenko, Lieutenant General V. G., 355, 369, 371–372
Rhine operation (1945), 387
Riazan', 382–383
Riga, 9–10, 12, 20, 22, 29
Rodimtsev, Major General A. I., 56, 65, 396 n.2, 397 n.13
Rognedino, 218
Romanenko, Senior Lieutenant N., 52, 54, 56, 426, 429
Romanushka, 241
Romashki, 276
Roslavl', 193, 214, 217, 219
Rossany, 290
Rossava, 277
Rossonsk, 290
Rotterdam, 40
Roztoki, 303
Rudenko, Colonel General S. I., 415 n.3
'Rumiantsev' (Belgorod–Khar'kov) operation (August 1943), 262
Russkaia Poliana, 283
Ruza River, 76
Rybalko, Lieutenant General P. S., 263
Rychagov, Lieutenant General P., 36
Rzhavets (airfield), 104, 108, 116, 119
Rzhev, 54, 78, 86, 88, 90–92, 108, 145–146, 187–188, 228–231
Rzhev operation (February 1942), 63, 228–231
Rzhishchev, 263, 269–270, 272–273, 279–280, 287

Safonovo, 136
Sagaidachnyi, Major N. I., 128, 426–427
Sakhalin Island, 320
Sakulino, 138–139
Salov, Major I. A., 178
Samarin, Major N. I., 427, 429
Samoilenko, Colonel Ia., 342, 353–357
Samok, 301
Samsonovo, 85
Sapovo, 159
Sapronovo, 183
Saratov, 56, 241, 408 n.18
Savinki, 159

Savino, 126–127, 131
Schensnovich, Colonel V., 339–340
Seidlitz, Major General Walter von, 234, 259
Selibka, 204, 207–209
Sekirna, 283–285
Seliger, Lake, 54, 228
Selishche, 192, 204, 270
Selivanovo, 132, 135
Semenkovo, 165
Semenovskoe, 127
Semlevo, 101, 125–127, 130
Semlevo Station, 132–133, 135–136, 138–139, 193
Sergeevo, 211
Sevastopol', 308–309
Shakhovskaia, 76, 91
Shandra, 280, 412 n.26
Shania River, 82, 85, 92, 94
Shansky Zavod, 82, 399 n.12
Sharov, Major V. N., 162, 166, 174, 428
Shchadrino, 209
Shcherbin, P. V., 428
Shchukino, 84
Shelakhov, Major General G. A., 318–319
Shilin, Lieutenant Colonel M. I., 213–214, 428
Shipp, Major W. E., 11
Shishkovo, 248
Shmelev, Colonel, 140, 185, 189, 208
Shtemenko, Colonel General S. M., 286
Shukin, Captain A. D., 428
Shuklin, Major, 198
Shumilin, 177
Shumilov-Bor, 242, 249
Shushmin, 148
Siaiulai, 44
Sidorchuk, Lieutenant Colonel P. M., 265, 268, 278–288, 411 n.38
Sidorenko, Colonel A. A., 354–356
Sidorovichi, 183
Sidorovskoe, 95
Siniavka (Belorussia), 50–51
Siniavka (Ukraine), 268, 270
Siniukovo, 95
Skorodumov, Major General I. A., 361
Slobodka, 172, 177, 179
Slovakia, 298–304
Slovak National Council, 298
Slovak operation (September 1944), 298–304
Slovak uprising (September 1944), 298–304, 403 n.15
Slutsk, 50–51
Smirnov, Captain M., 161, 166, 169, 174, 179, 198, 209–210, 428
Smosodino, 268, 274
Smolensk, 52, 55, 89, 92, 94, 04, 109, 112,

117, 119–120, 122–123, 125–126, 128–130, 136, 145, 193, 228, 262
Smolensk operation (July–August 1941), 52, 115
Smolensk operation (August 1943), 290
'Socialism in One Country', 3
Sofronov, G. P., xiv
Sokolov, Colonel S. V., 108, 111, 113, 126, 129, 134
Sokolovsky, Marshal V. D., 341, 347, 355
Soldatenko, Lieutenant M., 426
Soldatov, Major N. L., 79, 82, 84–85, 98, 100–101, 109, 112–113, 122, 129, 140, 181, 400 n.40, 401 n.33
Solntsev, Captain N. V., 426
Soloven'ki, 214
Solov'evo, 238, 242, 244, 246, 249
Solov'evka, 172
Sopil'nik, Lieutenant General A., 344–345
Sorokino, 207–208
Soviet–Finnish War, 38–39
Soviet Information Bureau (SOVINFORM BURO), 234
Spanish Civil War, 37
Spas-Demensk, 144, 150, 193, 219
Special Airborne Administration [*Vozdushno-desantnye voiska–VDV*], 44, 60
Spirin, Major General M., 387
Spirin, Major V. I., 209, 406 n.43, 426–427, 429
Squadrons, Soviet
  58th Separate Transport Aviation, 383
Stalin, I.V., 74, 89–90, 300, 322–323, 334, 336, 415 n.1
Stalingrad, 56, 64–65
Stalingrad operation (July–November 1942), 311, 314, 328, 389, 429
Stanichka, 315, 316
Stanishche, 132
Staraia Doroga, 51
Staraia Polianovo, 132
Staraia Russa, 65, 228, 231–232, 234, 236, 242
Starchak, Major I. G., 54, 60, 76, 79, 82, 84–85, 399 n.13, 428
Starniki, 294
Starintsa, 211
Staroe Askerovo, 194
Staroe Kalugovo, 199
Staroe Maslovo, 254–255
Staroe Prudische, 183
Staroe Tarasovo, 248, 253–255, 260
Starosel'e, 101, 181, 183
Starunin, Colonel A. I., 40–41
Starye Ladomiry, 253–254, 256
Stepantsy, 268, 270
Stogovo, 129, 132, 135–136

Stropkov, 299
Student, Major General Karl, 37, 46
Stupino Airfield, 241
Subbotniki, 165, 183
Sukhinichi, 52, 86, 88, 91, 92, 188, 228
Sukhorukhov, Colonel General D. S., xiv, 36, 361–362, 415 n.3
Sumy, 262
Sungari River, 318–319
Surzhik, Captain A. I., 79, 82, 84, 98, 100–101, 136, 138, 140, 428
Sutniki, 220
Suworschtsch (also spelled Suvorshch) River, 26
Svechin, A., 377
Sverdlov, F. D., 370–371
Sverdlovo, 308
Sverkhnaia Ilichebka, 308
Sverkhnoe Kaidakovo, 402 n.53
Svidivok, 283–287
Svinoroi, 249
Svintsovo, 159, 198
Sviridovo, 160
Svisloch, 51
Svisloch River, 14
Svoboda, General A., 301
Sychevka, 78, 90, 92, 108, 146

Tabory, 113, 115–116
Tadzhikistan, 4
Tagancha Forest, 280–281
Tagancha Station, 281
Talsky, Colonel V., 300
Taman Peninsula, 314
Tarasov, Lieutenant Colonel N. E., 36, 241–261
Tarasovo, 250
Tartarchenko, I. E., 9
Tat'ianino', 101, 160, 164, 178
Tat'ianitsa, 162
Temkino, 95, 100
Temnenskoe Swamp, 242, 244, 246
Temnyi Les Station, 52
Terekhovka, 196–197, 201
Tereshchenko, Senior Lieutenant P. V., 54, 160, 427–429
Teriaeva Sloboda operation (December 1941), 63, 75–78, 86
Tesnikovo, 125
Theaters of Military Operations (TVD), Soviet
  Far Eastern, 318
Tikhanov, Lieutenant General M. F., 64, 68, 427
Timoshenko, Marshal S. K., 39–41
Timkovichi, 50–51
Tkachenko, Lieutenant I., 426
Tkachev, Senior Lieutenant E. G., 281

Torop, 54, 56
Toropets, 228
Toropets–Kholm operation (January–February 1942), 228
Tractor Factory, 64
Training Centers, Soviet
  224th, 383
  242d, 383
Traktomirov, 268, 273
Trans-Caucasus, 381
Tri Duba Airfield, 300, 303–304
Triandafilov, V. K., 1
Trofimovo, 201
Troshino Station, 133
Trostianets, 14
Trostinets, 268, 270
Trudy, 298
Tsatskin, Lieutenant A., 426
Tukhachevsky, Marshal M. N., 1, 4, 6, 8–9, 13–14, 20, 23, 26–27, 37, 45, 385
Tula, 22, 57, 59, 86, 175, 303, 330, 382
Tuliava, 300
Tulitsy, 268, 270, 280
Tumanovka, 50
Tupliao, 319–320
Turkestan, 10
Turkish Wall, 309
Tutarinov, Lieutenant General I. V., 415 n.3
Tynovka, 101, 148, 160, 162, 165, 168, 171, 175, 177, 180, 404 n.52

Uborovich, I. P., 20–21
Ugra River, 146, 152, 171, 204, 207–208, 213, 220, 405 n.1
Ugra Station, 95, 101, 128–129, 140, 160, 152–163, 165, 181–183, 185, 189, 191–194, 196, 201, 204, 210
Ukhtomsky State Farm, 57
Ukraine, 6, 43, 67, 262, 263, 290, 305–306, 308, 328, 396 n.88
Ukrainian Partisan Staff, 298
Unified Military Doctrine, concept of, 3
United Nations, 377, 391
United States, 37
Usenko, Major General M. A., 56
Ushiachi, 293–294
Ustinov, Lieutenant Colonel, 258
Utvenko, Lieutenant General A. I., 64, 68
Uvarovo, 111
Uzlovka, 172

Valdai, 238
Varverovka, 92
Vasilenko, Lieutenant Colonel, 241, 247, 250, 253
Vasil'ev, Senior Lieutenant P., 162, 171, 427

Vasil'evka, 204, 315–316, 412 n.38
Vasilevsky, Marshal A. M., 74, 92, 318, 321
Vatolino, 238
Vatutin, Colonel General N. F., 246–249, 257, 263, 265, 268–270
Vekhotskoe, 111
Velikie Luki, 54, 242, 290
Velikopol'e, 95, 148, 159, 180
Velikopol'e–Zhelan'e operation (February 1942), 63, 148–227
Velikyi Bukrin, 69, 263, 265, 268–269, 273, 278
Verbulovo, 201
Vereia, 91
Vereteika, 241–242
Verterkhovo Station, 163, 165, 168, 178, 180, 192, 196, 201
Vertical Envelopment, 4
Veselaia Dubrava, 280
Veshki, 203
Vessiki, 244, 246, 249
Viaz'ma, 63, 78, 89–90, 92, 94–95, 100–101, 194–227, 229, 400 n.29, 405 n.1
Viaz'ma operation (February–June 1942), xv, 67, 72, 86, 91, 103, 104–227, 274, 286–289, 323, 387, 400 n.1, 424–425
Viaznikov (also spelled Vyaznikov), 22
Viazovets, 160, 192
Vietnam, 343, 349, 351, 356, 375
Vinogradov, Senior Lieutenant S., 426
Visiushii Bor, 257
Vitebsk, 29–30, 228, 289–290, 293, 297–298, 382
Vladislavovka, 309, 311
Vladivostok, 330
Vnukovo (airfield), 95, 98, 123, 152–153, 223
Vodneevka, 218
Volbovichi, 258
Volga River, 241, 408 n.18
Volochek (airfield), 210, 213
Volodarets, 129, 402 n.53
Volokolamsk, 76, 85–86, 90
Voloste Piatnitsa Station, 193
Vol'pe, A., 32
Vorob'ev, Major General I. N., 376
Voronezh, 5
Voronovo, 400 n.35
Vorontsovo, 118
Voroshilov, K. E., 8, 14, 20–23, 27
Voznesen'e, 191–192, 194, 196
Vskhody, 193, 204, 207–210
Vyderka, 253
Vypolsovo Station, 241

Vygor', 148, 160, 165, 175
Vysokoe, 139

Warsaw, 108, 113, 122, 146
Wavell, Major General A. P., 17
Western Dvina River, 294, 298
World War, First, 1, 3–4
Wongson, 319
Wyjesd, 23, 26

Yugoslavia, 387

Zabelin, Lieutenant Colonel I. N., 318
Zabnovo, 125, 129, 132, 135
Zabolot'e, 139, 248, 250
Zabrody, 230
Zaitsev Heights (Zaitseva Gora), 194, 196–198, 208
Zales'e, 256–258
Zamosh'e, 100
Zanoznaia, 183
Zarech'e, 100
Zarubentsy, 268, 273, 276
Zarubin, Captain I. P., 125, 429
Zatevakhin, Major General I. I., 36, 38, 68, 265
Zeltovka, 129
Zet'tsy, 308
Zhabo, Major V. V., 160, 176–177, 180, 182–183, 192–193, 196, 201, 204, 208, 210, 425
Zhadov, Colonel General A. S., 49, 396 n.2, 426
Zhashkovo (airfield), 104, 108, 113, 116, 118–119
Zhelan'e, 94–103, 108–109, 148, 152–153, 158, 161, 163, 168, 176, 201
Zhelan'e operation (January 1942), 63, 94–103
Zherdovka, 152, 160, 162–164
Zhilino, 217–218
Zhirkovo, 250
Zholydev, Major General B. G., 64
Zhukov, Marshal G. K., 38, 74, 78, 100, 104, 109, 111, 113, 119, 120–129, 132–133, 135, 138, 140, 145, 176, 180, 193–104, 198, 200, 269, 287, 336–337, 417 n.3
Zhukov reforms, 336–337
Zhukovka, 180, 189, 192, 196, 201
Zhurko, Major I., 427
Znamenka, 95, 98, 100–101, 103, 152, 160, 177, 179–180, 203–204, 226, 399 n.29, 400 n.29
Zubtsov, 92
Zusha River, 59
Zvolen, 303